UTILITARIANS AND RELIGION

THOEMMES

UTILITARIANS AND RELIGION

Edited and Introduced by
James E. Crimmins

Associate Professor of Political Theory and
Dean of the Faculty of Arts and Social Sciences
Huron College, University of Western Ontario

THOEMMES PRESS

This edition published by Thoemmes Press, 1998

Thoemmes Press
11 Great George Street
Bristol BS1 5RR, England

Thoemmes Press US office
22883 Quicksilver Drive
Sterling, Virginia 20166, USA

Hardback: 1 85506 570 3
Paperback: 1 85506 571 1

© James E. Crimmins, 1998

British Library Cataloguing-in-Publication Data
A CIP record of this title is available from the British Library

Printed in England by Redwood Books

UTILITARIANS AND RELIGION

*

PART ONE
Religious Utilitarians

*

PART TWO
Secular Utilitarians

For Johanne

Acknowledgements

For kind words of encouragement and advice in the early stages of this project I am indebted to Terence Ball and to the late Bob Fenn. Part Two was originally planned as a separate publication with Bob Fenn, but circumstances determined a different outcome. I am grateful to Anne Skoczylas for putting together the material for the biographical notes, her diligent proof-reading, and for compiling the index. Her work was funded by a grant from the Social Sciences and Humanities Research Council of Canada, to which I am obliged. Certain sections of the introductions to Parts One and Two, especially those on John Brown and Jeremy Bentham, are in part derived from earlier publications: (1) 'John Brown and the Theological Tradition of Utilitarian Ethics', *History of Political Thought*, 4/3 (1983), pp. 523–50, and (2) *Secular Utilitarianism: Social Science and the Critique of Religion in the Thought of Jeremy Bentham* (Clarendon Press, 1990).

As always, the work for this collection could not have proceeded without the patience and support of my companion in life, Johanne Lapensée-Crimmins. The book is dedicated to her.

J. E. C.
London, Ontario
December 1997

CONTENTS

**Part One
Religious Utilitarians**

Part Two
Secular Utilitarians

PART ONE
Religious Utilitarians

INTRODUCTION
Religious Advocates of the Utility Principle

The history of the relationship between religion and the principle of utility, and between utilitarians and religion, is often viewed as a neat chronology, with a gradual movement away from the religious form of utilitarianism towards a modernized, secular version.[1] There is a degree of cogency in this perspective. Initially, the relationship was harmonious, involving reinforcing elements within moral and political disquisition. Subsequently, utilitarianism and Christianity became antagonistic, if not always mutually exclusive, systems of thought. However, there are elements of the story which defeat the neatness of this chronology – secular elements which shape the religious version of utilitarian theory, and religious elements encompassed within the seemingly foreign secular variant of the doctrine. The writings in this collection illustrate several features of the history of utilitarian theory: (1) the utilitarian credentials of the eighteenth-century religious exponents, (2) the nature of the nineteenth-century secular utilitarian critique of the religion which underpinned the earlier version of the doctrine, and (3) the general interweaving of religious and secular elements within the British utilitarian tradition.

1

The term 'utilitarian' was coined by Jeremy Bentham in 1781, either in a letter to his friend George Wilson, in which he used the term to describe 'honest Joseph Townshend',[2] or as a result of a 'dream' he had about the same time while a guest at the Earl of Shelburne's country residence in Wiltshire. In this dream Bentham imagined himself 'a founder of a sect; of course a personage of great sanctity and importance. It was called the sect of the *utilitarians*.'[3] Is it anachronistic to apply the term 'utilitarian' to those advocates of utility as the standard of right and wrong who wrote before Bentham introduced the term? To answer this question we should

[1] This is the standard view, explained by Leslie Stephen, Ernest Albee, Elie Halévy, John Plamenatz, and others. It is still common practice to present utilitarianism as a secular theory; see Will Kymlicka, *Contemporary Political Philosophy: An Introduction* (Oxford 1990), p. 10.
[2] *The Correspondence of Jeremy Bentham* (CW = *The Collected Works of Jeremy Bentham*), iii, ed. I. R. Christie (London 1971), p. 57. Joseph Townshend (1739–1816).
[3] Bentham MSS., University College London (UCL) clxix. 79. The text of this 'dream' is given in full in James E. Crimmins, *Secular Utilitarianism: Social Science and the Critique of Religion in the Thought of Jeremy Bentham* (Oxford 1990), App. B, pp. 313–16.

first consider what Bentham meant when he employed the language associated with the utility principle.

It is generally understood that 'utilitarianism' can be understood (1) as a theory of ethics which provides a criterion for distinguishing between actions deemed right and wrong and an account of the nature of the moral judgements that characterise actions as right or wrong, and (2) as a movement or an ideology for legal, social and political reform which gained ground in the early nineteenth century largely due to the efforts of Bentham.[4] Bentham may well have had both meanings in mind when he dreamt of the utilitarian sect in 1781. However, since the 'religious utilitarians', whose writings constitute the first part of this volume, cannot be described as political reformers either in substance or disposition and certainly were not associated with Bentham in the reform movement, the latter meaning of the term cannot accurately be applied to them. Matters stand otherwise with the first, moral meaning of the term. The standard form of utilitarianism encompasses two essential elements: (1) the rightness/ wrongness of an action is determined by the goodness/badness of its consequences; (2) the only thing that is good in itself is pleasure and the only thing bad in itself is pain, and happiness is taken to be the sum of particular pleasures. Based on these elements, the doctrine is then expressed in the form of the greatest happiness principle, that is 'the rightness of an action is determined by its contribution to the happiness of everyone affected by it.'[5] These basic stipulations provide us with the essential ethical elements of utilitarian theory according to which the religious moralists represented in this collection count as 'utilitarians'.

Bentham's own history with the utility principle serves to underscore this contention. It is clear that he originally associated 'utility' with the pursuit of 'the greatest happiness of the greatest number'. In *A Fragment on Government*, published in 1776, he declared this 'a fundamental axiom', 'the measure of right and wrong', that '*utility* was the test and measure of all virtue', and that 'the obligation to minister to general happiness, was an obligation paramount to and inclusive of every other'.[6] In *An Introduction to the Morals and Principles of Legislation (IPML)*, printed in 1780 but not published until 1789, he introduced the notion of utility as a 'principle' when he titled the first chapter 'Of the Principle of Utility'.[7] *IPML* was then considered by Bentham to be the foundational text of his thought and his plans for future works were intended to elucidate the

---

[4]   Anthony Quinton, *Utilitarian Ethics* (1973; 2nd edn. La Salle, Illinois 1988), p. 1.

[5]   Quinton, *Utilitarian Ethics*, p. 1.

[6]   J. Bentham, *A Comment on the Commentaries and A Fragment on Government (CW)* ed. J. H. Burns and H. L. A. Hart (London 1977), pp. 393, 440–41 note. Henceforth FRAG (CW).

[7]   Jeremy Bentham, *An Introduction to the Principles of Morals and Legislation (CW)*, ed. J. H. Burns and H. L. A. Hart, With a New Introduction by F. Rosen (Oxford 1996), p. 11. Henceforth *IPML (CW)*.

practical application of the utility principle in the areas of civil law, penal law, judicial procedure, legislative 'reward', constitutional law, 'political tactics' (the mode of functioning in political assemblies), international law, finance, political economy, and 'universal jurisprudence' (a complete plan of a body of laws).[8] As a first principle used to establish everything else, the utility principle was not itself subject to proof: 'that which is used to prove everything else, cannot itself be proved: a chain of proofs must have their commencement somewhere'.[9] On the other hand, Bentham thought there to be sufficient testimony to the fact that it has always been generally accepted as the standard of right and wrong: 'By the natural constitution of the human frame, on most occasions of their lives men in general embrace this principle, without thinking of it: if not for the ordering of their own actions, yet for the trying of their own actions, as well as of those of other men.'[10] In the first two chapters of *IPML* Bentham put forward considerations designed to show that the utility principle is the only external standard of right of wrong which reasonable men could accept, and discarded a wide range of alternative principles and standards as capricious and just so many ways of avoiding appeal to an external common standard. The following are all peremptorily dismissed as deficient by comparison with utility: 'moral sense', 'common sense', 'understanding', 'rule of right', 'fitness of things', 'law of nature' (including 'law of reason', 'right reason', 'natural justice', 'natural equity', 'good order'), 'truth', 'doctrine of election', and the 'theological principle'.[11]

Two other features of Bentham's usage of the principle of utility in *IPML* are worth noting.[12] First, by this foundational principle Bentham meant to refer to a feeling or sentiment which served to approve the utility of an action. As he put it,

> The principle here in question may be taken from an act of the mind; a sentiment; a sentiment of approbation; a sentiment which, when applied to an action, approves of its utility, as that quality of it by which the measure of approbation or disapprobation bestowed upon it ought to be governed.[13]

Second, utility meant public utility, and the utility of the individual was that part of public utility in which the individual shared. Thus a person

---

[8]   Bentham, *IPML* (*CW*), pp. 5–6.
[9]   Bentham, *IPML* (*CW*), p. 13.
[10] Bentham, *IPML* (*CW*), p. 13.
[11] Bentham, *IPML* (*CW*), pp. 26–27 note, and 31; for the adherents to each of these alternative principles see the editorial notes in *IPML* (*CW*).
[12] For which see Bentham, *IPML* (*CW*), introduction by F. Rosen, p. liii, and D. G. Long, ' "Utility" and the "Utility Principle": Hume, Smith, Bentham, Mill', *Utilitas*, ii (1990), pp. 35–36.
[13] Bentham, *IPML* (*CW*), p. 12 note.

approved of an action or law (attached to it the 'sentiment of approbation') according to the degree to which the happiness of all the individuals involved in it is advanced. For Bentham, the relationship between happiness and pleasure and pain, mankind's 'two sovereign masters',[14] is straight-forward and does not require elaboration: pleasure contributes to happiness, while pain detracts from it. In these terms the public interest is constituted of the aggregate of individual interests, construed in terms of the balance of pleasures and pains experienced by each person: 'A thing is said to promote the interest, or to be *for* the interest, of an individual, when it tends to add to the sum total of his pleasures: or, what comes to the same thing, to diminish the sum total of his pains.'[15]

By the time the second edition of *A Fragment on Government* appeared in 1823 Bentham's preferred usage was 'the greatest happiness principle', having found the 'utility principle' and 'the greatest happiness of the greatest number' phrases subject to interpretations at odds with his original intention (although he continued to use both phrases on occasion).[16] He explained his difficulties with the phrase 'utility principle':

> The word *utility* does not so clearly point to the ideas of *pleasure* and *pain* as the words *happiness* and *felicity* do: nor does it lead us to the consideration of the *number*, of the interests affected: to the number, as being the circumstance which contributes, in the largest proportion, to the formation of the standard here in question; the *standard of right and wrong*, by which alone the propriety of human conduct, in every situation, can with propriety be tried.
>
> The want of a sufficiently manifest connection between the ideas of *happiness* and *pleasure* on the one hand, and the idea of *utility* on the other, I have every now and then found operating, and with but too much efficiency, as a bar to the acceptance, that might otherwise have been given, to this principle.'[17]

The gist of this explanation was reiterated at greater length in 1829, when Bentham turned his hand to relating the history of the utility principle in the 'Article on Utilitarianism'.[18] Despite the difficulties, however, on this occasion he states his preference for the term 'utility' due to its conjugates

---

[14] Bentham, *IPML* (CW), p. 11.

[15] Bentham, *IPML* (CW), p. 12.

[16] See Bentham, FRAG (CW), 2nd edn. 1823, *passim*.

[17] Bentham, FRAG (CW), Ch. I, sec. 48, p. 446, note z.

[18] Bentham alludes to misinterpretations of the utility principle and of the phrase 'the greatest happiness of the greatest number' in 'Article on Utilitarianism: Long Version' (1829), in *Deontology, together with A Table of the Springs of Action and the Article on Utilitarianism* (CW), ed. Amnon Goldworth (Oxford 1983), pp. 296–97. In particular, he discusses the problems associated with the potential exclusion of minority interests under the phrase 'the greatest happiness of the greatest number' (pp. 309–10).

'utilitarian' and 'utilitarianism': ' "utilitarian" for the class of persons by whom the principle is embraced and recognised as the source of right and wrong; "utilitarianism" for the system embraced in the doctrine taught by those same persons. From the locution, or say denomination, "the greatest happiness principle", no word to answer these two purposes can be deduced.'[19]

In line with Bentham's account, the religious moralists represented in this volume qualify as 'utilitarians': they held that the standard of right or wrong is general happiness and that actions are approved or disapproved depending on the degree and distribution of happiness produced; they construed general happiness in terms of the aggregate happiness of individuals; and they located the motivation to virtue in personal happiness. However, these moralists cannot be described as adherents of 'utilitarianism', if by that term is meant a radical legislative program of reform. 'Utilitarians' then, but not advocates of 'utilitarianism'.

The most notable religious utilitarians of the eighteenth century were John Gay (1699–1745), John Brown (1715–66), Soame Jenyns (1704–87), Edmund Law (1703–87), Abraham Tucker (1705–74), and William Paley (1743–1805). Gay, Brown, Law and Paley were each ordained clergy. All were educated at Cambridge, except Tucker, a lawyer educated at Merton College, Oxford. Gay, Brown, Jenyns, and Law were near contemporaries at Cambridge, and among their colleagues they could count David Hartley, Daniel Waterland, John Jortin, and Francis Blackburne. Hartley is an important figure in the development of utilitarian theory. He was acquainted with Gay at Cambridge, and tells us that Gay inspired him to examine 'the power of Association' and 'the Possibility of deducing all our intellectual Pleasures and Pains from Association'.[20] Though it was Hartley's more sophisticated and generalised version of the theory of association which came into philosophical currency in the second half of the eighteenth century, both Law and Tucker traced its origins to Gay (and before him to Locke). Brown and Law knew Gay's work and recommended it. Paley learnt from both Law and Tucker, dedicated his *Principles of Moral and Political Philosophy* (1785) to the first, and made a special point of acknowledging the work of the second. The philosophical and theological connections between these thinkers are extensive and clearly mark them off as adherents of a distinctive school.

There were earlier progenitors of this approach to morality.[21] In *De*

---

[19] 'Article on Utilitarianism: Long Version', in *Deontology* (*CW*), p. 300.

[20] David Hartley, *Observations on Man* (in two parts, London 1749), i. preface, pp. iii, v.

[21] The rudiments of the religious utilitarian view of the motivation supplied by the after-life are found in Locke's *Essay concerning Human Understanding* (Bk. II, Ch. 21, secs. 38 and 70), but it is hardly developed by him. Even so it is a fact of some interest that Locke ultimately failed to live up to the promise of his own maxim that 'Reason must be our last judge in everything' (Bk. IV, Ch. 19, sec. 14), to recommend a morality based on faith and revelation. See A. P. Brogan, 'John Locke and Utilitarianism', *Ethics*, 69/2 (1959), p. 87.

Legibus Naturæ Disquisitio Philosophica (1672) Richard Cumberland (1631–1718) defined right action in terms of the promotion of 'the greatest common good' of all rational beings (including God) and, against Hobbes, posited the notion that human nature was as much benevolent as it was self-interested. Cumberland raised the edict to pursue the common good (encompassing the happiness of the individual as well as the happiness of others) to the status of a natural law, for which there are divine punishments for non-compliance and rewards for compliance. In this scheme, however, it is the necessity of natural law which drives morality not the individual's motivation to seek his own personal happiness.[22] George Berkeley (1685–1753), the Bishop of Cloyne, set out the basic tenets of the religious version in his sermon *Passive Obedience, or the Christian Doctrine of not Resisting the Supreme Power, Proved and Vindicated upon the Principles of the Law of Nature* (1712), and in *An Essay Towards Preventing the Ruine of Great Britain* (1721) he surveyed the vice, recklessness, flippancy, and irreligion which he everywhere beheld with a predictable despondency, and bemoaned the absence of the discipline provided by religious belief.[23] However, Berkeley's moral theory is not unambiguous since he occasionally assumed the social nature of man *a priori*.[24] Joseph Butler (1692–1752), in 'Three Essays on Human Nature' (1726) and 'A Dissertation on the Nature of Virtue' (1736),[25] also outlined a rudimentary version of the doctrine, but argued that the consideration of consequences ought not to guide morality. Rather, the limitations of our knowledge require that we depend on the guidance provided by God's commands and the innate directions of 'conscience'; a utilitarian concern for happiness could not be taken to be the sole, or even the primary, principle of morality.

Other eighteenth-century moralists offered renditions of the basic principles of the religious version of utilitarian theory. Further into the eighteenth century Thomas Rutherforth set forth certain elements of the theory in his *Essay on the Nature and Obligations of Virtue* (1744), followed shortly after by James Long in *An Enquiry Into the Origins of the Human Appetites and Affections* (1747).[26] And, two years later, Josiah

---

22 See the excerpts from Cumberland's *De Legibus Naturæ* in *British Moralists 1650–1800*, 2 vols., ed. D. D. Raphael (1969; reprt. Indianapolis 1991), i. 79–102, and for a discussion see Linda Kirk, *Richard Cumberland and Natural Law* (Cambridge 1987).

23 Both essays are included in *The Works of George Berkeley, Bishop of Cloyne*, 9 vols., ed. A. A. Luce and T. E. Jesson (London 1948–57). Berkeley's gloomy forebodings in the second of these essays were later echoed by John Brown in *An Estimate of the Manners and Principles of the Times*, 2 vols. (London 1757, 1758).

24 Ernest Albee, *A History of English Utilitarianism* (1901; reprt. London 1957), p. 68.

25 Joseph Butler, 'Three Essays on Human Nature' in *Fifteen Sermons* (London 1726), and 'Dissertation on the Nature of Virtue,' in *The Analogy of Religion, Natural and Revealed, to the Constitution and Course of Nature. To which are added two brief Dissertations: I. Of Personal Identity. II. Of the Nature of Virtue* (London 1736).

26 For Rutherforth see Jacob Viner, *The Role of Providence in the Social Order: An Essay in Intellectual History* (Princeton 1972), pp. 71–73; for James Long see Paul McReynolds (ed.) *Four Early Works on Motivation* (Gainesville, FL 1969), introduction.

Tucker announced in *Two Dissertations on Certain Passages of Holy Scripture* (1749) that the 'master key' to the principles of government was a proper understanding of the distinction between individual entitlements and the public good. However, Tucker was less interested in questions of morality *per se*, and rather more concerned to establish the view that the magistrate was placed by God under a moral obligation to promote the public good.[27]

In contrast to these moralists, the religious utilitarians consistently employed the utilitarian language of happiness and its component parts. From Locke's *Essay concerning Human Understanding* (1690) they learnt that it is considerations of pleasure and pain that provide men with the impulse to action, and to this they added that the criterion of virtue is the standard of general happiness.[28] They all adhered to the hedonist psychology according to which individuals are motivated by considerations of pleasure and pain, and they were consequentialists who defined right conduct in terms of the resulting benefits which accrue to society. Necessarily, therefore, they were concerned with the problem of moral choice and with the best means to ensure the moral end of happiness in civil society. Moreover, they recognized the potential for conflict between interests in social and political life. It is the religious solution they offered to this potential conflict which distinguishes them. But by no means should this lead to doubts about their commitment to empiricism or their practical intent. Nor did they sacrifice logic for mysticism. Religion provided them with a solution to the problem of the harmonization of interests which (to use Halévy's sociological terminology) is neither 'natural' in the sense of an 'unintended consequence' or 'by-product' of individuals pursuing their own personal advantage, nor 'artificial' by which I mean the result of legislation ordering the actions of primarily self-interested citizens. The religious principle convinced them they had bridged the gap between self-interest and social interest, thereby solving one of the pivotal problems of eighteenth-century ethics. To the regulating agencies of providence without Church and legislation without divinity, they opposed a philosophy based on Christian beliefs and a recognition of the importance of the Established Church for the teaching of those beliefs. In sum, the general happiness is the criterion of virtue, the agent's own greatest happiness is the motive to the pursuit of virtue, and futurity provides the connecting link between

[27] Josiah Tucker, *Two Dissertations on Certain Passages of Holy Scripture* (London 1749); see also *Sermons on Political and Commercial Subjects, in Four Tracts with two Sermons* (Gloucester 1774) and *A Treatise Concerning Civil Government* (London 1781). For a discussion see Gregory I. Molivas, 'The Influence of Utilitarianism on Natural Rights Doctrines', *Utilitas*, 9/2 (1997), pp. 183–202, esp. pp. 184–85.

[28] See Brogan, 'John Locke and Utilitarianism', p. 79, where he argues that Locke formulated the basic theses of eighteenth-century utilitarianism. However, Brogan assumes that utilitarian ethics in the century after Locke was all of a kind, and that John Gay and others simply 'took Locke's theses and organized them into a systematic presentation'.

the two. There are two elements to the role of futurity in the account: on the one hand, individuals must consider their own happiness in this life *and* in the life to come and act accordingly, and on the other hand there is an accounting by God, with the rewards and penalties of the afterlife computed in proportion to the contribution each person has made to fulfilling the divine benevolent will and adding to the greatest happiness of others.

There are other elements of the writings of the religious utilitarians which encompass important 'secular' concepts and themes in the history of utilitarian thought: (1) the idea of virtue as a compound or mixed idea derived from Locke; (2) the habitual way in which individuals act in terms of the Hartleian conception of the association of ideas; (3) the importance of habit (or the consequential tendencies of actions) as the foundation of 'rule utilitarianism'; (4) the delineation of the sources of obligation in terms of natural, moral, civil or political, and religious sanctions; and (5) a general critique of competing moral theories, especially the arguments of the 'sentimentalists' (Shaftesbury and Hutcheson) and 'intellectualists' (Clarke and Wollaston). All these features are present in Gay's 'Preliminary Dissertation. Concerning the Fundamental Principle of Virtue or Morality' (1731) and exist in varying degrees of prominence in the work of the other religious utilitarians.

2

In the short, but influential 'Preliminary Dissertation' John Gay set out to discuss the two issues which divide 'Writers of Morality': (1) the '*Criterion of Virtue, viz.* what it is which denominates any Action virtuous', and (2) 'the *Principle* or Motive by which Men are induced to pursue Virtue'. (33)[29] He defined virtue as 'the Conformity to a Rule of Life, directing the Actions of all rational Creatures with respect to each other's Happiness; to which Conformity every one in all Cases is obliged: and every one that does so conform, is or ought to be approved of, esteemed and loved for so doing.' (37)[30] The idea of virtue 'includes either tacitly or expressly, not only the Idea of *Approbation* as the Consequence of it; but also that it is to every one, and in all Circumstances, an object of *Choice* . . .' (34)[31] Indeed, approbation and all other affections are 'finally resolvable into *Reason*, pointing out *private Happiness*' and 'whenever this end is not perceiv'd, they are to be accounted for from the *Association of Ideas*, and may properly enough be call'd *Habits*.' (35)[32] The issue to be resolved by moral theory is the apparent tension between the self-interested motive – '*the*

---

[29]   John Gay, 'Preliminary Dissertation. Concerning the Fundamental Principle of Virtue or Morality', prefixed to William King, *Essay on the Origin of Evil* [*De origine mali*, 1702], trans. Edmund Law (London 1731), p. xi. Henceforth 'Preliminary Dissertation'. Page numbers given in brackets () are references to the present volume (hence 33).

[30]   'Preliminary Dissertation,' p. xvii.

[31]   'Preliminary Dissertation', p. xiii.

[32]   'Preliminary Dissertation', p. xiv.

necessity of doing or omitting an Action in order to be happy' (37)[33] – and
the benevolent objective of morality. On the one hand, an action is said to
be right if it contributes to the happiness of others, while it is obligatory
only if it contributes to the happiness of the agent. The right action and the
action which is obligatory apparently coincide only through the religious
sanction (the hopes and fears related to the after-life).

Gay's starting point, then, is the essential benevolence of God who, by
his very nature, must will the happiness of his creatures. What men must
do is understand his will in order to know which actions promote the
happiness of mankind and thus what is morally required of them. Gay did
not explain how we can know the will of God, settling for the tautology
that God's benevolent will is manifest in his design for the general 'good
of mankind', thus pursuing this end *is* the will of God. However, in the
process of examining this question Gay anticipated two of the contributions
to the development of utilitarian moral theory most closely associated with
Bentham: (1) a statement of the four sanctions of morality (natural, virtuous, civil and religious), and (2) a view of happiness as the sum of
pleasures, between which only quantitative distinctions can be made.

3

The tenor of John Brown's remarks and choice of terminology in the second
of his three *Essays on the Characteristics of the Earl of Shaftesbury* (1751)
– 'On the Motives to Virtue, and the Necessity of Religious Principle' –
together with his own instruction to the reader to consult Gay's 'Preliminary
Dissertation' make the connection between their respective theories unquestionable.[34] Essentially, Brown follows Gay's manner of proceeding,
indicating the various definitions of virtue offered by others and the fact
that these stop short of grounding virtue in general happiness, before
considering the motive that truly obliges us to practice virtue. J. S. Mill
had exemplary praise for Brown's efforts (and for Soame Jenyns' similar
exposition of the utility principle),[35] and Albee declared Brown's essay 'in
some respects the best statement of the Utilitarian doctrine, from the distinctly theological point of view'.[36]

Despite their failure to define virtue, Brown held that in the writings of
previous moralists (he has in mind the 'moral sense' theorists, Shaftesbury
and Hutcheson, and the adherents of 'right reason', Clarke and Wollaston)
there were some indicators of its true nature, but that they were largely
obscured from view by a 'cloud of metaphysics'. Like Bentham, Brown

[33]   'Preliminary Dissertation,' p. xviii.
[34]   John Brown, 'On the Motives to Virtue, and the Necessity of Religious Principle', *Essays on the Characteristics of the Earl of Shaftesbury* (London 1751), pp. 109–239. Henceforth *Essays*.
[35]   J. S. Mill, 'Bentham' (1838), in *Collected Works of John Stuart Mill*, ed. J. M. Robson (Toronto 1969), x. 86–87.
[36]   Albee, *English Utilitarianism*, p. 90.

argued that as soon as moralists come to particulars they have no option but to have recourse to the standard of utility; they are inevitably forced to introduce the notion of happiness as integral to the characterization of actions. (62–64)[37] Brown's conclusion, for which he finds corroborating evidence in the work of the moralists he criticized; is that we cannot characterize an action without relating it to some external standard. It is the tendency of an action to produce happiness or misery, good or evil, which is the substance of this standard. Hence it is the nature of the effect or consequence of an action which gives us the idea of its beauty, fitness, truth or virtue and their opposites – terms which in themselves cannot provide the criterion whereby we universally evaluate the morality of actions. Indeed, 'common sense' has always shown us that the notion of virtue has never been fixed to any action, save where the tendency to produce happiness is apparent. (64)[38] Actions are classified as immoral when they afflict mankind, and they are considered virtuous when they facilitate the happiness of mankind. By this manner of reasoning Brown was led to define virtue as ' "the Conformity of our Affections with the public Good:" Or "the voluntary Production of the greatest Happiness." ' (65)[39]

But why is man obliged to practise virtue? The idea of obligation Brown thought was as much confounded by the moralists as the idea of virtue itself. What great purpose is served by claiming that we are obliged to pursue virtue because it is beautiful or good in itself, or because virtue is what is true, agreeable to nature or to the nature of things? All we gain from these is ' "that there is some Reason or other why we ought to practise Virtue; but that the particular Reason doth not appear, not withstanding all this refined Pomp of Affirmation." ' The only motive which can oblige us to practise virtue ' "must be the *Feeling* immediate, or the *Prospect* of future *private Happiness*" '. (74)[40] Brown expressed the classical utilitarian conception of motive: 'In one Sense a *Motive* is called *disinterested*; when it consists in a pure *benevolent* Affection, . . . In another, no Motive is *disinterested*: For even in acting according to these Impulses of Benevolence and Conscience, we gratify an Inclination, and act upon the Principle or *immediate Feeling* of *private Happiness*.' (74–75)[41] This observation lies at the heart of utilitarian ethics. It is the foundation upon which Brown based his view that the only motive to virtue is the immediate feeling or prospect of private happiness. For ' "a Motive, from its very Nature, must be something that affects *ourself*" ', and can that which affects ourself be anything

---

[37] *Essays*, ii. 129–32.
[38] *Essays*, ii. 133.
[39] *Essays*, ii. 136–37. The two parts of the definition do not have the same meaning, but Brown ignored the discrepancy.
[40] *Essays*, ii. 159.
[41] *Essays*, ii. 161.

other than 'the Feeling or Prospect of *Pleasure* or *Pain, Happiness* or *Misery?*' (75)[42]

This, of course, does not settle the matter of obligation; it only brings the problem into sharper focus. For, if the public or general happiness is the great object of virtue, how can this be pursued by men who are motivated to act solely by considerations of their own well being? Following Gay, Brown sought to solve the consequentialist dilemma of reconciling or harmonizing interests by invoking the Christian belief in the after-life with its accompanying hopes and fears. Religion provides the solution to the puzzle of how a person can will something which apparently conflicts with his personal interest, but which is for the good or benefit of others. The religious principle for Brown has two branches, the first of which is 'fear'. His defence of this aspect of religion against the insinuations of Shaftesbury is of little interest. Fear, and specifically the fear of divine punishment, being the passion which all men have the capacity to feel, constitutes the lowest base from which all men could begin to live the life of virtue. Even so, says Brown, there is nothing slavish in this; rather it 'implies a lively and habitual Belief, that we shall be hereafter miserable, if we disobey [God's] Laws', and this does no more than induce 'a *rational Sense*' of evil and the determination to avoid it. (95)[43] Of more interest is Brown's elucidation of the second branch of the religious principle since it is here that the positive character of the motive to virtuous action which Christianity supplies is to be found. This branch of the principle is ' "the Hope and Prospect of higher Degrees of future Happiness and Perfection:" . . .' (95)[44] To understand fully what Brown meant by this his theological position as a defender of orthodox beliefs must be borne in mind. Among the faithful of the day the spiritual dimension of the perfection of the soul was commonly held to be integral to the idea of personal happiness in its most encompassing sense. In Brown's Christian version of the utilitarian doctrine temporal happiness joined hands with the eternal happiness of the soul in pursuit of the ideal, the perfect harmony of virtue and happiness. For,

'Man is never so sincerely or heartily *benevolent*, as when he is truly happy in himself.' Thus the high Consciousness of his being numbered among the Children of GOD, and that his Lot is among the Saints; that he is destined to an endless Progression of Happiness, and to rise from high to higher Degrees of Perfection, must needs inspire him with that Tranquillity and Joy, which will naturally diffuse itself in Acts of sincere Benevolence to all his Fellow-Creatures, . . . (97)[45]

---

[42] *Essays*, ii. 163.
[43] *Essays*, ii. 214.
[44] *Essays*, ii. 215.
[45] *Essays*, ii. 221.

Only when man 'is truly happy in himself' can he be expected to progress in ever greater degrees toward perfection, and it is religious consciousness which affords man this happy disposition, making his own perfection and his contribution to the happiness of mankind possible. Neither happiness nor perfection on this view can be said to be the primary consideration for the true Christian, but each is essential for the possibility of the other. As Brown put it in the third of his essays on Shaftesbury, 'On Revealed Religion and Christianity',

> the whole *Weight* and *Energy* of the *Gospel* is employed in inforcing [sic] the Idea of *moral Perfection*, of our *nobler* SELF, of Self-Interest in the *higher* Sense, of the Necessity of extirpating every meaner Passion, and cherishing the great one of *unbounded Love*, as the necessary and only Discipline that can qualify us for future Happiness.[46]

Hence it is not that religion merely promises an extension or rectification of human justice, nor that the rewards and punishments of futurity are simply an addition to the imperfect rewards and punishments established by civil society. There is a specifically religious aspect which cannot be accounted for in such terms, something over and above the religious sanction which imparts to the doctrines of Christianity an undeniable efficacy. It is a spiritual quality which has nothing to do with visions or ecstasies, but everything to do with the will to be and to do good. The notion of posthumous rewards and punishments provides an aid to this moral endeavour, but it is in religion in its positive role – that which prompts a man not merely to refrain from evil but actually to do good, to love his fellow men and thus progress on the path to perfection – that the Christian finds himself most fully in accord with God's benevolent will.

While the rare few do not need the sanctions of religion, the rewards promised and the penalties threatened, to prompt them to practise virtue, to fulfil God's purpose, most men in their present condition of life are incapable of extensive benevolence. Because providence has not afforded every man this boon the Church, in its role as educator and moral guide, is an indispensable feature of social life. In the case of those who have made little progress in morality the teachings of Christianity are necessarily required for further progress. In religion, therefore, morality finds its chief agent of support.

4

Soame Jenyns' *A Free Inquiry into the Nature and Origin of Evil* (1757) gained notoriety through the celebrated review by Samuel Johnson in the

---

[46] *Essays*, iii. 329.

Literary Magazine.[47] Much of Jenyns' volume is devoted to the attempt to show that 'natural' evils are not real evils but rather the necessary inconveniences of God's benevolent order, which is described in hierarchical terms as a 'vast Chain, descending by insensible degrees from infinite perfection to absolute nothing.' (118)[48] The theory of optimism received prominence in William King's *Essay on the Origin of Evil* (1731; Latin edn. 1702),[49] which probably inspired Alexander Pope's *Essay on Man* (1733, 1734). As Jenyns' biographer has said, the *Inquiry* was 'one of numerous English theodicies adopting the notion that in spite of the presence of evil, this is indeed the best of all possible worlds, . . .'[50] In these terms, given God's benevolence and omnipotence, evil must serve a greater good. Beyond this Jenyns set out to erect a 'rational system of Ethicks'.[51] Johnson objected to the general tenor and substance of Jenyns' theory of evil, but begrudgingly recommended its ethics.[52] It might be noted, however, that Jenyns' recourse to the dictates of 'fate' as the basis for uncomplaining acceptance of one's lot in life in the expectation of future reward, epitomised the complacency Bentham found so anathema in the union between religion and the utility principle in moral theory.

Despite Jenyns' theological meanderings through the maze of evil, he is clear on the moral score. His consequentialism is expounded in similar terms to Gay's and Brown's. Actions should be judged virtuous or vicious, good or evil, based on their effects: 'It is the consequences . . . of all human actions that must stamp their value. So far as the general practice of any action tends to produce Good and introduce happiness into the world, so far we may pronounce it virtuous; so much Evil as it occasions, such is the degree of vice it contains.' (123)[53] The individual's motivation to pursue virtue is located in the prospect of his own personal happiness: 'happiness is the only real thing of value in existence,' everything else gains its importance 'as they contribute to its production,' and riches, power, wisdom, learning, strength, beauty, virtue, religion, 'even life itself' is 'desirable only

[47] *The Works of Samuel Johnson*, 11 vols. (Oxford 1825), vi. 47–76. Soame Jenyns, *A Free Inquiry into the Nature and Origin of Evil* (London 1757). Henceforth *Inquiry*.
  Leslie Stephen was highly critical of Jenyns' *Inquiry*: 'That this trifling should ever have been taken for an argument is rather surprising; and, in fact, it is chiefly memorable now for having given occasion to Johnson's celebrated review'; *History of English Thought in the Eighteenth Century*, 2 vols. (1876; 3rd edn. 1902; reprt. New York 1949), i. 388.
[48] *Inquiry*, p. 65. Arthur Lovejoy noted Jenyns' significance as a believer in the Great Chain of Being who tried to alleviate the consequences 'of the principle of continuity by dwelling upon the many degrees of intelligence found *within* the human species'; *The Great Chain of Being: A Study of the History of an Idea* (Cambridge, Mass. 1936), p. 197.
[49] See above note 29.
[50] Ronald Rompkey, *Soame Jenyns* (Boston 1984), p. 135.
[51] *Inquiry*, p. 2.
[52] Johnson refers to Jenyns' description of the 'chain of being' as 'little more than a paraphrase of Pope's epistles, or, yet less than a paraphrase, a mere translation of poetry into prose.' *Works*, vi. 49.
[53] *Inquiry*, p. 85.

as they tend to promote it.' (113)[54] Thus, assuming God's benevolent will, 'pain abstractly considered must have its uses' and 'those uses must be of the highest importance, tho' we have no faculties to conceive them.' (117)[55] It is only reasonable, Jenyns argues, to assume the existence of a future life, the doctrine of 'transmigration', and the proportionate adjustment of happiness commensurate with the past actions of men, the misery and happiness they have experienced in their temporal existence, and their contributions to virtue. (120)[56] The present life is 'the probation of Mankind,' affording men an opportunity to demonstrate their goodness in preparation for the life to come. It is in this respect a 'test of our obedience' to God's will. (123, 124)[57] Jenyns was the first of the religious utilitarians to posit a proportionate account of rewards and punishments in the afterlife as consistent with God's design, and was followed in this by both Tucker and Paley.

The difference between morality and religion is that 'Morality obliges Men to live honestly and soberly, because such behaviour is most conducive to publick happiness, and consequently to their own,' while religion enjoins men to the same course of action 'because [it is] conformable to the will of their Creator.' (124)[58] In this formulation the individual's personal happiness is the consequence of virtue, that is the performance of actions which serve the public happiness. But merit depends on faith in God and in his benevolent will. On this view of the matter moral action without faith is 'but wisdom, prudence, or good œconomy,' but does not merit God's reward. (124)[59] In this way Christianity stands alone among religions in setting 'in a right light these two material points, the Essence and the End of Virtue.' (124)[60] Law argued similarly, though Tucker objected to this caveat on the nature of 'good' actions.

5

Edmund Law's moral theory is essentially contained in his short essay 'On Morality and Religion', which immediately follows Gay's 'Preliminary Dissertation' at the front of the 1758 edition of King's *Essay on the Origin of Evil*. In a second short essay included in the same volume, entitled 'The Nature and Obligations of man, As a sensible and rational Being', Law explicitly referred to Gay's use of the associationist psychology (which he noted was derived from Locke, of whom he was a great admirer), and like

---

[54] *Inquiry*, p. 46.
[55] *Inquiry*, p. 62.
[56] *Inquiry*, pp. 74–75.
[57] *Inquiry*, pp. 88, 89.
[58] *Inquiry*, p. 90.
[59] *Inquiry*, p. 90.
[60] *Inquiry*, p. 91; see also pp. 154–60.

Brown, Tucker, and Paley, developed this aspect in his own work.[61] He was clear that the attainment of happiness and the avoidance of misery is the natural and reasonable end of 'a *Sensible* Being'. (147)[62] Further, Law was clear that the happiness of a person is the aggregate balance of his pleasures and pains, and made this reckoning a more transparent element of his theory than did Gay, Brown, Jenyns or Tucker. (142)[63] He defined virtue as '*The doing Good to Mankind, in Obedience to the Will of God, and for the Sake of everlasting Happiness.*' (153)[64] However, of all the religious utilitarians, Law presents us with the most extreme statement of the relation between religion and morality. Indeed, in the process of expounding it, he came very near to denying the basic consequential character of utilitarian ethics. For he wrote that if any actions 'are done for Profit, Honour, or out of mere Humour, nay not of the most disinterested Benevolence itself; so long as there is no Regard had to the Deity in them, they cannot be reckoned strictly Virtuous, nor claim a Place in Morals or Religion'. (153)[65] No other utilitarian moralist, with the possible exception of Jenyns, was prepared to go to this length to maintain the relation between religion and morality.

Law's view of the relationship between religion and utility reflects the text of Article XIII of the Thirty-nine Articles, 'Of Works before Justification,' which reads:

> Works done before the grace of Christ, and the Inspiration of his Spirit, are not pleasant to God, forasmuch as they spring not of faith in Jesus Christ, neither do they make men meet to receive grace, or (as the School-authors say) deserve grace of congruity: yea rather, for that they are not done as God hath willed and commanded them to be done, we doubt not but they have the nature of sin.[66]

This article always caused problems for Anglican theologians troubled by the apparently rigid distinction it draws between the actions of good and conscientious non-Christians and the actions of Christian believers.[67] Law, who wrote a tract arguing for a relaxation of the terms of subscription to the Articles,[68] seems to have understood Article XIII literally, and founded

[61] Edmund Law, 'On Morality and Religion' and 'The Nature and Obligations of Man, as a sensible and rational Being', prefixed to William King, *An Essay on the Origin of Evil*, 4th edn. (Cambridge 1758), xliii–lx.

[62] 'On Morality and Religion', p. xliii.

[63] 'The Nature and Obligations of Man', p. lv.

[64] 'On Morality and Religion', p. lii.

[65] 'On Morality and Religion', p. li.

[66] E. J. Bicknell, *A Theological Introduction to the Thirty-nine Articles of the Church of England* (1919; 3rd edn. rev. H. J. Carpenter, London 1955), pp. 207–8.

[67] Bicknell, *Thirty-nine Articles*, p. 208 note.

[68] Edmund Law, *Considerations on the Propriety of Requiring a Subscription to Articles of Faith* (Cambridge 1774).

his moral theory upon its central tenet: it is faith in Christ and obedience to His will that makes an action good in the sight of God. Thus, benevolence divorced from religious considerations will not bring the reward of God's grace and, therefore, not affect a person's prospects in the next life.

6

Abraham Tucker's *The Light of Nature Pursued* (1768, 1778) is a massive tome, which ranges across a broad canvas of philosophical and theological topics, sometimes returning to subjects already dealt with in other contexts, and interspersed with much anecdotal illustration and a few very odd visionary digressions.[69] In the realm of moral theory Tucker argued that both reason and revelation direct us to the pursuit of happiness, and the good of the individual is best pursued through actions designed to enhance the general good. Though Tucker recognized the practical and theoretical value of the sanction of religion to morality, he did not consider that calculations of rewards and punishments, immediate or in prospect, were indispensable to moral action. Heaven, Tucker explained, is that 'universal bank, wherein accounts are regularly kept, and every man debited or credited for the least farthing he takes out or brings in' (193),[70] but the good man will rarely need to entertain thoughts of futurity. Much like Brown, he explained that faith in the doctrines of Christianity will naturally awaken that disposition which disregards personal advantage in favour of the 'greater general good'. (174)[71] Aided by the belief in the immortality of the soul and the knowledge that it is God's will that we pursue the happiness of others, in time this happiness will itself become as much an object of our desire as our own happiness. Reason and religion lead to the same conclusion: God's commands 'terminate in two principal aims: to bring us into a hearty desire of one another's happiness equally with our own, and to inspire us with such just sentiments of himself as conduce most to our happiness.'[72]

In sum, Tucker's position is this: all action is directed by the idea of personal 'satisfaction' or pleasure, all satisfaction is one and the same in kind, moral notions are rooted in self-interested motives, general good is to be understood as the aggregate of happiness, virtue is rooted in 'prudence' (by which is meant the habit of weighing distant good and expedience in a fair balance with present pleasure), and it is the interest

---

[69] Abraham Tucker, *The Light of Nature Pursued*, first published in seven volumes (1768, 1778) under the pseudonym 'Edward Search'. A corrected 2nd edn. in 7 vols., with A life of Tucker by H. P. St John Mildmay (London, 1805), was reprinted in 2 vols. in 1834, and several times following. I quote from the 1834 reprt. of the 1805 edn. Henceforth *Light of Nature*.

[70] *Light of Nature*, i. 621.

[71] *Light of Nature*, i. 268.

[72] *Light of Nature*, i. 669.

in futurity which largely accounts for actions seemingly not based in considerations of temporal happiness.

Though he acknowledged Hartley's formulation of the theory of association, Tucker says he first learnt of it from Locke,[73] of whom he wrote 'I am so averse to differing from Mr. Locke, that whenever I cannot bring my notions to tally with his, I hunt about for all expedients to reconcile them, so that I may hold my own consistently with those he entertains.'[74] Tucker preferred to use the term 'translation' rather than 'association', and deployed it to explain the generation of our opinions and judgements in moral matters, including the connection between the ideas of personal and public happiness, self-interest and benevolence.[75] However, it is in Tucker's account of 'human nature' that Locke's impact is most evident, particularly his discussions of (1) the division of the faculties into thought and will, (2) the passivity of the mind and the construction of belief based on external impressions and internal reflection on such impressions, and (3) the composition of motives and the nature of their relationship to action.

Tucker's main contribution to the development of utilitarian theory lies in his argument that there are good utilitarian reasons for guiding action by general rules, rather than each action being dependent on a calculation of its likely consequences. Moral decisions by and large best proceed via an adherence to general rules, thus avoiding the risk of miscalculation. This is more than a refinement of the position taken by Gay and Brown, since Tucker introduces the notion as an explicit aid to virtue (not merely an implied description of the habitual nature of actions which tend to produce happiness or good). As Quinton points out, Tucker differs from both Gay and Brown in holding that the value to be realised by an action can only be impressionistic (in most instances) and not the product of mechanical arithmetic.[76] As he put it:

the necessity of rules and principles for our direction gives rise to a new species of prudence, which could not have had Being, were we capable of taking all our measures upon a full knowledge of their expedience: for it is not enough to consider the usefulness of an action, but we must likewise take into account how far it may either confirm or weaken the influence of some wholesome rule; because more good or harm may be done that way than by any direct consequences of the things we do.[77]

In the main, Tucker has the rules of religion in mind (197–99),[78] but what

[73] *Light of Nature*, i. 95.
[74] *Light of Nature*, i. 51.
[75] *Light of Nature*, i. pp. 150–53.
[76] Quinton, *Utilitarian Ethics*, p. 25.
[77] *Light of Nature*, i. 667.
[78] *Light of Nature*, ii. 589–90.

he says is equally applicable to the rules of rectitude, honour and prudence. None are good in themselves, rather 'they are only measures tending to a good beyond, they are expedients to make up for our short-sightedness, and supply the place of reason.' (199)[79] It is not that the adherence to rules always supersedes the use of private judgement, since there are times when rules and principles conflict, forcing us to decide in favour of one or the other. Moreover, it is frequently necessary to judge the best manner in which to apply rules in particular situations. In both instances judgement is based on a utilitarian calculation. In general, however, when rules have grown familiar and the practice of them spontaneous they foster habitual ways of acting not requiring further reflection. Just as 'those who speak correctly never deviate from the rules of grammar, yet never are guided by them nor once think of them,' so it is with religion, morality and prudence, where we first submit to rules but in due time the mind is brought to a habitual adherence to their edicts. (201)[80]

7

Paley's *Principles of Moral and Political Philosophy* (1785) and Bentham's *IPML* were published within four years of each other and were contemporaneous in production, their content being based on ideas formed in the late 1760s and early 1770s and brought to fruition in the 1780s.[81] William Whewell, who thought the quantitative character of utilitarian ethics fundamentally misconceived, believed the systems of Paley and Bentham to be in principle the same.[82] However, in modern discussions of the history of utilitarian thought they are compared usually to stress the distinctions between them.[83] At the heart of Bentham's *IPML* is a path-breaking examination of the motivation behind human activity and the relationship between this and legislation. By contrast, Paley's *Principles* is a synthesis of competing moral theories, with their essential elements related to or transformed into considerations of utility, an approach which betrays its origins in his university lectures of 1766–76.

The *Principles* is a much more extensive work than that of Gay, Brown, Jenyns or Law, and it is much more focused than Tucker's rambling and repetitive volumes. However, Paley owned that he had drawn upon many different sources for the Cambridge lectures upon which the book is based,

---

[79] *Light of Nature*, ii. 591.
[80] *Light of Nature*, ii. 592.
[81] William Paley, *Principles of Moral and Political Philosophy* (1785; 2nd edn. corrected 1786), in *The Complete Works of William Paley*, 4 vols., ed. Robert Lynam (London 1825), ii. Henceforth *Principles*.
[82] William Whewell, 'Bentham', in *Lectures on the History of Moral Philosophy* (Cambridge 1862).
[83] T. P. Schofield, 'A Comparison of the Moral Theories of William Paley and Jeremy Bentham,' *The Bentham Newsletter*, 11 (1987), pp. 4–22; James E. Crimmins, 'Religion, Utility and Politics: Bentham versus Paley,' in James E. Crimmins (ed.), *Religion, Secularization and Politics Thought: Thomas Hobbes to J. S. Mill* (London 1990), pp. 130–52.

and he particularly acknowledged a debt to Tucker.[84] Paley's biographer has argued that Tucker's influence was less than Paley suggests. But this is not to dismiss Paley's profession of gratitude as altogether misleading, since he 'accepted Tucker's general thesis, that reason and revelation support one another, that both bid us to be happy, and that the good of the individual is best promoted by promoting the general good, and so increasing the general stock of happiness'.[85] To this we can add that while both men recognized the practical and theoretical value of the sanction of religion to morality, neither considered that calculations of rewards and punishments, immediate or in prospect, were indispensable to moral action.

Paley was also influenced by his patron Bishop Law, from whom he took his definition of virtue: '*the doing good to mankind, in obedience to the will of God, and for the sake of everlasting happiness.*' (221)[86] In this definition is contained the matter or content, the criterion or rule, and the ultimate end of virtuous action. But this does not mean that each virtuous action involves the consciousness that it is to be performed for any one of these considerations. Following Tucker, Paley pointed out that men deliberate on few occasions; they act more from habit than reflection. (222)[87] A man confirmed in good habits will act in a virtuous manner without any further consideration, 'without having either the good of mankind, the will of God, or everlasting happiness, in his thought'. (223)[88] It is his disposition which determines his actions, and if the precepts of religion be inculcated at an early age they cannot help but issue in good habits in later life. Paley treated the rules of utilitarian duty as a code of Divine Law, adequately supported by religious sanctions. The making explicit the centrality of rules to the doctrine of utility distinguished Paley's theory from Bentham's, in which (legislation aside) the idea of rules taking the place of calculation is implied but not explicitly developed.

In this respect Paley did not lose sight of the significance of individual autonomy, without which moral choices are rendered nugatory. There are sanctions (fear of Hell and hope of Heaven) which will no doubt influence us to 'be good', as Paley says, but there is no necessary relationship between these sanctions and the actions of individuals. We are placed in this world to prove our worth in the sight of God, but this would be meaningless without moral agency. Each of us is to fathom God's will (the general good of mankind) and fulfil it whenever we can; in this manner we aspire to true happiness. But this, the Anglican Divine Thomas Gisborne argued, is precisely the flaw in Paley's reasoning. Paley stressed the ability of individuals to discover what is best-judged to maximize the happiness of others,

---

[84] *Principles*, p. 10.
[85] M. L. Clarke, *Paley: Evidences for the Man* (Toronto 1974), p. 58.
[86] *Principles*, p. 38.
[87] *Principles*, p. 39.
[88] *Principles*, p. 41.

yet their faculties are simply inadequate for the task. So much so, in fact, that Paley's theory is just as likely to provide a sanction for conduct contrary to Christian teaching as it is to promote God's will. It is for this reason, Gisborne admonished his fellow theologue, that revelation should not be relegated from its position as the cardinal dictate in settling questions of morality; men need a surer guide to conduct than utility.[89] Paley's doctrine requires that individuals know the good to be sought, but his denial of a moral sense leaves them incapable of so knowing. Later on the Anglican Richard Whately seized on this objection to condemn all versions of utilitarian morality.[90]

The notion of a life after death, the cornerstone of Paley's moral thought in the *Principles*, is a recurring theme in his work. In *A View of the Evidences of Christianity* (1794) he claimed that the assurance of a future life was the primary object of revelation, and in the *Natural Theology* (1802) he wrote of life on earth as a state of probation, preparatory to another world, and several of his sermons focused on related questions.[91] Although Paley admitted that the belief in an after-life was strictly a matter of faith, it provided his ethics with a powerful moral sanction readily apprehended by his fellow men. The religious element clearly distinguished Paley's theory from Bentham's secular variant of the doctrine. There are two other differences worth noting.

If it was true that Paley based happiness on maximising pleasure and minimising pain, with pleasures differing only in terms of their duration and intensity, he was also prepared to distinguish pleasures which contributed to happiness and those, which through repetition and habit, did not ultimately contribute to a person's happiness. The 'pleasures of sense' fell into this category: 'the animal gratifications of eating, drinking, and that by which the species is continued' as well as 'the more refined pleasures of music, painting, architecture, gardening, splendid shows, theatric exhibitions; and the pleasures, lastly, of active sports, as of hunting, shooting, fishing, etc.' (214)[92] Pleasures which invariably produced happiness included the prudent development of habits and the maintenance of good health, the exercise of the social affections, and the exercise of one's faculties in the service of the public. (217–21)[93] Bentham made no such judgements as to which pleasures contributed to a person's happiness. He classified

---

[89]   Thomas Gisborne, *The Principles of Moral Philosophy investigated, and briefly applied to the Constitution of Civil Society: together with remarks on the 'Principle' assumed by Mr Paley as the Basis of all Moral Conclusions, and other positions of the same Author* (1789; 3rd edn, London 1795), Part I, Chs. III and V.

[90]   Richard Whately, *Introductory Lectures in Political Economy* (London 1831), pp. 21–24, 68. Whately first attacked Paley in *Elements of Logic, Comprising the Substance of the Article in the Encyclopedia Metropolitana: with Additions, etc.* (London 1826).

[91]   See esp. Paley, *Sermons on Several Subjects*, XXVII, XXVIII, XXXIV, and XXXV, and *Sermons on Public Occasions*, VI, in *Complete Works*, iv. 199–210, 248–58, 329–40.

[92]   *Principles*, p. 27.

[93]   *Principles*, pp. 32–38.

pleasures, including those of sense, as an essential preliminary to the calculation of the contributions of pleasures to a person's happiness.[94] In Rosen's
account (which I have followed above) this means that Paley did not
consistently adhere to an empirical understanding of what pleasures people
actually feel. Furthermore, Paley ignored the fact that pleasures and pains
may differ from time to time, place to place, and society to society.[95] In
taking this position Paley points us in the direction of John Stuart Mill's
later refinement of utilitarian theory in which pleasures could be qualitat-
ively distinguished one from another. For Bentham, unlike Paley,
calculations of utility were strictly based on empirical evidence, and it could
not be predetermined which pleasures advanced happiness and which did
not. Bentham was so committed to this element of his theory that in *IPML*
he acknowledged the efficacy of the pleasures of religion,[96] even though he
was vehemently critical of their influence on the choices individuals make.

A further difference between Paley and Bentham is the very different
political positions they derived from the general happiness principle. We
might have expected Paley, who believed that expediency was the measure
of the value of social institutions, to have found a good deal in contemporary Britain that could be improved. In fact his attitude toward
established institutions, like that of the other religious utilitarians, was in
essence that of a political (albeit Whig) conservative. To be sure, Paley did
not regard the constitution as sacrosanct, but he found little about either
its ecclesiastical or secular wings bad enough to require reform. In sermons,
in pamphlets, and in his major work on ethics and politics, the *Principles*,
he vigorously supported a host of established practices and institutions on
the grounds of utility.[97] John Austin, who had many good things to say
about Paley and his work and who was far from being a radical reformer
himself, was convinced that Paley's position in the Church encouraged 'a
deal of shabby sophistry in defence or extenuation of abuses which the few
are interested in upholding'. Austin believed these elements of the *Principles*
to be inconsistent with the 'steady pursuit of the consequences indicated
by *general* utility', and in this respect 'the book [was] unworthy of the
man'.[98]

8

Paley's rendering of the utilitarian theory was influential in his own day
and in the century following.[99] In addition to Gisborne and Whately, con-

---

[94]   Bentham, *IPML* (CW), pp. 42–50.
[95]   Bentham, *IPML* (CW), introduction by F. Rosen, p. lv.
[96]   Bentham, *IPML* (CW), Ch. III.
[97]   For Paley's politics see Crimmins, 'Religion, Utility and Politics: Bentham versus Paley',
       passim.
[98]   John Austin, *The Province of Jurisprudence Determined*, ed. Wilfrid E. Rumble (1832;
       Cambridge 1995), pp. 72–73.
[99]   See Paley below, pp. 209–11.

temporary critics of Paley included Dugald Stewart, Edward Pearson, and Thomas Brown.[100] Against all these critics Paley was ably defended by Latham Wainewright.[101] Whether they supported or refuted him, nineteenth-century thinkers had to take Paley's philosophy into account. Thomas Malthus subscribed to Paley's version of the doctrine that public happiness, being the object of God's beneficent design, is the ultimate test of moral obligation and all schemes of social improvement.[102] Those Unitarian dissenters most closely associated with the radicals in the movement for social and political reforms also saw Paley and not Bentham as the fountainhead of the utilitarian doctrine. Indeed, the moral thought of Thomas Belsham, William Jevons, and W. J. Fox represents a deliberate effort by the dissenters within the ranks of the radicals to retain the Christian dimension of utilitarian theory.[103] As a mark of Paley's popularity, Brown denounced the 'Paleyans' not the Benthamites. And when Coleridge flung out his anti-utilitarian barbs it was Paley rather than Bentham who was uppermost in his mind. Paley's doctrine he found 'neither tenable in reason nor safe in practice'.[104]

Mossner noted the establishment on Paley's philosophy of what amounted to 'a Benthamite School' at Trinity College, Cambridge, around 1830.[105] Two years later when Cambridge witnessed a scathing attack on the *Principles* by the Woodwardian Professor of Geology, Adam Sedgwick, in a lecture subsequently published as 'A Discourse on the Studies of the University' (1833), it provoked a sympathetic response from J. S. Mill. Mill, who disliked Paley and dismissed his utilitarianism as ill-conceived,

---

[100] Dugald Stewart, *Elements of the Philosophy of the Human Mind*, 3 vols. (London 1792, 1814, 1827), and *The Philosophy of the Active and Moral Powers of Man*, 2 vols. (Edinburgh and London 1828); Edward Pearson, *Remarks on the Theory of Morals, in which is Contained an Examination of the Theoretical Part of Dr. Paley's 'Principles of Moral and Political Philosophy'* (Ipswich 1800); and Thomas Brown, *Lectures on the Philosophy of the Human Mind*, 4 vols. (Edinburgh 1820).

[101] Latham Wainewright, *A Vindication of Dr. Paley's Theory of Morals From the Principal Objections of Dr. Dugald Stewart; Mr. Gisborne: Dr. Pearson: and Dr. Thomas Brown. With an Appendix, Containing Strictures on some Remarks of Dr. Whately* (London 1830).

[102] See T. R. Malthus, *An Essay on the Principle of Population; Or, A View of its Past and Present Effects on Human Happiness* (1798; 2nd edn. enlarged 1803), ed. Donald Winch (Cambridge 1992), pp. xiv–viii.

[103] Thomas Belsham, *Elements of Philosophy of the Human Mind and of Moral Philosophy* (London 1801); William Jevons, *Systematic Morality, or a Treatise on the Theory and Practice of Human Duty, on the Grounds of Natural Religion*, 2 vols. (London 1827); and W. J. Fox, *Christian Morality* (London 1833). Bentham is mentioned only in passing by Belsham and Jevons.

[104] *The Collected Works of Samuel Taylor Coleridge*, ed. Barbara E. Rooke (London and Princeton 1969) iv, Pt. I, p. 314. For the comments of other notable contemporaries see Clarke, *Paley*, p. 128.

[105] Ernest Campbell Mossner, *Bishop Butler and the Age of Reason: A Study in the History of Thought* (New York 1971), p. 202.

arbitrary and shallow,[106] nevertheless recorded that Sedgwick's lecture 'had as its most prominent feature an intemperate assault on analytic psychology and utilitarian ethics, in the form of an attack on Locke and Paley. This had excited great indignation in my father and others, which I thought it fully deserved'.[107] It is also worth noting the continuance in the nineteenth century of the basic elements of Paley's religious utilitarianism in Austin's *The Province of Jurisprudence Determined* (1832) and, in an attenuated form, in James Fitzjames Stephen's *Liberty, Equality, Fraternity* (1873).[108] In short, the substantial impact of Paley's work bears ample testimony to the influence of the theory he expounded, and which had been developed and disseminated down through the eighteenth century by Gay, Brown, Jenyns, Law, and Tucker.

---

[106] D. L. Lemahieu, *The Mind of William Paley: A Philosopher and his Age* (Lincoln 1976), p. 161.
[107] John Stuart Mill, *Autobiography*, ed. Jack Stillinger and John M. Robson, *Collected Works of John Stuart Mill* (Toronto 1981), i. 208.
[108] See the introduction to Part Two, pp. 271–73.

JOHN GAY

'Preliminary Dissertation. Concerning the
Fundamental Principle of Virtue or Morality' (1731)

John Gay (1699–1745)

Biographical Note

Not much is known about John Gay. He was descended from a yeoman family in Frithelstock, Devon. His father, James (1655–1720), became rector of Upton Pyne, Devon, after graduation from St. John's College, Cambridge, in 1677–78. John was the second son of James and his wife, Elizabeth Hooper (d. 1732). After a grammar school education in Devon, Gay entered Sidney Sussex College, Cambridge, as Blundell scholar in 1718, taking his BA in 1721 (MA 1725). Various other Devonshire Gay relatives attended Cambridge colleges in the late seventeenth and early eighteenth centuries, including the poet, John Gay. Ordained a priest in 1723, Gay was elected a fellow of Sidney Sussex in 1724, becoming lecturer in Greek, Hebrew and ecclesiastical history.

During Gay's residence at Cambridge a significant number of other notable philosophical and theological figures were also present: Daniel Waterland, Magdalene 1699, Master, 1714–40; John Jortin, Jesus 1715, Fellow 1721–28; Edmund Law, St John's 1721, Fellow of Christ's 1726–27, Master of Peterhouse, 1756–87; John Taylor, St John's 1721, Fellow 1726–52; Soame Jenyns, St John's 1722–24; Francis Blackburne, Jesus 1723, Fellow 1728; David Hartley, Jesus 1726, Fellow 1727–30; John Brown, St John's 1732; and Richard Bentley, the classical scholar, was Master of Trinity from 1700 on and became Regius Professor of Divinity in 1717.[1] As Greek lecturer, Gay may have been acquainted with Bentley. In 1732 Gay resigned his fellowship to become Vicar of Wilshampstead, Bedfordshire, and in 1739, Vicar of Hawnes. His wife was another Elizabeth by whom he had two sons and four daughters. Gay died on 18 July 1745, and was buried at Wilshampstead.

While at Cambridge Gay composed his celebrated 'Preliminary Dissertation. Concerning the Fundamental Principle of Virtue and Morality', which Edmund Law published as a preface to his translation of William King's *Essay on the Origin of Evil* (1731). David Hartley identified Gay, whom he knew well, as the author of the 'Preliminary Dissertation' in the preface to his *Observations on Man* (1749), and the attribution has remained unquestioned.

The impact of the 'Preliminary Dissertation' on the development of

---

[1]   John Venn and J. A. Venn (compilers), *Alumni Cantabrigienses. Biographical List of all known students . . . to 1900*, 10 vols., Pt 1, vol. 2: *From the Earliest Times to 1751* (Cambridge 1922), p. 160.

utilitarian theory is commonly acknowledged. It is generally agreed that Gay was 'the true founder of the new philosophy'.[2] Albee thought that 'the whole outline of Utilitarianism in its first complete and unencumbered form is to be found in Gay's Preliminary Dissertation'.[3] Cragg also argued that all the essentials of utilitarianism were in Gay's brief treatise. In a chain of thought which ran from Locke through Shaftesbury, Pope, Akenside and Gay, Cragg argued, utilitarianism became 'the characteristic moral doctrine of the century'.[4] Humphreys viewed Gay as representing Augustan optimism, as expressed in the belief that God was keenly interested in the happiness of his creatures.[5] Hartley owned that Gay provided the hint which led to his theory of association.[6] The connection between Brown's essay on virtue and Gay's work has already been noted in the Introduction above.[7] The 'Preliminary Dissertation' was known by David Hume who had read the 1731 edition of King's *Essay on the Origin of Evil*. According to Mossner:

> Scrutiny of Hume's five notes on 'King' indicates that he was using the 1731 translation and was, therefore, exposing himself to the ideas of Law and Gay, as well as of King. This fact is of importance, for example, because Gay's short dissertation is the earliest known reconcilement of ethical utilitarianism with psychological associationism, two doctrines that were to be employed by Hume himself.[8]

William Paley, in his memoir of Law, also acknowledged Gay's importance.[9]

Though published anonymously, the 'Preliminary Dissertation' is the only generally accepted publication by Gay. However, there has been some speculation concerning what else Gay may have written and published. Selby-Bigge and Elmer Sprague attribute to Gay 'A Dissertation upon the Argument *a Priori* for proving the Existence of a First Cause',[10] which was appended to Edmund Law's *Enquiry into the Idea of Space, Time, Immensity, and*

---

2 Elie Halévy, *The Growth of Philosophic Radicalism* [*La formation du radicalisme philosophique*, 1901–4], trs. Mary Morris (1928; New Jersey 1972), p. 7 (referring to utilitarianism in general and not merely to the religious version).

3 Ernest Albee, *A History of English Utilitarianism* (1901; reprt. London 1957), p. 83.

4 Gerald R. Cragg, *Reason and Authority in the Eighteenth Century* (Cambridge 1964), p. 279.

5 A. R. Humphreys, *The Augustan World: Life and Letters in Eighteenth-Century England* (1954; 2nd edn. London 1964), pp. 164, 188.

6 David Hartley, *Observations on Man*, 2 pts. (London 1749), i. iii; see also Leslie Stephen, *History of English Thought in the Eighteenth Century*, 2 vols. (1876; 3rd edn. reprt. New York 1949), ii. 63.

7 Part One, Introduction, p. 11; see also Brown below, p. 65 note.

8 Ernest Campbell Mossner, *The Life of David Hume* (Austin 1954), p. 80.

9 George Wilson Meadley, *Memoirs of William Paley, D. D.*, 2nd edn. (Edinburgh 1810), p. 356.

10 L. A. Selby-Bigge, (ed.), *British Moralists: Being Selections from Writers Principally of the Eighteenth Century*, 2 vols. (Oxford 1897), ii. 388; and Elmer Sprague's entry on Gay in Paul Edwards (ed.), *Encyclopedia of Philosophy* (New York 1967), iii. 274.

Eternity (1734). However, the *National Union Catalogue* attributes this to Daniel Waterland. Spadafora suggests from the evidence of the titles and some phrases that Gay also wrote *An Introduction Towards an Essay on the Origin of the Passions* (1741) and *An Enquiry into the Origin of the Human Appetites and Affections* (1747).[11] No one else has claimed Gay as the author of the first of these tracts; Spadafora's evidence is circumstantial and not convincing. The second tract has occasioned some discussion.

Selby–Bigge believed the *Enquiry* to be the work of Hartley not Gay, and Ferg supports this view in 'Two Early Works by David Hartley'.[12] On the other hand, Passmore did not think either Gay or Hartley wrote the *Enquiry*.[13] McReynolds has reprinted the *Enquiry* and discussed the issue of authorship in his introduction, noting that William Scott in his biography of Hutcheson considered Gay to be the author of the *Enquiry*.[14] McReynolds says that a comparison of Gay's 'Dissertation' and the *Enquiry* 'makes it clear that the author of the latter was either Gay himself or someone else very familiar with the *Dissertation*'. However, on balance, the fact that the *Enquiry* was not published until two years after Gay's death lessened the likelihood of his being the author, since there is no suggestion that it is a posthumous work. McReynolds remained uncertain, but claimed James Long as the author on the authority of the *Dictionary of Anonymous and Pseudonymous English Literature* and the *Catalogue of the British Museum*.[15]

Note on the Text

Gay's 'Preliminary Dissertation. Concerning the Fundamental Principle of Virtue and Morality' was prefixed to Edmund Law's translation of William King's *Essay on the Origin of Evil* (1731). King's seminal work had originally appeared in Latin as *De origine mali* in 1702. Gay's 'Preliminary Dissertation' was subsequently included in the second (1732), third (1739), fourth (1758), and fifth (1781) editions of the English translation of that work. The text following is taken from the first English edition of 1731, printed for W. Thurlbourn of Cambridge and sold by R. Knaplock, J. and J. Knapton, and W. Innis of St. Paul's Church Yard in London.

[11] David Spadafora, *The Idea of Progress in Eighteenth-Century Britain* (New Haven and London 1990), pp. 142, 143 and note.
[12] Selby-Bigge (ed.), *British Moralists*, ii. 389; and Stephen Ferg, 'Two Early Works by David Hartley', *Journal of the History of Philosophy*, 19 (1981), pp. 173–89.
[13] J. A. Passmore, 'The Malleability of Man in Eighteenty-Century Thought', in Earl R. Wasserman (ed.), *Aspects of the Eighteenth Century* (Baltimore 1965), p. 37 note.
[14] William Robert Scott, *Francis Hutcheson: His Life, Teaching and Position in the History of Philosophy* (Cambridge 1900).
[15] Paul McReynolds (ed.), *Four Early Works on Motivation* (Gainesville, FL 1969), introduction, pp. xxvii–xxix.

PRELIMINARY DISSERTATION
Concerning the Fundamental Principle of Virtue or Morality.

Tho' all Writers of Morality have in the main agreed what particular Actions are virtuous and what otherwise; yet they have, or at least seem to have differ'd very much, both concerning the *Criterion* of Virtue, *viz.* what it is which denominates any Action virtuous; or, to speak more properly, what it is by which we must try any Action to *know* whether it be virtuous or no; and also concerning the *Principle* or Motive by which Men are induced to pursue Virtue.

As to the former, some have placed it in *acting agreeably to Nature*, or *Reason*; others in the *Fitness of things*; others in a Conformity with *Truth*; others in promoting the *Common Good*; others in the *Will of God*, &c. This Disagreement of Moralists concerning the Rule or Criterion of Virtue in general, and at the same time their almost perfect Agreement concerning the particular Branches of it, would be apt to make one suspect, either that they had a different Criterion (tho' they did not know or attend to it) from what they profess'd; or (which perhaps is the true as well as the more favourable Opinion) that they only talk a different Language, and that all of them have the same Criterion in reality, only they have express'd it in different Words.

And there will appear the more room for this Conjecture, if we consider the Ideas themselves about which Morality is chiefly conversant, *viz.* that they are all *mixed Modes*, or compound Ideas arbitrarily put together, having at first no Archetype or Original existing, and afterwards no other than that which exists in other Mens Minds. Now since Men, unless they have these their compound Ideas, which are signify'd by the same Name, made up precisely of the same simple ones, must necessarily talk a different Language; and since this difference is so difficult, and in some Cases impossible to be avoided, it follows that greater Allowance and Indulgence ought to be given to these Writers than any other: and that (if we have a mind to understand them) we should not always take their Words in the common Acceptation, but in the Sense in which we find that particular Author which we are reading used them. And if a Man interpret the Writers of Morality with this due Candor, I believe their seeming Inconsistencies and Disagreements about the Criterion of Virtue, would in a great measure vanish; and he would find that *acting agreeably to Nature*, or *Reason*, (when rightly understood) would perfectly coincide with the *Fitness of things*; the Fitness of things (as far as these Words have any meaning) with *Truth*; Truth with the *Common Good*; and the Common Good with the *Will of God*.

But whether this Difference be real, or only verbal, a Man can scarce avoid observing from it, that Mankind have the Ideas of most particular Virtues, and also a confused Notion of Virtue in general, before they have any Notion of the Criterion of it, or ever did, neither perhaps can they, deduce all or any of those Virtues from their Idea of Virtue in general, or upon any rational Grounds shew how those Actions (which the World call Moral, and most, if not all Men evidently have Ideas of) are distinguish'd from other Actions, or why they approve of those Actions call'd Moral ones, more than others.

But since the Idea of Virtue among all Men (however they differ in other respects) includes either tacitly or expresly, not only the Idea of *Approbation* as the Consequence of it; but also that it is to every one, and in all Circumstances, an Object of *Choice*; it is incumbent on all Writers of Morality, to shew that *that* in which they place Virtue, whatever it be, not only always will or ought to meet with Approbation, but also that it is always an Object of *Choice*; which is the other great Dispute among Moralists, *viz.* What is the Principle or Motive by which Men are induced to pursue Virtue.

For some have imagin'd that that is the only Object of Choice to a rational Creature, which upon the whole will produce more Happiness than Misery to the Chooser; and that Men are and ought to be guided wholly by this Principle; and farther, that Virtue will produce more Happiness than Misery, and therefore is always an Object of Choice: and whatever is an Object of Choice, that we approve of.

But this, however true in Theory, is insufficient to account for Matter of Fact, *i. e.* that the generality of Mankind do approve of Virtue, or rather virtuous Actions, without being able to give any Reason for their Approbation; and also, that some pursue it without knowing that it tends to their own private Happiness; nay even when it appears to be inconsistent with and destructive of their Happiness.

And that this is matter of Fact, the ingenious Author of the *Enquiry into the Original of our Idea of Virtue* has so evidently made appear by a great Variety of Instances, that a Man must be either very little acquainted with the World, or a mere *Hobbist* in his Temper to deny it.

And therefore to solve these two Difficulties, this excellent Author has supposed (without *proving*, unless by shewing the insufficiency of all other Schemes) a *Moral* Sense to account for the former, and a *public or benevolent Affection* for the latter: And these, *viz.* the Moral Sense and Public Affection, he supposes to be implanted in us like *Instincts*, independent of Reason, and previous to any instruction; and therefore his Opinion is, that no account can be given, or ought to be expected of them, any more than we pretend to account for the Pleasure or Pain which arises from Sensation; *i. e.* Why any particular Motion produced in our Bodies should be accompany'd with Pain rather than Pleasure, and *vice versa*.

But this Account seems still insufficient, rather cutting the Knot than untying it, and if it is not a-kin to the Doctrine of *Innate Ideas*, yet I think it relishes too much of that of *Ocult Qualities*. This ingenious Author is certainly right in his Observations upon the Insufficiency of the common Methods of accounting for both our *Election* and *Approbation* of Moral Actions, and rightly infers the Necessity of supposing a Moral Sense (*i. e.* a Power or Faculty whereby we may perceive any Action to be an Object of Approbation, and the Agent of Love) and public Affections, to account for the principal Actions of human Life. But then by calling these *Instincts*, I think he stops too soon, imagining himself at the Fountain-head, when he might have traced them much higher, even to the true Principle of all our Actions, our own *Happiness*.

And this will appear by shewing, that our Approbation of Morality, and all Affections whatsoever, are finally resolvable into *Reason*, pointing out *private Happiness*, and are conversant only about things apprehended to be means tending to this end; and that whenever this end is not perceiv'd, they are to be accounted for from the *Association of Ideas*, and may properly enough be call'd *Habits*.

For if this is clearly made out, the Necessity of supporting a Moral Sense, or public Affections to be implanted in us, since it ariseth only from the Insufficiency of all other Schemes to account for human Actions, will immediately vanish. But whether it be made out or no, we may observe in general, that all Arguments *ad Ignorantiam*, or that proceed *a Remotione* only (as this, by which the Moral Sense and public Affections are establish'd to be Instincts, evidently does) are scarce ever perfectly satisfactory, being for the most part subject to this Doubt, *viz.* Whether there is a full Enumeration of all the Parts; and liable also to this Objection, *viz.* That tho' I cannot account for Phænomena otherwise, yet possibly they may be otherwise accounted for.

But before we can determine this Point, it will be necessary to settle all the Terms: We shall in the first place therefore enquire what is meant by the *Criterion* of Virtue.

Sect. I.
Concerning the Criterion *of Virtue*

The Criterion of any thing is a Rule or Measure by a Conformity with which any thing is known to be of this or that sort, or of this or that degree. And in order to determine the Criterion of any thing, we must first know the thing whose Criterion we are seeking after. For a Measure presupposes the Idea of the thing to be measured, otherwise it could not be known (since what is the proper Measure of one thing is not so of another) whether it was fit to measure it or no. Liquids, Cloth, and Flesh, have all different Measures; Gold and Silver different Touchstones. This is very intelligible, and the Method of doing it generally clear, when either the Quantity or Kind of any particular Substance is thus to be ascertain'd.

But when we extend our Enquiries after a Criterion for abstract, mix'd Modes, which have no Existence but in our Minds, and are so very different in different Men; we are apt to be confounded, and search after a Measure for we know not what. For unless we are first agreed concerning the thing to be measur'd, we shall in vain expect to agree in our Criterion of it, or even to understand one another.

But it may be said, if we are exactly agreed in any mix'd Mode, what need of any *Criterion*, or what can we want farther? What we want farther, and what we mean by the Criterion of it is this; *viz.* to know whether any inferior or particular thing do belong to his mix'd Mode or no. And this is a very proper Enquiry. For let a Man learn the Idea of Intemperance from you never so clearly, and if you please let this be the Idea, *viz.* the Eating or Drinking to that degree as to injure his Understanding or Health; and let him also be never so much convinc'd of the Obligation to avoid it; yet it is a very pertinent Question in him to ask you, How shall I know when I am guilty of Intemperance?

And if we examine this thoroughly, we shall find that every little difference in the Definition of a mix'd Mode will require a different Criterion, *e. g.* If Murder is defined the *wilful* taking away the Life of another, it is evident, that to enquire after the Criterion of Murder, is to enquire how we shall know when the Life of another is taken away *wilfully*; i. e. when one who takes away the Life of another does it with that malicious Design which is implied by *Wilfulness*. But if Murder be defined the *Guilty* taking away the Life of another, then to enquire after the Criterion of Murder, is to enquire how it shall be known when *Guilt* is contracted in the taking away the Life of another. So that the Criterion of Murder, according to one or other of these Definitions, will be different. For Wilfulness perhaps will be made the Criterion of Guilt, but Wilfulness itself, if it want any, must have some farther Criterion, it being evident that nothing can be the Measure of itself.

If the Criterion is contain'd in the Idea itself, then it is merely *nominal*, e. g. If Virtue is defined, The acting agreeably to the Will of God: To say the Will of God is the Criterion of Virtue, is only to say, what is agreeable to the Will of God is *call*'d Virtue. But the *real* Criterion, which is of some use, is this, How shall I know what the Will of God is in this respect?

From hence it is evident, that the Criterion of a mix'd Mode is neither the Definition of it, nor contain'd in it. For, as has been shewn, the general

Idea is necessarily to be fix'd; and if the *Particulars* comprehended under it are fix'd or known also, there remains nothing to be measured, because we measure only things unknown. The general Idea then being fix'd, the Criterion which is to measure or determine Inferiors, must be found out and proved to be a proper Rule or Measure, by comparing it with the *general Idea* only, independent of the inferior things to which it is to be apply'd. For the truth of the Measure must be proved independently of the Particular to be measured, otherwise we shall prove in a Circle.

To apply what has been said in general to the Case in hand. Great Enquiry is made after the Criterion of *Virtue*; but it is to be fear'd that few know distinctly what it is they are enquiring after; and therefore this must be clearly stated. And in order to this, we must (as has been shewn) first fix our Idea of Virtue, and that exactly; and then our Enquiry will be, how we shall know this or that less general or particular Action to be comprehended under Virtue. For unless our Idea of Virtue is fix'd, we enquire after the Criterion of we know not what. And this our Idea of Virtue, to give any Satisfaction, ought to be so general as to be conformable to that which all or most Men are supposed to have. And this general Idea, I think, may be thus express'd.

Virtue is the Conformity to a Rule of Life, directing the Actions of all rational Creatures with respect to each other's Happiness; to which Conformity every one in all Cases is obliged: and every one that does so conform, is or ought to be approved of, esteemed and loved for so doing. What is here express'd, I believe every one, or most, put into their Idea of Virtue.

For Virtue, among all, or most, does imply some relation to *others*: where *Self* is only concern'd, a Man may be *prudent* but not virtuous; and an Action which relates immediately to *God*, is stiled *Religious*.

I think also that all Men, whatever they make Virtue to consist in, yet always make it to imply *Obligation* and *Approbation*.

The Idea of Virtue being thus fix'd, to enquire after the Criterion of it, is to enquire what that Rule of Life is to which we are oblig'd to conform or how that Rule is to be found out which is to direct me in my Behaviour towards others, which ought always to be pursued, and which, if pursued, will or ought to procure me Approbation, Esteem, and Love.

But before I can answer this Enquiry, I must first see what I mean by *Obligation*.

Sect. II.
Concerning Obligation

Obligation is the necessity of doing or omitting any Action in order to be happy: i. e. when there is such a relation between an Agent and any Action that the Agent cannot be happy without doing or omitting that Action, then the Agent is said to be *obliged* to do or omit that Action. So that Obligation is evidently founded upon the prospect of *Happiness*, and arises from that necessary Influence which any Action has upon present or future Happiness or Misery. And no greater Obligation can be supposed to be laid upon any *free Agent* without an express Contradiction.

This Obligation may be consider'd four ways, according to the four different manners in which it is induced: First, that Obligation which ariseth from perceiving the natural Consequences of things, *i. e.* the Consequences of things acting according to the fix'd Laws of Nature, may be call'd *Natural*. Secondly, that arising from Merit or Demerit, as producing the Esteem and Favour of our Fellow-Creatures, or the contrary, is usually stiled *virtuous*. Thirdly, that arising from the Authority of the Civil Magistrate, *Civil*. Fourthly, that from the Authority of God, *Religious*.

Now from the Consideration of these four sorts of Obligation (which are the only ones) it is evident that a full and complete Obligation which will extend to all Cases, can only be that arising from the Authority of *God*; because God only can in all Cases make a Man happy or miserable: and therefore, since we are *always* obliged to that conformity call'd Virtue, it is evident that the immediate Rule or Criterion of it is the Will of God. But is the *whole* Will of God the Criterion of Virtue? No. For tho' the whole Will of God is equally obligatory; yet, since Virtue was defined to be the conformity to a Rule directing my Behaviour with respect to my *Fellow-Creatures*, the Will of God can be no farther concern'd about Virtue, than as it directs me in that Behaviour.

The next Enquiry therefore is, what that Will of God in this particular is, or what it directs me to do?

Now it is evident from the Nature of God, *viz.* his being infinitely happy in himself from all Eternity, and from his Goodness manifested in his Works, that he could have no other Design in creating Mankind than *their* Happiness; and therefore he wills their Happiness; therefore the means of their Happiness: therefore that my Behaviour, as far as it may be a means of the Happiness of Mankind, should be such. Here then we are got one Step farther, or to a new Criterion: not to a new Criterion of Virtue *immediately*, but to a Criterion of the *Will of God*. For it is an Answer to the Enquiry, How shall I know what the Will of God in this particular is? Thus the Will of God is the immediate Criterion of Virtue, and the Happiness of Mankind the Criterion of the Will of God; and therefore the Happiness of Mankind may be said to be the Criterion of Virtue, but *once removed*.

And since I am to do whatever lies in my Power towards promoting the Happiness of Mankind, the next Enquiry is, what is the Criterion of this *Happiness*: *i. e.* how shall I know what in my Power is, or is not, for the Happiness of Mankind?

Now this is to be known only from the *Relations* of things, (which Relations, with respect to our present Enquiry, some have call'd their *Fitness* and *Unfitness*.) For some Things and Actions are apt to produce Pleasure, others Pain; some are convenient, others inconvenient for a Society; some are for the good of Mankind, others tend to the detriment of it: therefore those are to be chosen which tend to the good of Mankind; the others to be avoided.

Thus then we are got one step farther, *viz.* to the Criterion of the Happiness of Mankind. And from this Criterion we deduce all particular Virtues and Vices.

The next Enquiry is, How shall I know that there is this Fitness and Unfitness in things? or if there be, how shall I discover it in particular Cases? And the Answer is, Either from Experience or Reason. You either *perceive* the Inconveniencies of some Things and Actions when they happen; or you *foresee* them by contemplating the Nature of the Things and Actions.

Thus the Criterion of the Fitness or Unfitness of things may in general be said to be *Reason*: which Reason, when exactly conformable to the things existing, *i. e.* when it judges of things as they are, is called *Right Reason*. And hence also we sometimes talk of the *Reason of things*, i. e. properly speaking, that Relation which we should find out by our Reason, if our Reason was right.

The expressing by outward Signs the Relations of things as they really are, is called *Truth*; and hence, by the same kind of Metaphor, we are apt to talk of the *Truth*, as well as *Reason of things*. Both Expressions mean the same: which has often made me wonder why some Men who cry up *Reason* as the Criterion of Virtue, should yet dislike Mr. *Wollaston*'s Notion of *Truth* being its Criterion.

The Truth is, all these just mention'd, *viz.* the Happiness of Mankind; the Relations, or Fitness and Unfitness of things; Reason and Truth; may in some sense be said to be Criterions of Virtue; but it must always be remember'd that they are only *remote* Criterions of it, being gradually subordinate to its immediate Criterion, the Will of God.

And from hence we may perceive the Reason of what I suggested in the beginning of this Treatise, *viz.* That the Dispute between Moralists about the Criterion of Virtue, is more in Words than Meaning; and that this Difference between them has been occasion'd by their dropping the immediate Criterion, and choosing some a more remote, some a less remote one. And from hence we may see also the Inconvenience of defining any mix'd Mode by its Criterion. For that in a great measure has occasion'd all this Confusion, as may easily be made appear in all the pretended Criterions of Virtue above-mention'd.

Thus those who either expresly exclude, or don't mention the Will of God, making the immediate Criterion of Virtue to be the Good of Mankind; must either allow that Virtue is not in all Cases *obligatory* (contrary to the

Idea which all or most Men have of it) or they must say that the Good of Mankind is a sufficient Obligation. But how can the Good of Mankind be any Obligation to *me*, when perhaps in particular Cases, such as laying down my Life, or the like, it is contrary to my Happiness.

Those who drop the Happiness of Mankind, and talk of Relations, the Fitness and Unfitness of Things, are still more remote from the true Criterion. For Fitness without relation to some *End*, is scarce intelligible.

Reason and Truth come pretty near the Relations of things, because they manifestly presuppose them; but are still one step farther from the immediate Criterion of Virtue.

What has been said concerning the Criterion of Virtue as including our Obligation to it, may perhaps be allow'd to be true, but still it will be urg'd, that 'tis insufficient to account for matter of Fact, *viz.* that most Persons, who are either ignorant of, or never consider'd these Deductions, do however pursue Virtue themselves, and approve of it in others. I shall in the next place therefore give some account of our Approbations and Affections.

Sect. III.
Concerning Approbation *and* Affection.

Man is not only a *sensible* Creature, not only capable of Pleasure and Pain, but capable also of *foreseeing* the Pleasure and Pain in the future consequences of Things and Actions; and as he is capable of knowing, so also of *governing* or directing the Causes of them, and thereby in a great measure enabled to avoid the one and procure the other: whence the Principle of all Action. And therefore, as Pleasure and Pain are not indifferent to him, nor out of his Power, he pursues the former and avoids the latter; and therefore also those things which are *Causes* of them are not indifferent, but he pursues or avoids them also, according to their different Tendency. That which he pursues for its own sake, which is only Pleasure, is called an *End*; that which he apprehends to be apt to produce Pleasure, he calls *Good*, and approves of, *i. e.* judges a proper means to attain his end, and therefore looks upon it as an Object of choice; that which is pregnant with Misery he disapproves of and stiles *Evil*. And this Good and Evil are not only barely approved of, or the contrary, but whenever view'd in Imagination (since Man considers himself as existing hereafter, and is concern'd for his Welfare then as well as now) they have a *present Pleasure* or Pain annex'd to them, proportionable to what is apprehend to follow them in real Existence; which Pleasure or Pain arising from the prospect of future Pleasure or Pain is properly call'd *Passion*, and the Desire consequent thereupon, *Affection*.

And as by reflecting upon Pleasure there arises in our minds a *Desire* of it; and on Pain, an *Aversion* from it (which necessarily follows from supposing us to be sensible Creatures, and is no more than saying, that all things are not *indifferent* to us) so also by reflecting upon Good or Evil, the same Desires and Aversions are excited, and are distinguish'd into *Love* and *Hatred*. And from Love and Hatred variously modify'd, arise all those other Desires and Aversions which are promiscuously stiled Passions or Affections; and are generally thought to be implanted in our Nature *originally*, like the Power of receiving Pleasure or Pain. And when placed on inanimate Objects, are these following, Hope, Fear, Despair and its opposite, for which we want a Name.

Sect. IV.
Approbation and Affection consider'd with regard to Merit, *or the* Law of Esteem.

If a Man in the pursuit of Pleasure or Happiness (by which is meant the Sum total of Pleasure) had to do only with inanimate Creatures, his Approbation and Affections would be as described in the foregoing Section. But, since he is dependent with respect to his Happiness, not only on these, but also on rational Agents, Creatures like himself, which have the Power of governing or directing Good and Evil, and of acting for an End; there will arise different means of Happiness; and consequently different Pursuits, tho' tending to the same End, Happiness; and therefore different Approbations and Affections, and the contrary; which deserve particularly to be consider'd.

That there will arise different means of Happiness, is evident from hence, *viz.* that Rational Agents, in being subservient to our Happiness, are not passive but voluntary. And therefore since we are in pursuit of that to obtain which we apprehend the concurrence of their Wills necessary, we cannot but approve of whatever is apt to procure this Concurrence. And that can be only the Pleasure or Pain expected from it by them. And therefore, as I perceive that my Happiness is dependent on others, I cannot but judge whatever I apprehend to be proper to excite them to endeavour to promote my Happiness, to be a means of Happiness: *i. e.* I cannot but *approve it*. And since the annexing Pleasure to their Endeavours to promote my Happiness is the only thing in my power to this end, I cannot but approve of the annexing Pleasure to such Actions of theirs as are undertaken upon my account. Hence to approve of a Rational Agent as a means of Happiness, is different from the Approbation of any other means, because it implies an Approbation also of an Endeavour to promote the Happiness of that Agent, in order to excite him and others to the same concern for my Happiness for the future.

And because what we approve of we also desire (as has been shewn above) hence also we *desire* the Happiness of any Agent that has done us good. And therefore *Love* or *Hatred*, when placed on a rational Object, has this difference from the Love and Hatred of other things, that it implies a desire of, and consequently a pleasure in the Happiness of the Object beloved; or, if hated, the contrary.

The Foundation of this Approbation and Love (which, as we have seen, consists in his voluntarily contributing to our Happiness) is called the *Merit* of the Agent so contributing, *i. e.* that whereby he is entitled (upon supposition that we act like rational, sociable Creatures, like Creatures whose Happiness is dependent on each other's Behaviour) to our Approbation and Love: *Demerit* the contrary.

And this Affection or Quality of any Action which we call *Merit* is very consistent with a Man's acting *ultimately* for his own private Happiness. For any particular Action that is undertaken *for the sake of another*, is *meritorious*, i. e. deserves Esteem, Favour, and Approbation from him for whose sake it was undertaken, towards the Doer of it. For the presumption of such Esteem, *&c.* was the only Motive to that Action; and if such Esteem, *&c.* does not follow, or is presum'd not to follow it, such a Person is reckon'd unworthy of any favour, because he shews by his Actions that he is incapable of being *obliged* by Favours.

The Mistake which some have run into, *viz.* that Merit is inconsistent with acting upon *private Happiness*, as an ultimate End, seems to have arisen from hence, *viz.* that they have not carefully enough distinguish'd between an inferior and ultimate End; the end of a particular Action, and the end of Action in general: which may be explained thus. Tho' Happiness, private Happiness, is the proper or ultimate End of all our Actions whatever, yet that particular means of Happiness which any particular Action is chiefly adapted to procure, or the thing chiefly aim'd at by that Action; the thing which, if possess'd, we would not undertake that Action, may and generally is call'd the *End* of that Action. As therefore Happiness is the general End of all Actions, so each particular Action may be said to have its proper and peculiar End: Thus the End of a Beau is to please by his Dress; the End of Study, Knowledge. But neither pleasing by Dress, nor Knowledge, are ultimate Ends, they still tend or ought to tend to something farther; as is evident from hence, *viz.* that a Man may ask and expect a Reason why either of them are pursued: Now to ask the *Reason* of any Action or Pursuit, is only to enquire into the *End* of it: But to expect a Reason, *i. e.* an End to be assign'd for an *ultimate* End, is absurd. To ask why I pursue Happiness, will admit of no other Answer than an Explanation of the Terms.

Why *inferior Ends*, which in reality are only Means, are too often look'd upon and acquies'd in as *ultimate*, shall be accounted for hereafter.

Whenever therefore the *particular* End of any Action is the Happiness of another (tho' the Agent design'd thereby to procure to himself Esteem and Favour, and look'd upon that Esteem and Favour as a means of private Happiness) that Action is meritorious. And the same may be said, tho' we design to please God by endeavouring to promote the Happiness of others. But when an Agent has a view in any particular Action distinct from my Happiness, and that view is his *only Motive* to that Action, tho' that Action promote my Happiness to never so great a Degree yet that Agent acquires no *Merit*; *i. e.* he is not thereby entitled to any Favour and Esteem: Because Favour and Esteem are due from me for any Action, no farther than that Action was undertaken upon my account. If therefore my Happiness is only the pretended End of that Action, I am imposed on if I believe it real, and thereby think myself indebted to the Agent; and am discharg'd from any Obligation as soon as I find out the Cheat.

But it is far otherwise when my Happiness is the sole End of that particular Action, *i. e.* (as I have explain'd myself above) when the Agent endeavours to promote my Happiness as a Means to procure my Favour, *i. e.* to make me subservient to his Happiness as his ultimate End: Tho' I know he aims at my Happiness only as a means of his own, yet this lessens not the Obligation.

There is one thing, I confess, which makes a great alteration in this Case, and that is, whether he aims at my Favour *in general*, or only for some particular End. Because, if he aim at my Happiness only to serve himself in some particular thing, the Value of my Favour will perhaps end with his obtaining that particular thing: And therefore I am under less Obligation (*cæteris paribus*) the more *particular* his Expectations from me are; but under Obligation I am.

Now from the various Combinations of this which we call Merit, and its contrary, arise all those various Approbations and Aversions; all those Likings and Dislikings which we call *Moral*.

As therefore, from considering those Beings which are the *involuntary* means of our Happiness or Misery, there were produced in us the Passions or Affections of Love, Hatred, Hope, Fear, Despair, and its contrary: So from considering those Beings which *voluntarily* contribute to our Happiness or Misery, there arise these following. Love and Hatred, (which are different from that Love or Hatred placed on involuntary Beings; that placed on involuntary Beings being only a Desire to possess or avoid the thing beloved or hated; but this on voluntary Agents being a Desire to give Pleasure or Pain to the Agent beloved or hated) Gratitude, Anger, (sometimes call'd by one common Name, Resentment) Generosity, Ambition, Honour, Shame, Envy, Benevolence: and if there be any other, they're only, as these are, different Modifications of Love and Hatred.

Love and *Hatred*, and the Foundation of them, (*viz.* the Agent beloved or hated being apprehended to be instrumental to our Happiness) I have explain'd above. *Gratitude* is that Desire of promoting the Happiness of another upon account of some former Kindness receiv'd. *Anger*, that Desire of thwarting the Happiness of another, on account of some former Diskindness or Injury received. And both these take place, tho' we hope for, or fear nothing farther from the Objects of either of them, and this is still consistent with acting upon a Principle of *private Happiness*.

For tho' we neither hope for, nor fear any thing farther from these particular Beings; yet the Disposition shewn upon these Occasions is apprehended to influence the Behaviour of other Beings towards us; *i. e.* other Beings will be moved to promote our Happiness or otherwise, as they observe how we resent Favours or Injuries.

Ambition is a Desire of being esteem'd. Hence a Desire of being *thought* an Object of Esteem; hence of *being* an Object of Esteem, hence of doing *laudable*, i. e. useful Actions. *Generosity* and *Benevolence* are Species of it. Ambition in too great a Degree is called *Pride*, of which there are several Species. The Title to the Esteem of others, which ariseth from any meritorious Action, is called *Honour*. The Pleasure arising from Honour being paid to us, *i. e.* from others acknowledging that we are entitled to their Esteem, is with out a Name. *Modesty* is the fear of losing Esteem. The Uneasiness or Passion which ariseth from a Sense that we have lost it, is called *Shame*. So that *Ambition*, and all those other Passions and Affections belonging to it, together with *Shame*, arise from the Esteem of others: which is the Reason why this Tribe of Affections operate more strongly on us than any other, *viz.* because we perceive that as our Happiness is dependent on the Behaviour of others, so we perceive also that that Behaviour is dependent on the Esteem which others have conceiv'd of us; and consequently that our acquiring or losing Esteem, is in effect acquiring or losing Happiness, and in the highest Degree. And the same may be said concerning all our other Affections and Passions, to enumerate which, what for want of Names to them, and what by the confusion of Language about them, is almost impossible.

Envy will be accounted for hereafter, for a Reason which will then be obvious.

Thus having explain'd what I mean by *Obligation* and *Approbation*; and shewn that they are founded on and terminate in *Happiness*: having also pointed out the Difference between our Approbations and Affections as placed on involuntary and voluntary Means of Happiness; and farther, that these Approbations and Affections are not innate or implanted in us by way of *Instinct*, but are all *acquired*, being fairly deducible from supposing only sensible and rational Creatures dependent on each other for their Happiness, as explain'd above: I shall in the next place endeavour to answer a grand Objection to what has here been said concerning Approbations and Affections arising from a prospect of private Happiness.

The Objection is this.

The Reason or End of every Action is always known to the Agent; for nothing can move a Man but what is perceiv'd: but the generality of Mankind love and hate, approve and disapprove, immediately, as soon as any moral Character either occurs in Life, or is proposed to them, without considering whether their private Happiness is affected with it, or no: or if they do consider any Moral Character in relation to their own Happiness, and find themselves, as to their private Happiness, unconcern'd in it, or even find their private Happiness lessen'd by it in some particular Instance, yet they still approve the Moral Character, and love the Agent; nay they cannot do otherwise. Whatever Reason may be assign'd by speculative Men why we should be grateful to a Benefactor, or pity the Distressed; yet if the grateful or compassionate Mind never thought of that Reason, it is no Reason to him. The Enquiry is not why he *ought to be* grateful, but why he *is* so. These after-reasons therefore rather shew the Wisdom and Providence of our Maker in implanting the immediate Powers of these Approbations (*i. e.* in Mr. *Hutcheson*'s Language, *a Moral Sense*) and these Public Affections in us, than give any satisfactory account of their Origin. And therefore these Public Affections, and this Moral Sense, are quite independent on private Happiness, and in reality act upon us as mere Instincts.

Answer.

The Matter of Fact contain'd in this Argument, in my Opinion, is not to be contested; and therefore it remains either that we make the matter of Fact consistent with what we have before laid down, or give up the Cause.

Now, in order to shew this Consistency, I beg leave to observe, that as in the pursuit of Truth we don't always trace every Proposition whose Truth we are examining, to a first Principle or Axiom, but acquiesce, as soon as we perceive it deducible from some known or presumed Truth; so in our Conduct we do not always travel to the ultimate End of our Actions, *Happiness*: but rest contented, as soon as we perceive any Action subservient to a known or presumed *Means* of Happiness. And these presumed Truths and Means of Happiness, whether real or otherwise, always influence us after the same manner as if they were real. The undeniable Consequences of Prejudices are as firmly adhered to as the Consequences of real truths or arguments; and what is subservient to a false (but imagin'd) means of Happiness, is as industriously pursued as what is subservient to a true one.

Now every Man, both in his Pursuit after Truth, and in his Conduct, has settled and fixed a great many of these in his Mind, which he always acts upon, as upon *Principles*, without examining. And this is occasion'd by the Narrowness of our Understandings: We can consider but a few things at once; and therefore, to run everything to the Fountain-head would be tedious, thro' a long Series of Consequences. To avoid this we choose out certain Truths and means of Happiness, which we look upon as RESTING PLACES, which we may safely acquiesce in, in the Conduct both of our Understanding and Practice, in relation to the one, regarding them as *Axioms*; in the other, as *Ends*. And we are more easily inclined to this by imagining that we may safely rely upon what we call *Habitual* Knowledge, thinking it needless to examine what we are already satisfy'd in. And hence it is that Prejudices, both Speculative and Practical, are difficult to be rooted out, *viz.* few will examine them.

And these RESTING PLACES are so often used as Principles, that at last, letting that slip out of our Minds which first inclined us to embrace them, we are apt to imagine them, not as they really are, the *Substitutes* of Principles, but Principles themselves.

And from hence, as some Men have imagin'd *Innate Ideas*, because forgetting how they came by them; so others have set up almost as many distinct *Instincts* as there are *acquired Principles* of acting. And I cannot but wonder why the *Pecuniary* Sense, a Sense of *Power* and *Party*, &c. were not mention'd, as well as the *Moral*, that of *Honour, Order*, and some others.

The Case is really this. We first perceive or imagine some real Good, *i. e.* fitness to promote our Happiness in those things which we love and approve of. Hence (as was above explain'd) we annex Pleasure to those things. Hence those things and Pleasure are so ty'd together and associated in our Minds, that one cannot present itself but the other will also occur. And the *Association* remains even after that which at first gave them the Connection is quite forgot, or perhaps does not exist, but the contrary. An Instance or two may perhaps make this clear. How many Men are there in the World who have as strong a taste for *Money* as others have for Virtue; who count so much Money, so much Happiness; nay, even sell their Happiness for Money; or, to speak more properly, make the *having* Money, without any Design or Thought of using it, their ultimate End? But was this Propensity to Money born with them? Or rather, did not they at first perceive a great many Advantages from being possess'd of Money, and from thence conceive a Pleasure in having it, thence desire it, thence endeavour to obtain it, thence receive an actual Pleasure in obtaining it, thence desire to preserve the Possession of it? Hence, by dropping the intermediate Means between Money and Happiness, they join Money and Happiness immediately together, and content themselves with the phantastical Pleasure of having it, and make that which was at first pursued only as a *Means*, be to them a real *End*, and what their real Happiness or Misery consists in. Thus the Connection between Money and Happiness remains in the Mind; tho' it has long since ceased between the things themselves.

The same might be observ'd concerning the Thirst after Knowledge,

Fame, &c. the delight in Reading, Building, Planting, and most of the various Exercises and Entertainments of Life. These were at first enter'd on with a view to some farther End, but at length become habitual Amusements; the Idea of Pleasure is associated with them, and leads us on still in the same eager Pursuit of them, when the first Reason is quite vanish'd, or at least out of our Minds. Nay, we find this Power of *Association* so great as not only to transport our Passions and Affections beyond their proper bounds, both as to Intenseness and Duration; as is evident from daily Instances of Avarice, Ambition, Love, Revenge, &c. but also, that it is able to transfer them to improper Objects, and such as are of a quite different Nature from those to which our Reason had at first directed them. Thus being accustom'd to resent an Injury done to our Body by a Retaliation of the like to him that offer'd it, we are apt to conceive the same kind of Resentment, and often express it in the same manner, upon receiving hurt from a Stock or Stone, whereby the hatred which we are used to place on voluntary Beings, is substituted in the Room of that Aversion which belongs to involuntary ones. The like may be observ'd in most of the other Passions above-mention'd.

From hence also, *viz.* from the continuance of this *Association* of Ideas in our Minds, we may be enabled to account for that (almost diabolical) Passion called *Envy*, which we promis'd to consider.

Mr. *Locke* observes, and I believe very justly, that there are some Men entirely unacquainted with this Passion. For most Men that are used to Reflection, may remember the very time when they were first under the dominion of it.

Envy is generally defined to be that Pain which arises in the Mind from observing the Prosperity of others; not of *all* others indefinitely, but only of some particular Persons. Now the examining who those particular Persons whom we are apt to envy are, will lead us to the true Origin of this Passion. And if a Man will be at the Pains to consult his Mind, or to look into the World, he'll find that these particular Persons are always such as upon some account or other he has had a *Rivalship* with. For when two or more are Competitors for the same thing, the Success of the one must necessarily tend to the Detriment of the other, or others: hence the Success of my Rival and Misery or Pain are joined together in my Mind; and this connection or association remaining in my Mind, even after the Rivalship ceases, makes me always affected with Pain whenever I hear of his Success, tho' in Affairs which have no manner of Relation to the Rivalship, much more in those that bring that to my Remembrance, and put me in mind of what I might have enjoy'd had it not been for him. This may possibly cast some Light upon the black Designs and envious Purposes of the fallen Angels. For why might not they have formerly had some Competition with their Fellows? and why may not such Associations be as strong in them as us?

Thus also we are apt to envy those Persons that refuse to be guided by our Judgments and persuaded by us. For this is nothing else than a Rivalship about the Superiority of Judgment; and we take a secret Pride both to let the World see, and in imagining ourselves, that we were in the right.

There is one thing more to be observ'd in answer to this Objection, and that is, that we do not always (and perhaps not for the most part) *make* this Association ourselves, but *learn* it from *others: i. e.* that we annex Pleasure or Pain to certain Things or Actions because we see others do it, and acquire Principles of Action by imitating those whom we admire, or whose Esteem we would procure: Hence the Son too often inherits both the Vices and the Party of his Father, as well as his Estate: Hence *National* Virtues and Vices, Dispositions and Opinions: And from hence we may observe how easy it is to account for what is generally call'd the *Prejudice of Education*; how soon we catch the Temper and Affections of those whom we daily converse with; how almost insensibly we are *taught* to love, admire or hate; to be grateful, generous, compassionate or cruel, *&c.*

What I say then in answer to the Objection is this: 'That it is necessary in order to solve the principal Actions of human Life to suppose a Moral Sense (or what is signify'd by that Name) and also public Affections; but I deny that this Moral Sense, or these public Affections are innate, or *implanted* in us: they are acquired either from our own *Observation* or the *Imitation* of others.' But whether I have rightly deny'd it or no must depend upon the Arguments, and the Reader is to judge impartially for himself. I think this Matter deserves a fair Examination; and if what has been said already put others upon thinking of it I have my End.

JOHN BROWN

'On the Motives to Virtue, and the Necessity
of Religious Principle' (1751)

John Brown (1715–1766)

Biographical Note

Brown's family originated in the Scottish town of Haddington. His father, an episcopalian minister, served as curate of Rothbury, Northumberland, where John was born 5 November 1715. Shortly afterwards the family moved to the living of Wigton. John was educated at Wigton Grammar School. In 1732 he matriculated at St. John's College, Cambridge, receiving his BA with distinction in 1735 (MA 1739). There is evidence that Brown was acquainted with Francis Blackburne who, it is said, 'knew something of him at different times of his life'.[1] At Cambridge he may also have met theologians such as Waterland and Taylor. After taking orders, Brown was appointed minor canon and lecturer at Carlisle Cathedral. He proved himself a good Whig, serving in 1745 at the siege of Carlisle, and preaching sermons demonstrating his Whig principles. In 1747 Bishop Osbaldison of Carlisle appointed him one of his chaplains. When censured for omitting the Athanasian creed (doubtfully an inadvertent omission), Brown established his orthodoxy by reading the Creed, then resigned his chaplaincy.

Through William Warburton, the celebrated Bishop of Gloucester, Brown was entertained at Prior Park by Ralph Allen, to whom he dedicated his first major treatise, *Essays on the Characteristics of the Earl of Shaftesbury* (1751). Impressed by Brown's poem, *An Essay on Satire occasion'd by the Death of Mr Pope* (1745), it was Warburton who suggested that a critique of Shaftesbury would be welcomed. At Prior Park Brown met Charles Yorke, brother of Philip Yorke, Earl of Hardwicke (1690–1764). Despite public censure of clerical playwrights (Brown's plays *Barbarossa* and *Athelstane* were published and performed in 1754 and 1756) Hardwicke, on the recommendation of Warburton to Yorke, presented Brown in 1756 to the living of Great Horkesley, near Colchester. The Hardwicke connection might have brought him into contact with Soame Jenyns. Again Brown resigned his living, supposedly because his flattery of Pitt and Hardwicke in the otherwise pessimistic *An Estimate of the Manners and Principles of the Times* (2 vols. 1757, 1758) did not gain him further patronage, although a more complicated course of events is suggested by Rompkey which

---

[1] John Nichols, *Illustrations of the Literary History of the Eighteenth Century consisting of Authentic Memoirs and original Letters of Eminent Persons*, 8 vols. (1858; reprt. New York 1966), iii. 715.

involved an anonymous defence of Pitt and attack on Jenyns in the *Monitor*.[2]

Brown's success with the *Estimate*, his unexpectedly popular attack on the public morals of England's higher ranks, occasioned a rift with Warburton, who was jealous of his protegé. Thereafter Brown became uneasy about his ties to the Bishop, commenting 'I cannot bring myself to give up the freedom of my mind to Warburton and therefore we do not agree'.[3] He denied Bishop Lowth's charge of being obsequious to Warburton. Archdeacon Blackburne blamed those who had led Brown into intimacy with Warburton, saying 'No arts or allurements were omitted to attach him to a party, which easily found the means to consign him to contempt the moment it was suspected that he was uneasy in his bonds'.[4]

David Garrick acted in both Brown's plays – *Barbarossa* and *Athelstane* – but also managed to fall out with Brown. On this occasion Warburton acted as an intermediary, commenting to Garrick that Brown had 'too much honesty for a successful court chaplain, and too much sense and sobriety for a city preacher'.[5] As Andrew Kippis later remarked, Brown 'did not excel in the part of preserving his friends'.[6] Brown also managed to irritate David Hume by a comment in the *Estimate*, in which he accused 'a certain historian of our own times' of seeking popular acclaim and financial gain by disgracing religion. He quoted Hume as having implied, in a reply to the accusation that he expressly inserted irreligious passages in his *History of England*, that it had been done so that 'his book might sell'.[7] Mossner thought Brown's accusations 'malevolent', and quoted Josiah Tucker's condemnation of Brown's action in which he called him 'that superficial Creature'.[8] Hume expressed his puzzlement at Brown's attack on him to his publisher, Andrew Millar, wondering 'what I wrote that coud give him any handle for his Calumny'.[9]

In 1761 Osbaldison presented Brown to the living of St Nicholas, Newcastle, where he remained until his death in 1766. The circumstances of Brown's death are curious. Following the publication of *Thoughts on Civil*

2   *The Monitor, or British Freeholder*, No. 187, (17 Feb. 1759). Ronald Rompkey, *Soame Jenyns* (Boston 1984), p. 24; see also Jenyns below, p. 109. Rompkey relates that Brown resigned from the living of Great Horkesley when Hardwicke learnt that he was the author of the attack on Jenyns. However, the claim that Brown was the author in question does not find support in Donald D. Eddy's comprehensive *A Bibliography of John Brown* (New York 1971).

3   A. W. Evans, *Warburton and the Warburtonians: A Study in some Eighteenth-Century Controversies* (London 1932), p. 201.

4   Letter, 16 Oct. 1766, printed in *The St. James's Chronicle*, republished in Nichols, *Literary History*, iii. 715–18, quote at p. 715.

5   Evans, *Warburton and the Warburtonians*, pp. 200–1.

6   Andrew Kippis, *Biographia Britannica*, 5 vols., 2nd edn. (London 1780), ii. 660.

7   *The Letters of David Hume*, 2 vols., ed. J. Y. T. Greig (Oxford 1932), i. 249.

8   Ernest Campbell Mossner, *The Life of David Hume* (Austin 1954), pp. 308–9; see also *Letters of David Hume*, i. 270.

9   *Letters of David Hume*, i. 249.

Liberty, On Licentiousness and Faction (1765) he planned to go to Russia to assist the Empress Catherine in setting up a school system. Catherine forwarded £1000 to her London ambassador to facilitate Brown's journey to St Petersburg. Brown's friends persuaded him to abandon the idea, ostensibly because of his failing health. He had long suffered from gout and rheumatism, and had renewed attacks at this time.[10] In August 1766 Brown wrote to Catherine accounting for his expenses and explaining his situation. Soon after, on 23 September, he committed suicide by cutting his throat. After his death, a contemporary writer suggested that the proposal to send Brown to Russia was an 'egregious farce', the object of which was to render him 'perfectly ridiculous'.[11] Horace Walpole said that Brown 'ended his life deplorably by his own hand in a fit of illness and madness, having been invited to Russia to assist the Czarina in some of her ostentatious projects on legislation, and being oppressed, either with imaginary glory, or despondence of supporting his reputation'.[12] On Brown's suicide, Kippis quoted Mrs. Gilpin of Carlisle, who knew Brown from his days in Carlisle, about his long-term tendency to 'frenzy'. About his death, however, she stated:

> It was no pre-meditated purpose in him; for he abhorred the thought of self-murder, and, in bitterness of soul, expressed his fears to me, that, one time or another, some ready mischief might present itself to him, at a time when he was wholly deprived of his reason.[13]

Though a frequent critic of Brown, Walpole tempered his views in writing to Thomas Gray on Brown's death, 'poor Dr B. The unfortunate man apprehended himself going mad, and two nights after cut his throat in bed'.[14] In a letter to William Cole in 1780 Walpole could not resist his usual criticisms of Brown, but added 'poor Dr. Brown was mad; and therefore might be in earnest, whether he played the Fool or the Reformer'.[15] For his part, Cole felt more kindly towards Brown, replying that one should not be 'too hard on Dr Browne [sic], whose works deserve the highest encomia, whatever his self-sufficiency and arrogance may take away from their merit'.[16] He told Walpole, 'I can't help having a predilection

---

[10] Kippis, *Biographia Britannica*, ii. 667.
[11] Nichols, *Illustrations of the Literary History*, iii. 718.
[12] Horace Walpole, *Memoirs of the Reign of King George III*, first published by Sir Denis Le Marchand, Bart., re-edited by G. F. Russell Barker, 4 vols. (1894; New York 1971), ii. 57.
[13] Kippis, *Biographia Britannica*, ii. 673.
[14] *Horace Walpole's Correspondence with Thomas Gray, Richard West and Thomas Ashton*, ed. W. S. Lewis, L. Lam and Charles H. Bennett (London 1948), [*The Yale Edition of Horace Walpole's Correspondence*, ed. W. S. Lewis], xiv. 159.
[15] *Horace Walpole's Correspondence with the Rev. William Cole*, ed. W. S. Lewis and A. Dayle Wallace (London 1937), [*Yale Edition*], ii. 187.
[16] *Walpole's Correspondence with the Rev. William Cole*, ii. 190.

for his *Estimate* and *Essays on the Characteristics*, as tending to a worthy purpose'.[17] On the other hand, Walpole considered *Thoughts on Civil Liberty* 'a servile tract', and its author, 'the ape of Pope'.[18]

In addition to the works already mentioned, Brown's major publications include *A Dissertation on the Rise, Union, and Power, the Progressions, Separations and Corruptions, of Poetry and Music, To which is prefixed, The Cure of Saul* (1763), *Sermons on Various Subjects* (1764), and *The History of the Rise and Progress of Poetry, through Several Species* (1764).

Note on the Text

'On the Motives to Virtue, and the Necessity of Religious Principle' is the second of Brown's three *Essays on the Characteristics of the Earl of Shaftesbury* (1751). The other essays are 'On Ridicule considered as a Test of Truth' and 'On revealed Religion, and Christianity'. Between 1751 and 1764 six more 'editions' of the *Essays* appeared (little more than reprints of the original volume), including two in Dublin in 1751 and 1752. The text of the second essay reproduced here is from the first edition of the *Essays*, printed for C. Davis of Holborn in London.

---

[17] *Walpole's Correspondence with the Rev. William Cole*, ii. 196.
[18] Walpole, *Memoirs of the Reign of King George III*, ii. 57.

ESSAY II.
On the Motives to VIRTUE, and the Necessity of Religious Principle.

Section I.

HAVING considered the noble Writer's two first Treaties, so far as they regard the *Use of Ridicule*, we now come to his *Soliloquy*, or *Advice to an Author*. And here, bating only a few accidental Passages, which will be occasionally pointed out hereafter, we shall have little more to do, than to approve and admire: The whole Dissertation being, in its general Turn, one continued Instance of its Author's Knowledge and refined Taste in Books, Life, and Manners. I could dwell with Pleasure on the Beauties of this Work, if indeed they needed an Explanation: But that noble Union of Truth and Eloquence which shines through the whole, as it supersedes, so it would disgrace any Attempt of this Kind. To the Work itself therefore I recommend the Reader.

THE noble Writer having thus prepared us for the Depths of Philosophy, by enjoining an unfeigned and rigorous *Self-Examination*; proceeds to that highest and most interesting of all Subjects, *The Motives to virtuous Action*. And here it will probably appear, that with a Variety of useful Truths, he hath blended several plausible Mistakes, which, when more nearly viewed, seem to be attended with a Train of very extraordinary Consequences. What he hath given us on this Subject, lies chiefly in the two Treaties, which compose his second Volume: But as he frequently refers us to the other Parts of his Writings, where he hath accidentally treated the same Points in a more explicit Manner; so the same Liberty of comparing one Passage with another, will, I apprehend, be judged reasonable by the candid Reader. Thus we shall more effectually penetrate into his true Scope and Intention; and draw off, as far as may be, that Veil of *Mystery*, in which, for Reasons best known to himself, he hath so often wrapped his Opinions.

Section II.

'TIS no uncommon Circumstance in Controversy, for the Parties to engage in all the Fury of Disputation, without precisely instructing their Readers, or truly knowing themselves, the Particulars about which they differ. Hence that fruitless Parade of Argument, and those opposite Pretences to Demonstration, with which most Debates, on every Subject, have been inserted. Would the contending Parties first be sure of their own Meaning (a Species of Self-Examination which, I think, the noble Writer hath not condescended to mention) and then communicate their Sense to others in plain Terms and Simplicity of Heart, the Face of Controversy would soon be changed: And real Knowledge, instead of imaginary Conquest, would be the noble Reward of literary Toil.

In the mean Time, a History of *Logomachies*[a] well executed, would be no unedifying Work. And in order to open a Path to so useful an Undertaking, I will venture to give the present Section as an Introduction to it: For sure, among all the Questions which have exercised the Learned, this concerning *the Motives to Virtue* hath given Rise to the greatest Profusion of loose Talk and ambiguous Expression. The Argument hath been handled by several of great Name: And it might possibly be deemed Presumption to differ from any of them, had they not so widely differed among themselves. Much hath been said, and various have been their Opinions concerning our *Motives to Virtue*; but little hath been said in any definitive Manner, on the previous and fundamental Question, *What Virtue is?* By which I do not mean, what Actions are called Virtuous, for, about that, Mankind are pretty well agreed; but, what that *characteristic Circumstance* is, on Account of which, these Actions are called *virtuous*. Till we have determined this with all possible Precision, we cannot determine 'upon what Foundation Mankind can be moved to the Practice of them.' Our first Enquiry therefore must be, concerning the *Nature of Virtue:* In the Investigation of which, the Moralists of most Ages seem to have been remarkably defective.

Let us first consider what our noble Author hath said on this Subject. He tells us, 'The Mind cannot be without its Eye and Ear; so as to discern Proportion, distinguish Sound, and scan each Sentiment and Thought which comes before it. It can let nothing escape its Censure. It feels the soft and harsh, the agreeable and disagreeable in the Affections; and finds a *foul* and *fair*, an *harmonious* and a *dissonant*, as really and truly here, as in any musical Numbers, or in the outward Forms and Representations of sensible Things. Nor can it withold its Admiration and Extasy, its Aversion and Scorn, any more in what relates to one, than to the other of these Subjects. So that to deny the common natural Sense of a *sublime* and *beautiful* in Things, will appear an *Affectation* merely to any one who considers duly of this Affair[b].' The Perception of this Beauty he calls the *moral Sense* or *Taste*; and affirms, that Virtue consists in 'a perfect Conformity of our Affections and Actions with this supreme Sense and Symmetry of Things.'

---

[a]   A Strife about Words.
[b]   *Inquiry concerning Virtue*, Part iii. § 3.

Or, to use his own Words, 'The Nature of Virtue consists in a certain just Disposition or proportionable Affection of a rational Creature towards the *moral Objects of Right and Wrong*[c].'

THE next Writer I shall mention is the learned and amiable Dr. CLARKE. He thinks it necessary to reject this Idea of Virtue, which the noble Writer had established; and as a surer Foundation, than what mere *Affection*, *Sense*, or *Taste* could produce, lays the Basis of Virtue in *Reason*: And insists, that its true Nature lies in 'a Conformity of our Actions, with certain eternal and immutable Relations and Differences of Things. That from these, which are necessarily perceived by every rational Agent, there naturally arise certain *moral Obligations*, which are of themselves incumbent on all, antecedent to all positive Institution, and to all Expectation of Reward or Punishment[d].'

AFTER these, comes an ingenious and candid Writer, and in Opposition to both these Schemes of Moral, fixes the Nature of Virture in 'a Conformity of our Actions with *Truth*.' He affirms, that 'no Act, whether Word or Deed, of any Being, to whom moral Good and Evil are imputable, that interferes with any *true* Proposition, or *denies* any thing to be as it is, can be *right*. That, on the contrary every Act is right which does not contradict Truth, but treats every thing as being what it is[e].'

THERE are, besides these, several other philosophical Opinions concerning the Nature of Virtue: as, that it consists in following *Nature* – in avoiding all *Extremes* – in the Imitation of the *Deity*. But these are still more loose and indeterminate Expressions, if possible, than the former. If therefore the first should appear vague and ineffectual, the latter must of Course fall under an equal Censure.

Now it will appear, that all the three Definitions of Virtue, which Lord SHAFTESBURY, Dr. CLARKE, and Mr. WOLLASTON have given us, in designed Opposition to each other, are equally defective; 'Because they do not give us any more particular or determinate Ideas, than what we have from that *Single Word*, which with so much fruitless Labour they attempt to define.'

LET us first examine the noble Writer's Definition in this View. He says, that 'Virtue consists in a Conformity of our Affections with our natural Sense of the Sublime and Beautiful in Things, or with the moral Objects of Right and Wrong.' – Now, what new Idea do we gain from this pompous Definition? Have we not the same general Idea from the Word *Virtue*, as from the more diffused Expression of *the Sublime and Beautiful of Things*? And cannot we gather as much from either of these, as from the subsequent Phrase, 'the *moral Objects of Right and Wrong*?' – They are all general Names, relative to something which is yet unknown, and which is no more explained by the pretended Definition, than by the Word which is attempted

[c]   *Inquiry concerning Virtue*, Part iii § 1.
[d]   Clarke's *Demonst.* passim.
[e]   Wollaston's *Rel. of Nat.* § 1. passim.

to be defined. Indeed, when his Lordship further affirms, that to relieve the Needy, or help the Friendless, is an Instance of this Sublime and Beautiful of Things, we then obtain a more determinate Idea, with Regard to that particular Case. But still we are as much as ever at a Loss for a general *Criterion* or *Test*, by which the Virtue of our other Actions is to be determined. To say, therefore, that Virtue consists in acting according to the *fair*, the *handsome*, the *sublime*, the *beautiful*, the *decent*, the *moral Objects* of *Right* and *Wrong*, is really no more than ringing Changes upon Words. We might with equal Propriety affirm, 'that *Virtue* consists in *acting virtuously*.' This Deficiency Mr. WOLLASTON clearly saw. 'They, says he, who reckon nothing to be (*morally*) good, but what they call *honestum*, may denominate Actions according as that is, or is not the Cause or End of them: But then, what is *honestum*? Something is still wanting to measure Things by, and to separate the *honesta* from the *inhonesta*[f].'

DR. CLARKE's Definition seems not to include any thing more precise or determinate, than the noble Writer's. He affirms, that 'Virtue consists in a Conformity of our Actions with right Reason, or the eternal and immutable Relations and Differences of Things.' Here then a parallel Question ariseth, 'What is *right Reason*, and what these *eternal Relations* which are affirmed, by the learned Writer, to be the Test or Criterion of Virtue?' And 'tis observable, that when he comes to prove the Truth and Reality of these *Relations*, he is forced to resolve it into a *self-evident* Proposition. 'These Things, saith he, are so notoriously plain and *self-evident*, that nothing but the extremest Stupidity of Mind, Corruption of Manners, or Perverseness of Spirit, can possibly make any Man entertain the least Doubt concerning them[g].' Thus too, his ingenious *Advocate*, when pushed by his Adversary to declare, whether he perceives the Truth of these Relations by *Proof* or *Intuition* confesses 'they may be looked upon as *self-evident*[h].' Here then we may observe a strong Coincidence between the noble Writer's System of Expression, and this of Dr. CLARKE: For as the one affirms, that the *Sublime* and *Beautiful* of Things is *self-evident*, so the other affirms the same of the *Fit* and *Reasonable*. And as the *Sublime* and *Beautiful* give us no more determinate Ideas, than the *Virtuous*, so neither can we obtain any additional Information from the *Fit* and *Reasonable*. We are equally at a Loss to know what is *fit* and *reasonable*, as to know what is *virtuous*: Therefore the *one* can never be an adequate Definition of the other. Here too, Mr. WOLLASTON plainly saw the Want of Precision. As to those, he saith, 'who make *right Reason* to be a Law – it is true, that whatever will bear to be tried by right reason, is right; and that which is condemned by it, wrong: – But the Manner in which they have delivered themselves, *is not yet explicit enough*. It leaves Room for so many Disputes and *opposite*

[f]   *Rel. of Nat.* p. 22.
[g]   *Demonst.* p. 50.
[h]   Balguy's *Tracts*, 2[d] Part, of *Mor. Goodness*, p. 10.

right Reasons, that nothing can be settled, while every one pretends that *his* Reason is right[i].'

Now it will doubtless appear a Circumstance of Singularity, that Mr. WOLLASTON, who saw the essential defects of these two Definitions, should himself offer a *third*, which is precisely liable to the same Objection. 'Virtue, faith this learned Writer, consists in a Conformity of our Actions with Truth; in treating everything as being what it is.' Well: be it so. Yet the Question still recurs, what is *moral Truth?* And this demands a *Definition* no less than *Virtue*, which was the Thing to be defined. Had Lord SHAFTESBURY lived to see this new Theory proposed, how naturally would he have retorted Mr. WOLLASTON's Objection? 'You, Mr. WOLLASTON, reckon nothing to be *morally Good*, but what you call *Truth:* And you may indeed denominate Actions, according as that is, or is not, the Cause or End of them: But then, what is *Truth?* Something further is still wanting to measure Things by, and to separate *Truth* from *Falsehood*.' – Thus too would Dr. CLARKE have naturally replied: "Tis true, that whatever will bear to be tried by *Truth*, is right; and that which is condemned by it, wrong: But the Manner in which you have delivered yourself, is not yet explicit enough. You have rather confounded my Definition, than given a new one of your own: All that you have added, is an Impropriety of Speech. I speak of the *Rectitude* of Actions, you of the *Truth* of Actions; which I call an Impropriety of Speech, because *Truth* relates to *Affirmations*, not to *Actions*; to what is *said*, not to what is *done*. But supposing the Propriety of your Expression, what further Criterion have you gained? You confess, that *Truth* is discovered by *Reason* only; for you say, that *to deny Things to be as they are, is the Transgression of the great Law of our Nature, the Law of Reason*[k]. If so, then Reason is as good a Guide as Truth: We can as certainly know what is *right Reason*, as what is *Truth*. If therefore my Definition is defective, yours must be so too. If mine leaves Room for so many Disputes and *opposite right Reasons*, that nothing can be settled, while every one pretends that his Reason is *right*; yours must of Necessity be liable to the same Objection, must leave Room for so many Disputes and *opposite Truths*, that nothing can be settled, while every one pretends that his Idea of *Truth* is the *right* one. Truth, then, can never be a better Criterion than Reason, because our Idea of *Truth* must always *depend* upon our *Reason*.'

THUS it should seem, that our three celebrated Writers have not given the Satisfaction which might have been expected in an Affair of such philosophical Importance. Their common Attempt is to define the Nature, or fix the Criterion of Virtue: To this End, the first affirms, it consists in a Conformity of our Actions to the *Fair* and *Handsome*, the *Sublime* and

[i]   *Rel. of Nat.* p. 23.
[k]   *Rel. of Nat.* p. 15.

Beautiful of Things: The Second, the *Fitness*, *Reasons*, and *Relations* of Things: The Third, the *Truth* of Things. But inasmuch as these general Terms of *Beauty*, *Fitness*, *Truth*, convey not any more determinate Idea, than that of *Virtue*, which they are brought to define; the several pretended Definitions are therefore *inadequate* and *defective*[1].

WHAT then is *Virtue*? Let us consider its true Nature in the following Section.

Section III.

THERE are few among Mankind, who have not been often struck with Admiration at the Sight of that Variety of Colours and Magnificence of Form, which appear in an Evening *Rainbow*. The *uninstructed* in Philosophy consider that splendid Object, not as dependent on any other, but as being possessed of a *self-given* and *original Beauty*. But he who is led to know, that its Place and Appearance always varies with the Situation of the *Sun*; that when the latter is in his Meridian, the former becomes an inconsiderable Curve skirting the Horizon; that as the Sun descends, the Rainbow rises; till at the Time of his *Setting*, it encompasses the Heavens with a glorious Circle, yet *dies* away when he *disappears*; the Enquirer is then convinced, that this gay Meteor did but shine with a *borrowed* Splendor, derived from the Influence of that mighty *Luminary*.

THUS, in like Manner, though the *Beauty*, *Fitness*, *Truth*, or Virtue, of all those Actions which we term *morally Good*, seem at first View to reside in the several Actions, in an original and independent Manner; yet on a nearer Scrutiny we shall find, that, properly speaking, their Nature ariseth from their *Ends* and *Consequences*; that as these *vary*, the Nature of the several Actions *varies* with them; that from these alone, Actions gain their *Splendor*, are denominated *morally Good*, and give us the Ideas of *Beauty*, *Fitness*, *Truth*, or *Virtue*.

THE first Proofs in Support of this Opinion shall be drawn from those very Writers who most zealously oppose it. And here 'tis first remarkable, that 'while they attempt to fix their several Criterions of absolute, independent Beauty, Fitness, and Truth; they are obliged to admit *Exceptions*,

---

[1]   Let it be observed once for all, that the Definitions here censured as defective, are little more than direct Transcripts of what the old *Greek* Philosophers, and *Tully* after them, have said on the same Subject. To shew how generally this Kind of Language infects the Writers on Morality, we need only transcribe the subsequent Passage from a Follower of the noble Writer, 'We need not therefore be at a Loss, said he, for a *Description* of the sovereign Good – We may call it *Rectitude* of Conduct. – If that be too contracted, we may enlarge, and say, 'tis – to live perpetually selecting and rejecting according to *the Standard of Our Being*. If we are for still different Views, we may say, 'tis – to live in the Discharge of *Moral Offices* – to live *according to Nature* – To live *according to Virtue* – to live according to *just Experience* of those Things which happen around us.' Three Treatises by *J. H.* Treat. 3ᵈ, p. – 07.

which effectually destroy what they design to establish.' The following Instance, from one of these celebrated Writers, is equally applicable to the other two.

MR. WOLLASTON speaks in the following Manner: 'To talk to a Post, or otherwise treat it as if it was a Man, would surely be reckoned an *Absurdity*, if not *Distraction*. Why? Because this is to treat it as being what it is not. And why should not the converse be reckoned as bad; that is, to treat a Man as a Post? As if he had no Sense, and felt not Injuries which he doth feel; as if to him Pain and Sorrow were not Pain; Happiness not Happiness[m].' Now, you see that on his Scheme of absolute irrelative Truth, the Absurdity of *talking to a Post* is precisely of the same Nature with that of *injuring a Man*: For in both Cases, we treat the Post and the Man, as being *what they are not*. Consequently, on this Philosophy, if it be morally Evil to *injure* a *Man*, 'tis likewise morally Evil to *talk* to a *Post*. Not that I suppose Mr. WOLLASTON would have maintained this Consequence. He knew that the First of these Absurdities would only deserve the Name of *Folly*; the latter, of a *Crime*. As therefore he allows that Truth is equally violated in either Case; as there is something *highly immoral* in the one, and *nothing immoral* in the other, here is an Exception which overturns his Principle: which proves that the Morality or Immorality of Actions depends on something *distinct* from mere abstract, irrelative *Truth*.

THE same Exception must be admitted on Dr. CLARKE's System of Expression. For sure, 'tis neither *fit* nor *reasonable*, nor agreeable to the Relations of Things, that a Man should talk to a Post. Yet, although it be admitted as *irrational* and *absurd*, I do not imagine, any of Dr. CLARKE's Defenders would say it was *immoral*. So again, with regard to Lord SHAFTESBURY, 'tis clear there can be nothing of the *Sublime* or *Beautiful* in this Action of talking to a Post: On the contrary, there is (to use his own Manner of Expression) an apparent Indecency, Impropriety, and *Dissonance* in it. Yet, although his Admirers might justly denominate it *incongruous*, they would surely be far from branding it as *vile*. Here then the same Exception again takes place, which demonstrates that *Virtue* cannot consist either in *abstract Fitness* or *Beauty*; but that something further is required in order to constitute its Nature.

POSSIBLY therefore, the Patrons of these several Theories may alledge, that Actions which relate to *inanimate Beings* only, can properly be called no more than *naturally* beautiful, fit, or true: But that *moral* Fitness, Beauty, or Truth, can only arise from such Actions as relate to Beings that are *sensible* or *intelligent*. Mr. BALGUY expresly makes this Exception: He affirms, that 'moral Actions are such as are knowingly directed towards some Object intelligent or sensible[n].'

[m] *Rel. of Nat.* p. 15.
[n] *First Treat. on Moral Goodness*, p. 28.

AND so far indeed this Refinement approaches towards the Truth, as it excludes all *inanimate* Things from being the Objects of moral Good and Evil. Yet even this Idea of moral Beauty, Fitness, or Truth, is highly indeterminate and defective: Because innumerable Instances may be given, of Actions directed towards Objects sensible and intelligent, some of which Actions are manifestly *becoming, fit*, or *true*, others as manifestly *incongruous, irrational*, and *false*, yet none of them, in any Degree, *virtuous* or *vicious, meritorious* or *immoral*. Thus to speak to a Man in a Language he understands, is an Action *becoming, fit*, or *true*; 'tis treating him according to the Order, Relations, and Truth of Things; 'tis treating him according to *what he is*. On the contrary, to speak to him in a Language he understands not, is an Action neither *becoming, fit*, nor *true*; 'tis treating him according to *what he is not*; 'tis treating him *as a Post*. But although the first of these Actions be undeniably becoming, fit, or true, who will call it *Virtue?* And though the latter be undeniably incongruous, irrational, and false, who will call it *Vice?* Yet both these Actions are directed towards a Being that is sensible and intelligent. It follows therefore, that an Action is not either morally Good or Evil, merely because it is conformable to the Beauty, Fitness, or Truth of Things, even though it be directed towards an Object both *sensible* and *intelligent*; but that something still further, some more distinguishing and characteristic Circumstance is necessary, in order to fix its real Essence.

WHAT this peculiar Circumstance may be, we come now to enquire. And the first Lights in this Enquiry shall be borrowed from these very celebrated Writers, whom we have here ventured to oppose. For such is the Force and Energy of Truth, that, while they are attempting to involve her in a Cloud of Metaphysics, she breaks through the mystic Veil they had prepared and woven for her with so much Art, and diffuseth a Stream of genuine Lustre, which the most obdurate Prejudice can hardly withstand.

AND first, though the *noble* Writer every where attempts to fix an original, independent, moral Beauty of Action, to which every thing is to be referred, and which itself is not to be referred to any thing further[o]: Yet when he comes to an Enumeration of those *particular* Actions, which may be called morally Beautiful, he always singles out such as have a direct and necessary Tendency to *the Happiness of Mankind*. Thus he talks of the Notion of *a public Interest*[p], as necessary towards a proper Idea of Virtue: He speaks of public Affection in the same Manner; and reckons Generosity, Kindness, and Compassion, as the Qualities which alone can render Mankind truly Virtuous. So again, when he fixes the Bounds of the social Affections, he evidently refers us to the same End of human Happiness. 'If Kindness or Love of the most natural Sort be immoderate, it is undoubtedly

[o]   *Essay on Wit – Soliloquy – Enquiry – Moralists – Miscellanies –* passim.
[p]   *Enqu.* B. i. p. 2. § 3.

vicious. For thus over-great Tenderness *destroys the Effect of Love*; and excessive Pity renders us incapable of giving Succour[q].' When he fixes the proper Degrees of the *Private Affections*, he draws his Proof from this one Point, 'that by having the Self-Passions too intense or strong, a Creature becomes miserable[r].' Lastly, when he draws a Catalogue of such Affections, as are most opposite to Beauty and moral Good, he selects '*Malice, Hatred of Society – Tyranny – Anger – Revenge – Treachery – Ingratitude*[s].' In all these Instances, the Reference to human Happiness is so particular and strong, that from these alone an unprejudiced Mind may be convinced, that the Production of *human Happiness* is the great universal Fountain, whence our Actions derive their *moral Beauty*.

THUS again, though the excellent Dr. CLARKE attempts to fix the Nature and Essence of Virtue in certain Differences, Relations, and Fitnesses of Things, to which our Actions ought ultimately to be referred; yet in enumerating the several Actions which he denominates *morally Good*, he mentions none, but what evidently promote the same great End, 'the Happiness of Man.' He justly speaks of the *Welfare* of the *Whole*, as being the *necessary* and most *important* Consequence of *virtuous* Action. He tells us, 'that it is *more fit* that GOD should regard the *Good* of the *whole* Creation, than that he should make the Whole continually miserable: That all Men should endeavour to promote the *universal Good* and *Welfare* of all; than that all Men should be continually contriving the *Ruin* and *Destruction* of all[t].' Here again, the Reference is so direct and strong to *the Happiness of Mankind*, that even from the Instances alledged by the worthy Author, it appears, that a Conformity of our Actions to this great End, is the very Essence of *moral Rectitude*.

MR. WOLLASTON is no less explicit in this particular: For in every Instance he brings, *the Happiness* of Man is the single End to which his Rule of Truth verges in an unvaried Manner. Thus in the Passage already cited, though he considers the *talking to a Post* as an *Absurdity* he is far from condemning it as an *immoral* Action: But in the same Paragraph, when he comes to give an Instance of the Violation of *moral* Truth, he immediately has recourse to *Man*; and not only so, but to the *Happiness* of Man. 'Why, saith he, should not the converse be reckoned as bad; that is, to treat a *Man* as a *Post*; as if he had no *Sense*, and *felt* not *Injuries*, which he doth *feel*; as if to him *Pain* and *Sorrow* were not *Pain*; *Happiness* not *Happiness*?' At other Times he affirms, that 'the *Importance* of the Truths on the one and the other Side should be diligently *compared*[v].' And I would gladly know, how one Truth can be more important than another,

---

[q] *Enqu.* B. i. p. 2. § 3.
[r] Ibid.
[s] Ibid.
[t] *Demonst.* p. 45, &c.
[v] *Rel. of Nat.* p. 19.

unless upon this Principle, and in Reference to *the Production of Happiness*. Himself indeed confirms this Interpretation, when he speaks as follows: 'The Truth violated in the former case was, B had a Property in that which gave him such a Degree of *Happiness*: That violated in the latter was, B had a Property in that which gave him a *Happiness* vastly *superior* to the other: The Violation *therefore* in the latter Case was *upon this Account* a vastly *greater* Violation than in the former[x].'

THESE Evidences may seem sufficient: But that all possible Satisfaction may be given in a Circumstance which is of the greatest Weight in the present Question, these further Observations may be added.

As therefore these celebrated Writers give no Instances of moral Beauty, Fitness, or Truth, but what finally relate to the Happiness of Man; so, if we appeal to the common Sense of Mankind, we shall see that the Idea of Virtue hath never been universally affixed to any Action or Affection of the Mind, unless where this Tendency to produce Happiness was at least *apparent*. What are all the black Catalogues of Vice or moral Turpitude, which we read in History, or find in the Circle of our own Experience, what are they but so many Instances of *Misery produced?* And what are the fair and amiable Atchievments of *Legislators*, *Patriots*, and *Sages* renowned in Story, what but so many Efforts to raise Mankind from Misery, and establish the public Happiness on a sure Foundation? The first are *vicious*, *immoral*, *deformed*, because there we see Mankind *afflicted* or *destroyed*: The latter are *virtuous*, *right*, *beautiful*, because here we see Mankind *preserved* and *assisted*.

BUT that *Happiness* is the last Criterion or Test, to which the moral Beauty, Truth, or Rectitude of our Affections is to be referred, the two following Circumstances *demonstrate*: First, 'those very Affections and Actions, which, in the ordinary Course of Things, are approved as virtuous, do change their Nature, and become vicious in the strictest Sense, when they contradict this fundamental Law, of the greatest publick Happiness.' Thus, although in general it is a Parent's Duty to prefer a Child's Welfare, to that of another Person, yet, if this natural and just Affection gain such Strength, as to tempt the Parent to violate the *Public* for his Child's *particular* Welfare; what was before a *Duty*, by this becomes immoderate and *criminal*. This the noble Writer hath allowed: 'If Kindness or Love of the most natural Sort be *immoderate*, it is undoubtedly *vicious*[y].' And hence, he says, 'the Excess of motherly Love is owned to be a vicious Fondness[z].' The same *Variation* takes Place with regard to every other Relation between Man and Man. Insomuch, that the superior Regards which we owe to our Family, Friends, Fellow-Citizens, and Countrymen – Regards which, in their proper Degree, aspire to the amiable and high Names of *domestic*

[x]　*Rel. of Nat.* p. 21.
[y]　*Enq. on Virtue.*
[z]　*Enq. on Virtue.*

Love, *Friendship*, *Patriotism* – when once they desert and violate the grand Principle of *universal Happiness*, become a *vicious* Fondness, a mean and odious *Partiality*, justly stigmatized by all, as ignominious and *unworthy*.

SECONDLY, with such uncontrouled Authority does this great Principle command us; that 'Actions, which are in their own Nature most shocking to every *humane* Affection, lose at once their moral Deformity, when they become subservient to the general Welfare; and assume both the Name and the Nature of Virtue.' For what is more contrary to every gentle and kind Affection, that dwells in the human Breast, than to shed the Blood, or destroy the Life of Man? Yet the ruling Principle above-mentioned, can reconcile us even to *this*. And when the Necessity of public Example compels us to make a Sacrifice of this Kind; though we may lament the *Occasion*, we cannot condemn the *Fact*: So far are we from branding it as *Murder*, that we approve it as *Justice*: and always defend it on this great Principle alone, *that it was necessary for the public Good*.

THUS it appears, that those Actions which we denominate Virtuous, Beautiful, Fit, or True, have not any absolute and independent, but a relative and reflected Beauty: And that their Tendency to produce Happiness is the only Source from whence they derive their Lustre. Hence therefore we may obtain a just and adequate Definition of Virtue: Which is no other than 'the[a] Conformity of our Affections with the public Good:' Or 'the voluntary Production of the greatest Happiness.'

Section IV.

IT may possibly seem strange that so much has been thought necessary to be opposed to these metaphysical *Refinements* concerning the Nature of Virtue: But in Reality, 'tis a Point of the utmost Consequence: For these Refinements have given rise to a plausible Objection, which hath been retailed in a popular Manner by a late wordy Writer; whose least merit it is to have supplied our modish Coffee-house Philosophers with such a Variety of fashionable Topics, that they have never felt the least Want of that antiquated Assistance derived from Knowledge, Parts, and Learning.

THIS Gentleman taking Advantage of these metaphysical Refinements, and particularly of the noble Writer's imaginary Scheme of *absolute, irrelative* Beauty, 'the Hunting after which (he elegantly affirms) is not much

---

[a] The Gentlemen above examined seem to have mistaken the *Attributes* of Virtue for its *Essence*. Virtue is procuring Happiness: To procure Happiness is *beautiful, reasonable, true*; these are the Qualities or Attributes of the Action: But the Action itself, or its *Essence*, is procuring Happiness.

The Reader who is curious to examine further into this Subject, may consult the *Prelim. Dissert, to Dr. Law's Translation of KING's Origin of Evil*: Together with several Passages in the Translator's *Notes*, where he will find *Sense* and *Metaphysics* united in a very eminent and extraordinary Degree.

better than a wild Goose Chase[b];' attempts from hence to demonstrate, for the *Benefit* of his *Country*, that we are utterly mistaken, when we 'look upon Virtue and Vice as permanent Realities, that must ever be the same in all Countries and all Ages[c]:' And thus he prosecutes his Argument.

THE Worth or Excellence of every thing he says, varies according to Fancy or Opinion. 'Even in human Creatures, what is beautiful in one Country, is not so in another. – Three hundred Years ago, Men were shaved as closely as they are now; since that, they have wore Beards. – How mean and comical a Man looks, that is otherwise well-dressed, in a narrow-brimed Hat, when every body wears broad ones: And again, how monstrous is a very great Hat, when the other Extreme has been in Fashion for a considerable Time? – The many Ways of laying out a Garden judiciously are almost innumerable; and what is called Beautiful in them, varies according to the different *Taste* of Nations and Ages[d].' Thus capricious and uncertain, he tells us, are our Ideas of natural Beauty; and these he brings home to the Point of Morals. 'In Morals there is no greater Certainty: Plurality of Wives is odious among *Christians*, and all the Wit and Learning of a great Genius in Defence of it, has been rejected with Contempt. But Polygamy is not shocking to a *Mahometan*. What Men have learnt from their Infancy enslaves them, and the Force of Custom warps Nature, and at the same Time imitates her in such a Manner, that it is often difficult to know, which of them we are influenced by. In the East formerly, Sisters married Brothers, and it was meritorious for a Man to marry his Mother. Such Alliances are abominable: But it is certain, that whatever Horror we conceive at the Thoughts of them, there is nothing in Nature repugnant against them, but what is built upon Mode and Custom. A religious *Mahometan* may receive as great an Aversion against Wine[e].' Hence, with great Stretch of Reasoning he concludes, 'that Virtue and Vice are not permanent Realities,' but vary as other Fashions, and are subject to no other Law, than that of *Fancy* and *Opinion*.

AND so far indeed, this Gentleman seems to have argued justly, while he contends that mere *Approbation* and *Dislike*, the mere Idea of *Beauty* and *Deformity*, *Truth* or *Rectitude*, without Reference to some further *End*, can never constitute a real or permanent Foundation of *Vice* or *Virtue*. For, as he hath observed, there *have* been considerable Differences of Opinion upon *some Kinds* of moral Beauty and Deformity, in the different Nations and Ages of the World: And each Age and Nation hath ever been alike positive in asserting the Propriety of its own. Therefore, unless we have some further Test, some other distinguishing and characteristic Circumstance to refer to, besides that of mere *Approbation* and *Dislike*, how shall

[b]   *Fable of the Bees*, vol. i. p. 380; Oct. Ed.
[c]   *Fable of the Bees*, p. 372.
[d]   P. 376.
[e]   *Fable of the Bees*, p. 377, 379.

we ever know, which of these *anomalous* Opinions are *right* or *wrong*? If we have nothing further to appeal to, than the mere Propriety of *Taste*, though each may be thoroughly satisfied of the Justness of his own; yet he ought in Reason to allow the same Right of Choice to the rest of Mankind in every Age and Nation: And thus indeed, *moral Beauty* and Deformity, *Virtue* and *Vice*, could have no other Law, than that of *Fancy* and *Opinion*.

But when the great end of public Happiness is ultimately referred to, as the *one*, *uniform* Circumstance that constitutes the *Rectitude* of human Actions; then indeed, *Virtue* and *Vice* assume a more *real* and *permanent* Nature: The common *Sense*, nay, the very *Necessities* of Mankind, will urge them to make an unvaried and just *Distinctio*: For *Happiness* and *Misery* make too strong an Appeal to all the Faculties of Man, to be borne down by the *Caprice* of Fancy and Opinion. That it was either an accidental or a designed Inattention to the great Principle of *Happiness*, that gave this coarse Writer an Occasion to call in Question the permanent *Reality* of Vice and Virtue, the following Considerations may sufficiently convince us.

Should any one ask, whether *Health* and *Sickness* are two different Things, no Doubt we should answer in the Affirmative: And would surely suspect any Man's Sincerity, who should tell us, that what was accounted Health in one Age or Nation, was accounted Sickness in another. There are likewise such Things as wholesome Food and Poisons: Nor would we entertain a much better Opinion of him who should affirm, that *all* depends upon *Fancy*; that *Bread* or *Milk* are nourishing or destructive, that *Arsenic* and *Sublimate* are wholesome or poisonous, as *Imagination* and *Opinion* dictate. On the contrary we know, their Nature with Respect to Man, is *invariable*: The one, universally wholesome, the other, poisonous. Further: we know there have been Debates among Physicians, about *Regimen* and *Diet*: That some have maintained the Wholesomeness of *animal*, others of *vegetable* Food: Some recommended the Drinking of *Water*, others of *Wine*. Yet none was ever so weak as to conclude from these different Opinions about wholesome *Diet*, that the nourishing Qualities of *Bread* or the noxious ones of *Arsenic*, were not *permanent* Realities with regard to Man; or, that the first could be made *poisonous*, the latter, *wholesome*, by Dint of *Fancy* and *Opinion*.

Now, the Case we are debating is exactly parallel. For sure, the *Happiness* and *Misery* of Mankind are Things as distinct as *Health* and *Sickness*: Whence it follows, that certain Actions, under the same Circumstances, must universally produce Happiness or Misery, as naturally as Food produceth Health, or Poison, Sickness and Death. We have already seen, that whatever tends to the Good of all, is, by the consent of all, denominated *Virtue*; that whatever is contrary to this great End, is universally branded as *Vice*; in the same Manner, as whatever nourishes the Body is called *Food*; whatever destroys it, *Poison*. Accordingly, we find the Agreement among Mankind as uniform on the one Subject, as on the other. All

Ages and Nations having without Exception or Variance maintained, that Humanity, Fidelity, Truth, Temperance, and mutual Benevolence, do as naturally produce Happiness, as Food gives Health to the Body: That Cruelty, Treachery, Lying, Intemperance, Inhumanity, Adultery, Murder, do as naturally give Rise to Misery, as Poison brings on Sickness and Death.

BUT hath not this Author given such Instances as prove, that what is detested as *Vice* in one Country, is applauded as *Virtue* in another? That *Polygamy* and *incestuous Marriages* have been in some Nations reputed *lawful*, in others *meritorious?* And if one Virtue or Vice be imaginary or *variable*, doth it not clearly follow that *all* are so?

Now a Man of a common Turn of Thought would be apt to make a very different Inference. If from the *Variety* of Opinions among Mankind as to *some* Virtues or Vices, he concluded *these* were *variable*; then from the universal *Agreement* of Mankind with regard to *other* Virtues and Vices, he would conclude *these* were *fixed* and *invariable*. The *Consent* of Mankind in the *one*, proves as much as their *Disagreement* in the *other*. And 'tis evident that both their Consent and Disagreement arise from the same Principle: A Principle which destroys the Tenets, which this Author labours to establish. For, to resume our Illustration, as the various Opinions concerning the superior Wholesomeness of this or that kind of *Diet*, does not change the Nature of *Bread* or *Poison*; so neither can the various Opinions concerning *Polygamy* or *Incest*, affect or change the Nature of *Benevolence* and *Generosity*, *Adultery* and *Murder*. 'Tis plain, these various Opinions have been formed 'upon such Actions only, as are not universally and clearly connected with the Happiness or Misery of Mankind.' As these Actions have been deemed productive of the *one* or the *other*, they have been regarded as *Virtues* or *Vices*: But this Variety of Opinions does no more unsettle the Nature of those Actions, whose *Tendency* is clear and *certain*; than the Debates on the superior Wholesomeness of animal or vegetable *Diet* can change the Nature of *Bread* and *Poison*. Hence it appears, that Virtue and Vice are permanent Realities, and that their Nature is fixed, certain, and *invariable*.

THUS one Extreme produceth another. For the noble Writer and this Gentleman, through a strong Dislike of each other's Systems, have *both* endeavoured to prove *too much*, and in Consequence have proved *nothing*. The one, contending for the permanent *Reality* of Virtue, and, not content to fix it on its proper Basis, attempts to establish certain *absolute* and *immutable* Forms of Beauty, without Regard to any *further End*; and thus, by laying a chimerical Foundation, *betrays* the Cause which he so gener-ously defends. The other, intent on destroying the permanent Reality of Virtue and Vice, and perceiving how weak a Basis the noble Writer had laid for their Establishment, after proving *this* to be imaginary, as wisely as honestly infers, there is no real one in Nature. We now see the Folly of these Extremes: That as on the one Part, *Virtue* and *Vice* are Things merely *relative* to the *Happiness* of Man; so on the other, while Man continues what he is, all those *Relations* which concern his *Happiness*, and arise from his present Manner of Existence, are likewise *permanent* and *immutable*.

Section V.

BUT this idle Objection against the permanent *Reality* of Virtue and Vice, is not the only one which the Writer last mentioned hath laboured, for the Destruction of Religion and Virtue. For the main Drift and Intention of his Book is to prove no less a Paradox than this, that 'private Vices are public Benefits.' Now, till this Objection be removed, our Idea and Definition of Virtue can never be thoroughly established. For if *private Vices* be *public Benefits*, then private *Virtues* are public *Mischiefs*. And if so, what becomes of our *Definition*?

THE first notable Circumstance in this formidable Assertion of Dr. MANDEVILLE, is its utter Inconsistency with all that he hath advanced in order to destroy the Reality of Vice and Virtue. For if indeed these be mere *Names*, the Creatures of Fancy and Opinion, how can they be attended with any *uniform* Effects? How can they be either public *Benefits*, or public *Evils?* – If on the contrary, they really produce certain uniform Effects, as he hath attempted to prove, how can they be mere *Non-Entities*, the Creatures of Fancy and Opinion? Here lies a gross and palpable Incoherence: Take which of his two Theories you please, the other absolutely destroys it. If Vice be a public *Benefit*, it must be a permanent *Reality*: If it is not a permanent *Reality*, it cannot be a public *Benefit*.

LET us now examine the Foundations on which he hath built this strange Hypothesis. His Book may be analysed into four different Principles, which he hath variously combined, or rather jumbled together, according as each in their Turn would best serve his Purpose.

THE first Principle he lays down, or rather takes for granted, is, 'that Man is a Compound of evil Passions:' In other Words, 'that the Gratification of the natural Appetites is in itself a Vice.' There are in his Book, at least a hundred Pages of the lowest common-place Declamation, all founded on this one Principle, brought from the *Solitary Caves* and *Visions* of the *Desart*. Thus the Desire of being esteemed by others, he stigmatizes with the Name of *Pride:* The natural Desire of social Converse between the two Sexes, he distinguisheth by a *grosser* Appellation. In a word, through the whole Course of his Argument, he *supposes* that every *selfish* Appetite (that is, every Appetite which hath regard to *ourself*) is in its own Nature vile and abominable. This the candid Reader will probably think a little hard upon human Nature: That no Man can be *virtuous*, while he endeavours to be *esteemed*, while he loves to quench his Thirst, minister to Posterity, or eat his Dinner. On the Weight of these plain Instances, the Value of this first Principle may be safely left to any Man's impartial Trial.

HAVING thus branded every Gratification of the natural Appetites; he gains from hence a proper Foundation for the second *Pillar* of this *Temple* of Vice. For he acquaints us with great Solemnity, that, of all other Vices, that of *Luxury* is most beneficial to a State: And that if this were banished the Nation, all Kinds of manual Occupations would immediately languish and decay[f]. He says indeed, that *Pedants* make Objections to this Vice of Luxury, and tell you, that it *enervates* a People: But he adds, that 'since he has seen the World, the Consequences of Luxury to a Nation, seem not so dreadful to him as they did[g].' Had he left the Matter here, we should have been at a Loss to know how he would have made out this strange Tale: But the Riddle is cleared up at once, when we hear him say, that 'every thing is Luxury, that is not immediately necessary to make Man subsist as he is a living Creature[h].'

WE should have been startled perhaps had he assured us, that he had a *Wind-mill* which laid *Eggs*, and bred *young* ones: But how easily had he reconciled us to his Veracity in only saying, that by a *Wind-mill* he meant a *Goose*, or a *Turkey*?

THUS, when he affirms that Luxury produceth public Happiness, we stand ready for some deep and subtile Speculation, to support so wondrous a Paradox. But when he poorly tells us, 'that every thing is Luxury that is not immediately necessary to make Man subsist as he is a living Creature[99];' we laugh not so much at his Impudence, as at our own Folly in giving Ear to so idle a Prater, who, when we thought we had him reforming States, and new-modeling Philosophy, is all the while playing at *Crambo*.

LEST it should be suspected, that the Features of this Man's Folly are here aggravated, take a Copy of his Countenance in one Instance out of many that might be given. 'The Consequences, saith he, of this Vice of Luxury to a Nation, seem not so dreadful to me as they did.' – For 'clean Linen weakens a Man no more than Flannel[i].' Now from these Passages laid together, it appears; first, that Luxury is a Vice; secondly, that to wear clean Linen is Luxury; and, therefore, it comes out as clear as the Day, 'that *to wear clean Linen* is a Vice.'

SERIOUSLY: The Sophistry here employed, is such an Insult as hath been but seldom offered to the human Understanding. Did ever any Man before – except only a Set of wrong-headed Enthusiasts, whose Visions he is here obliged to adopt – did ever any Man maintain, that to use the Bounties of Nature, or enjoy the Conveniences of Life was a criminal Indulgence? Did ever any Man maintain, that *he* could be *viciously* luxurious, who neither

---

[f]   *Fable of the Bees*, passim.
[g]   Ibid. p. 247.
[h]   Ibid. p. 108.
[i]   *Fable of the Bees*, p. 119.

hurt his *Neighbour* nor *himself?* At this Rate, by an arbitrary Use of Words, and putting one Expression for another, we might boldly advance the most palpable Contradictions, and maintain that Dr. M——D—LE was a Man of Modesty and Virtue.

THUS far we have seen this Writer endeavouring to throw the *false* Colours of *Vice* upon the *natural Passions*, and such a *Use* of the Gifts of Nature as is really *Innocent*. In examining his two remaining Principles, we shall find him acting a Part the very *reverse*; and with the same Effrontery, endeavouring to throw the *false* Colours of *public Utility* on such *Actions* and *Affections* as are really *criminal* and *destructive*.

To this Purpose he boldly selects some of the most flagrant Crimes; and assures us, that without their happy Influence the Public would suffer exceedingly. Who had ever dreamt, that Mankind receives Benefit from *Thieves* and *House-breakers*? Yet he tells us, that 'if all People were strictly honest, half the Smiths in the Nation would want Employment[k].'

HIGHWAYMEN too, and *Robbers* are useful in their Generation. For 'if a Miser should be robbed of five hundred or a thousand Guineas[l], it is certain, that as soon as this Money should come to circulate, the Nation would be the better for the Robbery, and receive the same and as real a Benefit from it, as if an Archibishop had left the same Sum to the Public[m].'

HE is abundantly rhetorical on 'the large Catalogue of solid Blessings that accrue from, and are owing to intoxicating Gin[n].' Insomuch, that if the Drunkenness and Frenzy arising from the excessive Use of this salutary Liquor were curbed by the Magistrate, he seems to foretel the soft fatal Consequences to the Public Wealth and Welfare.

HERE then he enumerates several real Crimes, which are *necessarily* attended with *great Evils*; and these he demonstrates, are *accidently* productive of *some Good*. And this indeed is the only Part of his Argument, that is attended with any Degree of Plausibility: For here, it must be owned, there is Room for a dishonest Mind to *confound*, though by no Means to *convince* an impartial Reader. Because the Consequences of these Crimes being of a various and *discordant* Nature, some having the Appearance of *Good*, and others of *Ill* to Society; a *rhetorical* Display of the *former* may possibly induce a superficial Enquirer, who is caught by a Glare of Eloquence, to doubt whether *these* do not really *predominate*. But a moderate

---

[k] *Fable of Bees*, p. 82.
[l] There is a common Error with regard to *Misers*, on which this pretended Argument is built. They are generally accounted the greatest Enemies of *Society*, because they *hoard* the *Wealth* which ought to *circulate*. Now, to give even a *Miser* his due, this is really a groundless Charge: For they seldom *hoard* more than certain useless Papers, in the Shape of *Notes*, *Bonds*, and *Mortgages*: While the Wealth which they thus *hoard* in *Imagination*, circulates *freely* among all Ranks of People. The Guilt of the Miser's Passion lies in its being essentially destructive both of Justice and Benevolence.
[m] *Fable of the Bees*, p. 83
[n] Ibid. p. 89.

Share of Attention will convince us, that this is impossible. Because all the real Vices he mentions, though they be accidentally productive of some Good; yet 'tis such as might effectually be obtained without them. Thus the Money taken wrongfully by Stealth or Robbery, is only of Service to the Public by its Circulation: But Money may circulate without Stealth or Robbery; and therefore 'tis neither the Stealth nor Robbery that is of Service to the Public. On the other part, there are great and substantial Evils, which these Crimes, and these alone give Rise to. On this Occasion one might be very large on the Terrors and Distress, the Murders, and consequent Miseries, which the Villanies patronized by this Writer do necessarily produce. One who was Master of Dr. MANDEVILLE's *Town-Experience*, might draw a striking Picture of honest and industrious Families rowzed from Sleep at Midnight, only to be plundered and destroyed; of the horrid Attempts of abandoned Wickedness, let loose from Fear by the Security of Darkness; the Shrieks of ravished Maids and Matrons; the dying Groans of Brothers, Fathers, Husbands, weltring in their Blood; the Cries of innocent and helpless Orphans weeping over their murdered Parents, deprived at once of all that were dear to them, of all that could yield them Consolation or Support; and suffering every vile Indignity, that unrelenting Villainy can suggest or perpetrate. And how, think you, does this Scene of domestic Horror change its original Nature, and rise at length into a public Blessing? Why, because the Adventurers, having made off with their Booty, may possibly 'lay it out upon a *Harlot*, or squander it in a *Night-Cellar*, or a *Ginshop*°.' And thus the Money circulates through the Nation. But, in the mean Time, our Philosopher hath forgot the helpless Family reduced to Beggary by the Prowess of his *nocturnal Heroes:* He hath forgot that the fond and indulgent Parent might no less probably have laid out the Money in the temperate Maintenance and liberal Education of his Children, which is now squandered in unprofitable *Riot* and *Excess:* That these Destroyers of other Mens Happiness and these own, had they been employed in honest Labour, in the Cultivation of *Lands,* or the Improvement of *Manufactures*, might have done substantial Services to the Public and themselves, without the guilty *Alloy* of unprovoked Mischief. From these Circumstances, impartially compared, 'tis evident, that the only essential Consequence of private Vice, is public Misery: And thus our Author's new fashioned System of Morals falls back again into nothing.

His fourth Principle is much less plausible. Indeed he never applies to this, but when reduced to the last Necessity: When therefore every other Foundation fails him, he attempts to impose upon his Reader's Negligence or Simplicity, by representing Vice as a *Cause*, where in Reality 'tis a *Consequence*. Thus he tells us, 'Great Wealth and foreign Treasure will ever scorn to come among Men, unless you'll admit their *inseparable*

°   *Fable of the Bees*, p. 84, 85.

Companions, Avarice and Luxury: Where Trade is considerable, Fraud will *intrude*. To be at *once well-bred* and *sincere*, is no less than a Contradiction: And therefore whilst Man advances in Knowledge, and his Manners are polished, we must expect to see at the same Time his Desires enlarged, his Appetites refined, and his *Vices increased*[p].' So again, having been driven from his other strong Holds by certain impertinent Remarkers, whom he wisely dismisseth with an Air of Superiority and Contempt, he takes Refuge in the same ambiguous Phrases: As that 'Vice is *inseparable* from great and potent Societies, in the same Manner as *dirty Streets* are a necessary Evil, inseparable from the *Felicity* of *London*[q].'

Now, though this happy *Simile* may work Wonders in a *Coffee-House*, amongst those who see every *dirty Alley* pregnant with Demonstration; yet, 'tis to be hoped, more serious Readers may distinguish better. And be enabled to tell him, that before they grant his Position, *that private Vice is public Benefit*, they expect he should prove, 'that the Dirt in *London* Streets, is the Cause or Instrument whereby *London* becomes a populous and flourishing City:' A Proposition almost as remote from common Apprehension, as that *Tenterden Steeple* is the *Cause* of *Goodwin Sands*. Thus, we see how dextrously he puts the Change upon the unwary Reader; and while he pretends to exhibit an *essential Cause*, slurs him off with an *accidental Consequence*.

Into these four Principles, all evidently *False* or *Foreign* to the Purpose, his whole Book may be justly analysed. Nor is there one Observation in the Compass of so many hundred Pages, which tends to support the pernicious Falsehood that disgraceth his *Title-Page*, but what will naturally resolve itself into one or other of these wretched *Sophisms*. 'Tis therefore unnecessary to lead the Reader through all the *Windings* of this immense *Labyrinth* of Falsehood; 'tis enough, to have given the *Clue* which may safely conduct him through them.

Section VI.

HAVING at length gained an adequate Idea of Virtue, and found that it is no other than 'the voluntary Production of the greatest public Happiness;' we may now safely proceed to consider, 'what are the *Motives* by which Mankind can be induced to the Practice of it?'

And here we shall find another metaphysical *Cloud* resting upon *this* Path, in itself plain and easy to all Mankind. For the very Notion of the *Motives* to Virtue hath been as much confounded by moral Writers, as the Idea of *Virtue* itself. And here we might travel through another System

p *Fable of the Bees*, p. 201.
q *Fable of the Bees*, Preface p. 9, &c.

of *Logomachies*; while one asserts, that we ought to be *moved* to *love* and *pursue* Virtue, because *she* is *beautiful*; another, because Virtue is *good*; another, because Virtue is *good in itself*; a fourth, because Virtue is *Truth*; a fifth, because it is *agreeable to Nature*; a sixth, because it is agreeable to the *Relations of Things*.

BUT 'tis supposed that the intelligent Reader, from a Review of the first Section of this Essay, may be convinced, that all these *amusing* Expressions amount to no more than this, 'that there is some Reason or other why we ought to practise Virtue; but that the particular Reason doth not appear, notwithstanding all this refined Pomp of Affirmation.' And as it hath already been made evident, that the *Essence* of Virtue consists in a Conformity of our Affections and Actions, with the greatest *public Happiness*; so it will now appear, that 'the only *Reason* or *Motive*, by which Individuals can possibly be *induced* to the Practice of Virtue, must be the *Feeling* immediate, or the *Prospect* of future *private Happiness*.'

DOUBTLESS, the noble Writer's Admirers will despise and reject this, as an unworthy Maxim. For so it hath happened, that in the Height of their Zeal, for supporting his Opinions, they generally stigmatize *private Happiness*, as a Thing scarce worth a wise Man's inquiring after. Indeed, the many ambiguous Phrases of their Master have contributed not a little to this *vulgar Error*. For in one Place, he brands the modern Philosophers and Divines with the Name of Sophisters and Pedants, for 'rating Life by the Number and Exquisiteness of the pleasing Sensations[r].' At other Times he speaks of *Pleasure*, with all the Contempt of an ancient *Stoic*[s]. In the same high Style of the *Athenian Porch*, he passeth Judgment on the Hopes of the Religious: 'They have made Virtue so mercenary a Thing, and have talked so much of its *Rewards*, that one can hardly tell what there is in it, after all, which can be *worth* rewarding[t].' So again, he derides those 'modern Projectors, who would new frame the human Heart; and have a mighty Fancy to reduce all its Motions, Balances, and Weights to that one Principle and Foundation of a cool and deliberate *Selfishness*: And thus, Love of one's Country, and Love of Mankind, must also be *Self-Love*[u].'

Now ere we proceed further, it may be necessary to remark, that in some Degree there hath been a *Strife about Words* in this Particular too. For these Expressions of *Selfishness* and *Disinterestedness* have been used in a very *loose* and *indeterminate* Manner. In one Sense a *Motive* is called *disinterested*; when it consists in a pure *benevolent* Affection, or a Regard to the *moral Sense*. In another, no Motive is *disinterested*: For even in acting according to these Impulses of Benevolence and Conscience, we gratify an Inclination, and act upon the Principle or *immediate Feeling* of

---

[r]   *Wit and Hum.* Part iii. §4.
[s]   *Moral.* Part iii. § 3.
[t]   *Wit*, Part ii. § 3.
[u]   Ib.

private Happiness. Thus when we say, 'We love Virtue for Virtue's Sake;' 'tis only implied, that we find immediate Happiness from the Love and Practice of Virtue, without Regard to external or future Consequences.

ANOTHER Source of mutual Misapprehension on this Subject hath been 'the Introduction of *metaphorical* Expressions instead of *proper* ones.' Nothing is so common among the Writers on Morality, as 'the Harmony of Virtue' – 'Proportion of Virtue.' So the noble Writer frequently expresseth himself. 'But his favourite Term, borrowed indeed from the Ancients, is 'the BEAUTY of Virtue.' – *Quæ si videri posset, mirabiles excitaret amores*[w]. Of this our Author and his Followers, especially the most ingenious of them[x], are so *enamoured*, that they seem utterly to have forgot they are *talking in Metaphor*, when they describe the Charms of this *sovereign Fair.* Insomuch, that an unexperienced Person, who should read their *Encomiums*, would naturally fall into the Mistake of him, who asked the Philosopher, 'Whether the Virtues were not living Creatures[y]?' Now this *figurative* Manner, so essentially interwoven into philosophical Disquisition, hath been the Occasion of great Error. It tends to mislead us both with regard to the Nature of Virtue, and our Motives to the Practice of it. For first, it induceth a Persuasion, that Virtue is *excellent* without Regard to any of its Consequences: And secondly, that he must either want Eyes, or common Discernment, who doth not at first Sight fall in Love with this *matchless Lady.*

THEREFORE setting aside, as much as may be, all ambiguous Expressions, it seems evident, that 'a Motive, from its very Nature, must be something that affects *ourself.*' If any Man hath found out a Kind of Motive which doth not affect *himself,* he hath made a deeper Investigation into the 'Springs, Weights, and Balances' of the human Heart, than I can pretend to. Now what can possibly affect *ourself,* or determine us to Action, but either the Feeling or Prospect of *Pleasure* or *Pain, Happiness* or *Misery*?

BUT to come to the direct Proof: 'Tis evident, even to Demonstration, that no *Affection* can, in the strict Sense, be more or less *selfish,* or *disinterested* than another; because, *whatever* be its *Object,* the *Affection* itself is *still* no other than a *Mode* either of *Pleasure* or of *Pain*; and is therefore *equally* to be referred to the *Mind* or *Feeling* of the *Patient,* whatever be its *external Occasion.* Indeed, a late Writer of Subtilty and Refinement hath attempted to make a Distinction here. He says, 'It hath been observed, that every Act of Virtue or Friendship is attended with a secret *Pleasure*; from whence it hath been concluded, that Friendship and Virtue could not be disinterested. But the Fallacy of this is obvious. The virtuous Sentiment or Passion *produces* the Pleasure, and does not *arise* from it. I feel a Pleasure in doing good to my Friend, *because* I love him: but I do not love him for

---

[w] Cicero.
[x] Mr. Hutcheson.
[y] Senecæ Epist. cxiv.

the Sake of that Pleasure[z].' Now to me, the Fallacy of *this* is obvious. For in Fact, neither the *Passion*, nor the *Pleasure*, are either the *Cause* or the *Consequence* of each other; they neither *produce* nor *arise* from each other; because, in Reality, they are the *same Thing* under *different Expressions*. This will be clear, if we state the Case as follows: 'To *love* my Friend, is to *feel a Pleasure* in *doing him Good*:' And conversely; 'to feel a *Pleasure* in *doing Good* to my Friend, is to *love him*.' Where 'tis plain that the *Terms* are *synonymous*. The *Pleasure* therefore is the very *Passion itself*; and neither *prior* nor *posterior* to it, as this Gentleman supposeth.

AGAIN, that the Pleasures of Benevolence, and the moral Sense, are strictly *Selfish*, in this Sense of the Word, like every other Enjoyment, seems evident from some parallel Concessions of the noble Writer. For these seemingly disinterested Pleasures he perpetually sets on a Level with the Perceptions of natural Beauty, Order, Harmony, and Proportion. These last are, by all, acknowledged to be of the selfish Kind; therefore the other are so too; being only a *higher Order of the same*, and expresly called so by the noble Writer[a].

THE Reasons why the great universal Principle of *private Happiness* hath not been so clearly seen in the *Benevolent*, as in the *Self-Passions*, seem to be these. First, Ambiguous Expressions, such as have been remarked above. 2*dly*, Perhaps some Degree of *Pride*, and Affectation of *Merit*; because *Merit* seems to appear in what is called *Disinterest*. 3*dly*, And perhaps principally, because in the Exercise of the benevolent Passions, the Happiness is essentially *concomitant* with the Passion itself, and therefore is not easily separated from it by the *Imagination*, so as to be considered as a *distinct End*. Whereas in the Passions called *Selfish*, the Happiness sought after is often *unattainable*, and therefore easily and necessarily distinguished by the Imagination as a *positive End*. This Circumstance of Union however, as is judiciously remarked by one of the noble Writer's Followers[b] proves the great Superiority and Excellence of the benevolent Affections, considered as a Source of Happiness, beyond the Passions and Appetites, commonly called the *Selfish*.

BUT although these Observations be necessary, in order to clear up an Affair, which hath been much perplexed with philosophical, or *unphilosophical* Refinements; yet, on a closer Examination, it will appear, in the most direct Manner, from the noble Writer himself, that 'there is no other Principle of human Action, but that of the *immediate* or *foreseen* Happiness of the Agent:' That all these amusing Speculations concerning the *Comely*, *Fit*, and *Decent*; all these *verbal* Separations between *Pleasure, Interest, Beauty*, and *Good*, might have been sunk in one *precise* and plain Disquisition, concerning such Actions and Affections as yield a *lasting*, and such

---

[z]   Hume's *Essays, Mor.* and *Polit.* p. 125.
[a]   *Moralists*, Part ii.
[b]   Three Treaties, by *J. H.* Treat. 3[d]. *On Happiness*, p. 189.

as afford only a *Short* and transient *Happiness*. For thus, after all, his Lordship explains himself: 'That *Happiness* is to be pursued, and, in Fact, is always sought after; that the Question is not, who *loves himself*, and who *not*; but who *loves* and *serves himself* the *rightest*, and after the *truest* Manner. – That 'tis the Height of *Wisdom*, no doubt, to be *rightly Selfish*' – 'Even to leave Family, Friends, Country, and Society – in good Earnest, *who would not*, if it were *Happiness* to do so^c?'

THESE Expressions are so strongly pointed, as to leave no further Doubt concerning the noble Writer's Sentiments on this Subject. Indeed, they are the natural Dictates of common Sense, unsophisticated with false Philosophy. In every subsequent Debate therefore, wherein his Lordship's Opinions are concerned, we may safely build on this as an acknowledged and sure Foundation, 'that the Motives of Man to the Practice of Virtue, can only arise from a Sense of his *present*, or a Prospect of his *future Happiness.*'

Section VII.

NOW this Conclusion will carry us to another Question of a very interesting and abstruse Nature: That is, 'How far, and upon what Foundation, the uniform Practice of Virtue, is *really* and *clearly* connected with the Happiness of every Individual?' For so far, as we have seen, and no further, can every Individual be naturally moved to the Practice of it.

THIS is evidently a Question of *Fact*: And as it relates to the *Happiness* of *Man*, can only be determined by appealing to his *Constitution*. If *this* be indeed *uniform* and *invariable*; that is, if every Individual hath the same Perceptions, Passions, and Desires; then indeed the Sources of Happiness must be *similar* and *unchangeable*. If, on the contrary, different Men be differently constituted; if they have *different* Perceptions, Passions, and Desires; then must the Sources of their Happiness be equally *various*.

IT should seem therefore, that 'while Moralists have been enquiring into human Happiness, they have generally considered it, as arising from one *uniform* and *particular* Source, instead of tracing it up to those various Fountains whence it really springs; which are indefinitely various, combined, and indeterminable.' And this seems to have been the most general Foundation of Error.

IF we speak with Precision, there are but three Sources in Man, of Pleasure and Pain, Happiness and Misery: These are *Sense, Imagination*, and the *Passions*. Now the slightest observation will convince us, that these are associated, separated, and combined in Man, with a Variety almost infinite. In some, the Pleasures and Pains of *Sense* predominate; Imagination

^c   *Wit and Hum.* Part iii. § 3.

is dull; the passions inactive. In others, a more delicate Frame awakens all the Powers of Imagination; the Passions are refined; the Senses disregarded. A third Constitution is carried away by the Strength of Passion: The Calls of Sense are contemned; and Imagination becomes no more than the necessary Instrument of some further Gratification.

FROM overlooking this plain Fact, seems to have arisen the Discordance among Philosophers concerning the Happiness of Man. And while *each* hath attempted to exhibit one favourite Picture, as the *Paragon* or *Standard* of human Kind; they have *all* omitted some Ten thousand other Resemblances which actually subsist in Nature.

THUS, most of the *Epicurean* Sect, tho' not the Founder of it[d], have discarded *Benevolence* and *Virtue* from their System of *private* Happiness. The modern Patronizers of this Scheme, Mr. HOBBES, Dr. MANDEVILLE, and several *French* Writers, after heaping up a Collection of sordid Instances, which prove the *sensual* Inclinations and *Selfishness* of Man, leap at once to their desired Conclusion, that the pretended public Affections are therefore no more than the same low Passions in Disguise. That *Benevolence* makes no Part of Man's Nature; that the human Kind are absolutely unconnected with each other in Point of Affection: And that every Individual *seeks* and *finds* his *private* Happiness in and *from himself alone*.

THE noble Writer, on the contrary, viewing the brighter Parts of human Nature, through the amiable Medium of the *Socratic* Philosophy; and fixing his Attention on the *public Affections*, as the Instruments both of public and private Happiness; rejects the *Epicurean's* Pretences with Disdain: And, fully conscious of the high Claims and Energy of Virtue, affirms that the *private Affections* are, by no means, a Foundation for *private Happiness*: That, on the contrary, we must universally promote the Welfare of others, if we would effectually secure our own: And that in every Case, '*Virtue* is the *Good*, and *Vice* the *Ill* of every one[e]'

'TIS plain, no two Systems of Philosophy can be more *discordant* than these; yet each of them have obtained a Number of Partizans in all Ages of the World. The Question relates to a *Fact*, and the Fact lies open to the *personal Examination* of all Mankind. Whence then can so strange an opposition of Sentiments arise?

THIS seems to have arisen, not from a *false*, but a *partial* View and Examination of the Subject. The *Stoic* Party dwell altogether on the *social* or *public*, the *Epicurean* no less on the *private selfish* Affections: On

---

[d]   Επικουρος ο φιλοσοφος επι ταις, &c. *Epicurus* Philosophus, in libro quem Ratas opiniones inscribit, vitam cum *Justitia* conjunctam *perturbatione vacare* pronunciat; *injustam* vero *perturbatione* quamplurima *refertam* esse. Brevi dicto multæ veræ sententiæ, et ut summatim dicatur, id quod hominum improbitatem probe corrigere queat, complexus. Injustitia enim metropolis omnium malorum, non infime tantum conditionis hominibus, sed semel ut comprehendamus omnia, etiam gentibus, et civitatum populis et regibus, maximas producit calamitates. *Diodorus Sic. Eclog.* 1. 25.

[e]   *Enquiry concerning Virtue*, passim.

these respectively they declaim; so that according to the one, Mankind are naturally a Race of *Demi-Gods*; according to the other, a Crew of *Devils*. *Both* forgetting, what is unquestionably the Truth, that these *social* and *private* Affections are blended in an endless Variety of Degrees, and thus form an infinite Variety of Inclinations and of Characters. Many of the particular Facts, therefore, which these two Sects alledge, are true: But the *general* Consequence they draw from these *particular* Facts, is groundless and imaginary. Thus, 'tis true, that Mankind reap high Enjoyments from the Senses, Imagination, and Passions, without any regard to the public Affections: But the Consequence which the *Epicurean* would draw from hence, that 'therefore the public Affections are never, in any Case, a Source of private Happiness;' this is entirely void of Evidence: It supposeth Mankind to be *one uniform* Subject, while it is a Subject infinitely *various*; that every Individual has the same Feelings, Appetites, Fancies, and Affections, while, in Fact, they are mixed and combined in an endless Variety of Degrees. So, on the contrary, it must appear to every impartial Observer, that 'The Exercise of the public Affections is a Source of the highest Gratification to many Individuals.' But the *Stoic's* Conclusion, that 'therefore the uniform Exercise of the public Affections, in Preference to every other, is the only Source of Happiness to every Individual;' this is a Conclusion equally void of Evidence. For, like its opposite Extreme, it supposeth Mankind to be one uniform Subject, while, in Fact, it is a Subject in finitely various. It supposes that every Individual has the same Feelings, Appetites, Fancies, and Affections, while, in Reality, they are mixed and combined in an endless Variety of Degrees.

LET us now assign the most probable Foundation, on which these *narrow* and *partial* Systems have been so commonly embraced. For, that two Theories so opposite, and so devoid of all rational Support, should have made their Way in the World, without some *permanent* Cause beyond the Instability of mere *Chance*, seems hardly credible.

IT should seem therefore, that 'while the Patronizers of these two Systems have attempted to give a general Picture of the human Species, they have all along taken the Copy from themselves: And thus their Philosophy, instead of being a true History of Nature, is no more than the History of their own *Imaginations* or *Affections*.' – This Truth may receive sufficient Confirmation from the Lives and Conduct of all the old Philosophers, from the *elegant* PLATO walking on his rich *Carpets*, to the *unbred* CYNIC snarling in his *Tub*. As every Man's *Constitution* led him, so he adopted this or that Sect of *Philosophy*, and reasoned concerning *Fitness*, *Decency*, and *Good*. Read the Characters of CATO and CESAR, and you will clearly discover the true Foundation on which the one became a rigid *Stoic*, the other, a gross *Epicurean*. The first, yet a *Boy*, discovered such an *inflexible* Adherence to the Privileges of his Country, that he refused his Assent to what he thought a Violation of them, though threatened with immediate Death[f]. The *latter*, yet unpractised in the Subtilties of Philosophy, and under the sole Dominion of natural Temper, discovered, at his first Appearance in the World, such Traits of *Art*, *Spirit*, and *Ambition*, that SYLLA declared, he saw something more formidable than MARIUS rising in him[g]. To bring down the Observation to modern Times; 'tis evident, that the Patronizers of these two Systems inlist themselves according to the secret Suggestions of their several Passions. 'Tis well known, that the Writer of the *Fable of the Bees* was neither a *Saint* in his Life, nor a *Hermit* in his Diet: He seems to have been Master of a very considerable *Sagacity*, much Knowledge of the World, as it appears in populous *Cities*, extremely sensible to all the grosser *bodily* Enjoyments; but for *Delicacy* of Sentiment, Imagination, or Passion, nor an exquisite *Taste* either in *Arts* or *Morals*, he appears to have been *incapable* of it. – The noble Writer is known to have been of a Frame the very Reverse of this: His *Constitution* was neither more nor less opposite to Dr. MANDEVILLE's, than his Philosophy. His sensual Appetites were weak; his Imagination all alive, noble, and capacious; his Passions were accordingly refined, and his public Affections (in *Fancy* at least) predominant. To these Instances, a moderate Share of Sagacity and Knowledge of the World may add others innumerable, in observing the Temper and Conduct of the Followers of these two Systems; who always take Party according to the Biass of their own Constitution. Among the *Epicureans* we ever find Men of high Health, florid Complexions, firm Nerves, and a Capacity for Pleasure: Of the *Stoic* Party are the delicate or sickly Frames, Men incapable of the grosser sensual Enjoyments, and who either *are*, or *think* themselves, *virtuous*. Now from these accumulated Proofs we may be convinced, that 'they who give us these *uniform* Pictures of a Subject so *various* as *Mankind*, cannot have drawn them from *Nature*: That, on the contrary, they have copied them from their own *Hearts* or *Imaginations*; and fondly erected *themselves* into a general Standard of the *human Species*.'

BUT although these Observations may afford sufficient Proof, that the *Stoic* and *Epicurean* Pictures of Mankind are equally partial; yet still it remains to be enquired how far, upon the whole, the human Kind in Reality leans towards the *one* or the *other*: That is, 'how far, and in what Degree, the uniform Practice of Virtue constitutes the Happiness of Individuals?' Now the only Method of determining this Question, will be to select some of the most striking *Features* of the human Heart: By this Means we may *approach* towards a real *Likeness*, though from that infinite Variety which subsists in Nature, the *Draught* must ever be inadequate and *defective*.

To begin with the lowest Temperature of the human Species; 'there are

---

[f]   Plutarchi *Cato Utic.*
[g]   Suetonii *Julius Cesar.*

great Numbers of Mankind, in whom the *Senses* are the chief Sources of Pleasure and Pain.' To the Harmony of Sounds, the Beauty of Forms, the Decorum of Actions, they are utterly insensible. They are sagacious and learned in all the Gratifications of Sense; but if you talk to them of the public Affections, of Generosity, Kindness, Friendship, Good-will, you talk in a Language they understand not. They seem, in a Manner, unconnected with the rest of their Kind; they view the Praises, Centures, Enjoyments, and Sufferings of others, with an Eye of perfect Indifference. To Men thus formed, how can Virtue gain Admittance? Do you appeal to their *Taste* of Beauty? They have none. To their acknowledged Perceptions of *Right* and *Wrong?* These they measure by their private *Interest*. To the Force of the public *Affections?* They never felt them. Thus every Avenue is foreclosed, by which *Virtue* should enter.

THE next remarkable Peculiarity is, 'where not the Senses, but *Imagination* is the predominant Source of Pleasure.' Here the Taste always runs into the elegant Refinements of polite Arts and Acquirements; of Painting, Music, Architecture, Poetry, Sculpture: Or, in Defect of this truer Taste, on the false Delicacies of Dress, Furniture, and Equipage. Yet Experience tells us, that this Character is widely different from the virtuous one: That all the Powers of Imagination may subsist in their full Energy, while the *public Affections* and *moral Sense* are weak or utterly inactive. Nor can there be any necessary Connection between these different Feelings; because we see Numbers immersed in all the finer Pleasures of Imagination, who never once consider them as the Means of *giving Pleasure* to *others*, but merely as a *selfish* Gratification. This the noble Writer seems to have been aware of; and, not without great Address, endeavours to convert the Fact into a Proof of his main Theory, though, in Reality, it affords the strongest Evidence against him. 'The *Venustum*, the *Honestum*, the *Decorum* of Things, will force its Way, They, who refuse to give it Scope in the nobler Subjects of a rational and moral Kind, will find its Prevalency elsewhere, in an inferior Order of Things – as either in the Study of common *Arts*, or in the Care and Culture of mere mechanic *Beauties*. – The *Spectre* still will *haunt* us, in *some Shape or other*; and when driven from our cool Thoughts, and frighted from the *Closet*, will meet us even at Court, and fill our Heads with Dreams of Grandeur, Titles, Honours, and a false Magnificence and Beauty[h].' All this is ingenious and plausible: And the very elegant Allusion, of 'the Spectre still haunting us in some Shape or other,' seems at first View to imply, that even the most obstinate Endeavours to get rid of the Force of moral Beauty, are ineffectual and vain. But a nearer Examination will convince us, that the noble Writer applies here to *Eloquence*, rather than *Argument*; and puts us off with a *Metaphor* instead of a *Reason*. For the Pleasures of Imagination, whether they run in the Channel of polite Arts,

[h]   *Wit. and Hum.* Part iv. § 2.

Furniture, Planting, Building, or Equipage, are indeed no *Spectres*, but independent *Realities* fairly existing in the Mind: They have no immediate or necessary Connexion with the Happiness of Mankind, which is often and *designedly* violated in order to gain the Possession of them. 'Tis true, the Pleasures of Imagination and Virtue are often *united* in the same Mind; but 'tis equally true, that they are often *separate*; that they who are most sensible to the *one*, are entire Strangers to the *other*; that one Man, to *purchase* a fine *Picture*, will *oppress* his Tenant; that another, to *relieve* his distressed Tenant, will *sell* his Statues or his Pictures. The Reason is evident: The one draws his chief Pleasure from *Imagination*; the other from *Affection* only. 'Tis clear therefore, that 'where *Imagination* is naturally the predominant Source of Pleasure,' the Motives to Virtue must be very *partial* and *weak*, since the chief Happiness ariseth from a Source entirely distinct from the *benevolent Affections*.

ANOTHER, and very different Temperature of the Heart of Man is that 'wherein neither Sense nor Imagination, but the PASSIONS are the chief Sources of Pleasure and Pain.' This often forms the *best* or the *worst* of Characters. As it runs either, First, Into the Extreme of Selfishness, Jealousy, Pride, Hatred, Envy, and Revenge; or, 2*dly*, Into the amiable Affections of Hope, Faith, Candour, Pity, Generosity, and Goodwill; or, 3*dly*, Into a various Mixture or Combination of these; which is undoubtedly the most common Temperature of human Kind.

Now to the first of these Tempers, how can we affirm with Truth, that there is a natural Motive to Virtue? On the contrary, it should seem, that, if there be any Motive, it must be to *Vice*. For 'tis plain, that from the Losses, Disappointments, and Miseries of Mankind, such vile Tempers draw their chief Felicity. The noble Writer indeed, in his Zeal for Virtue, considers these black Passions as *unnatural*, and brands them as a Source of *constant Misery*[i]. And sure it would be matter of Joy to all good Men, to find his Proofs convincing. But if indeed this be not a true Representation of the Case, I see not what Service can be done to the Interests of *Virtue*, by *disguising Truth*. 'Tis not the Part of a Philosopher to write *Panegyrics*, but to *investigate* the real State of human Nature; and the only Way of doing this to any good Purpose, is to do it *impartially*: For with regard to human Nature, as well as Individuals, 'Flattery is a Crime no less than Slander.'

WHEN therefore the noble Writer calls these Affections *unnatural*, he doth not sufficiently explain himself. If indeed by their being unnatural, he means, that 'they are such in their Degrees or Objects as to violate the public Happiness, which is the main Intention of Nature;' in this Sense, 'tis acknowledged, they are *unnatural*. But this Interpretation is foreign to the Question; because it affects not the *Individual*. But if, by their being

---

[i]   *Enquiry.*

unnatural, he would imply, that they are 'a Source of constant Misery to the Agent;' this seems a Proposition not easy to be determined in the Affirmative.

FOR the main Proof which he brings in Support of this Assertion is, 'that the Men of *gentlest Dispositions*, and *best of Tempers*, have at some time or other been sufficiently acquainted with those Disturbances, which, at ill Hours, even small Occasions are apt to raise. From these slender Experiences of Harshness and ill Humour, they fully know and will confess the ill Moments which are passed, when the Temper is ever so little galled and fretted. How must it fare therefore with those, who hardly know any better Hours in Life; and who, for the greatest Part of it, are agitated by a thorow *active Spleen*, a close and settled Malignity and Rancour[k]?'

Now, this Instance is by no means sufficient to support the Affirmation. For 'tis plain, that in the Case of the 'Men of gentlest Dispositions, and best of Tempers, occasionally agitated by ill Humour,' there must be a strong Opposition and Discordance, a violent Conflict between the habitual Affections of Benevolence, and these accidental Eruptions of Spleen and Rancour which rise to obstruct their Course. A Warfare of this Kind must indeed be a State of complete Misery, when all is Uproar within, and the distracted Heart set at Variance with itself. But the Case is widely different, where 'a thorow active Spleen prevails, a close and *settled* Malignity and Rancour.' For in this Temper, there is no parallel Opposition of contending Passions: Nor therefore any similar Foundation for inward Disquiet and intense Misery. So much the noble Writer himself is obliged to own elsewhere. 'Is there that sordid Creature on Earth, who does not prize his own Enjoyment? – Is not *Malice* and *Cruelty* of the *highest Relish* with some Natures[l]?' Again, and still more fully to the Purpose: 'Had we Sense, we should consider, 'tis in Reality the *thorow* Profligate, the very *complete unnatural Villain* alone, who can any way *bid* for *Happiness* with the honest Man. True Interest is wholly on the one Side or the other. All between is Inconsistency, Irresolution, Remorse, Vexation, and an Ague-fit[m].' Neither is this Acknowledgement peculiar to himself: 'To be *consistent* either in Virtue or in Vice,' was the farthest that some of the most penetrating among the Ancients could carry the Point of *Morals*[n]. Thus where the *selfish* or *malevolent* Affections happen to prevail, there can be no internal *Motive* to *Virtue*.

ON the contrary, where the amiable Affections of Hope, Candour, Generosity, and Benevolence predominate, in this best and happiest of Tempers, Virtue hath indeed all the Force and Energy, which the noble Writer attributes to her Charms. For where the Calls of Sense are weak, the Imagination

k   *Enquiry*, Book ii. Part ii. § 3.
l   *Moralists*, Part i.
m   *Wit and Hum*, Part iv. § I.
n   See Arrian. *Epict.* lib. iii. c. 15.

active and refined, the public Affections predominant; there the *moral Sense* must naturally reign with uncontrouled Authority; must produce all that Self-Satisfaction, that Consciousness of merited Kindness and Esteem, in which, his Lordship affirms, the very Essence of our Motives to Virtue doth consist. This shall with Pleasure be acknowledged, nay asserted, as 'the happiest of all Temperaments,' whenever it can be *found* or *acquired*. To a Mind thus formed, Virtue doth indeed bring an *immediate* and *ample Reward* of perfect Peace and sincere Happiness in all the common Situations of Life. It may therefore be with Truth affirmed, that a Temper thus framed must indeed be naturally and internally *moved* to the uniform Practice of Virtue.

THERE are, besides these, an endless Variety of Characters formed from the various Combinations of these essential *Ingredients*; which are not designed as a full *Expression* of all the Tempers of Mankind: They are the Materials only, out of which these Characters are formed. They are no more than the several Species of *simple Colours* laid, as it were, upon the *Pallet*; which, variously *combined* and associated by the Hand of an experienced Master, would indeed call forth every striking *Resemblance*, every changeful Feature of the *Heart* of *Man*.

NOW, among all this infinite Variety of Tempers which is found in Nature, we see there cannot be any uniform Motive to Virtue, save only 'where the Senses are weak, the Imagination refined, and the public Affections strongly predominant.' For in every other Character, where either the Senses, gross Imagination, or selfish Passions prevail, a natural Opposition or Discordance must arise, and destroy the uniform Motive to Virtue, by throwing the Happiness of the Agent into a different Channel. How seldom this sublime Temper is to be found, is hard to say: But this may be affirmed with Truth, that every Man is not *really* possessed of it in the Conduct of Life, who *enjoys* it in *Imagination*, or *admires* it in his Closet, as it lies in the *Enquiry concerning Virtue*. A Character of this supreme Excellence must needs be *approved* by most: And the *Heart* of Man being an unexhausted Fountain of *Self-Deceit*, what it *approves*, is forward to think itself possessed of. Thus a lively *Imagination* and unperceived *Self-Love*, fetter the Heart in certain *ideal* Bonds of their own creating: Till at length some turbulent and furious Passion arising in its Strength, breaks these fantastic Shackles which Fancy had imposed, and leaps to its Prey like a *Tyger* chained by *Cobwebs*.

Section VIII.

FROM these different Views of human Nature, let us now bring this Argument to a Conclusion.

THE noble Writer's Scheme of Morals therefore, being grounded on a

Supposition, which runs through the whole Course of his Argument, that 'all Mankind are naturally capable of attaining a *Taste* or *Relish* for *Virtue*, sufficient for every Purpose of social Life,' seems essentially defective. For, from the Enquiry already made into the real and various Constitution of Man, it appears, that a great Part of the Species are naturally incapable of this *fancied* Excellence. That the various Mixture and Predominancy of *Sense*, *Imagination*, and *Passion*, give a different Cast and Complexion of Mind to every Individual: That the *Feeling* or *Prospect* of Happiness can only arise from this Combination: That consequently, where the benevolent Affections and moral Sense are weak, the selfish Passions and Perceptions headstrong, there can be no internal Motive to the *consistent* Practice of Virtue.

THE most plausible Pretence I could ever meet with, amidst all the Pomp of Declamation thrown out in Support of this *All-Sufficiency* of a *Taste* in Morals, is this: 'That although the Force and Energy of this Taste for Virtue appears not in every Individual, yet the Power lies dormant in every human Breast; and needs only be called forth by a *voluntary Self-Discipline*, in order to be brought to its just Perfection. That the Improvement in our Taste in Morals is parallel to the Progress of the Mind in every other Art and Excellence, in *Painting, Music, Architecture, Poetry*: In which, a *true* Taste, however *natural* to Man, is not born with him, but formed and brought forth to Action by a proper *Study* and *Application*.'

THE noble Writer hath innumerable Passages of this Kind: So many indeed, that it were Labour lost to transcribe them[o]. And one of his Followers hath affirmed in still more emphatical Expressions, if possible, than his Master, that 'the Height of *Virtuoso-ship* is VIRTUE[p].'

Now this State of the Case, though at first View it carries some Degree of Plausibility, yet, on a closer Examination, destroys the whole System. For if, as it certainly is, the *Capacity* for a Taste in *Morals*, be similar to a *Capacity* for a Taste in *Arts*; 'tis clear, that the most assiduous Culture or Self-Discipline can never make it even *general*, much less *universal*. One Man, we see, hath a Capacity or Genius for Painting, another for Music, a third for Architecture, a fourth for Poetry. Torture each of them as you please, you cannot infuse a Taste for any, but his own *congenial* Art. If you attempt to make the Poet an Architect, or the Painter a Musician, you may make a pretending *Pedant*, never an accomplished *Master*. 'Tis the same in Morals: Where the benevolent Affections are naturally strong, *there* is a *Capacity* for a high *Taste in* Virtue: Where these are *weak* or *wanting*, there is in the same Proportion, *little* or *no Capacity* for a *Taste* in Virtue. To harangue, therefore, on the superior Happiness attending the Exercise of the public Affections, is quite foreign to the Purpose. This

---

[o] *Charact.* passim.
[p] *Letters of Hydaspes to Philemon*, Let. vi.

superior Happiness is allowed, where the public Affections can be *found*, or *made*, predominant. But how can any Consequence be drawn from hence, so as to influence those who never felt the Impulse of public Affection? Are not the Pleasures of Poetry, Painting, Music, sublime, pure, and lasting, to those who *taste* them? Doth it therefore follow, that all Mankind, or any of them, can be harangued into a *Taste* and *Love* of these elegant Arts, while the very Capacity of receiving Pleasure from them is *wanting*? Thus in Morals, where a similar Incapacity takes Place through the natural Want of a lively Benevolence, no Progress can ever be made in the *Taste* or *Relish* for virtuous Enjoyment. Though therefore you should prove, as indeed one of Lord SHAFTESBURY's Followers hath done, 'that Virtue is accommodate to all Places and Times, is *durable, self-derived*, and *indeprivable*[r],' whence he concludes, it has the best Title to the Character of the sovereign Good; yet all the while, the main Point in Debate is taken for granted, that is, 'whether the Possession of it be any *Good* at all.' Now to those who receive no Increase of *internal* Happiness from it, it cannot be a *Good:* And where there is a natural *Defect* of benevolent Affection, it can give no *internal* Happiness: Consequently, though it have all the other Characters of the *Summum Bonum*, though it be *durable, self-derived*, and *indeprivable*, it can never, by such, be regarded as the *sovereign Good*.

'TIS pleasant enough to observe the Argumentation of the Writer last mentioned. After describing 'the fairest and most amiable of Objects, the true and perfect Man, that Ornament of Humanity, that god-like Being, without Regard either to Pleasure or Pain, uninfluenced either by Prosperity or Adversity, superior to the World, and its best and worst Events' – He then raiseth an Objection – 'Does not this System border a little upon the Chimerical?' – On my Word, a shrewd Question, and well worth a good Answer; and thus he clears it up. – 'It seems to require, said I, a Perfection to which no Individual ever arrived. That very Transcendence, said he, is an Argument on its behalf. Were it of a Rank inferior, it would not be that Perfection which we seek. Would you have it, said I, beyond Nature? If you mean, replied he, beyond any particular or individual Nature, most undoubtedly I would[r].' 'Tis not therefore to be wondered at, that this Gentleman, wrapped up in *Visions* of ideal Perfection, should express 'his Contempt of those superficial Censurers, who profess to refute what they want even Capacities to comprehend[s].' Doubtless he means those *groveling* Observers, who draw their Ideas of Mankind 'from particular or individual Natures,' and have not yet risen to 'the *beatific Vision*[t] of the perfect Man.'

---

[o]   Three Treat. by *J. H*. Treat. 3[d]. *On Happiness*.
[r]   Three Treat. by *J. H*. Treat. 3[d]. *On Happiness*, p. 215.
[s]   Ibid, p. 108.
[t]   Ibid.

Indeed, the Gentleman frankly owns, 'that Practice too often *creeps*, where Theory can *soar*[u].' And this I take to be a true Account of the Matter.

THUS, as according to these Moralists, the *Relish* or *Taste* for Virtue is similar to a Taste for Arts; so what is said of the Poet, the Painter, the Musician, may in this Regard with equal Truth be said of the Man of Virtue – *Nascitur, non fit*. Hence it is evident, that the noble Writer's System, which supposeth all Men capable of this exalted Taste, is chimerical and groundless.

BUT even supposing all Men capable of this high Taste in Morals, there would arise an unanswerable Objection against the Efficacy of this refined Theory. Though it were allowed, that all Mankind have the same delicate Perception of *moral*, as some few have of *natural* Beauty, yet the Parallel would by no means hold, that 'as the *Virtuoso* always pursues his Taste in Arts *consistently*, so the Man of *Virtue* must be equally *consistent* in *Action* and *Behaviour.*' For the *Virtuoso* being only engaged in mere *Speculation*, hath no opposite Affections to counteract his Taste: He meets with no Obstructions in his Admiration of Beauty: His Enthusiasm takes its unbounded Flight, not retarded by any Impediments of a discordant Nature. But the Man of *Virtue* hath a different and more difficult Task to perform: He hath often a numerous Train of Passions, and these perhaps the most violent to oppose: He must labour through the surrounding Demands and Allurements of selfish Appetite: Must subdue the Sollicitations of every the most natural Affection, when it opposes the Dictates of a pure Benevolence. Hence even supposing the most refined Taste for Virtue common to all, it must ever be retarded in its Progress, often baffled and overthrown amidst the *Struggle* of contending *Passions*.

THIS seems to be a full and sufficient Reply to all that can be urged in Support of this fantastic System from a View of *human Nature*. But as the noble Writer hath attempted to confirm his Theory by some collateral Arguments of another Kind, it may be proper here to consider their real Weight.

HE urges, therefore, the Probability at least, if not the certain Truth of his Hypothesis from hence, 'That it would be an Imputation on the Wisdom of the Deity to suppose that he had formed Man so imperfect, that the true Happiness of the Individual should not always coincide with that of the whole Kind[w].' And beyond Question, the Assertion is true: But the Consequence he draws from it, 'that therefore human Happiness must always consist in the immediate Feeling of virtuous Enjoyment,' is utterly groundless. This Inference seems to have been drawn from a View of the *Brute* Creation; in which we find, *Instincts* or *immediate Feelings* are the only Motives to Action; and in which, we find too, that these immediate Propen-

[u]   Three Treat. by *J. H.* Treat. 3[d]. *On Happiness*, p. 108.
[w]   *Enquiry*.

sities are *sufficient* for all the Purposes of their Being. In this Constitution of Things the Creator's Wisdom is eminently displayed; because, through a Defect of *Reason* or *Reflexion*, no other Kind of Principle could possibly have taken Place. But the Conclusion drawn from thence, 'that Man must have a similar Strength of Instinct implanted in him, in order to direct him to his supreme Happiness,' this is without Foundation: Because the Deity hath given him not only *present* Perceptions, but *Reason, Reflexion,* and a *Foresight of future* Good and Evil, together with a sufficient Power to obtain the one, and avoid the other. As therefore Man hath sufficient Notices of the *moral Government* of GOD, which will at length produce a perfect Coincidence between the *virtuous* Conduct and the *Happiness* of every Individual, it implies no essential Defect of Wisdom in the Creator, to suppose that he hath not given this *universal* and *unerring* Biass towards Virtue to the whole human Species. Man is enabled to pursue and obtain his proper Happiness by *Reason*; Brutes by *Instinct*.

AGAIN, the noble Writer often attempts to strengthen his Argument, by 'representing the *external Good* which naturally *flows* from *Virtue*, and the *external* Evils which naturally *attend* on Vice.'ˣ But sure this is rather deserting than confirming his *particular* Theory; which is, to prove that Happiness is *essential* to *Virtue*, and *inseparable* from it: 'That Misery is *essential* to *Vice*, and inseparable from it.' – Now, in bringing his Proofs from Happiness or Misery of the *external* Kind, he clearly deserts his original Intention: Because these *Externals* are not *immediate*, but *consequential*; not *certain*, but *contingent*. They are precisely of the Nature of *Reward* and *Punishment*; and therefore can have no Part in the Question now before us; which relates solely to 'that Happiness or Misery arising from the inward State of the *Mind, Affections,* and *moral Sense*, on the Commission of Vice, or the Practice of *Virtue*.' And this hath been already considered at large.

HOWEVER, that nothing may be omitted which can even remotely affect the Truth; we may observe, in passing, that after all the laboured and *well-meant* Declamation on this Subject, 'tis much easier to prove, 'that *Vice* is the Parent of *external* Misery, than that *Virtue* is the Parent of *external* Happiness.' 'Tis plain, that no Man can be vicious in any considerable *Degree*, but he must suffer either in his *Health*, his *Fame*, or *Fortune*. Now the Generality of Moralists, after proving or illustrating this, have taken it for granted, as a certain Consequence, that the external Goods of Life are, by the Law of Contraries, in a similar Manner annexed to the Practice of Virtue. But in Reality the Proof can reach no further than to shew the happy Consequences of *Innocence*, which is a very different Thing from *Virtue?* for *Innocence* is only the *abstaining* from *Evil*; *Virtue*, the actual Production of *Good*. Now 'tis evident indeed, that by *abstaining* from *Evil*

ˣ   *Enquiry*, B. ii. P. i. § 3.

(that is, by *Innocence*) we *must* stand clear of the Miseries to which we expose ourselves by the *Commission* of it: And this is as far as the Argument will go. But if we rigorously examine the external Consequences of an *active* Virtue, in such a World as this; we shall find, it must be often maintained at the Expence both of *Health*, *Ease*, and *Fortune*; often the Loss of Friends, and Increase of Enemies; not to mention the unwearied Diligence of *Envy*, which is ever watchful and prepared to blast distinguished Merit. In the mean time, the *innoxious* Man sits unmolested and tranquil; *loves* Virtue, and *praiseth* it; avoids the *Miseries* of *Vice*, and the *Fatigue* of *active* Virtue; offends no Man, and therefore is beloved by all; and for the rest, makes it up by fair *Words* and civil Deportment. 'Thus *Innocence*, and not *Virtue*; *Abstinence* from *Evil*, not the *Production* of Good, is the furthest Point to which Mankind in general can be carried, from a Regard to the *external* Consequences of Action.'

But whenever Appearances grow too strong against the noble Writer's System, he takes Refuge in an – *apage Vulgus!* – As he had before allowed, that 'the Vulgar may swallow any sordid Jest or Buffoonry,' so here he frequently suggests, that among the same Ranks, 'any kind of sordid Pleasure will go down.' But 'as it must be a finer Kind of Wit that takes with the Men of Breeding,' so in Morals 'the *Relish* or *Taste* for Virtue, is what naturally prevails in the higher Stages of Life: That the *Liberal* and *polished* Part of Mankind are disposed to treat every other Principle of Action as groundless and *imaginary*: But that among these, the *Taste* in Morals, if properly cultivated, must needs be sufficient for all the Purposes of Virtue[y].'

In reply to this, which is perhaps the weakest Pretence of all that the noble Writer hath alledged, we need only observe, that those who are born to *Honours*, *Power*, and *Fortune*, come into the World with the same *various* Mixture and *Predominancy* of *Sense*, *Imagination*, and *Affections*, with the *lowest* Ranks of Mankind. So that if they really enjoy better Opportunities of being completely virtuous, these must arise not from their internal *Constitution*, but their external *Situation* in Life. Let us examine how far this may give a Biass either towards Vice or Virtue.

Now 'tis plain that, with regard to the *Senses* or bodily *Appetites*, the Possession of Power and Fortune must be rather hurtful than favourable to Virtue. Wealth gives Opportunity of *Indulgence*, and Indulgence naturally *inflames*. Hence the Habits of *sensual* Inclination must in general be stronger in the *Lord* than the *Peasant*: Therefore, as nothing tends so much to imbrute the Man, and sink every nobler Affection of the Mind, as a servile Attendance on sensual Pleasure; so in this Regard, the Possession of Power and Fortune is rather *dangerous* than favourable to Virtue.

The same may be affirmed in respect to the *Passions* or *Affections*. Can

[y] See Misc. 3[d] c. 2. and many other detached Passages.

any thing tend so much to render any Passion ungovernable, as to know that we *need not* govern it? That our Power, Riches, and Authority, raise us *above Controul?* That we can hate, oppress, revenge, with *Impunity?* Are not the *Great*, of all others, most obnoxious to *Flattery?* Does not this tend to produce and nourish an *overweening* Opinion of *themselves*, an unjust *Contempt* of *others?* And is not *true Virtue* more likely to be *lost* than improved, amidst all these surrounding Temptations?

THE *Imagination* indeed is often refined, and *Reason* improved, in the higher Ranks of Life, beyond the Reach of the *mere Vulgar.* But they are little acquainted with human Nature, who think that *Reason* and *Imagination*, among the Bulk of Mankind, are any thing more than the *Ministers* of the *ruling Appetites* and *Passions:* Especially where the Appetites and Passions are inflamed by the *early* and *habitual* Possession of Honours, Power, and Riches.

BUT still it will be urged, that the *Great* are under the Dominion of a powerful Principle, which is almost unknown among the *Vulgar:* – The Principle of HONOUR – which is a perfect *Balance* against all these surrounding Difficulties, and a full *Security* to *Virtue.*

WITH regard to this *boasted* Principle, a very material Distinction must be made. By *Honour*, is sometimes meant 'An Affection of Mind determining the Agent to the Practice of what is right, without any Dependance on other Mens Opinions.' Now this is but the *moral Sense*, under a new Appellation: It ariseth too, not from any particular *Situation* of Life, but from the natural *Constitution* of the Mind. Accordingly, it is not confined to any one Rank of Men, but is seen promiscuously among the *Great* and *Vulgar.* 'Tis therefore entirely beyond the present Question, which only relates to such Circumstances as are peculiar to *high Life.*

THE other, and more common Acceptation of the Word *Honour*, and in which alone it belongs peculiarly to the *Great*, is 'an Affection of the Mind determining the Agent to such a Conduct, as may gain him the *Applause* or *Esteem* of those whose good Opinion he is fond of.' Now this Love of *Fame*, and Fear of *Disgrace*, though, as a *Secondary* Motive to Action, it be often of the highest Consequence in Life; though it often *counterfeits*, sometimes even *rivals* Benevolence itself; yet as a *principal* Motive, there cannot be a more *precarious* Foundation of Virtue. For the *Effects* of this Principle will always depend on the *Opinions* of others: It will always take its particular Complexion from *these*, and must always *vary* with them. Thus 'tis a Matter of mere *Accident*, whether its Consequences be *good* or *bad*, *wholesome* or *pernicious*. If the *applauded Maxims* be founded in *Benevolence*, the Principle will so far lead to *Virtue:* If they be founded in *Pride*, *Folly*, or *Contempt*, the Principle will lead to *Vice.* And, without any designed Satire on the *Great*, it must be owned, the latter of these hath ever been the *predominant* Character of *Honour.* It were false indeed to affirm, that the Principle hath no Mixture of *benevolent* Intention; yet 'tis equally clear, that its *chief* Design is not so much to secure the *Happiness* of *all*, as to maintain the *Superiority* of a *few*: And hence this Principle hath ever led its Votaries to abhor the Commission, not so much of what is *unjust*, as of what is *contemptible*. Thus it is clear, that the Principle of *Honour*, as distinguished from *benevolent* Affection and the *moral Sense*, can never be a sufficient Foundation for the *uniform* Practice of *Virtue*.

THESE are the main Arguments by which the noble Writer hath attempted to support this imagined *All-sufficiency* of the *Relish* or *Taste* in *Morals*. Had human Nature been indeed that *uniform* and *noble* Thing, which he seems to have *thought* it, he had surely been right in fixing the *Motives* to *Virtue*, on so generous and amiable a Principle. But as on Examination it appears, that he hath all along supposed this human Nature to be *what it is not*, his System is *visionary* and *groundless*; and his applauded Theory only fit to find a Place with the boasted Power of the great old *Geometer*, when he said – δος ωγ ςω, και τιω γιω κινησω[z].

MOST full indeed and clear to this Purpose are the Words of the noble Writer himself: Who, in his *miscellaneous* Capacity, and in a *merry* Mood, seems to have spoken more of Truth, than I believe he would care to stand to – 'Such has been of late our dry Task. No wonder if it carries, indeed, a *meagre* and *raw* Appearance. It may be looked on in Philosophy, as worse than a mere *Egyptian* Imposition. For to make Brick without Straw or Stubble, is perhaps an easier Labour, than to prove Morals without a World, and establish a Conduct of Life, without the Supposition of any Thing living or extant besides our *immediate Fancy*, and World of *Imagination*[a].'

THESE Sallies might possibly have seemed difficult to account for, had not the noble Writer himself saved us the Labour of this Task. For he elsewhere tells us, that 'all sound *Love* and Admiration is ENTHUSIASM: The Transports of Poets, Orators, Musicians, Virtuosi; the Spirit of Travellers and Adventurers; Gallantry, War, Heroism; all, all Enthusiasm! 'Tis enough: I am content to be this new ENTHUSIAST[b].' – And thus in another Place he describes the Effects of this high Passion: That '*Enthusiasm* is wonderfully powerful and extensive: – For when the Mind is *taken up in Vision*, – its Horror, Delight, Confusion, Fear, *Admiration*, or *whatever passion* belongs to it, or is uppermost on this Occasion, will have something *vast*, *immane*, and, as Painters say, BEYOND LIFE. And this is what gave Occasion to the Name of *Fanaticism*, as it was used by the Ancients in its original Sense, for *an* APPARITION *transporting the* MIND[c].'

---

[z]   Give me but a *Place* to set my Foot on, and I will move the whole Earth.
[a]   *Misc.* iv, c. 2.
[b]   *Moralists*, sub fin.
[c]   *Letter on Enthusiasm.*

Section IX.

HAVING sufficiently evinced the *flimzy*, though curious, Contexture of these *Cobweb* Speculations *spun* in the *Closet*, let us now venture abroad into the World; let us proceed to something applicable to Life and Manners; and consider what are the real Motives, by which Mankind may be sway'd to the *uniform* Practice of *Virtue*.

AND first, in Minds of a *gentle* and *generous* Disposition, where the sensual Appetites are weak, the Imagination refined, and the benevolent Affections naturally predominant; these very Affections, and the *moral Sense* arising from them, will in all the common Occurrences of Life secure the Practice of Virtue. To these fine Tempers thus happily formed, the inward Satisfaction of a virtuous Conduct exceeds that of every outward Acquisition; and affords to its Possessor a more true and lasting Happiness, than Wealth, or Fame, or Power can bestow.

SECONDLY, Where the same Degrees of public Affection subsist, but stand opposed by sensual or selfish Passions of equal Violence, even here the Agent may rise to very high Degrees of Virtue, but not without the Aids of *Discipline* and *Culture*. Yet 'tis observable, that the Virtues of such a Temper are rather *conspicuous* than *consistent*: Without some strengthening Assistance, the Progress of the Mind towards Perfection is often broke by the Sallies of disordered Passion.

THERE is yet another Character, essentially different from these, but seldom distinguished, because generally taken for the *first*. Many esteem themselves, and are esteemed by others, as having arrived at the most *Consummate Virtue*, whose Conduct never merits a higher Name than that of being *innoxious*. This is generally the Case of those who love *Retreat* and *Contemplation*, of those whose Passions are naturally *weak*, or carefully *guarded* by what the World calls *Prudence*. Now, as in the last mentioned Character, a *Curb* from *Irregularity* was requisite, so here a *Spur* to *Action* is equally necessary for the Support and Security of Virtue.

As we descend through more common and inferior Characters, the internal Motives to virtuous Actions grow less and less effectual. *Weak* or *no* Benevolence, a moral Sense proportionably *dull*, strong sensual *Appetites*, a clamorous Train of *Selfish* Affections, these mixed and varied in endless Combinations, form the real Character of the *Bulk* of Mankind: Not only in *Cottages*, but in *Cities*, *Churches*, *Camps*, and *Courts*. So that some stronger Ties, some Motives more efficacious are necessary, not only for the Perfection of *Virtue*, but the Welfare, nay, the very Being of *Society*.

'TIS not denied, nay, 'tis meant and insisted on, that among all these various Characters and Tempers, the Culture of the benevolent Affections ought to be assiduously regarded. For though we have seen that the Design of introducing an universal high *Relish* or *Taste* for Virtue be *visionary* and *vain*, yet still a lower, or a lower Degree may *possibly* be instilled. We have only attempted to prove, that the Capacity for this high Taste in Morals is not universally or essentially intervoven with the human Frame, but dispensed in various Degrees, in the same Manner as the Capacity for a Taste in *inferior* Beauties, in *Architecture*, *Painting*, *Poetry*, and *Music*.

To remedy this *Defect* of *unerring* Instinct in Man, by which he becomes a Creature so much less consistent than the Brute Kinds, Providence hath afforded him not only a Sense of *present*, but a Foresight of *future Good and Evil*.

HENCE the Force of human Laws; which being established by common Consent, for the Good of all, endeavour, so far as their Power can reach, by the Infliction of Punishment on Offenders, to establish the general Happiness of Society, by making the *acknowledged Interest* of every *Individual* to coincide and unite with the *public* Welfare.

BUT as human Laws cannot reach the *Heart* of Man; as they can only inflict *Punishment* on Offenders, but cannot bestow *Rewards* on the Obedient; as there are many Duties of *imperfect* Obligation which they cannot recognize; as *Force* will sometimes *defy*, and *Cunning* often *elude* their Power; so without some further Aids, some Motives to Action more *universally* interesting, Virtue must still be left betrayed and deserted.

Now as it is clear from the Course of these Observations, that nothing can work this great Effect, but what can produce 'an entire and universal Coincidence between private and public Happiness;' so is it equally evident, that nothing can effectually convince Mankind, that their own Happiness universally depends on *procuring*, or at least *not violating* the Happiness of others, save only 'the lively and active Belief of an all-seeing and all-powerful GOD, who will hereafter make them happy or miserable, according as they designedly promote or violate the Happiness of their Fellow-Creatures.' And this is the *Essence* of RELIGION.

THIS, at first View, should seem a Motive or *Principle* of Action, sufficient for all the Purposes of Happiness and Virtue. Indeed the Bulk of Mankind seem agreed in this Truth. Yet refining Tempers, who love to quit the common Tracks of Opinion, have been bold enough to call even this in Question. Among these, the noble Writer hath been one of the most diligent: It will therefore be necessary to consider the Weight of his Objections.

To prevent Misinterpretation, it may be proper to observe, that Lord SHAFTESBURY sometimes talks in earnest of the *Nobleness* and *Dignity* of *Religion*. But when he explains himself, it appears, he confines his Idea of it to that Part which consists solely in Gratitude to, and Adoration of the supreme Being, without any Prospect of future Happiness or Misery. Now, though indeed this be the noblest Part, yet it is beyond the Reach of all, save only those who are capable of the most *exalted* Degrees of Virtue. His Theory of *Religion* therefore is precisely of a Piece, with his Theory of the *moral Sense*; not calculated for Use, but Admiration; and only existing in the Place where they had their Birth; that is, as the noble Writer well expresseth it, in a *Mind taken up in Vision*.

He sometimes talks, or seems to talk, in earnest too, on the *Usefulness* of *Religion*, in the common Acceptation of the Word. With Regard to which 'tis only necessary to observe, that whatever he hath said on this Subject I readily assent to: But this is no Reason why it may not be necessary to obviate every thing he hath thrown out to the contrary, to prejudice common Readers against Religion, through the Vanity of being thought *Original*. To *invent* what is *just* or *useful*, is the Character of *Genius*: 'Tis a far *different* thing, to broach *Absurdities*.

First, therefore, he often asserts, that 'the Hope of future Reward and Fear of future Punishment is utterly unworthy of the free Spirit of a Man, and only fit for those who are destitute of the very first Principles of common Honesty: He calls it *miserable, vile, mercenary*: And compares those who allow it any Weight, to *Monkies* under the Discipline of the Whip[d].'

In Answer to these general Cavils (probably aimed chiefly at *Revelation*) which are only difficult to confute, as they are vague and fugitive, let it be observed, first; that whatever can be objected against *religious* Fear, holds good against the Fear of *human* Laws. They *both* threaten the Delinquent with the Infliction of Punishment, nor is the Fear of the one more unworthy, than of the other. Yet the noble Writer himself often speaks with the highest Respect of *Legislators*, of the Founders of *Society* and *Empire*, who, by the Establishment of wise and wholesome Laws, drew Mankind from their State of natural Barbarity, to that of cultivated Life and Social Happiness: Unless indeed he supposes that Orpheus and the rest of them did their Business *literally* by *Taste* and a *Fiddle*. If therefore the just Fear of *human* Power might be inforced without insulting or violating the *Generosity* of our Nature, whence comes it, that a just Fear of the *Creator* should so miserably degrade the Species? The religious Principle holds forth the same Motive to Action, and only differs from the other, as the Evil it threatens is infinitely greater and more lasting.

Further: If we consider the religious Principle in its true Light, there is nothing in it either *mean, slavish*, or *unworthy*. To be in a *Fright* indeed, to live under the Suggestions of *perpetual Terror* (in which, the noble Writer would persuade us, the religious Principle consists) is far from an amiable Condition. But this belongs only to the *Superstitious* or the *Guilty*. The first of these are *falsely* religious; and to the last, I imagine the noble Writer's most zealous Admirers will acknowledge, it *ought* to belong. But to the rest of Mankind, the *religious* Principle or *Fear* of GOD is of a quite different Nature. It only implies a lively and habitual Belief, that we shall be hereafter miserable, if we disobey his Laws. Thus every wise Man, nay,

---

[d]   *Wit and Humour – Enquiry – &c.*

every Man of common Understanding, hath a *like Fear* of every *possible Evil*; of the destructive Power of natural Agents, of *Fire, Water, Serpents, Poison*: Yet none of these Fears, more than the religious one, imply a State of *perpetual* Misery and Apprehension: None of them are inconsistent with the most generous Temper of Mind, or truest Courage. None of them imply more than a *rational Sense* of these several Kinds of Evil; and from that Sense, *a Determination to avoid them*. Thus the noble Writer himself, when it answers a different Purpose, acknowledges that 'a Man of Courage may be *cautious* without real Fear^e.' Now the Word *Caution*, in its very Nature, implies a Sense of a Possibility of Evil, and from that Sense a Determination to avoid it: Which is the very Essence of the religious Principle or the *Fear* of GOD.

AND as to the other Branch of religious Principle, 'the Hope and Prospect of higher Degrees of future Happiness and Perfection:' – What is there of *mean, slavish*, or *unworthy* in it? Are all Mankind to be blown up into the *Mock-majesty* of the *kingly* STOIC, seated on the Throne of *Arrogance*, and *lording* it in an *empty* Region of CHIMÆRA's? Is not the Prospect of Happiness the great universal Hinge of human Action? Do not all the Powers of the Soul centre in this one Point? Doth not the noble Writer himself elsewhere acknowledge this^f? And that our Obligations to Virtue itself can only arise from this one Principle, that it gives us real Happiness? Why then should the Hope of a happy Immortality be branded as *base* and *slavish*, while the Consciousness or Prospect of a happy Life on Earth is regarded as a just and honourable Motive?

THE noble Writer indeed confesseth, that 'if by the Hope of Reward, be understood the Love and Desire (he ought to have said, the *Hope*) of *virtuous Enjoyment*, it is not derogatory to Virtue.' But that in every other Sense, the indulged Hope of Reward is not only mean and mercenary, but even *hurtful* to Virtue and common *Humanity*: 'For in this religious Sort of Discipline, the Principle of *Self-Love*, which is *naturally so prevailing* in us *(indeed?)* being no way moderated or restrained, but rather improved and made stronger every Day, by the Exercise of the Passions in a Subject of more extended Self-Interest; there may be reason to apprehend lest the Temper of this kind should extend itself in general through all the Parts of Life.'

THIS, to say the best of it, is the very *Phrenzy* of Virtue. Religion proposeth true Happiness as the End and Consequence of virtuous Action: This is granted. It proposeth it by such Motives as must influence Self-Love, and consequently hath given the best Means of procuring it. Yet, it seems, Self-Love being not restrained, but made stronger, will make Mankind miss of true Happiness. That is, by leading Self-Love into the

---

^e *Enquiry*, B. ii. Part ii. § 3.
^f See above, Sect. VI. of this *Essay*.

Path of *true* Happiness, Religion will inevitably conduct it to *false*; by commanding us to *cherish* our *public* Affections, it will certainly *inflame* the *private* ones; by assuring us, that if we would be happy hereafter, we must be *virtuous* and *benevolent*, it will beyond Question render us *vile* and *void* of *Benevolence*. But this Mode of Reasoning is common with the noble Writer.

HOWEVER, at other Times his Lordship can descend to the Level of common Sense; and prosecute his Argument by Proofs diametrically opposite to what he here advanceth. For in displaying the Motives to Virtue, after having modelled the inward State of the human Mind according to his own Imagination, he proceeds to consider the *Passions* which regard *ourselves*, and draws another, and indeed a stronger Proof from *these*. – He there proves[g] the Folly of a vicious Love of Life, 'because Life itself may often prove a Misfortune.' So of *Cowardice*, 'because it often robs us of the Means of Safety.' – Excessive *Resentment*, 'because the Gratification is no more than an Alleviation of a racking Pain.' – The Vice of Luxury 'creates a Nauseating, and Distaste, Diseases, and constant Craving.' He urges the same Objections against intemperate Pleasure of the amorous kind. He observes that Ambition is ever 'suspicious, jealous, captious, and uncapable of bearing the least Disappointment.' He then proceeds thro' a variety of other Passions, proving them all to be the Sources of some internal or external Misery. Thus he awakens the same Passions of *Hope* and *Fear*, which, in a religious View, he so bitterly inveighs against. Thus he exhibits a Picture of future *Rewards* and *Punishments*, even of the most *selfish* Kind: He recommends the Conformity to Virtue, on the Score both of present and future *Advantage*: He *deters* his Reader from the Commission of Vice, by representing the Misery it will produce. And these too, such *Advantages* and such *Miseries*, as are entirely distinct from the mere Feeling or virtuous Affection or its contrary: From the Considerations of Safety, Alleviation of *bodily* Pain, the Avoidance of *Distaste*, and *Diseases*, Now doth not his own Cavil here recoil upon him? 'That in this Sort of Discipline, and by exhibiting such Motives as these, the Principle of Self-Love must be made stronger, by the Exercise of the Passions in a Subject of more extended Self-Interest: And so there may be Reason to apprehend, lest the Temper of this Kind should extend itself in general through all the Parts of Life.' Thus the Objection proves equally against both: In Reality, against neither. For, as we have seen, the *Sense*, or *Prospect* of Happiness, is the only possible Motive to Action; and if we are taught to believe that *virtuous Affection* will produce *Happiness*, whether the expected Happiness lies in *this* Life, or *another*, it will *tend*, and *equally* tend, to produce *virtuous* Affection. The noble Writer, therefore, and his Admirers, might as well attempt to remove Mountains, as to prove that the *Hope* and

---

g   *Enquiry*, B. ii. Part ii. § 3.

Prospect of a happy Immortality, can justly be accounted more servile, mercenary, or *hurtful*, than the View of those transient and earthly Advantages, which his Lordship hath so rhetorically and honestly display'd, for the Interest and Security of *Virtue*. In Truth, they are precisely of the same Nature, and only differ in Time, Duration, and Degree. They are both established by our Creator for the same great End of Happiness. And what GOD hath thus *connected*, it were *absurd*, as well as *impious*, to attempt to *separate*[h].

THERE is yet another Circumstance observable in human Nature, which still further proves, that the Hope of a happy Immortality hath no Tendency to produce selfish Affection, but its contrary. For let the *stoical* Tribe draw what Pictures they please of the human Species, this is an undoubted Truth, 'that *Hope* is the most universal Source of human *Happiness*: And that Man is never so sincerely and heartily *benevolent*, as when he is truly *happy* in himself.' Thus the high Consciousness of his being numbered among the Children of GOD, and that his Lot is among the Saints; that he is destined to an endless Progression of Happiness, and to rise from high to higher Degrees of Perfection, must needs inspire him with that Tranquillity and Joy, which will naturally diffuse itself in Acts of sincere Benevolence to all his Fellow-Creatures, whom he looks upon as his Companions in this Race of Glory. Thus will every noble Passion of the Soul be awakened into Action: While the joyless Infidel, possessed with the gloomy Dread of Annihilation, too naturally contracts his Affections as his Hopes of Happiness decrease; while he considers and despiseth himself, and his Fellow-Creatures, as no more than the Beasts that perish.

THE noble Writer indeed insinuates, that there is 'a certain Narrowness of Spirit, occasioned by this Regard to a future Life, peculiarly observable in the *devout* Persons and *Zealots* of almost every religious Persuasion[i].' In reply to which, 'tis only necessary to affirm, what may be affirmed with Truth, that with Regard to *devout* Persons the Insinuation is a *Falsehood*. It was prudently done indeed, to join the *Zealots* (or *Bigots*) in the same

---

[h] Hence we may see the Weakness and Mistake of those *falsely religious*, who fall into an *Extreme* directly *opposite* to this of the noble Writer; who are *scandalized* at our being determined to the Pursuit of Virtue through any Degree of Regard to its happy Consequences in this Life; which Regard they call *wordly, carnal, profane*. For it is evident, that the religious Motive is precisely of the same Kind; only *stronger*, as the Happiness expected is *greater* and more *lasting*. While therefore we set the *proper* and *proportioned* Value upon each, it is impossible we can act irrationally, or offend that GOD who established *both*.

This naturally leads to a further Observation, which shews the Danger, as well as Folly, of *groveling* in *Systems*. Virtue, we see, comes recommended and enforced on three Principles. It is attended with *natural* and *immediate Pleasure* or Advantage: – It is commanded by human *Laws*: – It is enjoined by *Religion*. – Yet the *Religionists* have often decry'd the first of these Sanctions: The *fanatical Moralists*, the *last*: And even the *second* hath not escaped the Madness of an *enthusiastic* Party; which, however, never grew considerable enough in this Kingdom, to merit Confutation.

[i] *Enquiry*, B. i. Part iii. § 3.

Sentence; because it is true, that *these*, being under the Dominion of *Superstition*, forget the true Nature and End of *Religion*; and are therefore *scrupulously* exact in the Observation of outward *Ceremonies*, while they neglect the superior and *essential* Matters of the Law, of *Justice, Benevolence*, and *Mercy*.

AND as to the Notion of confining the Hope of future Reward to 'that of virtuous Enjoyment only:' This is a *Refinement* parallel to the rest of the noble Writer's System; and, like all Refinements, contracts instead of enlarging our Views. 'Tis allowed indeed, that the Pleasures of Virtue are the highest we know of in our present State; and 'tis therefore commonly supposed, they may constitute our chief Felicity in another. But doth it hence follow, that no other Sources of Happiness may be dispensed, which as yet are utterly unknown to us? Can our narrow and partial Imaginations set Bounds to the Omnipotence of GOD? And may not our Creator vouchsafe us such Springs of yet untasted Bliss, as shall exceed even the known Joys of Virtue, as far as *these* exceed the Gratifications of Sense? Nay, if we consider, what is generally believed, that our Happiness will arise from an Addition of new and higher Faculties; that in the present Life, the Exercise of Virtue itself ariseth often from the *Imperfection* of our State; if we consider these Things, it should seem highly probable, that our future Happiness will consist in something quite beyond our present Comprehension: Will be 'such as Eye hath not seen, nor Ear heard, neither hath it entered into the Heart of Man to conceive.'

Section X.

BUT beyond these Objections, the noble Writer hath more than once touched upon another, which merits a particular Consideration. For he affirms, that 'after all, 'tis not merely what we call *Principle*, but a *Taste*, which governs Men.' That 'even Conscience, such as is owing to religious Discipline, will make but a slight Figure, where this Taste is set amiss[k].'

THE Notion here advanced is not peculiar to himself. He seems to have drawn it from a much more considerable Writer, who hath endeavoured to support the same Proposition by a great Variety of Examples[l]. Several Authors of inferior Rank have borrowed the same Topic, for popular Declamation. Nay, one hath gone so far as to assert, 'that Man is so unaccountable a Creature, as to act most commonly against his Principle[m].'

THE Objection, indeed, carries an Appearance of Force: Yet on a near Examination it entirely vanisheth.

IT must be owned, that in most Countries, a considerable Part of what

[k]   *Misc.* iii. c. 2.
[l]   BAYLE, *Pens. sur une* Comete.
[m]   *Fable of the Bees.*

is called *Religion*, deserves no other Name than that of *Absurdity* made *sacred*. And it were strange indeed, should *Bigotry* and *false* Religion produce that Uprightness of Heart, that Perfection of Morals, which is the genuine Effect of *Truth*.

IT must be owned, that with Regard to religious Principle, as well as moral Practice, every Man has the Power of being a *Hypocrite*. That Knaves, in order to be accounted *honest*, may appear *devout*. And we may reasonably suppose, if we consider the innumerable Artifices of Villainy, that the outward Profession of Religion becomes a frequent *Disguise* to an *atheistical* and *corrupted* Heart.

BUT though these Circumstances may sufficiently account for the Appearance in many particular Cases, yet, with Regard to the *general* Fact, *here* seems to lie the proper Solution of the Difficulty. 'That even where true Religion is known, professed, and in Speculation *assented* to, it is seldom so thoroughly *inculcated* as to become a Principle of Action.' We have seen that Imagination is the universal Instrument of human Action; that no Passion can be strongly excited in the Soul by mere Knowledge or Assent, till the Imagination hath formed to itself some kind of Picture or Representation of the Good or Evil apprehended[n]. Now the Senses and their attendant Passions are continually urging their Demands, through the immediate Presence of their respective Objects: So that nothing but the *vivid Image* of some greater Good or Evil in Futurity can possibly resist and overbalance their Sollicitations. The *Idea* therefore of future Happiness and Misery must be strongly impressed on the Imagination, ere they can work their full Effects, because they are *distant* and *unseen*: But this *Habit* of *Reflexion* is seldom properly fixed by *Education*; and thus for want of a proper Impression, 'religious Principle is seldom *gained*, and therefore seldom operates.'

BUT where a sincere and lively Impression takes place; where the Mind is convinced of the Being of a GOD; that he *is*, and is a *Rewarder* of them that diligently seek him; where the *Imagination* hath gained a Habit of connecting this great Truth with every Thought, Word, and Action; there it may be justly affirmed, that Piety and Virtue cannot but *prevail*. To say, in a Case of this Nature, that Man will not act according to his Principle, is to contradict the full Evidence of known Facts. We see how true Mankind commonly are to their Principle of *Pride*, or mistaken Honour; how true to their Principle of *Avarice*, or mistaken Interest; how true to their Principle of a Regard to *human* Laws. Why are they so? Because they have strongly and habitually connected these Principles in their Imagination with the Idea of their own Happiness. Therefore, whenever the religious Principle becomes in the same Manner habitually connected in the Imagination, with the Agent's Happiness; that is, whenever the religious Principle takes Place

---

[n] See above, *Essay* I. § 3.

at all, it must needs become infinitely more powerful than any other; because the *Good* it promiseth, and the *Evil* it threatens, are infinitely greater and more lasting. Hence it appears, that the Corruption of Mankind, even where the purest Religion is *professed*, and in Theory *assented* to, doth not arise from the *Weakness* of religious Principle, but the *Want* of it.

AND indeed on other Occasions, and to serve different Purposes, the noble Writer and his Partizans can allow and give Examples of all that is here contended for. Nothing is so common among these Gentlemen, as to declaim against the terrible Effects of *priestly Power*. 'Tis their favourite Topic, to represent Mankind as groaning under the Tyranny of the *Sacred Order*. Now what does this Representation imply, but 'the Force of religious Principle improperly directed?' If Mankind can be swayed by religious Hope and Fear, to resign their Passions and Interests to the *Artifice*, or Advantage of the *Priest*, why not to the *Benefit* of *Mankind*? 'Tis only impressing a different Idea of *Duty*: The Motive to Action is in both Cases the same, and consequently must be of equal Efficacy. Thus if religious Principle were void of *Force*, the Priesthood must be void of *Power*. The Influence therefore of the Priesthood, however dishonestly applied, is a Demonstration of the Force of *religious Principle*.

THIS therefore seems to be the Truth. Although, by timely and continued Culture, the religious Principle might be made more universally predominant; yet even as it is, though not so thoroughly inculcated as to become generally a consistent Principle of Action; in Fact it hath a frequent and *considerable*, though *partial* and imperfect Influence. None but the thoroughly Good and Bad act on continued or consistent Principles; all the intermediate Degrees of Good and Bad act at different Times on various and inconsistent Principles; that is, their *Imaginations* are by turns given up to *impressions* of a *different*, or even *contrary* Nature. This explains the whole Mystery: For, hence it appears that the consistent or inconsistent Conduct of Men depends not on the Nature of their Principles, but on having their Principles, whatever they are, *counteracted* by opposite ones. Although therefore, through a Failure of timely Discipline, Numbers of Men appear to be of that capricious Temper as not to be steddy to any Principle, yet still the religious one will *mix* with the rest, and naturally *prevail* in its *Turn*. This is certainly a common Circumstance among the *looser* and more *inconsiderate* Ranks of Men; who, although by no Means uniformly swayed by the Precepts of Religion, are yet frequently struck with Horror at the Thought of Actions *peculiarly* vile and deterred by the Apprehension of an all-seeing GOD from the Commission of Crimes *uncommonly atrocious*.

HERE then lies the essential Difference between the Efficacy of *Taste*, and *religious* Principle: That the first, being a Feeling or Perception dispensed in various Degrees, and in very weak ones to the Bulk of Mankind, is incapable, even through the most assiduous Culture, of becoming an uni-versal or consistent Motive to Virtue: But the religious Principle, arising from such Passions as are common to the whole Species, must, if properly inculcated, *universally* prevail.

'TIS evident therefore, that in the very first Dawns of Reason, religious Principles ought to be impressed on the Minds of Children; and this early Culture continued through the succeeding Stages of Life. But as the noble Writer hath strangely attempted to ridicule and dishonour Religion in every Shape; so here, he hath endeavoured to throw an Odium on this Method of religious Discipline, by representing it as the Enemy to true Morals and practical Philosophy, as it fetters the Mind with early Prejudices. 'Whatever Manner in Philosophy happens to bear the least Resemblance to that of *Catechism*, cannot, I am persuaded, of itself seem very inviting. Such a smart Way of questioning ourselves in our Youth, has made our Manhood more averse to the *expostulatory* Discipline: And though the metaphysical Points of our Belief, are by this Method with admirable Care and Caution instilled into tender Minds; yet the Manner of this *anticipated* Philosophy may make the After-work of Reason, and the inward Exercise of the Mind at a riper Age, proceed the more heavily, and with greater Reluctance. – 'Tis hard, after having by so many pertinent Interrogatories and decisive Sentences, declared *who* and *what* we are; to come leisurely in another, to enquire concerning our *real Self* and *End*, the Judgment we are to make of *Interest*, and the Opinion we should have of *Advantage* and *Good*: Which is what must necessarily determine us in our *Conduct*, and prove the leading Principle of our Lives°.'

IN reply to this *most philosophical* Paragraph, let it be observed; that it is not the Design of Religion to make *Sophists*, but *good Subjects* of Mankind. That Man being designed, not for *Speculation*, but *Action*, religious Principle is not to be instilled in a *philosophical*, but a *moral* View: Therefore with Regard to *Practice*, nothing can be more fit and rational than to impress acknowledged *Truths* at an Age when the *Recipient* is incapable of their *Demonstrations*; in the same Manner as we teach the *Mechanic* to *work* on *Geometric* Principles, while the Proofs are *unknown* to him.

BUT then, the *Prejudices of Education* – yes, these are the great *Stum-bling-block* to a modern *Free-thinker*. It still runs in his Head, that all Mankind are born to dispute *de omni scibili*ᵖ. Let therefore this *minute* Philosopher reflect, first, that a *Prejudice* doth not imply, as it generally supposed, the *Falsehood* of the Opinion instilled; but only that it is taken up and held without its proper *Evidence*. Thus a Child may be prejudiced in Favour of Truth, as well as Falsehood; and in him neither the one nor

---

°   *Advice*, &c. Part iii § 2.
ᵖ   On all Subjects.

the other can properly be called more than an *Opinion*. Further: The human Mind cannot remain in a State of *Indifference*, with regard either to *Opinion* or *Practice*: 'Tis of an *active* Nature; and, like a *fertile* Field, if by due Cultivation it be not made to produce good *Fruit*, will certainly spring up in *Tares* and *Thistles*. Impressions, Opinions, *Prejudices*, of one kind or other a Child will inevitably contract, from the Things and Persons that *surround* him: And if rational Habits and Opinions be not infused, in order *to anticipate* Absurdities; Absurdities will rise, and *anticipate* all rational Habits and Opinions. His *Reason* and his *Passions* will put themselves in *Action*, however untoward and inconsistent, in the same Manner as his *Limbs* will make an Effort towards progressive *Motion*, however awkward and absurd. The same Objection therefore that lies against instilling a *salutary Opinion*, will arise against *teaching* him to walk *erect*. For this, too, is a kind of '*anticipating* Philosophy:' And sure, a Child left to his own *Self-Discipline*, 'till he could come *leisurely* to enquire concerning his *real Self* and *End*,' would stand as fair a Chance to *grovel* in Absurdity, and bring *down* his Reason to the sordid *Level* of Appetite, as to *crawl* upon all *four*, and dabble in the *Dirt*. Thus the noble Writer's Ridicule would sweep away the whole System of Education along with the religious Principle: Not an Opinion or Inclination must be controuled, or so much as controverted; 'lest by this *anticipating* Philosophy, the Work of Reason, and the inward Exercise of the Mind, at a *riper* Age, should proceed the more heavily, and with greater Reluctance.' The Caprice of Infancy must rule us, till the very *Capacity* of Improvement should be *destroyed*; and we must turn *Savages*, in order to be made perfect in the *Sovereign Philosophy*!

'Tis no difficult Matter therefore to determine, whether a Child should be left to the Follies of his own *weak* Understanding and *nascent* Passions; be left to imbibe the Maxims of corrupt Times and Manners; Maxims which, setting aside all Regard to their speculative Truth or Falsehood, do lead to certain Misery; or, on the other hand, shall be happily conducted to embrace those religious Principles, which have had the Approbation of the best and wisest Men in every Age and Nation; and which are known and allowed to be the only Means of true Happiness to Individuals, Families, and States.

This therefore ought to be the early and principal Care of those who have the Tuition of Youth: And they will soon find the happy Effects of their Instruction. For as the Child's Understanding shall improve, what was at first instilled only as an *Opinion*, will by Degrees be embraced as *Truth*: Reason will then assume her just Empire; and the great, universal, religious Principle, a rational Obedience to the Will of God, will raise him to his utmost Capacity of moral Perfection; will be a wide and firm Foundation, on which the whole Fabric of Virtue may rise in its just Proportions; will *extend* and *govern* his *Benevolence* and *moral Sense*; will strengthen them, if weak; will confirm them, if strong; will supply their Want, if naturally defective: In fine, will direct all his *Passions* to their proper *Objects* and *Degrees*; and, as the great *Master-Spring* of Action, at once *promote* and *regulate* every Movement of his *Heart*.

IT must be owned, the noble Writer's Caution against this 'anticipating Philosophy' hath of late been deeply imbibed. In Consequence of it, we have seen *religious Principle* declaimed against, ridiculed, lamented. The Effect of this hath been, an abandoned Degree of Villainy in one Class of Mankind; a lethargic Indifference towards Virtue or Vice in another; and in the third, which boast the Height of modern Virtue, we seldom see more than the first natural. Efforts, the mere *Buddings* of Benevolence and Honour, which are too generally blasted ere they can ripen into *Action*. This Contempt of Religion hath always been a fatal *Omen* to *free* States. Nor, if we may credit Experience, can we entertain any just Hope, that this fantastic Scheme, this boasted *Relish* for Beauty and Virtue, can ever give Security to Empire, without the more solid Supports of religious Belief. For it is remarkable, that in the Decline of both the *Greek* and *Roman* States, after Religion had lost its Credit and Efficacy, this very *Taste*, this *sovereign Philosophy* usurped its Place, and became the common Study and Amusement (as it is now among ourselves) both of the *Vile* and *Vulgar*. The Fact, with Regard to *Greece*, is sufficiently notorious; with Regard to *Rome*, it may seem to demand a Proof. And who would think, that QUINTILIAN in the following Passage was not describing our own Age and Nation? 'Nunc autem quae velut propria philosophiae asseruntur, passim tractamus *omnes*: Quis enim modo de JUSTO, AEQUO, AC BONO, non et VIR PESSIMUS loquitur[q]?' – '*What was formerly the Philosopher's Province only, is now invaded by all: We find every wicked and worthless Fellow, in these Days, haranguing on* VIRTUE, BEAUTY, *and* GOOD.' What this *Leprosy* of *false* Knowledge may end in, I am unwilling to say: But this may be said with Truth, because it is justified by Experience; that along with the Circumstance now remarked, every other *Symptom* is rising among us, that hath generally attended the dark and troubled *Evening* of a *Commonwealth*.

DOUBTLESS, many will treat these Apprehensions with *Derision*: But this *Derision* is far from being an Evidence of their Falsehood. For no People ever sell a Sacrifice to themselves, till *lulled* and infatuated by their own Passions. *Blind Security* is an essential Characteristic of a People devoted to Destruction. The Fact is equally undeniable, whether it ariseth from the moral Appointment of Providence, or the Connexion of natural Causes. Though this is seen and acknowledged by those who are conversant with the History of Mankind; yet 'tis hard to convey this Evidence to those who seldom extend their Views beyond their own short Period of Existence; because they see the Prevalence of the *Cause* assigned, while yet the pre-

---

[q] *Quint. Prœmium.*

tended *Consequence* appears not. But they who look back into ancient Time are convinced, that the *public* Effects of *Irreligion* have never been sudden or *immediate*. One Age is *falsely* polite, *irreligious*, and *vile*; the next is sunk in *Servitude* and *Wretchedness*. This is analogous to the Operation of other Causes. A Man may be intemperate for twenty Years, before he feels the Effects of Intemperance on his Constitution. The Sun and Moon raise the Tides; yet the Tides rise not to their Height, till a considerable Time after the Conjunction of these two Luminaries. We cannot therefore justly decide concerning the future *Effects* of Irreligion, from its present State. The *Examples* of former Times are a much better *Criterion*: And these are such, as ought to make every Man among us, that regards Posterity, tremble for his Posterity while he reads them.

FOR this is but too just an *Epitome* of the Story of Mankind. That TYRANNY and SUPERSTITION have ever gone Hand in Hand; mutually supporting and supported; taking their Progress, and fixing their Dominion over all the Kingdoms of the Earth; overwhelming it in one general Deluge, as the Waters cover the Sea. Here and there a happy Nation *emerges*; breathes for a while in the enlightened Region of KNOWLEDGE, RELIGION, VIRTUE, FREEDOM: 'Till, in their appointed Time, IRRELIGION and LICENTIOUSNESS appear; *mine* the Foundations of the *Fabric*, and sink it in the general Abyss of IGNORANCE and OPPRESSION.

POSSIBLY the fatal Blow may yet be averted from us. 'Tis surely the Duty of every Man, in every Station, to contribute his Share, however *inconsiderable*, to this great End. This must be my Apology for opposing the noble Writer's fantastic System; which by exhibiting a false Picture of human Nature, is, in Reality an *Inlet* to *Vice*, while it seems most *favourable* to *Virtue*: And while it pretends to be drawn from the *Depths* of *Philosophy*, is, of all others, *most unphilosophical*.

SOAME JENYNS

A Free Enquiry into the Nature and Origin of Evil (1757)

Letter III. On Natural Evils
Letter IV. On Moral Evils

Soame Jenyns (1704–1787)

Biographical Note

Soame Jenyns was the son of Sir Roger Jenyns (d.1740) and his second wife, Elizabeth Soame (c.1662–1728), daughter of Sir Peter Soame, Bart., of Heydon, Essex. He was born in London either on 31 December 1703 or 1 January 1704. In the seventeenth century the Jenyns family were speculators in the drainage of Bedford Level in the Fens, and remained active in the management of the Bedford Level until the nineteenth century. Roger was knighted by William III, and shortly afterwards bought an estate near Bottisham, between Cambridge and Newmarket. His brother, John Jenyns, was elected to Parliament in 1710.

Soame Jenyns' early education was provided by his mother Elizabeth, then by two clergymen, Rev. W. Hill and Rev. Stephen White. In 1722 he entered St John's College, Cambridge as a Fellow-Commoner under Dr William Edmunson as tutor. He matriculated in 1724, but left Cambridge the next year without taking a degree. There is little information on his university career. However, since Jenyns was at Cambridge at the same time as other men with philosophical interests,[1] it seems likely that he would have received some intellectual stimulation during his time there.

By arrangement between their two families, in 1726 Jenyns married Mary Soame, his cousin and illegitimate daughter of Colonel Edmund Soame of Dereham Grange, Norfolk. The marriage proved unsuccessful. In 1742 Mary eloped with a Tory MP, William Levinz, living separately in London where she seems to have had a son who died at birth in 1750. She died there in 1753, and was buried in the family vault at Bottisham. In 1754 Jenyns married another cousin, Elizabeth Gray. An early biographer, Charles Nalson Cole, said that she had no looks, no fortune, and was 'pretty far advanced in years'.[2] She and Jenyns, however, were clearly devoted and remained happily married, although they had no children.

Jenyns was likable but said to be ugly, and a flattering portrait painted by Reynolds in 1757 caused entertainment to society. Horace Walpole commented, 'It is proof of Sir Joshua's art, who could give a strong resemblance of so uncouth a countenance without leaving it disagreeable'.[3] Jenyns was popular in the London salons because of his inoffensive and droll sense of humour. Later in life he was a favourite of the 'bluestocking' intellectual

---

[1]   See Gay above, p. 29.
[2]   Ronald Rompkey, *Soame Jenyns* (Boston 1984), p. 8.
[3]   Rompkey, *Soame Jenyns*, p. 19.

ladies such as Elizabeth Montagu, Hannah More and Susanna Dobson. Richard Cumberland, who knew Jenyns at the Board of Trade, left a favourable picture of Jenyns' character: physically ugly, dressed in 'all the colours of the jay', Jenyns was nevertheless 'the charm of the circle, and gave a zest to every company he came into'.[4] The only time Cumberland heard him being unkind was in the notorious 'Epitaph on Johnson'. Otherwise, 'His pleasantry ... was like the bread to our dinner; you did not perhaps make it the whole, or principal part, of your meal, but it was an admirable and wholesome auxiliary to your other viands'.[5]

After leaving Cambridge Jenyns divided his time between London and Bottisham. He became a political supporter of the Earl of Hardwicke, head of the influential Yorke family, who was a friend of the Duke of Newcastle and who served as Lord Chancellor after 1737. Jenyns' loyalty to his patrons, which led Walpole to call him 'the poet laureate of the Yorkes',[6] was rewarded by the provision of safe seats in the Commons for nearly forty years and by a place on the Board of Trade, where he served industriously from 1755 to 1780. In 1741 the Yorkes asked Jenyns to sit for Cambridgeshire, which he held until 1754. When it became clear that he would not be successful in the election of that year, the Yorkes found him a seat at Dunwich as a consolation. In 1758 Jenyns was elected one of the members for the town of Cambridge, a seat he held until 1780 when he chose to retire from public life. Nevertheless, he became involved in the 1780 election riots, causing Walpole to comment that 'Poor Mr Soame Jenyns was near being trampled to death by the mob: his face was much bruised. He is not made for mixing with a riotous mob. He rejoices at the thoughts of no more entering St Stephen's Chapel'.[7]

In 1757 Jenyns' *A Free Inquiry into the Nature and Origin of Evil* appeared, and was roundly criticized by the Tory Samuel Johnson.[8] Though a Whig, Jenyns could still launch an attack on William Pitt, in a privately circulated poem which was subsequently published (without his knowledge) in the *London Chronicle* and other newspapers in 1759 under the title 'A Simile'. The verse ridiculed Pitt's foreign policy of 1757–58, and the Tories who had acquiesced in it.[9] Walpole tells us that 'Pitt was grievously hurt; and it required all the intercession and protection of Lord Hardwicke to save Jenyns from being turned out of the Board of Trade'.[10] A week after

[4]   Richard Cumberland, *Memoirs of Richard Cumberland written by himself. Containing an account of his Life and Writings* (London 1806), pp. 247, 248.
[5]   Cumberland, *Memoirs*, p. 248.
[6]   Horace Walpole, *Memoirs of King George II*, 3 vols., ed. John Brooke (New Haven and London 1985), ii. 114.
[7]   *Horace Walpole's Correspondence with the Rev. William Cole*, ed. W. S. Lewis and A. Dayle Wallace (London 1937), [*The Yale Edition of Horace Walpole's Correspondence*, ed. W. S. Lewis], ii. 219.
[8]   See Introduction above p. 15 and note.
[9]   Rompkey, *Soame Jenyns*, p. 23.
[10] Walpole, *Memoirs of King George II*, iii. 55.

the poem was published a reply appeared in the *Monitor*, defending the agreement between Pitt and the Tories as essential to national security, poking fun at Jenyns' *Inquiry* for attempting to prove 'the *necessity of corruption*' in the governors of a free country, and criticising his sinecure appointment at the Board of Trade.[11] It has been suggested that John Brown, another of the beneficiaries of Hardwicke's favours, was the author of this reply.[12]

Hume considered Jenyns one of the literary arbiters of his day. In 1759 he told Adam Smith that he had sent a copy of *The Theory of Moral Sentiments* (1759) to several important moulders of opinion in London. These were the Duke of Argyle, Lord Lyttelton, Horace Walpole, Soame Jenyns and Edmund Burke.[13] Hume told Smith in his next letter, 'I am not acquainted with Jennyns [sic]; but he spoke very highly of the Book to Oswald, who is his Brother in the Board of Trade. . . . Mr Yorke was much taken with it as well as several others who had read it'.[14]

Johnson's critical review of Jenyns' *Inquiry* no doubt served to broaden the audience for his writings. Not surprisingly, Boswell did not think so highly of Jenyns' literary attainments, and quoted a poem by John Court-enay to this effect.[15] The unfortunate publication of Jenyns' private thoughts on Johnson (written before his death) provided fuel to keep alive the Jenyns–Johnson controversy:

> Here lies SAM JOHNSON: – Reader, have a care,
> Tread lightly, lest you wake a sleeping Bear:
> Religious, moral, generous, and humane
> He was; but self-sufficient, proud, and vain,
> Fond of, and overbearing in dispute,
> A Christian, and a Scholar – but a Brute.[16]

After Johnson's death, Jenyns gave a revised version of his epitaph to his blue-stocking friends, and again it was published without his consent. It now ended:

> Would you know all his wisdom and his folly,
> His actions, sayings, mirth and melancholy,
> Boswell and Thrale, retailers of his wit,
> Will tell you how he wrote and talk'd and cough'd and spit!

11 *The Monitor, or British Freeholder*, No. 187 (17 Feb. 1759).
12 See Rompkey, *Soame Jenyns*, p. 24, and Brown above, p. 52 and note.
13 *The Letters of David Hume*, 2 vols., ed. J. Y. T. Greig (Oxford 1932), ii. 303.
14 *Letters of David Hume*, p. 312.
15 James Boswell, *Boswell's Life of Johnson* (1952; reprt. London 1957), p. 224.
16 Rompkey, *Soame Jenyns*, p. 25.

The incensed Boswell then produced a nasty riposte '*Prepared for a Creature* not quite dead *yet*', published in the *Gentleman's Magazine*:

> Here lies a little ugly nauseous elf,
> Who judging only from its wretched self,
> Feebly attempted, petulant and vain,
> The 'Origin of Evil' to explain.
> A mighty Genius at this elf displeas'd.
> With a strong critick grasp the urchin squeez'd.
> For thirty years its coward spleen it kept,
> Till in the dust the mighty Genius slept;
> Then stunk and fretted in expiring snuff,
> And blink'd at Johnson with its last poor puff.[17]

Courtenay continued the defence of Johnson with an insulting review of Jenyns' career in which he poured scorn on his literary reputation.[18] Jenyns did not respond to the attacks of Boswell and Courtenay. However, his fame as an ironic wit made it difficult for his contemporaries to take him seriously. Johnson was typical in commenting, 'What Soame Jenyns says upon this subject is not to be minded, he is a wit'.[19] Nevertheless, both the *Inquiry into the Nature and Origin of Evil* and Jenyns' *A View of the Internal Evidence of the Christian Religion* (1776) were serious works. The latter caused Walpole to write to Mason,

> Soame Jenyns has published a confirmation of the Christian religion from internal evidence. Pray was not his *Origin of Evil* a little heterodox? I have dipped into this new piece, and thought I saw something like irony, but to be sure I am wrong, for the *ecclesiastical court* are quite satisfied.[20]

Jenyns' adherence to rational religion was typical of his day, and the ethical emphasis of *A View of the Internal Evidence of the Christian Religion* prompted Paley to announce he would willingly transcribe its remarks on the morality of the gospel into his own *A View of the Evidences of Christianity* (1794), since he was in perfect accord with Jenyns on the matter.[21] In addition to the philosophical and theological *Inquiry into the Nature and Origin of Evil* and *A View of the Internal Evidence of the Christian*

---

[17] *Gentleman's Magazine*, No. 56 (1786), p. 696; see Richard B. Schwartz, *Samuel Johnson and the Problem of Evil* (Madison 1975), pp. 89–90 and note.

[18] John Courtenay, *A Poetical Review of the Literary and Moral Character of the Late Samuel Johnson, L.L.D.* (London 1786), p. 15.

[19] Boswell, *Boswell's Life of Johnson*, p. 750.

[20] *Horace Walpole's Correspondence with William Mason*, eds. W. S. Lewis, Grover Cronin Jr., and Charles H. Bennett (London 1955) [*Yale Edition*], xxviii. 269.

[21] Rompkey, *Soame Jenyns*, p. 144.

Religion, Jenyns published a number of political works: *Gentle Reflections upon the Short but Serious Reasons for a National Militia* (1757), *The Objections to the Taxation of our American Colonies, by the Legislature of Great Britain, briefly consider'd* (1765), *Thoughts on the Causes and Consequences of the Present High Price of Provisions* (1767), *A Scheme for the Coalition of Parties, Humbly Submitted to the Publick* (1772), and *Thoughts on Parliamentary Reform* (1784). Shortly after his death Jenyns' writings were collected and published in four volumes in 1790.[22]

Note on the Text

Jenyns' *A Free Enquiry into the Nature and Origin of Evil* was first published in London in 1757, and three more editions appeared before the end of 1758. The *Enquiry* was later translated into French by Antoine de Rivarol and published in Paris in 1791. The *Enquiry* is presented in the form of six letters to an unnamed correspondent, as follows:

Letter I.   On Evil in General
Letter II.   On Evils of Imperfection
Letter III.   On Natural Evils
Letter IV.   On Moral Evils
Letter V.   On Political Evils
Letter VI.   On Religious Evils

Letters III and IV are reproduced here from the first edition of the *Enquiry* (pp. 45–120), printed for R. and J. Dodsley of London.

---

[22] *The Works of Soame Jenyns, Esq. in Four Volumes. Including Several Pieces Never Before Published. To Which are Prefixed, Short Sketches of the History of the Author's Family, and also of his Life; by Charles Nalson Cole,* 4 vols. (London 1790).

LETTER III.

On Natural EVILS.

SIR,

I shall now lay before you my free sentiments concerning the Origin of Natural Evils, by which I understand the sufferings of sensitive Beings only; for tempests, inundations, and earthquakes, with all the disorders of the material World, are no farther Evils than as they affect the sensitive: so that under this head can be only comprehended pains of body, and inquietudes of mind. That these are real Evils, I readily acknowledge; and if any one is philosopher enough to doubt of it, I shall only beg leave to refer him to a severe fit of sickness, or a tedious law-suit, for farther satisfaction.

The production of Happiness seems to be the only motive that could induce infinite Goodness to exert infinite Power to create all things: for, to say truth, Happiness is the only thing of real value in existence; neither riches, nor power, nor wisdom, nor learning, nor strength, nor beauty, nor virtue, nor religion, nor even life itself, being of any importance but as they contribute to its production. All these are in themselves neither Good nor Evil; Happiness alone is their great end, and they desirable only as they tend to promote it. Most astonishing therefore it must appear to every one who looks round him, to observe all creatures bless'd with life and sensation, that is, all creatures made capable of Happiness, at the same time by their own natures condemned to innumerable and unavoidable miseries. Whence can it proceed, that Providence should thus seem to counteract his own benevolent intentions? To what strange and invisible cause are all these numerous and invincible Evils indebted for their Existence? If God is a good and benevolent Being, what end could he propose from creation, but the propagation of Happiness? and if Happiness is the end of all existence, why are not all creatures that do exist happy?

The true solution of this important question, so long and so vainly searched for by the philosophers of all ages and all countries, I take to be at least no more than this, That these real Evils proceed from the same source as those imaginary ones of Imperfection before treated of, namely, from that subordination, without which no created system can subsist; all subordination implying Imperfection, all Imperfection Evil, and all Evil some kind of inconvenience or suffering: so that there must be particular inconveniences and sufferings annexed to every particular rank of created Beings by the circumstances of things, and their modes of existence. Most of those to which we ourselves are liable may be easily shewn to be of this kind, the effects only of human nature, and the station Man occupies in the universe: and therefore their Origin is plainly deducible from necessity; that is, they could not have been prevented without the loss of greater good, or the admission of greater Evils than themselves; or by not creating any such creatures as Men at all. And tho' this, upon a general view of things, does not so forcibly strike us; yet, on a more minute inspection into every grievance attendant on human nature, it will most evidently appear. Most of these, I think, may be comprehended under the following heads: poverty, labour, inquietudes of mind, pains of body, and death; from none of which we may venture to affirm Man could ever have been exempted, so long as he continued to be Man. God indeed might have made us quite other creatures, and placed us in a world quite differently constituted; but then we had been no longer Men; and whatever Beings had occupied our stations in the universal System, they must have been liable to the same inconveniences.

Poverty, for example, is what all could not possibly have been exempted from, not only by reason of the fluctuating nature of human possessions, but because the world could not subsist without it; for had all been rich, none could have submitted to the commands of another, or the necessary drudgeries of life; thence all governments must have been dissolved, arts neglected, and lands uncultivated, and so an universal penury have over-whelmed all, instead of now and then pinching a few. Hence, by the by, appears the great excellence of Charity, by which Men are enabled by a particular distribution of the blessings and enjoyments of life, on proper occasions, to prevent that poverty which by a general one Omnipotence itself could never have prevented: so that, by inforcing this duty, God as it were demands our assistance to promote universal happiness, and to shut out Misery at every door, where it strives to intrude itself.

Labour indeed God might easily have excused us from, since at his command the Earth would readily have poured forth all her treasures without our inconsiderable assistance: but if the severest Labour cannot sufficiently subdue the malignity of human nature, what plots and machi-nations, what wars, rapine, and devastation, what profligacy and licentiousness, must have been the consequences of universal idleness! So that Labour ought only to be looked upon as a task kindly imposed upon us by our indulgent Creator, necessary to preserve our health, our safety, and our innocence.

Inquietudes of mind cannot be prevented without first eradicating all our inclinations and passions, the winds and tides that preserve the great Ocean of human life from perpetual stagnation. So long as Men have pursuits, they must meet with disappointments; and whilst they have disappoint-ments, they must be disquieted; whilst they are injured, they must be inflamed with anger; and whilst they see cruelties, they must be melted with pity; whilst they perceive danger, they must be sensible of fear; and whilst they behold beauty, they must be inslaved by Love: nor can they be exempted from the various anxieties attendant on these various and turbulent passions. Yet without them we should be undoubtedly less happy and less safe; for without anger we should not defend ourselves, and without pity we should not assist others; without fear we should not preserve our lives, and without love they would not be worth preserving.

Pains of body are perhaps but the necessary consequences of the union of material and spiritual essences; for matter being by nature divisible, when endued with sensibility, must probably be affected by pains and pleasures by its different modifications: wherefore, to have been freed from our sufferings, we must have been deprived of all our sensual enjoyments; a composition by which few surely would be gainers. Besides, the pains of our bodies are necessary to make us continually mindful of their preservation; for what numberless lives would be lost by neglect in every trifling pursuit, or flung away in ill humour, was the piercing of a sword no more painful than the tickling of a feather?

> Death, the last and most dreadful of all Evils, is so far from being one, that it is the infallible cure for all others.
>
> To die, is landing on some silent shore, Where billows never beat, nor tempests roar. Ere well we feel the friendly stroke, 'tis o'er.
>
> GARTH.

For, abstracted from the sickness and sufferings usually attending it, it is no more than the expiration of that term of life, God was pleased to bestow on us, without any claim or merit on our part. But was it an Evil ever so great, it could not be remedied but by one much greater, which is by living for ever; by which means our wickedness, unrestrained by the prospect of a future state, would grow so insupportable, our sufferings so intolerable by perseverance, and our pleasures so tiresome by repetition, that no Being in the Universe could be so compleatly miserable as a species of immortal Men. We have no reason therefore to look upon Death as an Evil, or to fear it as a punishment, even without any supposition of a future life: but if we consider it as a passage to a more perfect state, or a remove only in an eternal succession of still improving states (for which we have the strongest reasons) it will then appear a new favour from the divine munificence; and a man must be as absurd to repine at dying, as a traveller would be, who proposed to himself a delightful tour thro' various unknown countries, to lament that he cannot take up his residence at the first dirty Inn which he baits at on the road. The instability of human life, or the hasty changes of its successive periods, of which we so frequently complain, are no more than the necessary progress of it to this necessary conclusion; and are so far from being Evils deserving these complaints, that they are the source of all novelty, from which our greatest pleasures are ever derived. The continual succession of Seasons in the human life, by daily presenting to us new scenes, render it agreeable, and, like those of the year, afford us delights by their change, which the choicest of them could not give us by their continuance. In the Spring of Life, the gilding of the sunshine, the verdure of the fields, and the variegated paintings of the Sky, are so exquisite in the Eyes of Infants at their first looking abroad into a new World, as nothing perhaps afterwards can equal. The heat and vigour of the succeeding Summer of Youth ripens for us new pleasures, the blooming maid, the nightly revel, and the jovial chace: the serene Autumn of compleat Manhood feasts us with the golden harvest of our worldly pursuits: nor is the hoary Winter of old age destitute of its peculiar comforts and enjoyments, of which the recollection and relation of those past are perhaps none of the least; and at last Death opens to us a new prospect, from whence we shall probably look back upon the diversions and occupations of this world with the same contempt we do now on our Tops and Hobbyhorses, and with the same surprise, that they could ever so much entertain or engage us.

Thus we see all these Evils could never have been prevented even by infinite Power, without the introduction of greater, or the loss of superior good, they being but the necessary consequences of human Nature; from which it can no more be divested, than matter from extension, or heat from motion, which proceed from the very modes of their existence.

If it be objected, that, after all that has been said, there are innumerable miseries entailed upon all things that have life, and particularly on Man; many diseases of the body, and afflictions of mind, in which Nature seems to play the Tyrant, ingenious in contriving torments for her children; that we cannot avoid seeing every moment with horror numbers of our fellow-creatures condemned to tedious and intolerable miseries, some expiring on racks, others roasting in flames, some starving in dungeons, others raving in mad houses; some broiling in fevers, others groaning whole months under the exquisite tortures of gout and stone. If it be said further, that some men being exempted from many calamities with which others are afflicted, proves plainly that all might have been exempted from all; the charge can by no means be disputed, nor can it be alledged that infinite Power could not have prevented most of these dreadful calamities. From hence therefore I am persuaded, that there is something in the abstract nature of pain conducive to pleasure; that the sufferings of individuals are absolutely necessary to universal happiness; and that, from connections to us inconceivable, it was impracticable for Omnipotence to produce the one, without at the same time permitting the other. Their constant and uniform concomitancy thro' every part of Nature with which we are acquainted, very much corroborates this conjecture, in which scarce one instance, I believe, can be produced of the acquisition of pleasure or convenience by any creatures, which is not purchased by the previous or consequential sufferings of themselves or others; pointing out, as it were, that a certain allay of pain must be cast into the universal mass of created Happiness, and inflicted somewhere for the benefit of the whole. Over what mountains of slain is every mighty Empire rolled up to the summit of Prosperity and Luxury, and what new scenes of desolation attend its fall? To what infinite toil of Men, and other animals, is every flourishing City indebted for all the conveniences and enjoyments of Life, and what vice and misery do those very enjoyments introduce? The pleasures peculiar to the continuing our species are severely paid for by pains and perils in one Sex, and by cares and anxieties in both. Those annexed to the preservation of ourselves are both preceded and followed by numberless sufferings; preceded by the massacres and tortures of various animals preparatory to a feast, and followed by as many diseases lying wait in every dish to pour forth vengeance on their destroyers. Our riches and honours are acquired by laborious or perilous occupations, and our sports are pursued with scarce less fatigue or danger, and usually attended with the distresses and destruction of innocent animals. This universal connection of pain with pleasure seems, I think, strongly to intimate, that pain abstractedly considered must have its uses; and since we may be assured, that it is never admitted but with the reluctance of the supreme Author, those uses must be of the highest importance, tho' we have no faculties to conceive them.

The human mind can comprehend but a very small part of the great and astonishing whole: for any thing we know, the sufferings (and perhaps the crimes producing those sufferings) of the Inhabitants of this terrestrial Globe may some way or other affect those of the most distant planet, and the whole animal world may be connected by some principle as general as that of attraction in the corporeal, and so the miseries of particular Beings be some way necessary to the happiness of the whole. How these things operate, is indeed to us quite inconceivable; but that they do operate in some such extensive manner is far, I think, from improbable.

All Ages and Nations seem to have had confused notions of the merits of sufferings abstracted from their tendency to any visible good, and have paid the highest honours to those who have voluntarily endured them, as to their common benefactors. Many in Christian Countries have formerly been sainted for long fasting, for whipping or tormenting themselves, for sitting whole years in uneasy postures, or exposing themselves to the inclemency of the weather on the tops of pillars. Many at this day in the East are almost deified for loading themselves with heavy chains, bending under burthens, or confining themselves in chairs stuck round with pointed nails. Now, if these notions are not totally devoid of all reason and common sense, (and few, I believe, are so which become universal) they can be founded on no other principle than this, of the necessity of pain to produce happiness, which seems another weighty instance of the probability of this ancient and universal opinion, tho' the reasons for it are forgot or unknown, and the practices derived from it big with the most absurd and ridiculous superstitions.

One cause, I think, from which many of our severest sufferings may be derived, may be discovered by analogical reasoning, that is, by assimilating those things which are not objects of our understandings, to others which lye within their reach. Man is one link of that vast Chain, descending by insensible degrees from infinite perfection to absolute nothing. As there are many thousands below him, so must there be many more above him. If we look downwards, we see innumerable species of inferior Beings, whose happiness and lives are dependent on his will; we see him cloathed by their spoils, and fed by their miseries and destruction, inslaving some, tormenting others, and murdering millions for his luxury or diversion; is it, not therefore analogous and highly probable, that the happiness and life of Man should be equally dependent on the wills of his superiors? As we receive great part of our pleasures, and even subsistence, from the sufferings and deaths of lower animals, may not these superior Beings do the same from ours, and that by ways as far above the reach of the most exalted human understandings, as the means by which we receive our benefits are above the capacities of the meanest creatures destined for our service? The fundamental Error in all our reasonings on this subject, is that of placing ourselves wrong in that presumptuous climax of Beast, Man, and God; from whence, as we suppose falsely, that there is nothing above us except the Supreme Being, we foolishly conclude that all the Evils we labour under must be derived immediately from his omnipotent hand: whereas there may be numberless intermediate Beings, who have power to deceive, torment, or destroy us, for the ends only of their own pleasure or utility, who may be vested with the same privileges over their inferiors, and as much benefited by the use of them, as ourselves. In what manner these benefits accrue to them, it is impossible for us to conceive; but that impossibility lessens not the probability of this conjecture, which by Analogy is so strongly confirmed.

Should you, Sir, have been lately employed in reading some of those sublime Authors, who, from pride and ignorance, delight to puff up the dignity of Human Nature, the notions here advanced may appear to you absurd and incredible, because inconsistent with that imaginary dignity; and you may object, that it is impossible that God should suffer innocence to be thus afflicted, and reason thus deceived; that tho' he may permit animals made solely for the use of Man to be thus abused for his convenience or recreation; yet that Man himself, the sole possessor of reason, the Lord of this terrestrial globe, his own ambassador, vicegerent, and similitude, should be thus dependent on the will of others, must be utterly inconsistent with the divine Wisdom and Justice. But pray, Sir, what does all this prove, but the importance of a Man to himself? Is not the justice of God as much concerned to preserve the happiness of the meanest Insect which he has called into being, as of the greatest Man that ever lived? Are not all creatures we see made subservient to each others uses? and what is there in Man, that he only should be exempted from this common fate of all created Beings? The superiority of Man to that of other terrestrial animals is as inconsiderable, in proportion to the immense plan of universal Existence, as the difference of climate between the north and south end of the paper I now write upon, with regard to the heat and distance of the Sun. There is nothing leads us into so many Errors concerning the works and designs of Providence, as that foolish vanity that can persuade such insignificant creatures that all things were made for their service; from whence they ridiculously set up Utility to themselves as the Standard of Good, and conclude every thing to be Evil which appears injurious to them or their purposes. As well might a nest of Ants imagine this Globe of Earth created only for them to cast up into hillocks, and cloathed with grain and herbage for their sustenance; then accuse their Creator for permitting spades to destroy them, and plows to lay waste their habitations; the inconveniences of which they feel, but are utterly unable to comprehend their uses, as well as the relations they themselves bear to superior Beings.

It is surprising that none of those Philosophers, who were drove to the supposition of two first Causes, and many other absurdities, to account for the Origin of Evil, should not rather have chosen to impute it to the ministration of intermediate Beings; and, when they saw the happiness of all inferior animals dependent on our wills, should not have concluded, that the good order and well-being of the Universe might require, that ours should be as dependent on the wills of superior Beings, accountable like ourselves to one common Lord and Father of all things. This is the more wonderful, because the existence and influence of such Beings has been an article in the Creed of all Religions that have ever appeared in the World. In the beautiful system of the Pagan theology, their Sylvan and Houshold Deities, their Nymphs, Satyrs, and Fawns, were of this kind. All the barbarous nations that have ever been discovered, have been found to believe and adore intermediate spiritual Beings, both good and evil. The Jewish religion not only confirms the belief of their existence, but of their tempting, deceiving, and tormenting mankind; and the whole system of Christianity is erected entirely on this foundation.

Thus, Sir, you see the good order of the whole, and the happiness it receives from a proper subordination, will sufficiently account for the sufferings of individuals; and all such should be considered but as the necessary taxes, which every member of this great Republick of the Universe is obliged to pay towards the support of the community. It is no derogation from the divine Goodness, that these taxes are not always imposed equally in the present state of things; because as every individual is but a part of the great whole, so is the present state but a part of a long, or perhaps an eternal succession of others; and, like a single day in the natural life, has reference to many more, both past and to come. It is but as a page in a voluminous accompt, from which no judgment can be formed on the state of the whole: but of this we may be assured, that the ballance will some time or other be settled with justice and impartiality. The certainty therefore of a future state, in which we, and indeed all Creatures endued with sensation, shall some how or other exist, seems (if all our notions of Justice are not erroneous) as demonstrable as the Justice of their Creator; for if he is just, all such Creatures must have their account of happiness and misery somewhere adjusted with equity, and all Creatures capable of virtue and vice must, according to their behaviour, receive rewards and punishments; and, to render these punishments; consistent with infinite goodness, they must not only be proportioned to their crimes, but also some way necessary to universal Good; for no Creatures can be called out of their primitive nothing by an all-wise and benevolent Creator, to be losers by their existence, or to be made miserable for no beneficial end, even by their own misbehaviour: so that all future misery, as well as present, must be subservient to happiness, or otherwise infinite Power, joined with infinite Goodness, would have prevented both vice and punishment.

For this reason, amongst all the shortsighted conjectures of Man into the dispensations of Providence and a future State, the ancient doctrine of Transmigration seems the most rational and most consistent with his wisdom and goodness; as by it all the unequal dispensations of things so necessary in one Life may be set right in another, and all creatures serve the highest and lowest, the most eligible and most burthensome offices of life by an equitable kind of rotation; by which means their rewards and punishments may not only be well proportioned to their behaviour, but also subservient towards carrying on the business of the Universe, and thus at the same time answer the purposes both of justice and utility. But the pride of Man will not suffer us to treat this subject with the seriousness it deserves; but rejects as both impious and ridiculous every supposition of inferior creatures ever arriving at its own imaginary dignity, allowing at the same time the probability of human Nature being exalted to the angelick, a much wider and more extraordinary transition, but yet such a one as may probably be the natural consequence, as well as the reward of a virtuous life: nor is it less likely that our vices may debase us to the servile condition of inferior animals, in whose forms we may be severely punished for the injuries we have done to Mankind when amongst them, and be obliged in some measure to repair them, by performing the drudgeries tyrannically imposed upon us for their service.

From what has been said, I think, it plainly appears that numberless Evils do actually exist, which could not have been excluded from the works of infinite goodness even by infinite power; and from hence it may be concluded, that there are none which could; but that God has exerted all his omnipotence to introduce all possible happiness, and, as far as the imperfection of created things would permit, to exclude all misery, that is, all natural Evil, from the universal system; which notwithstanding will introduce itself in many circumstances, even in opposition to infinite Power.

The Origin of Moral Evil lies much deeper, and I will venture to assert has never yet been fathomed by the short line of human understanding. That I shall be able to reach it, I have by no means the vanity to imagine: but, laying aside all preconceived opinions and systematical prejudice, I will in my next endeavour to come as near it as lies in the power of, SIR, &c.

LETTER IV.

On Moral EVILS.

SIR,

I must now leave that plain and easy road thro' which I have hitherto conducted you, and carry you thro' unfrequented paths, and ways untrodden by philosophical feet. Already, I think, the existence of Natural Evil has been sufficiently accounted for, without any derogation from the power, wisdom, or goodness of God. What next remains to be cleared up, is the Origin of Moral Evil; which, consistently with the same Divine Attributes, I have never seen accounted for by any Author, ancient or modern, in a manner that could give tolerable satisfaction to a rational Inquirer. Nor indeed can this be ever effectually performed, without at the same time taking into consideration all those most abstruse speculations concerning the nature of Virtue, Free-will, Fate, Grace, and Predestination, the debates of ages, and matter of innumerables folios. To attempt this, therefore, in the compass of a Letter, would be the highest presumption, did not I well know the clear and ready comprehension of the person to whom it is addressed; and also, that the most difficult of these kinds of disquisitions are usually better explained in a few lines, than by a thousand pages.

In order therefore to find out the true Origin of Moral Evil, it will be necessary, in the first place, to inquire into its nature and essence; or what it is that constitutes one action Evil, and another Good. Various have been the opinions of various Authors on this Criterion of Virtue; and this variety has rendered that doubtful, which must otherwise have been clear and manifest to the meanest capacity. Some indeed have denied that there is any such thing, because different ages and nations have entertained different sentiments concerning it: but this is just as reasonable as to assert, that there are neither Sun, Moon, nor Stars, because Astronomers have supported different systems of the motions and magnitudes of these celestial bodies. Some have placed it in conformity to truth, some to the fitness of things, and others to the will of God. But all this is merely superficial: they resolve us not why truth, or the fitness of things, are either eligible or obligatory, or why God should require us to act in one manner rather than another. The true reason of which can possibly be no other than this, because some actions produce happiness, and others misery: so that all Moral Good and Evil are nothing more than the production of Natural.

This alone it is that makes truth preferable to falsehood, this that determines the fitness of things, and this that induces God to command some actions, and forbid others. They who extol the truth, beauty, and harmony of Virtue, exclusive of its consequences, deal but in pompous nonsense; and they who would persuade us, that Good and Evil are things indifferent, depending wholly on the will of God, do but confound the nature of things, as well as all our notions of God himself, by representing him capable of willing contradictions; that is, that we should be, and be happy, and at the same time that we should torment and destroy each other; for injuries cannot be made benefits, pain cannot be made pleasure, and consequently vice cannot be made virtue by any power whatever. It is the consequences therefore of all human actions that must stamp their value. So far as the general practice of any action tends to produce Good, and introduce happiness into the world, so far we may pronounce it virtuous; so much Evil as it occasions, such is the degree of vice it contains. I say the general practice, because we must always remember in judging by this rule, to apply it only to the general species of actions, and not to particular actions; for the infinite wisdom of God, desirous to set bounds to the destructive consequences which must otherwise have followed from the universal depravity of mankind, has so wonderfully contrived the nature of things, that our most vitious actions may sometimes accidentally and collaterally produce Good. Thus, for instance, robbery may disperse useless hoards to the benefit of the publick; Adultery may bring heirs, and good humour too, into many families, where they would otherwise have been wanting; and Murder free the world from tyrants and oppressors. Luxury maintains its thousands, and Vanity its ten thousands. Superstition and Arbitrary Power contribute to the grandeur of many nations, and the liberties of others are preserved by the perpetual contentions of avarice, knavery, selfishness, and ambition: and thus the worst of vices, and the worst of Men, are often compelled by Providence to serve the most beneficial purposes, contrary to their own malevolent tendencies and inclinations; and thus private vices become publick benefits by the force only of accidental circumstances. But this impeaches not the truth of the Criterion of Virtue before mentioned, the only solid foundation on which any true system of ethicks can be built, the only plain, simple, and uniform rule by which we can pass any judgment on our actions; but by this we may be enabled, not only to determine which are good, and which are evil, but almost mathematically to demonstrate the proportion of Virtue or Vice which belongs to each, by comparing them with the degrees of happiness or misery which they occasion. But tho' the production of happiness is the Essence of virtue, it is by no means the End: the great End is the probation of Mankind, or the giving them an opportunity of exalting or degrading themselves in another state by their behaviour in the present. And thus indeed it answers two most important purposes; those are, the conservation of our happiness, and the test of our obedience: for had not such a test seemed necessary to God's infinite wisdom, and productive of universal Good, he would never have permitted the happiness of Men, even in this life, to have depended on so precarious a tenure, as their mutual good behaviour to each other. For it is observable, that he who best knows our formation, has trusted no one thing of importance to our reason or virtue: he trusts only to our appetites for the support of the Individual, and the continuance of our species; to our vanity, or compassion, for our bounty to others; and to our fears for the preservation of ourselves; often to our vices for the support of Government, and sometimes to our follies for the preservation of our Religion. But since some test of our obedience was necessary, nothing sure could have been commanded for that end so fit and proper, and at the same time so useful, as the practice of virtue; nothing have been so justly rewarded with happiness, as the production of happiness in conformity to the will of God. It is this conformity alone which adds merit to virtue, and constitutes the essential difference between Morality and Religion. Morality obliges Men to live honestly and soberly, because such behaviour is most conducive to publick happiness, and consequently to their own; Religion, to pursue the same course, because conformable to the will of their Creator. Morality induces them to embrace virtue from prudential considerations; Religion, from those of gratitude and obedience. Morality therefore, entirely abstracted from Religion, can have nothing meritorious in it; it being but wisdom, prudence, or good œconomy, which, like health, beauty, or riches, are rather obligations conferred upon us by God, than merits in us towards him; for tho' we may be justly punished for injuring ourselves, we can claim no reward for self-preservation; as suicide deserves punishments and infamy, but a Man deserves no reward or honours for not being guilty of it. This I take to be the meaning of all those passages in our Scriptures in which Works are represented to have no merit without Faith; that is, not without believing in historical facts, in creeds, and articles; but without being done in pursuance of our belief in God, and in obedience to his commands. And now, having mentioned Scripture, I cannot omit observing, that the Christian is the only religious or moral Institution in the world, that ever set in a right light these two material points, the Essence and the End of Virtue; that ever founded the one in the production of happiness, that is, in universal benevolence, or, in their language, Charity to all Men; the other, in the probation of Man, and his obedience to his Creator. Sublime and magnificent as was the philosophy of the Ancients, all their moral systems were deficient in these two important articles. They were all built on the sandy foundations of the innate beauty of virtue, or enthusiastick patriotism; and their great point in view was the contemptible reward of human glory; foundations which were by no means able to support the magnificent structures which they erected upon them; for the beauty of virtue, independent of its effects, is unmeaning nonsense; patriotism which injures mankind in general for the sake of a particular country, is but a more extended selfishness, and really criminal; and all human glory but a mean and ridiculous delusion. The whole affair then of Religion and Morality, the subject of so many thousand volumes, is in short no more than this: The Supreme Being, infinitely good, as well as powerful, desirous to diffuse happiness by all possible means, has created innumerable ranks and orders of Beings, all subservient to each other by proper subordination. One of these is occupied by Man, a creature endued with such a certain degree of knowledge, reason, and free-will, as is suitable to his situation, and placed for a time on this globe as in a school of probation and education. Here he has an opportunity given him of improving or debasing his nature, in such a manner as to render himself fit for a rank of higher perfection and happiness, or to degrade himself to a state of greater imperfection and misery; necessary indeed towards carrying on the business of the Universe, but very grievous and burthensome to those individuals, who, by their own misconduct, are obliged to submit to it. The test of this his behaviour, is doing good, that is, co-operating with his Creator, as far as his narrow sphere of action will permit, in the production of happiness. And thus the happiness and misery of a future state will be the just reward or punishment of promoting or preventing happiness in this. So artificially by this means is the nature of all human virtue and vice contrived, that their rewards and punishments are woven as it were into their very essence; their immediate effects give us a foretaste of their future, and their fruits in the present life are the proper samples of what they must unavoidably produce in another. We have Reason given us to distinguish these consequences, and regulate our conduct; and, lest that should neglect its post, Conscience also is appointed as an instinctive kind of monitor, perpetually to remind us both of our interest and our duty.

When we consider how wonderfully the practice of Virtue is thus inforced by our great Creator, and that all which he requires of us under that title is only to be happy, that is, to make each other so; and when at the same time we look round us, and see the whole race of mankind thro' every successive generation tormenting, injuring, and destroying each other, and perpetually counteracting the gracious designs of their Maker, it is a most astonishing paradox how all this comes to pass; why God should suffer himself to be thus defeated in his best purposes by creatures of his own making; or why Man should be made with dispositions to defeat them at the expence of his own present and future happiness; why infinite Goodness should form creatures inclined to oppose its own benevolent designs, or why infinite Power should thus suffer itself to be opposed.

The usual solution applied to this difficulty by the ablest Philosophers and Divines, with which they themselves, and most of their readers, seem perfectly satisfied, is comprehended in the following reasoning: That Man came perfect out of the hands of his Creator, both in virtue and happiness, but it being more eligible that he should be a Free-agent than a mere machine, God endued him with Freedom of will; from the abuse of which freedom, all Misery and Sin, that is, all natural and moral Evils, derive their existence: from all such therefore the Divine Goodness is sufficiently justified, by reason they could not be prevented without the loss of superior Good; for to create Men free, and at the same time compell them to be virtuous, is utterly impossible.

But whatever air of demonstration this argument may assume, by whatever fam'd Preachers it may have been used, or by whatever learn'd Audiences it may have been approved, I will venture to affirm, that it is False in all its Principles, and in its Conclusion also; and I think it may be clearly shewn, that God did not make Man absolutely Perfect, nor absolutely Free; nor, if he had, would this in the least have justified the introduction of Wickedness and Misery.

That Man came Perfect, that is indued with all possible Perfections, out of the hands of his Creator, is evidently a false notion derived from the Philosophers of the first ages, founded on their ignorance of the Origin of Evil, and inability to account for it on any other Hypothesis: they understood not that the universal System required Subordination, and consequently comparative Imperfections; nor that in the Scale of Beings there must be somewhere such a creature as Man with all his infirmities about him: that the total removal of these would be altering his very Nature; and, that as soon as he became Perfect, he must cease to be Man. The truth of this, I think, has been sufficiently proved; and besides the very supposition of a Being originally perfect, and yet capable of rendering itself wicked and miserable, is undoubtedly a Contradiction, that very power being the highest Imperfection imaginable.

That God made Man perfectly Free is no less false; Men have certainly such a degree of Free-will as to make them accountable, and justly punishable, for the abuse of it; but absolute and independent Free-will is what, I believe, no created Being can be possessed of. Our actions proceed from our Wills, but our wills must be deriv'd from the natural dispositions implanted in us by the Author of our Being: Wrong elections proceed from wrong apprehensions, or unruly passions; and these from our original Frame or accidental Education: these must determine all our actions, for we have no power to act differently, these previous circumstances continuing exactly the same. Had God thought proper to have made all Men with the same heads, and the same hearts, which he has given to the most virtuous of the species, they would all have excelled in the same virtues: or had the Byas implanted in Human Nature drawn as strongly towards the good side, as it now apparently does towards the bad, it would have operated as successfully, and with as little infringement on human Liberty: Men, as well as all other animals, are exactly fitted for the purposes they are designed for; and have inclinations and dispositions given them accordingly: He, who implanted patience in the lamb, obedience in the Horse, fidelity in the dog, and innocence in the dove, might as easily have inspired the breast of Man with these and all other virtues; and then his actions would have certainly corresponded with his Formation: therefore, in the strict philosophical Sense, we have certainly no Free-will; that is, none independent of our Frame, our Natures, and the Author of them.

But were both these propositions true, were Men originally created both perfect and free, yet this would by no means justify the introduction of moral Evil; because, if his Perfection was immediately to be destroyed by his Free-will, he might as well never have been possest of the one, and much better have been prevented from making use of the other: let us dispute therefore as long as we please, it must eternally be the same thing, whether a Creator of infinite power and knowledge created Beings originally wicked and miserable, or gave them a power to make themselves so, foreknowing they would employ that power to their own destruction.

If moral Evil therefore cannot be derived from the Abuse of Free-will in Man, from whence can we trace its origin? Can it proceed from a just, a wise, and a benevolent God? Can such a God form creatures with dispositions to do Evil, and then punish them for acting in conformity to those evil dispositions? Strange and astonishing indeed must this appear to us, who know so little of the universal Plan! but is far, I think, from being irreconcileable with the justice of the Supreme disposer of all things: for let us but once acknowledge the truth of our first great proposition, (and most certainly true it is) that natural Evils exist from some necessity in the Nature of things which no power can dispense with or prevent, the expediency of moral Evil will follow on course: for if misery could not be excluded from the works of a benevolent Creator by infinite power, these miseries must be endured by some creatures or other for the good of the whole: and if there were none capable of wickedness, then they must fall to the share of those who were perfectly innocent. Here again we see our difficulties arise from our wrong notions of Omnipotence, and forgetting how many difficulties it has to contend with: in the present instance it is obliged either to afflict Innocence or be the cause of Wickedness; it has plainly no other Option: what then could infinite Wisdom, Justice and Goodness do in this situation more consistent with itself, than to call into being Creatures formed with such depravity in their dispositions, as to induce many of them to act in such a manner as to render themselves proper subjects for such necessary sufferings, and yet at the same time indued with such a degree of Reason and Free-will to put in the power of every individual to escape them by their good behaviour: Such a Creature is Man; so corrupt, base, cruel and wicked as to convert these unavoidable miseries into just punishments, and at the same time to sensible of his own depravity and the fatal consequences of guilt, as to be well able to correct the one and to avoid the other. Here we see a substantial Reason for the

Depravity of Man, and the admittance of moral Evil in these circumstances seems not only compatible with the justice of God, but one of the highest instances of his consummate wisdom in ordering and disposing all things in the best manner their imperfect natures will admit.

There is undoubtedly something farther in the general Depravity of Mankind than we are aware of, and probably many great and wise ends are answered by it to us totally incomprehensible. God, as has been shewn, would never have permitted the existence of natural Evil, but from the impossibility of preventing it without the loss of superior Good: and on the same principle the admission of moral Evil is equally consistent with the divine Goodness: and who is he so knowing in the whole stupendous system of Nature, as to assert, that the Wickedness of some Beings may not, by means unconceivable to us, be beneficial to innumerable unknown Orders of others? or that the Punishments of some may not contribute to the Felicity of numbers infinitely superior?

But let us not forget that this Necessity of Vice and Punishment, and its subserviency to publick Good, makes no alteration in their natures with regard to Man; for, tho' the wisdom of God may extract from the wickedness of Men some remote benefits to the Universe; yet that alters not the case with regard to them, nor in the least extenuates their Guilt. He has given them reason sufficient to inform them, that their injuries to each other are displeasing to him, and Free-will sufficient to refrain from such actions, and may therefore punish their disobedience without any infringement of justice: He knows indeed, that though none are under any compulsion to do Evil, yet that they are all so framed, that many will certainly do it; and He knows also that incomprehensible secret why it is necessary that many should: but His knowledge having no relation to their determinations renders not their vices less criminal, nor the punishment of them less equitable: for, tho', with regard to God, Vice may be perhaps the consequence of Misery; that is, Men may be made inclined to Vice, in order to render them proper objects of such a degree of Misery as was unavoidably necessary, and previously determined for the sake of publick Good; yet, in regard to Man, Misery is the consequence of Vice; that is, all human Vices produce Misery, and are justly punished by its infliction.

If it be objected that this makes God the Author of Sin, I answer, God is, and must be the Author of every thing; and to say that any thing is, or happens, independent of the first Cause, is to say that something exists, or happens, without any Cause at all. God is the Author, if it may be so expressed, of all the natural Evils in the Universe; that is, of the fewest possible in the Nature of things; and why may he not be the Author of all moral Evil in the same manner and on the same principle? If natural Evil owes it existence to Necessity, why may not moral? If Misery brings with it its Utility, why may not Wickedness?

'If storms and earthquakes break not Heav'ns design,
Why then a Borgia or a Cataline!'

Wherefore it ought always to be considered, that, tho' Sin in Us, who see no farther than the Evils it produces, is Evil, and justly punishable; yet in God, who sees the causes and connections of all things, and the necessity of its admission, that admission is no Evil at all, and that necessity a sufficient vindication of his Goodness.

From this important proposition, that all Natural Evil derives its existence from necessity, and all Moral from expediency arising from that necessity; I say, from this important proposition, well considered and pursued, such new lights might be struck out as could not fail, if directed by the hands of Learning and Impartiality, to lead the human Mind thro' unknown regions of speculation, and to produce the most surprising and useful discoveries in Ethicks, Metaphysicks, and in Christianity too: I add Christianity, because it is a Master-key, which will, I am certain, at once unlock all the mysteries and perplexing doctrines of that amazing Institution, and explain fairly, without the least assistance from theological artifice, all those abstruse speculations of Original Sin, Grace and Predestination, and vicarious punishments, which the most learned have never yet been able to make consistent with Reason or Common-sense.

In the first place, for instance, the Doctrine of Original Sin is really nothing more than the very System here laid down, into which we have been led by closely pursuing Reason, and without which the Origin of Moral Evil cannot be accounted for on any principle whatever. Indeed, according to the common notions of the absolute Omnipotence of God, and the absolute Free-will in Man, it is most absurd and impious, as it represents the Deity, voluntarily bringing Men into Being with depraved Dispositions, tending to no good purposes, and then arbitrarily punishing them for the sins which they occasion with torments which answer no ends, either of their reformation or utility to the Universe: but when we see, by the foregoing explanation, the difficulties with which Omnipotence was environed, and that it was obliged by the necessity of Natural Evils to admit Moral, all these absurdities at once vanish, and the Original Depravity of Man appears fairly consistent with the Justice and even Goodness of his Creator.

The Doctrines of Predestination and Grace as set forth in the Scriptures, on the most impartial interpretation, I take to be these: that some Men came into the world with dispositions so invincibly bad, that God foreknows that they will certainly be guilty of many crimes, and in consequence be punished for them; that to others He has given better dispositions, and moreover protects them from Vice by a powerful but invisible influence, in the language of those writings called Grace: this Scheme has appeared to many so partial and unjust that they have totally rejected it, and endeavoured, by forced interpretations, to explain it quite out of the Bible, in contradiction to all the sense of language and the whole tenour of those writings: and indeed, on the old plan of God's absolute Omnipotence, uncontrouled by any previous necessity, in the nature of things, to admit both Natural and Moral Evil, it is highly derogatory from His wisdom and goodness; but, on the supposition of that previous Necessity, there appears nothing incredible in it, nor the least inconsistent with divine Justice; because, if God was obliged by the nature of things, and for the good of the whole, to suffer some to be wicked, and consequently miserable, he certainly might protect others both from guilt and punishment. He in this light may be compared to the commander of a numerous army, who, tho' he is obliged to expose many to danger, and some to destruction, yet protects others with ramparts and covert-ways; but so long as he exercises this power for the good of the whole, these distinctions amongst individuals ought never to be imputed to Partiality or Injustice.

The Doctrine of Sacrifice, or Vicarious Punishment, is the most universal, and yet the most absurd, of all religious Tenets that ever entered into the Mind of Man: so absurd is it, that how it came to be so universal is not easy to be accounted for: Pagans, Jews and Christians, have all agreed in this one point, tho' differing in all others; and have all treated it as a self-evident principle, that the Sins of one Creature might be attoned for by the Sufferings of another: but from whence they derived this strange opinion none of them have pretended to give any account, or to produce in its defence the least Shadow of a Reason: for that there should be any manner of connection between the Miseries of one Being and the Guilt of another; or, that the punishing the Innocent, and excusing the Guilty, should be a mark of God's Detestation of Sin; or, that two acts of the highest Injustice should make one of Justice, is so fundamentally wrong, so diametrically opposite to common-sense, and all our ideas of justice, that it is equally astonishing that so many should believe it themselves or impose it upon others. But on the foregoing plan this also may be a little cleared up, and will by no means appear so very inconsistent with Reason: for if a certain quantity of Misery in some part of the Universal System is necessary to the Happiness and Well-being of the Whole; and if this necessity arises from its answering some purposes incomprehensible to the human Understanding; I will ask any impartial Reasoner, Why the Sufferings of one Being may not answer the same Ends, or be as effectual towards promoting Universal Good as the Sufferings of another? If the Miseries of Individuals are to be looked upon as taxes which they are obliged to pay towards the support of the Publick, why may not the Sufferings of one Creature serve the same purposes. or absolve as much of that necessary tax as the Sufferings of another, and on that account be accepted as a payment or satisfaction for their Sufferings; that is, for the Sufferings due to the Publick Utility from the punishment of their crimes, without which the Happiness of the whole could not subsist, unless they should be replaced by the Suffferings of others? As we are intirely ignorant why Misery has any existence at all, or what interest it serves in the general System of things, this may possibly be the case for any thing we know; and that it is not, I am certain no one can affirm with Reason: Reason indeed cannot inform us that it is so, but that it may be, is undoubtedly no contradiction to Reason.

From what has been here said, I think, it is evident that the Origin of Evil is by no means so difficult to account for as at first sight it appears; for it has been plainly shewn that most of those we usually complain of are Evils of Imperfection, which are rather the absence of comparative Advantages than positive Evils, and therefore, properly speaking, no Evils at all; and as such ought to be intirely struck out of the Catalogue. It has likewise been made appear, that of natural Evils, which are the Sufferings of sensitive Beings, many are but the consequences naturally resulting from the particular circumstances of particular ranks in the scale of Existence, which could not have been omitted without the destruction of the Whole; and that many more are in all probability necessary, by means to us incomprenhensible, to the production of Universal Good. Lastly, it has been suggested, that from this necessity of Natural Evils may arise the expediency of Moral, without which those necessary Sufferings must have been with less justice inflicted on perfect innocence; and moreover that it is probable that Moral Evil, as well as Natural, may have some ultimate tendency to the Good of the Whole; and that the crimes and punishments of some Beings may, by some way or other, totally beyond the reach of our narrow capacities, contribute to the Felicity of much greater Numbers.

This plan, Sir, I am persuaded is not far distant from the truth; and on this Foundation, if I mistake not, a System of Morality and Religion, more compleat and solid, more consistent with Reason, and with Christianity too, might be erected than any which has yet appeared: I heartily wish that some person of more learning, abilities and leisure than myself, (and much more, I am sure, of all it would require) encouraged by your Favour, and assisted by your Sagacity, would undertake it, and condescend to fill up these out-lines so inaccurately sketched out by,
SIR, &c.

EDMUND LAW

'The Nature and Obligations of Man,
as a sensible and rational Being'

and

'On Morality and Religion' (1758)

Edmund Law (1703–1787)

Biographical Note

The Laws were yeomen from Askham, Westmorland. Law's paternal grand-parents were Edmund Law of Carhullan and Measand (will dated 1689) and Elizabeth Wright of Measand. Their son Edmund – Law's father – was the curate of Staveley-in-Cartmel, Lancashire, and schoolmaster there 1693–1742. He married Patience Langvaine, of Kirkby-Kendal, on 29 November 1701, and two years later, on 6 June 1703, she gave birth to the subject of this biography, another Edmund Law. Law received his early education at Cartmel School, and later attended Kendal Free Grammar School. On 6 April 1720 he became a sizar at St John's College, Cambridge. After taking his BA in 1723–24, he received his MA from Christ's College in 1727. In his 1749 public 'exercise' for his DD, Law defended the doctrine of psychopannychism, or the sleep of the soul between death and the Resurrection. This Reformation heresy was seen as Socinian by many, which led to doubts about Law's degree. Law received support from Francis Blackburne in the ensuing controversy. In return, after Blackburne advocated further reformation of the English Church in 1750, Law wrote to congratulate him 'on the good work of reformation on which he was so happily engaged'.[1] In 1726–27 Law was a Fellow of Christ's and remained at Cambridge until 1737. His Cambridge friends included Daniel Water-land, John Jortin, and John Taylor. Waterland, a notable champion of orthodoxy, was considered by Stephen 'a utilitarian so far as regards the criterion of morality, and he lays it down as a principle that we are to test the relative importance of divine commands . . . by asking what depends upon our conscientious obedience to them; or, in other words, which is most conducive to the general good'.[2] Jortin, a historian and biographer of Erasmus, and Taylor, an eminent Classical scholar, are thought to have had Unitarian tendencies, and Law may have been influenced by this.

Law's clerical career began on 5 June 1726, when he was ordained deacon. On 24 September 1727 he was ordained priest. From 1737 to 1746 he was rector of Greystoke, Cumberland, a living in the gift of

---

[1] Charles J. Abbey, *The English Church and its Bishops 1700–1800*, 2 vols. (London 1887), ii. 246; see also William Paley, 'A Short Memoir of Edmund Law, D. D., Lord Bishop of Carlisle', in George William Meadley, *Memoirs of William Paley*, 2nd edn. (Edinburgh 1810), pp. 356–57.

[2] Leslie Stephen, *History of English Thought in the Eighteenth Century*, 2 vols. (1876; 3rd edn. reprt. New York 1949), ii. 107.

Cambridge University. About 1737 Law married Mary Christian of Unerigg, Cumberland. Mary died either in 1772 or more likely 1762.[3] They had eight sons and four daughters. Law was Archdeacon of Carlisle from 1743 to 1756, and rector of Great Salkeld from 1746 to 1787. Elected Master of Peterhouse College, Cambridge, in 1754, he continued to serve in this capacity until 1787.[4] For a year in 1755–56 Law was also Vice-Chancellor of Cambridge University. A note in Meadley's edition of the *Memoir* says that this was 'In consequence of his mastership of Peterhouse'. From 1760–69 Law was University Librarian, or *proto-bibliothecarius*. In 1764 he became Knightsbridge Professor of Moral Theology or Casuistical Divinity, with the duty of giving four Latin lectures a term and a stipend of £60–70 annually.[5] Between 1763 and 1766 Law was Archdeacon of Stafford. He was also at various times a member of the cathedral chapters of Litchfield, Lincoln and Durham. Most of these offices were presentations from influential former pupils. Finally, from 1769 until his death, Law was Bishop of Carlisle.

According to William Paley, a close friend of Law's son John (later Bishop of Elphin), Law always spent the summer months in the residence of the Bishop of Carlisle, Rose Castle, although his main home was the Lodge at Peterhouse. Paley described him as 'a man of great softness of manners, and of the mildest and most tranquil disposition'. Law enjoyed books and literary conversation. His main fault, says Paley, was 'too great a degree of inaction and facility in his public station'.[6] Law died at Carlisle 14 August 1787, and was buried in Carlisle Cathedral.

Law's translation of William King's *Essay on the Origin of Evil* (1731), to which he added John Gay's 'Preliminary Dissertation', gained an influential readership at Cambridge. Spadafora suggests that Law may have assisted Gay in writing the 'Preliminary Dissertation', and notes that he had been interested in the theory of association while at Cambridge with Gay. Law had studied Hartley's work, and referred to the principle of association as ' "a universal *Law of our Nature*" that had no less "extent and influence in the intellectual World, than that of Gravity . . . in the Natural" '.[7] Law's commitment to Lockean sensationalism is evident in the two essays he added to the 1758 edition of King's *Essay on the Origin of Evil*: 'On Morality and Religion' and 'The Nature and Obligation of Man, as a sensible and rational Being'. In *Considerations on the State of the World with Regard to the Theory of Religion* (1745) Law argued the case for

---

3 Paley, 'A Short Memoir of Edmund Law', pp. 359–60.
4 Paley, 'A Short Memoir of Edmund Law', p. 359; and M. L. Clarke, *Paley: Evidences for the Man* (London and Toronto 1974), p. 311.
5 D. A. Winstanley, *Unreformed Cambridge: A Study of Certain Aspects of the University in the Eighteenth Century* (Cambridge 1935), p. 137.
6 Paley, 'A Short Memoir of Edmund Law', pp. 364, 365.
7 David Spadafora, *The Idea of Progress in Eighteenth-Century Britain* (New Haven and London 1990), p. 344.

believing in the continuous progress of human society.[8] He was convinced that his countrymen enjoyed 'the blessing of *liberty* in that perfection which had been unknown to former ages', and which 'includes every thing valuable in life'.[9]

Law's religious convictions have occasioned some discussion. His views on the state of the soul after death produced a series of refutations by contemporary theologians, but in other respects his views were in accord with sentiments expressed by moderate reformers within the Church. Nichols quotes a letter from the Rev. Thomas Pyle to Archbishop Thomas Herring of Canterbury in 1749, in which Pyle says:

> I read everything, and make use of the glorious prerogative of private judgment, the birthright of Protestants. I pass free sentiment upon Middleton. . . . So I shall upon what he is going to say on the only piece of that great man Law, that ever gave me pleasure. I read 'Disquisitions;' and, when I've done, fall to my prayers and wishes, that the good thing desired may be put into the hands of the able, knowing, and impartial, that no Church-*tinkers* may be suffered to mend some few holes and leave others open, at which some vital part of the noble Christian scheme may run out and be lost.[10]

Stephen called Law a leader of the Cambridge school of which Paley was a product.[11] J. C. D. Clark has taken a more critical look at Law's position, believing that 'The cause of heterodox theology and the abolition of subscription within the Church was associated, above all, with Newcastle's henchman in Cambridge university politics, Edmund Law'. According to Clark, Peterhouse produced men whose radicalism was based on Socinian doctrines propagated by Law: 'Law was the patriarch of a heterodox interest, and numbered among his associates and admirers Paley . . . Richard Watson and Gilbert Wakefield. . . . Edmund Law represented the survival of Samuel Clarke's doctrines among the grandly beneficed of the Anglican intelligentsia'.[12] While it seems unlikely that Law was in any real sense a Unitarian, he and his friends were certainly active in the anti-subscription movement, encouraging Blackburne to write *The Confessional* (1766).[13]

According to the *Gentlemen's Magazine* (June 1772) between 1766 and

[8] Abbey, *The English Church and its Bishops 1700–1800*, ii. 250; Stephen, *History of English Thought in the Eighteenth Century*, i. 406.
[9] Quoted in Spadafora, *The Idea of Progress in Eighteenth-Century Britain*, p. 228.
[10] John Nichols, *Literary Anecdotes of the Eighteenth Century*, 9 vols. (London, 1814; reprt. New York 1966), ix. 439.
[11] Stephen, *History of English Thought in the Eighteenth Century*, i. 406.
[12] J. C. D. Clark, *English Society 1688–1830* (Cambridge 1985), p. 313, and pp. 311–12.
[13] Martin L. Clarke, *Paley: Evidences for the Man* (London and Toronto 1974), p. 18.

1772 the 'Subscription Controversy' was debated in over forty pamphlets.[14] The controversy heightened in 1771 when Blackburne drew up proposals for a petition for relief of Dissenters to be presented to Parliament. In essence, it was a plea for a relaxation of the terms of subscription to the Thirty-nine Articles. This became known as the 'Feathers Tavern Petition'. Of the 250 subscribers to the petition who met under Blackburne's leadership at the Feathers Tavern in London only a few were laymen; the overwhelming majority were beneficed clergymen and Fellows of the University of Cambridge.[15] The latter group included Law, Richard Watson, the Regius Professor of Divinity, Paley, then a tutor at Christ's College, James Lambert, the Regius Professor of Greek, and Dr Plumptre, the President of Queens' College. All the fellows of Queens' supported their President,[16] but in February of the following year the House of Commons rejected the petition by a vote of 271 to 71.[17] The failure of the petition did not signal the end of the affair, and for another two years a gentlemanly but vigorous debate ensued at the universities. Law was encouraged to set down his own views in support of reform in the anonymously published *Considerations on the Propriety of Requiring a Subscription to Articles of Faith* (1774). He received a swift response from Thomas Randolph, President of Corpus Christi, Oxford, in *The Reasonableness of Subscription to Articles of Religion* (1774). Law's involvement in the debate also gave rise to this invective:

> But chief, O Law, to thee be honours paid.
> Well sits the mitre on thy hoary head:
> Wonder of bishops! still pursue thy plan,
> Man to a brute, and God degrade to man.
> How can I count the labours of thy life?
> With creeds and articles at constant strife;
> With Blackburne leagued, in many a motley page,
> Immortal war with Mother Church to wage; . . .[18]

Paley, who had inexplicably refused to sign the Feather's Tavern petition, entered the debate to answer Law's detractors in *A Defence of the 'Con-*

---

[14] For a discussion of the controversy see Winstanley, *Unreformed Cambridge*, pp. 301–16; Caroline Robbins, *The Eighteenth Century Commonwealthmen* (Cambridge, Mass. 1961), 324–35; Clarke, *Paley: Evidences for the Man*, pp. 17–23; and D. L. LeMahieu, *The Mind of William Paley: A Philosopher and His Age* (Lincoln 1976), pp. 16–19.

[15] Abbey, *The English Church and its Bishops*, ii. 124.

[16] Winstanley, *Unreformed Cambridge*, pp. 303–5.

[17] Even so there shortly followed at Cambridge (23 June 1772) the substitution of a declaration of *bona fide* Church membership for subscription to the three articles of the 36th Canon; A. V. Dicey, *Lectures on the Relation between Law and Public Opinion in England during the Nineteenth Century* (1905; 2nd edn. London 1962), p. 479.

[18] Abbey, *The English Church and its Bishops*, ii. 247–48.

siderations on the Propriety of Requiring a Subscription to Articles of Faith' (1774).[19]

Paley had for long been attached to Law, theologically and politically. In 1776 Paley contributed 'Observations on the Character and Example of Christ' and an 'Appendix on the Morality of the Gospel' to a new edition of Law's *Reflections of the Life and Character of Christ* (originally published with *Considerations on the State of the World* in 1745), and in 1785 he dedicated his *Principles of Moral and Political Philosophy* to Law, praising him as an industrious defender of Christianity.

In addition to the writings already mentioned, Law's other major publications were *An Enquiry into the Ideas of Space, Time, Immensity and Eternity* (1734), and an edition of *The Works of John Locke* with a preface and life of the author (1777).

Note on the Text
The essays 'On Morality and Religion' and 'The Nature and Obligations of Man, as a sensible and rational Being', were included by Law in the fourth edition of his translation of William King's *An Essay on the Origin of Evil* (1758), which he had first published with John Gay's 'Preliminary Dissertation' in 1731 (King's original Latin text appeared in 1702). Immediately following Gay's 'Preliminary Dissertation' there is a note introducing Law's essays:

> As the following Papers, which were originally printed in the *Weekly Miscellany No. 7, 8, 9*, are upon the same Subject with the foregoing Dissertation, and may possibly serve to illustrate it, the Author has thought proper to insert them in this fourth Edition, together with some hints that he has met with in relation to the *Origin of our Ideas*, which may help to Explain Mr. *Locke's* Principles, and determine the Controversy about an *innate Moral Sense*, and which are therefore here proposed for a more full Consideration.

Law's two essays are here presented in the reverse order from which they were originally published. Thus the argument of the second essay, that moral philosophy is properly founded on natural philosophy, comes before the essay in which Law states the component elements of his moral theory. The texts of the two essays are taken from Law's fourth edition of King's *Origin of Evil* printed for W. Thurlbourn & J. Woodyer in Cambridge, and J. Beecroft in Pater-noster-Row, London.

---

[19] See Paley below, p. 209.

THE
Nature and Obligations of MAN,
As a sensible and rational BEING

1. ALL our primary, simple Ideas proceed from Sensation, external or internal; the latter of which may be extended through most parts of the Vessels of the Human Body, and is extremely complicated; and will be found perhaps upon examination to produce much greater and more various Effects than we are commonly aware of. From the one or the other of these we receive continual impressions while we are awake; and from the united force of several such impressions, may arise a new species of Sensation, or an Idea different from any that appear'd in any of the individuals. Thus various liquors, meats, and medicines producing a general agitation or composure in what is call'd the nervous System, raise as general a kind of rapturous gaity, or tranquil delight: and *v. v.* which bears so near a resemblance to some intellectual operation, that it is often mistaken for such; and in reality is as distinct from the mere *Taste* of all such liquors &c. as any objects of the Sense and Intellect are from each other.

2. By our faculties of repeating and enlarging, of comparing, and compounding, or abstracting these and their several Objects we raise a secondary set of Ideas, still more mixt and diversify'd, but yet of the same general nature; which often go under the name of *intellectual*, from the intellect's being so evidently employ'd about them; but all grow out of the old Stock, all flow from the same Source, *i. e.* are originally form'd from Sense and wholly grounded in it: as may in part appear from the *words* we use in describing them, *v. g.* to *apprehend, comprehend, conceive*, &c. which are (as Mr. *Locke* observes) words manifestly *taken from the operation of sensible things, and apply'd to certain modes of thinking.* B. 3. C. 1. §. 5.

3. The contemplation of these very Faculties, by which we mold and modify the original materials of our knowledge, produces a third set of Ideas, still more remote from the first origin; and therefore term'd Ideas of *pure* Intellect, as more immediately arising from and terminating in the reflex view of these same intellectual and active powers, and of their several operations: *v. g.* perceiving that we do perceive, &c. considering what it is to compare, compound &c. and what these and the like powers extend to and infer. Whence we form all the notion we have of a *Spirit*.

4. Man is a compound of corporeal Organs, (most of them conveying

sensitive impressions, as observ'd above) and the distinct powers of *perception* (in the latter sense of that word) or *Thinking* in general, and voluntary *Action* in close union with these.

5. We may observe likewise that these latter, which are generally stiled active powers, are not always in exercise, any more than some of the passive, sensitive ones are; their Exercise being manifestly suspended during some bodily disorders, and altogether ceasing in the intervals of what is called *sound* Sleep. Whence it appears that Thought and voluntary Action cannot in strictness be essential, or immutably necessary to any one part of our Constitution; but rather is connected with and dependent on a certain disposition of the whole frame, or a regular State of the chief branches of it.

6. Some of these sensible Ideas are in certain respects agreeable to us, others the contrary; the former being, in all probability, such as tend to the preservation of each individual, the latter to its destruction.

7. A foresight of them likewise, or of their several *Causes*, has the same effect in some degree; nay sometimes may be so form'd as to produce it in a higher degree than the objects themselves would, were they present. Thus may the Imagination crowd the pleasures or pains of a day, a year, an age into one moment, and thereby make the impressions of these two last Classes far more general and extensive, as well as more intense and exquisite, than any of the particular sensitive ones of which they are composed.

8. And as a prospect of these and their causes is productive of the same kind of pleasure or pain that attends the presence of each, so the *pursuit* of the former and avoidance of the latter becomes also agreeable, and all that as sensible and rational Beings we can be concerned about; since the sum total, or the aggregate of these same pleasures or pains, is our supreme, ultimate *Happiness* or *Misery*; the attainment of the one, and security from the other, our most *perfect* State: the necessary means of attaining to which End compose our *natural Good*, and in the regular intended pursuit of it consists our *moral Goodness*.

9. Now as most of these means of Happiness lie in the power of others, who being of the same nature with ourselves, can only be induced to contribute to it, or to co-operate with us in procuring it, by a settled disposition in us of doing the like to them on all occasions; hence the contracting of such disposition, and a regard to their good in the general course of our actions becomes necessary to our own; in the design'd prosecution of which lies the *formal*, and in the actual production of it the *material* part of Virtue; both which in common acceptation constitute the whole of our *merit* with respect to each other.

10. Not that the promoting of another's Happiness is ever of itself immediately, or by any kind of natural or innate Principle, productive of our own: as well might one feel by another's Senses, or be made happy by

his Feelings without any real participation of them; as well might we suppose a man to act entirely on another's motives, as judge any thing good, right and fit for him to do, or to communicate to another, merely because that thing is good and fit for the other to receive, or pleasant to enjoy, except that same enjoyment is in some measure relative to his own proper Rule or End, or can be made right and reasonable for him to pursue by some such medium as connects it with his natural Principle, that constant and invariable ground of Action, *i. e.* his own Happiness.

11. Nor is it difficult to find or form such a Connection from what was hinted above; *Reason* discovers it, as well from the natural Consequence of things; benevolent affections in each person being apt to generate correspondent ones in others, and each beneficent act to engage a return of like good offices; as from the positive appointment of the Deity, who designs the common Happiness or perfection of all rational Beings, according to the nature he has given them, and the Circumstances under which he has placed them; having made them with no other view that we can conceive, than in order to have this communicated to them in the most effectual manner; and who must consequently approve of every instance of their co-operation with him in the same design, and assuredly reward each regular course of Action in his Creatures that tends to promote it.

12. His *will* in this respect is therefore the general *Rule* or true *Criterion* of Morality, as what infallibly must, and what alone can, effectually secure to us our ultimate End, Happiness upon the whole; Happiness in some certain *State*, above and beside the natural consequence of all our virtuous Acts and Habits; and who will in that State make us most ample amends for whatever pains we take here, or whatever loss and inconvenience we can possibly undergo in prosecuting of them; and thereby makes such prosecution an invariable Duty to us, or constitutes a perfect and perpetual *obligation* thereto.

13. The same thing may be either traced out thus by Reason and demonstrated, or come at in a more compendious way, which yet will have equally strong and permanent Effects upon our Constitution, nay commonly more sudden and more striking ones; on which account it is often mistaken for self-evidence or intuition: – I mean the power of ASSOCIATION, which was just hinted at by Mr. *Locke*, but apply'd to the present purpose more directly by the Author of the foregoing *Dissertation*, and from him taken up and consider'd in a much more general way by Dr. *Hartley*, who has from thence solv'd many of the Principal appearances in Human Nature, the sensitive part of which, since Mr. *Locke*'s Essay, had been very little cultivated, and is perhaps yet to the generality a *terra incognita*; how interesting soever, as well as entertaining, such Enquiries must be found to be: on which account it is much to be lamented that no more thoughtful persons are induced to turn their minds this way; since so very noble a foundation for improvements has been laid by both these excellent Writers,

especially the last: whose work is, I beg leave to say, in the main, notwithstanding all its abstruseness, well worth studying; and would have been sufficiently clear and convincing had he but confined his observations to the plain *Facts* and Experiments on which it was first founded, without ever entering minutely into the *Physical Cause* of such Phenomena; as the great *Newton* wisely did in the point of *Gravitation*, throwing his whole Theory of that same *Æther* and its Vibrations, into some modest *Queries*: notwithstanding his very probable supposition that both Gravitation in the greater Orbs, and all sensation and muscular Motion in all animal Bodies, might depend upon it.

14. Nor will perhaps this Principle of *Association* appear of less extent and influence in the intellectual World, than that of Gravity is found to be in the Natural. It is already discovered to be an universal *Law of our Nature*, intimately connected with the mutual operations of the Mind and Body, notwithstanding the odd whimsical appearance it first made in Mr. *Locke*'s Essay, (though he applied it to better purposes in his *Conduct of the Understanding*, §. 40.) and its being so often slighted as a *vague, confused* Principle by later Writers; particularly Dr. *Hucheson. System of Moral Philosophy*, p.55, *& c*. And though we may possibly never comprehend the Cause that actuates it, or the instrument by which it is exerted (any more than we can hope to see the Bond of Union between Mind and Body; though this, by the bye, may seem a fair step towards it) yet 'tis enough for our present purpose if the Principle itself has been so far explained by the worthy Author abovementioned, as thence to demonstrate that the Moral sense may be wholly generated from sensitive Pleasures, and supported by them: which I apprehend to be done effectually. See his *Observations on Man*, V. 2. p. 471, *&c*.

15. If the forementioned account of our acquiring this Moral Sense be admitted, it is shewn in reality to be no more than a *Habit*, which is never of itself a sure and sufficient Rule, but wants some other regulation; and like all other habits should be grounded on some solid Principles of Reason, and ever subject to them.

16. But whether this account be admitted or not, Mr. *Locke* has plainly proved that it must be acquired some how or other, since there are no kind of *practical principles innate*, or so much as *self-evident*; nor can our knowledge of any moral Propositions be *intuitive; since it requires discourse and reasoning to discover the certainty of their truth*, B. 1. C. 3. § 1. *which plainly depends upon some other truth antecedent to them, and from which they must be deduced*, ibid. *and Men may very justly demand a Reason for every one of them*, ib. § 4. which reason lies in another province, and must be fetched from the *natural relations* of the things and persons that surround us, *i. e.* from sensitive pleasure and pain, on which hinge all our Passions turn, and from whence must be derived the great Rule of our Actions, *ib.* § 3.6, *&c*. and B. 2. C. 20.

17. The same judicious writer (Mr. *Locke*) has accounted for that *variety of Moral Rules* visible amongst Men, *from the different sorts of Happiness they have a prospect of*, § 6. as also from their *Education, Company and Customs of their Country*, § 8. any of which serves to set *Conscience* on work, and thereby tends to diversify their moral rule; which if it were innate, or (what comes to the same thing) any natural Sense or Instinct, must one would think be uniform and invariable: but whether any such be found among our Species is after all *a matter of Fact* determinable only by those who are well conversant in the early education of Children, and duly qualified to make just observations on their original frame and native dispositions. If this had been more carefully attended to, with what the same able Writer has delivered concerning the true History of the Human Mind, I fancy a right Theory of Morals might long ago have been laid down with more success; and in particular we should have been satisfied that any such Principle as will perpetually influence and effectually induce us to promote the Happiness of others absolutely and entirely independent of our own, can never be wrought out of our original Feelings; or spring from that primary and purely native stock of our Ideas, on which are grounded all the Tribe of natural Appetites, and the whole Furniture of the Human Mind. It must therefore either be superinduced by Reason, in view of attaining our great End, as observed above; or come in under the Head of *Association*, and by way of Habit, without any ultimate End or distinct view at all. Those of the other side of the Question may chuse which of these two they like best.

18. From the whole it will appear, that there is properly but *one original source* of our Ideas, i. e. *Sensation*; nor any original pleasures or pains beside sensitive ones, however variously combined, abstracted or enlarged: and therefore any innate intellectual determination, or Moral Principle wholly underived from and naturally independent of these, seems an *impossibility*. The Intellect perceives only what is in things, and if there be nothing in the Mind originally beside these same sensitive Pleasures or Pains, then can it constitute no other Class fundamentally different from these, and much less opposite to them, whatever alterations or improvements may be made amongst them: and the *Medicina Mentis* will, like that of the *Body*, be all composed of the same sort of Ingredients, however mixed and altered in the Composition.

If Mr. *Locke*'s plan were once rightly understood we should have little room for any dispute about the different natures of these two, or the distinct Principles that actuate and govern them. We should soon find that all sound Philosophy in *Morals* is entirely built on *Natural* Philosophy, and never to be separated from it. But we seem not yet to have followed this great Author up to his first Principles, or duly traced the consequences of his System, notwithstanding his having been so long and justly admired amongst us; and most of the inveterate prejudices that used to attend his confutation of the old idle Doctrine of innate Ideas and Instincts be now well nigh worn out. Though perhaps even yet there may be left enow to prevent an impartial examination of his Scheme; the aim and tendency whereof is no other than to reduce the foundations of our Knowledge, and our Happiness, to that original *Simplicity* which Nature seems to observe in all her Works.

On
Morality and Religion

THE very Notion of a reasonable Creature implies, that he propose to himself some *End*, and act in pursuit of it. The only Enquiry then can be, What End does Reason direct him to pursue, and by what *Means* shall he attain it? Now a *Sensible* Being, or one that is made capable of Happiness or Misery, can reasonably propose to himself no other End than the Perfection of this Being, *i.e.* The Attainment of the one, and Avoidance of the other. He can have no Reason or Motive to pursue that which does not at all relate to him; and it is evident that nothing does relate to him, but that which has relation to his Happiness. If he be also endowed with *Liberty* of Will, it is impossible that any thing else should move or affect him; nor can any other Influence or Obligation be laid upon him without an express Contradiction. If therefore right Reason can only shew him to be what he is, and direct him to act accordingly, it is plain it can propose to him no other End but *his own Happiness*, beyond or beside which he can have no real Concern to know, to act, or to be.

Having seen the true End of Man consider'd as a sensible rational, and free Being; we will in the next Place enquire after the Means of attaining this End. Now as Man is also *dependent* on other Beings for that Happiness of which he is made capable, the only Means of attaining it must be to recommend himself to the Favour of those several Beings on whom he does depend, and in Degrees proportioned to that Dependence. But as himself and all other Beings depend absolutely upon the Deity, who alone has their Happiness or Misery always in his Power, it is plain the Favour of God will be the only adequate and effectual Means to attain his End, *i. e.* Happiness upon the Whole: And therefore, whatever tends to procure the Divine Favour, will be of perpetual Obligation, and ought to be the principal Aim of all his Actions. As all Obligation is founded on the Desire of Happiness, and all our Happiness entirely depends on God, it is evident that his Will must be always Obligatory, and what alone is able to make any thing else so. And though he has framed and disposed the World in such a Manner that certain Actions will generally recommend us to the Favour of those other Beings to whom we stand related, and so may be said to become Duties to us, and if Universally followed, would bring universal Happiness; yet since all my Reason for pursuing them can only be their Fitness to bring Happiness to me, which in the present State of

Things they are not always fit and likely to do, the Will of God must necessarily intervene, to inforce these Duties upon me, and make them universally binding.

As far indeed as certain Dispositions and Affections will recommend us to the Favour and Esteem of all those Persons with whom we are or may be concerned, and thereby bring more Happiness than Misery to us, so far we have a good Reason to indulge and exercise them; but when (upon what Account soever) they have not this Effect, but the Contrary, or at least have it not in so high a Degree as some other Dispositions and Affections would have (as is very often the Case; What Principle in Nature will oblige us to the Exercise of them in such Circumstances? Nay, what Reason can we find to justify us in it, but only our Dependence on the Deity, who requires it; and who, we are assured, will either defend and support us here in the Exercise of them, or make us ample Amends hereafter for what we lose by them.

It is not then any *Relations* of Things which in themselves, and abstract-edly consider'd, oblige us to the Practice of that which we call moral Virtue; but the Will of God which enjoins it, and which alone affords an *eternal and immutable Reason* for the Practice of it. We are able to conceive no kind of Reason or Obligation to act, but what is founded on Happiness, nor any fix'd and permanent Happiness, but what is founded on the Will of God: 'Tis therefore his Will properly and ultimately which we follow in the Practice of Virtue, and Virtue only, as it is agreeable to, and an Indi-cation of his Will; wherein its Worth consists, and from whence it derives its Power of obliging.

And therefore to set aside the Deity in the Consideration of Virtue, must be to relax it from its true Principle, to take it off its only Foundation: and to endeavour to exalt Morality into an Independency on his Will, is to undermine and destroy it. Any other Principle but this, will either come short of the Mark, or carry us from it.

Thus they who teach that Virtue is to be practis'd for its *native Loveliness* and *intrinsic Worth*, must either affirm that it is lovely and valuable they know not for what, or why; *i. e.* have no distinct Ideas to these fine Words; or must mistake the Means for the End. Virtue, we find, is lovely for its good Effects, and truly valuable on account of the Consequences that will certainly attend it, either by the Laws of Nature, or positive Appointment; therefore they will call it *lovely in itself*, or *absolutely* so; and tell us it is to be pursued purely *for its own sake*, and exclusively of all the aforesaid Consequences; *i. e.* exclusively of every thing that is good and valuable in it.

They who follow Virtue for the immediate *Pleasure* which attends the Exercise of it, must either take it for granted that we have some innate Instinct or Affection, which at all times infallibly directs, and forcibly inclines us to what is Right, (all which is as false as Fact can make it) or else they practice Virtue for a Reason which is common to any other

Practice, and will equally lead them to any; a Motive which accompanies every strong Persuasion or settled Habit of Mind, whatever may be its future unforeseen Consequences. To do what either our Judgment approves, or we have chose and set our Hearts upon, will give us this immediate Pleasure in any Course of Life; especially in one, which we can pursue without external Disturbance, or which happens to have the Vogue of the Place, or Esteem of our Acquaintance, to encourage and confirm us in our Pursuit.

They who describe Virtue to be *following Nature*, go upon a Principle near akin to the foregoing, and full as bad: For if our Nature, as far as it concerns Morals, be in a great measure of our own making, as we have Reason to suppose; if it may be greatly corrupted and perverted, as all allow; this will be a very erroneous, at least an absolutely uncertain Guide. It will amount to no more than this, Do always what you like best; or, Follow your present Humour.

They who practice Virtue for present *Convenience*, *Interest*, or *Reputation*, stand upon more solid Ground; which nevertheless will often fail them, as we have seen above. The like has been observ'd concerning *Reason*, and the *Relation of Things*.

IN our last, we endeavoured to establish the following Conclusions. Private Happiness, upon the Whole, is the ultimate End of Man: This absolutely depends on, and can effectually be secured only by the Will of God; the Will of God therefore is our only adequate Rule of Action, and what alone includes perpetual Obligation.

We shall here endeavour more distinctly to point out the Reason and Necessity for such a Rule, and shew what kind of Conformity to it will secure the End proposed. The End of all, we said, was private Happiness. Now as we are assured that the Deity had no other Design in framing the World at first, nor can have any End in continuing to preserve and govern it, but to lead us all to as much Happiness as we are capable of; his Will and our Happiness become perfectly co-incident, and so many safely enough be substituted one for the other. He proposes only the Good of his Creatures by being obeyed, and makes it the Rule and Reason of all that he enjoins; and knows the most effectual Methods of attaining it: An absolute implicit compliance with his Will may therefore not improperly be called our ultimate End; nay, ought to be esteemed and acted on as such in all particular Cases. As it is an infallible Rule and adequate Measure of our Duty, it must oblige us to an Action when we can see no farther Reason for it; and it is highly necessary and fit it should. Our Knowledge of the Nature of ourselves, and those about us, is very short and imperfect; we are able to trace our Happiness but a few Steps through the various Consequences of Things, and Reasons of Action; and are frequently apt to deviate from the

Paths of Truth into Error and Absurdity. We stand in need therefore of some *Rule* on which we may constantly depend, which will always guide and direct us in our Pursuit; and this, as we have seen, can only be the Will of that Being in whose Hands we always are, and who is both able and inclined to reward us to the uttermost. Our next Enquiry then must be, how we shall secure this Reward to us, or what will certainly obtain his Favour; and that is, in one Word, *Obedience*, the having a Regard to his Will in all our Actions, and doing them for this Reason only, because they are well pleasing to him, and what he requires of us.

That this must be the only Means of recommending ourselves to his Favour, the only true Principle which can make our Actions properly virtuous or rewardable by him, is very plain: For nothing can in Reason entitle me to a Reward from another, which has no manner of Relation to him; and nothing can have any relation to the Deity, but what is done *on his Account*, in obedience to his Command, or with an Intent to please him. The *Matter* of the Act can neither be of Advantage nor Disadvantage to him; therefore the *Intention* is all that can make it bear any Relation to him. In one Sense indeed the material Part of the Act may relate to the Deity, *viz*. As it tends in its own Nature to further or oppose the Designs of his Government: But this will never relate to him in such a manner, as to make the Agent a proper Subject either of Reward or Punishment for it. To make one a Subject of Reward for any particular Action, his Will must be concerned in it so far as to intend to merit the Reward which is annexed to the Performance of it, or at least to will and intend the Performance of that Action as so proposed. To be a proper Subject of Punishment, a Person must intend the Breach of some Law, or at least the Neglect and Disregard of it; or the Commission of such an Act as he knows, or might know, if he desired, to be a Breach of it. Consequently it is the Aim and Design of an Action only which makes Guilt or Merit imputable to the Agent; and in that Aim and Design does the Guilt or Merit of it wholly consist. From hence then we may compute the Value or Defect of any particular Action in a Moral or Religious Account. As far as it is intended to obey the Will of God, and advance the Ends of his Government, in Preference of or Opposition to any other Interest or Inclination; so far it is meritorious with or acceptable to him: As far as it is done in compliance with any particular Interest or Inclination, in opposition, to, or with a greater Regard had to it than to the Will of God, or in actual Disregard of that Will; so far, and in such Circumstances it is offensive or injurious to him: As far as it is done without any distinct End, or any distinct Consideration of the Will of God in that End, so far it is at best purely indifferent, and of no moral or religious Account at all. If the End of any particular Action terminate in ourselves *immediately*, and we have no farther View in it than the Attainment of some temporal Advantage, Honour, or the like; the Action can but be innocent at best; we serve not God herein, but ourselves; and when we attain the natural good Effects thereof in this Life, we have our Reward. Nothing can intitle us to any supernatural and extraordinary Recompence from the Deity in another State, but what was done purely on his account; in Obedience to his Will, or in order to recommend us to his Favour. And though we cannot properly *merit* any thing of God, by reason of those innumerable Benefits received from him, which we shall never be able to repay; by reason of our manifold Transgressions which our good Works cannot attone for; and because of the many Defects attending even the best of them; which render them not so good as they might and ought to be; though for these Reasons, I say, we cannot properly *merit* any thing of God; yet nevertheless by *Covenant* and *Promise* we may be certainly entitled to his Favour, so far as we comply with those Terms of Salvation which he has proposed, and perform such Duties as he has commanded, purely in *Obedience* to him; which is the only Principle (as we have seen) that can make any thing rewardable by him.

Not that it is necessary that we should always have this Principle explicitly in view, and be able to deduce every particular Action immediately from a Consideration of the Will of God, in order to make it acceptable to him. It may, it is hoped, be sufficient, if we have a general Intent of serving him in the whole of any considerable Undertaking, and an express Regard to him whenever he appears to be more immediately concerned in any Part of it. Our imperfect Understanding will not allow us to trace up every thing to our ultimate End; we find it necessary therefore to fix several inferior and subordinate ones, wherein we are forced to acquiesce, both in our Knowledge and our Practice; and it is sufficient to recommend and justify an Action, if it can be fairly deduced from any of these subordinate Ends, and have some Connection or other with what is manifestly our Duty. Nay farther, some Actions which are directed to no distinct End at all, though in themselves indeed they be no proper Subjects of Reward (as was observed) yet they may become such by virtue of certain *Habits*, whereof they are Consequences, and for which Habits we are properly accountable: and the Reason of this is evident. As we cannot have our main End constantly in view, it is necessary for us to acquire such Habits of acting as may lead us almost insensibly to it, and carry us on our Journey, even when we are not thinking of it. These Habits therefore, if they be rightly founded and directed, must intitle us to a Reward for all the several Actions which flow from them, even when the first Foundation is forgot. Thus a Servant sufficiently deserves both the Title and Reward of being faithful and obedient, if he have acquired such Habits of constant Diligence in his Master's Business, as will carry him regularly through it, though he seldom consider the End of all his Labour, or think of his Master in it.

WE have, in two former Papers, considered the true *End* of human Actions, and the Means of attaining it. We have laid down the only adequate *Rule* or Criterion of Morality, as also removed some of the false and insufficient ones usually proposed. We have inquired into the Motive, Ground, or *Principle* on which Virtue ought to be pursued, and pointed out the proper Method of applying it. To compleat our Design upon this Subject, we shall now examine the *material* Part of Virtue, and obviate some Mistakes that have arisen, and may still arise on that Head.

The most common one is to put the *Matter* of any Duty for the whole Duty. Thus some have defined moral Goodness to be nothing more than chusing, willing, or procuring *Natural Good*, including both Private and Publick: Others make it to consist in producing the greatest Degree of *Pleasure*, i. e. in the Agent himself; or in pursuing *private Happiness*: But except these Writers intend to treat only of the *material Part* of Virtue, whenever they describe it in such Terms, their Descriptions are evidently partial and defective. Moral Goodness, or Moral Virtue in Man is not merely chusing or producing Pleasure or Natural Good, but chusing it without View to present Rewards, and in Prospect of a future Recompence only. For, observe how the Case stands. The greatest Natural Good of all is so provided for by God himself, by the strong Appetites he has implanted in Men, or the Necessities he has laid them under, that there is no Moral Goodness, no Virtue at all in chusing it. The greatest Natural Good I call what concerns the Being of the Moral World; and the second greatest, what concerns their *Well-being*. Now God has taken care to preserve the World in Being, to continue both the Species and Individual. 1. By implanting a very strong Love of Life in every Man. 2. By the Appetites of Hunger and Thirst. 3. By warm Desires for propagating the Species. 4. By the Στοργὴ of Parents towards their Offspring. 5. By necessitating Men to unite in Society, and mutual Offices of Trade, *&c.* Upon these five Articles depends the very Being of Mankind: And God would not trust such weighty Things as those to the weak Reason of Man, but has provided for them by never failing Appetites and Necessities; insomuch that there is no Virtue in chusing those Actions, but in regulating or moderating them.

There is no Moral Goodness in eating and drinking, though a Natural Good, necessary to keep up Life: No Moral Goodness in propagating the Species, though that also must come under the Notion of chusing Natural Good: No Moral Goodness in pursuing the Στοργὴ before-mentioned, nor in carrying on any Trade for the Service of the World; though without these Things the World could not subsist. Moral Goodness therefore lies not in chusing the greatest Natural Good, but in chusing any Natural Good, when not impelled to it by *Necessity*, nor moved by *present* Pleasure or Reward. Eating and Drinking is not Virtue, because we do it to satisfy Hunger and Thirst, and to please the Appetite: But the Virtue is in regulating and moderating the Appetite, that that very Appetite which is necessary for the Being of the World, may not be carried to such an Excess as to disturb its Well-being. The like may be said of the rest.

The Case is the same in Acts of the most immediate beneficial Tendency, whether they be directed to the Publick in general, to inferior Societies or particular Persons: To defend, assist, relieve a Friend or Fellow-Citizen; to serve and support him in his Credit or Fortunes, Body or Mind: If this, which commonly goes by the Name of Moral Goodness, proceed from selfish Views, or no distinct View at all; from a Prospect of future Advantage in this Life, or from the present Pleasure of performing it; it is nothing. To preserve the Rights, Laws and Liberties of our Country, to improve and reform a whole Nation, to engage in Enterprizes that will be of universal Benefit to Mankind; any or all such Actions, though never so good in their Effects, and right as to the *Matter* of them, yet if they be wanting in Point of Principle; if they are done for Profit, Honour, or out of mere Humour, nay out of the most disinterested Benevolence itself; so long as there is no Regard had to the Deity in them, they cannot be reckoned strictly Virtuous, nor claim a Place in Morals or Religion.

Moral Goodness therefore is not barely the willing or producing *Natural Good*, whether private or publick. This would be denominating the Whole from a Part; the Fault of all those Definitions formerly mentioned. Thus they who describe it to be *following Nature*, neither settle the *Matter*, nor establish any determinate *Rule*; and if they have a *Principle*, it is either false or inadequate, as was before observed. They who determine it to be acting according to *Reason, Truth*, or the *Relations of Things*, at most lay down only the *Rule*, and *Matter*; but give us neither any distinct *Principle*, nor *End*. They who define it to be *Obedience to the Will of God* only, leave out the material Part, *i. e.* Do not shew what the Will of God requires, or wherein it consists: Neither do they sufficiently inform us *why* we ought to obey it, or direct us to what we call our ultimate End. A compleat Definition of Virtue, or Morality, should take in all these Particulars, and can be only this: *The doing Good to Mankind, in Obedience to the Will of God, and for the Sake of everlasting Happiness.*

E. L.

ABRAHAM TUCKER

The Light of Nature Pursued
(1768, 1778; 3rd edn. 1834)

*

I. Human Nature
Ch. XX
Ch. XXVII
Ch. XXXVI

*

II. Theology
Ch. XXVIII

*

III. Lights of Nature and Gospel Blended
Ch. XXXV, secs. 1–5

Abraham Tucker (1705–1774)

Biographical Note

With the exception of John Gay, far less is known about Abraham Tucker than any of the other eighteenth-century religious utilitarians. He was the son of a London merchant, whose family was originally from Somerset, and of Judith, daughter of Abraham Tillard. Born 2 September 1705, following the early deaths of his parents Tucker was brought up by his uncle, Sir Isaac Tillard. Tillard was a kind and cultured guardian, who advised his ward to model his letters on those of St Paul. After school in Bishops Stortford, in 1721 Tucker attended Merton College, Oxford, as a gentleman commoner. He studied philosophy, mathematics, French, and Italian, and developed a talent for music. In 1724 he entered the Inner Temple to learn law. Never called to the Bar, Tucker used his legal knowledge as a landowner and Justice of the Peace. In 1727 he purchased Betchworth Castle, near Dorking, with an extensive estate. Following this, Tucker studied agriculture, collecting books on the subject, toured parts of England and Scotland, and spent one vacation in France and Flanders. On 3 February 1736 he married Dorothy (d. 7 May 1754), daughter of Edward Barker of East Betchworth, cursitor baron of the exchequer. They had two daughters, Judith (d. 26 November 1794) and Dorothea Maria (d. 5 March 1768) who married Sir Henry Paulet St John of Dogmersfield Park, Hampshire, and had one son, H. P. St John Mildmay, MP. The latter was to re-edit Tucker's major work *The Light of Nature Pursued* (1768, 1778), which he published with a life of his grandfather in 1805. After the death of his wife, Tucker devoted himself to educating his daughters and to writing. Although frequently asked to stand for Parliament, he refused.[1]

Tucker completed the first four volumes of *The Light of Nature Pursued* in 1768, when they appeared under the pseudonym 'Edward Search', a name he had already employed on the title-page of *Free Will, Knowledge and Fate* (1763). The latter was a selection of extracts from the manuscripts which he eventually published in more complete form in 1768. In 1771 Tucker began to go blind and created a machine to guide his hand to write legibly. During his final years his daughter Judith transcribed his work for the press and learned Greek to be able to read original sources to him. The final three volumes of *The Light of Nature Pursued* were edited from Tucker's manuscripts by Judith and published posthumously in 1778, four

---

[1]   John Fyvie, *Noble Dames and Notable Men of the Georgian Era* (New York 1911), p. 208.

years after his death. This is the work upon which Tucker's reputation as
a theologian and a utilitarian moral philosopher rests.

Leslie Stephen admired Tucker, calling him 'the ablest and most original
exponent of this [the utilitarian] theory',[2] in spite of the fact that 'he utterly
ignores the principle that the secret of being tedious is to say everything'.[3]
Tucker's principal influence was on Paley, who admitted his debt in *The
Principles of Moral and Political Philosophy* (1785).[4] Indeed, Stephen considered that Tucker's and Paley's theories were 'nearly identical'.[5] However,
in the opinion of LeMahieu, Stephen overstated the debt and was unfair
to Paley.[6] Fyvie adds that Tucker influenced Archbishop Whately in his
Bampton Lectures, and that Mackintosh praised *The Light of Nature
Pursued*, regretting its neglect. Though he offered little to support the point,
he considered that Tucker anticipated much of the utilitarian doctrine of
Bentham and Mill.[7]

Tucker published little of consequence aside from the voluminous *The
Light of Nature Pursued*. There were several short miscellaneous pieces,
like *The Country Gentleman's Advice to his Son on the Subject of Party
Clubs* (1755), *Man in Quest of Himself* (by 'Cuthbert Comment', 1763),
and *Vocal Sounds* (by 'Edward Search', 1773). William Hazlitt recognized
the value of Tucker's philosophy and tried to make it accessible to a wider
audience in *An Abridgment of the Light of Nature Pursued* (1807).

Note on the Text

Tucker began writing *The Light of Nature Pursued* in 1756. He published
the first four volumes in 1768, and these were followed by volumes 5–7
posthumously in 1778 (prepared for the press by Tucker's daughter Judith).
All seven volumes appeared under the pseudonym 'Edward Search'.
Employing the same pseudonym, Tucker had earlier published a series of
extracts from the original manuscripts under the title *Free Will, Knowledge
and Fate: A Fragment* in 1763. A second edition of *The Light of Nature
Pursued*, edited by Sir H. P. St John Mildmay, Tucker's grandson, appeared
in seven volumes in 1805 with a life and an additional chapter restored
from the original manuscripts. This material was omitted by Judith Tucker
on the grounds that her father's views on the construction of the first
four verses in the Gospel according to St John might be misconstrued as
unorthodox. In his brief biography of Tucker at the front of the 1805

---

2   Leslie Stephen, *History of English Thought in the Eighteenth Century*, 2 vols. (1876; 3rd
    edn. 1902; reprt. New York 1949), ii. 110.
3   Stephen, *History of English Thought in the Eighteenth Century*, ii. 111.
4   See Introduction above, pp. 20–21.
5   Stephen, *History of English Thought in the Eighteenth Century*, ii. 121.
6   D. L. LeMahieu, *The Mind of William Paley: A Philosopher and His Age* (Lincoln 1976),
    p. 124.
7   Fyvie, *Noble Dames and Notable Men of the Georgian Era*, pp. 203, 248.

edition Mildmay argued that this reasoning had now lost its force. Mildmay's edition of *The Light of Nature Pursued* subsequently appeared in a more accessible two-volume version in 1834 (the restored material is Chapter XXII of the second volume, titled 'Word or Logos'). The two-volume edition was reprinted in 1836, 1837, 1842, 1848, and 1852, and several American editions appeared throughout the nineteenth century. The extracts which follow are taken from the first two-volume edition of 1834, published in London by Thomas Tegg and Son.

I. Human Nature

CHAP. XX.
INTRODUCTION OF MOTIVES.

SENSATION first moves us to action, in order to continue it if pleasant, or remove it if painful: thus the taste of victuals urges children to take more of them into their mouths, and the smart of a pin to catch away their hands from it. When they have gotten competent stores of reflection, these too affect them in like manner with sensation, and sometimes overpower it; for you may draw off a child's notice from any little pain or craving of appetite, by diverting it with play-things. As imagination becomes worked into trains, the notice, being put into one by some particular object, will run on to other ideas very different from those the object exhibited. Nor does imagination fail to suggest fancies of her own motion, without any object to introduce them: of what kind they shall be, depends greatly upon constitution, the present state of our animal spirits, or disposition of mind, inclining us either to seriousness or gaiety, business or diversion. Habits, too, attract the notice to follow them inadvertently by that ease there is in giving way to the little transient desires they present rather than restraining them. And when experience has brought us acquainted with the properties of things external, and the command we have over the ideas of our mind, which knowledge gives us the use of our understanding, we can then procure motives for ourselves; either by application of such objects as will raise any particular desire, or by putting reflection upon the hunt for something that will please us, or suggesting inducements to strengthen us in our purpose, or by resolution to banish some intruding ideas, and fix our whole attention upon others.

2. Thus there are three causes contributing to introduce motives into the scale: the action of the mind, impulse of external objects, and mechanical play of our organs; and these three mutually influence one another. The mind operates two ways, either by design or inadvertently; for when she turns her notice upon an idea, though with no other view than for the present amusement it affords, this occasions it to lead in a train of its associates, and often awakens a desire that would have lain dormant without such attention. Therefore, if we have any hurtful inclination belonging to us, it is very dangerous to let our thoughts run upon objects relative thereto; for we may raise a disturber we did not expect, nor can quiet again whenever we please: and perhaps desire scarce ever rises to any high pitch, unless assisted by some action of the mind tending to foment

it. But when the mind acts with design, nevertheless she has that design suggested by something happening to her from without, or by the spontaneous working of imagination; to which sources she must have recourse in search for motives of her conduct, or gathering encouragements to support her in an undertaking. Even in the most arbitrary exercises of her power, as when she endeavours to attain her purpose by dint of resolution, she uses some instrument to do her work. A man that holds his hand near a roasting fire, must have some reason for so doing, either to cure a burn, under the notion of fire driving out fire, or to try how long he can hold it there, or for some other purpose which appears satisfactory at the time, or else it would never have put him upon the attempt: this satisfactory purpose, then, he strives to retain in full vigour, without suffering it to fluctuate or fade, and withdraws his notice from that uneasiness the smart of the fire would throw upon him. Herein he acts upon the mental eye much in the same manner as we do upon the bodily, when we wink against a glaring light, or stretch our nerves to observe some obscure object that cannot be discerned without straining; or as we do upon the organs of hearing, when of two persons talking to us at once, we disregard the one, and attend wholly to the other. And in all cases of resolution, we may perceive the like method practised: we do not annex the idea of Best to what had it not before, but among opposite subjects, whereto that idea is already annexed, we hold one under contemplation, and exclude the rest, or strengthen it with other considerations, from whence that idea may be transferred.

Things external are made to operate upon us either by natural causes, or the situation we stand in, or the company we consort with: but what effect they shall produce in us depends greatly upon the cast of our imagination. For we have observed before, that the same objects affect people variously, exciting different judgments, and suggesting different motives in one from what they do in another: nor does the mind want a power many times of applying or removing objects, and of increasing or diminishing in some measure the impression of those before her by an operation upon her organs.

In like manner the spontaneous courses of our ideas, although depending chiefly upon habit, and running into those trains of thought to which we have been accustomed, yet may be diverted by objects occurring, or drawn aside by the force of sympathy, or controlled by the power of the mind, so as to take another track than they would have followed of their own accord.

3. If we examine our proceedings carefully, we shall find in all of them a mixture of volition and machinery, and perhaps the latter bearing a greater share than the former. We never enter upon an undertaking without some purpose starting up in our thoughts, or recommended by the present occasion as expedient or agreeable: we choose the measures for accomplishing it from among the stores presented by our understanding;

and though we perform the work by our own activity, yet our manner of proceeding is such as former practice has made ready to us, and the minute steps necessary for completing it rise mechanically in our imagination. Our latent motives, which bear so great a sway in the behaviour of most men, cannot owe their appearance to the mind, because they escape her observation when she would discover them: and our minute motives prompting us to inadvertent actions, which are far more numerous than commonly supposed, must take rise from some other spring, because the mind perceives them not the moment before they operate, nor remembers them the moment after. Nor are the grosser parts of our machine without their influence upon our actions; the natural temperament of our constitution, the accidental condition of our humours, the brisk or slow circulation of our animal spirits, the circumstances of health or sickness, freshness or weariness, fulness or emptiness, render the mind alert or unapt for exercise, turn imagination into different trains, excite desires of various kinds, and in great measure model the shape of our behaviour.

4. What is the particular structure of our machine, how the several parts of it communicate, or in what manner they operate upon one another, we cannot pretend to describe, and therefore must express ourselves by figures. Sometimes we talk of characters imprinted, or traces engraven in the memory, sometimes of roads and tracks worn in the imagination, of weights hanging in the balance, springs impelling to action, wheels resembling those of clock-work, images striking upon the mental eye, or streams and currents running in various channels. Those expressions, if intended for a physical account of our interior frame, could not all be admitted, as being inconsistent with one another: but when we speak figuratively of a matter we cannot describe directly, we may vary our images without inconsistency, for the same will not answer in every case, therefore it is allowable to take any that shall afford the greatest resemblance according to the present occasion for which we want to apply it.

But if we may guess at the internal texture of our machine by the grosser parts of it discoverable upon dissection, they will lead us to imagine that our ideas are conveyed by a multitude of little tubes affecting us variously according to the motions excited in them, or according to the courses of some subtle fluid they contain: or should we, with Doctor Hartley, suppose the nerves to be solid capilaments, and the business performed by an ether surrounding them on the outside, this will amount to the same thing; because a number of these small strings placed close together will form tubes of the interstices between them, which may serve as channels for the foresaid ether to pass along. Therefore, if I were to compare the human machine to any of our contrivances of art, I should choose for my foundation a large Organ; wherein the bellows answer to the animal circulation, the pipes to the organs of sensation and reflection, and the organist to the mind. But the organist here does not make all the music: for the pipes are so contrived as to sound with the striking of things external upon them, or by the mere working of the bellows, which plays as it were by clockwork without a blower. Yet is this but an imperfect representation of the natural machine: to make our comparison more complete, we must suppose other sets of pipes for conveying objects of the other senses; besides innumerable smaller ones returning an echo to the larger, and new modulating the sounds or lights received from them, which supplies us with our ideas of reflection. These little vessels are so soft and flexible, that they will change their form and run into various contextures with one another, whereon depend our inclinations and stores of knowledge: for as a pipe will give a different sound according to the length or other dimensions it consists of, so objects affect us differently according to the disposition of the channels through which they pass. Nor must we omit the many conveyances necessary for distributing the alimentary juices, which serve like oil to moisten and supple the works or to repair the waste made by continual use. Add to this a multitude of other pipes which dilate and shorten upon inflation, and thereby draw certain strings fastened to their extremities: from whence proceeds muscular motion, and the power of acting upon the several parts of our machine, as well the grosser as the finer. And all this infinite variety of works, so complicated with one another, and yet so exactly disposed as not to interfere with each other in their play, Nature has stowed within the narrow compass of a human body; which if an artist were to endeavour to imitate by constructing an engine that should perform those few of the human movements that art can imitate, it would require an immense fabric to contain everything necessary for executing his purpose. But the most wonderful circumstance of all is, that our organist sits in utter darkness with respect to the nearest parts of his instrument, which are to be the immediate subjects of his action, having no notice of anything but what comes to him through his pipes: he knows not the situation of his keys, on which hand lies the base or the treble; nevertheless, after a competent practice in his trade, he acquires such an unaccountable expertness, that he never touches the wrong key, but takes his measures exactly, without perceiving what they are, and upon an idea only of some remote consequence they will produce.

5. Since there is so close a connection between the parts of our machine acted upon by the mind and those moved by the animal circulation, it follows that each must have an influence upon the other. Our vital spirits, according as they stand disposed, force a particular kind of ideas upon the mind, and the latter in every exertion of her power causes an alteration in the courses of the former: sometimes designedly, but oftener as a natural consequence of something else she intends. He that runs means only to arrive the sooner at the place whither he would go; but besides this he quickens his pulse, heats his flesh, and puts himself out of breath, effects which he did not think of, nor perhaps should have ensued had it been at

his option to have helped them. The like happens on other exercises of our activity, which propagate a motion to the several parts of our body corresponding respectively with the organs employed in those exercises; and these parts, by frequently receiving such motions, become disposed to fall into them again mechanically, or upon the slightest touch, and thereby excite the same ideas that generated them. From hence arise our habits, which though learned at first by single, but perhaps inadvertent acts of the mind, yet recur upon us aftewards involuntarily. Hence likewise spring the passions, which I take to be only a stronger sort of habits acquired early in our childhood, when the matter of our composition being tender and pliable, may be worked easily into new channels wherein the animal spirits may flow more copiously. For I do not imagine that nature gave us passions: she may indeed have made each man more susceptible of one sort than another, but they are brought into form by the action of the mind bending her notice continually to particular sets of objects. Just as nature may have prepared one man for a dancer by giving him strength and suppleness in his joints, or another for a singer by giving a clear and sonorous voice: but it is art and practice that invest them with the respective faculties of dancing or singing.

CHAP. XXVII.
ULTIMATE GOOD.

FOR so I choose to translate the Summum Bonum of the ancients, as much and as unsuccessfully sought after as the philosopher's stone, rather than call it the Chief Good, as it is vulgarly termed. For the inquiry was not to ascertain the degrees of goodness in objects, or determine what possessed it in the highest pitch beyond all others; but, since the goodness of things depends upon their serviceableness towards procuring something we want, to discover what was that one thing intrinsically good which contented the mind of itself and rendered all others desirable in proportion as they tended directly or remotely to procure it. Good, says Mr. Locke, is that which produces pleasure, and if we understand it thus strictly, in the true original sense, our inquiry were vain: for then the very expression of good in itself would be absurd, because nothing good could be ultimate, the pleasure it produces lying always beyond. But it is customary to call that good which stands at the very end of our wishes, and contents the mind without reference to anything further: and in this common acceptation the term will be applicable to our present purpose.

2. Upon perusal of the chapter of satisfaction, and those of the four classes of motives, whoever shall happen to think they contain a just representation of human nature, need not be long in seeking for this summun bonum: for he will perceive it to be none other than pleasure or satisfaction, which is pleasure taken in the largest sense, as comprising

every complacence of mind together with the avoidance of pain or uneasiness. Perhaps I shall be charged with reviving the old exploded doctrine of Epicurus upon this article, but I am not ashamed of joining with any man of whatever character in those parts of it, where I think he has truth on his side: though whether I do really agree with him here, is more than I can be sure of, for I find great disputes concerning what he called pleasure. If he confined it to gross sensual delights or imaginations relative thereto, as his adversaries charged him with, and the bulk of his followers seem to have understood him, I cannot consent to shut myself up within such narrow limits: for though these things may afford a genuine satisfaction sometimes and when sparingly used, yet it is to be had more plentifully elsewhere. Therefore, being regardless whether my sentiments tally or no with those of Epicurus, I shall not trouble myself to examine what he really thought, but endeavour as far as I am able to explain what this satisfaction is, which I suppose the summum bonum or ultimate end of action. And this I cannot do better than by referring, as I have done before in the chapter upon that article, to every man's experience of the condition of mind he finds himself in when anything happens to his wish or good liking; when he feels the cool breezes of a summer evening or the comfortable warmth of a winter fire; when he gains possession of something useful or profitable; when he has done anything he can applaud himself for or will redound to his credit with persons he esteems.

3. But to consider satisfaction physically, it is a perception of the mind, residing in her alone, constantly one and the same in kind, how much soever it may vary in degree: for whether a man be pleased with hearing music, seeing prospects, tasting dainties, performing laudable actions, or making agreeable reflections, his complacence and condition of mind will be the same if equal in degree, though coming from different quarters. But this complacence, and indeed every other perception, the mind never has, unless excited in her by some external object striking upon her bodily senses, or some idea giving play to her mental organs. We have supposed there may be some certain fibre whose peculiar office it is to affect the mind in this manner, and our organs please or not by their motion according as, in the natural texture or present disposition of our frame, they stand connected with this spring of satisfaction. Whether there really be such a particular spring or no is not very material to know, for if we could ascertain its existence we cannot come at it either with the finger or surgeon's probe so as to set it a working for our entertainment. Since then we cannot touch this spring directly, we must endeavour to convey an impulse to it by those channels that nature has provided us with for the purpose: for common experience testifies that there are a variety of sensations and reflections qualified to excite satisfaction in the mind when we can apply them. But our attention usually reaching no further than to these causes, for if we can procure them the effect will follow of course, we give the name of

pleasure to those sensations and scenes of imagination which touch us in the sensible part: hence pleasure becomes an improper term to express the summum bonum by, because objects or ideas that have pleased may not do so again; therefore if we were to recommend it as the end of action, we might be misunderstood, or mislead some unwary person already inclined that way into the pursuit of a wrong object; for pleasure in the vulgar acceptation will not always please. If Epicurus understood it in this sense, I renounce communion with him as a heretic; but if by pleasure he meant the very complacence of mind generated by agreeable objects of any kind whatever, I cannot refuse him my assistance against all opponents; and the rather for fear this may prove the only point whereon we shall ever have an opportunity of joining forces together.

4. Nor can it be doubted that satisfaction is proposed to our pursuit by nature, when we reflect how universally and perpetually it engages all mankind, how steadily volition follows the prospect of immediate satisfaction, as has been shown in the foregoing inquiry, if one may be said to show a thing that was before sufficiently manifested by Mr. Locke. The man and the child, the civilized and the savage, the learned and the vulgar, the prudent and the giddy, the good and the wicked, constantly pursue whatever appears most satisfactory to them in their present apprehension: and if at any time they forego an immediate pleasure for sake of a distant advantage, it is because they conceive a greater satisfaction in the prospect of that advantage or uneasiness in the thought of missing it. Therefore, those who can content themselves with the enjoyments of to-day without feeling an actual concern for the morrow, will never be moved to action by anything future, how fully soever they acknowledge the expedience of it: and when pain rises so high as that the mind cannot find any contentment under it, it will overpower the best grounded resolutions. Neither is there any more room to doubt of satisfaction being the ultimate end than of its being a natural good, because all other goodness centres in that: the gratifications of pleasure, the rules of prudence and morality, are good, only as they tend by themselves or in their consequences to satisfy the mind: one may give a reason for all other things being good, but for that alone no reason can be given, for experience not reason must recommend it. Why is knowledge good? because it directs us to choose the things that are most useful. Why are useful things good? because they minister to the supply of our wants and desires. Why is this supply good? because it satisfies the mind. Why is satisfaction good? here you must stop, for there lies nothing beyond to furnish materials for an answer: but if anybody denies it, you can only refer him to his own common sense, by asking how he finds himself when in a state of satisfaction or disquietude, and whether of them he would prefer to the other.

In short, the matter seems so clear that one may be thought to trifle in spending so many words to prove it: and after all, what is the upshot of the whole but to show that satisfaction satisfies? a mere identical proposition adding nothing to our knowledge, but the same as if one should say that plenitude fills, that heat warms, that hardness resists and softness yields to the touch. Yet as trifling as the proposition may appear, Mr. Locke has bestowed a great deal of pains in proving the value and efficacy of satisfaction: nor have there been wanting persons of no small reputation with whom such pains were necessary, who out of their extravagant zeal for virtue denied that all other pleasures conferred anything towards bettering the condition of the mind. Had they pronounced them cloying, unstable, often delusive of the expectation, and productive of greater mischiefs, they had said right, and enough to answer their main purpose: but this would not do; they insisted that when we see a man actually pleased with trifles, wanting nothing else, but fully contended with the condition of mind they throw him into, nevertheless he was miserable at the very instant of enjoyment without regard to consequences. What is this but undertaking to prove that satisfaction does not satisfy, which whoever can accomplish may rise to be a cardinal, for he need not fear being able to demonstrate transubstantiation. Our divines talk more rationally when they admit that the pleasures of sin may satisfy for a moment, but are too dearly bought when purchased with disease, shame, remorse, and an incapacity for higher enjoyments.

5. One remark more concerning the summum bonum, viz. that though a noun of the singular number, nevertheless it is one in species only, containing a multitude of individuals. For our perceptions are fleeting and momentary, objects strike successively upon our organs, and ideas rise incessantly in our imagination, which thereby throw the mind into a state of complacence or disquietude, corresponding with the manner of their impulse, which has no duration: therefore satisfaction cannot continue without a continual application of satisfactory causes. This gains another name for the summum bonum, and makes us entitle it Happiness, which is the aggregate of satisfactions. For though this term be sometimes applied to the enjoyment of a single moment, and then is synonymous with satisfaction, yet it more generally and properly denotes the surplus and successes a man has met with or may expect over and above his disappointments: if the surplus be anything considerable, we pronounce him happy; if his disquietudes greatly exceed, we style him miserable. Ovid understood it in this sense when he laid down that we can never pronounce a man happy before his death, because the fortune of life being uncertain, whatever enjoyments we see him possessed of we can never be sure they may not be overbalanced by evils to come: and Milton the same, in his apostrophe to our first parents, Sleep on, blest pair, yet happy if ye seek not other happiness and know to know no more. But sound sleep, being a state of insensibility, is capable neither of satisfaction nor uneasiness: therefore the

sleeping pair were happy only in respect to that ample store of unmingled pleasures lying in reserve for them against they awoke.

Thus happiness relates to the whole tenor of our lives, but multitudes of our actions do not reach so far as to affect our condition so long as we have our being: this breaks happiness again into smaller portions corresponding with the length or extent of their influence. It may be all one after dinner whether I eat mutton or chicken, but if one will please me better during the time of eating and the indulgence will do me no harm, why should not I take that I like best? When we lay out a day's diversion by some little excursion abroad, we regard what will entertain us most for the day, notwithstanding some trifling inconveniences of sloppy roads or indifferent accommodations at a paltry inn. If we take a house we consider, not what will be the most easy for the first month, but most commodious during the whole lease. And when a father puts his son to school, he might supply him with more enjoyment at home than can be expected during the seven years of schooling; but he considers that learning will enable him to pass his life afterwards more agreeably and usefully. Thus upon several occasions proposed to our option, that is always the best which will add most to our happiness as far as its consequences extend.

6. Our satisfactions come sometimes from causes operating of their own accord, as upon change of weather from chill or sultry to moderate, or upon hearing joyful news unexpectedly; but for the most part we must procure them for ourselves by application of proper means. Now since we are prompted to use our activity by desire, since the good things occurring spontaneously would have been objects of our desire had we known of them beforehand, or our intervention been wanted, therefore may justly be styled desirable; and since desire of itself renders objects satisfactory which would otherwise have been indifferent, therefore it is the first rule of happiness to procure the gratification of our desires; nor shall I scruple to recommend this as the proper business of life. Let every man by my consent study to gratify himself in whatever suits his taste and inclination, for they vary infinitely: one man's meat is another man's poison; what this person likes the next may abhor; what delights at one time may disgust at another; and what entertains when new may grow stale and insipid afterwards. Our appetites and fancies prompt us fast enough to this gratification, to choose objects suited to our particular tastes and to vary them as we find our relish change: but the misfortune is that desire often defeats her own purpose, either by mistaking things for satisfactory which are not, as when a child goes to play with the flame of a candle; or by a more common mistake apprehending gratification to lie in a single point, whereas this, like happiness, consists in the sum aggregate of enjoyments. He that indulges one desire to the crossing of many others, ought no more to be thought pursuing gratification than he can be thought to pursue profit who takes twenty pounds to-day for goods that he might have sold to-morrow

for forty: a true lover of money will reject it when offered upon such terms, and a true lover of gratification who knows what he is about will reject it upon the like. Therefore there is no occasion to persuade men out of their senses, and face them down that gratification adds nothing to their satisfaction, no not for a moment: on the contrary, we may exhort them to pursue it as a thing most valuable, and therefore to pursue it in the same manner as they would other valuable things, that is, not to take a little in hand in lieu of more they might have by and by. Any trifle that hits our fancy suffices to content the mind, and if we could enjoy it for ever with the same relish, it would answer our whole purpose; for I know of no weariness, no satiety, no change of taste in the mind; these all belong to the organs bodily and mental. When a glutton sits down to a well-spread table with a good appetite, if he ever has any, he possesses as much of the summum bonum as can be obtained within the time; and if he had victuals continually supplied him, a hole in his throat to discharge them as fast as swallowed, and nothing in the world else to do, he might attain it completely: but this cannot be: yet if he can prolong appetite beyond its stretch by high sauces, until he has overcharged himself, still I can allow him in a state of enjoyment during the repast, for he has a desire, and he gratifies it. But has he none other desires that will solicit him by and by? has he not a desire of being free from sickness of stomach, or distemper; nothing else he wants to do with his money; no diversion, no business that requires alertness of spirits, no regard for his credit, the good word of his friends, or his own peace of mind; if he has other desires that must suffer by indulging this one, he is a very bad accomptant in the article of gratification. Thus the very interests of our desires sometimes require self denial, which is recommendable only on that account: nor would I advise a man ever to deny himself, unless in order to please himself better another time.

7. Since then our desires mislead us so grossly, sometimes mistaking their own intention, and at other times starving one another, let us have recourse to reason to moderate between them, and to remedy the inconveniences they would bring upon us: and this, upon observing the opposition among them, will quickly discover that there are two ways of attaining gratification, one by procuring the objects we desire, the other by accommodating desire to the objects before us, or most convenient for us upon the whole. Either of these methods would answer our purpose, if we could pursue it effectually: were it possible to command everything with a wish, and supply fuel to our desires as fast as they start up, still varying their objects, as they themselves vary; or could we carry our heart in our hands, moulding it like wax, to the shape of every circumstance occurring, we need never feel a moment's uneasiness. But neither of these is possible: many things that would please us, lie out of our reach, some of them never to be obtained, others only now and then, as opportunity favours, but the greater part of them satiate, before desire abates: on the other hand, there are

some natural desires we can never totally eradicate, some necessaries, without which we cannot sustain our bodies in vigour, nor our spirits in alertness, to serve us upon any occasion. Therefore we must drive the nail that will go, use our understandings in surveying the stock of materials for gratification, either generally or at any particular time in our power, and examining the state of our desires, which among them are most attainable, or least contradictory to others, or what we can do towards blending them to ply most suitable to our convenience.

The former of these methods, that of procuring objects to our fancy, is the most obvious, therefore most commonly practised. We see men run eagerly after whatever their present desire urges them to, in proportion to the strength of their inclination; yet even here they must often call in consideration to their aid. For our pleasures, even those of them which are attainable, do not always hang so close within our reach, as that we can gather them whenever so disposed, but there are many things preparatory to the obtaining them; materials to be provided for supplying them, skill to be learned, dexterity to be acquired for the making and properly applying of that provision. This gives rise to the common rules of prudence, to all arts and sciences, directing or enabling men to make advances in fortune, honour, elegance, or other principal object they have set their hearts upon, and supplying the world with the conveniences and entertainments of life. The preparatories to pleasure will by translation become themselves objects of desire sufficient to move us, without the reference they bear to their end: and it is necessary they should, or else we must miss of the benefit they will do us. For as a traveller must not keep his thoughts constantly intent upon the place he wishes to arrive at, if he would make any dispatch in his journey, but having once taken the right road, fixes his eye upon the nearest parts of it as he goes along; so neither can we always contemplate the enjoyments we are providing for ourselves without interrupting our progress. Our capacities are too short to hold the whole line of our pursuit in view, but we must rest upon some part of it most convenient for our present direction: nor indeed could we always see to the end of our line if we were to strain ever so much, therefore must trust to others, or to our own former determination, for an assurance that it will lead us the way we would wish. Thus happiness, although the ultimate end of action, yet is not always, perhaps I might say, very seldom, our ultimate point of view: for our road lies through lanes and hedges, or over an uneven, hilly country, where we can see very little way before us: nay, sometimes we must seemingly turn our backs upon it, and take a compass round in the plain beaten track, to avoid impracticable morasses, or other obstacles intervening. Hence we may learn why pleasure is so deceitful a guide to happiness, because it plunges us headlong forward through thick and thin, fixing our eyes upon a single point, and taking them off from the marks leading to that aggregate of satisfactions whereof happiness consists. Wherefore he that resolves to please himself always will scarce ever do so, for by perpetually indulging his desires he will destroy or lose the means of indulging them.

8. For the skill of providing materials to gratify our desires, we must consult common prudence and discretion, or resort to the professors of arts and sciences containing the several branches of it: but the other method of gratification by managing the mind itself and bringing desire to the most convenient ply, belongs properly to the moralist; whose business lies not so much in informing you how to procure what you want, as how to forbear wanting what you cannot have, or would prove hurtful to you. But want cannot be removed without aid of some other want; for as you can never bring a man to assent to a proposition unless by means of some premises whereto he does already assent, so you can never bring him to any desire, unless by showing the connection it bears with something he already desires. The desire of happiness would suffice for this purpose, if we had it stronger infixed than we find in our breasts: but though all have this desire, so far as that they would be willing enough to receive happiness, if they could get it upon asking for; yet, being an aggregate, and therefore always in part at least distant, they prefer the present gratification of other desires before it. Therefore the moralist will begin with striving to inculcate this desire of happiness into himself and others as deeply as possible. But since this can hardly ever be done so effectually as one would wish, for we can never raise so vivid an idea of remote objects, as to equal those standing close to us, he will examine all other propensities belonging to us in order to encourage those which are most innocent, most satisfactory, most compatible together, and best promoting his principal aim. These he will endeavour to render habitual, so as that they may start up to the thought uncalled, and gather strength enough to overpower others he wishes to eradicate. As we cannot upon every occasion see to the end of our proceedings, he will establish certain rules to serve as landmarks for guiding us on the way. These rules, when he has leisure and opportunity for mature consideration, he will build on one another, erecting the whole fabric upon the basis of summum bonum before described. But because their reference to the ultimate end cannot be continually kept in mind, he will inure himself and everybody within his reach, by such methods as he shall find feasible, to look upon them as good in themselves, that they may become influencing principles of action. The outer branches of these rules, calculated for ordinary occasions, will of course vary according to those occasions or to the tempers, abilities, situations, and needs of different persons, to particularize all which would be endless and impracticable; but there are a few general rules universally expedient, as being the stem whereout the rest are to grow. The first seems to be that of habituating ourselves to follow the dictates of judgment in preference to any impulse of passion, fancy, or appetite, and forbear whatever our reason disapproves as being wrong: for

there is nothing more evident than that the knowledge of right and wrong can do us no benefit while resting in speculation alone and not reduced into practice; which it can never be unless become habitual, and striking with the force of an obligation or an object of desire.

CHAP. XXXVI.
LIMITATION OF VIRTUE.

I HOPE what has been hitherto delivered, may be found tending to recommend virtue as the most desirable object a man can pursue, to rest it upon the solid foundation of human nature, instead of those airy notions of an essential beauty wherein some have placed it, and to purify it from those extravagancies wherewith it has been loaded by the indiscretion of zealots. But to deal ingenuously and aim at truth, rather than saving the credit of our performance, let us not suppress an exception there lies against it, as limiting and confining the obligation of virtue within a certain compass which ought to extend to all cases universally. For it may be urged, that if satisfaction, a man's own satisfaction, be the groundwork of all our motives; if reason can furnish no ends of her own, but serves only to discover methods of accomplishing those assigned her by sense; if she recommends virtue and benevolence solely as containing the most copious sources of gratification: then are virtue and benevolence no more than means, and deserve our regard no longer than while they conduce towards their end. So that upon an opportunity offering wherein a man may gain some pleasure or advantage slily and safely without danger of after damage to himself, though with infinite detriment to all the world beside, and in breach of every moral obligation, he will act wisely to embrace it.

2. I cannot deny that the consequence follows in speculation upon the case above supposed, but I conceive such case can never happen in fact, so long as a man has any prospect of good and evil to come. For we must take into account, not only the advantage accruing from an action, but likewise the benefits or mischiefs of the disposition of mind giving birth to it: and if this will lead us into evils overbalancing the present profit of the action, we cannot be said to do it without danger of after damage to ourselves. The virtues belong to the heart rather than the head, or to speak in our own style, their residence lies in the imagination not the understanding; and to be complete must direct out inadvertent motions as well as our deliberate, that is, must become appetites impelling to action without standing to consider their expedience. Now whoever resists their impulse soberly and premediately upon consideration of their being inconvenient to his private purposes, will thereby make such a breach upon their authority and give such a crooked turn to his mind, as must unavoidably draw him into evils greater than any immediate advantage he may gain. All vice, says Juvenal, stands upon a precipice, and if we once step over

the brink, nobody can tell how far we shall go down: one of these two things must necessarily follow, either we shall continue sliding until we fall into destruction, or must put ourselves to infinite trouble in climbing the precipice, a trouble far exceeding the pleasure we may have felt at first in the ease of a downhill motion. He that cheats when he can do it safely will want to cheat at other times, and consequently must suffer, either by a self-denial or the mischiefs of an indulgence: so that it had been more for his benefit to have adhered inviolably to his rule of honesty. The ultimate end we have assigned for a reasonable creature to act upon was not present pleasure or profit but the aggregate of enjoyments: and we have laboured, I hope not unsuccessfully, to prove from a survey of human nature that nothing adds so largely to that aggregate as a right disposition of mind. We have indeed placed enjoyment in gratification, but then have put those who will lend us an ear in mind, that gratification depends more upon bending desire to such a ply as that it may fasten upon things attainable and convenient, than upon procuring the objects of every desire starting up in our fancy. Now the habits of moral prudence and benevolence alone can bring desire to the proper ply: but those habits cannot retain their influence with him who shall wilfully and upon principle permit his other desires to break in upon them. Therefore though the common rules of virtue may lawfully be dispensed with upon an honest regard to her interests and a judicious discernment of the greater general good, for this strengthens our attachment to those objects whereon the rules were founded: yet we may never infringe them upon any other consideration of pleasure or selfishness, for this would be introducing another principle of action incon-sistent with the former. But it would be the most imprudent thing in the world for a man to allow himself in such liberties as must destroy a principle of conduct that prudence and reason have recommended, so long as there remains any prospect of his receiving future benefit from its influence.

3. Nevertheless, it must be confessed that when life draws near to an end, if it should be urged upon us that then the obligations to virtue must cease, I should not know what to answer. For since they arise from expedience, they must drop of course when there is no longer a possibility of that expedience taking place. We have laid down before, that a man need never deny himself in anything unless in order to please himself better another time; if then he shall never see that other time, there is no reason why he should deny himself at all: but he may without scruple gratify whatever desires he finds in his heart, since there is no room for any bad consequences to follow upon them; nor need he fear their subverting a principle he has found all along of excellent use to guide him in his conduct, when he has no further course to run wherein that principle may direct him. Why should he restrain his extravagance when he has enough to last him the little time he expects to live? why should he forbear intemper-

ance when it cannot have time to fill him with diseases? why should he scruple to cheat when he shall slip out of harm's way before a discovery can overtake him? why should he trouble himself with what becomes of the world when he is upon the point of leaving it: or do anything for the benefit of others, when he can receive no returns from them, nor in any manner gather the fruits of his labours.

4. But notwithstanding this concession, it does not necessarily follow that a man must quit the practice of virtue when he sees his dissolution approaching; for this will depend upon the turn of mind he has already taken. If indeed he has pursued it hitherto by constraint, and still finds in himself strong propensities to gluttony, debauchery, gallantry, and other inordinate desires, I have suggested no arguments which might induce him to restrain them, nor offered advantages he can reap sufficient to compensate the trouble of a self-denial. For as physicians permit a patient, whom they have absolutely given over, to eat and drink whatever he pleases, because when nothing can do him good nothing can hurt him; so the moralist will think it in vain to prescribe a regimen for diseases of the mind, when there is no time to work a cure, nor any enjoyment of health to be expected. Our motives of action are not to be changed presently, nor can we give a new turn to desire as easily as put on our clothes; therefore, when the glass is almost run out, it is too late to think of taking up a set of fresh inclinations, but every one must be left to make the most of those he already possesses. But this very consideration will engage the man who has spent his days in a virtuous course to persevere in it to the last: not indeed now from obligation or expedience, but for the ease and pleasure he finds in pursuing an habitual track. We observed just now that the virtues to be complete must have fixed their residence in the heart, and become appetites impelling to action, without further thought than the gratification of them; so that after their expedience ceases, they still continue to operate by the desire they raise. Nor is it unusual in other cases for men to continue the courses they have been accustomed to, after the reasons upon which they began them are no more. I knew a mercer, who having gotten a competency of fortune, thought to retire and enjoy himself in quiet, but finding he could not be easy without business, was forced to return to the shop and assist his former partners gratis, in the nature of a journeyman. Why then should it be thought strange that a man, long inured to the practice of moral duties, should persevere in them out of liking, when they can yield him no further advantage? To tell him that he may squander without fear of poverty, gluttonize without danger of distempers, and bring a secret mischief upon others without hazard of its ever coming round upon himself, were no temptation to him: for he has no relish to such divertisements, his appetites having been long since set upon what is just, and becoming, and beneficent. So that though prudence has no further commands, he will employ himself in the same exercises she used to enjoin,

as the most agreeable way wherein he can lay out his few remaining moments.

5. Upon this occasion, I cannot avoid entering the lists once more on behalf of Epicurus, to vindicate him against a charge of inconsistency, laid by Tully in his second de Finibus, Cap. 30, 31. Epicurus it seems had written a letter, on the last day of his life, to one Hermachus, earnestly recommending his pupils, the children of his deceased friend, Metrodorus, to his tuition. And had directed by will, that his executors should provide an entertainment, yearly, on his birth-day, and on the like day of every month, for such as used to study philosophy with him, in order to preserve alive in their minds the remembrance of himself and of the said Metrodorus. Now this friendly concern for the name and family of Metrodorus, and this careful provision for keeping up the spirit of the sect, by bringing them together once a month, Tully thinks acting out of character in one who referred all things to pleasure, and held that whatever happens after our decease is nothing to us. But whoever observes the motions of the human mind, may see that many things which are nothing to us when they happen, are yet a great delight to us in the prospect and contemplation. How often do people please themselves with laying schemes for raising a family, or spreading their fame to future ages, without any probable assurance that they shall enjoy the successes of their family, or have any knowledge of what the world shall say of them a hundred years hence? but the thought of what shall then happen affords them a present entertainment, and therefore they follow pleasure as much in promoting those schemes as they should do in pursuit of any favourite diversion. I would fain know how Tully would have had Epicurus dispose of his last day to have acted in character: should it have been spent in the enjoyment of nice dainties, exquisite wines, or fine women? this he might have expected had he had the same notion of Epicurus that we have of an epicure. La Fontaine's glutton having eaten up a whole salmon all but the jowl, so surfeited himself therewith, that his physicians declared him past all hopes of a recovery: well, says he, since the case is so, then bring me the rest of my fish. Now this man we must own behaved consistently with himself throughout: but why must other people follow his example who have not the same fondness for salmon? Let us give everybody their due, whether we like them or not: it appears from what accounts have been handed down to us, and which Tully was not ignorant of, that nobody was less of an epicure than Epicurus himself. He had carefully studied the sources of pleasure and found nothing more conducive thereto than temperance, patience, benevolence, and all the moral virtues; we may suppose he had so full a persuasion of this their tendency, and so inured himself to the practice of them, that he had gotten an habitual liking to them, and could not turn his hand to anything else with equal relish. Imagine then a man of this turn arrived at the last morning of his existence, and considering

how to pass his only remaining day with most satisfaction to himself: how could he do it better than by continuing that course which he had constantly found most pleasurable and best suited to his taste? There is no occasion to suppose the love of probity, friendship, and public spirit, to be innate: for the perpetual experience and contemplation of their advantageousness is enough to make them objects of desire.

6. But though I have thus much to allege in favour of Epicurus, towards showing that his conduct might be all of a piece when he wrote the letter and made the will above mentioned, notwithstanding his referring all things to pleasure: yet I cannot so easily justify Regulus against all imputation of imprudence upon the like principle. For it is one thing to contrive how we shall lay out the day in a manner most agreeable to our liking, when nothing we do therein can affect us to-morrow, and quite another to take our measures wisely when it depends upon our present behaviour whether we shall have a morrow or no. There is nothing more glaringly evident than that the end of Being must put an end to enjoyment: therefore, he that takes a course, how satisfactory soever to his own mind, which must destroy him, acts imprudently, as he consults present satisfaction rather than the aggregate of it, wherein happiness properly consists. Nor am I moved with those ranting exclamations of the Stoics, that there is more joy in a day well spent than in years of sensual delights: I am sensible our pleasures are not all equal in degree, but I cannot conceive how so much enjoyment can be crowded into a small space of time as to make it worth our while to neglect years to come for the sake of it; for our organs can neither bear nor contain so large a measure. Such outcries are in the style of the dissolute and inconsiderate, as encouraging the same disregard to the future with the maxim they proceed upon, a short life and a merry. But the most fatal mistake men are apt to fall into, lies in their estimating pleasures according to the degree of them: for it has been made appear under the article of Pleasure, that we are much more beholden to those of the gentler kind, as adding more largely to the aggregate of satisfactions, than to the intense. Even our common diversions please more by the engagement of some pursuit they put us upon than by the joy of an acquisition. Nor shall we see cause to lay so much stress upon the raptures of virtue, when we reflect how many less worthy objects can give them as well for a time; a sudden turn of good fortune, a title of honour, a ribbon, whether blue, green, or red, the smiles of a mistress, a kind word, a delusive promise, the veriest trifle, will do it in proportion to the fondness there is for them: so that a day spent in the accomplishment of any eager desire carries as much intrinsic weight, abstracted from all considerations of the future, as a day spent in the exercise of virtue. Wherefore the preferableness of virtue does not arise so much from the transports she occasions as from the calm serenity and steady complacence of mind she insures, the satisfactory reflections she gives scope to, the attainableness of the desires

she raises, their compatibleness with one another, and their clearness from mischievous consequences: all which regard the time to come, and therefore cannot consist with whatever renders us incapable of good or evil for the future.

7. Yet neither can it be certainly concluded from men's enduring patiently for a good cause, that they feel those transports in supporting it which shall keep their minds in a state of continual enjoyment: for we may remember, that objects operate no less by the want than the desire of them; by our unwillingness to miss them than by the pleasure of moving towards them: and that there is an abhorrence of vice as well as a love of virtue When motives act this way they fall under the class of necessity, which always throws the mind into a state of uneasiness; nor is her condition instantly bettered upon doing well while it is done out of obligation, nor until we can come to do it upon liking. If this were Regulus' case, we must certainly pronounce him to have acted imprudently, and that Epicurus could not have done the same consistently with his principles, since he gave up all those enjoyments he might have expected in a longer life without receiving even present pleasure in exchange: and it had been for his benefit to have had no such strong attachment to his obligations. But not to derogate from the character of Regulus, let us suppose the utmost that can be supposed in his favour: let us allow him to have felt so great satisfaction in the nobleness of his conduct as drew out the sting of every evil that could befal him, and to have ended his days in exquisite delight amidst all the cruel torments that were inflicted upon him. Still this delight, how high soever in kind, must necessarily fall short in duration; and he had better have contented himself with smaller pleasures which might have compensated by their continuance for what they wanted in weight. Perhaps it may be said he had contracted so strong a detestation of treachery and abhorrence of infamy that he could not support himself in any quiet of mind under the reflection of them: so that being no longer capable of enjoying life with pleasure he chose to end it in a manner that might prove most satisfactory. But what brought him under this incapacity besides his own disposition of mind which could find a relish in nothing but what was just, becoming, and laudable? Another who had not the same squeamish disposition might have found enjoyments enow under general censure and self-reproach to make life desirable. Nor will it suffice to allege that he had good grounds at first for acquiring this disposition, which having once taken up it was not in his power to lay down again at pleasure: for it is not our business to find excuses for him in the weakness of human nature, which cannot suddenly change a rooted habit of acting or liking that we have long accustomed ourselves to, but to inquire whether this procedure of his were a weakness or no. And for this purpose we must imagine to ourselves a man who should have an absolute command over his inclinations to turn them this way or that as he saw proper, and consider how

such an one would use his power in the situation of Regulus. We cannot well suppose otherwise than that such a person would keep his eye constantly fixed upon the original rule of rectitude which drives solely at happiness. He would establish upon that bottom certain maxims of conduct and morality as he judged them conducive thereto: but he would never suffer himself to be enslaved by the maxims himself had established, nor let any subordinate means lead him away from his ultimate end. He would know that what is good and laudable at one time, may become mischievous and blameable by a change of circumstances. He might encourage in himself a love of probity and honour as yielding the largest income of satisfaction, yet if matters came to that pass as to make it appear they must have a contrary tendency, he would throw aside his scruples and turn his thoughts to such enjoyments as were to be had without them.

8. Upon the whole we are forced to acknowledge that hitherto we have found no reason to imagine a wise man would ever die for his country or suffer martyrdom in the cause of virtue, how strong propensity soever he might feel in himself to maintain her interest. For he would never act upon impulse nor do anything without knowing why: he would cultivate a disposition to justice, benevolence, and public spirit, because he would see it must lead him into actions most conducive to his happiness, and would place such confidence in his rules as to presume they carried that tendency in particular instances wherein it did not immediately appear. But it is one thing not to see directly that measures have such a tendency, and another to discern clearly that they have a contrary: and when they take away all capacity of further enjoyment, this is so manifest a proof of their inexpedience as no presumption whatever can withstand. Therefore he will never let his love of virtue grow to such an extravagant fondness as to overthrow the very purposes for which he entertained it.

9. I am apprehensive this conclusion will give offence to many as seeming to undo all we had done before in the service of virtue, by thus deserting her at last in time of greatest need when she is entering upon her most arduous undertakings. Yet I know not wherein we have acted unfairly either in the choice of our premises or deduction of inferences from them. We have searched every corner of the human breast, and found that all our motives derive either immediately or remotely from our own satisfaction and complacence of mind. Nature has given us this spring as the first mover of all our actions and ultimate object of all our contrivances. We have seen that reason cannot work upon her own bottom, but must fetch materials from elsewhere, for there is no reasoning unless from premises already known before we enter upon the consultation: therefore how far soever she may investigate her principles upon one another she must at last rest in such as she finds assigned her by sense and appetite, her office being only to correct their errors in the prosecution of their aims, to take better measures than they do, and lead to the same point discreetly and effectually

which they drive at preposterously and vainly. We have shown that the rules of morality stand on the foundation of happiness, that all notions of them which have not this basis to rest upon are fantastic and unstable: from whence it will follow that whenever, by the unlucky circumstances of our situation, this support happens to be withdrawn from under them, they must necessarily fall to the ground. Thus if our premises lead us to a conclusion we do not like, we may say with Doctor Middleton, that we cannot help it: for it was not our business to hunt for arguments in support of any cause whatsoever, but to take a careful survey of nature without prejudice or prepossession, and gather such observations as should appear resulting therefrom.

10. But it will be said that we have made only a partial and imperfect survey; for if we had availed ourselves of all the light nature would have afforded, we might have discovered that the end of life is not the end of Being, that our dissolution is but a removal from this sublunary stage to act upon some other, where our good works shall follow us and yield a plentiful harvest of happiness which had not time to ripen here: therefore a man does not act imprudently who perseveres in his virtues to the very last, although they manifestly tend to cut him off from life with all its enjoyments, and promise him nothing but pain and torment for the little time he has to continue upon earth. All this, consistently with the nature of my work, I can regard yet only as a suggestion, having found nothing in the progress of these researches to convince us of another life, or show the tendency of what we do here to affect us hereafter: yet neither have I found anything to disprove them, so that they remain proper matter of further inquiry. And since I find them maintained by persons of the greatest learning and judgment, and almost universally received among mankind, since they are in themselves matters of the utmost importance, and we see the limits of virtue cannot be ascertained without them, it would be inexcusable to pass them over unregarded, or without a thorough and careful examination; which not being easily dispatched, so as to settle those points to our satisfaction, I shall reserve them for the subject of another volume. Therefore it may be considered that I am but in the midway of my journey and what I may learn in the succeeding stages of it is yet uncertain; no because it is said in § 4 that I have suggested no arguments to induce vicious man near the end of his days to restrain his desires, and in this section, that I have found nothing to convince us of another life, ought it to be inferred from thence that I may not in my further progress? He that has a good opinion of religion, as having a rational and solid foundation to stand upon, ought to believe that I shall find such arguments and grounds of conviction as have not hitherto occurred, when prosecuting the subject with a fair and careful examination; and may presume that what now appears the most exceptionable part of my doctrine will then become capable of being turned to the advantage of religion, by showing its absolute

necessity to make the system of morality complete. In the meanwhile he cannot surely blame me for attempting to prove that the practice of virtue is the wisest course a man can follow to attain happiness even in this world; and to abate the scandal he might take at the exception made of a person in Regulus's situation, to whom a strong attachment to virtue would be a misfortune, he may please to reflect it is not unsimilar to a declaration of St. Paul's, that if in this life only we had hope we were of all men the most miserable. But one who is proceeding on a course of inquiries can take nothing for granted beforehand, he can draw his inferences only from the premises already collected, and must shape them in such manner as they shall naturally lead him. So that I must still adhere to my present conclusion, until seeing cause to alter it, for I cannot yield to any authority how great or general soever: this would be to depart from the plan I proposed at setting out, which was to try what lights I could strike out by the exercise of my reason, without calling in foreign aids; the extent of that, be it greater or be it less, is the line I am to run; and when I am come to the end of this line I must stop short, unless by another effort of reason I can chance to catch hold of another clue.

11. Nevertheless, I am very loath to leave the scrupulous reader with an ill impression of me upon him, though but for a season, and yet I do not know how to efface it myself, but must trust to his candour to do the best he can for me. Perhaps his good nature may suggest to him, that if this conclusion I pretend to abide by were my real ultimate opinion, I should not be so inconsistent with myself as to divulge it. For the discovery that a man's own safety will supersede all obligations, is of a nature not to be communicated without lessening its value to the owner: he may believe then I should have locked it carefully up, as a precious deposit to be reserved for private use, that if ever the case should so happen as that I cannot obey the dictates of honour and conscience, without endangering my person, I might avail myself of this secret to slip any own neck out of the collar: but it would certainly be for my interest to persuade the world that the duties of virtue are indispensable, and they ought to sacrifice everything for the good of the public, whereof I am a member, and must consequently share in the fat of their sacrifices. Therefore I think it is no unreasonable favour to expect, that he will suppose I have already run over in my own mind the matters I am to present him with by-and-by, and foresee something will occur among them, which will oblige me to recant the odious part of my doctrine, and come over to his sentiments. Let us then take leave in good hopes, that however we may part a little out of humour for the present, we shall grow better satisfied with one another upon our next conversation.

II. Theology

CHAP. XXVIII.
GENERAL GOOD.

IT has been frequently said, that if horses knew their own strength, they would never submit to all the drudgeries and hardships they are made to undergo. But it might with better justice be said, that if men knew the force of that reason and discretion in their power to exert, they would never submit to all those inconveniences, troubles, and vexations, they might relieve themselves from by a proper application of these talents. For there is industry and contrivance enough in quantity throughout the world, to supply all our wants and desires; they fail only through misapplication. We see daily how indefatigable men are in their several pursuits, how vigilant in watching opportunities to gratify a predominant passion, how attentive and sagacious in practising little artifices to compass a favourite purpose. But the misfortune is, that they spend their industry for the most part upon trifles, or in the service of some fond humour suggested accidentally by fancy, or at best for the accomplishment of narrow views, terminating solely upon themselves. Whereas the most beneficial enterprises can only be achieved by the united endeavours of many, concurring in some work that may redound to the advantage of them all. We see this exemplified in the benefits of society, where the operations of war, the conveniencies of commerce, and regulations of civil policy, are promoted by the persons concerned acting in partnership and concert. The common transactions of life go on more easily, and conversation becomes more agreeable, for a readiness to assist and oblige.

Nature designed the whole species for one society, as we may judge from the variety of productions serviceable to all, the different materials and opportunities for cultivating the art and sciences, which she has distributed about among the countries upon earth: so that no one of them furnishes the accommodations of life completely without communication with the rest. But folly, selfishness, and passion, have prevented our growing into a vigorous healthy body; we are a disjointed multitude, each caring only for himself, and thereby losing those innumerable advantages we might work out by our unanimity. Whose place is ill supplied by succedaneums, such as the desire of riches or honour, the lash of necessity or dread of dangers too glaring to escape our dull optics: which prove a feeble cement to join us into those partial societies and temporary engagements conveying the blessings we do enjoy. Nay, what is worse, our greediness and ill humour often drive us to endeavour the damage and displeasure of one another: which occasions a double waste of industry, by obliging others, who might employ it better, to apply theirs in relieving or defending themselves against our attacks. But unanimity cannot subsist without universal charity and unreserved good will, which nothing can better promote than the persuasion of there being a real connection of interests and mutual dependence of happiness among mankind, and this persuasion our doctrine of equality seems particularly well suited to propagate.

2. It was with a view to bring men better disposed towards one another that I entered upon my task. For how much soever I may have seemed to trifle and play the wanton sometimes, I have all along had grand designs in my eye, being no less than to contribute so far as in me lay, towards exciting a general concern and mutual benevolence among my fellow creatures. For I cannot help being persuaded that if this could be completely effected, so as that every man should become a friend and hearty well-wisher to every man, this alone would restore a paradise upon earth; although earthquakes should still continue to overthrow, tempests to sweep away, blights to destroy, and wild beasts to devour as usual: for I doubt not that the united skill and labours of mankind might remove all intolerable evils, and teach the art of bearing easily all that could not be avoided. Yet I am not so romantic as to think of completing this design, or even making any large stride towards it. But Rome was not built in a day, nor by the hands of a single laborer: yet years and ages are composed of days, and the most stupendous works performed by numbers made up of single labourers.

The world seems growing more humanized, more enlarged in their notions, and readier to take concern in distant joys and sorrows, than they were in former times: and as these advances are made insensibly by particular persons, each contributing a little towards promoting them, it becomes every one to lend a helping hand to so salutary a work, in such way as he finds himself best suited to take. As I have not much intercourse among mankind, nor acquired an expertness in the management of topics prevailing with the Many: it seemed that I could not do better than address myself to the thinking and studious, by collecting a chain of observations which might serve as a hint for them to improve, towards bringing themselves into a conformity of sentiment and openness of temper. For if, instead of entering the lists as adversaries contending for victory, they would consider one another as persons consulting together upon the methods of accomplishing a purpose they all had at heart: however they might vary for a while, they could not be long without discerning which were the best. And if they would employ their talents sincerely for the public good, in preference to any private views or favorite schemes or pre-contracted prejudices, they must quickly draw the rest of the world after them. For the multitude are ready enough to follow their leaders; nor ever desert them, unless enticed away by opposite leaders.

But to deal with the sagacious and deep-thinking one must go to the bottom of things, for they will not take up with strong assertions nor superficial appearances, how shining soever: but to bring them into one mind one must proceed upon premises they can examine themselves and approve of. Therefore they fail in their transactions among one another by dealing too much in abstractions, ideal differences of right and wrong, of laudable and blamable, and intrinsic value of rules and qualities: which as men's ideas vary infinitely, being modelled according to their several turns of thought, they can never settle to mutual satisfaction. For this reason I have endeavored to dig down to a foundation they will all agree strong enough to bear a superstructure: for I suppose the most righteous and unprejudiced will allow it commendable for a man to do what he can for himself, provided he do no hurt to another thereby, nor thwart any rule of Religion or duty. Therefore self-interest of itself is a proper consideration to put us upon action: and I have taken this for my basis to work upon. It must be owned indeed that all others propose happiness and truest interest, as the ultimate aim to be attained by the several systems: but then they either carry their road through the wilds of abstraction, or take large leaps from stage to stage, by which methods they do not render the continuity visible even to one another. Therefore I have been careful to keep my feet all along upon the solid ground of experience, employing such abstractions and reasonings from time to time as could be drawn thereupon, and attempting to trace the connection, step by step, from self-interest to the virtues: so that whoever thinks fit to follow me may do it without leaping hedges or flying in the air, and judge for himself in what particulars I have been defective. Only I must desire he will distinguish between excursions I make for illustration or for removing obstructions that would stop my passage or for other particular purposes, and the main parts of my road conducting directly towards the journey's end.

I have examined human nature and found that Satisfaction, every man's own satisfaction, is the spring that actuates all his motions. I have investigated the sources of satisfaction, which is conveyed for the most part through the channel of desire; observed that desire may be turned into new courses by good management; inquired what turns of desire afford the most copious stream; and shown that the ideas exciting desire, derive, nearly or remotely, from external and prior causes. I have then proceeded to the contemplation of external nature; and from thence attempted to rise to the Author of nature, together with so much as can be discovered from his works concerning his attributes and character: wherein there appears no weakness nor humour, no spark of arbitrary or inequitable disposition, but unreserved and unniggardly goodness. From this height I have returned downwards, to show that all causes in act derive their efficacy

and destination from the act of the First, exerted with certain foreknowledge and deliberate design of whatever should follow thereupon. I have
likewise scrutinized minutely the motions of freewill, explained the difference between necessity and certainty, and shown the consistence of liberty
with pre-appointment, whereby it appears that human action is among the
causes depending in a chain upon the First. From all this I have concluded
that all events, whether yielding enjoyment or trouble, effected as well by
the choice and activity of man as by chance or nature, were of the divine
provision: and this provision being made in perfect equity, that there is an
equality of happiness, upon the whole balance of good and evil, allotted
to every creature.

Thus far we have travelled already, and our next step shall be, from this
equality to deduce a reciprocal connection of interests among the creation;
from whence will naturally flow an universal charity and steady attention
to the general good. As to the methods whereby this is most effectually
promoted, these are copious enough to supply materials for another work,
if we should have strength and opportunity to undertake it: it is enough
that we furnish ourselves here with a fundamental and ruling principle of
action, in lieu of that we had established before. For we set out at first
with the position, that a man has nothing else to do than pursue his own
interests in such a way as his judgment shall represent most feasible and
effectual: nor need we still recant our opinion, but having found our own
interest indissolubly connected with that of others, we may discard our old
aim securely, and take up this, as answering the very purpose driven at by
the former; keeping our eye constantly upon it as a mark to direct us in
all our proceedings.

3. For if the accounts of all are to be set even, we can get nothing by
obtaining a little advantage at the expense of greater damage to another;
and lose nothing by submitting to some pain for procuring him a greater
pleasure. Because in the former case we depress his balance more than we
raise our own, and thereby cut ourselves off from so much of the expectations we were entitled to by the rule of equality as the difference amounts
to: in the latter we raise his balance more than we depress our own, and
thereby increase our future expectations in like proportion. For so if there
be two merchants in partnership, each of them during the course of trade
would think himself interested in the balance appearing from time to time
upon the other's books: and would judge it prudent to throw any branch
of trade into the other's hands, if it would turn to greater profit there than
in his own. Nor would it alter his measures, that his partner had a larger
balance of cash in hand already; for while he could supply himself by his
own industry, he would choose to do it that way rather than draw out of
what lay elsewhere in reserve for his future occasions.

Now it is the rule of equality, entitling each adventurer to a share in the
whole profits of the business, that constitutes a partnership; whether

imposed by the authority of a superior, or settled by mutual compact. For if a merchant sends his sons with a competent stock to trade in different parts of the globe, upon condition that when they return home, the gains of all shall be divided equally among them; this is a partnership as much as if they had entered into it by voluntary agreement: and the King's frigates ordered out upon a joint cruize, are as much partners as a company of privateers.

Therefore the universe may be justly regarded as an innumerable host of partners dealing together in the traffic of happiness: and it is our business to apply all our contrivance and industry towards improving the common stock, and adding to the quantity of enjoyments in nature wherever we can. It is no matter whether we do this in the hands of another or of ourselves, we shall advance our own benefit either way alike; because our share or interest must always rise and fall proportionably with that of the public. But there are disbursements to be made in all traffic: labour, trouble, danger, disappointment, self-denial, pain, and punishment, are the disbursements necessary in the commerce of nature; and the prudent merchant will grudge no expense likely to yield a larger return. Only he will manage parsimoniously, driving his bargains hard, that the cost may not run higher than the occasion absolutely requires; nor yet will he scruple to advance any sums because the returns may fall into other hands, for the common stock will be the object he has constantly at heart, as knowing himself so much the richer man as that can be made to increase.

4. Thus the general good becomes the root whereout all our schemes and contrivances, all our rules of conduct and sentiments of honour are to branch: and the centre whereto all our particular lines of direction are to point. But this general good, although much in men's mouths, seems but little understood, being supposed always to imply something redounding to the benefit of the whole community; whereas we are too inconsiderable to do any good whereof the universe may partake. Nevertheless, let it be remembered that the whole is made up of individuals; so that every pleasure we do our neighbour, is an addition to the quantity of happiness in nature. Just as a merchant, sending goods to one partner, which may be disposed of to great advantage, thereby enlarges the common stock, although the rest of the company should know nothing of the matter. Therefore whatever good we do to any particular creature, we do to the universe: agreeably to that expression of him who represented a community as their head. What ye have done unto one of the least of these my brethren, ye have done unto me.

But though universal good be promoted by the good of any single person, yet it is more promoted by what redounds to the benefit of numbers; which therefore deserves the preference whenever opportunity serves, or the two come into competition: and this is so evident, that nobody can doubt of it. Hence the mighty bustle commonly made with public spirit, which as bandied about in the world, is become an empty sound, with nothing of spirit in it; or used as a pretence to varnish over selfish designs; or employed as an artifice to bring others into a disinterested zeal, which those who recommend it laugh at in their sleeve as a weakness. But if such as have abilities would set themselves in earnest to trace the relation between self-interest and general through the channels of nature and Providence, in the manner I have attempted, they might perhaps clear the passage more demonstratively: and by their greater sagacity and skill in casting light upon objects, might render the connection visible to common apprehensions, so as to make them intimately persuaded of its reality, and embrace it as a practical principle of action. Nevertheless, to take off from their trouble as much as I can, since men are remarkably ingenious at starting objections against the best evidenced truths they do not like, I shall endeavour to obviate such as I apprehend may arise against this rule now laid down as the most prudential.

5. It may be alleged that the quantity of good and evil in nature is such and none other than God in his wisdom and bounty has thought proper to make it: and consequently the portion of each individual must be such precisely as falls to his share, according to the number of creatures existent, beyond the power of any thing to alter it. Therefore it matters not what good or hurt they bring upon their neighbour, because they cannot diminish the portion of either allotted to him, they can only anticipate the times of his receiving it: for if they do the former, he has so much less to expect; if the latter, so much less to fear, in the remainder of his period.

Now this allegation might have some colour of reason, if we knew the precise portion assigned to each creature, or if it were to be ascertained by an unalterable fatality: but we know not the one, and know the other, from our experience, not to be the case. So that whenever we do good, we see the immediate benefit of it; but we cannot see, nor rationally conclude, that some remote loss or damage shall ensue from it. And with respect to the portion, the whole measure of that is secured no otherwise than the several articles composing it, and the times of their being given: that is, not by a fatality, but by a provision of adequate causes. Let but men turn the tables, and they will see the hollowness of their excuse: for if another goes to hurt them, or debar them from taking the pleasures in their power, they will not bear to be told, it is only an anticipation or retardment of what they must receive some time or other. And in gratifications of desire or self-interest, they will not hear of a fatality; whereas in reality these matters are as much under appointment by the provision of causes as anything else whatever. Therefore let them only raise their desire to its proper object to wit, the advancement of good wherever feasible, and their objection will vanish of itself. I have endeavoured to make appear in the last Chapter but one, that the secret Will of God can be no guide to our conduct which we are to form upon the declared Will, evidenced to us by our reason judging upon the consequences of measures, or by rules built upon our former experience or upon the authority of those who know the tendency of actions better than ourselves; therefore we have nothing to do with appointments any further than as manifested to our apprehension. For the decree or determination of God is nothing else than the provision of causes adapted to each particular event; and the operation of those causes is requisite to execute the decree; but in matters within our power, our own deliberation and industry are among those causes; wherefore we must think and strive for ourselves notwithstanding the decree.

This is apparent in common affairs of life: for who that lives in plenty does not see that he has his daily bread appointed him by having the means in his hands of procuring it, for which he ought to be thankful? yet does not see at the same time that this appointment by no means supersedes his cares in sending to market and ordering his family? Thus, although the portion of happiness be of divine appointment, yet the application of our cares and industry, for conveying the parts of it administered by our own agency, is requisite and advisable. In these instances the Will of God is done by our Will: but that Will orders all things for the best. Yet though whatever we shall do must therefore be agreeable to his Will, and best to be done, because done: still this does not take away the use of judgment and deliberation to direct our choice between the several measures of conduct. If a man having it in his power to do something whereby he should get a thousand pounds seven years hence, should be told that whether he did it or let it alone, either way would be the best he could take: I make no doubt he would prefer that which afforded him a visible gain, rather than depend upon the unknown profit to arise from his rejecting it. So if, however we conduct ourselves, we shall unerringly pursue that unknown Best appointed by divine provision, it behoves us to take the way apparently best to our own judgment.

But men never employ these sophisms unless in justification of their gratifying some present fancy; whereas if they had any weight, they must avail against inclination as well as judgment, the omission of either being alike the best thing could have been done, whenever done: so that all choice and preference of any kind whatever will be taken away, and a total stagnation of activity ensue. But if between things equal in themselves, liking and fancy may cast the balance, surely the weights of reason and prudence are greater. Yet we cannot allow them intrinsically equal, for our fortunes in futurity, as well as present time, are in great measure of our own making: therefore if we hurt them by misconduct, what remains will be the quantity thought best to be allotted us by Divine Wisdom; and if we improve them, the quantity so increased will likewise be that thought best by the same wisdom. Thus the best we may attain by the road of virtue and discretion will be (if I may so speak) a better Best, than any we can arrive at through the paths of folly and indulgence.

6. Another handle may be taken for cavilling, from our having laid down that every evil is to be considered as the payment for a purchase of something more valuable: from whence it may be inferred that by plaguing and hurting another, we do him no injury, for we only compel him thereby to make an advantageous purchase. Or if the value of the estate and the price be settled by divine appointment, we only call upon him for a part of his payment, which it is all one whether he makes to-day or to-morrow, since he must have made it some time or other. But this may be answered in the same manner with the former; for we know not either the certain value of the estate or the price, nor whether one shall be enhanced in proportion to the other: therefore by doing hurt we visibly increase the payment, without knowing whether we shall increase the purchase.

Besides, by this rule it would be incumbent upon every man to make himself as miserable as possible, because by so doing he would purchase a larger fund of happiness: but I believe no man in his sober senses and dispassionate moods, ever run himself wilfully into miseries upon this account; nor unless called thereto by some rule of duty, which was a particular assurance that the sufferings he submitted to were worth his while to undergo. We know not what proportion of evil is necessary for the services of the universe, therefore ought to use all means in our power for lessening it, being well assured that we cannot reduce it lower than the sum imposed for the necessary services. The public taxes are a payment for the protection afforded by the state: yet he that should compel his neighbour to pay a shilling in the pound more than the law demands, or than he knows the exigencies of the state require, would be deemed to do an injury. So he who puts another to a pain or trouble from whence he sees not the benefit resulting, does him a wrong; by exacting a payment he cannot be assured would ever have been demanded.

7. But the most plausible exception lying against the expedience of labouring for the general good, arises from our inability to contribute so much towards it as to make our share worth the consideration. For it may be urged, if you had it in your power to do something that would make a thousand people happy for fifty years together: though this would seem a vast addition to the common stock of enjoyment, yet when you reflect what prodigious multitudes it is to be divided amongst, your own part will scarce amount to the value of once smelling at a rose. So there is no inducement to bestir yourself, because with your utmost endeavours you cannot make an addition to your own fortune sufficient to be perceived.

But let us consider, that if this doctrine were to prevail, most of the blessings of nature, the benefits of society, and conveniences of life, would be lost: the most valuable of which are procured by the operation of feeble, inconsiderable agents. The planets are holden in their orbits by the attraction of minute particles, undiscernible with a microscope, composing the body of the sun: the earth is clothed with pasture by little seeds, each whereof cannot throw up herbage enough to make a bite for a sheep: if we admit a Mundane Soul, the worlds are formed and the courses of nature kept in order, by spirits which singly could not heave a mote in the Sun beams. What is a single soldier in those armies that have kept the mightiest potentates in awe? If he lag behind you do not stop for him, or if he be slain you do not miss him. What is a private person's quota to those immense supplies supporting our armaments in all quarters of the globe? If he has not wherewithal to pay, the operations go on as before, and none but the collector or his nearest neighbours know anything of his failure. Yet a wise man, finding himself to have courage and ability for the service, would not desert in time of battle although there were no courts martial to overawe him: nor withhold his proportion of the taxes although his goods were liable to no distress. For he would regard what he contributes by his person or his pocket as entitling him to a share of the advantages procured by all the others he joins with: an object well worth his contemplation. Nor let it be made a discouragement that some unreasonable creatures refuse their helping hand: for there are enow concurring some way or other in the public service to render the benefits worked out by them a sufficient inducement to become one of their number.

8. But we need not undervalue our particular services because they yield but little profit: for though the performance of them cannot do much good, yet it may prevent great mischiefs which might have ensued upon the omission. The negligence of a single sentinel may give the enemy an opportunity of surprising a whole camp, and a little carelessness in placing a candle may produce a fire that shall burn down a whole town. Therefore we can never be too vigilant, because we can never know what waste of destruction may ensue upon the want of it. What though our persons be single and our efforts small, nobody can say what multitudes they may not affect, nor what tides of industry they may not excite. It is notorious of how spreading a nature both the virtues and the vices are: for example and sympathy diffuse the stream to all quarters from a single fountain: and a man may sometimes find that in his power wherein all mankind shall have concern in the consequences. Noah built his ark to save his little family consisting of eight persons: but in so doing he saved all the generations of men that have since overspread the earth. The founders of Religions and sects in philosophy, inventors of arts and sciences, though imparting their thoughts to a few, have thereby opened channels which overflowed whole nations and countries. And as we know not how far the people of the intermediate state stand affected by what passes here, nor what effect their transactions have upon the spiritual substance; it is not impossible nor improbable, that a single person may do that which shall be felt by the whole universe.

It may be said this might happen perhaps to extraordinary persons once in an age, but a private man never stands in a situation to work consequences that can possibly extend beyond the narrow circle of his acquaintance. But I would ask him how he knows that? For we have shown in our Chapter of Providence, that the affairs of the world are all complicated and interwoven among one another into one tissue: that the greatest events depend upon the minutest, and the constitution of the Roman empire, together with that of the kingdoms branched out from thence, might be determined by some such inconsiderable circumstance as the wearing a particular coloured riband upon a certain festival. So that there is no such thing as trifle in nature, every little incident and sudden fancy being provided for by perfect wisdom with a regard to the whole. For how narrow soever the views of creatures may be, God beholds the universe, and directs every little stroke in his all-comprehensive plan, so as to contribute its share towards the general good. Or if there be such things as trifles, they are so intermingled among the imperceptible springs of important events, that the most prying eye cannot distinguish them apart.

Therefore we ought always to stand upon our guard, and shape our minute motions by such discretion and regard to rectitude as is proper upon the occasion, for the chance of effecting what unseen good or escaping what unthought of evil may possibly depend upon them. For the chain of causes and effects runs to such immeasurable lengths and divides into so many unperceivable threads, that no man can be sure his manner of stirring the fire or buttoning his coat shall not be attended with consequences greater than he is aware of. But it would be in vain to take his measures upon consequences that human sagacity cannot investigate: therefore he has nothing to do with them, nor with anything else besides the rules of prudence, charity, propriety, and innocence, so far as in the present circumstances of the case he can discern them. For since the wisest men have always maintained that moral good is the ready road to natural, while he follows the best lights of his judgment, he may trust Providence for leading him unknowingly into all those secret advantages possible in his situation to be attained. For though God no doubt has appointed each of us his certain portion, yet he deals out to us, perhaps the whole, or at least a great part of it, by our own or one another's hands. For we have seen more than once before, that things certain may nevertheless depend upon human contrivance and industry. Therefore it behoves us to use the proper degree of circumspection as well in matters of trifle as of moment: because according to our conduct in either, our portion will be better or worse; and that in a measure greater than we think of, and large enough to deserve our notice and overpay the trouble of the acquisition.

9. Yet even supposing this was not the case, but that it were impossible for us, either directly or in consequence, to add so largely to the general fund as may raise the least perceivable difference in each private share; still there would not want encouragement to bestir ourselves: for it is not necessary that every particular profit must be divided among the whole

company, because the members may have equal shares, though assigned them out of different funds. Were there a million of traders dispersed up and down in different quarters, and destined to make the same fortunes, they might be divided into distinct partnerships of ten in a company, who might traffic and settle their balances from time to time among themselves, without intercourse among the other decads. Equality might still be preserved, provided there were an able superintendent of the whole, who should take care there were the like opportunities of trade among the several decads, or that particular persons were removed in due order from a less to a more gainful fellowship. And, in fact, we find the creation, so far as our experience reaches, divided into distinct species and limited societies, the effects of whose actions extend no further than to a certain number of those with whom they have intercourse. Nor can we presume otherwise of those unseen consequences depending upon the secret concatenation of causes, which however they may in part extend to innumerable multitudes, are likely to affect some particular class of beings principally, with whom we stand nearest concerned. And upon removal into a new fellowship, the rule of equality will require that the place assigned us should be such as may secure to us the balance due upon our former account. For though these changes be brought about by natural courses, yet God, being the author and disposer of nature, establishes all her provisions in equity; as well those respecting the changes from one state into another, as those regulating accounts in the same. So that by our diligence in the branch of trade before us, we determine what interest we shall have in the branches to be allotted us hereafter. Thus, in every stage of being, the main of what profits we can make will accrue to the benefit of such a competent number as that our proportion shall remain weighty enough to be felt in our hands.

Or even if we suppose all the gains accruing thrown into the general fund upon account of the whole partnership, there is no necessity they should be drawn out again by little fractions from each, so minute as to reduce them below our notice. Could a man raise a profit of a thousand pounds, to receive it again by a farthing a year, he might despise the addition of a farthing to his annual income; but if it came by fifties or hundreds of pounds at a time, he would find the convenience of them for his occasions. So the share of happiness we earn by some effort of our industry, being dealt out to us in serviceable portions, will answer our future wants some time or other, without detriment to our fellow-creatures receiving theirs in like manner. This would evidently be the case upon admitting an universal rotation: for then every person falling in some part of his course into the place of every other, must receive the very same good, both in kind and quantity, as he does to his neighbour; and if he can do that which redounds to many, he will reap the benefit of it so many times as there are persons to whom he has done service. But should there be no such exact retaliation in kind, yet equity requiring that the good befalling one should likewise befall another, there must be a compensation equal in value. Therefore, though we do not receive just the same sized notes, or the same species of coin we carried in, we shall be sure of receiving the full amount in good negotiable cash.

So that since the allegory of books has been employed by the best authorities, we may consider the provisions of Heaven as an universal bank, wherein accounts are regularly kept, and every man debited or credited for the least farthing he takes out or brings in. All the good we procure to another, the labour and self-denial we go through prudently, and evil we suffer unavoidably, are written down as articles in our favour; all the evil we do, the fond indulgences we give into, or good we receive, entered per contra as so much drawn out of our cash. Perhaps something may be taken out for the public services, but then we have the benefit of this in the public conveniences and protection whereof we partake; but the remainder lies placed to each private account for answering our calls or supplying our occasions.

And this is a better bank than that of England to keep our current cash; I shall not say, for its greater security, because the monied men of this and foreign nations think the other secure enough; but the Bank of England give no interest upon their notes, whereas the Bank of the Universe improve what we have lying there to immense advantage, far beyond what could be made in script by any Jew or clerk in the secretary office let into secrets; and the application to our several occasions lies under wiser management than our own. If I have an account with the Bank of England, and should take it into my head, because other folks are fond of the like, to throw away a large sum in punch and ale for gaining me the huzzas of a drunken mob, and procuring me an opportunity of serving my country which I want abilities to use; or to buy a horse of noble lineage descended from Turkish or Barbarian ancestors to run at Newmarket: upon applying to the cashier in Threadneedle-street for a thousand pounds, he will instantly order payment without asking questions: though I may want the money grievously next year to make up a portion for my Serena or my Sparkler. Or should I chance on some distant journey to be reduced low in pocket, if I have no checked paper along with me, I cannot draw for a single six-pence to buy me a little bread and cheese.

But the directors of the bank above have constant intelligence from all parts of the universe, and their runners traversing to and fro among their customers: so that whatever I have belonging to me there, if I call for a sum to squander away upon some vice or folly, though I beg and pray never so hard, the cashier will not issue me a farthing, because he knows it had better be kept in reserve for more necessary occasions. But if I chance to fall into distress in any disconsolate spot of nature, where a supply would do me real service, though I should not see the danger of my situation, nor have sent advice with the needful per post, I shall have the runner angel privately slip the proper sum into my hand at a time when I least expect it. So we have no need to trouble ourselves about the improvement of our money there, or the laying it out for our particular uses: it is our business to use all our judgment and industry and vigilance for throwing as much as we can continually into bank. Yet this does not hinder us from taking present enjoyments from time to time, where innocent and lying properly within our reach: for though this be a lessening of our future demands, yet the future were of no avail if it were never to be present; nor is money good for anything but to be spent, provided it be spent prudently, and no more given for things than they are worth.

10. Nor have we concern only with the articles of our own account, but with those likewise of other persons; from whence we may receive a pleasure not to be found in the ordinary course of worldly commerce. If on attending at the earthly accountant office, the eye, while the clerks turn over the leaves of their books, happens to catch upon somebody else's balance, which appears ten times larger than our own, one may be mortified to find oneself so inconsiderable in point of riches, compared with him.

But in the accounts of Providence, a like discovery could prove no such mortification: for we dealing all in partnership, the profits whereof are to be made equal to each in some shape or other in some part of our period, whatever virtues, talents, or successes we see elsewhere, adding more largely to the common stock than we can do ourselves, must become matter of rejoicing rather than vexation. Because the rule of equality insures to us that we shall either immediately partake of the fruits gathered therefrom, or at some future time be instated in a branch of trade we see to be more profitable than that now under our management.

And this consideration, duly attended to, must put an end to that humour of depreciating the characters, the abilities, and the enjoyments of other creatures, so generally prevailing among mankind. For as the more good, so the less evil we can find in others, the better it is for ourselves. For my part, I am so far from any temptation to believe myself the happiest of my species, that I would thank anybody who should prove me the most miserable creature in the universe: I do not mean, who should bring mischief upon me, or discover misfortunes in store which I do not know of, for this would be madness to desire: but should show the condition I now stand in, such as it is, inferior to that of every other being: so that the common labourer, the galley-slave, the negro, the flea, the mite, and every departed soul, possessed greater enjoyments than those within my reach. Such a discovery would afford me a most ravishing prospect of nature, and without hurting me in present, give me more hopeful expectations for the future: for since I am not always to continue in the same state, I could make no change unless for the better.

But I am too sensible of the blessings vouchsafed me, to be persuaded into this imagination: on the contrary, when I behold miseries anywhere appearing far greater than anything I ever underwent, which yet I have found troublesome enough; it raises, besides a fellow feeling for the sufferer, a melancholy reflection to think that the lot of existence is subjected to so severe a condition. However, my partiality to wish it easier makes me ready to embrace every evidence that offers for believing it so: and it is with pleasure I find alleviations, from custom, difference of apprehension or insensibility, for every natural evil; and extenuations from ignorance, inadvertency, and surprise, for every moral. Or if this cannot be done, find benefits resulting therefrom; enjoyments and advantages compensating them.

Thus the doctrine of equality tends directly to nourish benevolence, mutual esteem, good wishes, and favourable judgments, between fellow-creatures; and how much soever it may appear at first sight to encourage indolence, by making men trust to the diligence of their partners, yet when fairly examined, it proves as strong a recommendation and solid ground of care and industry in particular persons, as any principle whatever. Therefore, those who should not admit it, might yet allow it excuse for sake of the desirable ends aimed at by proposing it to their consideration.

III. Lights of Nature and Gospel Blended

CHAP. XXXV.
RULE, CUSTOM, AND FASHION

As much as we may affect to define Man a reasonable creature, daily experience will manifest to him that observes it attentively, that reason has a very small share in our motions: it can only direct some of the principal of them, but the intermediate spaces are occupied by trains of ideas and impulses rising mechanically in our imagination: and it is well if the principal be directed by reason, for the further we can extend its authority so much the happier for us; but with all our diligence we can never make it complete, but the machine will still retain a greater influence upon our conduct than we can gain for ourselves. For we many times enter upon courses of action unthinkingly, and in the prosecution of them proceed scarce with any consciousness of the minute steps we take; if reflection does plainly mark out our path, we do not always follow it, being hurried a quite contrary way by the impetuosity of passion or fondness of desire; and when best disposed to take the benefit of our understanding, it proves but an imperfect guide. For the proper goal for reason to lead us to, is the greater good, or balance of enjoyment to result from all the consequences of an action; but these it is seldom quick-sighted enough to discern so as to make a fair computation among them.

This being our constitution, it is in vain to think of setting our understanding to lead the active powers continually by the hand, or expect to hold in contemplation the whole expedience of every measure we take; the exercises of that faculty are best bestowed in habituating the internal wheels of the machine to run spontaneously in such trains as appear most eligible when the lights of reason shine clearest, or the eye of Contemplation has the fullest, distinctest prospect in view; and in storing up rules, maxims, and judgments in the memory, which may serve occasionally for immediate direction in shaping our conduct.

For in time of action we have not leisure to examine the expedience of things, we should make no despatch among them if we were to go about it, but must follow implicitly the rule resolved on, or the judgment occurring; besides that, what reflection we are masters of is little enough to guide us in making application of them to the particular circumstances before us: so that when we act most rationally we cannot so properly be said to know why, as to remember that we formerly did know, nor do we march immediately under the banner of reason, but under the leading of those subaltern impulses which she has chosen for our governors.

Since then this is the case with men of the best natural and improved understandings, what can be expected from the bulk of mankind who want capacity or leisure to trace the long and intricate line of expedience? to tell them of a perpetual dependence upon their reason is the same as bidding them be different creatures than they were made: they must have a clue put into their hands by which they may find their goal without knowing where it lies, for their goal is happiness, but their clue will sometimes lead into labour, trouble, and uneasiness, a road by which they little think to find it: and it behoves every man so far as he is able, to lend a helping hand towards spinning the clue. For we were neither born nor talented for ourselves alone, we are citizens of the universe, inhabitants of the little corner thereof; the dirty pellet where we are now stationed, and whatever we can do for her compatriot reptiles crawling about us, is the best thing to be done for ourselves.

But rule, custom, and fashion are the engines by which men may be drawn into an expedience they do not discern: therefore we ought to be very cautious of weakening the authority of a good rule because we may fancy it needless for ourselves, much less because it lies under some present inconvenience. It were to be wished, that rules could be formed attended with no inconvenience or mischief; but in this elementary globe, the off-spring of a chaos not yet grown to perfect symmetry of parts, we must expect to find nothing good without its alloy, so shall do wisely to take the good with the bad; better submit to one, than lose the other.

2. Rule is the substitute of reason to direct in times of darkness when there are not lights, a blaze sufficient for informing the understanding, and to restrain the rovings of appetite by its authority: but to do the latter there must be an attachment to it, and it must itself have grown into something of an appetite, for else it will remain an unavailing speculation which can only serve to make our errors wilful, because it is the departure from a known rule which renders a procedure faulty; agreeably to what St. Paul has remarked, that where there is no law there can be no transgression.

But it is necessary there should be many rules to answer the several exigencies that may occur, for where they are few, they will be too general to serve for direction in particular cases, without a greater strength of reason than we have to employ: but when numerous, it is unavoidable that they must sometimes clash, and hence arise the perplexities we meet with in the practice of morality; for where there is but one rule applicable to the business in hand, the road is plain, so that we cannot miss of it unless by want of resolution to execute what we know; but when two rules point to opposite measures, it is not always easy to know whether we have taken the right, or the wrong.

A man is urged by his benefactor to what he thinks not quite expedient for the public, his service is due to both, which then shall he prefer? why the public undoubtedly, whose interests he lies under a higher obligation of pursuing than those of any single person whoever: so you think here is a clear decision of the point if he have but virtue enough to follow it; and indeed there is in matters of importance, but is the decision equally clear in things of smaller concern? what if his friend desires French wine, must he not gratify him for fear of encouraging a trade detrimental to the public? for a man may be faultily scrupulous, as well as laudably conscientious: but who can distinguish precisely in all cases between trifles, and matters of consequence to the public, which no rules of civility, custom, or private obligation ought ever to supersede? and in common transactions there is a rule of justice and of equity requiring an exact impartiality to all, yet something is due to favour and to private prudence; but it is hard to settle the precise boundaries between them so as never to stand at a loss in what instances we are to side with a friend, or deal equitably with a stranger, to take care of ourselves in a bargain, or proceed with an honest, open simplicity.

These difficulties have been made the subject of declamations wherewith to exercise scholars in the art of prudence; and we may find some of them canvassed in Tully's offices: but it is impossible to smooth them all, nor should we be much gainers if they could be totally removed, because they put us upon exerting our understanding to extricate ourselves out of them. Experience shows the little avail of those tomes of casuistry which have been compiled in former times, attempting to frame rules for every occasion that can happen, rules for governing the exceptions to be made in those rules, and settling the precedence among them: if such a scheme could be completed so as to suit every one's apprehension, we should then live by apprehension alone, having no use for our rational faculty to deliberate, to weigh, to balance, and strike out new lights for ourselves.

But we have all some little portion of understanding given us which will admit of improvement by continual use, and though we can seldom act entirely by reason we may often take assistance from it in the construction and application of our rules, in comparing them together, penetrating into the spirit of them, and trying them by the more general from whence they branched.

If whenever the eye sees double so that the point of rectitude appears on opposite sides, we could look along the line of expedience to its origin the greater good, we might then infallibly distinguish the reality from the appearance: but since opportunities for such large discernment very rarely happen, the sole remedy to supply the want of it lies in determining the precedency of our rules, and settling the degrees of authority among them, so that we may know which ought to supersede another by the shock we should feel upon breaking through it: but then great care must be taken, that some secret prejudice do not intrude in the decision, and the vexation of disappointing some favourite inclination be not mistaken for the shock of an offence against rectitude; for it is very common for self-interest to pervert judgment, and for desire to assume the garb and likeness of a rule.

Therefore it is the part of every man to add what he can to the sanction of salutary rules, and preserve the subordination among them, which he may be encouraged to do for his own sake as well as that of the generality; for nobody can attain a thorough knowledge of all points necessary for his conduct so as to proceed by science in all the several branches of it, but he that is able to prescribe in some things may be glad to follow the leading of his neighbours in others. Nor how well soever he may be qualified in point of skill to prescribe, has any of us authority enough to attempt it with probability of success; therefore we shall be most serviceable by joining in with our example and recommendation to add weight to the best of those which are already prevailing.

3. But as the best plants are apt to luxuriate if not carefully watched and skilfully tended, so the attachment to rules sometimes grows too strong, making them a clog instead of a help to our motions; the hunger and thirst after righteousness turns into a vitiated appetite producing righteousness overmuch, and the love of rectitude becomes a preciseness and rigidity unpliant to the common occasions of life. This indeed seldom happens, and then it is by an attachment to one or two favourite rules in neglect of all the rest, for while we pay a due regard to them all they will moderate one another, or submit to the moderation of sober judgment. But as they are not all to be learned at once, for knowledge comes by slow degrees, I should wish to see young people a little overscrupulous in adhering to the few they are acquainted with, for the same reason that Cicero liked better to find his scholar in rhetoric exuberant than barren; because luxuriance is much easier cured than sterility, as a vigorous plant may be pruned with less trouble than you can nourish up a weakly. For the overstrict will run themselves into inconveniences which must teach them experience to correct their error, but the licentious can never be made sensible, how severely soever they suffer by their licentiousness, because having no observation they cannot profit by experience; besides in one case you will have appetite, the natural propensity to ease and pleasure, and the world to assist you, whereas in the other they will all join strongly with the enemy.

The greatest mistakes spring from an apprehension of intrinsic value in rules, whereas neither the rules of religion, nor of rectitude, nor of honour, nor of prudence, are good in themselves: they are only measures tending to a good beyond, they are expedients to make up for our short-sightedness, and supply the place of reason; therefore, when recourse can be had to the principal, the authority of the substitute is superseded. So it behoves us to study the uses of our several rules, and where they can be discerned, no attachment to the letter ought to withhold us from procuring the spirit, or gaining the end, proposed therein by any methods most effectual for the purpose.

But then the discernment ought to be very clear, for the presumption lies always strongly on the side of received rules; nor must the judgment be passed upon a single inconvenience, but computation likewise be made of the mischiefs that may ensue at other times, either to the public or ourselves, upon invalidating their force. Such discernment is most likely to be had where it appears evidently there has been an alteration of circumstances, which may render a rule hurtful that was highly beneficial before, or where it has been palpably misunderstood, or where there is a peculiarity of situation incompatible with the practice of it.

But though rules ought to be founded on reason, sometimes the reason is none other than for regularity and method sake, in which case they may be so far arbitrary or accidental as to give a preference between forms perfectly indifferent before. If there be a long causeway with a hollow way by the side, it is all one whether the passengers going and coming give each other the right hand or the left, yet when one has been pitched upon, it would cause great confusion to break into it. Men acting in concert can perform much more than if each were left to take his own way, but there is no uniting forces unless all will submit to some rule: and a single person may dispatch his work quicker by adhering to the method he had prescribed himself at first, though perhaps there are a hundred other methods which might have answered his purpose as well. One principal benefit of government and subordination is that the words of a superior may be a rule to his dependants, whereby numbers are made to join in the same work, and act as effectually as if the strength of all could be gathered into a single person.

4. The proper sanction of rules is fear, shame, or obligation; there is always something irksome and restrictive in them which we do not choose, but submit to through necessity: to rule is the same as to govern, and the ruling passion does not deserve its appellation for the pleasure it gives when followed with full acquiescence and consent of mind, but because it acts as an imperious tyrant driving upon difficulties and fatigues, and forcing us to do things against our judgment. Indeed, while we can hold the benefits attainable by a rule strongly in contemplation, the desire of them may take out all spice of irksomeness belonging to it, yet still the end remains the sole object of our choice, and we pursue the means because obliged thereto by their being necessary to compass our end. When rules are grown familiar and the practice of them spontaneous, so that it becomes easier to follow them than abstain, they lose their essence though they retain their name; being now no longer rules governing the conduct, but habits or ways of acting fallen currently into, without care or reflection.

But the language of mankind is not so accurate as to keep the terms always strictly to the same signification, therefore it is usual to call those habits by the name of rules which were first contracted under the idea of obligation, by the necessity of escaping some mischief or insuring some desirable benefit. Hence comes it that there is a wide difference between leading a regular life, and living by rule; the one is pleasant, easy, smooth, and dispatchful, the other unengaging, toilsome, stiff, and generally wasteful both of time and strength.

Persons who live by rule, though of their own framing, and many times whimsical enough, are not esteemed to pass their time the most pleasurably while they make a point of proceeding in certain particular forms and methods, for they still act under an obligation though imposed by themselves; their movements are not a whit the less a task for being a task of their own setting. Wherefore prudence should incline us to set ourselves such tasks as may grow into engaging and profitable habits, for then we may get into a course of acting according to rule without being restrained by it: that this is possible, appears in matters of language; those who speak correctly never deviate from the rules of grammar, yet never are guided by them nor once think of them: it is well known how laborious are the exercises of schoolboys while forced to put their words together by rules, but when the structure of phrase has become familiar to them, there is an end of rule, whose use ceases in proportion as a regularity of diction grows to be habitual: and we learn upon the authority of Cicero, that the rules taught by rhetoricians were not of their own invention but drawn from observation upon the ways of managing an argument practised by orators. So that the purpose of rules is nothing more than to lead into that regularity of speech, and of working the springs of persuasion, which was first acquired without any rule at all; and the effect of proficiency in learning is to get rid of the necessity of rules.

The same it is with the arts of religion, morality and prudence; we must submit to rules at first, some of them irksome and rigorous enough to the novice, and this is the thorny way leading into virtue; but trouble is not wisely undertaken unless for the sake of that ease which is the child of expertness, therefore our business is by a steady adherence to salutary rules to bring the mind as fast as possible into a liking of them and turn them into habits; for then imagination will be disciplined to run spontaneously in regular trains most conducive to our benefit, and desire will anticipate judgment by prompting continually to the very courses which that would recommend: and then are we past the thorny way, and arrived in the delightful champaign, where all is smooth, and clear, and engaging.

Nevertheless, while grovelling in this vale of mortality, we shall still find many quarters of the country beset with the like thorns, through which we must open ourselves a passage by the like resolution and perseverance, striving to work as many beaten roads as we can, that we may range about in pursuit of our own advantages and those of our neighbour, with the better ease and dispatch.

5. There is an affinity between rule, habit, and custom, for they all tend to produce a uniformity of conduct, to prevent our motions from being desultory, and join them together into certain courses. Rule, as I said before, is generally founded on obligation, and begun with some degree of reluctance; but custom is oftener fallen into accidentally, or introduced by convenience, or if it were sometimes imposed by rule, the origin is usually forgotten, and men follow it without other reason than because they see it followed.

There is often a very strong attachment to customs, not only for the trouble and awkwardness found in going an unbeaten road, but for the veneration they are had in, which raises a kind of a scruple of conscience against departing from them; they are conceived to be good in themselves, to make a rectitude; for it is a constant argument among the common people, that a thing must be done, and ought to be done, because it always has been done. History produces instances of insurrections that have been raised by endeavouring to put people out of an insignificant, and perhaps inconvenient custom; and every nation esteems its own customs wise, becoming, and laudable, but those of other countries absurd and ridiculous. Many forms in religion have been held sacred and stickled for, tooth and nail, without other reason assigned, than their ancient and general usage, and you may observe people, very different with respect to the principles of their sect, submit to many inconveniences, rather than be put out of the way they have been accustomed to.

Nor does the prevalence stop at actions, it reaches to the sentiments too; for men have as high a veneration for their usual ways of thinking as of behaviour; what they never questioned in their own minds, and never heard questioned, passes for an innate principle, a self-evident truth, needing no evidence to support it, and which no evidence can overthrow. It was upon this foundation I suppose that Lucretius asserted so roundly that nothing except body can touch or be touched, and that there can be no understanding unless in a human shape, because he had never seen an intelligent creature in any other. And this I suspect lies at the bottom of all speculative atheism; for being constantly accustomed to the operations, and to seek for the causes of all phenomena in the qualities of matter, men cannot bring their imagination to depart from its customary track so far as to conceive any other power to operate.

This likewise makes it so extremely hard to distinguish between creation and composition, or change of form, between essence and existence, between the accession of quality and production of substance, because it has been always customary to apprehend things by their qualities, to give them new names when in assortment which they had not while separate, and esteem them different Beings from their constituent parts. This keeps men so little acquainted with their real selves, and wherein their personality consists, because they have been constantly accustomed to denominate the person by the bodily appearance or the character, and because they never remember themselves existing without organs, therefore count the organs component parts of themselves.

Nevertheless custom has its uses, and those not inconsiderable, as well for thinking as acting; our surest reasonings proceed upon principles already known and never doubted of, some customary apprehensions must serve for the basis even of those discoveries which wean us from others; our knowledge of an immaterial agent springs from having constantly observed upon every close examination into the operations of matter, that it never begins nor increases an impulse, but only transmits precisely the same it had received from elsewhere.

Custom begets expertness and renders things easy which were difficult and irksome before; it gives us our erect posture, for nature made us prone like the beasts, and endows us with speech which one cannot suppose the first men learnt, nor can you teach your children by rule and grammar; it cements society, for nothing knits men so firmly together as a communion of usages, and if you know the customs of a country you may know where to find company, and how to join with them in their ways of proceeding; it is the retailer to dispense the useful imports of science among the vulgar, in whom many practices of Religion, of good polity, the management of their children, and measures of private prudence, are mere custom, though introduced originally by wisdom, extensive discernment, and mature deliberation; nor is there any merchant in knowledge of so universal correspondence as to import commodities of all kinds, but must still resort to the shop of general usage for some things, nor has a better reason to give for many of his proceedings, than because other people do the like: it multiplies engagements, and gives currency to the business of life, for most men would stand idle unless when some urgent desire is afloat, utterly at a loss how to dispose of themselves if there were not certain customary methods of employing their time. Though it influences by attraction without addressing to the reason, yet it always carries the presumption of reason on its side, for nobody would begin a pernicious or inconvenient custom; and sometimes it makes reason, for where there are several roads of equal length leading to the same place, the beaten is always the smoothest, the safest, and the most sociable.

But customs may become bad by an alteration of characters or circumstances, or may have been fallen into unthinkingly without sufficient information on the inconveniences attending them: therefore it is dangerous to contract such an attachment for old usages, as no experience nor consideration can loosen, for nothing ought to supersede the authority of reason when the judgments of it are clear: to follow any inferior guide implicitly is slavery, not discipline: but then we ought to be very sure of having a good warrant for the liberties taken with prevailing customs, for the burden of the proof lies strongly upon him that would impeach them; no man is justified in breaking them, because he does not see their expedience, nor unless he plainly sees a mischief attending them.

WILLIAM PALEY

The Principles of Moral and Political Philosophy
(1785; 2nd edn. 1786)

Bk. I, Chs. VI–VII

Bk. II, Chs. I–IX

Bk. VI, Ch. III

William Paley (1743–1805)

Biographical Note

Paley's paternal family came from Langcliffe, in the parish of Giggleswick, Yorkshire. In 1734 his father, William (c. 1710–1799), graduated from Christ's College, Cambridge, the traditional place of learning for Paley men since the early seventeenth century. The following year he was appointed vicar of Helpston, Northants., and went to live in nearby Peterborough where he was a minor canon of the cathedral. In July 1742 the elder Paley married Elizabeth Clapham (d. 1796) of Stackhouse, Giggleswick. Their eldest son, William, was born in July 1743, and was followed by three daughters. In 1745 Paley's father was appointed headmaster of Giggleswick School, where his son received his early schooling and, later, a scholarship to attend Christ's College. In November 1758 Paley was admitted as a sizar at Christ's, matriculated the next year, and graduated with a BA in 1763 as Senior Wrangler, after studying under Anthony Shepard (mathematics and natural philosophy) and Backhouse (logic, metaphysics and moral philosophy, largely discussing Locke, Clarke and Hutcheson).[1] In his examination, he argued against capital punishment, and discussed whether eternal punishment was contradictory to the divine attributes.

From 1763 to 1766 Paley was a schoolmaster and tutor in Greenwich. He sustained an early interest in law by attending trials at the Old Bailey. In 1765 he won a Cambridge prize for a dissertation in Latin prose, arguing that Epicurean philosophy was 'far more favourable to virtue and happiness, than the rigid doctrines' of the Stoics.[2] According to LeMahieu 'this critique of the ancient moralists . . . revealed a nascent utilitarianism'.[3] On taking his MA in 1766 Paley became a Fellow of Christ's, where he remained for ten years. In 1768 he became a tutor, teaching Backhouse's old courses. His fellow tutor was John Law, the son of Edmund Law and a friend since 1762. Paley lectured on Locke in the first year, then went on to Clarke's *Being and Attributes of God*, lectures which anticipated his *Natural Theology: or, Evidences of the Existence and Attributes of the Deity, collected from the Appearances of Nature* (1802).[4] The moral lec-

---

[1] George Wilson Meadley, *Memoirs of William Paley, D.D.*, 2nd edn., corrected and enlarged (Edinburgh 1810), p. 11.
[2] Meadley, *Memoirs of William Paley, D.D.*, p. 41.
[3] D. L. LeMahieu, *The Mind of William Paley: A Philosopher and His Age* (Lincoln 1976), p. 10.
[4] Meadley, *Memoirs of William Paley, D.D.*, pp. 77–78.

tures which he gave in the third year formed the basis for *The Principles of Moral and Political Philosophy* (1785).[5] A student later said that as a lecturer Paley made everything interesting, and notes from his lectures were highly sought after.[6] He became Senior Dean in 1775. On 6 June 1776 Paley married Jane Hewitt (d. 1791), the daughter of a Carlisle spirit merchant. They produced a family of four sons and four daughters. In 1789 Paley refused the offer of the Mastership of Jesus College, Cambridge. He was granted a DD in 1795 after the publication of *A View of the Evidences of Christianity* (1794). In December of that year Paley married Catherine Dobinson of Carlisle.

In his clerical career Paley was a noted pluralist, ostensibly because this was the only way to finance his family. Paley once remarked 'though I am a pluralist in preferment, I am a much greater pluralist in children'.[7] He was ordained by the Bishop of London on 21 December 1767. After 1769, he was chaplain to Bishop Edmund Law of Carlisle, and became the Whitehall preacher 1771–76. Thanks to Law, from 1775 to 1805 Paley was Rector of Musgrave, Westmorland, where he attended only rarely to preach a sermon. Between 1776 and 1793 he was vicar of Dalston, near Carlisle, as well as being vicar of Appleby from 1777 to 1789.[8] In 1780 Paley was appointed to a stall in Carlisle Cathedral, and from 1782 to 1805 he was Archdeacon of Carlisle and Rector of Great Salkeld, Cumberland. His main publications followed this appointment, but did not lead to the bishopric anticipated by his clerical contemporaries. Paley received several other clerical sinecures which augmented his income, estimated at £900, out of which he had to pay his curates.[9] In 1795 he became Rector of Bishop Wearmouth, Durham, this final preferment bringing him an additional £1200 a year. For the last ten years of his life, he spent nine months in Durham, and the three spring months at Lincoln, where he was sub-dean of the Cathedral.[10]

Paley's Yorkshire background remained with him. Thrifty, humorous and down to earth, in old age he shocked an intellectual visitor, Henry Digby Best, by complaining about the discomfort of a small rush-seated chair thus: 'I hate these nasty little chairs, they sink in the middle and *throost*

5 British Library Add. Mss. 12,079, Paley's notes on moral and political thought, partly reproduced in Edmund Paley's edition of *The Works of William Paley*, 7 vols. (London 1825), i. 142–61; see LeMahieu, *The Mind of William Paley*, p. 10, and Meadley, *Memoirs of William Paley, D.D.*, p. 79.

6 LeMahieu, *The Mind of William Paley*, p. 10.

7 Meadley, *Memoirs of William Paley, D.D.*, p. 161.

8 Citing the episcopal register, Martin L. Clarke says 1777–1785; *Paley: Evidences for the Man* (London and Toronto 1974), p. 30.

9 Clarke, *Paley: Evidences for the Man*, p. 32.

10 Ernest Barker, 'Paley and His Political Philosophy', in *Traditions of Civility* (Cambridge 1948), p. 206.

one's goots up into one's *brains*.[11] Paley died on 25 May 1805 at Lincoln, and was buried in Carlisle Cathedral.

As a fellow at Cambridge Paley belonged to the Hyson Club, a latitudinarian group formed in 1757 or 1758.[12] Other members included John Law, John Jebb, and Richard Watson. All were interested in education and the reformation of the Cambridge system. They also shared utilitarian sentiments. Law wrote favourably of John Gay's utilitarian definition of virtue, and Richard Watson, whose liberal attitudes condemned him to remain Bishop of Llandaff longer than any other man in British history, argued in one of his tracts that 'there is not a single precept in the Gospel . . . which is not calculated to promote our happiness'.[13] In addition, they each agreed that rational inquiry and tolerance in religious matters should be promoted and free discussion encouraged.[14] Members of the Hyson Club became involved in the controversy over subscription to the Thirty-Nine Articles. In 1766 Francis Blackburne published *The Confessional*, while five years later John Jebb was at the forefront of the meetings held at the Feather's Tavern. The subsequent petition was signed by almost all the Club members. Although Paley, claiming that he could not afford a conscience, did not sign the petition, he defended Edmund Law against the criticisms of Thomas Randolph in *A Defence of the 'Considerations on the Propriety of Requiring a Subscription to Articles of Faith', in Reply to a Late Answer from the Clarendon Press* (1774).[15] The arguments contained in this pamphlet stand as a summary of the position of the reformers, and were repeated later by Paley in a brief chapter on subscription included in the *Principles*.[16] Paley's arguments for toleration were later used by Lord Grey and Charles James Fox in the House of Commons.[17]

Apart from Paley's importance as the prime representative of eighteenth-century theological utilitarianism, he remained a significant influence through the use of his works by Cambridge students. According to Le-Mahieu, through Paley the nineteenth century received a 'unified corpus of thought that embodied many of the most treasured assumptions of the Enlightenment in England'.[18] From 1786 into the early nineteenth century the *Principles* was mandatory for Cambridge examinations, and from 1822

---

[11] LeMahieu, *The Mind of William Paley*, p. 5.
[12] LeMahieu, *The Mind of William Paley*, p. 11, and Clarke, *Paley: Evidences for the Man*, p. 26.
[13] Richard Watson, *A Collection of Theological Tracts*, 6 vols. (Cambridge 1785), i. ix, quoted by LeMahieu, *The Mind of William Paley*, p. 15.
[14] Meadley, *Memoirs of William Paley, D.D.*, p. 80.
[15] See Law above, p. 138.
[16] William Paley, *The Principles of Moral and Political Philosophy* (1785; rev. edn. London 1786), Bk. III, Pt. I, Ch. XXII. Here, and in his defence of Law, Paley adopted the same line as he had previously argued in his Cambridge lectures, evident from his extant lecture notes (BL Add. Mss 12079/113–14); Clarke, *Paley: Evidences for the Man*, p. 21.
[17] Barker, *Traditions of Civility*, p. 213.
[18] LeMahieu, *The Mind of William Paley*, p. 154.

to 1920 *A View of the Evidences of Christianity* was on the required list for the Previous, or Little-go, examination for all second year undergraduates. By 1814 twenty English editions of the *Principles* had appeared, and the text remained on the syllabus until 1920, providing an education in ethics and Christian political economy for several generations of university graduates.[19] Writers throughout the century produced abridgements and analyses of Paley's work for students.[20] These included rhyming versions, such as the anonymous *Rhymes for all the Authors quoted by Paley in the first eight Chapters* and *Paley's Verses, by Paley's Ghost* by C. W. Empson, the latter containing the gem:

> Which is more likely, Hume asketh of you,
> The testimony false or the miracles true?
> Go tell him that twelve men of sense and of wit
> May fairly be reckoned the truth to have hit.[21]

Darwin, who entered Christ's College in 1828, wrote of `A View of the Evidences of Christianity* and *Natural Theology*, 'The careful study of these works . . . was the only part of the Academical Course which . . . was of the least use to me in the education of my mind'.[22] In these works Paley posited a rationally ordered, purposeful and divinely legitimated universe, assumptions which later appeared in the Bridgewater Treatises of the 1830s.

Modern commentators have found reason to point to Paley as marking a philosophical era. Sykes believed that 'Paley's importance indeed lay in the exactitude with which he represented the *zeitgeist*' of the utilitarianism of the eighteenth century English establishment.[23] Cragg agreed, considering him 'the last great representative of the Whig and latitudinarian spirit', who 'represented the Indian summer of eighteenth-century assumptions'.[24] Keynes classed Paley with Locke, Hume, Smith, Bentham, Darwin, and Mill in a tradition of lucid, humane science, motivated by disinterested public spirit.[25] In LeMahieu's account, 'The coherence of Paley's philosophy, its synthetic quality, reflected an ideological consensus among British intellectuals in the eighteenth century. . . . Paley distilled and crystallized the strategic ideas of his predecessors into a philosophy whose very comprehen-

---

[19] Ernest Campbell Mossner, *Bishop Butler and the Age of Reason: A Study in the History of Thought* (New York 1971), p. 201. For Paley's Christian political economy see A. M. C. Waterman, 'The Ideological Alliance of Political Economy and Christian Theology, 1798–1833', *Journal of Ecclesiastical History*, 34/2 (1983), pp. 231–44.

[20] LeMahieu, *The Mind of William Paley*, pp. 155, 162–63.

[21] Clarke, *Paley: Evidences for the Man*, pp. 130, 131.

[22] LeMahieu, *The Mind of William Paley*, p. 178.

[23] Norman Sykes, *Church and State in the XVIIIth Century* (1934; Hamden, Conn. 1962), p. 326.

[24] Gerald Cragg, *Reason and Authority in the Eighteenth Century* (Cambridge 1964), pp. 213, 215.

[25] Clarke, *Paley: Evidences for the Man*, p. 134.

siveness justified its modest claims to originality'.[26] Leslie Stephen raised one of the few dissenting voices, judging that Paley was merely 'a condenser and a compiler' in moral philosophy, following in paths previously well-beaten by Locke, Waterland and Law.[27] Clarke thought Stephen's strictures too severe, noting that in 1877, the year following Stephen's comments, another edition of Paley's *Works* was published, proving his lasting influence.[28]

In addition to the *Principles*, *A View of the Evidences of Christianity*, and *Natural Theology*, Paley's other major publication was *Horæ Paulinæ, or the Truth of the Scripture History of St Paul evinced, by a Comparison of the Epistles which bear his name, with the Acts of the Apostles and with one another* (1790), numerous editions of which appeared throughout the nineteenth century. Several editions of Paley's works have appeared, including two in 1825, by his son Edmund Paley and by Robert Lynam.[29]

Note on the Text

Paley's *Principles of Moral and Political Philosophy* was first published in 1785, and dedicated to his patron Edmund Law, Bishop of Carlisle. A corrected second edition appeared the following year. Eleven more London editions were published between 1786 and 1799, with many more English and American editions in the following century. A French translation was published in 1789. The extracts following are taken from the second volume of Robert Lynam's edition of *The Complete Works of William Paley*, 4 vols. (London 1825). Lynam's text of the *Principles* is the revised second edition of 1786.

---

[26] LeMahieu, *The Mind of William Paley*, p. 152.
[27] Leslie Stephen, *History of English Thought in the Eighteenth Century*, 2 vols. (1876; 3rd edn. reprt. New York 1949), ii. 121.
[28] Clarke, *Paley: Evidences for the Man*, p. 126.
[29] For Edmund Paley's edition see above note 5, and for Lynam's edition see Note on the Text following.

The Principles of Moral and Political Philosophy

BOOK I.

CHAP. VI.
HUMAN HAPPINESS.

THE word *happy* is a relative term: that is, when we call a man happy, we mean that he is happier than some others, with whom we compare him; than the generality of others; or than he himself was in some other situation: thus, speaking of one who has just compassed the object of a long pursuit, – 'Now,' we say, 'he is happy;' and in a like comparative sense, compared, that is, with the general lot of mankind, we call a man happy who possesses health and competency.

In strictness, any condition may be denominated happy, in which the amount or aggregate of pleasure exceeds that of pain; and the degree of happiness depends upon the quantity of this excess.

And the greatest quantity of it ordinarily attainable in human life, is what we mean by happiness, when we inquire or pronounce what human happiness consists in.[1]

In which inquiry I will omit much usual declamation on the dignity and capacity of our nature; the superiority of the soul to the body, of the rational to the animal part of our constitution; upon the worthiness, refinement, and delicacy, of some satisfactions, or the meanness, grossness, and sensuality,

---

[1] If any *positive* signification, distinct from what we mean by pleasure, can be affixed to the term 'happiness,' I should take it to denote a certain state of the nervous system in that part of the human frame in which we feel joy and grief, passions and affections. Whether this part be the heart, which the turn of most languages would lead us to believe, or the diaphragm, as Buffon, or the upper orifice of the stomach, as Van Helmont thought; or rather be a kind of fine network, lining the whole region of the præcordia as others have imagined; it is possible, not only that each painful sensation may violently shake and disturb the fibres at the time, but that a series of such may at length so derange the very texture of the system, as to produce a perpetual irritation, which will shew itself by fretfulness, impatience, and restlessness. It is possible also, on the other hand, that a succession of pleasurable sensations may have such an effect upon this subtile organization, as to cause the fibres to relax, and return into their place and order, and thereby to recover, or, if not lost, to preserve, that harmonious conformation which gives to the mind its sense of complacency and satisfaction. This state may be denominated happiness, and is so far distinguishable from pleasure, that it does not refer to any particular object of enjoyment, or consist, like pleasure, in the gratification of one or more of the senses, but is rather the secondary effect which such objects and gratifications produce upon the nervous system, or the state in which they leave it. These conjectures belong not however to our province. The comparative sense, in which we hve explained the term Happiness, is more popular, and is sufficient for the purpose of the present chapter.

of others; because I hold that pleasures differ in nothing, but in continuance and intensity: from a just computation of which, confirmed by what we observe of the apparent cheerfulness, tranquility, and contentment, of men of different tastes, tempers, stations, and pursuits, every question concerning human happiness must receive its decision.

It will be our business to shew, if we can,

I. What Human Happiness does not consist in:
II. What it does consist in.

First, then, Happiness does not consist in the pleasures of sense, in whatever profusion or variety they be enjoyed. By the pleasures of sense, I mean, as well the animal gratifications of eating, drinking, and that by which the species is continued, as the more refined pleasures of music, painting, architecture, gardening, splendid shows, theatric exhibitions; and the pleasures, lastly, of active sports, as of hunting, shooting, fishing, &c. For,

1st, These pleasures continue but a little while at a time. This is true of them all, especially of the grosser sort of them. Laying aside the preparation and the expectation, and computing strictly the actual sensation, we shall be surprised to find how inconsiderable a portion of our time they occupy, how few hours in the four-and-twenty they are able to fill up.

2dly, These pleasures, by repetition, lose their relish. It is a property of the machine, for which we know no remedy, that the organs by which we perceive pleasure, are blunted and benumbed by being frequently exercised in the same way. There is hardly any one who has not found the difference between a gratification, when new, and when familiar; or any pleasure which does not become indifferent as it grows habitual.

3dly, The eagerness for high and intense delights takes away the relish from all others; and as such delights fall rarely in our way, the greater part of our time becomes, from this cause, empty and uneasy.

There is hardly any delusion by which men are greater sufferers in their happiness, than by their expecting too much from what is called pleasure; that is, from those intense delights, which vulgarly engross the name of pleasure. The very expectation spoils them. When they do come, we are often engaged in taking pains to persuade ourselves how much we are pleased, rather than enjoying any pleasure which springs naturally out of the object. And whenever we depend upon being vastly delighted, we always go home secretly grieved at missing our aim. Likewise, as has been observed just now, when this humour of being prodigiously delighted has once taken hold of the imagination, it hinders us from providing for, or acquiescing in, those gently soothing engagements, the due variety and succession of which are the only things that supply a vein or continued stream of happiness.

What I have been able to observe of that part of mankind, whose professed pursuit is pleasure, and who are withheld in the pursuit by no restraints of fortune, or scruples of conscience, corresponds sufficiently with this account. I have commonly remarked in such men, a restless and inextinguishable passion for variety; a great part of their time to be vacant, and so much of it irksome; and that, with whatever eagerness and expectation they set out, they become, by degrees, fastidious in their choice of pleasures, languid in the enjoyment, yet miserable under the want of it.

The truth seems to be, that there is a limit at which these pleasures soon arrive, and from which they ever afterward decline. They are by necessity of short duration, as the organs cannot hold on their emotions beyond a certain length of time; and if you endeavour to compensate for this imperfection in their nature by the frequency with which you repeat them, you suffer more than you gain, by the fatigue of the faculties, and the diminution of sensibility.

We have said nothing in this account, of the loss of opportunities, or the decay of faculties, which, whenever they happen, leave the voluptuary destitute and desperate; teased by desires that can never be gratified, and the memory of pleasures which must return no more.

It will also be allowed by those who have experienced it, and perhaps by those alone, that pleasure which is purchased by the encumbrance of our fortune, is purchased too dear; the pleasure never compensating for the perpetual irritation of embarrassed circumstances.

These pleasures, after all, have their value; and as the young are always too eager in their pursuit of them, the old are sometimes too remiss, that is, too studious of their ease, to be at the pains for them which they really deserve.

Secondly; Neither does happiness consist in an exemption from pain, labour, care, business, suspense, molestation, and 'those evils which are without;' such a state being usually attended, not with ease, but with depression of spirits, a tastelessness in all our ideas, imaginary anxieties, and the whole train of hypochondriacal affections.

For which reason, the expectations of those who retire from their shops and counting-houses, to enjoy the remainder of their days in leisure and tranquillity, are seldom answered by the effect; much less of such, as, in a fit of chagrin, shut themselves up in cloisters and hermitages, or quit the world, and their stations in it, for solitude and repose.

Where there exists a known external cause of uneasiness, the cause may be removed, and the uneasiness will cease. But those imaginary distresses which men feel for want of real ones (and which are equally tormenting, and so far equally real), as they depend upon no single or assignable subject of uneasiness, admit oftentimes of no application of relief.

Hence a moderate pain, upon which the attention may fasten and spend itself, is to many a refreshment: as a fit of the gout will sometimes cure the spleen. And the same of any less violent agitation of the mind, as a literary controversy, a lawsuit, a contested election, and, above all, gaming; the passion for which, in men of fortune and liberal minds, is only to be accounted for on this principle.

Thirdly; Neither does happiness consist in greatness, rank, or elevated station.

Were it true, that all superiority afforded pleasure, it would follow, that by how much we were the greater, that is, the more persons we were superior to, in the same proportion, so far as depended upon this cause, we should be the happier; but so it is, that no superiority yields any satisfaction, save that which we possess or obtain over those with whom we immediately compare ourselves. The shepherd perceives no pleasure in his superiority over his dog; the farmer, in his superiority over the shepherd; the lord, in his superiority over the farmer; nor the king, lastly, in his superiority over the lord. Superiority, where there is no competition, is seldom contemplated; what most men are quite unconscious of.

But if the same shepherd can run, fight, or wrestle, better than the peasants of his village; if the farmer can shew better cattle, if he keep a better horse, or be supposed to have a longer purse, than any farmer in the hundred; if the lord have more interest in an election, greater favour at court, a better house, or larger estate, than any nobleman in the county; if the king possess a more extensive territory, a more powerful fleet or army, a more splendid establishment, more loyal subjects, or more weight and authority in adjusting the affairs of nations, than any prince in Europe; in all these cases, the parties feel an actual satisfaction in their superiority.

Now the conclusion that follows from hence is this; that the pleasures of ambition, which are supposed to be peculiar to high stations, are in reality common to all conditions. The farrier who shoes a horse better, and who is in greater request for his skill, than any man within ten miles of him, possesses, for all that I can see, the delight of distinction and of excelling, as truly and substantially as the statesman, the soldier, and the scholar, who have filled Europe with the reputation of their wisdom, their valour, or their knowledge.

No superiority appears to be of any account, but superiority over a rival. This, it is manifest, may exist wherever rivalships do; and rivalships fall out amongst men of all ranks and degrees. The object of emulation, the dignity or magnitude of this object, makes no difference; as it is not what either possesses that constitutes the pleasure, but what one possesses more than the other.

Philosophy smiles at the contempt with which the rich and great speak of the petty strifes and competitions of the poor; not reflecting that these strifes and competitions are just as reasonable as their own, and the pleasure which success affords, the same.

Our position is, that happiness does not consist in greatness. And this position we make out by shewing, that even what are supposed to be the peculiar advantages of greatness, the pleasures of ambition and superiority, are in reality common to all conditions. But whether the pursuits of ambition be ever wise, whether they contribute more to the happiness or misery of the pursuers, is a different question; and a question concerning which we may be allowed to entertain great doubt. The pleasure of success is exquisite: so also is the anxiety of the pursuit, and the pain of disappointment; – and what is the worst part of the account, the pleasure is short-lived. We soon cease to look back upon those whom we have left behind; new contests are engaged in, new prospects unfold themselves; a succession of struggles is kept up, whilst there is a rival left within the compass of our views and profession; and when there is none, the pleasure with the pursuit is at an end.

II. We have seen what happiness does not consist in. We are next to consider in what it does consist.

In the conduct of life, the great matter is to know beforehand, what will please us, and what pleasure will hold out. So far as we know this, our choice will be justified by the event. And this knowledge is more scarce and difficult than at first sight it may seem to be: for sometimes, pleasures, which are wonderfully alluring and flattering in the prospect, turn out in the possession extremely insipid; or do not hold out as we expected: at other times, pleasures start up which never entered into our calculation; and which we might have missed of by not foreseeing: whence we have reason to believe, that we actually do miss of many pleasures from the same cause. I say, to know 'beforehand;' for, after the experiment is tried, it is commonly impracticable to retreat or change; beside that shifting and changing is apt to generate a habit of restlessness, which is destructive of the happiness of every condition.

By the reason of the original diversity of taste, capacity, and constitution, observable in the human species, and the still greater variety which habit and fashion have introduced in these particulars, it is impossible to propose any plan of happiness, which will succeed to all, or any method of life which is universally eligible or practicable.

All that can be said is, that there remains a presumption in favour of those conditions of life, in which men generally appear most cheerful and contented. For though the apparent happiness of mankind be not always a true measure of their real happiness, it is the best measure we have.

Taking this for my guide, I am inclined to believe that of happiness consists,

I. In the exercises of the social affections.

Those persons commonly possess good spirits, who have about them many objects of affection and endearment, as wife, children, kindred, friends. And to the want of these may be imputed the peevishness of monks, and of such as lead a monastic life.

Of the same nature with the indulgence of our domestic affections, and equally refreshing to the spirits, is the pleasure which results from acts of bounty and beneficence, exercised either in giving money, or in imparting, to those who want it, the assistance of our skill and profession.

Another main article of human happiness is,

II. The exercise of our faculties, either of body or mind, in the pursuit of some engaging end.

It seems to be true, that no plenitude of present gratifications can make the possessor happy for a continuance, unless he have something in reserve, – something to hope for, and look forward to. This I conclude to be the case, from comparing the alacrity and spirits of men who are engaged in any pursuit which interests them, with the dejection and *ennui* of almost all, who are either born to so much that they want nothing more, or who have *used up* their satisfactions too soon, and drained the sources of them.

It is this intolerable vacuity of mind, which carries the rich and great to the horse-course and the gaming-table; and often engages them in contests and pursuits, of which the success bears no proportion to the solicitude and expense with which it is sought. An election for a disputed borough shall cost the parties twenty or thirty thousand pounds each, – to say nothing of the anxiety, humiliation, and fatigue, of the canvass; when a seat in the house of commons, of exactly the same value, may be had for a tenth part of the money, and with no trouble. I do not mention this, to blame the rich and great (perhaps they cannot do better), but in confirmation of what I have advanced.

Hope, which thus appears to be of so much importance to our happiness, is of two kinds; – where there is something to be done towards attaining the object of our hope, and where there is nothing to be done. The first alone is of any value; the latter being apt to corrupt into impatience, having no power but to sit still and wait, which soon grows tiresome.

The doctrine delivered under this head, may be readily admitted; but how to provide ourselves with a succession of pleasurable engagements, is the difficulty. This requires two things: judgment in the choice of *ends* adapted to our opportunities; and a command of imagination, so as to be able, when the judgment has made choice of an end, to transfer a pleasure to the *means*: after which, the end may be forgotten as soon as we will.

Hence those pleasures are most valuable, not which are most exquisite in the fruition, but which are most productive of engagement and activity in the pursuit.

A man who is in earnest in his endeavours after the happiness of a future state, has, in this respect, an advantage over all the world: for, he has constantly before his eyes an object of supreme importance, productive of perpetual engagement and activity, and of which the pursuit (which can be said of no pursuit besides) lasts him to his life's end. Yet even he must have many ends, besides the *far end*; but then they will conduct to that, be subordinate, and in some way or other capable of being referred to that, and derive their satisfaction, or an addition of satisfaction, from that.

Engagement is every thing: the more significant, however, our engagements are, the better: such as the planning of laws, institutions, manufacturers, charities, improvements, public works; and the endeavouring, by our interest, address, solicitations, and activity, to carry them into effect: or, upon a smaller scale, the procuring of a maintenance and fortune for our families by a course of industry and application to our callings, which forms and gives motion to the common occupations of life; training up a child; prosecuting a scheme for his future establishment; making ourselves masters of a language or a science; improving or managing an estate; labouring after a piece of preferment; and lastly, *any* engagement, which is innocent, is better than none; as the writing of a book, the building of a house, the laying out of a garden, the digging of a fish-pond, – even the raising of a cucumber or a tulip.

Whilst our minds are taken up with the objects or business before us, we are commonly happy, whatever the object or business be; when the mind is *absent*, and the thoughts are wandering to something else than what is passing in the place in which we are, we are often miserable.

III. Happiness depends upon the prudent constitution of the habits.

The art in which the secret of human happiness in a great measure consists, is to *set* the habits in such a manner, that every change may be a change for the better. The habits themselves are much the same; for, whatever is made habitual, becomes smooth, and easy, and nearly indifferent. The return to an old habit is likewise easy, whatever the habit be. Therefore the advantage is with those habits which allow of no indulgence in the deviation from them. The luxurious receive no greater pleasure from their dainties, than the peasant does from his bread and cheese; but the peasant, whenever he goes abroad, finds a feast; whereas the epicure must be well entertained, to escape disgust. Those who spend every day at cards, and those who go every day to plough, pass their time much alike; intent upon what they are about, wanting nothing, regretting nothing they are both for a time in a state of ease; but then, whatever suspends the occupation of the card-player, distresses him; whereas to the labourer, every interruption is a refreshment: and this appears in the different effects that Sunday produces upon the two, which proves a day of recreation to the one, but a lamentable burden to the other. The man who has learned to live alone, feels his spirits enlivened whenever he enters into company, and takes his leave without regret; another, who has long been accustomed to a crowd, or continual succession of company, experiences in company no elevation of spirits, nor any greater satisfaction, than what the man of a retired life finds in his chimney-corner. So far their conditions are equal; but let a change of place, fortune, or situation, separate the companion from his circle, his visitors, his club, common-room, or coffee-house; and the difference and advantage in the choice and constitution of the two habits will shew itself. Solitude comes to the one, clothed with melancholy; to the other, it brings liberty and quiet. You will see the one fretful and restless, at a loss how to dispose of his time, till the hour come round when he may forget himself in bed; the other easy and satisfied, taking up his book or his pipe, as soon as he finds himself alone; ready to admit any little amusement that casts up, or to turn his hands and attention to the first business that presents itself; or content, without either, to sit still, and let his train of thought glide indolently through his brain, without much use, perhaps, or pleasure, but without *hankering* after any thing better, and without irritation. – A reader, who has inured himself to books of science and argumentation, if a novel, a well-written pamphlet, an article of news, a narrative of a curious voyage, or a journal of a traveller, fall in his way, sits down to the repast with relish; enjoys his entertainment while it lasts, and can return, when it is over, to his graver reading, without distaste. Another, with whom nothing will go down but works of humour and pleasantry, or whose curiosity must be interested by perpetual novelty, will consume a bookseller's window in half a forenoon: during which time he is rather in search of diversion than diverted; and as books to his taste are few, and short, and rapidly read over, the stock is soon exhausted, when he is left without resource from this principal supply of harmless amusement.

So far as circumstances of fortune conduce to happiness, it is not the income which any man possesses, but the increase of income, that affords the pleasure. Two persons, of whom one begins with a hundred, and advances his income to a thousand pounds a year, and the other sets off with a thousand, and dwindles down to a hundred, may, in the course of their time, have the receipt and spending of the same sum of money; yet their satisfaction, so far as fortune is concerned in it, will be very different; the series and sum total of their incomes being the same, it makes a wide difference at which end they begin.

IV. Happiness consists in health.

By health I understand, as well freedom from bodily distempers, as that tranquillity, firmness, and alacrity of mind, which we call good spirits; and which may properly enough be included in our notion of health, as depending commonly upon the same causes, and yielding to the same management, as our bodily constitution.

Health, in this sense, is the one thing needful. Therefore no pains, expense, self-denial, or restraint, to which we subject ourselves for the sake of health, is too much. Whether it require us to relinquish lucrative situations, to abstain from favourite indulgences, to control intemperate passions, or undergo tedious regimens; whatever difficulties it lays us under, a man, who pursues his happiness rationally and resolutely, will be content to submit.

When we are in perfect health and spirits, we feel in ourselves a happiness independent of any particular outward gratification whatever, and of which we can give no account. This is an enjoyment which the Deity has annexed to life; and it probably constitutes, in a great measure, the happiness of infants and brutes, especially of the lower and sedentary orders of animals, as of oysters, periwinkles, and the like; for which I have sometimes been at a loss to find out amusement.

The above account of human happiness will justify the two following conclusions, which, although found in most books of morality, have seldom, I think, been supported by any sufficient reasons: –

First, That happiness is pretty equally distributed amongst the different orders of civil society:

Secondly, That vice has no advantage over virtue even with respect to this world's happiness.

CHAP. VII.
VIRTUE.

VIRTUE is '*the doing good to mankind, in obedience to the will of God, and for the sake of everlasting happiness.*'

According to which definition, 'the good of mankind' is the subject; the 'will of God,' the rule; and 'everlasting happiness,' the motive, of human virtue.

Virtue has been divided by some moralists into *benevolence, prudence, fortitude*, and *temperance. Benevolence* proposes good ends; *prudence* suggests the best means of attaining them; *fortitude* enables us to encounter the difficulties, dangers, and discouragements, which stand in our way in the pursuit of these ends; *temperance* repels and overcomes the passions that obstruct it. *Benevolence*, for instance, prompts us to undertake the cause of an oppressed orphan; *prudence* suggests the best means of going about it; *fortitude* enables us to confront the danger, and bear up against the loss, disgrace, or repulse, that may attend our undertaking; and *temperance* keeps under the love of money, of ease, or amusement, which might divert us from it.

Virtue is distinguished by others into two branches only, *prudence* and *benevolence: prudence*, attentive to our own interest; *benevolence*, to that of our fellow-creatures: both directed to the same end, the increase of happiness in nature; and taking equal concern in the future as in the present.

The four CARDINAL virtues are, *prudence, fortitude, temperance*, and *justice.*

But the division of virtue, to which we are in modern times most accustomed, is into duties; –

Towards *God*; as piety, reverence, resignation, gratitude, &c.

Towards *other men* (or relative duties); as justice, charity, fidelity, loyalty, &c.

Towards *ourselves*; as chastity, sobriety, temperance, preservation of life, care of health, &c.

More of these distinctions have been proposed, which it is not worth while to set down.

I shall proceed to state a few observations, which relate to the general regulation of human conduct; unconnected indeed with each other, but very worthy of attention; and which fall as properly under the title of this chapter as of any future one.

I. Mankind act more from habit than reflection.

It is on few only and great occasions that men deliberate at all; on fewer still, that they institute any thing like a regular inquiry into the moral rectitude or depravity of what they are about to do; or wait for the result of it. We are for the most part determined at once; and by an impulse, which is the effect and energy of pre-established habits. And this constitution seems well adapted to the exigencies of human life, and to the imbecility of our moral principle. In the current occasions and rapid opportunities of life, there is oftentimes little leisure for reflection; and were there more, a man, who has to reason about his duty, when the temptation to transgress it is upon him, is almost sure to reason himself into an error.

If we are in so great a degree passive under our habits, Where it is asked is the exercise of virtue, the guilt of vice, or any use of moral and religious knowledge? I answer, In the *forming and contracting* of these habits.

And hence results a rule of life of considerable importance, *viz.* that many things are to be done and abstained from, solely for the sake of habit. We will explain ourselves by an example or two. – A beggar, with the appearance of extreme distress, asks our charity. If we come to argue the matter, whether the distress be real, whether it be not brought upon himself, whether it be of public advantage to admit such application, whether it be not to encourage idleness and vagrancy, whether it may not invite impostors to our doors, whether the money can be well spared, or might not be better applied; when these considerations are put together, it may appear very doubtful, whether we ought or ought not to give any thing. But when we reflect, that the misery before our eyes excites our pity, whether we will or not; that it is of the utmost consequence to us to cultivate this tenderness of mind; that it is a quality, cherished by indulgence, and soon stifled by opposition; when this, I say, is considered, a wise man will do that for his own sake, which he would have hesitated to do for the petitioner's; he will give way to his compassion, rather than offer violence to a habit of so much general use.

A man of confirmed good habits, will act in the same manner without any consideration at all.

This may serve for one instance; another is the following. – A man has been brought up from his infancy with a dread of lying. An occasion presents itself where, at the expense of a little veracity, he may divert his company, set off his own wit with advantage, attract the notice and engage the partiality of all about him. This is not a small temptation. And when he looks at the other side of the question, he sees no mischief that can ensue from this liberty, no slander of any man's reputation, no prejudice likely to arise to any man's interest. Were there nothing farther to be considered, it would be difficult to shew why a man under such circumstances might not indulge his humour. But when he reflects that his scruples about lying have hitherto preserved him free from this vice; that occasions like the present will return, where the inducement may be equally strong, but the indulgence much less innocent; that his scruples will wear away by a few transgressions, and leave him subject to one of the meanest and most pernicious of all bad habits, – a habit of lying, whenever it will serve his turn: when all this, I say, is considered, a wise man will forego the present, or a much greater pleasure, rather than lay the foundation of a character so vicious and contemptible.

From what has been said, may be explained also the nature of *habitual* virtue. By the definition of virtue, placed at the beginning of this chapter, it appears, that the good of mankind is the subject, the will of God the rule, and everlasting happiness the motive and end, of all virtue. Yet, in fact, a man shall perform many an act of virtue, without having either the good of mankind, the will of God, or everlasting happiness, in his thought. How is this to be understood? In the same manner as that a man may be a very good servant, without being conscious, at every turn, of a particular regard to his master's will, or of an express attention to his master's interest; indeed, your best old servants are of this sort: but then he must have served for a length of time under the actual direction of these motives, to bring it to this: in which service his merit and virtue consist.

There are *habits*, not only of drinking, swearing, and lying, and of some other things, which are commonly acknowledged to be habits, and called so; but of every modification of action, speech, and thought. Man is a bundle of habits.

There are habits of industry, attention, vigilance, advertency; of a prompt obedience to the judgment occurring, or of yielding to the first impulse of passion; of extending our views to the future, or of resting upon the present; of apprehending, methodizing, reasoning; of indolence and dilatoriness; of vanity, self-conceit melancholy, partiality; of fretfulness, suspicion, captiousness, censoriousness; of pride, ambition, covetousness; of overreaching, intriguing, projecting: in a word, there is not a quality or function, either of body or mind, which does not feel the influence of this great law of animated nature.

II. The Christian religion hath not ascertained the precise quantity of virtue necessary to salvation.

This has been made an objection to Christianity; but without reason.

For, as all revelation, however imparted originally, must be transmitted by the ordinary vehicle of language, it behoves those who make the objection, to shew that any form of words could be devised, that might express this *quantity*; or that it is possible to constitute a standard of moral attainments, accommodated to the almost infinite diversity which subsists in the capacities and opportunities of different men.

It seems most agreeable to our conceptions of justice, and is consonant enough to the language of Scripture,[2] to suppose, that there are prepared for us rewards and punishments, of all possible degrees, from the most exalted happiness down to extreme misery; so that, 'our labour is never in vain;' whatever advancement we make in virtue, we procure a proportionable accession of future happiness; as, on the other hand, every accumulation of vice is the 'treasuring up so much wrath against the day of wrath.' It has been said, that it can never be a just economy of Providence, to admit one part of mankind into heaven, and condemn the other to hell; since there must be very little to choose, between the worst man who is received into heaven, and the best who is excluded. And how know we, it might be answered, but there may be as little to choose in the conditions?

Without entering into a detail of Scripture morality, which would anticipate our subject, the following general positions may be advanced, I think, with safety.

1. That a state of happiness is not to be expected by those who are conscious of no moral or religious rule: I mean those who cannot with truth say, that they have been prompted to one action, or withholden from one gratification, by any regard to virtue or religion, either immediate or habitual.

There needs no other proof of this, than the consideration, that a brute would be as proper an object of reward as such a man, and that, if the case were so, the penal sanctions of religion could have no place. For, whom would you punish, if you make such a one as this happy? – or rather indeed religion itself, both natural and revealed, would cease to have either use or authority.

2. That a state of happiness is not to be expected by those, who reserve to themselves the habitual practice of any one sin, or neglect of one known duty.

---

[2]　'He which soweth sparingly, shall reap also sparingly; and he which soweth bountifully, shall reap also bountifully.' 2 Cor. ix. 6. – 'And that servant which knew his Lord's will, and prepared not himself, neither did according to his will, shall be beaten with many stripes; but he that knew not, shall be beaten with few stripes.' Luke xii. 47, 48. – 'Whoever shall give you a cup of water to drink in my name, because ye belong to Christ; verily I say unto you, He shall not lose his reward;' to wit, intimating that there is in reserve a proportionable reward for even the smallest act of virtue. Mark ix. 41. – See also the parable of the pounds, Luke xix. 16, &c.; where he whose pound had gained ten pounds, was placed over ten cities; and he whose pound had gained five pounds, was placed over five cities.

Because, no obedience can proceed upon proper motives, which is not universal, that is, which is not directed to every command of God alike, as they all stand upon the same authority.

Because such an allowance would in effect amount to a toleration of every vice in the world.

And because the strain of Scripture language excludes any such hope. When our *duties* are recited, they are put *collectively*, that is, as all and every of them required in the Christian character. '*Add* to your faith virtue, and to virtue knowledge, and to knowledge temperance, and to temperance patience, and to patience godliness, and to godliness brotherly kindness, and to brotherly kindness charity.' (2 Pet. i. 5–7.) On the other hand, when vices are enumerated, they are put *disjunctively*, that is, as separately and severally excluding the sinner from heaven. '*Neither* fornicators, nor idolators, nor adulterers, nor effeminate, nor abusers of themselves with mankind, nor thieves, nor covetous, nor drunkards, nor revilers, nor extortioners, shall inherit the kingdom of heaven.' (1 Cor. vi. 9, 10.)

Those texts of Scripture, which seem to lean a contrary way, as that 'charity shall cover the multitude of sins;' (1 Pet. iv. 8.) that 'he which converteth a sinner from the error of his way, shall hide a multitude of sins;' (James v. 20.) cannot, I think, for the reasons above mentioned, be extended to sins deliberately, habitually, and obstinately, persisted in.

3. That a state of mere unprofitableness will not go unpunished.

This is expressly laid down by Christ, in the parable of the talents, which supersedes all farther reasoning upon the subject. 'Then he which had received one talent, came and said, Lord, I knew thee that thou art an austere man, reaping where thou hast not sown, and gathering where thou hast not strawed: and I was afraid, and hid thy talent in the earth; lo, there thou hast that is thine. His lord answered and said unto him, Thou wicked and *slothful* servant, thou knewest (or, knewest thou?) that I reap where I sowed not, and gather where I have not strawed; thou oughtest therefore to have put my money to the exchangers, and then at my coming I should have received mine own with usury. Take therefore the talent from him, and give it unto him which hath ten talents: for unto every one that hath shall be given, and he shall have abundance; but from him that hath not, shall be taken away even that which he hath: *and cast ye the unprofitable servant into outer darkness, there shall be weeping and gnashing of teeth.*' (Matt. xxv. 24, &c.)

III. In every question of conduct, where one side is doubtful, and the other side safe, we are bound to take the safe side.

This is best explained by an instance; and I know of none more to our purpose than that of suicide. Suppose, for example's sake, that it appear doubtful to a reasoner upon the subject, whether he may lawfully destroy himself. He can have no doubt, that it is lawful for him to let it alone. Here therefore is a case, in which one side is doubtful, and the other safe.

By virtue therefore of our rule, he is bound to pursue the safe side, that is, to forbear from offering violence to himself, whilst a doubt remains upon his mind concerning the lawfulness of suicide.

It is *prudent*, you allow, to take the safe side. But our observation means something more. We assert that the action concerning which we doubt, whatever it may be in itself, or to another, would in *us*, whilst this doubt remains upon our minds, be certainly sinful. The case is expressly so adjudged by St. Paul, with whose authority we will for the present rest contented. – 'I know and am persuaded by the Lord Jesus, that there is nothing unclean of itself; but *to him that esteemeth any thing to be unclean, to him it is unclean.* – Happy is he that condemneth not himself in that thing which he alloweth; and he that doubteth, is damned (*condemned*) if he eat, for whatsoever is not of faith (*i. e.* not done with a full persuasion of the lawfulness of it) is sin.' (Rom. xiv. 14. 22, 23.)

BOOK II

CHAP. I.
THE QUESTION 'WHY AM I OBLIGED TO KEEP MY WORD?'
CONSIDERED.

WHY am I obliged to keep my word?

Because it is right, says one. – Because it is agreeable to the fitness of things, says another. – Because it is conformable to reason and nature, says a third. – Because it is conformable to truth, says a fourth. – Because it promotes the public good, says a fifth. – Because it is required by the will of God, concludes a sixth.

Upon which different accounts, two things are observable: –

First, that they all ultimately coincide.

The fitness of things, means their fitness to produce happiness: the nature of things, means that actual constitution of the world, by which some things, as such and such actions, for example, produce happiness, and others misery: reason is the principle, by which we discover or judge of this constitution: truth is this judgment expressed or drawn out into propositions. So that it necessarily comes to pass, that what promotes the public happiness, or happiness on the whole, is agreeable to the fitness of things, to nature, to reason, and to truth: and such (as will appear by and by) is the Divine character, that what promotes the general happiness, is required by the will of God; and what has all the above properties, must needs be *right*; for, right means no more than conformity to the rule we go by, whatever that rule be.

And this is the reason that moralists, from whatever different principles they set out, commonly meet in their conclusions; that is, they enjoin the same conduct, prescribe the same rules of duty, and, with a few exceptions, deliver upon dubious cases the same determinations.

Secondly, it is to be observed, that these answers all leave the matter *short*; for the inquirer may turn round upon his teacher with a second question, in which he will expect to be satisfied, namely, *Why* am I obliged to do what is right; to act agreeably to the fitness of things; to conform to reason, nature, or truth; to promote the public good, or to obey the will of God?

The proper method of conducting the inquiry is, FIRST, to examine what we mean, when we say a man is *obliged* to do any thing; and THEN to shew *why* he is obliged to do the thing which we have proposed as an example, namely, 'to keep his word.'

CHAP. II.
WHAT WE MEAN WHEN WE SAY A MAN IS 'OBLIGED' TO DO A THING.

A MAN is said to be *obliged*, '*when he is urged by a violent motive resulting from the command of another.*'

First, 'The motive must be violent.' If a person, who has done me some little service, or has a small place in his disposal, ask me upon some occasion for my vote, I may possibly give it him, from a motive of gratitude or expectation: but I should hardly say that I was *obliged* to give it him; because the inducement does not rise high enough. Whereas if a father or a master, any great benefactor, or one on whom my fortune depends, require my vote, I give it him of course: and my answer to all who ask me why I voted so and so, is, that my father or my master *obliged* me; that I had received so many favours from, or had so great a dependance upon, such a one, that I was *obliged* to vote as he directed me.

Secondly, 'It must result from the command of another.' Offer a man a gratuity for doing any thing, for seizing, for example, an offender, he is not *obliged* by your offer to do it; nor would he say he is; though he may be *induced, persuaded, prevailed upon, tempted*. If a magistrate or the man's immediate superior command it, he considers himself as *obliged* to comply, though possibly he would lose less by a refusal in this case, than in the former.

I will not undertake to say that the words *obligation* and *obliged* are used uniformly in this sense, or always with this distinction; nor is it possible to tie down popular phrases to any constant signification: but wherever the motive is violent enough, and coupled with the idea of command, authority, law, or the will of a superior, there, I take it, we always reckon ourselves to be *obliged*.

And from this account of obligation it follows, that we can be obliged to nothing, but what we ourselves are to gain or lose something by; for nothing else can be a 'violent motive' to us. As we should not be obliged to obey the laws, or the magistrate, unless rewards or punishments, pleasure or pain, somehow or other, depended upon our obedience; so neither should we, without the same reason, be obliged to do what is right, to practise virtue, or to obey the commands of God.

CHAP. III.
THE QUESTION 'WHY AM I OBLIGED TO KEEP MY WORD?' RESUMED.

LET it be remembered, that to be *obliged*, is 'to be urged by a violent motive, resulting from the command of another.'

And then let it be asked, Why am I *obliged* to keep my word? and the answer will be, Because I am 'urged to do so by a violent motive (namely, the expectation of being after this life rewarded, if I do, or punished for it, if I do not), resulting from the command of another' (namely, of God).

This solution goes to the bottom of the subject, as no farther question can reasonably be asked.

Therefore, private happiness is our motive, and the will of God our rule.

When I first turned my thoughts to moral speculations, an air of mystery seemed to hang over the whole subject; which arose, I believe, from hence, – that I supposed, with many authors whom I had read, that to be *obliged* to do a thing, was very different from being *induced* only to do it; and that the obligation to practise virtue, to do what is right, just, &c. was quite another thing, and of another kind, than the obligation which a soldier is under to obey his officer, a servant his master; or any of the civil and ordinary obligations of human life. Whereas, from what has been said it appears, that moral obligation is like all other obligations; and that *obligation* is nothing more than an *inducement* of sufficient strength, and resulting, in some way, from the command of another.

There is always understood to be a difference between an act of *prudence* and an act of *duty*. Thus, if I distrusted a man who owed me a sum of money, I should reckon it an act of prudence to get another person bound with him; but I should hardly call it an act of duty. On the other hand, it would be thought a very unusual and loose kind of language, to say, that, as I had made such a promise, it was *prudent* to perform it; or that, as my friend, when he went abroad, placed a box of jewels in my hands, it would be *prudent* in me to preserve it for him till he returned.

Now, in what, you will ask, does the difference consist? inasmuch, as, according to our account of the matter, both in the one case and the other, in acts of duty as well as acts of prudence, we consider solely what we ourselves shall gain or lose by the act.

The difference, and the only difference, is this; that, in the one case, we consider what we shall gain or lose in the present world; in the other case, we consider also what we shall gain or lose in the world to come.

They who would establish a system of morality, independent of a future state, must look out for some different idea of moral obligation; unless they can shew that virtue conducts the possessor to certain happiness in this life, or to a much greater share of it than he could attain by a different behaviour.

To us there are two great questions:

I. Will there be after this life any distribution of rewards and punishments at all?

II. If there be, what actions will be rewarded, and what will be punished?

The first question comprises the credibility of the Christian religion, together with the presumptive proofs of a future retribution from the light of nature. The second question comprises the province of morality. Both questions are too much for one work. The affirmative therefore of the first, although we confess that it is the foundation upon which the whole fabric rests, must in this treatise be taken for granted.

CHAP. IV.
THE WILL OF GOD.

As the will of God is our rule; to inquire what is our duty, or what we are obliged to do, in any instance, is, in effect, to inquire what is the will of God in that instance? which consequently becomes the whole business of morality.

Now there are two methods of coming at the will of God on any point:

I. By his express declarations, when they are to be had, and which must be sought for in Scripture.

II. By what we can discover of his designs and deposition from his works; or, as we usually call it, the light of nature.

And here we may observe the absurdity of separating natural and revealed religion from each other. The object of both is the same – to discover the will of God, – and, provided we do but discover it, it matters nothing by what means.

An ambassador, judging by what he knows of his sovereign's disposition, and arguing from what he has observed of his conduct, or is acquainted with of his designs, may take his measures in many cases with safety, and presume with great probability how his master would have him act on most occasions that arise: but if he have his commission and instructions in his pocket, it would be strange not to look into them. He will be directed by both rules: when his instructions are clear and positive, there is an end to all farther deliberation (unless indeed he suspect their authenticity): where his instructions are silent or dubious, he will endeavour to supply or explain them, by what he has been able to collect from other quarters of his master's general inclination or intentions.

Mr. Hume, in his fourth Appendix to his Principles of Morals, has been pleased to complain of the modern scheme of uniting Ethics with the

Christian Theology. They who find themselves disposed to join in this complaint, will do well to observe what Mr. Hume himself has been able to make of morality without this union. And for that purpose, let them read the second part of the ninth section of the above essay; which part contains the practical application of the whole treatise, – a treatise, which Mr. Hume declares to be 'incomparably the best he ever wrote.' When they have read it over, let them consider, whether any motives there proposed are likely to be found sufficient to withhold men from the gratification of lust, revenge, envy, ambition, avarice; or to prevent the existence of these passions. Unless they rise up from this celebrated essay with stronger impressions upon their minds than it ever left upon mine, they will acknow-ledge the necessity of additional sanctions. But the necessity of these sanctions is not now the question. If they be *in fact established*, if the rewards and punishments held forth in the gospel will actually come to pass, they *must* be considered. Such as reject the Christian religion, are to make the best shift they can to build up a system, and lay the foundation of morality, without it. But it appears to me a great inconsistency in those who receive Christianity, and expect something to come of it, to endeavour to keep all such expectations out of sight in their reasonings concerning human duty.

The method of coming at the will of God, concerning any action, by the light of nature, is to inquire into 'the tendency of the action to promote or diminish the general happiness.' This rule proceeds upon the presumption, that God Almighty wills and wishes the happiness of his creatures; and, consequently, that those actions, which promote that will and wish, must be agreeable to him; and the contrary.

As this presumption is the foundation of our whole system, it becomes necessary to explain the reasons upon which it rests.

CHAP. V.
THE DIVINE BENEVOLENCE

WHEN God created the human species, either he wished their happiness, or he wished their misery, or he was indifferent and unconcerned about both.

If he had wished our misery, he might have made sure of his purpose, by forming our senses to be so many sores and pains to us, as they are now instruments of gratification and enjoyment: or by placing us amidst objects so ill-suited to our perceptions, as to have continually offended us, instead of ministering to our refreshment and delight. He might have made, for example, every thing we tasted, bitter; every thing we saw, loathsome; every thing we touched, a sting; every smell a stench; and every sound a discord.

If he had been indifferent about our happiness or misery, we must impute to our good fortune (as all design by this supposition is excluded) both the capacity of our senses to receive pleasure, and the supply of external objects fitted to produce it. But either of these (and still more both of them) being too much to be attributed to accident, nothing remains but the first supposition, that God, when he created the human species, wished their happiness; and made for them the provision which he has made, with that view, and for that purpose.

The same argument may be proposed in different terms, thus: Contrivance proves design; and the predominant tendency of the contrivance indicates the disposition of the designer. The world abounds with contrivances; and all the contrivances which we are acquainted with, are directed to beneficial purposes. Evil, no doubt, exists; but is never, that we can perceive, the object of contrivance. Teeth are contrived to eat, not to ache; their aching now and then, is incidental to the contrivance, perhaps inseparable from it: or even, if you will, let it be called a defect in the contrivance; but it is not the *object* of it. This is a distinction which well deserves to be attended to. In describing implements of husbandry, you would hardly say of the sickle, that it is made to cut the reaper's fingers, though, from the construction of the instrument, and the manner of using it, this mischief often happens. But if you had occasion to describe instruments of torture or execution, This engine, you would say, is to extend the sinews; this to dislocate the joints; this to break the bones; this to scorch the soles of the feet. Here, pain and misery are the very *objects* of the contrivance. Now, nothing of this sort is to be found in the works of nature. We never discover a train of contrivance to bring about an evil purpose. No anatomist ever discovered a system of organization calculated to produce pain and disease; or, in explaining the parts of the human body, ever said, This is to irritate; this to inflame; this duct is to convey the gravel to the kidneys; this gland to secrete the humour which forms the gout: if by chance he come at a part of which he knows not the use, the most he can say is, that it is useless: no one ever suspects that it is put there to incommode, to annoy, or to torment. Since then God hath called forth his consummate wisdom to contrive and provide for our happiness, and the world appears to have been constituted with this design at first; so long as this constitution is upholden by him, we must in reason suppose the same design to continue.

The contemplation of universal nature rather bewilders the mind than affects it. There is always a bright spot in the prospect, upon which the eye rests; a single example, perhaps, by which each man finds himself more *convinced* than by all others put together. I seem, for my own part, to see the benevolence of the Deity more clearly in the pleasures of very young children, than in any thing in the world. The pleasures of grown persons may be reckoned partly of their own procuring; especially if there has been any industry, or contrivance, or pursuit, to come at them; or if they are founded, like music, painting, &c. upon any qualification of their own acquiring. But the pleasures of a healthy infant are so manifestly provided for by *another*, and the benevolence of the provision is so unquestionable, that every child I see at its sport, affords to my mind a kind of sensible evidence of the finger of God, and of the disposition which directs it.

But the example, which strikes each man most strongly, is the true example for him: and hardly two minds hit upon the same; which shews the abundance of such examples about us.

We conclude, therefore, that God wills and wishes the happiness of his creatures. And this conclusion being once established, we are at liberty to go on with the rule built upon it, namely, "that the method of coming at the will of God, concerning any action, by the light of nature, is to inquire into the tendency of that action to promote or diminish the general happiness."

CHAP. VI.
UTILITY

So then actions are to be estimated by their tendency.[1] Whatever is expedient, is right. It is the utility of any moral rule alone, which constitutes the obligation of it.

But to all this there seems a plain objection, *viz.* that many actions are useful, which no man in his senses will allow to be right. There are occasions, in which the hand of the assassin would be very useful. The present possessor of some great estate employs his influence and fortune, to annoy, corrupt, or oppress, all about him. His estate would devolve, by his death, to a successor of an opposite character. It is useful, therefore, to despatch such a one as soon as possible out of the way; as the neighbourhood will exchange thereby a pernicious tyrant for a wise and generous benefactor. It might be useful to rob a miser, and give the money to the poor; as the money, no doubt, would produce more happiness, by being laid out in food and clothing for half a dozen distressed families, than by continuing locked up in a miser's chest. It may be useful to get possession of a place, a piece of preferment, or of a seat in parliament, by bribery or false swearing: as by means of them we may serve the public more effectually than in our private station. What then shall we say? Must we admit these actions to be right, which would be to justify assassination, plunder, and perjury; or must we give up our principle, that the criterion of right is utility?

It is not necessary to do either.

[1]   Actions in the abstract are right or wrong, according to their *tendency*; the agent is virtuous or vicious, according to his *design*. Thus, if the question be, Whether relieving common beggars be right or wrong? we inquire into the *tendency* of such a conduct to the public advantage or inconvenience. If the question be, Whether a man, remarkable for this sort of bounty, is to be esteemed virtuous for that reason? we inquire into his *design*, whether his liberality sprang from charity or from ostentation? It is evident that our concern is with actions in the abstract.

The true answer is this; that these actions, after all, are not useful, and for that reason, and that alone, are not right.

To see this point perfectly, it must be observed that the bad consequences of actions are twofold, *particular* and *general*.

The particular bad consequence of an action, is the mischief which that single action directly and immediately occasions.

The general bad consequence is, the violation of some necessary or useful *general* rule.

Thus, the particular bad consequence of the assassination above described, is the fright and pain which the deceased underwent; the loss he suffered of life, which is as valuable to a bad man, as to a good one, or more so; the prejudice and affliction, of which his death was the occasion, to his family, friends, and dependants.

The general bad consequence is the violation of this necessary general rule, that no man be put to death for his crimes but by public authority.

Although, therefore, such an action have no particular bad consequences, or greater particular good consequences, yet it is not useful, by reason of the general consequence, which is of more importance, and which is evil. And the same of the other two instances, and of a million more which might be mentioned.

But as this solution supposes, that the moral government of the world must proceed by general rules, it remains that we shew the necessity of this.

CHAP. VII.
THE NECESSITY OF GENERAL RULES.

You cannot permit one action and forbid another, without shewing a difference between them. Consequently, the same sort of actions must be generally permitted or generally forbidden. Where, therefore, the general permission of them would be pernicious, it becomes necessary to lay down and support the rule which generally forbids them.

Thus, to return once more to the case of the assassin.

The assassin knocked the rich villain on the head, because he thought him better out of the way than in it. If you allow this excuse in the present instance, you must allow it to all who act in the same manner, and from the same motive; that is, you must allow every man to kill any one he meets, whom he thinks noxious or useless; which, in the event, would be to commit every man's life and safety to the spleen, fury, and fanaticism, of his neighbour; – a disposition of affairs which would soon fill the world with misery and confusion; and ere long put an end to human society, if not to the human species.

The necessity of general rules in human government is apparent: but whether the same necessity subsist in the Divine economy, in that distribution of rewards and punishments to which a moralist looks forward, may be doubted.

I answer, that general rules are necessary to every moral government: and by moral government I mean any dispensation, whose object is to influence the conduct of reasonable creatures.

For if, of two actions perfectly similar, one be punished, and the other be rewarded or forgiven, which is the consequence of rejecting general rules, the subjects of such a dispensation would no longer know, either what to expect or how to act. Rewards and punishments would cease to be such – would become accidents. Like the stroke of a thunderbolt, or the discovery of a mine, like a blank or a benefit-ticket in a lottery, they would occasion pain or pleasure when they happened; but, following in no known order, from any particular course of action, they could have no previous influence or effect upon the conduct.

An attention to general rules, therefore, is included in the very idea of reward and punishment. Consequently, whatever reason there is to expect future reward and punishment at the hand of God, there is the same reason to believe, that he will proceed in the distribution of it by the general rules.

Before we prosecute the consideration of general consequences any farther, it may be proper to anticipate a reflection, which will be apt enough to suggest itself, in the progress of our argument.

As the general consequence of an action, upon which so much of the guilt of a bad action depends, consists in the *example*; it should seem, that if the action be done with perfect secrecy, so as to furnish no bad example, that part of the guilt drops off. In the case of suicide, for instance, if a man can so manage matters, as to take away his own life, without being known or suspected to have done so, he is not chargeable with any mischief from the example; nor does his punishment seem necessary, in order to save the authority of any general rule.

In the first place, those who reason in this manner do not observe, that they are setting up a general rule, of all others the least to be endured; namely, that secrecy, whenever secrecy is practicable, will justify any action.

Were such a rule admitted, for instance in the case above produced; is there not reason to fear that people would be *disappearing* perpetually?

In the next place, I would wish them to be well satisfied about the points proposed in the following queries:

1. Whether the Scriptures do not teach us to expect, that, at the general judgment of the world, the most secret actions will be brought to light?[2]

2. For what purpose can this be, but to make them the objects of reward and punishment?

---

[2] 'In the day when God shall judge the secrets of men by Jesus Christ.' Rom. xi. 16. – 'Judge nothing before the time until the Lord come, who will bring to light the hidden things of darkness, and will make manifest the counsels of the heart.' 1 Cor. iv. 5.

3. Whether, being so brought to light, they will not fall under the operation of those equal and impartial rules, by which God will deal with his creatures?

They will then become examples, whatever they be now; and require the same treatment from the judge and governor of the moral world, as if they had been detected from the first.

CHAP. VIII.
THE CONSIDERATION OF GENERAL CONSEQUENCES PURSUED.

THE general consequence of any action may be estimated, by asking what would be the consequence, if the same sort of actions were generally permitted. – But suppose they were, and a thousand such actions perpetrated under this permission; is it just to charge a single action with the collected guilt and mischief of the whole thousand? I answer, that the reason for prohibiting and punishing an action (and this reason may be called the *guilt* of the action, if you please) will always be in proportion to the whole mischief that would arise from the general impunity and toleration of actions of the same sort.

'Whatever is expedient, is right.' But then it must be expedient on the whole, at the long run, in all its effects, collateral and remote, as well as in those which are immediate and direct; as it is obvious, that, in computing consequences, it makes no difference in what way or at what distance they ensue.

To impress this doctrine on the minds of young readers, and to teach them to extend their views beyond the immediate mischief of a crime, I shall here subjoin a string of instances, in which the particular consequence is comparatively insignificant; and where the malignity of the crime, and the severity with which human laws pursue it, is almost entirely founded upon the general consequence.

The particular consequence of coining is, the loss of a guinea, or of half a guinea, to the person who receives the counterfeit money: the general consequence (by which I mean the consequence that would ensue, if the same practice were generally permitted) is, to abolish the use of money.

The particular consequence of forgery is, a damage of twenty or thirty pounds to the man who accepts the forged bill: the general consequence is, the stoppage of paper currency.

The particular consequence of sheep-stealing, or horse-stealing, is a loss to the owner, to the amount of the value of the sheep or horse stolen: the general consequence is, that the land could not be occupied, nor the market supplied, with this kind of stock.

The particular consequence of breaking into a house empty of inhabitants is, the loss of a pair of silver candle-sticks, or a few spoons: the general consequence is, that nobody could leave their house empty.

The particular consequence of smuggling may be a deduction from the national fund too minute for computation: the general consequence is, the destruction of one entire branch of public revenue; a proportionable increase of the burden upon other branches; and the ruin of all fair and open trade in the article smuggled.

The particular consequence of an officer's breaking his parole is, the loss of a prisoner, who was possibly not worth keeping: the general consequence, that this mitigation of captivity would be refused to all others.

And what proves incontestably the superior importance of general consequences is, that crimes are the same, and treated in the same manner, though the particular consequence be very different. The crime and fate of the house-breaker is the same, whether his booty be five pound or fifty. And the reason is, that the general consequence is the same.

The want of this distinction between particular and general consequences, or rather, the not sufficiently attending to the latter, is the cause of that perplexity which we meet with in ancient moralists. On the one hand, they were sensible of the absurdity of pronouncing actions good or evil, without regard to the good or evil they produced. On the other hand, they were startled at the conclusions to which a steady adherence to consequences seemed sometimes to conduct them. To relieve this difficulty, they contrived the τὸ πρεπον, or the *honestum*, by which terms they meant to constitute a measure of right, distinct from utility. Whilst the *utile* served them, that is, whilst it corresponded with their habitual notions of the rectitude of actions, they went by *it*. When they fell in with such cases as those mentioned in the sixth chapter, they took leave of their guide, and resorted to the *honestum*, The only account they could give of the matter was, that these actions might be useful; but, because they were not at the same time *honesta*, they were by no means to be deemed just or right.

From the principles delivered in this and the two preceding chapters, a maxim may be explained, which is in every man's mouth, and in most men's without meaning, *viz.* 'not to do evil, that good may come:' that is, let us not violate a general rule, for the sake of any particular good consequence we may expect: which is for the most part a salutary caution, the advantage seldom compensating for the violation of the rule. Strictly speaking, that cannot be 'evil,' from which 'good comes;' but in this way, and with a view to the distinction between particular and general consequences, it may.

We will conclude this subject of *consequences* with the following reflection. A man may imagine, that any action of his, with respect to the public, must be inconsiderable; so also is the agent. If his crime produce but a small effect upon the *universal* interest, his punishment or destruction bears a small proportion to the sum of happiness and misery in the creation.

CHAP. IX.
OF RIGHT.

RIGHT and obligation are reciprocal; that is, wherever there is a right in one person, there is a corresponding obligation upon others. If one man has a 'right' to an estate; others are 'obliged' to abstain from it. – If parents have a 'right' to reverence from their children; children are 'obliged' to reverence their parents; – and so in all other instances.

Now, because moral *obligation* depends, as we have seen, upon the will of God; *right*, which is correlative to it, must depend upon the same. Right therefore signifies, *consistency with the will of God*.

But if the Divine will determine the distinction of right and wrong, what else is it but an identical proposition, to say of God, that he acts *right?* or how is it possible to conceive even that he should act *wrong?* Yet these assertions are intelligible and significant. The case is this: By virtue of the two principles, that God wills the happiness of his creatures, and that the will of God is the measure of right and wrong, we arrive at certain conclusions; which conclusions become rules; and we soon learn to pronounce actions right or wrong, according as they agree or disagree with our rules, without looking any farther: and when the habit is once established of stopping at the rules, we can go back and compare with these rules even the Divine conduct itself; and yet it may be true (only not observed by us at the time) that the rules themselves are deduced from the Divine will.

Right is a quality of persons or of actions.

Of persons, as when we say, such a one has a 'right' to this estate; parents have a 'right' to reverence from their children; the king to allegiance from his subjects; masters have a 'right' to their servants' labour; a man has not a 'right' over his life.

Of actions; as in such expressions as the following: it is 'right' to punish murder with death; his behaviour on that occasion was 'right;' it is not 'right' to send an unfortunate debtor to jail; he did or acted 'right,' who gave up his place, rather than vote against his judgment.

In this latter set of expressions, you may substitute the definition of right above given, for the term itself; *e.g.* it is 'consistent with the will of God' to punish murder with death; – his behavior on that occasion was 'consistent with the will of God;' – it is not 'consistent with the will of God' to send an unfortunate debtor to jail; – he did or acted 'consistently with the will of God,' who gave up his place, rather than vote against his judgment.

In the former set, you must vary the construction a little, when you introduce the definition instead of the term. Such a one has a 'right' to this estate, that is, it is 'consistent with the will of God' that such a one should have it; – parents have a 'right' to reverence from their children, that is, it is 'consistent with the will of God' that children should reverence their parents; – and the same of the rest.

BOOK IV.

CHAP. III.
THE DUTY OF SUBMISSION TO CIVIL GOVERNMENT EXPLAINED.

THE subject of this chapter is sufficiently distinguished from the subject of the last, as the motives which actually produce civil obedience, may be, and often are, very different from the reasons which make that obedience a duty.

In order to prove civil obedience to be a moral duty, and an obligation upon the conscience, it hath been usual with many political writers (at the head of whom we find the venerable name of Locke) to state a compact between the citizen and the state, as the ground and cause of the relation between them; which compact, binding the parties for the same general reason that private contracts do, resolves the duty of submission to civil government into the universal obligation of fidelity in the performance of promises. This compact is twofold:

First, An *express* compact by the primitive founders of the state, who are supposed to have convened for the declared purpose of settling the terms of their political union, and a future constitution of government. The whole body is supposed, in the first place, to have unanimously consented to be bound by the resolutions of the majority; that majority, in the next place, to have fixed certain fundamental regulations; and then to have constituted, either in one person, or in an assembly (the rule of succession, or appointment, being at the same time determined), a *standing legislature*, to whom, under these pre-established restrictions, the government of the state was thenceforward committed, and whose laws the several members of the convention were, by their first undertaking, thus personally engaged to obey – This transaction is sometimes called the *social compact*, and these supposed original regulations compose what are meant by the *constitution*, the *fundamental laws of the constitution*; and form, on one side, the *inherent indefeasible prerogative of the crown;* and, on the other, the inalienable, imprescriptible *birthright* of the subject.

Secondly, A *tacit* or *implied* compact, by all succeeding members of the state, who, by accepting its protection, consent to be bound by its laws; in like manner as, whoever *voluntarily enters* into a private society is understood, without any other or more explicit stipulation, to promise a conformity with the rules and obedience to the government of that society, as the known conditions upon which he is admitted to a participation of its privileges.

This account of the subject, although specious, and patronised by names the most respectable, appears to labour under the following objections: that it is founded upon a supposition false in fact, and leading to dangerous conclusions.

No social compact, similar to what is here described, was ever made or entered into in reality; no such original convention of the people was ever actually holden, or in any country could be holden, antecedent to the existence of civil government in that country. It is to suppose it possible to call savages out of caves and deserts, to deliberate and vote upon topics, which the experience, and studies, and refinements, of civil life alone suggest. Therefore no government in the universe *began* from this original. Some imitation of a social compact may have taken place at a *revolution*. The present age has been witness to a transaction, which bears the nearest resemblance to this political idea, of any of which history has preserved the account or memory: I refer to the establishment of the United States of North America. We saw the *people* assembled to elect deputies, for the avowed purpose of framing the constitution of a new empire. We saw this deputation of the people deliberating and resolving upon a form of government, erecting a permanent legislature, distributing the functions of sovereignty, establishing and promulgating a code of fundamental ordinances, which were to be considered by succeeding generations, not merely as laws and acts of the state, but as the very terms and conditions of the confederation; as binding not only upon the subjects and magistrates of the state, but as limitations of power, which were to control and regulate the future legislature. Yet even here much was presupposed. In settling the constitution, many important parts were presumed to be already settled. The qualifications of the constituents who were admitted to vote in the election of members of congress, as well as the mode of electing the representatives, were taken from the old forms of government. That was wanting, from which every social union should set off, and which alone makes the resolution of the society the act of the individual, – the unconstrained consent of all to be bound by the decision of the majority; and yet, without this previous consent, the revolt, and the regulations which followed it, were compulsory upon dissentients.

But the original compact, we are told, is not proposed as a *fact*, but as a fiction, which furnishes a commodious explication of the mutual rights and duties of sovereigns and subjects. In answer to this representation of the matter, we observe, that the original compact, if it be not a fact, is nothing; can confer no actual authority upon laws or magistrates; nor afford any foundation to rights which are supposed to be real and existing. But the truth is, that in the books, and in the apprehension, of those who deduce our civil rights and obligations *à pactis*, the original convention is appealed to and treated of as a reality. Whenever the disciples of this system speak of the constitution; of the fundamental articles of the constitution; of laws being constitutional or unconstitutional; of inherent, inalienable, inextinguishable rights, either in the prince, or in the people; or indeed of any laws, usages, or civil rights, as transcending the authority of the subsisting legislature, or possessing a force and sanction superior to what belong to the modern acts and edicts of the legislature; they secretly refer us to what passed at the original convention. They would teach us to believe, that certain rules and ordinances were established by the people, at the same time that they settled the charter of government, and the powers as well as the form of the future legislature; that this legislature consequently, deriving its commission and existence from the consent and act of the primitive assembly (of which indeed it is only the standing deputation), continues subject, in the exercise of its offices, and as to the extent of its power, to the rules, reservations, and limitations, which the same assembly then made and prescribed to it.

'As the first members of the state were bound by express stipulation to obey the government which they had erected; so the succeeding inhabitants of the same country are understood to promise allegiance to the constitution and government they find established, by accepting its protection, claiming its privileges, and acquiescing in its laws; more especially, by the purchase or inheritance of lands, to the possession of which, allegiance to the state is annexed, as the very service and condition of the tenure.' Smoothly as this train of argument proceeds, little of it will endure examination. The native subjects of modern states are not conscious of any stipulation with the sovereigns, of ever exercising an election whether they will be bound or not by the acts of the legislature, of any alternative being proposed to their choice, of a promise either required or given; nor do they apprehend that the validity or authority of the laws depends at all upon *their* recognition or consent. In all stipulations, whether they be expressed or implied, private or public, formal or constructive, the parties stipulating must both possess the liberty of assent and refusal, and also be conscious of this liberty; which cannot with truth be affirmed of the subjects of civil government, as government is now, or ever was, actually administered. This is a defect, which no arguments can excuse or supply: all presumptions of consent, without this consciousness, or in opposition to it, are vain and erroneous. Still less is it possible to reconcile with any idea of stipulation the practice, in which all European nations agree, of founding allegiance upon the circumstance of nativity, that is, of claiming and treating as subjects all those who are born within the confines of their dominions, although removed to another country in their youth or infancy. In this instance certainly, the state does not presume a compact. Also, if the subject be bound only by his own consent, and if the voluntary abiding in the country be the proof and intimation of that consent, by what arguments should we defend the right, which sovereigns universally assume, of prohibiting, when they please, the departure of their subjects out of the realm?

Again, when it is contended that the taking and holding possession of land amounts to an acknowledgment of the sovereign, and a virtual promise of allegiance to his laws, it is necessary to the validity of the argument to prove, that the inhabitants who first composed and constituted the state, collectively possessed a right to the soil of the country; – a right to parcel it out to whom they pleased, and to annex to the donation what conditions they thought fit. How came they by this right? An agreement amongst themselves would not confer it; that could only adjust what already belonged to them. A society of men vote themselves to be the owners of a region of the world: – does that vote, unaccompanied especially with any culture, enclosure, or proper act of occupation, make it theirs? does it entitle them to exclude others from it, or to dictate the conditions upon which it shall be enjoyed? Yet this original collective right and ownership is the foundation for all the reasoning by which the duty of allegiance is inferred from the possession of land.

The theory of government which affirms the existence and the obligation of a social compact, would, after all, merit little discussion, and, however groundless and unnecessary, should receive no opposition from us, did it not appear to lead to conclusions unfavourable to the improvement and to the peace of human society.

1st. Upon the supposition that government was first erected by, and that it derives all its just authority from, resolutions entered into by a convention of the people, it is capable of being presumed, that many points were settled by that convention, anterior to the establishment of the subsisting legislature, and which the legislature, consequently, has no right to alter, or interfere with. These points are called the *fundamentals* of the consti-tution; and as it is impossible to determine how many, or what they are, the suggesting of any such serves extremely to embarrass the deliberations of the legislature, and affords a dangerous pretence for disputing the authority of the laws. It was this sort of reasoning (so far as reasoning of any kind was employed in the question) that produced in this nation the doubt, which so much agitated the minds of men in the reign of the second Charles, whether an act of parliament could of right alter or limit the succession of the crown.

2dly. If it be by virtue of a compact that the subject owes obedience to civil government, it will follow that he ought to abide by the form of government which he finds established, be it ever so absurd or inconvenient. He is bound by his bargain. It is not permitted to any man to retreat from his engagement, merely because he finds the performance disadvantageous, or because he has an opportunity of entering into a better. This law of contracts is universal: and to call the relation between the sovereign and the subjects a contract, yet not to apply to it the rules, or allow of the effects, of a contract, is an arbitrary use of names, and an unsteadiness in reasoning, which can teach nothing. Resistance to the *encroachments* of the supreme magistrate may be justified upon this principle; recourse to arms, for the purpose of bringing about an amendment of the constitution, never can. No form of government contains a provision for its own dissol-ution: and few governors will consent to the extinction, or even to any abridgment, of their own power. It does not therefore appear, how despotic governments can ever, in consistency with the obligation of the subject, be changed or mitigated. Despotism is the constitution of many states: and whilst a despotic prince exacts from his subjects the most rigorous servitude, according to this account, he is only holding them to their agreement. A people may vindicate, by force, the rights which the constitution has left them; but every attempt to narrow the prerogative of the crown, by new limitations, and in opposition to the will of the reigning prince, whatever opportunities may invite, or success follow it, must be condemned as an infraction of the compact between the sovereign and the subject.

3dly. Every violation of the compact on the part of the governor, releases the subject from his allegiance, and dissolves the government. I do not perceive how we can avoid this consequence, if we found the duty of allegiance upon compact, and confess any analogy between the social compact and other contracts. In private contracts, the violation and nonperformance of the conditions, by one of the parties, vacates the obligation of the other. Now the terms and articles of the social compact being nowhere extant or expressed; the rights and offices of the administrator of an empire being so many and various; the imaginary and controverted line of his prerogative being so liable to be overstepped in one part or other of it; the position, that every such transgression amounts to a forfeiture of the government, and consequently authorizes the people to withdraw their obedience and provide for themselves by a new settlement, would endanger the stability of every political fabric in the world, and has in fact always supplied the disaffected with a topic of seditious declamation. If occasions have arisen in which this plea has been resorted to with justice and success, they have been occasions in which a revolution was defensible on other and plainer principles. The plea itself is at all times captious and unsafe.

Wherefore, rejecting the intervention of a compact as unfounded in its principle, and dangerous in the application, we assign for the only ground of the subject's obligation, THE WILL OF GOD AS COLLECTED FROM EXPEDIENCY.

The steps by which the argument proceeds, are few and direct. – 'It is the will of God that the happiness of human life be promoted:' – this is the first step, and the foundation not only of this, but of every moral conclusion. 'Civil society conduces to that end:' – this is the second proposition. 'Civil societies cannot be upholden, unless, in each, the interest of the whole society be binding upon every part and member of it:' – this is the third step, and conducts us to the conclusion, namely, 'that so long as the interest of the whole society requires it, that is, so long as the established government cannot be resisted or changed without public inconveniency, it is the will of God (which *will* universally determines our duty) that the established government be obeyed,' – and no longer.

This principle being admitted, the justice of every particular case of resistance is reduced to a computation of the quantity of the danger and grievance on the one side, and of the probability and expense of redressing it on the other.

But who shall judge this? We answer, 'Every man for himself.' In contentions between the sovereign and the subject, the parties acknowledge no common arbitrator; and it would be absurd to refer the decision to *those* whose conduct has provoked the question, and whose own interest, authority, and fate, are immediately concerned in it. The danger of error and abuse is no objection to the rule of expediency, because every other rule is liable to the same or greater; and every rule that can be propounded upon the subject (like all rules indeed which appeal to, or bind, the conscience), must in the application depend upon private judgment. It may be observed, however, that it ought equally to be accounted the exercise of a man's own private judgment, whether he be determined by reasonings and conclusions of his own, or submit to be directed by the advice of others, provided he be free to choose his guide.

We proceed to point out some easy but important inferences, which result from the substitution of *public expediency* into the place of all implied compacts, promises, or conventions whatsoever.

I. It may be as much a duty, at one time, to resist government, as it is, at another, to obey it; to wit, whenever more advantage will, in our opinion, accrue to the community from resistance, than mischief.

II. The lawfulness of resistance, or the lawfulness of a revolt, does not depend alone upon the grievance which is sustained or feared, but also upon the probable expense and event of the contest. They who concerted the Revolution in England, were justifiable in their counsels, because, from the apparent disposition of the nation, and the strength and character of the parties engaged, the measure was likely to be brought about with little mischief or bloodshed; whereas it might have been a question with many friends of their country, whether the injuries then endured and threatened would have authorized the renewal of a doubtful civil war.

III. Irregularity in the first foundation of a state, or subsequent violence, fraud, or injustice, in getting possession of the supreme power, are not sufficient reasons for resistance, after the government is once peaceably settled. No subject of the British empire conceives himself engaged to vindicate the justice of the Norman claim or conquest, or apprehends that his duty in any manner depends upon that controversy. So likewise, if the house of Lancaster, or even the posterity of Cromwell, had been at this day seated upon the throne of England, we should have been as little concerned to inquire how the founder of the family came there. No civil contests are so futile, although none have been so furious and sanguinary, as those which are excited by a disputed succession.

IV. Not every invasion of the subject's rights, or liberty, or of the constitution; not every breach of promise, or of oath; not every stretch of prerogative, abuse of power, or neglect of duty, by the chief magistrate, or by the whole or any branch of the legislative body; justifies resistance, unless these crimes draw after them public consequences of sufficient magnitude to outweigh the evils of civil disturbance. Nevertheless, every violation of the constitution ought to be watched with jealousy, and resented as *such*, beyond what the quantity of estimable damage would require or warrant; because a known and settled usage of governing affords the only security against the enormities of uncontrolled dominion, and because this security is weakened by every encroachment which is made without opposition, or opposed without effect.

V. No usage, law, or authority whatever, is so binding, that it need or ought to be continued, when it may be changed with advantage to the community. The family of the prince, the order of succession, the prerogative of the crown, the form and parts of the legislature, together with the respective powers, office, duration, and mutual dependency, of the several parts, are all only so many *laws*, mutable like other laws, whenever expediency requires, either by the ordinary act of the legislature, or, if the occasion deserve it, by the interposition of the people. These points are wont to be approached with a kind of awe; they are represented to the mind as principles of the constitution settled by our ancestors, and, being settled, to be no more committed to innovation or debate; as foundations never to be stirred; as the terms and conditions of the social compact, to which every citizen of the state has engaged his fidelity, by virtue of a promise which he cannot now recall. Such reasons have no place in our system: to us, if there be any good reason for treating these with more deference and respect than other laws, it is either the advantage of the present constitution of government (which reason must be of different force in different countries), or because in all countries it is of importance that the form and usage of governing be acknowledged and understood, as well by the governors as by the governed, and because, the seldomer it is changed, the more perfectly it will be known by both sides.

VI. As all civil obligation is resolved into expediency, what, it may be asked, is the difference between the obligation of an Englishman and a Frenchman? or why, since the obligation of both appears to be founded in the same reason, is a Frenchman bound in conscience to bear any thing from his king, which an Englishman would not be bound to bear? Their conditions may differ, but their *rights*, according to this account, should seem to be equal: and yet we are accustomed to speak of the *rights* as well as of the happiness of a free people, compared with what belong to the subjects of absolute monarchies; how, you will say, can this comparison be explained, unless we refer to a difference in the compacts by which they are respectively bound? – This is a fair question, and the answer to it will afford a farther illustration of our principles. We admit then that there are many things which a Frenchman is bound in conscience, as well as by coercion, to endure at the hands of his prince, to which an Englishman would not be obliged to submit: but we assert that it is for these two reasons alone: *first*, because the same act of the prince is not the same grievance, where it is agreeable to the constitution, as where it infringes it; *secondly*, because redress in the two cases is not equally attainable. Resistance cannot be attempted with equal hopes of success, or with the same prospect of receiving support from others, where the people are reconciled to their sufferings, as where they are alarmed by innovation. In this way, and no otherwise, the subjects of different states possess different civil rights; the duty of obedience is defined by different boundaries; and the point of justifiable resistance placed at different parts of the *scale* of suffering; all which is sufficiently intelligible without a social compact.

VII. 'The interest of the whole society is binding upon every part of it.' No rule, short of this, will provide for the stability of civil government, or for the peace and safety of social life. Wherefore, as the individual members of the state are not permitted to pursue their private emolument to the prejudice of the community, so is it equally a consequence of this rule, that no particular colony, province, town, or district, can justly concert measures for their separate interest, which shall appear at the same time to diminish the *sum* of public prosperity. I do not mean, that it is necessary to the justice of a measure, that it profit each and every part of the community (for, as the happiness of the whole may be increased, whilst that of some parts is diminished, it is possible that the conduct of one part of an empire may be detrimental to some other part, and yet just, provided one part gain more in happiness than the other part loses, so that the common weal be augmented by the change); but what I affirm is, that those counsels can never be reconciled with the obligations resulting from civil union, which cause the *whole* happiness of the society to be impaired for the conveniency of a *part*. This conclusion is applicable to the question of right between Great Britain and her revolted colonies. Had I been an American, I should not have thought it enough to have had it even demonstrated, that a separation from the parent-state would produce effects beneficial to America; my relation to that state imposed upon me a farther inquiry, namely, whether the whole happiness of the empire was likely to be promoted by such a measure: not indeed the happiness of every part; that was not necessary, nor to be expected; – but whether what Great Britain would lose by the separation, was likely to be compensated to the joint stock of happiness, by the advantages which America would receive from it. The contested claims of sovereign states and their remote dependencies may be submitted to the adjudication of this rule with mutual safety. A public advantage is measured by the advantage which each individual receives, and by the number of those who receive it. A public evil is compounded of the same proportions. Whilst, therefore, a colony is small, or a province thinly inhabited, if a competition of interests arise between the original country and their acquired dominions, the former ought to be preferred; because it is fit that, if one must necessarily be sacrificed, the less give place to the greater: but when, by an increase of population, the interest of the provinces begins to bear a considerable proportion to the *entire* interest of the community, it is possible that they may suffer so much by their subjection, that not only theirs, but the whole happiness of the empire, may be obstructed by their union. The rule and principle of the calculation being still the same, the *result* is different: and this difference begets a new situation, which entitles the subordinate parts of the state to more equal terms of confederation, and, if these be refused, to independency.

PART TWO
Secular Utilitarians

INTRODUCTION
Secular Utilitarian Critics of Organized Religion

Jeremy Bentham (1748–1832) is frequently cited as the founder of modern utilitarian theory. In the path-breaking *Introduction to the Principles of Morals and Legislation (IPML)*, published in 1789, he set about delineating the component parts of the theory, with the aim of founding a comprehensive science of morals and legislation upon the principle of utility.[1] No previous moralist could lay claim to such ambition or to the precision that Bentham brought to the task. Nonetheless, in the light of the writings published by the eighteenth-century religious utilitarian (included in Part One) Bentham's claim to being the founder of the theory is subject to qualification. Certainly, Bentham himself was cognisant that he had been preceded in several fundamental respects by other theorists, and he was familiar with the writings of several of the religious utilitarians. There were even occasions when, for tactical purposes, he allied himself with the religious proponents in a unified front against the critics of the utility principle.[2] However, the primary influences shaping his own version of the theory came from the anti-clerical and, in some cases, atheistic philosophes of France.[3] Repelled by what he perceived as the ascetic and complacent implications of religious utilitarianism, Bentham drew substantially upon the rationalist strand of the enlightenment, promoted a secularized form of the principle of utility, and launched a far-reaching onslaught on its religious affiliation. James Mill (1773–1836) and John Stuart Mill (1806–73), as well as Bentham, developed critiques of religious belief and religious institutions from the perspective of their own version of utilitarianism. However, if Bentham and the Mills herald the secular phase of the history of the theory, there are also 'religious' remnants in their thought which run contrary to this neat chronology, and which indicate a more complex relationship between utilitarianism and religion in the nineteenth century.

[1] Jeremy Bentham, *An Introduction to the Principles of Morals and Legislation* (CW), ed. J. H. Burns and H. L. A. Hart, With a New Introduction by F. Rosen (Oxford 1996). Henceforth *IPML* (CW).

[2] Discussed in James E. Crimmins, 'Religion, Utility and Politics: Bentham versus Paley,' in James E. Crimmins (ed.), *Religion, Secularization and Political Thought: Thomas Hobbes to J. S. Mill* (London 1990), pp. 130–52.

[3] For a discussion of the influences on the development of Bentham's philosophy see James E. Crimmins, *Secular Utilitarianism: Social Science and the Critique of Religion in the Thought of Jeremy Bentham* (Oxford 1990), Ch. 1.

1

Bentham's published writings on religion were the culmination of nearly a lifetime's reflection on its supposed fictions, absurdities, and evil consequences. The lengthy examination of the Anglican Church, its creed, institutions, and politics, in *Church-of-Englandism and its Catechism Examined* (1818) was followed by the briefer and more thoughtfully contrived dissection of Christianity's fundamental beliefs in *An Analysis of the Influence of Natural Religion on the Temporal Happiness of Mankind* (1822), and the bombastic polemic on Paley's version of the life and miracles of St Paul in *Not Paul, but Jesus* (1823).[4] Bentham was in his seventies when these works appeared in print. However, the basic tenets of this critique of religion were already a part of his philosophy when *IPML* appeared over forty years before.

Early in his intellectual development Bentham became aware of the attraction of the religious version of the doctrine of utility to his Christian contemporaries. He opposed it on both metaphysical and moral grounds. Materialism and nominalism dictated that the ideas of the soul, of a future state, and of an all-seeing omnipotent God were fictions irreducible to 'real' entities. Bentham's descriptive theory of language, with its attendant classificatory and paraphrastic techniques, revealed that these ideas, lacking physical referents, could not be made intelligible to the human understanding.[5] This did not change the fact that the religious sanction influenced the actions of individuals and, like John Gay, Bentham included it as one of the four forms of sanctions – together with the physical, political or legal, moral or popular sanctions – capable of giving binding force to any law or rule of conduct.[6] At the same time, his emerging vision of the rational utilitarian society did not require the continuance of an institution so obviously detrimental to the greatest happiness. This was made plain in the pages of *IPML*,[7] and Bentham's convictions on this question remained fixed for the remainder of his life.

In the second decade of the new century Bentham's critique of religion became part of his general assault on England's political establishment. In the *Plan of Parliamentary Reform* (1817), which he started to write in 1809, he gave a sketch of the 'temporal' nature of the constitution and expounded the democratic causes of annual parliaments, secret and uni-

---

[4]   Jeremy Bentham, *Church-of-Englandism and its Catechism Examined* (London 1818), *Analysis of the Influence of Natural Religion on the Temporal Happiness of Mankind*, by 'Philip Beauchamp' [ed. G. Grote] (London 1822), and *Not Paul, but Jesus*, by 'Gamaliel Smith' (London 1823). Henceforth *Church-of-Englandism*, *Analysis*, and *Not Paul*, respectively.

[5]   For Bentham's discussion of the soul and of the nature of God see 'A Fragment on Ontology', in *The Works of Jeremy Bentham, Published under the Superintendence of his Executor, John Bowring*, 11 vols. (Edinburgh, 1838–43), viii. 196 and note. Henceforth Bowring. For a discussion see Crimmins, *Secular Utilitarianism*, pp. 52–60.

[6]   Bentham, *IPML* (CW), p. 34.

[7]   Bentham, *IPML* (CW), Ch. II, esp. pp. 18, 31–32 and note.

versal male suffrage. In *Church-of-Englandism* he promised to tackle the 'spiritual' nature of the constitution.[8] In the event he went to extraordinary lengths to point out all the absurdities inherent in both the structure and doctrines of the church. In its final form *Church-of-Englandism* presents us with a general exposé of the corruption and corrupting effect of the ecclesiastical establishment in England. Its nearly 800 pages are constituted of two prefaces, a detailed Plan of the Work, and three separate parts to the main text: (1) an Introduction in five parts on the 'exclusionary system' operated by the National Society for Promoting the Education of the Poor in the Principles of the Established Church (founded in 1811); (2) 'The Church of England Catechism Examined'; and (3) five appendices on various aspects of 'Church-of-Englandism', including suggestions for the reform of the Church leading to its 'euthanasia'. 'The Church of England Catechism Examined' – 'the body of the work', later published on its own in 1824 – provides us with several of the liveliest parts of *Church-of-Englandism*.[9]

Bentham's declared purpose in his examination of the Catechism was to expose its 'poisonous nature'. The use of the Catechism in the schools of the National Society was based on the argument that the Bible is complex and needs interpretation in order to be understood by children. However, to Bentham the Catechism is 'spurious matter' which children will not be any the better for having learnt by heart. Central to this argument is Bentham's distinction between the 'understanding' and the 'will'. The former is that to which argument appeals and which can be won over by the persuasion of reason; the latter is the source of the volitions upon which we act and is formed according to the motivation provided by the sanctions of pleasure and pain. The reasonable person will act according to the apparent reasonableness perceived in a proposed action; where reason does not prevail the will can be directed by the inducements of pleasure or the threat of pain, or a combination of the two. At the bottom of Bentham's charge against the Church's use of the Catechism in the National Society's schools is the acknowledgement that the episcopacy fully understood the human psyche and consciously employed methods calculated to influence, to shape and control it. What distinguishes sinister from benign influence is the difference between, on the one hand, the action of will on will and, on the other hand, the action of the understanding on understanding. In Bentham's ethics the appeal to rational argument, that is to consequentialist calculation, is the proper and acceptable mode by which one person may influence the mind and actions of another. By comparison, the over-powering of one will by another – save with the aid

[8] Bentham, *Church-of-Englandism*, Preface on Publication, pp. x–xi.
[9] Jeremy Bentham, *The Church of England Catechism Examined* (London 1824). Henceforth *Catechism Examined*.

of legal sanctions designed to further the public good – is an improper and thus a sinister mode of influence.[10]

That the Catechism contains matter tending to the 'prostration of understanding and will', Bentham was pleased to note, is openly avowed by William Howley, the Bishop of London, who expressly stated it to be the aim of the National Society and the reason for employing the Catechism in its schools. In his *Charge to the Clergy of London* (1815) Howley set forth the Church's position as follows: those of the nonconforming sects outside the pale of the Anglican Church are ' "generally" . . . men of some education, whose thoughts "have been little employed on the subject of religion; or who, *loving rather to question than learn*, have approached *the oracles of divine truth* without that *humble docility*, that *prostration of the understanding* and *will*, which are indispensable to proficiency in Christian instruction" '.[11] This lent credence to Bentham's claim that it is not the word of Christ, but the Church's scriptural 'interpretation' before which children are to prostrate themselves in the schools of the National Society. In this regard the Bishop stands condemned by his own words: to interpret the Scriptures, Bentham admonished, is 'arbitrarily imposing a meaning unwarranted by the usages of language'.[12] Yet, is this not exactly what the Catechism represents? It is clearly implied that the 'oracles of divine truth' are to be found here and not in the Bible. Hence it is not the case that the understanding and will are prostrate before God; they lie prostrate before the Church and its formulary – the prostration is of 'man before man', and a mind which is prostrate is 'a mind in the lowest state of debility'.[13]

Another of Bentham's complaints was that like subscriptions to articles of faith the Catechism fosters the habit of insincerity. To demand assent from a child too young to understand that to which he is assenting is to 'force him to *tell lies*', and consequently the child will 'contract the *habit* of lying'.[14] When a child subscribes to Church doctrines via the Catechism that child avows belief in all the articles of the Christian faith, and this is a promise to believe an innumerable host of things hardly any of which can be understood. (294)[15] This, Bentham claimed, strikes at the root of all religion and all morality: 'forasmuch as, in giving utterance to this mass

---

[10]   See L. J. Hume, *Bentham and Bureaucracy* (Cambridge 1981), p. 182, where he paraphrases Bentham on this topic from Bentham MSS, University College London (UCL) cxxv. 47–52. These mss. are headed 'Parliamentary Reform' and dated 1811.

[11]   William Howley, Bp of London, *A Charge to the Clergy of London at the Primary Visitation of that Diocese in the Year 1814* (London 1815), p. 23, quoted in *Church-of-Englandism*, App. I, p. 88. Bentham's emphases.

[12]   Howley, *A Charge to the Clergy of London*, p. 22, quoted in *Church-of-Englandism*, App. I, p. 92.

[13]   *Church-of-Englandism*, App. I, p. 89.

[14]   *Church-of-Englandism*, p. 12.

[15]   *Catechism Examined*, p. 17 [*Church-of-Englandism*, 'Catechism Examined', pp. 13–14]. Page numbers given in brackets () are references to the present volume (hence 294).

of absurdity, the child is forced to say that *he believes it*, – while, at his years, at any rate, to believe is not possible, – thus it is that the duty and practice of *lying* forms part of every Church of England child's first lesson'. (295)[16] Nor is this mendacity confined to the instance of avowal. It is something which stays with the child for life; it inculcates the habit of lying, of insincerity, the notion that it is acceptable to assent to doctrines which are not understood and hence cannot be believed.

The articles of belief contained in the Catechism which Bentham denounced as absurd are: the notion of the Devil as God's protagonist, the idea that God was conceived by the Holy Ghost, the claim that Christ was born of a virgin mother and that the son of God died a mortal death, and the doctrines of the Trinity and the Communion of Saints. In treating of these various propositions he turned his irony to good effect, but it is his theory of language which is the foundation of the analysis. Bentham's metaphysics dictates that words must correspond to objects, or they must be capable of reduction by paraphrasis to real entities. If in a given case neither is true or possible then the word in question is a fiction, likely to cause confusion and capable of misapplication in unscrupulous hands as a means of deception. Never could there have been a subject so open to an attack founded on the demand for definitions and clear and unambiguous language as the Church Catechism. We need not, however, follow Bentham through his entire critique of the Apostles' Creed (297–307);[17] its character is readily conveyed by a few brief examples.

The doctrine of the Trinity Bentham declared a glaring example of a proposition lacking any obvious sense, but in which children are expected to avow belief. Such an avowal is to utter 'sounds without sense; mere words without meaning'. If the Holy Ghost is the Holy Spirit of God, why do we need to profess belief in both God and his spirit? 'Believing in a man, what more do you do, by believing in his spirit likewise?' It is only to 'string words upon words, – and then, for every word, believe, or pretend to believe, that a correspondent really existing object is brought into existence'. (300)[18] The article of belief in 'the Holy Catholic Church' is similarly dealt with. Is it the Church of England that is meant here or is it the Roman Catholic Church – the Church of the Papists, who once persecuted English Protestants? What is it that makes the Church 'holy'? The article is a confused proposition to which no explanation is so much as hazarded. Bentham is sure that if the 'poor child' were to think upon the subject 'how distressing must be the perplexity into which he here finds

---

[16] *Catechism Examined*, pp. 18–19 [*Church-of-Englandism*, 'Catechism Examined', p. 15].
[17] *Catechism Examined*, pp. 23–40 [*Church-of-Englandism*, 'Catechism Examined', pp. 17–32].
[18] *Catechism Examined*, pp. 27, 28 [*Church-of-Englandism*, 'Catechism Examined', pp. 20, 22].

himself plunged?' (301–2)[19] He is made to declare 'that he believes in whatever is thus forced into his mouth, without knowing so much as *who* it is that put it where it is, much less *what* it is'. The only thing learnt from this mode of instruction is 'the art of *gratuitous assertion* – the art of speaking and writing without thinking – and the art of making *groundless inferences*'. (304)[20] Such are the pernicious consequences of 'catechitical instruction'.

Bentham's irony is unrestrained in his examination of the sacraments of baptism and communion. These, according to a literalist interpretation of the New Testament, are found to have received no sanction from Jesus; they are entirely the fabrication of the Church. (287–93, 316–31)[21] So far as baptism is concerned, Bentham suggests that Christ's example of washing the feet of his Apostles is a more instructive ceremony for the clergy to follow with their congregations, though he acknowledged that the bishops were hardly likely to stoop so low. (324–26)[22] For communion Bentham has particularly harsh words. The transubstantiation or metamorphosis of bread and wine into body and blood, he says, 'is the *pure* grimgribber of modern *technical* theology'. In Luther's reform of Roman Catholic theology the body and blood of Christ are said to accompany the bread and wine. This theory of consubstantiation Bentham called 'the *adulterated* grimgribber', and found in it a source of even greater confusion than in the theory of transubstantiation: 'on the *con* plan the mess has more matter in it than in the *trans*: and the more the worse'.[23] On either version the idea of communion is little better than 'cannibalism'. The trick in the explanation, Bentham explained, is to refer to the 'spiritual sense' of the proposition; this is the appeal to a purer sense, superior to the carnal or temporal sense. It is by this means that something false or absurd becomes true or reasonable. If there is a mind to subdue this is the way to accomplish the task, by introducing 'the *spiritual* sense – alias the *nonsensical* sense'. (328–31)[24]

---

[19] *Church Catechism*, pp. 30, 31 [*Church-of-Englandism*, 'Catechism Examined', pp. 23, 24].

[20] *Catechism Examined*, p. 35 [*Church-of-Englandism*, 'Catechism Examined', pp. 27, 28].

[21] *Catechism Examined*, pp. 4–14, 55–83 [*Church-of-Englandism*, 'Catechism Examined', pp. 2–11, 47–72]; see also *Church-of-Englandism*, pp. 238–45, and App. II, pp. 154–67.

[22] *Catechism Examined*, pp. 71–73 [*Church-of-Englandism*, 'Catechism Examined', pp. 62–63]; see also *Church-of-Englandism*, App. II, pp. 167–68.

[23] Art. XXVIII of the Thirty-nine Articles, 'Of the Lord's Supper', distinguishes the Anglican interpretation from the Roman Catholic belief in transubstantiation which, it is said, 'cannot be proved by Holy Writ; but is repugnant to the plain words of scripture, over-throweth the nature of the sacrament, and hath given occasion to many superstitions.' Bentham appears to confuse the Catholic and Anglican versions of the sacrament. On the Anglican view, 'The Body of Christ is given, taken, and eaten, in the Supper, only after an heavenly and spiritual manner. And the means whereby the Body of Christ is received and eaten in the Supper is Faith' (E. J. Bicknell, *A Theological Introduction to the Thirty-Nine Articles of the Church of England* (1919; 3rd edn. rev. H. J. Carpenter, London 1955), p. 382).

[24] *Catechism Examined*, pp. 78–83 [*Church-of-Englandism*, 'Catechism Examined', pp. 68–72].

According to Bentham, then, the 'avowed object' of the bishops in enforcing the use of the Catechism is neither more nor less than a system of intellectual and moral slavery. The schools of the National Society are the instruments of the 'tyrants and sub-tyrants' in the ecclesiastical hierarchy; the result is oppression and persecution.

Bentham's criticisms of natural and revealed religion received their most comprehensive treatment in the *Analysis* and *Not Paul*. In these works religion in general and Christianity in particular are by turns ridiculed, denounced as anti-intellectual, and condemned as socially pernicious. Bentham would have been well-pleased that from a reading of the *Analysis* Leslie Stephen concluded that utilitarianism 'logically implied the rejection of all theology'.[25] Here, in exhaustive manner, Bentham tested the belief in the after-life against a conception of the world based on the methodological premises, as he understood them, of natural science. In *Not Paul* Bentham set out to undermine the historical foundations of Christianity by revealing the subversive character of Paul's contribution, questioning his motives and indicating the contrast with the teachings of Christ. In the process he subjected the scriptural 'reports' of Paul's miracles to a close examination, founded on the same experiential arguments used in the *Analysis*.

The objective of the *Analysis* was to show that conflict between legitimate attempts at political reform, on the one hand, and arbitrary power, on the other, can only be resolved by setting aside all beliefs of a religious or otherworldly nature. Religion, Bentham declared (probably with Paley's religious version of the doctrine of utility in mind),

> has been affirmed to be the leading bond of union between the different members of a society – to be the most powerful curb on the immoral and unsocial passions of individuals – to form the consolation and support of misfortunes and declining life – in short it has been described as the most efficient prop both of inward happiness and of virtuous practice in this world. (345)[26]

The supposed truth of these assertions formed the subject-matter of Bentham's inquiry. His conclusions were predictable. He found that the inducements of Heaven and Hell provide no rule of guidance whatever for the pursuit of earthly happiness. On the contrary, they frequently suggest rules of action unconducive to the attainment of happiness. Moreover, such is human nature that fears of future punishment outweigh the hopes of future reward, and this produced an overall loss of happiness due to the disquietude that is occasioned by contemplating the prospect of death. Finally, the threat of God's wrath in the hereafter affects the conduct of

---

[25] Leslie Stephen, *The English Utilitarians*, 3 vols. (London 1950), ii. 40.
[26] *Analysis*, p. 1.

individuals in this life by preventing them from learning and obeying the rules which experience alone can teach them. In this respect religion introduced perplexity and confusion into the science of morality.

In applying the methods of natural science to theological questions Bentham believed he stood on firm ground and, despite the fact that the two men shared similar assumptions about human nature, beheld a recognizable enemy in the shape of William Paley. In Paley he encountered the classic statement of the argument from design, the principal prop of orthodox natural theology in the eighteenth century. The *a priori* argument for the existence of God based on intuition, effective where it fell in with commonly held beliefs, was unconvincing to the person who simply denied the existence of the intuition. In contrast, the argument from final causes purported to rest on common ground with the philosophy which demanded empirical proof. The existence of the Deity, it was thought, could be inferred from the ordered workings of Nature, in just the same manner that the existence of a watchmaker could be inferred from the existence of a watch. This was Paley's argument in *Natural Theology* (1802).

The classic critique of the argument from design is found in Hume's *Dialogues concerning Natural Religion*, published in 1779, over twenty years before Paley's *Natural Theology* appeared. Like Hume, Bentham met the argument on its own ground, that is to say, the world of experience. He denounced it as 'completely extra-experiential'; it describes the transition from confusion to order but no one has ever had experience of this 'preliminary chaos'. Nor is the original creative power of God certified by experience. Hence to introduce the notion of an 'omnipotent will' in order to explain the facts is really no explanation at all, but rather a collection of meaningless words. The argument from design sounds plausible because it applies reasoning which is undeniably valid when appropriately applied: the inference from a watch to a watchmaker is persuasive because we know what is meant by a watchmaker and sufficient of what is involved in making a watch. However, when the inference is that the world was created by an intelligent being, we infer the action of an incomprehensible being performing an incredible operation upon inconceivable materials. As such the inference is really illusory or else results in the assertion that the phenomenon is inexplicable.

The disjunction between the belief that the world was created by an intelligent agent and an individual's experience of the world itself required no further elaboration for Bentham.[27] He argued that there either is undeniable evidence to support a proposition or there is not; if there is not, then it is a belief which has nothing to do with the world of experience and as such is irrelevant to any discussion of the relationship between

---

[27] For David Hume's subtle reasoning on the same question see *Dialogues concerning Natural Religion*, ed. Norman Kemp Smith (1779; London 1947), p. 88, and the discussion in J. C. A. Gaskin, *Hume's Philosophy of Religion* (London 1978), pp. 130–39.

individuals and their world. However, Bentham was not so much concerned with the truth of the proposition that 'God created the world' as with the problem of what kind of world exists. Hence his discussion focused rather upon the supposed attributes of God.

Even if we grant, which Bentham does not, that the world was created by a designing intelligence, we are still not justified on his account of the matter in ascribing any intentions to its creator other than what are actually realized in the visible constitution of things. Insofar as nature and history testify to a certain degree of justice and beneficence in the distribution of pleasure and pain, the author of nature can be credited with justice and benevolence; but if on examination we perceive inequalities of fortune in the world irreconcilable with our notions of morality, we have no grounds for inferring that God's intentions have been thwarted in the execution. (355–56)[28] Bentham attempted to demonstrate the impossibility of individuals forming any other idea of God's attributes than a damning one. The less people know of something the more they feel threatened by it. In this case it is ignorance of the after-life which leads a person to fill the void by imagining its terrors. For fear is 'the never-failing companion and offspring of ignorance'. (347)[29] Only knowledge can protect us from these superstitious fancies, and 'wherever our knowledge fails us and we are reduced to a state of unprotected helplessness, all our sense of security, all anticipations of future ease, must vanish along with it'. An unknown future necessarily comes fraught with misery and torment. (347)[30] Added to this, because pain, measure for measure, is a stronger sensation than pleasure (Bentham ignores the difficulties this presents for calculation) so the idea of a posthumous existence is more likely to be conceived as a state of suffering rather than of enjoyment. This is the case because to those struggling to satisfy their needs 'pain alone, and want or uneasiness, which is a species of pain, are the standing provisions of nature'. Pleasure, on the other hand, is 'artificial and invented'. (348)[31]

It is our uncertainty about what is in store for us after death, then, that leads us to fear the worst. But even where the rewards of the after-life most readily come to mind it is, Bentham claimed, 'impossible to conceive an expectation more deplorably uncertain'. (372)[32] Though such expectations can be intense and durable to the utmost extent, this is the work of the imagination and not the result of experience. Naturally, given specific circumstances, one may imagine the consequences of a potential act and this could provide a legitimate motive to perform it.[33] But to visualize

[28] *Analysis*, pp. 19–20.
[29] *Analysis*, p. 5.
[30] *Ibid.*
[31] *Analysis*, p. 7.
[32] *Analysis*, p. 47.
[33] See Bentham's distinction between pleasures and pains 'in prospect' and pleasures and pains 'in esse' in *IPML* (CW), p. 98.

futurity is 'to exalt the conceptions of fancy to a level with real and actual experience, so that the former shall effect the mind as vividly as the latter', which, for Bentham, 'is the sole characteristic of insanity, and the single warrant for depriving the unhappy madman of his liberty'. (373)[34]

Experience is the touch-stone of this account and on these terms it dismayed Bentham that religion should exercise a significant influence upon human conduct. By contrast, the pleasures and pains of this life unavoidably affect our conduct and experience teaches us the actions to which they are attached. Such knowledge is simply not available to us in respect of a posthumous existence. Any conceptions we have of the character of this future world can only be based upon the conceptions we entertain of the character of the Deity, and these conceptions are notoriously distinguished by their failure to account for all the evidence. The predictable result of the 'fundamental data' should be no more or less than the conception of a capricious and tyrannical Being productive of 'extreme and unmixed fear'. (354)[35] To assume, as the religious exponents of utility do, that the Deity treats us with favour and kindness is a presumption entirely inconsistent with the evidence of experience. The actual conception of the Deity, according to Bentham, should really be a mixed one, perceived as fluctuating between good and evil 'but infinitely more as an object of terror than of hope'. (356)[36]

Of particular interest in *Not Paul* is the discussion of Paul's miracles, including his conversion on the road to Damascus. Here again Bentham employed the presuppositions of his social science, though the whole discussion is carried on in language more appropriate to a court room than to a philosophical or theological controversy. Bentham began the book disingenuously, by proposing that the reader should think of him as continuing the critical work begun by Conyers Middleton (1683–1750) in his celebrated *Free Inquiry into the Miraculous Powers* (1748).[37] Hume's first *Enquiry*, containing the section 'Of Miracles', was published in the same year as Middleton's *Free Inquiry*. Many years later Hume confessed his chagrin in his autobiographical 'My Own Life' (1777): 'On my return from Italy, I had the mortification to find all England in a ferment, on account of Dr Middleton's *Free Inquiry*, while my performance was entirely overlooked and neglected.'[38] There was every reason to compare the two investigations. Both tended to undermine the belief in miracles, but whereas Hume was raising methodological difficulties about the possibility of providing adequate historical proof of such occurrences, Middleton

---

[34] *Analysis*, pp. 48–49.
[35] *Analysis*, pp. 16–17.
[36] *Analysis*, p. 20.
[37] *Not Paul*, p. iii; Conyers Middleton, *A Free Inquiry into the Miraculous Powers* (1748; Dublin 1749).
[38] David Hume, 'My Own Life', in *An Inquiry Concerning Human Understanding*, ed. Charles W. Hendel (New York 1955), pp. 5–6.

concentrated principally on the kind of historical evidence actually available. In the first place, Middleton addressed his argument to those Protestants who believed in the occurrence of miracles, but who also held that the age of miracles was now past. He recognised this was a precarious position to take, since it was not readily apparent exactly where the dividing line should be drawn. Middleton sought to address this weakness, but in doing so, inadvertently perhaps, he could not help casting doubt upon the credibility of the miracles of the New Testament. Although he never ventured to question the miracles performed by the Apostles, he attacked the credibility of similar accounts in the early Christian Church. In a series of highly damaging quotations, he exposed the credulity of 'the primitive Fathers' including St Augustine, and went so far as to cite passages in which they appeared to be deliberately approving pious frauds. It was this aspect of Middleton's work that Bentham applauded. But, in truth, Bentham had more in common with Hobbes and Hume than with Middleton on miracles.

Though concerned to maintain the institutions of the Church under the political will of the sovereign, Hobbes was convinced that its revelatory foundations were less than secure. In *Leviathan* he argued that it is the ignorance of natural causes which inclines persons to believe in supernatural events and, additionally, that those who lack experience of human tricks are the most easily deceived.[39] Hume, too, in *The Natural History of Religion* (1757) ascribed the origin of religious beliefs to the ignorance of natural causes, adding that such beliefs were assisted by the incessant hopes and fears that actuate the human mind.[40] And in concluding the chapter of the *Enquiry* in which he had cast doubt on the belief in miracles he asserted that,

> the *Christian Religion* not only was at first attended with miracles, but even to this day cannot be believed by any reasonable person without one. Mere reason is insufficient to convince us of its veracity: And whoever is moved by *Faith* to assent to it, is conscious of a continued miracle in his own person, which subverts all the principles of his understanding and gives him a determination to believe what is most contrary to custom and experience.[41]

Bentham followed closely Hume's analysis, though his language was rather that of the propagandist than the enquiring philosopher.

---

[39]   Thomas Hobbes, *Leviathan* (London 1651), Pt. III, Ch. XXXVII.
[40]   David Hume, *The Natural History of Religion*, in *Essays Literary Moral, and Political* (London n.d. [1870?]), pp. 516–17.
[41]   David Hume, *An Enquiry Concerning Human Understanding*, in *Enquiries concerning Human Understanding and concerning the Principles of Morals*, ed. L. A. Selby-Bigge; 3rd edn. rev. by P. H. Hidditch (1748, 1751; Oxford 1975), sec. X, Pt II, p. 131.

Miracles, Bentham had written in the *Analysis*, are founded upon the extra-experiential belief that God interferes in earthly affairs, or more precisely, miracles are 'fictions by which the human intellect has . . . been cheated and overrun'.[42] Paul's revelation was a fraud of this nature, and Bentham believed that this could be established by reading Paul's own version of his conversion to Christianity. In the Epistle to the Galatians, for instance, Paul omitted to explain the circumstances of his revelation and this drew the retort from Bentham:

> Revelation? revelation from Jesus? from the Lord, speaking from heaven? from the Almighty? On what occasion, in what place, at what time, in what company (if in any,) was it thus received? To no one of these questions does he venture to furnish an answer – or so much as an allusion to an answer. Why? – even because he had none to give.[43]

The reason for Paul's omission, Bentham explained in his role of prosecutor, is because in attendance when this epistle was delivered were the Apostles and men acquainted with the Apostles, that is, 'men who would surely have denied what he said'.[44] In the eyes of the Apostles Paul's revelation was a fabrication and it is strange that modern Christians 'who . . . know nothing about it, take it for granted that it was all true'.[45]

Reviewing the scriptural testimony from Acts of the Apostles commonly cited to support Paul's miracles (391–411),[46] Bentham's analysis proceeded in typically peremptory and disdainful fashion. The blinding of Elymas the sorcerer (Acts xiii: 6–12) is explained in terms of an agreement between Paul and Elymas to their mutual benefit. The healing of the crippled Lystra (Acts xiv: 8–11) is accounted for by portraying Lystra as a vagrant hired 'for a few pence' to act a part designed by Paul. The exorcism of the Devil from Lydia (Acts xvi: 16–18) cannot be substantiated since nobody saw the Devil, not even the historian who recorded the deed. The earthquake at Philippi which created the opportunity for Paul and Silas to escape from prison (Acts xvi: 25–40) was brought about 'by means altogether natural'. Paul's vision at Corinth (Acts xviii: 7–11) cannot be verified since only he was a witness to it. The exorcisms at Ephesus (Acts xix: 1–20) have no evidence of persons, times or places to support them. The raising of Entychus from the dead (Acts xx: 7–12) is confuted by Paul's own account of the matter. The comforting of Paul by an angel (Acts xxvii: 20–25) is a lie formulated by Paul himself. His survival of a snake-bite (Acts xxviii: 1–6) is explained by the fact that the snake, at that moment, 'happened . . .

---

[42] *Analysis*, p. 103.
[43] *Not Paul*, p. 66.
[44] *Not Paul*, p. 68.
[45] *Not Paul*, p. 230.
[46] *Not Paul*, Ch. XIII, secs. 2–13, pp. 302–34.

not to be provided with a competent stock of venom' having 'already expended it upon some other object'. Finally, the curing of the father of Publius (Acts xxviii: 7–10) was not brought about by Paul's intervention but by the fever ceasing of its own accord.

Bentham's treatment of Paul's miracles is strictly in accord with his view that the Scriptures are to be read as any other texts of history, that is, according to methods applied in all other areas and periods of human history. If miracles, being events which transcend or violate the laws of nature, do occur then we cannot draw a line, as Middleton and others do, and admit the truth only of a special class of reports of miracles, denying on general historical grounds that any other reports down through the ages could possibly be true. If we do this we give up the possibility of writing history altogether. On the other hand, if we accept the presupposition of a connection between natural causes and natural events then we must deal not with miracles but with stories of miracles. This was clearly Bentham's position and, as we have seen, he found no difficulty in supplying an account of such 'stories'. His principal argument against the belief in miracles, however, is much like that given by Hume in the essay 'Of Miracles': the ultimate standard is always derived from experience and observation and the wise man will always proportion his belief to the evidence.[47] No amount of testimony in favour of belief in a miracle, Hume claimed, could conceivably balance, let alone outweigh, the evidence against it, or, what comes to the same thing, in favour of the law or laws of nature it allegedly violates.[48] In a similar vein Bentham claimed, if a miracle were reported today we should not be surprised if persons who heard of it were sceptical. Who can doubt that if Paul's exorcism of Lydia were 'spoken of in some newspaper, as having happened in the present year' that it would, 'by its disconformity to the manifest state of things, and the whole course of nature, be regarded as too absurd and flagrantly incredible to deserve to be entitled to a moment's notice'. (395)[49]

Bentham's legal training is evident throughout this discussion. What is believed to have happened at so many centuries distance is accepted on the authority of the testimony of witnesses, but for the most part such evidence is merely circumstantial. Reviewing the evidence supporting Paul's revelation, Bentham asks, 'would any judge fine a man a shilling?' And in an extraordinary outburst Bentham censured Locke and Newton for believing Paul's revelation when the evidence was so slight: 'O Locke! O Newton! where was your discernment!'[50] In the case of Paul's conversion, the evi-

---

[47] Hume, *An Inquiry Concerning Human Understanding*, in *Enquiries*, sec. X, Pt I, pp. 114, 110.

[48] For a discussion of the background to the eighteenth century controversy over miracles and Hume's role in it see Gaskin, *Hume's Philosophy of Religion*, Ch. 7.

[49] *Not Paul*, p. 308.

[50] *Not Paul*, p. 50.

dence (or lack of it) he thought especially damning. Paul was supposed to have been accompanied on his journey to Damascus but his is the only testimony to his conversion – there is no 'collateral evidence' from any independent witnesses.[51] Bentham did not think any more was needed to convince a rational reader.

As powerful and all-embracing a critique as Bentham mounted in *Church-of-Englandism*, the *Analysis*, and *Not Paul*, it is a curious element of his writing in general that he frequently employed religious terminology and referred to religious figures when describing his thought and its importance.[52] As noted in the introduction to Part One, in 1781 he dreamt of the founding of 'the sect of the utilitarians'. (3) Twenty years later, in a letter to his editor Étienne Dumont (28 June 1802) he rejected the application 'Benthamite' to describe his followers and the doctrine they held: 'What sort of animal is that?' Even so, he continued, 'a new Religion would be an odd sort of thing without a name: accordingly there ought to be one for it – at least for the professors of it. Utilitarian (Angl.) Utilitarien (Gall.) would be the more PROPRE'.[53] Not long after, in the *Rationale of Judicial Evidence*, Bentham fancied himself as the 'Luther of Jurisprudence' searching with 'penetrating eye and dauntless heart' into the cells and conclaves of the law.[54]

Others followed Bentham in so picturing the proselytizing character of his utilitarianism and its disciples, though Mazlish's description of Bentham as 'a very eccentric version of Jesus Christ' takes such comparisons too far.[55] To his American friend, John Neal, Bentham was 'the great high-priest of legislation'.[56] Matthew Arnold also alluded to the religious character of Bentham's utilitarianism and pictured 'the ardent longing of a faithful Benthamite, traversing an age still dimmed by the last mists of transcendentalism, to be spared long enough to see his religion in the full and final blaze of its triumph'.[57] J. S. Mill provided the most famous example of this manner of speaking of utilitarianism in his *Autobiography*, where he wrote of the effect upon him, in the winter of 1821–22, of his reading of Dumont's edition of Bentham's *Traités de législation*:

[51]   *Not Paul*, pp. 79, 89.
[52]   For a selection of representative examples see Charles F. Bahmueller, *The National Charity Company: Jeremy Bentham's Silent Revolution* (Berkeley 1981), pp. 66–67, 167.
[53]   *The Correspondence of Jeremy Bentham* (CW), vii, ed. J. R. Dinwiddy (Oxford 1988), p. 65.
[54]   Bowring, vi. 270 note.
[55]   Bruce Mazlish, *James and John Stuart Mill: Father and Son in the Nineteenth Century* (New York 1975), p. 132.
[56]   *Principles of Legislation from the Manuscripts of Jeremy Bentham*, ed. John Neal (Boston 1830), p. 14.
[57]   Arnold continues to relate that 'This respectable man . . . was, perhaps, in real truth, on a pious pilgrimage, to obtain from Mr. Bentham's executors, a sacred bone of his great dissected Master'; 'Preface to *Essays in Criticism*' (1865), in *Lectures and Essays in Criticism*, ed. R. H. Super (Ann Arbor, Mich. 1962), p. 289.

The reading of this book was an epoch in my life; one of the turning points in my mental history . . . The 'principle of utility' understood as Bentham understood it, and applied in the manner in which he applied it . . ., fell exactly into its place as the keystone which held together the detached and fragmentary component parts of my knowledge and beliefs. It gave unity to my conceptions of things. I now had opinions; a creed, a doctrine, a philosophy; in one among the best senses of the word, a religion; the inculcation and diffusion of which could be made the principal outward purpose of a life.[58]

That Bentham and others occasionally borrowed the language of religion to describe the utilitarian philosophy is perhaps not unusual for the period. However, to depict utilitarianism itself as a substitute religion, as Bentham and J. S. Mill did, suggests that they perceived a deficiency in the life of men consequent on the elimination (or absence) of conventional religion – a need requiring fulfilment. In the posthumous *Auto-Icon: Or Farther Uses of the Dead to the Living* (printed 1842, not published) Bentham went further still, to imagine a secular world in which churches of 'auto-icons' were centres for instruction in utilitarian ideas.[59] This remarkable discussion of the uses of corpses has affinities with the 'Dialogues of the Dead', so popular in the previous age, and with the versions of the Religion of Humanity expounded by Auguste Comte and John Stuart Mill. More especially, it suggests a mind from which the social utility functions of religion had not been entirely dismissed.

2

James Mill was ordained a minister in the Church of Scotland and often attended the debates in the General Assembly.[60] He remained a Christian at least until 1806, but several articles authored in the preceding five years reveal increasing doubts about revelation as the source of knowledge about God's attributes. Mill's extensive reviewing of theological works between 1806 and 1811 appears to have sharpened his thinking to the point where he became an agnostic. Bentham, whom he met in late 1808 and worked closely with thereafter, may also have influenced him, but Mill was already well down the path to infidelity by then. After 1811 he

---

[58] John Stuart Mill, *Autobiography*, ed. Jack Stillinger and John M. Robson, *Collected Works of John Stuart Mill* (Toronto 1981), i. 69; *Traités de legislation civile et pénale . . . Publiés en françois par Ét. Dumont*, 3 vols. (Paris 1802).

[59] Jeremy Bentham, *Auto Icon: Or Farther Uses of the Dead to the Living, A Fragment* (based on manuscripts principally dated 1831, printed 1842 but not published). I am grateful to the late Robert A. Fenn for a copy of his edited and annotated unpublished version of this tract. For a discussion of the often bizarre recommendations contained in this 'last work' see Crimmins, *Secular Utilitarianism*, pp. 292–302.

[60] R. A. Fenn, *James Mill's Political Thought* (New York 1987), p. 3.

wrote no more theological reviews. In all likelihood, by 1815 Mill was an atheist.[61]

It is likely, initially, that Mill's antagonism to the Church of England was fostered by his Presbyterian ecclesiology, which spurned the episcopal structure and pretensions of its Anglican counterpart, and which was noted for the diligence and commitment of its clergy. The contrast with the Church of England was striking, and from 1806 forward Mill made no secret of his distaste for its institutions and practices.[62] *In Schools for All, In Preference to Schools for Churchmen Only* (1812) Mill published his most well-known outraged attack on the Church's advocacy of sectarian schools, calling into question the political motives of the Church.[63] Mill's criticisms may well have helped sharpen Bentham's criticisms on the same subject. On the other hand, in later life he wrote several articles critical of established religion along the lines taken by Bentham, including two *Westminster Review* attacks in 1825 and 1826 on Robert Southey's history of the Church of England,[64] and 'The Church, and Its Reform', which appeared in the first number of the *London Review* in 1835, the penultimate year of his life.[65]

In the critique of Southey Mill adopted the position of the polemicist, condemning Southey's *Book of the Church* (1824) as 'an old woman's story-book' and unsparing in his disgust at the eulogy of Archbishop Laud it contained.[66] Mill's anticlericalism is underpinned by a Hobbesian logic. Beginning from 'the principle that men desire power', he argued that it is desired 'to make other men do what we please: to place their persons, their actions, and properties, to as great an extent as possible, at our disposal.' For Mill, as for Hobbes, this is 'one of the strongest propensities in human nature, and altogether insatiable.' In this respect the clergy are no different from other men, save that they function with the

---

[61]   In a letter to the atheist Francis Place (6–13 Sep. 1815) Mill refers to his review article on Dugald Stewart and the cunning manner in which he made 'a juggical [ie. Christian] review preach flat atheism', and 'prove that there is not an argument for the existence of God which will bear to be looked at for a moment.' The article is 'Stewart's Philosophy of the Human Mind,' *The British Review*, vol. VI, No. 11 (Aug. 1815), pp. 170–200. The letter to Place (BL Add. Mss. 35152, f.163v) is quoted by Fenn, *James Mill's Political Thought*, p. 34.

[62]   The earliest substantial indication of Mill's attitude is found in 'Van Mildert on Infidelity', *The Literary Journal*, n.s. vol. II, No. 4 (Oct. 1806), pp. 359–70; Fenn, *James Mill's Political Thought*, p. 89 note.

[63]   For a discussion see Fenn, *James Mill's Political Thought*, pp. 82–88.

[64]   James Mill, 'Southey's Book of the Church', *The Westminster Review*, No. 3 (5 Jan. 1825), pp. 167–212, and 'Ecclesiastical Establishments', *The Westminster Review*, No. 5 (10 Apr. 1826), pp. 504–48. Robert Southey, *The Book of the Church*, 2 vols (London 1824), and *Vindiciæ Ecclesiæ Anglicanæ* (London 1826).

[65]   James Mill, 'The Church, and Its Reform', *The London Review*, vol. 1, No. 2 (July 1835), pp. 257–95. For a discussion see Fenn, *James Mill's Political Thought*, pp. 45–50.

[66]   Mill, 'Southey's Book of the Church', pp. 167, 173–4, 187–98.

benefit of the power of the state, from which they draw their 'powers of persecution'.[67]

In 'The Church, and Its Reform' Mill highly recommended Bentham's *Church-of-Englandism* (430),[68] and the discussion is generally conducted on utilitarian premises, beginning with a cost-benefit analysis of the work and responsibilities of the clergy. Mill found nothing of worth in the rituals and ceremonies of the Church and was unequivocal in condemning its clergy as men who 'adhere to it either for the sake of the name, or for the good things which they owe to it, with a small proportion indeed of those in whose adherence to it regard for religion has any thing to do'. The Church is merely 'a state engine; a ready and ever-willing instrument in the hands of those who desire to monopolize the powers of government – that is, to hold them for the purpose of abusing them.' (436)[69] Mill quoted extensively from Pope's *Dunciad* to illustrate the stifling effects on the mind of the inculcation of dogmas (446–49,[70] and noted that the Church's 'new-born zeal for the religious education of the poor' is related to its realization that the acquisition of knowledge unaccompanied by religion poses a danger to it.' (449)[71]

Surprising though it may be, Mill did not follow Bentham in advocating the 'euthanasia' of the Church. Rather, he devoted himself to what the clergy could usefully do, with the goal of converting the Church 'from an instrument of evil into an instrument of much good' (438).[72] He urged the founding of a 'State religion' in which 'the whole population' might be united, a Church without dogmas or ceremonies. (451)[73] Toward this end Mill proposed that the clergy and bishops be appointed by a newly established government department, the Ministry of Public Instruction. Bishops – or 'inspectors' in Mill's nomenclature – would no longer sit in the House of Lords, tithes would be eliminated, parishes reorganized, and pay for the clergy and bishops standardized. (439–43)[74] Financial incentives were to be introduced to ensure the excellence and efficiency of the clergy in their new social and educative functions. Favourable results would be rewarded with 'annual premiums', with results measured in each parish in terms of the reduction in the number of crimes, law-suits, paupers, and uneducated

---

67 Mill, 'Ecclesiastical Establishments', pp. 506, 508.
68 'The Church, and Its Reform', p. 266. Mill defers to Bentham's *Church-of-Englandism* at several points in the article: (1) on the communion ceremony, (2) objections to the Bishop of London's *Charge to the Clergy of London*, (3) criticism of the ceremony of baptism – see pp. 264, 265, 270 (429, 430, 434).
69 'The Church, and Its Reform', p. 272.
70 'The Church, and Its Reform', pp. 283–6.
71 'The Church, and Its Reform', pp. 286.
72 'The Church, and Its Reform', p. 274.
73 'The Church, and Its Reform', p. 288.
74 'The Church, and Its Reform', pp. 275–80.

children, and increases in the numbers attending reading rooms and in the supply of the most instructive books. (452)[75]

The theological content of 'sermons' would be minimal, their aim being to establish in the minds of the congregation 'pure ideas of the moral character of God'. This is a concession by Mill to public opinion, since behind it stands Bentham's critique of the supposed attributes of God in the *Analysis*.[76] 'It is unavailing', Mill writes, 'to call the Almighty benevolent, when you ascribe to him lines of action which are entirely the reverse. It is vain to call him wise, when you represent him as moved by considerations which have weight only with the weakest of men.' To call the Almighty a loving God while at the same time attributing to him a propensity to punish offenders out of all proportion to the gravity of their offences is clearly a fallacious and pernicious practice. (432)[77] Not that the sermons should be weighed down by discussions of this kind; rather the objective is to enhance social utility. They should be calculated to impart 'as deeply as possible, all the impressions which lead to good conduct', and thereby 'lead us to rejoice in being the instruments of happiness to others'. (433)[78]

Apart from sermonizing, the 'clergy' were also to deliver 'useful lectures on various branches of art and science'. In this way craftsmen could be made acquainted with 'the mechanical powers', and the congregation as a whole might be exposed to edifying chemical experiments, acquire 'knowledge of the composition and decomposition of bodies', and receive instruction in the basics of botany and astronomy. To these might be added – a modern note here – 'lectures on the art of preserving . . . health'. (453)[79] In addition, the congregation should receive instruction in 'political science', from which they might learn something of 'the laws which determine the rate of wages' and 'by which the annual produce of the labours of the community is distributed'. In this manner – though one assumes a certain amount of irony was intended – Mill thought the people could be reconciled 'to that inequality of distribution which they see takes place, and which there are people ignorant or wicked enough to tell them, is a violation of their rights'. (453–54)[80] Finally, 'social amusements', such as music and dancing, were to supplement the educative aspects of Mill's Sunday programme. Churches are to function not only as centres of instruction but also as community centres where meetings, dances and communal meals can take place. (455–56)[81]

---

[75] 'The Church, and Its Reform', p. 289.
[76] Mill's notes on Bentham's *Analysis* are in the 'Commonplace Books of James Mill', 5 vols., London Library (unpublished, c. 1800–35), ii. 77–78, 74–75, 73, in that order.
[77] 'The Church, and Its Reform', p. 267.
[78] 'The Church, and Its Reform', p. 269.
[79] 'The Church, and Its Reform', p. 290.
[80] 'The Church, and Its Reform', p. 291.
[81] 'The Church, and Its Reform', p. 293–94.

Mill's disgust for the Church and its teachings is plainly stated in 'The Church, and Its Reform' and other essays. However, the constructive utilitarian elements of his critique – as impractical as they might be – are indicative of his reluctance to abandon the idea of religion as providing the nucleus of a social bond. This perspective on the potential of religion properly formed was developed further by the younger Mill in his own writings on religion.

3

John Stuart Mill, like his father, greatly approved of the general tendency of Bentham's *Analysis* and employed some of its arguments in his essay on the 'Utility of Religion'.[82] This was one of the essays Helen Taylor posthumously published as *Three Essays on Religion* (1874), the others being 'Nature' and 'Theism'.[83] 'Nature' and 'Utility of Religion' were written in 1854 and 'Theism' sometime between 1868 and 1870. The views on religion expressed in these essays are perfectly consistent with Mill's mature thoughts on the subject expressed elsewhere, most notably in *On Liberty* (1859) and *Auguste Comte and Positivism* (1865). F. E. L. Priestley has succinctly delineated the fundamental elements of Mill's position:

> His thinking is firmly rooted in empiricism; his whole concept of truth is strongly defined by the 'canons of induction' – truth is what can be proved by induction from empirical evidence. His concept of a true religion is consequently of a religion of naturalism, as opposed to one of supernaturalism, a religion of the this-worldly as opposed to one of the other-worldly. The sort of religion he can approve of he finds in Comte's Religion of Humanity. The ethical system dependent on this religion is the Utilitarian. And finally, he sees this religion as an instrument of progress, of an emergent ethical evolution.[84]

The empirical and inductive elements of Mill's assessment of natural religion are evident in the essay 'Nature'. This was a topic he had tackled

---

[82] Mill refers to the 'searching character' of the *Analysis*, which he says 'produced the greatest effect upon me' and 'contributed materially to my development'; *Autobiography*, in *Collected Works*, i. 73. In an earlier draft of the *Autobiography* Mill mentioned that 'the volume bearing the name of Philip Beauchamp [the pseudonym Bentham used for the *Analysis*], which was shown to my father in manuscript and by him given to me to read and make a marginal analysis of, as I had done of the *Elements of Political Economy*, made a great impression on me' (*Collected Works*, i. 72). It was suggested to me sometime ago by Professor R. A. Fenn that the 'marginal analysis' to which Mill refers may have been copied or employed in some fashion in the notes made on the *Analysis* by his father (see above note 76).

[83] John Stuart Mill, *Three Essays on Religion* (London, 1874). The essays on religion are included in Mill's *Collected Works*, vol. 10, ed. J. M. Robson (Toronto 1969), pp. 369–489. References are to the first edition of 1874, from which the text of 'Utility of Religion' presented in this volume is taken.

[84] *Collected Works*, i. introduction, p. lvi.

as a boy of fourteen in an analysis of Paley's *Natural Theology*, written under his father's instructions.[85] Its conclusion stands as a summary of its judiciously presented principal arguments:

> The scheme of Nature regarded in its whole extent, cannot have had, for its sole or even principal object, the good of human or other sentient beings. What good it brings to them, is mostly the result of their own exertions. Whatsoever, in nature, gives indication of beneficent design, proves this beneficence to be armed only with limited power; and the duty of man is to co-operate with the beneficent powers, not by imitating but by perpetually striving to amend the course of nature – and bringing that part of it over which we can exercise control, more nearly into conformity with a high standard of justice and goodness.[86]

Given the absence of concrete evidence, Mill did not think that anything other than a healthy scepticism was warranted when regarding the credibility of the proofs of God's providence provided by Nature.

Much of the argument about the kind of evidence offered by Nature for *a posteriori* discovery of the divine attributes suggest the more formal arguments presented in the later 'Theism'. The latter contains Mill's comprehensive examination of the being and attributes of God. Here he dismissed the *a priori* 'proofs' as 'unscientific'.[87] On the other hand, the *a posteriori* evidence that God governs the universe through invariable laws is at least subject to empirical test. The argument from design – an argument which proceeds through analogy – suggests 'the adaptations in Nature afford a large balance of probability in favour of creation by intelligence.' But it is 'certain that it is no more than a probability; . . .'[88] Allowing for the probability, however, Mill examined the supposed attributes of the Deity and in greater detail repeated the central argument of 'Nature', which is to say that assumptions of God's omnipotence and benevolence run contrary to the evidence available.[89] Revelation provides no better assurance for these assumptions. In particular, the existence of miracles cannot be used to prove the existence of God, since 'unless a God is already recognized, the apparent miracle can always be accounted for on a more probable hypothesis than that of the interference of a Being whose very existence it is supposed to be the sole evidence.'[90] Even if the existence of a God with the power to modify his own creation be allowed, the witnesses to miracles do not provide testimony of a kind that compels belief. Nevertheless, Mill

---

[85] Mill, *Autobiography*, in *Collected Works*, i. 74.
[86] Mill, 'Nature', p. 65.
[87] Mill, 'Theism', p. 139.
[88] Mill, 'Theism', p. 174.
[89] Mill, 'Theism', p. 192.
[90] Mill, 'Theism', p. 232.

admits that he cannot disprove the existence of miracles and, therefore, his arguments against them do not preclude anyone from hoping they are true.[91] In the concluding section of 'Theism' Mill maintains that scepticism toward the evidence of natural and revealed religion is 'the rational attitude of a thinking mind'.[92] But, with a far greater sensitivity to the value of religious sentiment than either his father or Bentham allowed, Mill argued that the moral benefits of belief in a morally perfect Being should not be underestimated: from it comes 'the habit of taking the approbation of such a Being as the *norma* or standard to which to refer and by which to regulate our own characters and lives.'[93] Such impressions (including those left to us by the historical Christ) are 'excellently fitted to aid and fortify that real, though purely human religion, which sometimes calls itself the Religion of Humanity and sometimes that of Duty.'[94]

This contrast with the elder utilitarians reminds us that as a critic of Bentham Mill holds a special fascination. As is well-known, following his mental crisis of 1826–27 Mill embarked on a reconsideration of the basic values of utilitarianism, out of which he emerged convinced that the human personality is a far richer ensemble than either Bentham or his father had supposed. He did not reject the doctrine of utility, but now thought that attention should be directed to the 'internal culture of the individual', to the cultivation of feeling and the development of the aesthetic sensibilities. Utilitarianism, as a science of society, should not be entirely preoccupied with the 'external culture', the purely rational mode of thought and behaviour. What this meant was that the external environment, and by implication the project to fashion the 'correct' conditioning factors originated by Helvétius, did not have the central importance for Mill which it had for Bentham.[95] From this perspective the importance of religious sentiment as an aspect of an individual's 'internal culture' could not be so easily dismissed.

At various times in his life Mill looked to Auguste Comte's Religion of Humanity to provide a focus for the religious and aesthetic sensibilities of a people that had been brought to understand the illusory nature of conventional religion. Mill viewed Comte as a devotee of the true experiential philosophy and an advocate of the happiness of mankind as the standard by which to measure the value of institutions and rules of action, and an opponent of the theological and metaphysical. There were, of course, important differences between Mill and Comte. The authoritarian tendencies he detected in Comte's plan to establish a 'salutary ascendancy

---

[91] Mill, 'Theism', p. 240.
[92] Mill, 'Theism', p. 242.
[93] Mill, 'Theism', p. 250.
[94] Mill, 'Theism', pp. 255–6.
[95] Gertrude Himmelfarb, *On Liberty and Liberalism: The Case of John Stuart Mill* (New York 1974), p. 7.

over opinion' exercised by an organized body of 'the most eminent thinkers' was anathema to the author of *On Liberty*.[96] Comte's stress on the need for unity and the suppression of self-regarding actions, together with the 'mania for regulation' demonstrated in the elaborate provisions for ceremony, ritual and doctrine, looked to Mill like a 'system for the total suppression of all independent thought'.[97] Later in life Mill denounced Comte's theory as 'the completest system of spiritual and temporal despotism, which ever yet emanated from a human being, unless possibly that of Ignatius Loyola'.[98] Even so, he never let go of the idea of a secular Religion of Humanity and a great part of 'Utility of Religion' is taken up with discussing it.

In this essay Mill set out to inquire whether religion – leaving aside the question of its truth – 'is really indispensable to the temporal welfare of mankind; . . . and whether the benefits which it yields might not be obtained otherwise, without the very large alloy of evil, by which, even in the best form of the belief, those beliefs are qualified.' (471)[99] The essay opens with a discussion of the *Analysis*. Mill recognized the worth of Bentham's criticisms of the fundamental beliefs of traditional Christianity and he followed him in emphasizing the danger of associating sound moral precepts with doctrines intellectually unsustainable. What is different, however, is that Mill is not completely negative: he thought parts of Bentham's argument were pressed too hard, and he allowed some value historically to religion as an aid to ethics. (472)[100] His real contribution in this respect is to present the Religion of Humanity as a suitable replacement for traditional Judaeo-Christian religions, as an equal to them in their best (most positive) manifestations and as their superior in everything else. Mill did not dispute the value of religion, neither in the past nor in the present, as a source of personal satisfaction and of elevated feelings. But he queried whether to obtain this goal it was necessary 'to travel beyond the boundaries of the world'. His thinking was that 'the idealization of our earthly life, the cultivation of a high conception of what it may be made', was capable of supplying 'a religion equally fitted to exact the feelings and (with the same aid from education) still better calculated to ennoble the conduct than any belief respecting the unseen powers'. Mill encouraged individuals to identify their feelings with 'the entire life of the human race'. (485, 486)[101] As Rome was to the Roman people and as Jehovah was to the Jews, so the human race – past, present and future – should be our object of devotion. Mill likened religion to patriotism, not a patriotism

---

[96] J. S. Mill, *Auguste Comte and Positivism* (1865), in *Collected Works*, x. 314.
[97] Mill, 'Auguste Comte and Positivism', *Collected Works*, x. 335, 321, 351.
[98] Mill, *Autobiography*, in *Collected Works*, i. 221.
[99] 'Utility of Religion', p. 74.
[100] 'Utility of Religion', p. 76. On the same page Mill informs us that he intends to make free use of the writings of Comte in this essay.
[101] 'Utility of Religion', pp. 104–5.

stirred by great crises but a continuing (educated and cultivated) patriotic concern to serve the world conceived in its broadest sense. This 'exalted morality', a morality which does not depend upon rewards for action, is in reality a religion (a 'real religion', Mill calls it). Qualifying his commitment to utilitarian theory, he explained that 'outward good works' are only a part of this religion, being 'rather the fruits of the religion than the religion itself'. (487)[102] His final, tantalizing pronouncement upon the matter stands thus:

> The essence of religion is the strong and earnest direction of the emotions and desires toward an ideal object, recognized as of the highest excellence, and as rightfully paramount over all selfish objects of desire. This condition is fulfilled by the Religion of Humanity in as eminent a degree and in as high a sense as by the supernatural religions even in their best manifestations, and far more so than in any of their others. (487)[103]

The object of this religion and, indeed, the rationale for its very existence, is a sense of unity with humanity and a deep feeling for the general good. Thus is the religious character of Mill's utilitarianism enunciated.

4

As I have observed elsewhere,[104] when Mill praised Brown's work on Shaftesbury in his essay on 'Bentham' (1838) his purpose, not necessarily needless, was to stress that the utilitarian doctrine did not originate with Bentham, but was a feature of the intellectual air of the age before he wrote.[105] But the real point to be made is that though the doctrine did not originate with Bentham he, more than anyone else, provided it with its secular character, and that this was a radical departure from the then prevailing version of utilitarian theory in Britain. By the time Mill wrote his celebrated essay, and as a direct result of the teaching of Bentham and his disciples, conventional religion was deemed at best to be needless baggage which the doctrine could do without. Even so, as we have seen, there are religious elements of the utilitarianism of Bentham and the Mills which serve to modify this view of the secular progression of the tradition. It is also worth noting the continuance in the nineteenth century of the earlier religious strand of utilitarian theory in the hands of supposedly secular theorists, most notably in the writings of John Austin and James Fitzjames Stephen.

Austin, commonly supposed to be a devoted disciple of Bentham, evi-

---

[102] 'Utility of Religion', pp. 108, 109.
[103] 'Utility of Religion', p. 109; see also pp. 109–22, where Mill discusses the points of superiority of the Religion of Humanity over traditional religion. (487–93)
[104] Crimmins, *Secular Utilitarianism*, p. 307.
[105] J. S. Mill, 'Bentham' (1838), in *Collected Works*, x. 86–87.

dently drew inspiration in his law lectures from Paley as well as from Bentham.[106] In the summer of 1827 he was appointed the first Professor of Jurisprudence at University College London – 'the infidel and godless college in Gower Street', as a contemporary summarily condemned it.[107] Prior to this, between 1823 and 1826 he was a member, with his brother Charles, of the Benthamite circle responsible for the collective editorship of the radical *Westminster Review*. Based on the lectures given at University College in 1828, Austin published *The Province of Jurisprudence Determined* (1832), in which he laid out a general doctrine of jurisprudence according to the principles of Bentham and discussed fundamental aspects of the law, including the nature of law itself, sovereignty, power, subjective right, duty, and so on. In this respect Austin is usually viewed as a straightforward educator and expositor, principally concerned with analytical jurisprudence and not at all interested in the Benthamic projects of legal reform and the codification of substantive and constitutional law.[108] Austin's conservativism is apparent in the theory of utility he espoused, which was much like Paley's. It is a theory rooted in his Christian convictions that it is the will of God that men be happy, and that the measure of right and wrong are divine laws. These divine laws, 'revealed' and 'unrevealed' (the latter 'set to that portion of mankind who are excluded from the light of Revelation'), are no more nor less than the utilitarian will of God.[109] In this respect, utility and divine will coincide and, if Bentham tested existing practices and institutions against the standard of utility and found them wanting, Austin tended to view established institutions and practices as embodying utility. However, it is indicative of a common misreading of the history of the development of utilitarian thought that Leslie Stephen should claim that Austin's utilitarianism was of 'the most rigid [Benthamite] orthodoxy'.[110] Only if Paley were also allowed into the ranks of the 'orthodox' could this be true.

In *Liberty, Equality, Fraternity* (1873) Stephen's 'orthodox' utilitarian brother, the jurist James Fitzjames Stephen, presented himself as a defender of Hobbes' and Bentham's theory of law and sovereignty. However, on the subject of religion he sided with the former against the latter. In Stephen's account, Bentham's utilitarianism suffered from its lack of provision for obligation to its moral and legal norms. He rejected Mill's Religion of Humanity as fanciful and was at times guarded about his own religious

---

[105] For evidence of Austin's religious beliefs see *Letters of George Cornewall Lewis*, ed. G. E. Lewis (London 1870), pp. 103–5.

[107] *Evening Standard* (19 June 1828), in Gordon Huelin, *King's College London: 1828–1978* (London 1978), p. 3.

[108] Michael Lobban, *The Common Law and English Jurisprudence, 1769–1850* (Oxford 1991), p. 223.

[109] John Austin, *The Province of Jurisprudence Determined*, ed. Wilfrid E. Rumble (1832; Cambridge 1995), p. 39.

[110] Stephen, *The English Utilitarians*, iii. 320.

convictions. Nonetheless, Stephen's solution was drawn from his reading of the second half of *Leviathan* – an admittedly unlikely source – where he took Hobbes to be arguing that obligation to law required belief in a rewarding and punishing God.[111] The 'truths' established by experience and reason are the result of scripture and remain dependent on the antecedent beliefs therein expounded. For utility to prevail, therefore, the state must actively promote and teach this religion and inculcate its beliefs. None of the eighteenth-century utilitarian moralists argued the issue more stridently than Stephen, and this is an eloquent testimony to the continuing presence in the Victorian mind of the religious version of utilitarian theory.

[111] James Fitzjames Stephen, *Liberty, Equality, Fraternity*, ed. Stuart D. Warner (1873; Indianapolis 1993), pp. 175–6.

JEREMY BENTHAM

I
The Church of England Catechism Examined (1824)

II
Analysis of the Influence of Natural Religion on the Temporal Happiness of Mankind (1822)

III
Not Paul, but Jesus (1823)

Jeremy Bentham (1748–1832)

Biographical Note

Born on 15 February 1748 in Houndsditch, London, Jeremy Bentham was the elder son of a London attorney, Jeremiah Bentham and his first wife, Alicia Groves (d. 1759). A second child, Samuel, was born in 1757. Jeremiah came from a middle class, London family and had prospered through speculations in real estate. A devout member of the Church of England, he was a calculating, purse-pinching man with social aspirations. When Jeremy proved to be a prodigy, he transferred his ambitions to him and set out to educate him to attain eminence in the worlds of law and politics. He personally taught Jeremy Latin and Greek. To ensure that the child grew up with the necessary social graces, Jeremiah arranged for instruction in music, art, drill, dancing and French. The physical exercises proved difficult because of Bentham's small stature and ill-health, but music and French were life-long sources of pleasure to him. Bentham's early French lessons were enlivened by reading from a book of fairy tales, and by study of Fenelon's *Télémaque*, which impressed him greatly. In contrast, the family library comprised only didactic volumes since both parents were convinced that children's books must be free from 'the poison of amusement'.[1] One biographer has suggested that while Jeremy found history exciting, he was depressed by the pious devotional works around him and that his 'hedonism had its origins in his father's library'.[2] Fortunately, during summer visits to his maternal grandmother, Bentham discovered books by a wider range of authors, including Defoe and Richardson.

Bentham attended Westminster School from 1755 to 1760. He hated the school, calling it 'a wretched place for instruction'.[3] Under-sized and apprehensive, Bentham was bullied by the other pupils. He commented later, 'I was a favourite, a timid child, who gave offence to nobody; and one more dutiful could not exist'.[4] At the age of twelve he was sent to Queen's College, Oxford, from which he obtained his BA in 1763 (MA 1766). His three years there were no more stimulating, but it left him with an interest in educational reform. He also acquired a deep distrust of oaths as a result of being forced to sign the Thirty-nine Articles. The necessity

---

[1]   Charles Warren Everett, *The Education of Jeremy Bentham* (New York 1931), p. 14.
[2]   Mary P. Mack, *Jeremy Bentham: An Odyssey of Ideas, 1748–1792* (London 1962), p. 35.
[3]   *The Works of Jeremy Bentham, Published under the Superintendence of his Executor, John Bowring*, 11 vols. (Edinburgh, 1838–43), x. 30. Henceforth Bowring.
[4]   Bowring, x. 20.

for subscription led him to consider the hypocrisy of the Church of England, and to reject established religion, as he later made clear in *Church-of-Englandism and its Catechism Examined* (1818). In November 1763 Bentham began his legal training by entering Lincoln's Inn and listening to the cases heard before Lord Mansfield in the Court of King's Bench, including the proceedings against John Wilkes. He returned briefly to Oxford to hear William Blackstone's lectures, but later pronounced the jurist's style 'cold and formal'.[5]

When Jeremiah Bentham remarried in 1766, he provided his elder son with comfortable chambers at Elm Court No. 1, Lincoln's Inn, along with property from his mother's estate which produced an income of about £100. Although Bentham was admitted to the bar in 1769, his active legal career was brief and unsuccessful. He remembered that year rather for his reading of Montesquieu, Barrington, Beccaria and Helvétius, writers who 'set me on the principle of utility'.[6] He found the current state of English law abhorrent and preferred to devote his energy to applying scientific principles to legislative reform.[7]

Bentham found the phrase 'the greatest happiness of the greatest number' in a pamphlet by Joseph Priestley in 1768.[8] Beccaria's *On Crimes and Punishments* (1764), translated into English in 1767, also contains the words 'the greatest happiness divided among the greatest number', and in his later Commonplace book, Bentham admitted to uncertainty as to which first influenced him.[9] Beccaria's enlightened views on the principles of law and punishment along with Helvétius' efforts at defining and analyzing moral terms helped Bentham in his search for a new science of legislation. His discovery of the French *philosophes* in 1769 led him to compose letters to Voltaire, d'Alembert, Morellet, and others.[10]

A trip to France with his father in 1764 had already given Bentham a favourable impression of the French people, although he found much that was backward in the country.[11] In 1785 he again travelled across France to Nice to join a vessel bound for Smyrna, but his shyness prevented him from visiting d'Alembert on his way through Paris. The object of the expedition was to spend some time with his brother, who was then employed by Prince Potemkin in Russia.[12] On this journey Bentham visited Italy, Constantinople, Bulgaria and Poland before entering the Ukraine, where he was to join Samuel at Potemkin's estate outside Kritchev.

---

[5]   Bowring, x. 45.
[6]   Bowring, x. 54.
[7]   Everett, *The Education of Jeremy Bentham*, p. 49.
[8]   Charles Milner Atkinson, *Jeremy Bentham: His Life and Work* (London 1905), p. 20.
[9]   Bowring, x. 142.
[10] See Mack, *Jeremy Bentham*, pp. 102–115. It is unlikely the letters to Voltaire and d'Alembert were sent.
[11] Bowring, x. 47.
[12] For details of the visit to Russia see Bowring, x. 149–71.

Catherine the Great visited the estate in 1787 during Bentham's stay. Typically, however, Bentham shrank from the opportunity of presenting her his juridical code, and remained secluded during the visit. He finally returned to England in 1788, taking the route through Poland, Germany and Holland.

While Bentham was in Russia, his friend George Wilson drew his attention to Paley's *Principles of Moral and Political Philosophy* (1785) as 'founded entirely on utility, or, as he chooses to call it, the will of God, as declared by expediency'.[13] Wilson feared that Bentham would be seen as plagiarizing when he published his own work. Bentham was busy with the *Defence of Usury* (1787), but on his return he hurried to prepare for the press a version of his own principles, *An Introduction to the Principles of Morals and Legislation* (1789; largely completed and printed 1780).

Out of Bentham's stay with Samuel came the architectural project which was to occupy his thoughts for many years – the Panopticon. This plan for an easily controlled model prison had been designed by Samuel and developed by Jeremy. The building of new prisons had been mandated by the Hard Labour Act of 1778, and Bentham's plans were in conformity with both the act and with Howard's vision of prison reform.[14] For over twenty years Bentham struggled to make this idea a reality, sinking considerable sums of his own money into it, with government encouragement. Only in 1812 was the scheme finally terminated, when Bentham was paid £23,000 to recompense him for the expenses which he had incurred. At the time of Bentham's interest in the new French judicial code he sent Brissot a copy of *Panopticon: or the Inspection-House* (1791), and the idea was discussed by the Legislative Assembly.[15]

Bentham's political convictions at this time have been widely discussed. Abandoning the Bentham family Jacobite leanings, the pragmatic Jeremiah supported the Hanoverian dynasty, and imbued in his son conservative monarchist opinions. However, Bentham's youthful conservatism gradually lessened as his democratic sympathies increased. Opinions differ on the timing of Bentham's conversion to democracy. Mary Mack argued for an early date at the time of the French Revolution.[16] Others consider Bentham's meeting with James Mill in late 1808 to have been the catalyst in his change of views.[17] What is certain, however, is that his examination of the English

[13] *The Correspondence of Jeremy Bentham* (CW), iii, ed. Ian R. Christie (London 1971), p. 490.

[14] Everett, *The Education of Jeremy Bentham*, pp. 176–77.

[15] J. H. Burns, 'Bentham and the French Revolution', *Transactions of the Royal Historical Society*, 5th Series, 16 (1966), p. 107–8.

[16] Mack, *Jeremy Bentham*, pp. 17, 432, 438.

[17] For example, Elie Halévy, *The Growth of Philosophic Radicalism* [*La formation du radicalisme philosophique*, 1901–4], trs. Mary Morris (1928; New Jersey 1972), p. 255; and J. R. Dinwiddy, 'Bentham's Transition to Political Radicalism, 1809–10', *Journal of the History of Ideas*, 36 (1975), pp. 683–700. A more complicated view, set in the context of the French Revolution, can be found in James E. Crimmins, 'Bentham's Political Radicalism Reexamined', *Journal of the History of Ideas*, 55/2 (1994), pp. 259–81.

legal system led him to consider constitutional problems.[18] When his theories were ignored in his own country, he tried to implement them elsewhere. In 1778 he had entered a contest to create a new criminal code for Russia,[19] and he saw the French Revolution as an opportunity to put his theories into practice. He sent pamphlets of suggestions to Mirabeau as early as 1788, and in 1790 wrote a *Draught* of a constitutional plan for France.[20] While the excesses of the Terror reinforced the doubts about natural rights which Bentham had felt in his teens when he heard Blackstone lecture, his experiences did not lessen his enthusiasm for utilitarian reform. His interest in French affairs at this time also served to bring him into greater contact with Étienne Dumont (1759–1829), the Swiss scholar who popularized his work in Europe through editions translated into French.[21] On 26 August 1792 Bentham was created an honorary citizen of France, along with such luminaries as Priestley, Paine, Wilberforce, Washington and Kosciusko.[22] In response to this honour Bentham wrote, 'The general good is everywhere the true object of all political action, – of all law'.[23] In his later years Bentham published *Leading Principles of a Constitutional Code for any State* (1823) with encouragement from the Cortes of Portugal.

Nevertheless Bentham never gave up working for legislative and constitutional reform in England. In 1823 he provided funds to start the *Westminster Review*, a periodical designed to air radical views. His last years were spent designing a detailed constitutional code enshrining his ideas on legislation and administration. During his final years he conducted a lengthy correspondence with the Irish reformer, Daniel O'Connell, hoping once again that his ideas might influence policy. His profound antagonism to Catholicism, and the differing relative importance which O'Connell placed on Irish rather than English reform eventually led to the end of the correspondence.[24]

Throughout his life Bentham maintained a circle of friends and admirers, despite often living away from society and in later years calling himself the hermit of Queen's Square Place.[25] He was particularly intimate with his younger brother Samuel, who had been his pupil and protegé as a boy and young man. Until Samuel went to Russia in 1780, Bentham had supervised his education and career. John Lind, a journalist and pamphleteer, was a close friend in the 1770s. George Wilson and James Trail, who had been

---

[18]   Mack, *Jeremy Bentham*, p. 43. See also Sir Leslie Stephen, who saw Bentham as coming to political radicalism through his disgust at the English legal system in *The English Utilitarians* (1900; London 1950), i. 276–82.

[19]   Mack, *Jeremy Bentham*, p. 61.

[20]   Burns, 'Bentham and the French Revolution', pp. 97, 103–5.

[21]   Burns, 'Bentham and the French Revolution', p. 114.

[22]   Bowring, x. 280–81.

[23]   Bowring, x. 282.

[24]   James E. Crimmins, 'Jeremy Bentham and Daniel O'Connell: Their Correspondence and Radical Alliance, 1828–1831', *Historical Journal*, 40/2 (1997), p. 385.

[25]   John Dinwiddy, *Bentham* (Oxford 1989), p. 17.

fellow students at Lincoln's Inn, nursed him devotedly when he suffered from psychosomatic blindness in 1781.[26] He corresponded with his friend, Dr James Anderson, in Edinburgh, and enjoyed the company of John Howard, a man whom he greatly admired. After reading *A Fragment on Government* (1776), the Earl of Shelburne (1784 Marquis of Lansdowne) invited Bentham to stay at his country house, Bowood, in 1781. Through Shelburne Bentham entered the world of politics, meeting members of the government as well as Sir Samuel Romilly and Dumont. In his later years Bentham was surrounded by disciples who acted as secretaries and collaborators in his work. James Mill, John Stuart Mill and John Bowring all worked with Bentham in this way. Francis Place, George Grote and Edwin Chadwick shared his radical ideas. David Ricardo and Henry Brougham were also treasured acquaintances.

Although he never served in any official capacity, after 1781 Bentham had friends and correspondents in important positions. When some of these younger men became involved in a scheme to create an inexpensive non-sectarian educational system in England, James Mill interested Bentham in the idea. The result was an offer of land for a school and the publication of *Chrestomathia* (1815), a design for a 'new system of instruction to the higher branches of learning for the use of the middling and higher ranks in life'.[27] The curriculum was to be utilitarian in intent ('Chrestomathia' meant useful learning) and was to emphasize science and technology rather than the classics. While the school plan was never carried out, in 1828 the group succeeded in founding University College London, England's first secular university.

The death of Jeremiah Bentham in 1792 gave Bentham financial security and permitted his involvement in the Panopticon scheme. At that time he moved into his father's house in Queen's Square Place, which became his main residence for the rest of his life. His new affluence allowed him to provide cheap lodgings for friends such as James Mill, and to rent a country house for sustained periods of writing. In 1814 he moved to Ford Abbey, a massive Gothic and Tudor structure, where for some years the Mill family spent their summers with him. Bentham gave up the tenancy of Ford Abbey in 1818, and thereafter lived mainly in London.

Bentham never married. In 1775 he fell in love with a penniless young woman, precipitating a crisis in his life. His father disapproved of the match, and refused to increase his income. His friend, John Lind, suggested that he should marry in spite of this, and earn his living with his pen. Bentham finally decided against the marriage on the grounds that such circumstances were incompatible with his dedication to making his mark

---

[26] Mack, *Jeremy Bentham*, p. 336.
[27] Halévy, *Growth of Philosophic Radicalism*, p. 287.

as a legal reformer.[28] He later met and enjoyed the company of Caroline Fox at Lord Shelburne's house between 1781–91. In 1805 he proposed to her, but was rejected.

Although he died on the eve of the signing of the Reform Bill (6 June 1832), Bentham was a man of the eighteenth century – a *philosophe*. His understanding was rational and scientific. Legislative codes could be reformed on utilitarian lines which would be appropriate for an enlightened age. His total confidence in his own ideas was the result of his exceptionally wide early reading.

> What Bacon did was to proclaim – '*Fiat experimentum*'; but his own knowledge of Natural Philosophy was ignorance.
> What Locke did, was to destroy the notion of innate ideas.
> What Newton did, was to throw light on one branch of science.
> But I have planted the tree of Utility – I have planted it deep, and spread it wide.[29]

Convinced that even the dead could serve a utilitarian purpose, Bentham directed in his will that his body be dissected.[30] In a pamphlet, the *Auto-Icon; or Farther Uses of the Dead to the Living* (printed 1842, not published), written shortly before his death, Bentham proposed the display of mummified bodies for public instruction.[31] In accordance with this, he requested that his own body, dressed in his habitual garments, be displayed at University College.

Bentham's published and unpublished writings are extensive. There are large holdings of his manuscripts at University College London and the British Library, many of which have not been published.[32] In addition to the published works already mentioned, the following should be noted: *A Comment on the Commentaries*, *Of Laws in General*, *Scotch Reform*, *A Table of the Springs of Action*, *Plan of Parliamentary Reform, in the Form of a Catechism*, *Rationale of Judicial Evidence*, *Constitutional Code*, and *Deontology*. Several of these works were not published in Bentham's lifetime, but have appeared in modern editions. The first collection of Bentham's writings was published by the companion of his later years and literary executor, John Bowring, in eleven volumes, 1838–43.[33] A collection

---

[28] Charles Warren Everett, *Jeremy Bentham* (London 1966), pp. 24–6; see also Everett, *The Education of Jeremy Bentham*, pp. 72–92.

[29] Bowring, x. 588.

[30] Ross Harrison, *Bentham* (London 1983), pp. 5–7.

[31] See James Steintrager, *Bentham* (Ithaca, NY, 1977), p. 121; Harrison, *Bentham*, p. 22; and James E. Crimmins, *Secular Utilitarianism: Social Science and the Critique of Religion in the Thought of Jeremy Bentham* (Oxford 1990), pp. 296–99.

[32] For a description of the manuscripts at University College see A. T. Milne, *Catalogue of the Manuscripts of Jeremy Bentham in the Library of University College* (1937; 2nd edn. London 1962).

[33] See note 3 above.

of his economic writings appeared 1952–54.[34] More recently, the Bentham Committee based at University College London has overseen the production of the still to be completed *Collected Works of Jeremy Bentham*, including his correspondence.[35] The first volumes of this edition appeared in 1968, and it is planned to include Bentham's writings on religion.

Note on Text I

The Church of England Catechism Examined (1824) was a central part of the first of Bentham's published writings on religion, *Church-of-Englandism and its Catechism Examined* (1818). 'The Church of England Catechism Examined' constituted 'the body of the work' around which Bentham constructed a rambling and lengthy text of some 800 pages, in which he launched a wholesale attack on the Anglican establishment, concluding with detailed arguments for its 'euthanasia'. It is clear that Bentham conceived this part of the original work as a separate entity from its other sections. Publishing it on its own made eminent sense, especially given the poor reception the full work on the church had received when first published in 1818 (largely due to its cumbersome length and sometimes tediously constructed arguments). *Church-of-Englandism* was never published again in its entirety, but six extracts subsequently appeared: three editions of *The Church of England Catechism Examined* (1824, 1868 and 1890), and three editions of the sections devoted to the 'vices' of the Church and the proposed remedies, the first two of the latter entitled *Mother Church Relieved by Bleeding* (1823 and 1825), and the third entitled *The Book of Church Reform* (1831).

Bentham's name is on the title-page of *The Church of England Catechism Examined*, which is described as 'A New Edition'. A comparison between this tract and the section of *Church-of-Englandism* in which Bentham examined the catechism reveals numerous amendments to the style and grammar, as well as corrections of typographical errors in the original. The text following is the tract as printed in 1824 for John and Henry L. Hunt of Tavistock Street in Covent Garden, London.

[34] *Jeremy Bentham's Economic Writings*, 3 vols., ed. Werner Stark (London 1952–54).
[35] *The Collected Works of Jeremy Bentham*, General Editors: J. H. Burns, John Dinwiddy, F. Rosen (London and Oxford 1968–), in progress.

JEREMY BENTHAM

I

The Church of England Catechism Examined (1824)

THE CHURCH OF ENGLAND CATECHISM EXAMINED.

Question 1. WHAT is your name?
Answer. (Pronouncing the child's name.)
Question 2. Who gave you that name?
Answer. My Godfathers and my Godmothers in my baptism (1); wherein I was made a member of Christ, the child of God, and an inheritor of the kingdom of heaven (2).

OBSERVATIONS.

(1). [*Godfathers and Godmothers in my baptism.*] – Thus far the answer appears not to stand exposed to any considerable objection; it being supposed that to this examination no child is subjected on whom the ceremony called *baptism* has not been performed. So far as this is true, the answer is nothing more than the statement of a matter of fact, of the existence of which, though, generally speaking, it is not possible the child should have any remembrance of it, it is but natural that he should feel himself assured by satisfactory and unsuspected evidence. But this blamelessness – it will soon be seen whether it be of any long continuance.

(2). [*Wherein I was made*, &c.] – Already the contempt of truth, pregnant with those incongruities of which that corrupt affection is so naturally productive, begins to manifest itself. In this formulary styled a *Catechism*, will be found involved, though many of them tacitly, in a manner and without any sufficient warning, a system of assertions, prodigious in extent and variety, contained in another formulary, being the verbal part of a ceremony of prior date, called *baptism*. Of this anterior ceremony, the *examinee*, a child, commonly but just able to speak – a child, in which the faculty of name has as yet scarcely begun to develop itself – a child completely incompetent to the forming of any *judgment*, or so much as a *conception*, in relation to the matter contained in it, is made to take upon himself to pronounce the effect.

Here, then, the first lesson which he is made to learn, and *that* under the notion of forming his mind to the sentiment of *piety*, is a lesson, which, if it amount to any thing and has any meaning, is a lesson of *insincerity*: and which, as far as it forms him to any thing forms him to insincerity. For hereby what is the declaration which he is made to utter? – a declaration, asserting in the character of a true fact, the fact of his entertaining a persuasion which in truth he does not entertain, and which that he should entertain, is, in the nature of the case, not possible. When by Rousseau, on the occasion of the stories commonly put into the hands of children under the name of *fables*, the practice, of thus drawing from the fountain of falsehood and misrepresentation the first aliment presented to the human mind, was held up to view, and the absurdity and mischievous tendency of it displayed, deep and extensive was the sensation produced by the remark, not less so the conviction and recognition of the justice of it. But if, in any such profane book of instruction, the admission of falsehood be incongruous, and the habit of regarding it not only with indifference but with approbation pernicious, how much more so in a book of religious instruction? – in a book professing to introduce men to the favour of the God of Truth?

Yes, if by misrepresentation – yes, if by falsehood, any real and *preponderant* good effect could be produced, such as could not be produced by any other means. But by this or any other of the falsehoods so plentifully strewed all over this Catechism, and which will successively be held up to view, in what imaginable shape can any good be seen to flow?

Question 3. – What did your Godfathers and Godmothers then for you?

Answer. – They did promise and vow three things in my name (1): First, that I should renounce the devil and all his works (2), the pomps and vanity of this wicked world (3), and all the sinful lusts of the flesh (4): Secondly, that I should believe all the articles of the Christian faith (5): And, thirdly, that I should keep God's holy will and commandments, and walk in the same all the days of my life (6).

OBSERVATIONS.

1. *Things* is the name given to the *courses of conduct* which are the subjects of the vow here spoken of. But, before we enter upon the consideration of these *things*, one *thing* presents itself as calling for consideration, – and that is the implied – the necessarily implied – assumption, that it is in the power of any person, – not only with the consent of the father or other guardian, but without any such consent, – to fasten upon a child at its birth, and long before it is itself even capable of giving consent to anything, with the concurrence of two other persons, alike self-appointed, load it with a set of obligations – obligations of a most terrific and appalling character – obligations of the nature of *oaths*, of which just so much and no more is rendered visible, as is sufficient to render them terrific – obligations, to which neither in quantity nor in quality are any limits attempted to be or capable of being assigned.

Every child, at its birth, is cast into bondage, under the power of three persons, who, for any provision that is made to the contrary, may have been self-chosen and in practice frequently are. Even though these bonds were not more coercive than those of *temporal* slavery – of slavery in the *temporal sense* – this surely would be bad enough: – the notion of a power derived from the Almighty to cast men into such bondage, absurd and indefensible enough. But such bondage, what is it in comparison of the bondage actually supposed to be thus imposable and imposed? It is as the space covered by human life to eternity: to that eternity, over which the effects, here supposed to be produced by this bondage, are here supposed to extend.

Oh but, by our wisdom and our care (say the lawgivers by whom this formulary was devised and imposed) – *by our wisdom and our care, against abuse of this power, provision – effectual provision – has in and by this very instrument been made* . . .

Answer – Yes; such provision as will be seen. But, in the mean time, and to authorize you to make this provision, what you have assumed, – and what for that purpose it was necessary for you to assume, – and *that* in the character of an universal proposition, is – that, by the Almighty, in consideration of that particular portion of wisdom which to *you in particular* it has happened to be blest with, such power not only is *fit to be* given to *rulers in general*, but *has actually been* given to them; – and this, be they who they may, to *all* rulers: and sure enough, if, to the extent to which, to the purpose of the argument, it is necessary it should be assumed, this general proposition is granted, every proposition necessary to the establishment of your own aptitude in particular may be thrown into the bargain, as not being worth disputing about.

But, any such power – when, and on what occasion, was it ever given? where is any the least evidence, of any such gift to be found?

A job for the casuists. – Here is an engagement taken – an engagement taken in the solemn and awful form of a vow – a vow made by the sponsors – that the child shall do so and so: a vow made by A, not that he himself, but that B, shall do so and so. B, in process of time, breaks the vow: for this transgression – for this breach of a *vow* – of a *promissory oath* – for this species of *perjury*, who is it that is to be punished? A or B? or some one else, and who else? If punished, in what *mode* and to what *amount* punished? by everlasting flames in hell, or by any and what milder punishment? – Questions these, which, whenever this formulary is considered as any thing better than a parcel of words without meaning, will surely, now that, perhaps, for the first time the suggestion is made, be regarded as having some claim to answers. The persons thus dealing out eventual punishment at their own pleasure – viz. *the sponsors* – are they the persons, by whom, in case of a breach of the vow, the punishment is to be borne, – suppose the ordinary one of everlasting burning in hell fire? – if so, quere, of the whole number of persons who have been inveigled into the taking upon themselves this office, what is the number that will be saved? – What is the number? – *Answer.* None. For, whether its being kept inviolate is not as far from being possible as from being desirable, is what any rational eye will presently be in a condition to perceive. Upon the person, whom, in a state of helpless infancy, under the direction of the Church of England hierarchy, they have thus fastened upon and loaded with this burthen – is it upon this Jonas, that the lot of punishment will fall? – What a case is his! and, in its effect, what sort of a boon is this, which is thus magnified!

II. – Thus much as to the *general principle* of the alleged engagement – now as to the subject matter of it.

Three, and but three, is the number here spoken of as the number of things vowed and promised. But, of these *three* things, the first-mentioned is of itself a TRIPLE one, speaking of three things, or sets of things, as so many things which are to be renounced, as so many things, for the renunciation of which the child (whatsoever be meant by *renunciation*) undertakers, under the name of *sponsors* (or the child can not be a Christian) must be found, that will pledge themselves.

Mean time, without stopping as yet to take any clear view of the preceding *things*, no sooner is the last of them brought to view, than a question very naturally presents itself. Supposing this engagement fulfilled, can any thing else be wanting? 'God's holy will and commandments' kept, can any thing more be necessary? Is it in the nature of the case that even God himself should will or desire any thing more? The terms of the phrase, it must be confessed, are *general* at the same time, for terms so comprehensive, few can be clearer or more easily intelligible. – 'A *commandment*' – what sort of a thing *that* is, is among those things, which, by daily and hourly reference, are made known to every body. Sure enough, if every thing else had been equally clear, no such commentary as the present would ever have made its appearance.

Come we now to those other '*things*' by which this last is so unnecessarily preceded.

In relation to these *first-mentioned* things, numbered first and second, the first observation that strikes the eye is – that, presented as they are in this manner to view, the child is bid to look upon them as so many distinct things – upon each of them as something which in its nature is distinct, and on this occasion specially contradistinguished, from the thing *last-mentioned*, viz. '*the keeping God's holy will and commandments.*' If all the days of his life so it is that a man has been keeping this holy will and these holy commandments, what he has thus been doing, is he to understand then that it will be accepted as sufficient? Not he, indeed: – remain for him to do all these other things, whatsoever they may be.

These things, whatever they are, if so it be that it is in *pursuance* as well as in consequence of the engagement thus taken, that they are to be done by him, then so it is that to his doing them one thing more is necessary; which is, that he understand what they are: unfortunately, there, it will be seen, lies the difficulty, – and *that*, to an ordinary understanding, not to speak of extraordinary ones, it is much to be feared, an insuperable one.

Among the three things, or sets of things, that are to be renounced, first come '*the Devil and all his works*.' – The *Devil*, who or what is *he*, and how is it that he is *renounced*? – The *works* of the Devil, what are *they*, and how is it that they are renounced? – Applied to the Devil, who or whatever he is, – applied to the Devil's works, whatever they are, – what sort of an operation is *renouncement* or *renunciation*?

To all these several words, – to one of them in particular, by which an idea no less terrific than obscure and indeterminate is wont to be excited, what tolerably distinct ideas can rationally be expected to be attached in the mind of infant simplicity and ignorance? When the holy person, whose name is next under the Sovereign's, seated on the pinnacle of theological science, – when the *Archbishop of Canterbury* himself is able to tell us who or what the Devil is, what are his *works*, and by what operation they are *renounced* – they being all the while things distinct, – all of them, – as well from 'the sinful lusts of the flesh' as from 'the pomps and vanity of this wicked world,' – then it is that it may be time enough to expect any tolerably clear and practically useful idea of all these mysteries to stand attached to these words in the infant mind, for the nourishment of which this composition, such as we see it, is the morsel first administered.

'*The Devil and all his works*.' – And in the first place, the Devil himself, – of whom so decided and familiar a mention, as of one whom every body knows, is made. – Where lives he? Who is he? What is he? The child itself, did it ever see him? by any one, to whom, for the purpose of the inquiry, the child has access, was he ever seen? The child, has it ever happened to it to have any dealings with him? Is it in any such danger as that of having, at any time, to his knowledge, any sort of dealings with him? – If not, then to what purpose is this *renouncement*? and, once more, what is it that is meant by it? Suppose him, however, to have actually renounced this Devil – that is, speaking of this Devil, to have said, *I renounce him* – in what condition is he, other than that which he would have been in had no such renouncement been made? – The engagement, whatever it be, if any, which by this renunciation has been taken, by what *act* or acts is it that it would be *violated*? – This is surely among the things that would be worth knowing, were it only that a man might have it in his power to avoid the violating – the breaking – of this his engagement, without knowing and for want of knowing what it is.

'*The Devil and all his works*!' – Exists there any where any real being to which this name is applicable? If yes, exists there any sufficient reason for supposing that he ever made his appearance upon this earth? – ever made his presence sensible to, exhibited his person to the senses of, any human being that ever lived?

Not by unbelievers only, but by many a pious Christian, is the existence of any such being not merely doubted of, but, for such reasons as to them have been satisfactory, utterly denied: – the sort of *being* mentioned under this name being, in their notion of the matter, no other than an *allegorical* one; the passages, in which mention is made of him, so many purely *allegorical* or *figurative* expressions.

Figurative, and nothing more, was and is, according to them, the existence of this personage: figurative, and upon a line with that of *Jupiter* and *Juno* and the other inhabitants of the classical heaven, subjects or colleagues to those celestial potentates.

True, say certain fathers of the primitive Christian church. Yes; most exactly indeed upon a par were and are the Devils, great and small, with those *Gods* and *Goddesses*, great and small – with those *Dii majorum gentium* – with those *Dii minorum gentium*. Strange, indeed, if they were not upon a par, when in truth they were and are the very same. Who? – yes – who were Jupiter and Juno and the rest of them? – Who, but so many *Devils*, who, applying their influence to the inhabitants of this earth, caused themselves to be respectively worshipped under those classic names.

In these later times, to men of the deepest learning, – though among them it probably would not be easy to find many, if any, to join their suffrages on this question with those of the above-mentioned fathers, – every thing relative to this personage, and in particular his existence, is matter of doubt and difficulty, and as between this and that one of them is matter of *dispute*. At the same time, even among babes and sucklings, there is not one who is not qualified to decide upon it, and so well qualified as in this our Church to be forced to decide upon it, and to decide upon it accordingly.

To any such tender mind how indeed should it be matter of doubt or difficulty! – when, besides being assured of the existence of this personage by the earliest of all lessons and highest of all authorities – (for that of *the Bible*, – a book of which the sense is to be taken upon the credit of this improved substitute, is but derivative) – not only his nature but his very form is brought to view and made known by those *portraitures*, which are to be seen every where, and in particular in so many copies of the Book of Common Prayer, of which this Catechism forms a part.

To the learned, as well as to the gay, among persons of riper years, such portraitures, with the infinite variety of tales connected with them, are either subjects of merriment of objects of indifference. But, to the multitude of the young and uninformed, whose learning begins and ends with this so highly magnified summary, serious indeed is the idea attached to that tremendous sound. How many, from whose minds the horrific being, – of which, from the most unquestionable authority the existence is thus certified, – is never absent! How many, to whom this his ideal presence is sufficient to render *solitude*, at least when coupled with *darkness*, a situation of never-ceasing torment?

(3). ['*The pomps and vanity of this wicked world.*'] – Pomps and vanity, *two* other sorts of things given here as *one* thing, – and that one, as well as the things preceding and succeeding, a thing to be '*renounced.*' Renounced? – By whom? – By every member of the Church of England without exception, and *that* with almost his earliest articulate breath.

As to the *vanity*, with or without the subjoined limitation, by which it is confined to '*this wicked world,*' being in itself the *vainest* of all *vain* words – so completely *vain* as to be void of all meaning – it may, with that character attached to it, be dismissed.

But the word *pomp* – to this word is attached by usage – unvaried usage – a meaning somewhat more determinate and intelligible. Under the word *pomp* are comprised all those factitious appendages by which factitious dignity, – when combined with the visible and tangible fruits and marks of opulence, – is, in the hands of the *ruling few*, employed to distinguish them from the *subject many*.

The *Monarch*, in the first place, is it not by *pomp* that he is intended and enabled to display and preserve his *dignity*, and therewith and thereby to maintain his *power*? The robes – the sceptre – the crown – the train of attendants, in so many forms and colours – armed and unarmed – if these be not the elements of *pomp*, what others are?

Not to speak of *Lords Temporal*, with their *titles*, their *coronets*, and their *armorial ensigns*, behold the Lords *Spiritual*, with the '*fine linen*' on their *shoulders*, the '*purple*' on their *liveries*, the *purple* and the *mitre* on their *equipages*. If not of *these* things, of *what* things is '*pomp*' made?

Of all these holy personages – these sitting and walking pageants – what one has there ever been, by whom all these *things* have not thus been solemnly *renounced*? – all these *things*, to which, disguised under the name of *decency*, they now cling with such fond and undisguised affection; – these *things*, of which the very essence of their order is, according to them, composed, and by the taking away of which *the Church* would, according to them, be laid in ruins, and along with it *the State*.

That this so much magnified instrument of theatrical piety is neither more nor less than a farce, – that nothing that is to be found in it need or ought to be considered as possessing any binding force, – that it is neither more nor less than so much sound without sense, – is not this the comment which, in that highest of all high places, the text receives from practice?

Such, then, being the judgment passed on it by the highest of all authorities, by what inferior authority – by what private individual – should any different judgment be passed upon it?

And this is the '*Instruction, which*' (as it says itself in and by its title) 'is to *be learned* of every person before he be brought to be confirmed by *the Bishop:*' – By the Bishop? and by what Bishop? – by the self-same Bishop, who by the '*pomps*,' whatever they are, by which he is surrounded, manifests the contempt with which, by himself, this same *Instruction* is regarded: and who, at the very time when the youthful votaries whom he beholds at his feet are passing examination under his eye, under his authority, in and by the words thus forced into their mouths, made to declare the knowledge which they have of its contents, and the sentiments of veneration with which, by these same contents, they have been impregnated, – is all the while, in relation to these same contents, making manifest, if not his deliberate contempt of them, at least his ignorance or negligence.

(4). '*Sinful lusts of the flesh.*' – In this may be seen the *third* and last of the three '*things*,' or sets of things, which with its scarce articulate accents the child, so lately in its cradle, is made to declare itself to have '*renounced*.' – Those '*lusts*,' which he has so decidedly '*renounced*' – those '*sinful lusts*' – what are they? – what, in his view of them, can they be? – Is it that the '*lusts of the flesh*' are *all* of them '*sinful*,' and as such to be comprised in the *renunciation?* or is it that, while there are *some* of them that *are* sinful, and such are to be '*renounced*,' others there are that are *not* sinful, and accordingly are *not* comprised in it? – These are among the secrets, which, howsoever here *mentioned*, are not here *made known*. But are they not *worth knowing?* – Are they not *necessary* to be known? – Are they not such as *must* have been known, ere the '*Instruction which is to be learned of* (meaning *by*) *every* person,' can to *any one* person be of any sort of use?

(5). '*Secondly, that I should believe all the articles of the Christian faith.*'
Behold here another subject for a promise – for a promise in the shape of a *solemn vow* – in the shape of that sacred sort of instrument, which is neither more nor less than an *oath*, applied and adapted to this particular purpose. A promise? – to do what? – *to believe:* – a promise to believe an innumerable host of things, – and that without knowing what they are. For, be it observed, the thing to be believed is – not simply *the Articles*, but *all* the Articles. Follows, indeed, the *Creed* called *the 'Apostles' Creed*,' the repetition of which is performed in answer to the presently following command – '*Rehearse the Articles of thy Belief.*' – But in this Creed are they all contained? Not they indeed. For if they are, what is the *Nicene* Creed, and what the *Athanasian?* – both of them comprised in the *Liturgy* – that massy compound which the child is condemned to gulp down after he has swallowed this Catechism; – each of them as much a part of the Church of England Liturgy, and thereby of what passes among Church of Englandists for the repository of the Christian faith, as that called the *Apostles' Creed* is.

Question 4. – Dost thou not think that thou art bound to believe and to do as they have promised for thee?

Answer. – Yes, verily; and by God's help, so I will. And I heartily thank our heavenly Father, that he hath called me to this state of salvation, through Jesus Christ our Saviour. And I pray unto God to give me his grace, that I may continue in the same to my life's end.

OBSERVATIONS.

Question. '*Dost thou not think,*' &c. – Answer. '*Yes, verily,*' &c. – Here then, not only do the authors of this formulary themselves advance this absurdity, but they compel the poor child, – as they have hitherto compelled so many millions – compelled, during so many successive generations, the far greater part of the population of the whole kingdom, and done what depended upon them towards compelling all future generations to the end of time, – to pronounce his assent to it and his approbation of it.

Now then, once more, if so it be that it is in the power of any three persons, under the name of *Sponsors*, to take possession of a child – a newborn child – and bind it, force it, to believe *this set* of Articles – how should it not be equally in their power to force it to believe any *other* set of Articles! – to believe, for example, the direct *reverse* of these same Articles? – If it be in their power thus to force a child, – to force as many children as they please, – to believe a set of Articles which *they* call '*the Christian faith,*' how should it not be in their power to force it to believe a set of Articles, for example, of *the Mahometan* faith?

Here then is a notion, which strikes – (for does it not strike?) – at the root of all religion as well as all morality: and, forasmuch as, in giving utterance to this mass of absurdity, the child is forced to say that *he believes it*, – while, at his years, at any rate, to believe it is not possible, – thus it is that the duty and practice of *lying* forms part of every Church of England child's first lesson. – Forms part? – Yes – forms a part, though but a part, of what he is *taught*, – but forms nearly the whole of what – let us hope at least – it is possible to him to *learn* from it.

Command, immediately following upon the fourth question – '*Rehearse the Articles of thy Belief.*'

Answer. – 'I believe in God, the Father Almighty, Maker of heaven and earth: And in Jesus Christ, his only Son our Lord, who was conceived by the Holy Ghost (1), born of the Virgin Mary (2), suffered under Pontius Pilate (3), was crucified, dead, and buried (4). He descended into hell (5); the third day he rose again from the dead. He ascended into heaven, and sitteth at the right hand of God the Father Almighty; From thence he shall come to judge the quick and the dead. I believe in the Holy Ghost (6); the Holy Catholic Church (7); the communion of Saints (8); the forgiveness of sins (9); the resurrection of the body, and the life everlasting. Amen.'

OBSERVATIONS.

The Apostles' Creed! This name, thus formally and universally applied – applied to a formulary, which, of those by whom in that character it is forced into the mouths of children, there is not one by whom any such notion is entertained, as that any one of those immediate disciples of Jesus had any, the smallest share in the formation of it!

Applied? – and by whom? – By the rulers of the English Church – of the Church of England, past and present – by that Bench of Bishops, whose name stands at the head of an Association, instituted for a set of purposes, of which the first in the order of time as well as of importance, is the causing the whole population to receive the formulary in that character.

An association, of which one main object is, to give currency to a *forgery!* to continue – and *that* for ever – to palm upon the rising generation as genuine an already exposed imposture. On the whole Bench sits there so much as a single individual, who will venture to declare that he believes it *not* to have been a forgery? that he believes any of those to have had a hand in it in whose name it is thus put upon the whole people?

To all those who do not, with a critical eye pointed to the questions of *verity* and *authenticity*, occupy themselves in the searching of the Scriptures, the immediate and sole looked-to evidence of that verity and authenticity consists in the implied evidence supposed to be bestowed upon it by those Right Reverend and well-paid witnesses. But here are these same witnesses, continually occupied in giving an attestation of authenticity to a document, of the seriousness of which they cannot but be, every one of them, fully conscious. If the religion of Jesus had no better ground to stand upon than this modern evidence, where would be the sort of regard due to it?

To give proofs, or so much as references to proofs, of its being a forgery – a generally exploded forgery – would be a mere waste of labour – *Pearson* – *Bishop Pearson* – whose comment on it is regularly included in the list of works studied by all Candidates for Church of England Ministry, into whose heads any such idea as that of rendering themselves, in an intellectual point of view, in any degree fit for their office, ever happens to find entrance, – *Pearson*, in styling it *the Creed*, knew it too well to venture, either in his title page or any where else, to style it *the Apostles' Creed;* or so much as, in the way of insinuation, to give it to be understood that the Apostles had, any of them, any thing to do with it. 'The Creed received in all ages of the Church,' (says he in his Epistle dedicatory): and thus far only did he venture to go beyond the truth in speaking of it, except by this, viz. 'it is (says his Preface) generally taken to comprehend all things necessary to be believed:' – *the* Creed – as if he had never heard of more Creeds than this one: as if that Liturgy, of which it forms a part, did not, lest confusion should not be thick enough, force into men's mouths two other Creeds – the *Nicene* and the *Athanasian* (yes, the Athanasian!) by the side of it.

For the first time – (pity the edition now on the table, though the *tenth,* does not enable any one to say exactly what time was) – for the first time – observing what sort of a thing this tissue of dark allusions, taken in its own state, was, – he formed the generous resolution of rendering it intelligible: and in this endeavour, no fewer than four hundred closely printed folio pages, with more of microscopic notes than text, are employed: 'so that every one, when he pronounceth the Creed, may know, (says the good Bishop) what he ought to intend and what he is understood to profess, when he so pronounceth it:' so that now, to all those in whose instance to the labour of studying this *Exposition*, and the faculty of buying or borrowing it, has been added the felicity of understanding it, the text, in so far as the enterprise undertaken by the comment has been successful, has been rendered intelligible.

Creed and Exposition together, of those who but for it would have been damned, how many will have been saved by it? Of those who, if they had had it, would have been saved, how many will have been damned for want of it? – those included who will not have been rich enough either to buy or borrow it. When to each of these questions a satisfactory answer has been provided, then it is that of its worth a correct estimate as well as conception will have been formed.

This, together with both the other Creeds, and together with the spirit and so large a portion besides of the substance of her Liturgy, was by the Church of England received from her Holy Mother: among whose histories that of the *pic-nic* formation of this Creed by its putative fathers the Apostles may be found in their proper places. The equally established Church of *Scotland* is wiser and honester than to teach any of these Creeds.

Of the three declarations of persuasion, which, under the name of *Creeds*, are all adopted into and make part of the Church of England Liturgy, this, – which by universal confession falsely (1), yet not the less universally, is called *the Apostles' Creed*, – is one.

In relation to this instrument, as here placed and employed, two questions naturally present themselves –

1. The set of opinions here stated as deduced from the text of holy writ, are they rightly deduced from holy writ? Do they in holy writ find a sufficient warrant?

If yes, is it right and useful to take the whole of the instrument as it stands, – and thus, at the tenderest age, force it into the mouths of children?

Of these questions, the first does not in any peculiar manner belong to this place: for the present, at least, it may therefore be dismissed.

In relation to the other question, a few observations may be not altogether without their use.

(1). [*Who was conceived by the Holy Ghost.*] – Not to dispute the matter of fact – the child – is it in the nature of the case that, of this *conception*, any conception at all should be entertained by the child by whom the answer is lisped?

(2). [*Born of the Virgin Mary.*] – The like question to this clause. – Born of a Virgin? – Yes: viz. of a woman who was once a virgin: but if *that* be what is here to be understood, so was every man that was ever born. Born without prejudice to her virginity? – she remaining after the birth as entirely a virgin as she was before? Is this a matter, the conception of which is, to a pupil, at such an age, in the number of things possible? – at such an age – not to speak of any less early age. Admitting the possibility, the attempt to convey an idea such as this, can it in any way be of use?

(3). [*Suffered under Pontius Pilate.*] – To a child at such an age the name of the Roman governor under whose government the suffering took place – the remembrance of it, is it of any particular use?

(4). [*Was crucified, dead and buried.*] – Crucifixion – burial – in neither of these two facts is there any thing but what, at a very early age, a child may be capable of comprehending without much difficulty – But death? the death of whom? – the death of a God? What! a God? a God *of our own* die? – Much about this time, perhaps a little earlier, perhaps a little later, it may have happened to the child to hear of the Gods of the *heathens* – Gods in multitudes – not one of them subject to death. In such a case, how inferior will this comparatively new God be apt to appear to him, in comparison of the least of these ancient ones! But if God the *Son* was thus mortal, what should preserve his Father from being mortal too? If it was the Son's turn to die at that time, may it not one of these days be the Father's turn? and then what is to become of the world and all that live in it?

For the removal of this difficulty, what answer is left, but the doctrine of the *two natures?* Jesus (the child must be told) had two natures – the human and the divine: he was a man and a God; that is *the* God – for there is but one God – at the same time. It was the man only that was crucified, and, dying under the operation, was then buried. The God did not die: in the case of God, no such thing as death took place: it is not in the nature of God, that is to say, of the one God, to die. Well, then, while one of these persons, viz. the man, was dying, the other of them, the God, the one God, whereabouts was he? – Have a care, child, what you say. Two persons? no such thing. Man one, God one: these one and one, which you in your ignorance take for two, are not two persons: they are but one. – How but one person? One man, is not that one person? and one God, is not that another person? One and one, do they not make two? – In answer to any such questions, nothing remains but to chide the poor child for his ignorance – to insist upon his understanding in this case the difference between a nature and a person, and thereupon to plague him till he declares himself satisfied, that though Jesus had two *natures*, he had but one *person*, and that, in that instance at least, so far as *personality* was concerned, *a God* – no, not *a God*, but God – yes, *God*, and man together, were one and the same.

Now, to any practical purpose, whether this or any part of it be true or no, is not, to child or man, worth inquiry. How should it be? For to human conduct, take it in any of these ways, what difference does it make? But, in regard to all this, or any part of this, to force a child to declare – to declare most solemnly and seriously, that he believes it, – believes it just as he believes in the existence of the person by whose words and gestures the words are forced into his mouth, and this in a case in which any such belief is as plainly impossible! – in this lies the mischief: – and, so long as in a habit of falsehood and insincerity, and that a universal one, there is any thing mischievous, this mischief will be as real as the pretended belief is false.

(5). [*He descended into hell.*] – Of the matter of fact here asserted, the truth being admitted – (though for the admitting it no warrant was ever so much as attempted to be found in any part of Scripture that bears any relation to Jesus, and though as well might it have been asserted, that, while a visit was then paid to *hell* by *Jesus*, a visit was at the same time paid to *heaven* by the *Devil*) – still, on this as on so many preceding and succeeding occasions, comes the question – supposing the fact ever so well established, to what possible good use force a child, as soon as it can speak, to say that it believes this, or so much as use any endeavours to cause it actually to believe any such thing?

When, against this proposition, the monstrous absurdity of it, coupled with its utter destituteness of all warrant from Scripture, is brought to view, the observation made by way of answer – and that probably enough a true one, is – that in this particular the *translation* is incorrect; for that in the original Greek the word rendered in English by *hell*, did not on this occasion mean that which on every other occasion it is commonly understood to mean – viz. the abode and place of torment of the damned.

But, besides that of this observation a necessary effect is to give birth to another question, – viz. if not *hell*, what other place then is on this occasion to be understood? – (a question, to which an answer would not, it is supposed, be very easy to be found) – another observation is, that in the case of at least nine hundred and ninety nine out of a thousand of those whose salvation is understood to be in so material a degree dependent – dependent, in some way or other – upon this Catechism, no such mistranslation is known or so much as suspected. In the conception of this vast majority, the place of torment appointed for the Devil and his angels, – *this* is the place to which the visit of this Son of God – himself God – was, in his own divine person, paid.

Of this perplexity, added to so many other perplexities, what is the result? That, in the minds of a very large proportion of the whole number – a very large proportion, if not the whole, of this discourse, called a *Creed* and *the Creed*, produces the same effect as, and no more than, so much inarticulate sound. Not but that if, in the instance of the whole number, such were the case with *the whole* of this same creed, it would be all the better; always excepted the mischief of the lie which the child is taught and compelled to utter, in thus seriously and solemnly declaring that he believes it.

(6). [*I believe in the Holy Ghost.*] – Mere sounds without sense: mere words without meaning: not only void of all meaning, which to any *such young* person can be of any *use* – not only void of all meaning which to *any* person can be of any use, – but without any thing attached to them that can be called *meaning*.

What is the *Holy Ghost?* – *Answer.* The same as the *Holy Spirit.*

What then is the *Holy Spirit?* – *Answer.* The Spirit of God.

What then is this Spirit of God, that, when you believe this God, this should not be enough, but that you must believe in this Spirit of God besides? Believing in a man, what more do you do by believing in his Spirit likewise?

'*The Lord be with you,*' says the Minister to the congregation in one part of our Liturgy. Not to be behind hand with him either in piety or politeness, nor yet to give him back his compliment without variation, as if for want of words, 'And *with thy Spirit,*' returns the *Chorus*, under the command of the clerk. In any such variation of the phrase, has imagination in its extravagance ever soared to such a height as to fancy itself to be possessing and employing a *re-agent*, having the effect of *decomposing* a human person, in such sort as to convert him, polypus like, into *two* persons, of which *himself* is one and his *spirit* the other?

If believing in God be not enough, without believing in the Spirit of God besides, how came *this* to be enough? To believe in the Spirit of God in addition to God himself, how can this be sufficient, when, besides the Spirit of God, according to the flowery texture of the same language and the same Scriptures, there are so many other things belonging to God, viz. the hand of God, the arm of God, the finger of God, the word of God, the power of God, the glory of God, and so forth: each of them not less susceptible, than the Spirit of God, of a separate existence – Oh, silly men – yes, if sincere, 'more silly than any sheep, which on the flowery plains shepherd did ever keep' – ye string words upon words, – and then, for every word believe, or pretend to believe, that a correspondent really existing object is brought into existence.

The Holy Ghost being, at the end of the account, something which is the same as God and at the same time distinct from God, – and being something in which, day by day, the child is obliged to say that he believes – by the sense of this obligation, should it happen to him to be induced to put himself upon the look-out for something determinate to believe in, – of such his inquiry, what, if any thing, will be the result?

In the same instructive prints which present to his view the *Devil* in the character of a black man, with horns on his head and a tail to his rump, he will behold a *pigeon*, hovering in a spot of light. This *pigeon*, which, however, he will be taught to call not by this name, but by its other and more poetical name, a *dove* – this *pigeon* it is, that if any thing will be the object of his belief.

Our God, whose picture *here* and *now* must not be drawn, but which when *here* it *was* drawn, *was* – and *there* where it is drawn, is – the picture of an *old man*; – *another God*, whose picture may be drawn, and is continually drawn, and when drawn is seen to be the picture of a *young man* – which God is likewise not only a God but also a man; – a *third* God, whose picture may be drawn, and being drawn, is seen to be the picture of the sort of *pigeon* called a *dove*, – these three Gods, who, man and *pigeon* included, make, after all, but one and the same object of belief, and that object *a God*, – these, when this system of instruction has been read, marked, learnt, and inwardly digested, comprise and constitute the *subject* of all this science – the *object* of the young child's belief – of that belief, of which he is forced to say that he entertains it. – That he entertains it? – why? – Even because, in an unthinking and half-hearing moment, three persons, under the rod of the law, – to save him from the endless and inscrutable mass of temporal inconvenience, attached to the non-performance of the ceremony, – undertook, by that which would be not only a *rash*, but a *flagitious*, were it any thing but a *senseless* vow, that, after having begun to entertain this belief, before he knew or cared what it was that he was thus entertaining, he would to the end of his life continue to entertain it.

(7). [*The Holy Catholic Church.*] – *The Holy Catholic Church*. – 'I believe in the Holy Catholic Church.' – Not to speak of former times, what is it that *at present* a child can understand himself to have spoken of himself as doing, when he has declared that he believes in *the Holy Catholic Church*? – *I believe in God*? – Yes, this is what he *may* conceive himself to understand. – I *believe* in God; i.e. I believe in the existence of a God – and so in regard to *Jesus Christ* and the *Holy Ghost*. But – *I believe in the existence of a Holy Catholic Church*? – For this same Church, of which, under the name of *the Holy Catholic Church* – one Holy Catholic Church, and no more than one – he is thus forced to speak, where is it that he is to look? If, by any such name as *the Catholic Church*, there be any thing that on any other occasion he has ever heard spoken of as being in existence, it will have been *the Roman Catholic Church* – a Church composed of

Roman Catholics, who are the same men that are sometimes called *Papists*, and who, when they were in power, burnt as many of the good people called *Protestants*, of whom he himself is one, as for that purpose they could lay hold of. Now, as to the *Holy Ghost*, in whom the child has just been declaring himself to believe, – whatsoever is or is not meant by *holiness*, – that *Ghost*, without any difficulty, is *holy*. But this Church, composed as it is of the barbarous men called *Papists*, is this too, *Holy*? – holy, even as the *Holy Ghost* is *Holy*? – On the part of the poor child, suppose any particle of thought to be bestowed upon the subject, how distressing must be the perplexity into which he here finds himself plunged? – But no: – before it has arrived thus far, the plain truth of the case is – that, whether in the breast of a child or in the breast of an adult, the faculty of thought, having found itself baffled and wearied out, has, in despair, withdrawn itself from the whole subject, leaving in the grasp of the conception and the memory nothing but a string of sounds and characters, void of all sense.

(8). [*The Communion of Saints.*] – *The Communion of Saints?* One more puzzle; a riddle which unhappily is not explicable, but which happily is not worth being explained.

The Communion of Saints – What is a *Communion?* What are *Saints?* – Saints, the poor child will soon have heard of. – There is St. Peter; there are the rest of the twelve Apostles, (Traitor *Judas* being excepted): there are Jesus's four *Biographers*, decorated with the title of *Evangelists*; all or most of them more or less known to him by their portraits; all of them striking likenesses; and, though last not least, there is St. *Paul*, whose beginning had borne but too near a resemblance to the latter end of *Judas*. In *the Communion*, – or, at any rate, in a communion, – the child may likewise ere long behold a thing which he has *heard of*, and moreover *heard* – a part of the Church service, called sometimes for shortness *the Communion* simply, at other times without abbreviation *the Communion Service*. – *Communion* – *Saints* – *belief* – putting together the ideas brought to view by these three words, – what in relation to this matter will be the little creature's belief? – something, perhaps, to this effect; viz. that, among the Apostles and whatever other holy men used to be called *Saints*, it was a custom to join together in the performance of the *Communion service*; of the Communion service – worded, as he has seen it, or is about to see it worded, viz. in the *Church of England Liturgy*.

If this be an error, well would it be for the successive generations by which the compound here analyzed is destined to be swallowed – not to speak of those by whom it *has been* swallowed, – if, of all errors contained in it, this were the most pernicious one.

Saints, whose portraits he has there been used to see – that, like good Saints as they were, they used, all of them, to join in the performance of the Communion service – this may do for a time. But to believe in the Communion of Saints, is to believe in the Saints themselves: – and who are these Saints? Any such question, should it ever happen to him to put to himself, what answer will he have to give? – Where shall he find it? – Where shall he look for it? – Sooner or later it may happen to him to look into the Calendar that stands at the commencement of his Common Prayer Book, more especially as it is there that he will have to look for Holidays. Looking into this treasury of consecrated idleness, he will find, that, to the original stock of Saints, he will have to add a list of modern ones; not to speak of Martyrs and Confessors, with whom this Catechism has happily abstained from burthening his memory and his conscience. Neither in this however will there be any great difficulty: and now, to his belief in the Devil will be added his belief in *Saint Dunstan*, whose Church is established still in Fleet-street, and whose Saintship consisted in pulling the unclean spirit by the nose. Here at any rate may be Saints enough to satisfy his believing appetite, so long as his studies are confined to the Common Prayer Book, of which this Catechism makes a part, and the Calendar by which it is commenced or preceded. But by the Holy Scriptures – should they ever carry him so far – how will those ideas, which by the Common Prayer Book he had been led to form of Saints, be enlarged, and at the same time confused and troubled? On this head, are the Holy Scriptures – is the New Testament – are the Acts of the Apostles, to be believed? If so, then is every one a Saint by whom the religion of Jesus is, or ever has been, or shall ever have been, professed. Read to this purpose the Acts of the Apostles; or, what is shorter, turn to any *Concordance*.

If this be so, then in the number of these holy subjects or objects of his belief, he may have to place not only St. *Peter* and St. *Paul* with their contemporaries, as above, with such of their successors as St. *Sutton*, and St. *Vernon*, and St. *Howell*, and St. *Burgess*, and St. *Eldon*, and St. *Sidmouth*, and St. *Harrowby*, and St. *Bailey*, and St. *Stevens*, and St. *Parke*, and St. *Wilberforce*, and St. *Bernard*, and St. *W. Milner* the Protestant, and St. *Milner* the Catholic, and St. *Hannah* and St. *Joanna*, – but St. *Napoleon*, moreover, and St. *George*, and St. *Ellenborough*, and St. *Yarmouth the Orangeman*, and St. *Headfort*, and St. *Dudley Bate*, and St. *Southey*, and St. *Anti-Jacobin*, and St. *Eclectic*, and St. *Quarterly Review*.

(9). [*The forgiveness of sins; the resurrection of the body; and the life everlasting.*] – On these several points, to the present purpose it seems scarcely necessary to bestow any very particular observations. Thus briefly and elliptically conceived, containing nothing but a mere indication of certain topics, as if touched upon in some other work, the phrases amount of themselves to nothing. The demand they present for explanation is obvious and undeniable; and in the whole body of that formulary, by not so much as a syllable in the way of explanation are they accompanied.

Nothing of that sort is there in the *Creed* itself; as little in this *Catechism*, into which, for the instruction of young children, it is engrafted.

As such they add to the number of propositions or subject-matters, in relation to which, while it is impossible the child should entertain any belief concerning them, he is thus forced to stand up with all solemnity, and say, '*I do believe.*'

As to these three last-mentioned subjects, compleat the proposition – what in each instance you have, and all that you have, is composed of so many allusions – mere allusions. In the mind of him, whoever he was, by whom this formulary was penned, they had doubtless, every one of them, a *subject-matter or object*, more or less determinate – every one of them accordingly a *meaning*. But in the mind of the so newly-born child, – in that mind, in which it is, generally speaking, impossible that the indeterminate portion of matter thus alluded to should have any place what meaning can they, any of them, have? At bottom, what then is it that he is thus forced to declare? What but this, viz. that he believes in whatever is thus forced into his mouth, without knowing so much as *who* it is that put it where it is, much less *what* it is?

Question 5th. – What dost thou chiefly learn in these articles of thy belief? –

Answer. – First, I learn to believe in God the Father, who both made me and all the word (1).

Secondly, in God the Son, who hath redeemed me and all mankind (2).

Thirdly, in the Holy Ghost, who sanctifieth me and all the elect people of God (3).

OBSERVATIONS.

To these three things may be added three others which, with a degree of correctness proportioned to the degree of the impregnation he has received from them, a child may make sure of learning; – and these are – the art of *gratuitous assertion* – the art of speaking and writing without thinking – and the art of making *groundless inferences.*

(1). [*Belief in God the Father.*] – Yes: this is among the things which, supposing them *noticed*, are not incapable of being *learnt* from it.

(2). [*Belief in God the Son?*] – Yes, and this likewise. – But belief *in God the Son, who redeemed me and all the world?* – As to the fact of the *redemption*, had it been taken for the subject of an independent article of belief, no objection would, *here* at least, have been made to it. But the Creed called the *Apostles'* Creed? – this just repeated Creed? – from this discourse is the belief of any such thing as *redemption* to be learnt? Look at it, reader, once more: examine it from top to bottom. Of no such thing – any the slightest intimation will you find in it.

But *mankind, all* of whom the child is thus made to say he believes to have been redeemed – redeemed, along with himself, by Jesus – *they*, on considering the condition in which they will be seen to be placed, present some claim to notice.

Of this *redemption*, the *universality* any more than the *fact* is not here meant to be disputed. But, whosoever has been made to declare himself to be a believer in it, it might not have been amiss, it should seem, had some little provision been made for preserving him from any such obligation as that of declaring, on an eventually subsequent occasion, a directly opposite belief: viz. that of declaring, in solemn form, his belief of and in the entire contents of that other formulary called the *Thirty-nine Articles*. – Of that test and treasury of Church of England orthodoxy, in *one* article, viz. the 18th, intituled, '*Of obtaining eternal salvation only by the name of Christ*,' 'Those (it is said) are to be held accursed, that presume to say that every man shall be saved by the law or sect which he professed, so that he be diligent to frame his life according to that Law and the Light of Nature. For Holy Scripture doth set out unto us (concludes the article) only the name of Jesus whereby men must be saved.'

Not to speak of any *former* portion of time, – of the whole number of human beings existing at *this* time upon this our earth, by far the greater number, it is manifest, can never have heard of any such person or name as *Jesus*. This great majority – are they capable of being saved, each of them '*diligently framing his life*,' in the terms of the article, 'according to the Law of Nature,' (i.e. it must be presumed, leading a virtuous life), or are they not?

Being, along with the rest of mankind, redeemed by Jesus, is a man *capable* of being '*saved*,' otherwise than 'by the name of Jesus?' – then is the article *false*. – Is he *incapable*? – then where is the use of such *redemption*, and what is a man the better for it?

Every man who takes what are called *Holy Orders* – every man, whose name is entered in the books of either University – declares in writing his belief in *all* these *Articles*. But, as hath been seen, no sooner does he thus declare, than, by such his declaration, he contradicts the belief thus expressed in and by this his *Catèchism*.

By parental authority – by the compulsion, inseparable from the exercise, however directed, of that authority, – in a word, by *force* – by any thing but *argument* or *reason* applied to the understanding, – during a long and uninterrupted course of years, he is made continually to declare this to be his belief: thereupon, when the time for the purchase of a ticket in the Ecclesiastical Lottery, and with it the time for *Subscription* comes, – all on a sudden he turns short round, casts from him this his belief, and embraces the reverse of it.

All this with the most perfect, and the most exemplary *regularity*: and thus it is that *order, good order, regularity, decency* – sounds so sweet to the

ears of *Orthodoxy, Despotism,* and their ever ready handmaid, *Mendacity* –
are preserved.

(3). [*Thirdly, in God the Holy Ghost, who sanctifieth me and all the elect
people of God.*] – In explanation of the function called, *sanctification,* thus
allotted to God the *Holy Ghost,* what, in this instrument, is there to be
found? – Just as much as in explanation of the function of *redemption,*
just allotted, as above, to God the *Son.*

Whence then all this elaborate distinction of functions? all the work thus
given to the carving knife? The Godhead being, as every body is supposed
to know, or at least made to say, composed of three persons, – and, on the
occasion in question, the plan being to give something to do for each, –
thereupon, the less plainly incomprehensible functions of *creation* and
redemption being already disposed of, – divided, as hath been seen, between
the two other persons of this undivided Trinity, comes the question – what
can we find for the Holy Ghost to do? – Answer. *Sanctification.* – Here,
then, whatsoever be the meaning of it, here was a sort of *employment*
found for him, every other being engaged.

Here, then, in this word, we have the name of a sort of *process,* which
the child is made to say is going on within him; going on within him at all
times – going on within him at the very instant he is giving this account of
it. This process, then, what is it? Of what feelings is it productive? By what
marks and symptoms is he to know whether it really is or is not going on
within him, as he is forced to say it is? How does he feel, now that the
Holy Ghost is *sanctifying* him? How is it that he would feel, if no such
operation were going on within him?

Too often does it happen to him, in some shape or other, to commit *sin*;
or something which he is told and regarded to believe is *sin*: an event which
cannot fail to be frequently, not to say continually, taking place, if that be
true, which in the Liturgy we are all made so decidedly to confess and
assert, – viz., that we are all – all of us without exception – so many
'*miserable sinners?*' In the *School-room,* doing what by this Catechism he
is forced to do, saying what he is forced to say, the child thus declares
himself, notwithstanding, a *sanctified* person. From thence going to church,
he confesses himself to be no better than '*a miserable sinner.*' If he is not
always this miserable sinner, then why is he always forced to say he is? If
he is always this same miserable sinner, then this sanctification, be it what
it may, which the Holy Ghost was at the pains of bestowing upon him,
what is he the better for it?

The child, into whose mouth these words are forced, does he not so
much as suppose himself to feel going on within him any process, to which
the word *sanctification* can be applied? If *not,* then what is it that this
same *sanctification* means? and why is it that he is made to speak of the

Holy Ghost, as performing or having performed it upon him, when he feels not any such thing, nor knows any thing about the matter?

Does he then feel or suppose any such particular operation going on within him? If so, then must this sanctification be the receiving of that inward light, which certain of the people called *Methodists* take upon them to speak of themselves as feeling within themselves. By the rulers of the Church and their adherents, these Methodists are spoken of as *schismatics*, and a species of heretics. Quere, such reprobation, how is it consistent with the declaration thus expressed and included in this Catechism?

To be *sanctified* is to be made *holy*. By the child, be he who he may, sooner or later, this point of information will have been received, if it has not been already. While giving this answer, *does* the child then feel itself *holy*? – If *not*, then why is it to be forced to say it does? If *yes*, then is it already a *Methodist* child: an arrant *Methodist*.

Question 6th. – You said that your Godfathers and Godmothers did promise for you that you should keep God's commandments. Tell me how many there be.

Answer. – Ten.

Question 7th. – Which be they?

Answer. – The same which God spake in the twentieth chapter of Exodus, saying, I am the Lord thy God, who brought thee out of the land of Egypt, out of the house of bondage.

I. Thou shalt have none other Gods but me.

Thereupon follow the other nine of these commandments.

OBSERVATIONS.

Upon the face of this introduction, an appearance rather unfortunate presents itself. The child in question is not a Jew: neither he nor any of his forefathers were ever, in the manner thus alluded to, '*brought out of the land of Egypt.*' But it is to the Jews, and to that race alone, – to those, and the progeny of those, who were thus brought out of the land of Egypt – that these Commandments are any where in the Bible represented as having been delivered.

How far, by a person professing the religion of Jesus, they ought to be considered as binding upon him, is a subject of controversy, upon which it is not proposed to enter in this place.

One observation however there is, which, even in this place, claims admission, – and *that* by a title which it seems not easy to dispute. This is – that, in a discourse, which is intended for the instruction of *Christian* children, and which has for one of its objects the causing these Commandments to be regarded as binding upon Christians, it seems not altogether congruous to that design to employ a form of words, upon the face of which it appears that no person, not being of Jewish lineage, and at the same time of the Jewish persuasion in matters of religion, and therefore no child for whose use this formulary was intended, is of the number of the persons to whom these Commandments were addressed.

In relation to this incongruity, what was the expectation, and consequent instruction, of the penners and establishers of this formulary? – that it *would* and *should*, or that it *would not* and *should not*, attract, in general, the notice, and engage the attention, of those who were destined to be impregnated with it? – impregnated with the *matter*, or at any rate, with the *words* of it? *If yes*, then the expectation and intention was, – that, by those, by whom the words of this formulary were got by heart, no reliance should be placed in the *words*, of which it was composed; but that for the sense of it, they were to refer themselves to whatever construction the person, to whose guidance it was meant they should stand subjected, might at any time be pleased to put upon it: – *if no*, then the expectation and intention was, – that in this part at least – (and if in *this* part, how should it be otherwise in any *other?*) the place it occupied in men's minds would and should be that of an insignificant assemblage of words: – of mere words, not accompanied by correspondent ideas, and therefore not capable of exercising any influence on human practice; – on the conduct of those upon whose memories it was to be impressed.

But, in relation to this matter, let the *expectation* and *intention* have been what they may, what is likely to be the *effect?* The incongruity, *will it* be perceived? then in so far will the unfitness of this formulary for its purpose be perceived. The incongruity, will it *not* be perceived? it will then be, because, – in this particular part, as in the whole together, – it is not of a nature to take on the understanding any efficient hold, nor therefore to produce on life and conduct any beneficial effect.

> Thou shalt not make to thyself any graven image, nor the likeness of any thing that is in heaven above, or in the earth beneath, or in the waters under the earth.

OBSERVATIONS.

Upon the face of this commandment, two branches of art and science stand condemned and prohibited; viz. the *graphic art* in all its various modifications; the graphic art, and thereby, in great measure, the science of *natural history*; two branches of art and science; and thereby, among *men*, those by whom those branches of art and science are respectively practised and cultivated: on the one hand, *painters* and other such *artists* – on the other hand, *natural philosophers*.

True it is that, immediately after the above, these are the words that follow: – '*Thou shalt not bow down to them, nor worship them.*' Well then (it has been said) by this it appears, that in so far as concerns manual operation in any shape, in addition to the act of *bowing down to* and *worshipping them*, all that was meant to be included in the prohibition was, not simply the act of *making* the sorts of things in question, but the act of making them for the *purpose* in question: *viz.* that of their being *bowed down to* and *worshipped*.

Yes, verily: in this may be seen a signification, which must per force be put upon these words, in so far as a resolution has been previously taken, that whatsoever were the real meaning of the prohibitory clause, the act of *making*, as applied to the class of articles in question, shall not be *considered* as included in it.

But, upon the face of the words, as they here stand, is this the *true*, the *natural*, the *proper* sense of them? If so, then are the words designative of the sort of act first mentioned, *viz.* the act of *making* – then are the words – '*Thou shalt not make to thyself*' – to be considered as words void of meaning: then is the whole passage to be understood, as it would be if no such words were there.

But, for the taking of any such liberty with this passage, where is the sufficient warrant? If with *this* passage, that sort of liberty may be taken, – taken at pleasure, by any man who finds a convenience in so doing, – why not with any other, and every other? – This is the way that, now-a-days, so many religions are made. By omission, by insertion, by substitution – by *amendment* in every shape – a man makes a Bible of his own; and thereupon, with intimations given of divine vengeance in case of refractoriness, he calls upon mankind to bow down and worship it.

The writer, inspired or not inspired, by whom this passage was originally penned, was he so much less skilled in the import and management of his own language, as not to be able to give expression to a prohibition, which he *did* intend *should* take effect, – not to be able to give expression to this prohibition, without adding to it another and still more extensive, – and that a useless and pernicious one, – which he *did not intend* should take effect? Inspired or uninspired, had he not foresight enough to foresee (and surely no such gift as that of supernatural prophecy was necessary to enable a man to foresee) that such as is here contended for would be the signification put upon these words, – and in consequence to do what was so perfectly easy to do, for preventing any such sense from being put upon them, *viz.* to forbear inserting the words by which this supposed real intention was so plainly counteracted, and which could not be either necessary or conducive to any other purpose than that of counteracting it.

In truth, according to the plain and only natural import of the words, here are two sorts of acts, perfectly distinct from and unconnected with each other, that are successively taken for the objects of so many successive prohibitory clauses. *One* is – the act of *worshipping* the natural objects therein described, the *other* is – the act of *making* visible representations of these same objects.

True it is, that it is not in *this* order that the two prohibitions follow one another: it is in the reverse order: the prohibition of *making* any likenesses of the objects in question – this is the prohibition that happens here to have been first. And in this collocation it is – in the relative position thus given to these two prohibitive clauses, which in this their situation are, however, upon the face of them, no less completely independent of one another, than in the opposite situation they would have been – in this circumstance, insignificant as it is, may be seen the only shadow of pretence that could be found for a change so violent – for a misrepresentation so manifest.

All this while, as every body knows in this country, in which the religion of Jesus is not only professed, but established, and even forced upon men by law, – under the same law the *making of graven images* is not only practised and allowed, but by public authority encouraged; as well as in all other imaginable ways, 'the likenesses' of all sorts of things that are 'in heaven above, or in the earth beneath, or in the water (whatsoever there is of it that is) under the earth.' In this state of law and universal practice, while such as above is manifestly the import of this commandment, – a commandment, exhibiting not only in the character of a *divine* one, but of a divine one, binding not only upon the Jews, to whom it was delivered, but upon Christians, to whom it was not delivered, – is it not deplorable, that, in this country in particular, every Christian belonging to the established religion, should thus be forced to declare his resolution to keep this commandment along with the rest – this commandment, which no such Christian ever *does* keep, or entertain so much as a thought of keeping? or, except in and by this formulary, addressed to young children only, is ever called upon to keep?

To engage in any such task as that of writing a commentary on this Jewish code, forms not any part of the design of the present tract. That part of this Catechism, which is composed of the remaining eight of these commandments, has therefore been omitted.

Question 8. – What dost thou chiefly learn by these commandments?

Answer. – I learn two things: my duty towards God, and my duty towards my neighbour.

OBSERVATIONS.

Of a *commentary*, be the subject what it may, a proper, – and (it should seem) where, as here, censure is out of the question, the only proper – use is – in so far as the text is, either with reference to all persons in general, or with reference to a particular description of persons, for whose use the commentary is intended, less perspicuous than might have been wished, to clear away the ambiguity or obscurity; – to wit, by bringing to view what, upon the consideration of the whole, presents itself as the true meaning

– the meaning intended by the person of whose discourse the text is composed.

On a subject such as the present, if, – besides exhibiting the meaning which it was in the mind and intention of the author of the original work to convey, – the author of the accessory work in question takes upon himself to draw inferences of his own, in so far it is rather a *sermon* than a *commentary*. Be that as it may, in this case what he ought to do is – carefully to avoid confounding with the consecrated ground-work his own unconsecrated inference: and, in particular, in giving expression to his own inference, he ought to employ for that purpose other words of his own, chosen by himself for that same purpose; and not any such words of the original text, as will have the effect of causing this inference of his to be regarded not as his inference, but as so much matter already and actually included in the text; i. e. as constituting a part of that meaning, which, by means of that text, it had been the intention of the author to convey to his expected readers.

Taken on the footing of an *independent* proposition, that in the main, at this time of day, it would be for the benefit of a professor of the religion of Jesus, to regard the above described duties as so many duties incumbent on himself, is not here less meant to be represented as a matter open to dispute. But that, in the character of *an inference* – an inference drawn from the tenor of the code here in question, any such proposition is correct, can not be admitted. The Jews – they and they alone – were the people to whom this code was addressed. In addressing himself, whether to his hearers or his readers, those, and those alone, were the people, which, on this occasion, could have been present to the mind of *Moses*, in such sort as to be considered as the people, with reference to whom the word *neighbour* was to be understood. But in those days, and on that occasion, who was *the neighbour of a Jew?* In general, every other Jew but most assuredly no person other than a Jew. On that occasion, had the benefit of these commandments been meant to be extended to men in general, the word correspondent to the word *man*, and *not* the word correspondent to the word *neighbour*, would have been the word employed. If by *Moses*, of all men, men *in general* – all men without distinction – had been meant, what should have been *his* inducement to discard this most obvious of all words, and substitute to it a different word, the effect of which, in so far as any effect is given to it, is – to designate, to the exclusion of the whole remainder of the species, a comparatively minute portion of it.

Neighbour being a *relative* term – a word of *reference* – no sooner is the *object* of reference changed, than, in this new case, it comes to be designative of a set of persons altogether different from those which in the first instance it was employed to designate. The sort of person, who, during the penning of the text, was in contemplation under the word *neighbour*, could be no other than a *Jew*. But, at this time of day, in so far as the word *neighbour* is used in its only proper sense, no Jew is the neighbour, much less the *only* sort of neighbour, of any child into whose mouth this formulary is forced. True it is that, when *Jesus* comes, he is represented as making *an amendment* to this code: declaring, on that occasion, that, by every one of *his* followers, not *Jews* alone, but every other man without exception, should, to the purpose of receiving the benefits proffered by him, be considered in the character of a *neighbour*. With this explanation, true it is that, to the particular purpose in question, in the vocabulary of a follower of Jesus, the word *neighbour* becomes synonymous to the word *man*: – understand with this explanation, given as it was by *Jesus*. But, to the explanation and extension, thus, at so vast a distance of time after the issuing of this code, given to it by Jesus, no reference is, in this formulary, to be found. In it the neighbour of the *Christian* is represented as being at all times the same sort of person as was the neighbour of the *Jew* in *Moses'* time; and the one as well as the other, as being the same sort of person as is designated by the word *man* at all times. Accordingly, presently after, *viz.* in the answer to the next question but one, the expression *all* men is slipt in, – and, without notice, is employed in the place of *neighbour*: as if the two words had all along the same meaning: and thus, instead of the clear light in which the whole matter might so easily have been placed, it is wrapt up in confusion and darkness.

Question 9. – What is thy duty towards God?

Answer. – My duty towards God is to believe in him, to fear him, and to love him with all my heart, with all my mind, with all my soul, and with all my strength; to worship him, to give him thanks, to put my whole trust in him, to call upon him, to honour his holy name and his word, and to serve him truly all the days of my life.

OBSERVATIONS.

On the subject of this answer, not a few are the questions that present themselves: – the questions, pregnant, all of them, with doubts, if not with objections, – some of them chargeable, as it should seem, with impertinence. But as the suggestions conveyed by them have not for their result any imputation on the *morality* of the discourse; – as, supposing them well grounded, nothing beyond its character for wisdom is affected by them, – to frame the answers is a task that will be left altogether to the reader: nor, upon any of the subjects thus touched upon, will any more words be employed than what have been found absolutely necessary for giving expression to the questions themselves.

1. Belief in God? what is it that is here meant by it? belief that God *exists*, or any thing, and what else?

2. Belief – an act of the understanding – ought it to be, or can it be made subject to the determination of the will?

3. If, in the mind in question, the existence of God is *already* the subject matter of *belief*, what need can there be to take it for a subject of *obligation*? – to rank it among *duties*?

4. If it be not, where can be the *effective ground* – the cause of fulfilment – in the case of the *obligation* thus supposed? Of what sort of matter can any such ground be composed?

5. In regard to *love*, on the supposition that, to the person in question, the object in question is not only an object of *fear*, but of a fear which is altogether boundless, in this case, of any such affection as is expressed by the word *love*, is the real existence, or any thing but the name and profession, compatible with such fear?

6. In particular, any such sentiment or affection as *love*, is it, in such a place as the human breast, producible by, or so much as compatible with, all this *straining*.

7. Wherein, except in words, consists on this occasion the difference between *heart* and *mind*, and *soul* and *strength*?

8. By this accumulation of words, thus heaped one upon another, is any other idea conveyed than that of the extreme difficulty of the task thus endeavoured to be imposed, *viz.* the task of *loving*?

9. Any such affection as that called love, where it really has place, does it ever happen to it to have for its accompaniment any such idea as that of *difficulty*?

10. Be the object what it may, be to whom the idea of *loving* it presents any such idea as that of difficulty, can he with truth be said to *love* it?

11. In the case of a young child – not to speak of maturer age – does it seem likely that, by all these words, any such *straining* should frequently be produced?

12. Supposing it produced, does it seem likely that any real good effects, with relation either to his own happiness, or to the happiness of those whose lot may have placed them within the field of his influence, will result from it?

13. Be the person who he may, a determination on his part to put his *whole* trust in God, is it, if carried into effect, compatible with the practice of putting any *part* of his trust in the known and perpetually experienced and unquestionable operation and efficiency of *second* causes?

14. A *total*, or even considerable, though it were but *partial*, disregard to the operation of such *second causes*, would it be in any degree compatible with personal safety – with the preservation of health, of life, or of any thing that is worth preserving, whether to the individual himself, or to any other person or persons whose lot it may be to stand in need of his assistance?

15. The exertions thus required, and per force undertaken to be employed,

in the endeavour to serve that *Being*, to whom all human service is '*unprofitable*,'[1] might they not with more profit be directed to the service of those weak creatures, whose need, of all the service that can be rendered to them, is at all times so urgent and so abundant?

Question 10. – What is thy duty towards thy neighbour?

Answer. – My duty towards my neighbour, is to love him as myself, and to do to all men as I would they should do unto me. To love, honour, and succour my father and mother. To honour and obey the king, and all that are put in authority under him. To submit myself to all my governors, teachers, spiritual pastors and masters. To order myself lowly and reverently to all my betters. To hurt nobody by word or deed. To be true and just in all my dealings. To bear no malice nor hatred in my heart. To keep my hands from picking and stealing, and my tongue from evil speaking, lying, and slandering. To keep my body in temperance, soberness, and chastity. Not to covet nor desire other men's goods; but to learn and labour, truly to get mine own living, and to do my duty in that state of life, unto which it shall please God to call me.

OBSERVATIONS.

Of this long and wordy formulary, had the whole contents been of a piece with the answer thus given to this question, assuredly it would never have been taken for the subject of a commentary, wearing any such complexion as that of the present, or having any such conclusions for its result and practical inference.

Throwing out the greater part, or the whole of the rest, adding or not adding any thing in the place of the matter thus discarded, – were it proposed to retain the substance of this answer, some such little changes might perhaps be suggested, as need not despair of being received in the character of *amendments*. But, taken even as it stands, especially when consideration is bad of the age in which it was penned, and above all, when comparison is made of it with the whole remainder of that of which it forms a part, – so beautiful does it appear, that the eye shrinks from any such task, as that of travelling over it in search of imperfections.

Question 10, (put immediately after *the Lord's Prayer*). – What desirest thou of God in this prayer?

Answer. – I desire my Lord God our heavenly Father, who is the giver of all goodness, to send his grace (1) unto me, and to all people.

---

[1]   Luke xvii, 10. – So likewise ye, when ye shall have done all those things which are commanded you, say, we are unprofitable servants; we have done that which was our duty to do.

OBSERVATIONS.

(1). [*Grace.*] – Here is the Prayer; and in the whole tenor of it, from beginning to end, about any such thing or word as *grace*, not so much as a single syllable.

The misrepresentation thus made, is it an innocent one? On the mind of every man by whom this formulary is regarded as unexceptionable, the effect of it – is it not – in conjunction with so many other causes which the same formulary sets to work, – to contribute towards the reconciling him to that convenient laxity of interpretation, which among religionists is so unhappily frequent, – and, with relation to all worldly interests, so convenient?

A subject-matter, of which every body sees that no mention is made in this Prayer – this subject-matter, a child, who sees that it is *not* there, is made to declare – to declare in the face of a clergyman, or other person, under whom he is passing this examination, – and who, as well as he, sees that it is *not* there, – to declare, and to declare most solemnly, that it is there.

The lesson thus forced into every Church-of-England mouth, suppose it to be productive of any fruits whatsoever, – is it possible that, under such instruction, a rooted and habitual depravation of the mental faculties, intellectual and moral, should not be of the number of those fruits? To repeat as if it were true that which with his own eyes he sees to be untrue, this is what from infancy a child is compelled to practise – this is what he is made to reckon among the number of his *duties*.

In addition to *grace*, another of the *things* which, they not being in this Prayer, the pupil is thus forced to declare himself to have found in it, is *death – everlasting death*. – Of *everlasting death*, what mention is there in this Prayer of Jesus? – Not any: nor yet so much as of what is commonly meant by *death*. Of *evil*, yes: and death (it may be said) everlasting death – is not this an evil? – Doubtless: at least if by *death* be meant – not the absence of all sufferance, but sufferance itself. But if this were a sufficient warrant for making the child say that Jesus spoke of *death*, when no such word as *death* is to be found in what he said, so would it be for speaking of all other things, one after another, to which, with any propriety, the word *evil* could be applied, and thereupon saying of each, that Jesus had spoken of it.

As to *grace* on this occasion, as on so many others – not to say *all* others – it is a mere *expletive*; adding nothing to the sense. Yet upon the ground of this expletive, systems have been built, controversies raised, swords drawn, and blood made to flow in torrents.

But of this disastrous expletive, more will be seen presently; *viz.* when the modern inventions, called *Sacraments*, come to be laid upon the table.

Question 11. – How many Sacraments hath Christ ordained in his Church?

Answer. – Two only (1), as generally necessary to salvation: that is to say, *Baptism* (2), and the *Supper of the Lord* (3).

OBSERVATIONS.

(1). [*Two only.*] – Of the word *only*, the use – so all commentators are agreed – was to put an exclusion upon a parcel of other ceremonies to which this revolted Church, the Church of England, had found the name of *sacrament* attached by the original Church from which she broke loose.

But as to *Christ*, the question being how many *sacraments* hath Christ ordained, the true answer would have been – none. For on what occasion, in the only language in which he spoke, is he represented as having employed any word to which the word *sacrament*, taken from the Latin *sacramentum*, corresponds in this our language?

Sacrament? what is it but a word of modern invention – a sort of metaphysical term, having certainly for its effect, probably for its object, the causing to be regarded as mysterious, two operations, in neither of which there was any mystery, – to be regarded as having a connexion with each other – and that connexion fraught with mystery – two objects, between which no such connexion, nor any connexion at all, had been established by Jesus.

(2). [1. *Baptism*] – This operation was a *ceremony:* a ceremony, having for its object the serving to establish, and upon occasion bring to mind, the fact of a man's having been aggregated into the society formed by Jesus: the religious society, of which – God or man, or both in one, – he was the teacher and the head.

In an unlettered community it was a sort of substitute for an entry in a *register* or *memorandum book.* By a too natural misconception, the mere *sign* or *evidence* of this aggregation was taken for the *efficient cause* of the benefits produced by it. Thereupon came questions, out of number, about the circumstances by which it should be accompanied: – 1. whether the application of the water should be *total* or *partial?* – 2. if partial, what fingers should be employed in it? – 3. and what the *form* should be that should be given to the wet mark made by it? &c. &c.[2] the principle of *nullity* – that inexhaustible source of uncertainty in all its excruciating shapes – that prime instrument of fraud and rapine – being borrowed from technical jurisprudence, and in the character of a necessary *consequence*, attached to every deviation from the arbitrarily imagined and endlessly

---

[2]   In the Russian Empire, by differences on this ground, persecutions and disastrous civil wars have been kindled. By the sect, which, in the sixteenth century, under the name of *Anabaptists*, to the determination of performing the humectation in the *total* way, as it was performed by Jesus, added other particulars, some of which were not only absurd but deplorably mischievous – peculiarities not regarding ceremony but morals – prodigious were the miseries inflicted and suffered.

diversified standard of rectitude. In the same spirit, had the literary, and more durable expedient of a *Register-book* been employed, questions might have been started – whether, for the validity of the appointment, the *quill* should be a *goose*-quill or a *crow*-quill; the *paper*, *demy* or *foolscap*; the *binding*, *calf* or *sheep*.

Christ *ordain* Baptism under the name and character of a *Sacrament*? If by *ordain* is meant the same as by *institute* – the same as *the having been the first to practise*, or *cause to be practised*, – he did not so much as *ordain* it in the character of a *ceremony*. Practise it indeed he did, and afterwards cause it to be practised. But, before he practised it, or caused it to be practised by or upon any one else, he submitted to have it practised upon himself, after it had been practised already upon multitudes. By John it had already been practised upon multitudes, before it was practised by him upon Jesus. – Those who are forced to say this Catechism, why are they so much as suffered to read the New Testament? Can they read it without seeing this?

By whomsoever first invented and put in practice, – in its character of a *succedaneum* to an entry in a *Register-book*, it was an operation in every respect well imagined. In the country in which it was thus practised, heat was plenty, water scarce, writing and reading still scarcer, money not over plenty. Baptism – whether by dipping, by sprinkling, or by both, – was then and there a pleasant operation. Wherever either a river ran, or a lake stood, it cost nothing. John took no surplice fees. Jesus took no surplice fees. Whenever the existence of the Devil is fully proved, it will be proved that by that Ghost it was that these priests' fees were instituted, exactly at the same time with Judges' fees. Surplice fees are unknown in Scotland. By the Church of England only, not by the Church of Scotland, do the poor behold the gates of heaven shut against them.

Question 12. – What meanest thou by the word Sacrament?

Answer. – I mean an outward and visible sign of an inward and spiritual grace, given unto us, ordained by Christ himself, as a means whereby we receive the same, and a pledge to assure us thereof.

OBSERVATIONS.

Here, as already observed – here may be seen another example, – shewing how a semblance of something may be manufactured out of nothing. Two transactions – the performance of the ceremony of *Baptism*, and the utterance of a few words, stated as having been uttered by Jesus on the occasion of a supper at which he was present – two transactions, – which, unless it be the identity of the person who bore the principal part in both, had nothing at all in common, – forced into conjunction; and a generic appellation – *the sacrament* – made to serve, as it were, for a box, for inclosing them, and keeping them together. – *Sacrament?* by whom was this word invented and made? By *Jesus?* – no more than it was by *Satan.* When thus made, what is the meaning given to this Rome-sprung vocable? In the English, and other dialects of the Teutonic, it is rendered by *holy:* it is *the holy thing.* And *a holy thing,* what is it? – *Holiness?* the word *holiness,* what is meant by it? As a property belonging to the thing itself, be the thing what it may, just nothing. By a thing – by any thing whatsoever, of which, by the principle of association, the idea has happened to become connected with the idea of the Almighty Creator, – a connexion of which any one created thing is, and ever has been, just as capable as any other, – by any thing – by every thing to which any such accident has happened, is this mysterious property thus acquired.

Thus then – such has been the course taken by the manufacturing process – by the invention of this so much worse than useless generic term, a branch of false science – a portion of wayward school logic – has been manufactured. Being made to pass examination in this science, the unfledged parrot takes in the words that are forced into its mouth, and declares itself to *understand,* where there is nothing to be understood.

Under the name of '*a grace,*' a something – and that something 'good' – given unto us – given to every body – given alike to every man, whatsoever be his conduct – given as a thing of course, – by the mere ceremony: a pretended something, which, when examined by an unsophisticated eye, turns out to be in itself exactly nothing, – and even by the name thus given to it, is but *a sign,* – yet, by the description at this same time given of it, it is an *efficient cause!*

The Almighty had hold of, and made to enter into a contract (under what penalty is not mentioned) pledging himself, binding himself, to give to this pretended *efficient cause* a pretendedly *real effect!* Thus it is that the sham science grows: thus it is that the wilderness is formed, in which the wits of those who are destined to travel in it, are destined to be lost.

Question 13th. – How many parts are there in a sacrament?

Answer. – Two: the outward visible sign, and the inward spiritual grace.

OBSERVATIONS.

A compound made out of a *real* and *visible ceremony,* to which, by the force of imagination, is attached an *invisible* and *unintelligible* effect – such is the *whole:* and now comes the unfledged parrot, and with his tongue is required to split it into two parts.

Question 14th. – What is the outward visible sign, or form in Baptism?

Answer. – Water (1); wherein the person is baptized (2) in the name of the Father, and of the Son, and of the Holy Ghost (3).

OBSERVATIONS.

(1). – Water the sign? No: – of itself water is not the sign of the thing in question – i.e. the transaction here in question – or of any thing else. Of the transaction in question, viz. aggregation to the society in question, the sign was a physical *operation:* not water itself, but the *application* of that liquid to the body of the person aggregated. For preserving the memory of the transaction in question, – instead of a transient operation, such as was the application of water to the body in question, suppose the object employed to have been an *entry* in a *Baptism book:* of the transaction in question what would have been the sign? – not the *leaf* of the book in its *blank* state, but the *mark made – the words written –* on that leaf.

In itself nothing can be more trifling than such an inaccuracy: the real matter of regret is – that in this body of pretended instruction, composed by a man who understood not what he wrote, a child should be forced to declare himself to understand, that which, neither to himself nor any one else, is any thing better than unintelligible.

(2). 'Where*in* the person is baptized' – not where*with*, but where*in* – Alas! alas! what a scene of horror presents itself to view! The baptism then must be by immersion – by a thorough dipping – or it is no baptism. The whole ceremony – all *null and void!* Of the myriads in a year, who, under the Church of England discipline, are *said* to be baptized, how many are the *really* baptized? – Not one!

All, all of us heathens! all a prey to Satan! – all children of wrath! (so we shall see the next answer saying) – all 'alive to sin!' – all 'dead to righteousness!' – the best works we ever do, or can do, no better than so many sins!!!

(3). [*In the name of the Father, and of the Son, and of the Holy Ghost.*] – Here we have a short string of sounds – sounds that are in use to perform the office of *names* – and, by the texture thus given to a mouthful of air, note well the effects produced! a human being rescued or not rescued from a state of endless torment! And, to such an operation, in the character of a *cause* – by whom – by what – have such effects been attached? – By the deluded or deluding imaginations of a set of presumptuous and domineering men. – Under the name of *magic*, or some such name, state the same conceit as issuing from a heathen brain, – execration or derision, instead of awe and veneration, are the sentiments it calls forth.

Question 15th. – What is the inward and spiritual grace?

Answer. – A death unto sin, and a new birth unto righteousness; for being by nature born in sin, and the children of wrath, we are hereby made the children of grace.

OBSERVATIONS.

Note well the sort of story that is here told. – The Almighty God, – maker of all things visible and 'invisible' – 'of heaven and earth, and all that therein is' – makes, amongst other things, a child; and no sooner has he made it, than he is *'wrath'* with it for being made. He determines accordingly to consign it to a state of endless torture. Meantime comes somebody, – and, pronouncing certain words, applies the child to a quantity of water, or a quantity of water to the child. Moved by these words, the all-wise Being changes his design; and, though he is not so far appeased as to give the child its pardon, vouchsafes to it a *chance* – no one can say *what* chance – of ultimate escape – And this is what the child gets by being 'made' – and we see in what way made – '*a child of grace.*'

Thereupon comes the sort of *wit*, ghostly and ghastly, which, on such occasions, has been so plentifully played off: there we have *death*, and here we have *new birth*: death unto sin, new birth unto righteousness. And in this wit we have a subject – not merely for *admiration*, but moreover for *belief*: – for belief, of the withholding of which, as if it were in the power of every man to believe or not believe what he pleased, the consequence is – what at every turn, and upon every occasion, stares us in the face – a state of endless torture.

Question 16th. – What is required of persons to be baptized?

Answer – Repentance, whereby they forsake sin; and faith, whereby they stedfastly believe the promises of God made to them in that sacrament.

OBSERVATIONS.

Obvious indeed are the observations suggested by this answer. But forasmuch as by the next question these observations are themselves undertaken to be obviated, let this next question, with the answers which it is employed to call forth, be first heard.

Question 17th. – Why then are infants baptized, when, by reason of their tender age, they cannot perform them?

Answer. – Because they promise them both by their sureties: which promise, when they come to age, themselves are bound to perform.

OBSERVATIONS.

[Perform *them?*] – Perform *what?* – Here may be seen a cloud of obscurity and ambiguity, derived from a sort of source – a purely grammatical one – such as in a composition so highly elaborated, and so abundantly examined, would not naturally have been looked for. Of such things as are in their nature capable of being '*performed,*' the *last* thing mentioned, – not to say the only thing, – is what is brought to view by the word *promises*. Yet, on a little reflection, these things, viz. *promises,* (it will be seen) can not be among the things here in view. – Why? – Answer Because *God* is the person *by* whom these promises were stated as being made. But, not even in such a composition as *this*, can it have been supposed or pretended, that when God is the person by whom a promise is made, the person by whom that promise is to be performed is an infant. An infant? Yea, *a just-born infant.* – the time allowed for performance being no longer than the interval between its birth and the age at which baptism is commonly administered: an interval commonly of between a week and a fortnight.

Look a little forwards however, and then a little backwards, and it will be sufficiently clear that, though the *things* to be performed are indeed *promises*, yet the *person, by whom* they are to be performed, is – not the least antecedent, viz. *God*, but the *infant*: the infant who is considered as the subject of the operation in question, viz. *baptism*. Why not *God* but the infant? – *Answer*, for this plain reason: – because the acts which are held up to view in the character of subjects of *promise* are '*Faith* and *Repentance*;' to wit, the Faith and Repentance above spoken of.

It is not, however, without some violence to *grammar* – some violation of the *rules* of grammar – that the language is here reconcileable to the rules of common sense. The *number* employed in the 16th question is the *singular* number. – 'What is required:' the number employed in the 17th question, by which, with its answer, the answer to that 16th question is undertaken to be explained, is the *plural* number: '*Perform them,*' says the 17th question: promise *them*, says the answer to it. And this promise *them*, of what is it the representative? Why – as turns out immediately after – of two things. Here then, between question the 16th (i. e. the question, to which, it being, and with so much reason, considered, that explanation is wanting, explanation, such as we see, is accordingly given) – between this 16th question and question 17th (i. e. the question employed to explain it) a contradiction exhibits itself. Believe the *explained* question, there is but *one* thing required: believe the *explaining* question, there are two things – two very different things, both, required: viz. the *faith* and the *repentance*. These are the *them* which, viz. by *their sureties*, the children *promised:* these are the *them* which, viz. *by themselves*, they are to perform. For so it is, that according to this law and this divinity, they themselves are thus to be sureties for their own sureties.

From the grammatical, return we now to the religious ground: and thereon to what remains of the task which the poor child has to go through with.

Two things, as above, he is required to do: and *that* because once upon a time, without knowing any thing about the matter, he promised to do them: *he* promised, that is, *other people* did, which comes to the same thing. These things are – to *repent* of *sin*, whether he has committed any or no: and to believe, – and that 'stedfastly,' whatever he may think of it, – what, for that purpose, is thereupon put into his hands. This is – that when, a few days after his birth, the Clergyman threw a little water on his face, – saying over him at the same time a few words without a meaning, – God was all the while making him *promises*, which promises might however as well have not been made, since nobody has so much as pretended to know what they were.

Another task, which his believing faculty is, at the same time, put to, – though without any express mention of it, – consists in the believing bad *principles* to be good *principles*, and bad *reasons* good *reasons*.

Example of bad *principles:* – that it is in the power of any *three* persons, two of them being of the one sex and one of the other, by making, in the name of a new-born infant, a parcel of *promises*, to saddle it with a load of *obligations:* amongst others, that of believing – how incredible soever, when the time comes, they may appear to him, – things upon things, which, had he not been thus saddled, he could *not* have believed.

Example of bad *reasons:* – that a man's having taken upon him to promise, that a child shall believe so and so, affords any reason for the child's believing as much, or so much as trying to believe it.

The point of *time*, at which these two exploits are to be performed – in this may be seen a point, in relation to which, if the babes and sucklings should, any of them, succeed in forming to themselves any thing like a clear conception, they will have done more than seems to have been done by the sages, by whom this task has been thus put into their hands.

'*What is required of persons* AFTER *they have been baptized?*' Had the question stood thus, the meaning would have been clear enough. Thus, however, it unfortunately does not stand: instead of so doing, it stands thus: – '*What is required of persons* TO BE *baptized?*' In this way of putting it, the child's having done these things, that are thus 'required' of him, is what, in the language of lawyers, is called *a condition precedent* to his being baptized. These things, then, which he is to do before he is baptized – that is, before he is a *fortnight*, or perhaps before he is a *week* old – what are they? – The question has been already answered. He is to *repent* – to repent of the sins which, in nobody can say what numbers, in his way from the breast to the cradle and back again, he has already committed: and he is to believe – to believe with all his might, all the fine things which for that purpose have been provided. All this while, if so it be, that a child, almost as soon as born, may *promise* by proxy, why not *repent* and *believe* by proxy? The sponsors, when they have *promised* for him, why not as well *perform* for him? Having undertaken for the *performances*, as they are all along called, – viz. a quantity of *repentance*, and moreover, a quantity of *faith*, – who so proper as *they* to execute these several performances?

To a child of a week or a fortnight old, the finding sins of its own to repent of, may not be altogether so easy a task, as on this occasion seems to have been supposed: – To the good men and woman, or the good man and women, by whom all these promises are made for it, the matter may, every now and then at least, be a matter of much less difficulty.

The *order* in which these same two performances are required and expected to succeed one another; – in this may be seen another exemplification of the muddiness of the fountain from which all this instruction flowed. In the natural course of things, the *motive* comes before the *act*. If the course here prescribed were to be pursued, the *act* would take the lead: and then, with a manifestation of humility, of which any example would not easily be found elsewhere, up comes in the train of it the generating and directing *motive*. According to the scheme of Jesus, faith was of course every where the seed, repentance one of the fruits of it: it was because a man believed – expected to experience the eventual fulfilment of the threats and promises held out to him – it was because a man believed that he was to repent, – not because he repented, that he was to believe.

Into the conception of any man besides this *Catechism-maker*, did any such idea ever enter, as that of addressing threats and promises to a man, to no other purpose than that of making him do what he had done already? But, if the mind, in which both these fruits were to be produced by the genial virtue of this ceremony, was a new-born infant's, either of them would be as ready to come forth as the other: and thus the *Catechism-maker* is justified.

Question 18*th*. – Why was the sacrament of the Lord's Supper ordained?

Answer. – For the continual remembrance of the sacrifice of the death of Christ, and of the benefits which we receive thereby.

OBSERVATIONS.

Of this answer, – keeping *in* that part for which a warrant is to be found in the text of the Gospel History, and leaving *out* of it that part which, no such warrant being to be found for it, has been the work of imagination, – inserting at the same time such words of limitation as may be necessary to confine the proposition within the limits designated by the sacred text, – of this answer the purport might (it should seem) have stood thus expressed: – 'For the continual remembrance . . . of the death of Christ,' to be preserved in the minds of such of his disciples as, – having been admitted by him into a state of peculiar intimacy, and, from time to time, sent out by him, from place to place, to preach his doctrine, – became distinguished by the appellation of his 'Apostles:' – Apostles, in the Greek (the only language in which the Gospel History, or any part of it, has been handed down to us) meaning neither more nor less than an *Emissary* or *Messenger*.

As to '*the benefits which we receive thereby*,' – what, in this Catechism, they are said to be – what the child is forced to say he believes them to be – will be seen presently.

Moreover, in the act of *receiving*, as brought to view by the word '*received*,' is implied the act of *delivering*: as also, that he, by whom the act of delivering is to be performed, is a different person from him by whom the act of receiving is to be performed. A foundation being thus laid, – and that foundation having, in the words of the sacred history, a sufficient support, – and that not exposed to dispute, – now comes the superstructure, which is the seat of the deception, and which has no such support. This is – that to the act of *delivering*, one sort of person and one alone, is competent: viz. *a Priest*: a person, on whom a corporeal ceremony has been performed: a ceremony from which a multitude of spiritual, supernatural, and mystical consequences are deduced: – the act of *receiving* – that alone is the *act*, whereunto, under the system, of which this Catechism makes a part, persons other than priests are competent: nor even to this are the profane multitude competent, but subject to *exceptions*, drawn out of an inexhaustible mine of exceptions, which has been opened for that purpose: – a mine capable, in its origin at least, of being dug into to any depth, which the interest of those who opened it could require.

And thus it is that, upon the ground of this *supper*, which, as the whole history declares, was neither more nor less than a mere social and farewel repast, taken with the utmost privacy; – a repast of which none were partakers, but the most confidential friends and disciples of the Master; – a repast, taken on the occasion of his foreseen and approaching fall; – upon this ground, and with so slender a stock of the most ordinary materials, has been erected a manufactory of *grace*: – of *grace*, – a commodity, which, being alike suited to every body's use, was to be sold to all who should be disposed to purchase it: a *manufactory*, carried on in different forms, under an imaginary perpetual patent, always for the benefit of the *patentees*.

Instead of domination for the purpose of degradation, – had useful instruction, and the melioration of moral disposition and conduct been the object, – and thereupon had some physical operation, performed by Jesus himself, and actually directed to that object, been looked out for, to be taken for a subject of imitation, and, for the above good purposes, converted into a ceremony, – in any such case, in the incident of the *feet-washing*, as related by Saint John, the founders of the Romish, and therein of the English Church, might have found what they wanted.

A little before the supper in question there was another; if indeed it was another, and not the same. Be this as it may, at the supper spoken of by *John* (by whom not the least intimation is given to the *bread-breaking*), the same select disciples being present, Jesus sees reason to give them a lesson of humility. He therefore in his own person and deportment sets them an example of that virtue. He insists on washing their feet. Put to shame by a manifestation so striking of a disposition with which their own formed so disadvantageous a contrast, Peter resists: vain however is all resistance, and, upon the feet of all the twelve, the operation is performed.

To give to this ceremony a real importance – a practical object, no arbitrary inferences – no additions – would have been necessary: never was design more plainly, more impressively expressed.[3]

While this comparatively insignificant one was sublimated into a *mystery* – that really instructive ceremony, how comes it to have been passed in such profound neglect? – How? – why for three perfectly intelligible reasons: –

1. Because it gave, to the self-created order of official persons, no privilege, no peculiar advantage.

2. Because the lesson which it so plainly gives, is to them a lesson of condemnation.

3. Because, to the inventors of the *drinking ceremony*, drinking wine while others looked on, was an operation more pleasant than would have been the washing the feet of those same spectators.

Here then are two contiguous suppers – two farewel suppers – or two incidents, related as having had place at the same supper. By the one, a lesson is given – a lesson pregnant with instruction as plain as it is salutary, – and one, the applicability of which, and with it the utility, will endure as long as man endures. In the other, what is visible to every eye is – an incident, naturally interesting indeed in no mean degree to the individuals then present, but having neither interest nor meaning, as applied to any

---

[3]   St John, Chap. XIII.

   1 Now before the feast of the Passover, when Jesus knew that his hour was come that he should depart out of this world unto the father, having loved his own which were in the world, he loved them unto the end.

   2 And supper being ended, the devil having now put into the heart of Judas Iscariot, Simon's son, to betray him;

   3 Jesus knowing that the father had given all things into his hands, and that he was come from God and went to God;

   4 He riseth from supper, and laid aside his garments; and took a towel, and girded himself.

   5 After that he poured water into a bason, and began to wash the disciples' feet, and to wipe them with the towel wherewith he was girded.

   6 Then cometh he to Simon Peter: and Peter said unto him, Lord, dost thou wash my feet?

   7 Jesus answered and said unto him, what I do thou knowest not now; but thou shalt know hereafter.

   8 Peter saith unto him, Thou shalt never wash my feet. Jesus answered him, if I wash thee not thou hast no part with me.

   9 Simon Peter saith unto him, Lord, not my feet only, but also my hands, and my head.

   10 Jesus saith unto him, he that is washed, needeth not, save to wash his feet, but is clean every whit; and ye are clean, but not all.

   11 For he knew who should betray him; therefore, said he, ye are not all clean.

   12 So after he had washed their feet, and had taken his garments, and was set down again, he said unto them, Know ye what I have done to you?

   13 Ye call me master and Lord; and ye say well, for so I am.

   14 If I, then, your Lord and master, have washed your feet; ye also ought to wash one another's feet.

   15 For I have given you an example that ye should do as I have done to you.

   16 Verily, verily, I say unto you, the servant is not greater than his Lord; neither he that is sent, greater than he that sent him.

   17 If ye know these things, happy are ye if ye do them.

other individual; nor of itself calculated or designed to convey instruction in any shape whatsoever. – The universally important transaction is passed over in universal silence and neglect, – the other is converted into a mystery, with damnation – universal damnation, or thereabouts – at the bottom of it!

Question 19. – What is the outward part or sign of the Lord's Supper?

Answer. – Bread and Wine, which the Lord hath commanded to be received.

OBSERVATIONS.

[*Hath commanded to be received?*] – Mark well the misrepresentation of which this phrase is the chief instrument: seldom has a plan of misrepresentation been more subtilely contrived.

Had the passage stood in these words, *Which the Lord . . . commanded to be received*, stood in these words, without the word *hath*, – the answer would, as far as it went, have been unobjectionable: as far as it went, it would have been conformable to the sacred text. Mark well – without the word *hath:* for in this short word lurks the poison – the seed of the deceit.

It is by this word *hath* that the transaction is represented as meant to be applied to the *indefinite present: i.e.* to every *point of time*, at which it shall have happened to this account of it to find a reader, and to every individual *person*, by whom, he being a believer in the religion of Jesus, it shall have happened to be heard or read.

Such is the conception, which, by the authors of this Catechism, composed in the sixteenth century after the birth of Jesus, is endeavoured to be impressed: *viz.* that to the effect just described, a command delivered by Jesus, in the intention of its being considered as obligatory, – obligatory with a force equal at least to that of any of his moral precepts, – was addressed to *all* persons, by whom the religion taught by him should come to be professed – to *all* of them, without distinction, to the end of the time.

Such is the conception which, by these men of yesterday, this part of the *history* of Jesus is represented as intended to convey. In *the history itself*, how is this same matter represented?

According to the history, who are the persons present? – a numerous assembly, as at the delivery of the sermon on the *Mount?* – No: – but a chosen few, sitting with him in a private chamber: the twelve disciples, whose condition had been distinguished from that of the general body of his followers by marks of peculiar confidence, and whose life had been interwoven with his own by habits of peculiar intimacy.

'Ever and anon, when I am no longer with you, and when after my departure it happens to you, to you the chosen among my disciples, to meet together on a convivial occasion as at present, – when the materials of the repast are before you, think of your departed master, think of this your last meeting (for such it will be) in my presence. Think of his now approaching death: think of the cause and fruit of it. When, for the purpose of the social repast, bread, such as that which I have thus broken, comes also to be broken, think of this body, which, for the part acted by me for your instruction, will, ere long, be broken and destroyed.'

'When the wine, whatever it be that stands before you, comes to be poured out, let it call to your remembrance his blood which will have been shed in that same cause' . . .

With this evident sense before them, will nothing satisfy men but the grossest nonsense? Of the multitude of figurative expressions, to which scanty and unformed languages in general – to which the Jewish language in particular, with its dialects – were necessitated, or at least were continually wont to have recourse, – is *this alone*, in spite of the plainest common sense, to be understood in the literal sense?

That, in his own hand Jesus held his own body, but in the first instance without the blood belonging to it; and having, by breaking it into eleven or twelve pieces, converted each of those *parts* into the *whole*, gave those his eleven or twelve bodies, one to each guest – he himself, with or without his body, looking on all the while to see them eat it, – and thereupon, immediately after gave to each of them the whole of his blood, *viz.* the wine which had just been poured out, and by him converted into blood, – the bodies, into which the bread had been converted, not having any blood in them, – that of all these self-contradictory extravagances the existence should be more probable than that, on an impassioned occasion, Jesus should have made use of a figurative expression – and that too in a language which scarce offered any other? In a barbarous age, and thence, under the influence of blind caprice, even in a more improved age, – under the Roman Catholic edition of the religion of Jesus . . . Yes: under such a system, in the admission given to any such style of interpretation, how little soever there may be of abstract, reason, there is but too much of consistency.

But, under a government calling itself *Protestant*, – and oppressing *Catholics*, because they are Catholics, and, for these very extravagances, branding them with the name of *Idolalers!* . . .

Believe that Jesus, having held his own body in his own hand, gave to each of twelve men, the whole of that same body, and then saw them eat it, &c. &c. – Believe this, because Jesus is related to have said so? – Well then – (not to speak of *a way*[4]) believe that Jesus was *a door* – a door always open for as many men as pleased to '*go in and out*' *through it:*[5] for this too is among the things, which, in the same sacred books, it is related

---

[4] John xiv. 6. Jesus saith unto him, I am the *way*, the truth, and the life: no man cometh unto
  the father but through me.

[5] John x. 9. I am the *door*; by me, if any man enter in, he shall be saved, and shall go in and
  out, and find pasture.

of him that he said. In the mouth of a Protestant, among Protestants, this argument, when addressed by them to Catholics, is relied on as conclusive. Conclusive? and against what? why, against this very cannibal story, of the truth of which every Church of England child is thus forced to declare itself persuaded.

Compared with this, the supposition about *the door* would be rational and probable. Consider *Bright* and *Lambert*: the least of these great men had quantity of matter enough in his body to admit of an aperture, through which, as through a door, a man of ordinary size might have passed without much difficulty. Believing and teaching the mystery of *Cannibalism*, will a man refuse to believe and teach this other mystery of the *door*? If so, what will his faith avail him? – When bread and wine, and body and blood, and every thing else is swallowed, still, unless he will swallow the *door* likewise, – still, if he is consistent, he is an *unbeliever*; he is still an *infidel*, and all that he has swallowed has been swallowed in waste.

Question 20. – What is the inward part, or thing signified?

Answer. – The body and blood of Christ, which are verily and indeed taken, and received by the faithful in the Lord's Supper.

OBSERVATIONS.

Body and Blood, *without* the Bread and Wine, the Bread and Wine being metamorphosed into Body and Blood, – in the *pure* grimgribber of modern *technical* theology – in the theology of the *Roman* school – this is *transubstantiation*. Body and Blood, *with* the Bread and Wine – in the *adulterated* grimgribber – the produce of *Luther's* unmatured attempts to throw off the load of pernicious rubbish heaped up by the Romish school – this is *consubstantiation*. In respect of absurdity, self-contradiction, and groundless inference, – between the *trans* and the *sub*, is there so much as a shade of difference worth thinking of? On the *con* plan the mess has more matter in it than in the *trans:* and the more the worse.

'*Verily and indeed!*' – Danger is here foreseen, – and, it being foreseen, provision is thus made against it: – the danger, lest, here or there, the stomach of this or that intractable and refractory child, should, in the midst of all this instruction, be tempted to listen, in preference, to the testimony of his own senses: lest, accordingly, not finding in his palate the taste and consistence of *flesh*, any more than, under his eyes, the colour of *blood*, he should thereupon, notwithstanding all *assurances*, and the threatenings that may be seen glittering in the back-ground, be perverse enough to harbour doubts of his own *Cannibalism*. Of the reiterated intensity of these *asseverations*, the object is – to keep out, if possible, all such *doubts*.

Question 21. – What are the benefits whereof we are partakers thereby?

Answer. – The strengthening and refreshing of our souls by the body and blood of Christ, as our bodies are by the bread and wine.

OBSERVATIONS.

In itself, a puzzling one indeed is the question here. But – answers such as this – let *these* be received as answers, no question can be a puzzling one. – Souls refreshed by a body and a quantity of blood? – Oh yes: if the body were but a *metaphorical* body, the blood but *metaphorical* blood, and the refreshment but *metaphorical* refreshment, in that case there would be no difficulty. By that which is *metaphorical, any thing* may be done: Yes, *any thing*; for that which is *metaphorical* is – *any thing*. But the body – is it then a metaphorical body? – Not it indeed. It is the *real* body: the blood is the *real* blood; – or how could they be '*verily and indeed taken?*' the *refreshment*, which a true Church of England soul takes by the *eating* of this *body*, and the *drinking* of this blood, is either no refreshment at all, or it is the same refreshment, that the soul of a New Zealander takes when he has been fortunate in battle: when, as a clergyman of the New Zealand religion, whatever it be, would phrase it, – 'the Lord has delivered the enemy into his hand.'

Nay, but it is only by that part of the meal which is composed of the bread and the wine, that our bodies (says somebody), *are here said to be 'refreshed.'* – True: but the *body* and the *blood* are not the less said to be *taken*: i. e. taken, if into any thing, into our bodies: '*verily*, (lest any thing like doubt on the subject should be suffered to remain) – '*verily and indeed taken.*' When thus *taken*, true indeed it is, that it is to the refreshing of our *souls*, that *that* part of the *chyle*, which is extracted *from* it, is applied. But, as to the *verily*, with which it must have been *taken*, the particular application thus made of it, makes not any difference: whatever part of man's person it goes to the refreshment of, – to produce this refreshment, whatever it is, *taken* it must be: – *taken?* yes, and *digested* likewise: – or how can any thing like *refreshment* be afforded by it?

To make all points not only *plain and clear*, but moreover smooth and easy, – on *this*, as on so many other occasions, the word *spiritual* is at hand. In a *carnal, temporal* sense, not exactly true, *conceditur*: but besides the *carnal, temporal* source, for this, as for all other words for which it is wanted, there is a *spiritual* sense: and, if in this *spiritual* sense the thing be, as it *is*, true, – then, in this same *spiritual* sense, it is not only *as well* as if it were true in the *carnal* sense, but much better: better, viz. by the amount of the *superiority* – the undeniable superiority – of *things spiritual* over *things temporal*: – not to speak of *persons*.

So convenient is the use – so admirable the virtue – of the word *spiritual*. By it whatsoever things are *false* may at pleasure be made *true*: false in a *carnal* – false in a *temporal* sense – yes, so let them be: – still, in a *spiritual* sense, they are not the less capable of being true: whereupon, in that purer and superior sense, if there be any *convenience* in their being true, true they are.

To perform this metamorphosis, you couple the word *spiritual*, as above, with the word *sense*. This done, take any proposition that you please, the more absurd the better: – a still more absurd one, than the above *cannibal* proposition, if – which it will hardly be found to do – the nature of things affords any where a more absurd one. – Proposed by itself, and without that support, which the adjunct in question has in store for every absurdity, the falsity of it is, in the mind of any man in his senses, too glaring to admit of its finding so much as a momentary acceptance. Thus it is with it in its *natural* sense. To the word *sense*, add the word *spiritual*, and now, instead of being absurd and *false* – false to a degree of palpable absurdity – it requires nothing but a simple assertion to render it true. Have you any such thing in hand as *a mind*, to subdue, – to soften, – to weaken? – a mind, which you want to convert into a species of wax, ready to be moulded at any time to your purpose, whatsoever that purpose be? – here then is your way to go to work upon it. Take in hand one of these absurd propositions – the more palpably absurd the better – try it upon the man in the first place, *without* subterfuge: try it upon him in its *natural* sense. If in that sense you find him swallowing it, so much the better: – but, if you find him giving it back to you immediately, unable or refusing to swallow it, – you then give it to him a second time, wrapped up in the words *spiritual* sense – a *spiritual* sense, (tell him) and no other, is the sense in which he is to understand it.

Alas! – the quantity of the good things of this wicked world, which, by men calling themselves *spiritual*, are every day consuming – would they but content themselves with the consuming of these same good things, in a *spiritual* sense, – leaving to the growers, and makers, and buyers, the consuming of them in a *carnal* sense, – how much less would there be to be seen of that *pauperism*, which, under the covering of prosperity, that glitters at and about the *head*, is, in the *heart* of the population, so plainly seen, as well as so severely felt!

Generally speaking, this *spiritual* sense – alias *nonsensical* sense – seems to be the opposite or negative of the *carnal* sense. Thus, for example, in this *cannibal* case; – viz. eating the body and blood of a man, or of a God, or of both together. – *Carnal* sense, *eating it: spiritual* sense, *not* eating it.

To this interpretation of the word *spiritual*, as applied to *sense*, give constancy and *consistency*, then, in so far as it is understood in this sense, there may be not much harm in it. – For, in that case, forasmuch as there is such a thing as *eating* the sort of food in question in a *spiritual* sense, so there will also be such a thing as *believing* in that same sense: and as, in a spiritual sense, *eating* is *not* eating, – so, in a spiritual sense, *believing* will be *not* believing.

On this plan, unspeakable will be the benefit both to *Faith* and to *Charity*: to *Faith*, because, on this plan, there is nothing whatsoever but may be believed – believed by all men and without difficulty: – to *Charity*, because, on this plan, throughout the whole field of divinity, the whole mass of any two men's opinions, – in a word, of all men's opinions, – may, on every imaginable point, be as opposite as possible, and brotherly love not in any the smallest degree lessened by it: – take any proposition whatsoever, A believes it in a carnal or temporal sense, B, and every body else that differs from A, believes it in a spiritual sense. Here then, if, by and with this mode of unity, *Faith* is satisfied, so still more easily and heartily is *Charity: Hope* need never quit them, and thus every thing is as it should be.

Question 22. – What is required of them who come to the Lord's Supper?

Answer. – To examine themselves, whether (1) they repent them truly of their former sins (2), stedfastly purposing to lead a new life (3), have a lively faith in God's mercy through Christ (4), with a thankful remembrance of his death (5), and be in charity with all men.

OBSERVATIONS.

Five distinguishable alleged *duties*, forming so many subjects of examination, are here observable: five *duties* or *obligations*, concerning which every child is forced to affirm and declare, that he is persuaded of their having been imposed by the Almighty – imposed upon the child himself, together with all his fellow Christians.

Concerning all these supposed duties, the first question that presents itself as proper to be made, is – in any one of the histories we have of *Jesus*, what ground is there for any such supposition, as that, in the character of duties to be performed on the occasion of any such ceremony, as that which, having been instituted by the Church of Rome, and retained by the Church of England, is here spoken of, – duties, to this effect, or to any other were by Jesus meant to be imposed upon any person whatsoever; and in particular upon any person, into whose mouth the declaration, to the effect that has just been seen, has ever been, or is ever destined to be forced? – *Answer.* – Not any. The ceremony itself, a mere modern invention; – the duties, thus attached to it, a mere fiction; – a fiction, put forth in the teeth of those undisputed and undisputable texts of Scripture, in which nothing that bears the smallest resemblance to it is to be found. In these texts, the persons addressed, no other than the *twelve* chosen disciples, distinguished by the name of *Apostles*, – no other disciples, or followers, being present, – or, so much as in the way of any the slightest and most general allusion, spoken of: even to these chosen few the act recommended, of such a nature, – a mere token and pledge of remembrance, – a social act of a purely convivial nature, – as scarcely to be capable of being taken for the subject of a duty. They *all* eat, they *all* drank: – thus say two of those three of his four biographers, by whom what passed at that supper is reported. At that same time, he (Jesus himself) eat with them, if *Luke* is to be believed: consequently, according to the orthodox interpretation, eat and drank along with them his thirteenth part of his own body and his own blood: which doing, he said to them, on that same occasion, according to that same Luke; '*This do in remembrance of me.*'[6] A duty, if a duty it can be called, plainly and expressly confined to *twelve* persons, then living and then present: and, in their instance, no such *accessory* duties as are here set up – no nor any other accessory duties – added to it; – such being the exact state of the case, – with the acknowledged standard of belief and practice before their eyes, up start a set of men, sixteen centuries after, – and, without deigning to assert, do more than assert – for they pretend to take for granted, – that, upon all that ever professed, or ever shall profess, the religion of Jesus, a whole swarm of duties, viz. the swarm thus confidently delivered, were, on that same occasion, imposed by him.

If, without support from any history, true or false, – and, on the contrary, in the teeth of so many histories, which now are, and then were in every body's hands – all of them recognized, as constituting, in relation to this very subject, the sole standard of belief and practice, – if, under such disadvantages, such palpable misrepresentation has been made – such gross impositions, not only attempted, but, by the arm of coercive power carried into effect with success, – what limits can there be to the impostures which, with the same support, may with like success have been attempted, on subjects, on which the power of imposture has found no such obstacle to check it? – *Tradition – Roman Catholic Tradition –* in this word – not to look any further – an indication is given of the sort of matter, in which an answer to this question may be found.

Under all these five heads of examination, and in particular under the first, – suppose however the answer were in the affirmative: on this supposition, various are the observations, which the answer would be apt to suggest, if considered in its several particular parts.

1. This supernatural recipe with what degree of frequency is it expected to be repeated? 2. Suppose it were *a week* – suppose it but once a *month* – suppose even the number of doses taken in a year still smaller – Each time, – let the times follow one another ever so quickly, – here is '*a new life*' undertaken to be led: – such at least is to be, on each occasion, the 'stedfast purpose.' But, of any such new life – (whatsoever may be meant by a new life) – what on any occasion, according to the string of intimations thus

---

[5] Luke xxii. 15. 'And he said unto them, With desire *I have desired to eat this passover* with you before I suffer: 16. For I say unto you, I will not *any more* eat thereof until it be fulfilled in the kingdom of God.' Such being his declared desire, and the means being at hand, and no obstacle at hand, of course that desire was fulfilled.

given, will be the fruit or use? – Each time there is to be *'repentance'* – each time the repentance is to be *'true* – yet, true as it is, each and every time it is to be of no effect: the penitent being, all along, in the same sad case, as if no repentance had taken place. Each time the *purpose*, how *'stedfast'* soever it be, is to be broken through, and the condition which the penitent is thereupon to be in, is to be exactly the same as if no such *'purpose'* had been resolved upon. For, if that purpose be to lead a life without sin, then, suppose the purpose adhered to, of what use would be the *new life*? – The *new* life – no: – the *old* life is on that supposition the only *good* one: – a *new* life? – whatsoever of *novelty* his life had in it, he would, on this supposition, be but so much the worse for it.

Mark well, that all the time this perpetual alternative of sinning and repentance is going on, 'lively' is to be the man's *'faith in God's mercy:'* lively, in other words, his assurance – that upon repentance, forgiveness will each and every time follow. Full of comfort, no doubt, for the time, will this assurance be. For time *present*, yes: – But on the *future*, on each such occasion, what, if any, will be, at all times, its *tendency*, and but too probably its effect? What but to give encouragement – and by encourage-ment birth – to sin?

In a word – to use a familiar, but not the less opposite, expression – at the end of each such supper, *a new score*, it appears, is to be considered as commenced; and, at the conclusion of each immediately succeeding one, such new score will, if the view thus given of the effect be a correct one, be considered as *rubbed off*. In an account of sins, any more than in an account of money, can there be any stronger, or indeed other encouragement to the running up of a fresh score, than the assurance of having it rubbed off *at pleasure*: rubbed off at any time, and at no other expense than that of a few words of course.

As to contrition, *grief, sorrow, penitence, repentance*, – whatever be the *words* employed, – for any such affection, what room does the nature of the case leave in the breast of a man, whose persuasion is – that he is dealing upon such terms? *Sin*, he may thus at all times have his bellyfull of: only one thing he must not forget, which is – that in some manner or other, between the time of his committing each such sin, and the time of the next supper of this sort that he partakes of, he must 'truly repent,' i.e. be sincerely sorry for it. – Take a mouthful of bread and a mouthful of wine – taking care that before they are swallowed, whatsoever sins it has happened to you to commit, since the *last* preceding mouthful of each was swallowed, are truly repented of, – vanished are all these sins: all these sinful acts are caused not to have happened, and every thing is as it should be. Such is the virtue of this bread, and of this wine: – if not this, then what else is it?

Under or over the *Church of Rome*, certain Popes used for some time to be selling this sort of licence (*indulgence* was in the language of technical theology, its appropriate name): and, in that Church, to a *Church-of-England* eye, it was of course every thing that was mischievous and abominable. By these Popes it was granted indeed, but in retail only, at so much per sin, and at high prices: and, the higher the prices, the smaller the number of those, in whose instance it could be obtained, and thereby become productive of its mischievous effects. But, if even under the Church of Rome this licensing system was a mischievous one, under the Church of England, how much greater must not be the mischievousness of it? Under the Church of England, at so small a price as that of the Table offering, *if* any such there be, it is put into every hand that can afford to pay that small price: and the whole mass of sins, which, between supper and supper, a man can see his convenience in committing – the whole mass, be they in spirit and number what they may, are thus included in one and the same *indulgence*.

Has it not *this* effect? – Well then, if it has *not*, *no* effect has it whatever: – and such, from beginning to end, is the perpetual alternative. *Justification*, – shadow of Justification, the case affords not any: *apology, palliation*, this is all that can be made or done for it. That, when all is said and done, things may, by a dispensation of God's providence, produced by an act of God's mercy, turn out to be in that same state, in which they would have been, had nothing of this sort been either said or done, – such is the most favourable result, of which, under the guidance of the most prejudiced judgment, the most sanguine imagination can entertain a hope.

And, in that most favourable case, can it really be said to be thus destitute of effect? – Yes: but in no other sense than that, in which, after having, for a length of time, been employed, dose after dose, without success, in the hope of curing some disease, *opium* may be said to have been destitute of effect. The non-existence of *particular* effect – viz. of the particular *good* effect hoped for – is but too true. But, of a *general* effect – and *that* a most disastrous one – the *existence* is at the same time but too true – a prostration of strength – an universal debility – 'that prostration of the understanding and will,' by which the constitution is destroyed.[7]

RECAPITULATION.

On recurring to the Observations contained in the preceding pages, the following are the *vices* which will, it is believed, be found to have been proved upon this formulary, the peccant matter of which is, with a diligence unhappily so successful, injected, by the hand of power, into the breasts of the great majority of the population, at the very first dawn of the reasoning faculty –

---

[7]   And the production of which is among the *declared* objects of the NATIONAL INSTITUTION according to the form given to it by the BENCH OF BISHOPS; and in particular of the BISHOP OF LONDON's labours in support of it.

I. BAD GRAMMAR. For a passage teaching bad grammar by example, see p. 64. [321; page numbers in brackets refer to the present text.]

II. BAD LOGIC; viz.

1. By inculcation of matter plainly useless. See p. 25 to 31. [299–302]
2. By inculcation of manifest surplusage. See p. 8, 9, 10. [290–291]
3. By inculcation of matter plainly unintelligible. See p. 8 to 16, 23 to 35, 38, 40. [290–294, 297–304, 306, 307]
4. By inculcation of propositions inconsistent with one another. See p. 14, 15, 16, 17. [293, 294]
5. By inculcation of instruction which is either erroneous, or at best useless. See p. 49, 50, 51, 52. [312, 313, 314]
6. By exemplification and consequent inculcation of the art and habit of gratuitous or unfounded assertion, and groundless inference. See p. 35, 36, 37, 46, 47, 48, 49. [304, 305, 306, 310, 311, 312]
7. By inculcation of matter, repugnant to those Thirty-nine Articles, to which the whole body of the Clergy – Bishops and Archbishops included – together with all other ruling and otherwise influential persons, – who become partakers of that course of education which is in highest repute, will, upon entrance into that course, after being thus impregnated with the repugnant matter of this formulary, be forced to declare their assent and approbation on record. See p. 36 to 37. [305–307]
8. By inculcation of matter savouring of Popery. See p. 75 to 80. [326–329]

III. Matter, the tendency of which is – to operate, in various *other* ways, to the depravation of the INTELLECTUAL part of man's frame, viz.

1. Matter, by which the principle of *vicarious obligation* is inculcated: i.e. by which children are commanded to believe, that it is in the power of two or three self-appointed persons, by agreeing together, to oblige a young child, in conscience, to pursue to the end of his life, any course of conduct, which, at that time, it may please them to prescribe. See p. 6, 7, 8. [288–290]
2. Matter, by which the young child is himself forced to utter *a rash promise*, binding him, during life, to pursue the course of conduct therein and thereby prescribed. See p. 17. [294]
3. Matter, by which the child is initiated in the art and habit of *lax interpretation*: i.e. of declaring, in relation to the discourse in question, whatever it may be, his persuasion, that such or such was the meaning, intended by the *author* to be conveyed by it: viz. whatever meaning it may at any time happen to suit the personal purpose of the *interpreter* so to convey, how wide soever of the import really so intended to be conveyed. See p. 53 to 57. [314–317]

4. Matter, by which the *intellectual* part of the child's frame is destined to be *debilitated* and *depraved* by groundless and useless *terrors*. See p. 12, 13, 14, 61. [291, 292, 293, 319]

IV. Matter, the tendency of which is to operate, in various other ways, to the DEPRAVATION of the MORAL part of man's frame: viz.
1. Matter, in the texture of which *Hypocrisy* is plainly discernible. See p. 15, 16. [293, 294]
2. Matter, by which *lying* is inculcated as a duty: – a duty, which the child is forced to declare himself bound to persevere in the performance of. See p. 4, 5, 18, 24, 25, 38, 39, 53, 54, 60. [287, 288, 295, 298, 299, 315, 318]
3. Matter, by which *Imposture* may be seen to be promoted. See p. 55 to 89. [316–334]
4. Matter, by which *Forgery* may be seen to be knowingly uttered. See p. 19, 20, 21. [295, 296, 297]
5. Matter, by which encouragement is given to sin and *wickedness in every shape*. See p. 86 to 89. [332–334]

V. Matter, the tendency of which is to operate, in an immediate way, to the injury of the SENSITIVE part of man's frame.
Matter, by which groundless and useless terrors are infused, as above.

Such, – on the grounds all along referred to, and plainly brought to view, – is the character and tendency herein *imputed* to this Church of England formulary, with the matter of which every English breast is, by the government at large, under the guidance of the ruling part of the Clergy, designed and endeavoured to be impregnated: *imputed*, and with what *justice*, let any person in whose eyes either the morals or the understanding of the whole people of England are objects worthy of regard, and who at the same time has courage to look in the face truth, however unwelcome, and opposed by prejudices ever so inveterate, lay his hand upon his heart and pronounce.

Ill will towards men, – towards all men, in whatsoever rank in life situated, with reference to him in whose breast the corrupt affection is evident – equal, superior, or inferior, – this, taking the whole together, may now be added to the list of those fruits, the seeds of which are so thickly sown by this machine. Ill will and, from ill will, oppression and persecution: – oppression the *chronical* disease, persecution, the *acute*: oppression, universal, habitual, and sluggish; persecution particular and casual; according as opportunity happens to be favourable.

The genealogy is in this wise: From *imaginary* grace, imaginary *mystery*, imaginary *sacrament*, come imaginary *blasphemy*, imaginary *sin*; from imaginary sin, comes *real antipathy*; and from men, in ruling and otherwise influential situations, *real oppression* and *real persecution*, on that one part; *real suffering* on the other: – for, by the imaginary sin, is produced, in the ruling breast, along with the antipathy, a pretence for gratifying it.

GOOD MEN, GOOD SUBJECTS, and GOOD CHRISTIANS – such, and in these very words, are the *goods*, which, – in giving the explanation of his truly admirable, and beyond doubt *ultimately* and highly useful, system of intellectual machinery, – over and over again, – and always, by means of a set of instruments, of which this formulary is the earliest and beyond comparison most extensively employed article, – over and over again: – and, as here, in *placard letters* – Dr. Bell undertakes for the manufacturing.

Good men and *Good Christians!* and by means of a thorough impregnation with the matter of this formulary! – Yes: if, of *Good men* and *Good Christians*, the characteristic qualities are – *hypocrisy, lying, imposture, forgery, sin* and *vice* in every other shape.

Good subjects? Yes: if the *goodness* of the subjection be in proportion to the *abjectness* of it: for, of abjectness in the subjection of the *subject many* to the dominion of the *ruling few*, can any more conclusive exemplification be exhibited, than that which is afforded, by the practice thus persevered in, of the swallowing of matter, thus poisonous to the whole moral texture of man's frame? – *Good Subjects?* – Yes: if the *Good Subject* be a character purposely selected to form a contrast with that of the *Good Citizen:* a description, by which – though now so studiously marked out for infamy as descriptive of an enlisted partizan of *anarchy* – no Frenchman, in the most despotic æra of the monarchy, ever scrupled to designate himself.

GOOD MEN, GOOD SUBJECTS, and GOOD CHRISTIANS! – Yes: let us not only wish, but hope, and even believe – that in and from the mind-turning mill, invented and worked by *Dr. Bell*, all these good articles will in conclusion be manufactured and issued out for use. Manufactured? – but by what instrument? – By this formulary? – No: – but, if at all, *in spite* of it.

The greater the efficiency of this admirable instrument – the more capable in its own nature of being, in all its efficiency, applied to the best uses – the greater in the breast of a true lover of mankind will be the regret at seeing it, in the very first application made of it, employed in thus thickly sowing in the mind, at the earliest dawn of reason, the seeds of depravity in every shape.

For consolation one hope remains: – and this is – that, after having, with whatsoever success, been thus employed in the introduction of the disease, it may, in a maturer state of the faculties – such is the nature of the instrument – be, still more effectually as well as more worthily, rendered conducive to the extirpation of it.

JEREMY BENTHAM

II

Analysis of the Influence of Natural Religion on the Temporal Happiness of Mankind (1822)

Part One

Jeremy Bentham

Note on Text II

To avoid running the risk of prosecution for blasphemy the *Analysis of the Influence of Natural Religion on the Temporal Happiness of Mankind* (1822) was given to the world under the pseudonym 'Philip Beauchamp'. Why this particular name was chosen remains a mystery. It was edited from Bentham's manuscripts by George Grote, then a young disciple. The British Library has four volumes of manuscripts which were sent by Bentham to Grote in the winter of 1821.[1] In the main the manuscripts are in the hand of John Colls, Bentham's amanuensis of the time, or in the hand of Bentham himself.

Bentham's intentions regarding the *Analysis* were first set out in a detailed Plan of the Work that he sent with the manuscripts to Grote under the general title 'The Usefulness of Religion in the Present Life Examined'. He projected not one but two or possibly three volumes or parts. The first book was to deal with the usefulness of natural religion and the remainder with revealed religion, particularly the doctrines of England's official religion.[2] This general approach was reiterated in a letter to Grote of 9 December 1821, where Bentham introduced the manuscripts for Grote's 'tactical powers' to 'make good use of', referring to them as 'a garden of good fruits'. The remainder of the letter is devoted to a general outline as to how Grote might set about his task. The first volume was to be an examination of the truth and utility of 'Natural Jug' (i.e. natural religion), which was to be supplemented 'if advisable' by an extension of the analysis to include the truth and utility of the 'alledged revealed Jug'.[3] 'Juggernaut' was Bentham's code for organized religion or, on occasion, Christianity in general. In a second letter to Grote, Bentham offered to look the manuscripts over and see whether it might be possible to 'do any thing more towards rendering the work more methodical, correct, clear, concise and comprehensive'. 'Should it be found necessary', he adds, 'grudge not the trouble of recomposing . . . [and] if any considerable additions be found requisite, nobody can be better qualified for making them than yourself'.[4]

---

[1] BL Add. Mss 29806–809, dated variously between 1811–21, mainly 1811, 1815, 1819, 1821.
[2] The Plan of the Work for *Analysis* is at BL Add. Mss 29807/157–62.
[3] Bentham to Grote (9 Dec. 1821), BL Add. Mss 29806/1.
[4] BL Add. MSS 29807/12–13.

It was in this manner that Bentham authorized the young and eager Grote to rewrite and, if necessary, to make additions to his original material.

In the event, neither Bentham nor Grote ever commented on their respective roles in the production of the book, raising questions about this for later commentators. The article on Grote in the *Dictionary of National Biography* records that a comparison between the finished work and the manuscripts 'shows the enormous amount of labour required to bring them into form', and comments that 'Grote had practically to write the essay leaving aside the greater part of the materials before him and giving to the remnant a shape that was his rather than Bentham's'.[5] Leslie Stephen concurred with this view.[6] On the other hand, Martin Clarke, Grote's biographer, argued 'that Grote conscientiously reproduced Bentham's arguments, and that there is nothing of his own in the substance of the book'.[7] More recently, David Berman has claimed that Grote was principally responsible for the work.[8] However, until a thorough study of the extant manuscripts housed in the British Library is conducted, we will not have a precise accounting of the balance of the work to be assigned to Grote, on the one hand, and to Bentham, on the other. It is no doubt true that Grote did have to put a large number of the manuscripts aside and it is his style rather than Bentham's in which the work is penned. But it is from Bentham's manuscripts that the substance of the work is drawn and it is according to his plan that the arguments were arranged. However important Grote's editorial duties, therefore, and these should not be underestimated given the great bulk of manuscripts he was asked to deal with, we can be sure that the *Analysis* truly reflects Bentham's opinions on the topic of the influence of the religious sanction on temporal happiness.

The book was eventually published in 1822 by the radical free thinker Richard Carlile, who was already serving a six year sentence in Dorchester Prison for publishing blasphemous literature and, hence, unlikely to be prosecuted further for this, his latest affront to the religious sensibilities of the English establishment. Though Bentham's authorship was not long a secret, Grote's hand in the work was not revealed until after his death. His wife Harriet made no mention of the book in her life of her husband, but one of the reviewers of this biography let the secret out in the *Edinburgh Review*. Confirmation eventually came by way of the 1875 edition of the *Analysis* and the French translation of that year, both of which make clear Grote's involvement, the latter describing it as 'd'apres les papiers de J.

---

5   *DNB*, viii. 728–29.
6   Leslie Stephen, *The English Utilitarians*, 3 vols. (1900; reprt. London 1950), i. 316.
7   Martin L. Clarke, *George Grote: A Biography* (London 1962), pp. 30–31.
8   David Berman, *A History of Atheism in Britain: From Hobbes to Russell* (London and New York 1990), pp. 191–94.

Bentham par George Grote'.[9] The extract following is taken from the first edition, printed and published by Carlile in 1822.

---

[9] *La Religion naturelle, son influence sur le bonheur du genre humain, d'apres les papiers de J. Bentham par George Grote* (Paris 1875).

Analysis of the Influence of Natural Religion on the Temporal Happiness of Mankind
Part One

CHAPTER I.
Preliminary Statements and Definition.
ON the truth of religion much has been urged; on its usefulness and beneficial tendency, comparatively little – little, at least, which can be termed
argumentative or convincing. But assumption is shorter than proof, and
the advocates of religion, though scarcely deigning to bestow any inquiry
or analysis upon the subject, have not failed to ascribe to it results of
supreme excellence and happiness. It has been affirmed to be the leading
bond of union between the different members of society – to be the most
powerful curb on the immoral and unsocial passions of individuals – to
form the consolation and support of misfortunes and declining life – in
short it has been described as the most efficient prop both of inward
happiness and of virtuous practice in this world. Whether these sublime
pretensions are well-founded or not, the following inquiry is destined to
ascertain.

The warmest partisan of natural religion cannot deny, that by the influence of it (occasionally at least) bad effects have been produced; nor can
any one on the other hand venture to deny, that it has on other occasions
brought about good effects. The question therefore is, throughout, only as
to the comparative magnitude, number, and proportion of each.

One course has indeed been adopted, by means of which religion has
been, in appearance, extricated from all imputation, of having ever given
birth to ill effects in any shape. So far as the results occasioned by it have
been considered as good, the producing cause has been termed *religion*: so
far as these results have been regarded as bad, this name has been discarded,
and the word *superstition* has been substituted. Or these injurious effects
have avowedly been thrown aside under the pretence that they are *abuses
of religion*; that the abuse of a thing cannot be urged against its use, since
the most beneficent preparations maybe erroneously or criminally applied.
By these false methods of reasoning the subject has been inconceivably
overclouded, and it is therefore essentially necessary to expose and guard
against such fallacies in the outset. From the former of these two sources
all deception will be obviated by an accurate definition of the term *religion*,
by strictly confining it to one meaning, and invariably introducing it when-

ever that meaning is implied. Against the latter principle, by which what are called the abuses of a thing are discarded from the estimate of its real importance and value, we declare open war. By the use of a thing, is meant the good which it produces; by the abuse, the evil which it occasions. To pronounce upon the merits of the thing under discussion, previously erasing from the reckoning all the evil which it occasions, is most preposterous and unwarrantable. Were this mode of summing up receipts and eluding all deduction of outgoings, admissible, every institution, which had ever produced any good effects at all, must be applauded as meritorious and useful, although its pernicious effects, which had been thrust out of the account, might form a decided and overwhelming balance on the other side.

By the term *religion* is meant the belief in the existence of an almighty Being, by whom pains and pleasures will be dispensed to mankind, during an infinite and future state of existence. And religion is called natural, when there exists no written and acknowledged declaration, from which an acquaintance with the will and attributes of this almighty Being may be gathered.

My object is therefore to ascertain, whether the belief of posthumous pains and pleasures, then to be administered by an omnipotent Being, is useful to mankind – that is, productive of happiness or misery in the present life.

I say, *in the present life*, for the distinction is exceedingly important to notice. Compared with an interminable futurity, the present life taken in its utmost duration, is but as a point, less than a drop of water to the ocean. Although, therefore, it should be demonstrated that religion, considered with reference to the present life, is not beneficial, but pernicious – not *augmentative* but destructive of human happiness – there might still remain ample motive to the observance of its precepts in the mind of a true believer.

CHAPTER II.
The Expectations of posthumous Pain and Pleasure, which Natural Religion holds out, considered simply and in themselves.

THE pains and pleasures, which are believed to await us in a posthumous existence, may be anticipated either as conditional, and dependent upon the present behaviour of the believer, or as unconditional dispensations, which no conduct on his part can either amend or aggravate. Though perhaps it is impossible to produce any case in which the belief has actually assumed this latter shape, yet it will be expedient to survey it in this most general and indeterminate form, before we introduce the particular circumstances which have usually accompanied the reception of it. A few considerations will suffice to ascertain whether expectations of posthumous pains and pleasures, considered in themselves and without any reference to the direction which they may give to human conduct, are of a nature to occasion happiness or misery to the believer.

Nothing can be more undeniable than that a posthumous existence, if sincerely anticipated, is most likely to appear replete with impending pain and misery. The demonstration is brief and decisive.

A posthumous state of existence is necessarily unknown and impervious to human vision. We cannot see the ground which is before us; we possess not the slightest means of knowing whether it resembles that which we have already trodden. The scene before us is wrapped in impenetrable darkness. In this state of obscurity and ignorance, the imagination usurps the privilege of filling up the void, and what are the scenes which she pourtrays? They are similar to those with which the mind is overrun during a state of earthly darkness – the product of unmixed timidity and depression. Fear is the never-failing companion and offspring of ignorance, and the circumstances of human life infallibly give birth to such a communion. For the painful sensations are the most obtrusive and constant assailants which lie in ambush round our path. The first years of our life are spent in suffering under their sting, before we acquire the means of warding them off. The sole acquisition applicable to this purpose is knowledge – knowledge of the precise manner and occasion in which we are threatened, and of the antidote which may obviate it. Still however the painful sensations are continually on the watch to take advantage of every unguarded moment; nor is there a single hour of our life in which the lessons of experience are not indispensably necessary for our protection against them.

Since then it is only to knowledge that we owe our respite from perpetual suffering; wherever our knowledge fails us and we are reduced to a state of unprotected helplessness, all our sense of security, all anticipations of future ease, must vanish along with it. Ignorance must generate incessant alarm and uneasiness. The regular œconomy of the universe, by which nature is subjected to general laws, and the past becomes the interpreter of the future, is often adduced as a reason for extolling the beneficence of the Deity; and a reliance on the stability of *events*, as well as in the efficacy of the provision we have made against the future, is justly regarded as the most indispensable ingredient in human happiness. Had we no longer any confident expectation that to-morrow would resemble yesterday – were we altogether without any rule for predicting what would occur to us after this night, how shocking would be our alarm and depression! The unknown future which was about to succeed, would be pregnant to our affrighted imaginations, with calamity from which we know not how to shelter ourselves. Infants are timorous to a proverb, and perhaps there is scarcely any man, possessed of vision, whom darkness does not impress with some degree of apprehension and uneasiness. Yet if a man fancies himself unsheltered, when only the visible prognostics of impending evil are effaced, while all his other means of foresight and defence remain inviolate, how much keener will be the sense of his unprotected condition, when all means of predicting or averting future calamity are removed beyond his reach? If in the one case his alarmed fancy peoples the darkness with unreal enemies, and that too in defiance of the opposing assurances of reason, what an array of suffering will it conjure up in the other, where the ignorance and helplessness, upon which the alarm is founded, is so infinitely magnified, and where reason cannot oppose the smallest tittle of evidence?

I have thus endeavoured to show that from the unintermitting peril to which human life is exposed, and the perpetual necessity of knowledge to protect ourselves against it, mankind must infallibly conceive an unknown future as fraught with misery and torment. But this is not the only reason which may be assigned for such a tendency. Pain is a far stronger, more pungent, and more distinct sensation than pleasure; it is more various in its shapes, more definite and impressive upon the memory, and lays hold of the imagination with greater mastery and permanence. Pain, therefore, is far more likely to obtrude itself upon the conceptions, where there exists no positive evidence to circumscribe their range, than pleasure. Throughout the catalogue of human suspicions, there exists not a case in which our ignorance is so profound as about the manner of a posthumous existence; and since no reason can be given for preferring one mode of conceiving it to another, the strongest sensations of the past will be perfectly sure to break in, and to appropriate the empty canvass. Pain will dictate our anticipation, and a posthumous life will be apprehended as replete with the most terrible concomitants which such a counsellor can suggest.

Besides, pain alone, and want or uneasiness, which is a species of pain, are the standing provisions of nature. Even the mode of appeasing those wants, is the discovery of human skill; what is called *pleasure* is a secondary formation, something superadded to the satisfaction of our wants by a further reach of artifice; and only enjoyable when that satisfaction is perfect for the present, as well as prompt and certain for the future. Want and pain, therefore, are natural; satisfaction and pleasure, artificial and invented: and the former will on this ground also be more likely to present itself as the characteristic of an unknown state, than the latter.

The preceding arguments seem to evince most satisfactorily, that a posthumous existence, if really anticipated, is far more likely to be conceived as a state of suffering than of enjoyment. Such anticipation, therefore, considered in itself, and without any reference to the direction which it gives to human conduct, will assuredly occasion more misery than happiness to those who entertain it.

Though believers in a posthumous existence seldom in fact anticipate its joys or torments as unconditionally awaiting them, and altogether independent of their present conduct, yet it is important to examine the effects and tendency of the belief, when thus entertained. We frequently hear the hope of immortality magnified as one of the loftiest privileges and blessings of human nature, without which man would be left in a state of mournful and comfortless destitution. To all these vague declamations, by which it is attempted to interest the partiality of mankind in favour of the belief in question, the foregoing arguments furnish a reply; they demonstrate that such anticipations, so far from conferring happiness on mankind, are certain to fasten in preference upon prospects of torments, and to occasion a large overplus of apprehension and uneasiness – at least, until some revelation intervenes to settle and define them, and to terminate that ignorance which casts so terrific a character over the expected scenes.

He who imagines himself completely mortal, suffers no apprehension or misery, in this life, from the prospect of death, except that which the pains attending it, and the loss of present enjoyments, unavoidably hold out. A posthumous existence, if anticipated as blissful, would doubtless greatly alleviate the disquietude which the prospect of death occasions. It cannot be denied that such a persuasion would prove the source of genuine happiness to the believer. But the fact is, that a posthumous existence is not, by the majority of believers, anticipated as thus blissful, but as replete with terrors. The principles of human nature, to which reference has been made in the foregoing arguments, completely warrant this conclusion, supposing no revelation at hand to instil and guarantee more consoling hopes. It is obvious therefore, that natural religion alone and unassisted, will to the majority of its believers materially aggravate the disquietude occasioned by the prospect of death. Instead of soothing apprehensions which cannot be wholly dispelled, it would superadd fresh grounds of uneasiness, wrapped up in an uncertainty which only renders them more painful and depressing.

Having thus ascertained, that posthumous anticipations, considered in themselves and in their capacity of feelings, occasion more unhappiness than benefit to the believer, I shall now examine them under that point of view in which they are commonly regarded as most beneficial and valuable.

CHAPTER III.
The Expectations of posthumous Pain and Pleasure, which natural Religion holds out, considered as conditional, and as exercising Influence upon human Conduct.

IT is in this mode that such expectations are commonly regarded as most beneficial to mankind. The anticipation of posthumous pleasure and pain, conditional upon the actions of the believer, is affirmed to imprint upon individual conduct a bias favourable to the public happiness. I shall now proceed to investigate the validity of this plea, which has hitherto been seldom challenged.

If natural religion contributes to human happiness, by means of the influence which it exercises on the conduct of men, such a result can be brought about only in one of these ways; either it must provide *a directive rule*, communicating the knowledge of the *right path* – or it must furnish *a sanction* or inducement for the observance of some directive rule, supposed to be known from other sources. Unless it thus either admonishes or impels, it cannot possibly affect in any way the course of human nature.

Section I. – Natural Religion Furnishes no Directive Rule Whatever.

It is obvious at first sight, that natural religion communicates to mankind no rule of guidance. This is the leading defect which revelation is stated to supply, by providing an authentic enumeration of those acts to which future pains and pleasures are annexed. Independent of revelation, it cannot be pretended that there exists any standard, to which the believer in a posthumous existence, can apply for relief and admonition. The whole prospect is wrapt in impenetrable gloom, nor is there a streak of light to distinguish the one true path of future happiness from the infinite possibilities of error with which it is surrounded.

Nor is the absence of any authoritative collection of rules, by which the believer might adjust his steps in all circumstances however difficult, the only defect to be remarked. Experience imparts no information upon the subject. That watchful scout, who on all other occasions spies out the snares and terrors of the march, and points out the path of comparative safety, here altogether deserts us. We search in vain for any witness who may enlighten this deplorable ignorance. The distribution of these pains and pleasures is completely unseen, nor does either the gainer or loser ever return to testify the mode of dispensing them. We cannot therefore pretend even to conjecture whether there is any general rule observed in awarding them; or if there be a rule, what are its dictates. It is impossible to divine what behaviour is visited with severity, what conduct leads to pleasurable results, during a state in which there is not a glimmering of light to guide us.

The natural religionist therefore is not only destitute of any previous official warning, by a compliance with which he may ensure safety or favour: he has not even the means of consulting those decisions according to which the pleasures and pains are actually awarded to actions already committed. Not only is there no statue law extant, distinguishing, with that strict precision which should characterise the legislator as he ought to be, the path of happiness from that of misery: even the imperfect light of common law is here extinguished – even that record of decisions is forbidden, from whence we might at least borrow some shadowy and occasional surmises, and learn to steer clear of the more excruciating lots of pain. The darkness is desperate and unfathomable; and as truth and rectitude can be but a single track amidst an infinity of divergent errors, the chances in favour of a wrong line of conduct are perfectly incalculable. Yet a false step, if once committed, is altogether without hope or remedy. For when the posthumous sufferings are inflicted, the hour of application and profit is irrevocably past, and the sufferer enjoys not even the melancholy consolation which he might derive from the hope of preventing any future repetition of the same torture.

It seems, therefore, almost unaccountable, that natural religion, how rich soever its promises, how terrible soever its threats, should exercise the least influence upon human conduct, since the conditions of its awards are altogether veiled from our sight. Why does the prospect of other pains affect our conduct? Because experience teaches us the actions to which they are specially attached. Until we acquire this knowledge, our behaviour cannot possibly be actuated by the anticipations which they create. How then can natural religion, shrouded as it is in such matchless obscurity, prove an exception to these infallible principles, and impel mankind without specifying a single benefit derivable from one course of action rather than another?

Since however it unquestionably does exercise some influence upon human conduct, this must be effected by providing inducements for some extraneous directive rule. I shall proceed to examine the nature of the precepts which it thus adopts and enforces, since there are none peculiarly suggested by itself.

Section II. – Natural Religion Indirectly Suggests, and Applies her Inducements to the Observance of, a Rule of Action very Pernicious to the Temporal Interests of Mankind.

In inquiring what extraneous rules of conduct are likely to promise either posthumous pleasure, or security from posthumous pain, we are unable to perceive, at first, how the believer should be led to any preference or conclusion upon the subject. So completely are we destitute of evidence, that it seems presumptuous to select any one mode of conduct, or, to exclude any other. Experience alone can announce to us what behaviour is attended with enjoyment or discomfort during this life; it is this guide alone who informs us that the taste of fruit will procure pleasure, or that contact with the fire will occasion pain, and if the trial had never been made, we should to this day have remained ignorant even of these trite and familiar facts. We could not have affirmed or denied anything about them. Suppose a species of fruit perfectly new to be discovered; if any one, before, either he himself, or some one else has tasted it, confidently pronounces that it is sweet and well flavoured, an assertion so premature and uncertified could be treated only with contempt. We should term it folly and presumption thus to prophecy the pleasure or pain consequent *in this life* upon any particular conduct, prior to any experimental test.

Whence comes it then, that the same certificate, which is allowed to be our only safeguard here against the dreams and chimeras of fancy, should be dismissed as superfluous and unnecessary in our anticipations of posthumous pain and pleasure? If a man ignorant of medicine is unable to point out a course of life which shall, if pursued in England, preserve him from liability to the yellow fever when he goes to Jamaica, how much more boldness is required to prescribe a preparatory course against consequences still further removed from the possibility of conjecture?

Rash, however, as such anticipations may seem to be, they have almost universally obtained reception, under some form or other. And it is highly important to trace the leading assumptions which have governed the prophecies of men on the subject of posthumous pain and pleasure – to detect those universal principles which never fail to stand out amidst an infinite variety of subordinate accompaniments.

Natural religion merely implants in a man the expectation of a posthumous existence, involving awards of enjoyment and suffering apportioned by an invisible Being. This we suppose it to assure and certify; beyond this, all is dark and undiscovered. But on a subject so dim and yet so terrible, the obtrusive conjectures of fancy will not be silenced, and she will proceed to particularise and interpolate without delay. The character of the invisible Being in whose hands these fearful dispensations are lodged, will present the most plausible theme for her speculations. If his temper, and the actions with which he is pleased or displeased, can be once discovered, an apparent clue to the secret sentences of futurity will be obtained. He will gratify those whose conduct he likes – injure those whose behaviour is disagreeable to him. But what modes of conduct will he be supposed to approve or disapprove?

Before we proceed to unfold the principles which govern our suppositions regarding his temper, it may be important to point out, in a few words, the insufficient basis upon which all anticipations of future enjoyment or suffering are built, independent of revelation. The pains and pleasures of a posthumous life are under the dispensation of the invisible Being. But so also are the pains and pleasures of this life. You do not found any expectations regarding the latter upon any assumed disposition of their invisible Dispenser. You do not pacify your ignorance of those causes which may create a tendency to the yellow fever, by conjecturing that certain actions are displeasing to his feelings. Predictions founded upon such wretched surmise would indicate the meanest imbecility. Why, then, should such evidence be considered as sanctioning anticipations of posthumous awards, when the commonest experience will not allow it to be employed to interpret the dispensations of the very same Being in the present life? In estimating the chances of life and death, of health and disease, no insurer ever inquires whether the actions of the applicant have been agreeable or disagreeable to the Deity. And the reasoning, upon which the trial by ordeal rests, is regarded with unqualified contempt, implying as it does, that this

Being approves or detests modes of action, and that he will manifest these feelings by dispensations in this life, of favour or severity. Yet this is merely a consistent application of the very same shift, for superseding the necessity of experience, on which the posthumous prophecies of natural religion are founded.

In this life, however, it may be urged, there are laws of nature which the Deity cannot or will not interrupt. But why should there not also be posthumous laws of nature, discoverable only by experience of them, and inviolable to the same extent? The presumption unquestionably is, that there are such posthumous laws, and that we can no more predict, from a reference to the attributes of the Deity, the modes of acquiring pleasure and avoiding pain in a posthumous life, than we can in this.

Amidst the dimness and distance of futurity, however, reason is altogether struck blind, and we do not scruple to indulge in these baseless antici-pations. The assumed character of the invisible Dispenser is the only ground on which fancy can construct her scale of posthumous promotion and disgrace. And thus the rule of action, to which natural religion will affix her inducements of future vengeance and remuneration, will be framed entirely upon the conceptions entertained regarding his character.

We thus find ourselves somewhat nearer to the object of the present inquiry, whether natural religion conduces to the happiness or misery of mankind during the present life. It appears that natural religion does not itself originate any rule of action whatever, and that the rule which it is supposed to second and enforce depends only upon conceptions of the temper of the Deity. If he is conceived to be perfectly beneficient – having no personal affections of his own, or none but such as are coincident with the happiness of mankind – patronising those actions alone which are useful, and exactly in the degree in which they are useful – detesting in a similar manner and proportion those which are hurtful – then the actions agreeable to him will be beneficial to mankind, and inducements to the performance of them will promote the happiness of mankind. If, on the other hand, he is depicted as unbeneficent – as having personal affec-tions seldom coincident with human happiness, frequently injurious to it, and almost always frivolous and exactive – favouring actions which are not useful at all, or not in the degree in which they are useful – disapproving with the same caprice and without any reference to utility – then the course of action by which his favour is to be sought, will be more or less injurious to mankind, and inducements to pursue it will in the present life tend to the production of unhappiness.

From this alternative there can be no escape. According to the temper of the Being whom we seek to please, will be the mode of conduct proper for conciliating his favour. To serve the devil is universally considered as implying the most abhorrent and detestable behaviour.

If we consult the language in which mankind speak of the Deity, we shall be led to imagine that he is in their conception a being of perfect and unsullied beneficence, uniting in himself all that is glorious and all that is amiable. Such is the tendency and amount of the words which they employ. Strange, however, as the inconsistency may appear, it will not be difficult to demonstrate, that mere natural religion invariably leads its votaries to ascribe to their Deity a character of caprice and tyranny, while they apply to him, at the same moment, all those epithets of eulogy and reverence which their language comprises. This discrepancy between the actual and pretended conception is an infallible result of the circumstances, and agreeable to the principles of human nature.

1. What are the fundamental data, as communicated by natural religion, respecting the Deity, from which his temper and inclinations are to be inferred? A power to which we can assign no limits – an agency which we are unable to comprehend or frustrate – such are the original attributes from which the disposition of the possessor is to be gathered.

Now the feeling which excessive power occasions in those who dwell under its sway, is extreme and unmixed fear. This is its appropriate and never-failing effect, and he who could preserve an undisturbed aspect in the face of a power against which he knew of no protection, and which might destroy him in an instant, would justly be extolled as a man of heroic firmness. But what is the temper of mind which fear presupposes in the object which excites it? A disposition to do harm. Now a disposition to do harm, conjoined to the power of effecting it at pleasure, constitutes the very essence of tyranny. Examine the fictitious narratives respecting men of extraordinary strength; you will find a Giant or a Cyclops uniformly pourtrayed as cruel in the extreme, and delighted with the scent of human blood. Such are the dispositions which the human fancy naturally imagines as guiding the employment of irresistible might. Our terrors (as Father Malebranche remarks) justify themselves, by suggesting appropriate persuasions of impending evil, and compel us to regard the possessor of unlimited powers as a tyrant.

The second characteristic of the Deity is an unknown and incomprehensible agency. Now an incomprehensible mode of behaviour, not reducible to any known principles, is in human affairs termed *caprice*, when confined to the trifling occurrences of life; *insanity*, when it extends to important occasions. The capricious or the insane are those whose proceedings we cannot reconcile with the acknowledged laws of human conduct – those whose conduct defies our utmost sagacity of prediction. They are incomprehensible agents endued with limited power. The epithets *capricious, insane, incomprehensible*, are perfectly convertible and synonymous.

Let experience now teach us the feelings with which mankind usually regard the mad, the wayward, and the unfathomable course of proceeding among themselves. They laugh at the caprices of a child; they tremble at the incoherent speech and gestures of a madman. Every one shrinks with dismay from the presence of the latter; the laws instantly enclose his body, and thrust upon it the invincible manacles of matter, since no known apprehension will act as a sufficient coercive upon his mind. Caprice and insanity, when accompanied even with the limited strength of a man, excite in us the keenest alarm, which is only heightened by the indefinite shape of the coming evil.

But let us suppose this object of our terror to be still farther strengthened. What if we arm the incomprehensible man with a naked sword! What if we figure him, like the insane Orlando of Ariosto, roaming about with an invulnerable hide, and limbs insensible to the chain! What if, still farther, he be entrusted with the government of millions, seconded by irresistible legions who stand ready at his beck! Can the utmost stretch of fancy produce any picture so appalling as that of a mad, capricious, and incomprehensible Being exalted to this overwhelming sway? Yet this terrific representation involves nothing beyond surpassing might, wielded by one whose agency is unfathomable. And these are the two attributes, the alliance of which, in a measure still more fearful and unlimited, constitutes the Deity, as pourtrayed by natural religion.

So complete is this identity between incomprehensible conduct and madness, that amongst early nations, the madman is supposed to be under the immediate inspiration and control of the Deity, whose agency is always believed to commence where coherent and rational behaviour terminates.

But the Deity (it will be urged) treats us with favour and kindness, and this may suffice to remove our apprehensions of him. I reply, that the most valuable gift could never efface them, while the proceedings of the donor continued to be entirely inconsistent and unintelligible. It is the very essence of caprice and madness, that present behaviour constitutes no security whatever for the future. Our disquietude for the future must therefore remain as oppressive as before, and can never be relieved by these occasional gusts of transient good-humour. As few men hope, and almost every one fears, in cases where no assured calculation can be framed, it is obvious that this irregular favouritism would still leave us in all the restlessness of suspense and uncertainty.

The actual conception, therefore, which mankind will form of the Deity, from the consideration of those original data which unassisted natural religion promulgates concerning him, seems now to be sufficiently determined. He will not be conceived as designing constant and unmixed evil, for otherwise his power would carry it into effect; nor, for the same reason, as meditating universal and unceasing good. While there exists good in the universe, such a power cannot be wielded by perfect malevolence; while there exists evil, it cannot be directed by consummate benevolence.[1] Besides, either of these two suppositions would destroy the attribute of incomprehensibility, and would substitute in their stead a consecutive and intelligible system of action. The Deity therefore will be conceived as fluctuating between the two; sometimes producing evil, sometimes good, but infinitely more as an object of terror than of hope. His changeful and incomprehensible inclinations will be supposed more frequently pernicious than beneficial to mankind, and the portrait of a capricious tyrant will thus be completed.

2. Unamiable, however, and appalling as this conception may actually be, it is equally undeniable that no language, except that of the most devoted reverence and eulogy, will ever be employed in describing or addressing the Deity. To demonstrate this, it will be necessary to revert to the origin of praise and blame.

Praise is the expression of goodwill and satisfaction towards the person who has occasioned us a certain pleasure. It intimates a readiness on our part to manifest this good will by some farther repayment. It supposes the performance of a service which we have neither the right to expect, nor the means of exacting. We bestow it in order to evince to the performer of the service and to the public in general, that we are not insensible to the favour received, and that we are disposed to view all who thus benefit us with peculiar complacency. Our praise therefore is destined to operate as a stimulus to the repetition of that behaviour by which we profit.

Blame, on the contrary, is the signal of dissatisfaction and wrath against the person who has caused us pain. It implies a disposition which would be gratified by inflicting injury upon him. It proclaims to him, and to every one else, our sense of the hurt, and the perils prepared for all who treat us in a similar manner. And we design, by means of it, to frighten and deter every one from conduct noxious to our welfare.

---

[1]　Plato tells us that the Deity is perfectly and systematically well intentioned, but that he was prevented from realizing these designs by the inherent badness and intractable qualities of matter. This supposition does indeed vindicate the intentions of the supreme Being, but only by grievously insulting his power and limiting his omnipotence. According to this theory, the Deity becomes a perfectly comprehensible person; and the attribute of incomprehensibility being taken away, all the preceding reasonings which are founded on it fall to the ground. But at the same time that he becomes perfectly comprehensible, he becomes a thorough dead letter with regard to all human desires and expectations. For by the supposition his power only extends to the production of the already existing amount of good. He can produce no more good – that is, he can be of no farther use to any one, and therefore it is vain to trouble ourselves about him.

But what evidence is there for this doctrine of Plato? Not the shadow of an argument can be produced in its favour, and where nothing is set up as a defence, one cannot tell where to aim an attack. The only mode of assailing it is by constructing a similar phantom on one's own side, in order to expose the absurdity of the first by its resemblance to the second. Conformably to this rule, I affirm that the Deity is perfectly and systematically malevolent, and that he was only prevented from realizing these designs by the inherent goodness and incorruptible excellence of matter. I admit that there is not the smallest evidence for this, but it is just as well supported, and just as probable as the preceding theory of Plato.

Such is the origin and such the intention of the language of encomium and dispraise. Each is a species of sanction, vested in the hands of every individual, and employed by him for his own benefit; the former *remuneratory*, and destined to encourage the manifestation of kindness towards him; the latter *punitory*, and intended to prevent injurious treatment.

Having thus unfolded the nature of praise and censure, it will not be difficult to explain the laws which govern their application; and to separate the circumstances in which a man will praise, from those in which he will blame.

Our employment of the punitory sanction, or of blame, is in exact proportion to our power; our employment of the remuneratory sanction, or of praise, is in a similar manner proportional to our weakness.

The man of extraordinary power, who possesses unlimited disposal of the instruments of terror, has not the slightest motive to praise. His blame, the herald and precursor of impending torture, is abundantly sufficient to ensure conformity to his will. The remuneratory sanction is in its nature comparatively feeble and uncertain; the punitory, when applied in sufficient magnitude, is altogether infallible and omnipotent. He who possesses an adequate command of the latter, will never condescend to make use of the former. He will regard himself as strictly entitled to the most unqualified subservience on the part of those whom he might in an instant plunge into excruciating torments. If he partially waives the exercise of this prerogative, he will consider it as an undeserved extension of mercy.

On the other hand, the man without strength or influence, who cannot hurt us even if he wished it, is cut off from the employment of the punitory sanction. His blame is an impotent murmur, threatening no future calamity, and therefore listened to with indifference. It would, under these circumstances, revolt and irritate us, or else provoke our derision. In either case, it would only render us less disposed to conform to his will, and policy therefore will induce him to repress it altogether. His sole method of influencing our behaviour is by a prodigal employment of the remuneratory sanction – by repaying the slightest favour with unbounded expressions of gratitude – by lavishing upon us such loud and devoted eulogy, as may impress us with his readiness to consecrate to our benefit all the energies of a human being, if we condescend to repeat our kindness. Such are the methods by which he endeavours to magnify and exaggerate the slender bounty which fortune permits him to apply in encouragement of the favours of mankind.

The most copious experience may be adduced in support of these principles. Does the planter, whom the law arms with unlimited power, bestow any eulogy upon his slave, in return for the complete monopoly of his whole life and services? He considers himself as entitled to *demand* all this, since he possesses the means of *extorting* its fulfilment. Let us trace the descending scale of power, and mark how the approach of weakness gradually unsheaths the remuneratory sanction. Were his free labourer (particularly in those lands where labour is scarce and highly paid) to work in his employment with an energy and devotion at all comparable to that which he exacts from his slave, the planter would be prompt in applying the stimulus and encouragement of eulogy. A slighter service, on the part of a friend of equal rank, will draw from him encomiums on the kind and generous temper by which he has benefited. But the merest civility, even a peculiar look or word, bestowed by the king or a superior, is sufficient to impress upon him the deepest esteem and reverence. He loudly extols the gracious deportment of a person upon whom he had no claim, and from whom he could have entertained no expectations.

If any one makes me a present of a considerable sum, I magnify his bounty to the skies; I recommend him to the public by all the epithets significant of kindly and beneficent feelings, and thus display the conspicuous return which I am ready to make for such treatment. But let the government grant me a claim upon his estate, however unjustly, and the premium of praise is no longer necessary when I am thus master of the engine of exaction. I no longer therefore bestow upon him, by whose labour I profit, those laudatory terms which promise good will on my part. 'Is it not enough for him' (said Charles I. when the death of Lord Northampton was commended to his sympathy) – 'Is it not enough that he has died for his king?' So thoroughly is the standing demand which any one makes upon his fellow-creatures, measured by the extent of his compulsory power. It is upon those services only, which overstep this limit, and which he possesses not the means of extorting, that he will expend the tribute of his praise, or waste the incentive which it offers to a future reproduction of favours. Charles I. would not have uttered such a sentence the day before his execution.

With the weak, again, the punitory sanction is completely silenced and annulled. A slave never dreams of announcing dissatisfaction at the conduct of his master. If he did so, the consequence would be an additional infliction of stripes. In despotic governments you hear not a murmur against the oppressor – at least, until excess of suffering produces desperation. The entire extinction of all free sentiment among dependants and courtiers has become proverbial. They dare not express even that indirect and qualified censure of their superior, which is implied in dissenting from his opinion. They tolerate his insults with a patience and complacency for which they reimburse themselves in their conversation with inferiors. Not only do they abstain from hinting that there is any censurable ingredient in his character, but they dare not even withhold their encomiums, lest they should seem to doubt his exalted merit. It is unnecessary to cite particular instances of a subservience and flattery so notorious.

In proportion as we raise the inferior into equality, his blame becomes more efficacious, and is proclaimed oftener and more freely. Advance him still higher, and his propensity to find fault will be still farther extended, until at last it becomes so exciteable and eruptive, as to disregard altogether the feelings of others, and to visit with merciless severity the most trivial defect of conformity to his wishes.

From this examination we may extract some important principles, which will materially elucidate the object of the present inquiry. It appears, first, that the employment of praise or blame bears an exact ratio to the comparative weakness or strength of the critic. Weakness determines praise, strength blame; and the force of either sentiment is measured by the extent of the determining quality. The greater the disparity of power, the more severe is the blame heaped upon the inferior, the more excessive the praise lavished upon the superior. Secondly, the employment of praise and blame is in an inverse ratio to each other. He who praises the most, blames the least; he who blames the most, scarcely praises at all. The man to whom the utmost praise is addressed, seldom hears any blame – and *vice versâ*. Thirdly, the application of praise and blame bears an inverse ratio to the services performed. The greater the service rendered, the more is the performer of it blamed; the less is he praised. There is no human being from whom the planter derives so much benefit as from his slave; there is none upon whom he expends so little eulogy, or pours so much reproach. On the contrary, it is towards him who had the largest power of inflicting evil upon us, and who confers on us the most insignificant favours, that our encomiums are the warmest, our censure the most gentle and sparing. A mere intermission of the whip, or perhaps an occasional holiday, will draw forth abundant expression of praise on the part of the slave. How gracious and beneficent is a sovereign styled, by him upon whom he has bestowed a single look of favour! The vehemence of our praise is thus not measured by the extent of the kindness bestowed, but by the superiority of the donor to the receiver, and implies only the dependence and disparity of the latter.

If the foregoing account of praise and blame be correct, it presents an entire solution of the apparent discrepancy which suggested itself at the commencement of the enquiry. It explains how the Deity, although actually conceived (from the mere data of natural religion) as a capricious despot, is yet never described or addressed without the largest and most prodigal encomiums. For where is the case in which so tremendous and exaltation of the agent above the subject can be pointed out? Where is the comparative weakness of the latter so deplorably manifest? The power of which we speak is unlimited, and therefore with respect to it, we are altogether prostrate and abject. It is, under such circumstances, the natural course, that we should abstain from all disparaging and provocative epithets, and repress every whisper which might indicate a tone of disaffection towards the Omnipotent. 'Personne n'aime à prendre une peine inutile, même un enfant,' observes Rousseau; and to proclaim an impotent hatred, besides being unmeaning and irrational, might prove positively noxious, by alienating any inclination to benefit us on the part of the Supreme. However painful may be the treatment which we experience at his hands, we must cautiously refrain from pronouncing our genuine sentiments of the injury, inasmuch as such a freedom might prolong or aggravate, but could never extenuate, our sufferings.

The same weakness will give birth to an extravagant and unsparing use of the remuneratory sanction. We know well how little our epithets really signify or promise, since the Deity stands in no need of our good offices; and therefore we endeavour to bestow force upon this host of unmeaning effusions by multiplying its numbers, and by piling up superlative upon superlative. We magnify the smallest crumb into a splendid benefaction, which merits on our part a return of endless devotion to his service. By thus testifying our own ready subservience – by applying to him terms significant of qualities morally good and beneficial to mankind, and thereby intimating that every one else owes to him a similar gratitude – we hope to constitute something like a motive for repeating the favour. This varied and exuberant flattery is the only mode of soothing the irritability of an earthly despot, and therefore we naturally apply it to one of still more surpassing might.

Suppose that any tyrant could establish so complete a system of espionage as to be informed of every word which any of his subjects might utter: It is obvious that all criticisms upon him would be laudatory in the extreme, for they would be all pronounced as it were in the presence of the tyrant, and *there* we know that no one dares to express even dissent of opinion. The unlimited agency of the Deity is equivalent to this universal espionage. He is conceived as the unseen witness of every thing which passes our lips – indeed even of our thoughts. It would be madness, therefore, to hazard an unfavourable judgment of his proceedings, while thus constantly under his supervision.

It seems, therefore, sufficiently demonstrated, that the same incomprehensible power, which would cause the Deity to be conceived as a capricious despot, would also occasion him to be spoken of only under titles of the loftiest eulogy. For language is not the sign of the idea actually existing in the mind of the speaker – but of that which he desires to convey to the hearer. In the present case these two ideas are completely at variance, as they must uniformly be where there is an excessive disparity of power.

It has been necessary to pursue the enquiry into the character of the Deity as pourtrayed by natural religion, to a length which may possibly seem tedious. But as the rule of conduct, to which natural religion applies her inducements, depends altogether on the conceptions framed of the invisible governor of a posthumous existence – it is of the highest moment to lay bare the actual conceptions of him, in order to ascertain whether a behaviour adjusted according to them will be beneficial or injurious to mankind.

Since the dispositions of the Deity are, in this unenlightened condition, supposed to be thus capricious and incomprehensible, it may seem extraordinary that mankind should have attempted to assign to them a definite boundary, by marking out any line of conduct as agreeable or disagreeable to him.

But the fact is, that the terms incomprehensible and unlimited are merely negative, and therefore have no positive meaning whatever: their actual import is, that the Deity is a being of whom we know less, and who has more power, than any other. We conceive him as differing only in degree from other possessors of power, and we therefore assimilate him the most closely to those earthly sovereigns in whom the most irresistible might resides.

We are thus furnished with a clue to the actions which unassisted natural religion will represent as agreeable and odious to the Deity. Experience announces to us what practices will recommend us to the favour of terrestrial potentates, and what will provoke their enmity. From this analogy (the nearest we can attain upon the subject) will be copied the various modes of behaviour which the Deity is imagined to favour or abominate. To pursue the former course and avoid the latter, will be the directive rule to which the inducements of natural religion affix themselves. This directive rule will indeed ramify into many accidental shapes, among different nations; but its general tenor and spirit will, throughout, be governed by the analogy just mentioned, since that is our nearest resource and substitute in the total silence of experience.

The central passion in the mind of a despot is an insatiate love of dominion, and thirst for its increase. All his approbation and disapprobation, all his acts of reward and punishment, are wholly dictated by this master-principle. I state this in a broad and unqualified manner; but I feel warranted by the amplest evidence, and by the concurrent testimony of political writers, almost all of whom stigmatise in the harshest language the unbridled government of a single man.

Pursuing this clue, it will not be difficult to distinguish those characters which he will mark out as estimable or hateful. The foremost in his estimation will be that man who most essentially contributes to the maintenance of his power: the greatest object of his hatred will be he who most eminently threatens its annihilation. Next in the catalogue of merit will be inserted the person who can impress upon his mind, in the most vivid and forcible manner, the delicious conviction of his supremacy – who can re-kindle this association continually, and strike out new modes of application to prevent it from subsiding into indifference. Next in the list of demerit will appear the name of him whose conduct tends to invalidate this consciousness of overwhelming might – whose open defiance or tardy conformity generates mistrust and apprehension – or who, at least, can contemplate with an unterrified and uninfluenced eye the whole apparatus of majesty. Such will be the most eminent subjects, both of favour and disgrace, on the part of the despot.

In all cases where the gratification of his love of power is allied with the happiness of his subjects, qualities conducive to that happiness will recommend themselves to his patronage. But it is a melancholy truth, that this coincidence *seldom*, we might say *never*, occurs. He who is thus absorbed in love of dominion, cannot avoid loving the correlative and inseparable event – the debasement of those over whom he rules; in order that his own supremacy may become more pointed and prominent. Of course he also has an interest in multiplying their privations, which are the symptoms and measure of that debasement. Besides, his leading aim is to diffuse among his subjects the keenest impressions of his own power. This is, in other words, to plant in their bosoms an incessant feeling of helplessness, insecurity and fear; and were this aim realized, everything which deserves the name of happiness must, throughout their lives, be altogether over shadowed and stifled.

Doubtless there will be occasions on which the view of prosperity will gratify him. Such will be the case when it is strongly associated with the exercise of his own creative fiat – and when its dependance upon and derivation from himself is so glaring as to blazon forth conspicuously the majesty of the donor. In order thus to affect the public mind, his benefits must be rare in their occurrence, bestowed only on a few, and concentrated into striking and ostentatious masses. All the prosperity, therefore, in which he will take an interest will be that of a few favourites; his own work, achieved by the easy process of donation. This munificence of temper, however, is not only not coincident with the happiness of the community, but is altogether hostile to it. The former, because the real welfare of the many is to be secured not by occasional fits of kindness, but by the slow and unobtrusive effect of systematic regulations, built upon this study of human nature, discoverable only by patient thought, and requiring perpetual watchfulness in their application: the latter, because these donatives are at the bottom mere acts of spoliation, snatching away the labours of the many for the benefit of a favoured few.

It thus plainly appears that the despot can never derive any pleasure from the general well-being of the community, though he may at times gratify himself by exalting individuals to sudden pre-eminence over the rest. Consequently the qualities conducive to the happiness of the community will not meet with the smallest encouragement from him. They will even be discouraged, indirectly at least, by the preference shown to other qualities not contributory to this end. But the personal affections of the despot have been shown to lead, in almost all cases, to the injury of the people. And therefore those mental habits, which tend to gratify these affections, will be honoured with his unqualified approval; those which tend to frustrate them, will incur his detestation. In the former catalogue will be comprised all the qualities which lessen and depress human happiness; in the latter, all which foster and improve it.

Such is the scale according to which the praise and censure, the rewards and punishments, of the earthly potentate, will be dispensed. By this model, the nearest which experience presents, the conceptions of mankind must be guided, in conjecturing the character and inclinations of the Deity.

The first place in the esteem of the Deity will, in pursuance of this analogy, be allotted to those who disseminate his influence among men – who are most effectually employed in rendering his name dreaded and reverenced, and enforcing the necessity of perpetual subjection to him. Priests, therefore, whose lives are devoted to this object, will be regarded as the most favoured class.

The largest measure of his hate will in like manner be supposed to devolve on those, who attempt to efface these apprehensions, and to render mankind independent of him, by removing the motives for their subjection. The most decisive way of effecting this is by presuming to call in question his existence – an affront of peculiar poignancy, to which the material despot is not exposed. Atheists, therefore, will be the persons whom he is imagined to view with the most signal abomination.

Immediately beneath the priests will be placed those who manifest the deepest and most permanent sense of his agency and power – in words, by the unceasing use of hyperbole, to extol the Deity and depress themselves – in action, by abstaining on his account from agreeable occupations, and performing ceremonies which can be ascribed to no other motive than the desire of pleasing him. Works, which can be ascribed to this motive alone, must from their very nature produce no good at all, or at least very little: for were they thus beneficial, they would be recompensed with the esteem and gratitude of mankind, and the performer of them might be suspected of having originally aimed at this independent advantage. Whereas he who whips himself every night, or prefaces every mouthful with a devotional formula, can hardly be supposed to have contemplated the smallest temporal profit, or to have had any other end in view, than that of pleasing the Deity. Such actions will be thought to convey to him the liveliest testimony of his own unparalleled influence, and the performers of them will be placed second in the scale of merit.

Next to Atheists, his highest displeasure will be conceived to attach to those who either avowedly brave his power, or tacitly slight and disregard it – who indulge in language of irreverent censure, or withhold the daily offering of their homage and prostration – who dwell careless of his supremacy, and decline altogether the endurance of privations from which no known benefit, either to themselves or others, can arise. Such persons assume an independence which silently implies that the arm of the Deity is shortened and cannot reach them; and they will, therefore, be considered as the next objects of his indignation.

These then are the qualities, which the natural religionist, guided by the experience of temporal potentates, will imagine the Deity to favour or dislike. To this extraneous directive rule, therefore, the inducements of natural religion, and the expectations of a posthumous life, will apply themselves. Nor can we doubt, for an instant, that such a rule is highly detrimental to human happiness in this life.

It cannot be otherwise, so long as nothing more is known of the Deity except that he possesses a super-human power, and that we cannot understand his course of action. It is the essence of power to exact obedience; and obedience involves privation and suffering on the part of the inferior. The Deity having power over all mankind, exacts an obedience co-extensive with his power; therefore all mankind must obey him, or, in other words, immolate to his supremacy a certain portion of their happiness. He loves human obedience; that is, he is delighted with human privations and pain, for these are the test and measure of obedience. He is pleased, when his power is felt and acknowledged: that is, he delights to behold a sense of abasement, helplessness, and terror, prevalent among mankind. If, under the earthly despot, rewards and punishments are undeniably distributed in a manner injurious to human happiness – under the God of unassisted natural religion, whose attributes must be borrowed from the despot, the case must be similar. There is indeed this difference which deserves to be remarked – that those deductions from human happiness which the temporal potentate requires, are altogether unproductive and final: while those exacted by the Deity, though embracing the very same period, are in comparison transient and preparatory, entitling the contracting party to the amplest posthumous reimbursement. In the former case, the expenditure of suffering is a dead loss; in the latter, it is a judicious surrender of present, in expectation of future, advantages.

But it may be urged in opposition, that the Deity is like a beneficent judge, and not like a despot – that he fetters individual taste no farther than is necessary for the happiness of the whole. Revelation may doubtless thus characterize him; but natural religion can never portray him under this amiable aspect. His power is irresistible, and therefore all limitations of it must be voluntary and self-imposed. How then can we venture to assume, that he will exact from individuals no more self-denial than is requisite for the benefit of the whole, unless it shall please him specially to communicate to us his recognition of such a boundary? We cannot possibly know what boundary he will select, until he informs us. Prior to revelation, therefore, the Deity can be conceived as nothing else but a despot – that is, the possessor of unrestricted sway. To compare him with a beneficient judge, is an analogy wholly fallacious and inadmissible. Why is the judge beneficent? Because his power is derivative, dependent, and responsible. Why does he impose upon individuals no farther sacrifices than are necessary to ensure the well-being of the society? Because all the compulsory force which he can employ is borrowed from the society, who will not permit it to be used for other purposes. Suppose these circumstances altered, and that the judge possesses himself of independent unresponsible power: the result is, that he becomes a despot, and ceases altogether to be beneficent. It is only when thus strengthened and unshackled that he becomes a proper object of comparison with the Deity – and then, instead of a judge, he degenerates invariably into an oppressor and a tyrant.

Amongst other expressions of reverence towards the Deity, doubtless the appellation of a judge, one of the most adorable functions which can grace humanity, will not be omitted. But we have already shown that the language of praise is not on this occasion to be considered as indicating the existence of truly valuable qualities in the object. Because that immensity of power, which is the distinguishing attribute of the Deity, distorts the epithets of eulogy, and terrifies us into an offer of them, by way of propitiation, whether deserved or not by any preceding service.

It seems clear then from the foregoing inquiry, that the posthumous hopes and fears held out by natural religion, must produce the effect of encouraging actions useless and pernicious to mankind, but agreeable to the invisible Dispenser, so far as his attributes are discoverable by unaided natural religion – and our conceptions of his character, are the only evidence on which we can even build a conjecture as to the conduct which may entail upon us posthumous happiness or misery. Whatever offers an encouragement to useless or pernicious conduct, operates indirectly to discourage that which is beneficial and virtuous. In addition, therefore, to the positive evil which these inducements force into existence of themselves, they are detrimental in another way, by stifling the growth of genuine excellence, and diverting the recompense which should be exclusively reserved for it.

CHAPTER IV.
Further Considerations on the temporal usefulness of that rule of action, which the inducements of Natural Religion enforce.

THOUGH the preceding argument, drawn from the character which unassisted reason cannot fail to ascribe to the Deity, seems amply sufficient to evince that the expected distribution of his favour and enmity is not such as to stimulate useful, and to discountenance pernicious conduct (regarding merely the present life); yet I shall subjoin a few considerations in addition, which may tend to corroborate and enforce my principles.

1. Suppose that by any peculiar perversion of reason, all belief in a God or in a future state should die away among the votaries of some Pagan system. Is it not perfectly unquestionable, that all which had been before conceived as the injunctions of natural religion, would at once be neglected and forgotten? We need not take any trouble to demonstrate this, partly

because it is so obvious a consequence, partly because it is always implied in the outcry raised against atheistical writings.

But the sources of pleasure and of pain, in this community, would still remain unaltered with regard to the present life, even in the state of impiety into which they had just plunged. What had been useful or pernicious to them before, would still continue to be so. They would have precisely the same motive to encourage the former and to repress the latter. Can any reason be given why their rewards and punishments should be insufficient to effect this end? There will still, therefore, remain in the bosom of each individual, ample motive to behaviour beneficial to the society – ample motive against conduct injurious to it.

To select a particular example. He who was, before the influx of disbelief, a skilful and diligent tradesman or physician, will he on a sudden become imprudent or remiss? Will he become indifferent to the acquisition of emolument and importance? It will not surely be contended, that any such alteration of character or conduct is to be anticipated. Apply a similar supposition to the same man in other capacities – as a father, a husband, a trustee, or any other function in which the happiness of some among his fellows depends upon his conduct. In neither of these cases will there be any motive for him to deviate from his former behaviour, supposing that to have been valuable and virtuous. But all the transactions, in which a man's conduct affects his fellow-creatures, may be comprised under some relation of this sort – and in none of these situations will he have any motive to exchange a beneficial for a noxious course of action. Consequently the expiration of religious belief will leave perfectly sufficient motive for the maintenance of conduct really useful to mankind.

If the practices enjoined by natural religion would expire without its support, this must be because there is no motive left to perform them. But to say that there is no such motive, proves that the practices produce no temporal benefit whatever: e converso, therefore, he who would maintain that pious works are temporally beneficial, must also affirm that there would be motive enough to perform them, supposing our earthly existence to terminate in annihilation. But no one ever thinks of asserting this: on the contrary, the vital necessity of implicit belief, as an incentive, is loudly proclaimed, and the certain extinction of all religious performances, if unbelief should become general, is announced and deplored. It is altogether inconsistent and contradictory, therefore, to maintain that there is any temporal benefit annexed to these practices – since this, if true, must constitute a motive common both to believers and unbelievers.

2. If natural religion consisted in the practice of actions beneficial to mankind in the present life, the actions enjoined by it would be the same all over the earth. The sources of human pleasure and pain are similar every where, and therefore the modes of multiplying both one and the other will be similar throughout. Take, for example, any particular branch

of behaviour which is justly extolled as highly conducive to human happiness: you will find justice, veracity, or prudence precisely the same in their nature, although practised with very different degrees of strictness, both in the East, and in the West. If therefore piety consisted of a collection of qualities calculated to produce temporal benefit, you would discover the same identity between Pagan and Christian piety, as there is between Pagan and Christian justice or veracity.

But the very reverse is most notoriously the fact. The injunctions and the practices of one religion are altogether different from those of every other. Believers in any one of them will view the rest with abhorrence. A Christian who visits a country where his religion has never been heard of, will doubtless expect to meet with just or veracious men, varying in frequency according to circumstances: but he will never once dream of discovering any Christians there. Christianity therefore does not consist in the manifestation of qualities which confer temporal benefit on mankind, since these are capable of universal growth in every climate.

A mere enquiry into the meaning of words will suffice to corroborate this. When we describe an individual as belonging to any particular religion, the epithet implies that he entertains a certain set of persuasions, attested either by his own confession, or by a conformity, besides, to a peculiar class of ceremonial practices which characterize the system. But by merely indicating the religion to which he adheres, no information has been conveyed as to his moral qualities, or whether his conduct is beneficial or noxious to his fellows. It may be either one or the other, whatever be the religion he adopts or believes in. In order to state with which class it ought to be ranked, we must employ a very different language. We must describe him as a good Pagan or a bad Pagan – a just or an unjust Mussulman – veracious or a liar.

Consequently an adherence to the injunctions of religion is something entirely different from an habitual performance of beneficial actions. For the latter are everywhere uniform and identical, while the mandates of religion are infinitely various: and farther, in mentioning the system of religion to which any individual belongs, we do not at all state whether his conduct is beneficent or pernicious – therefore an adherence to the system is perfectly consistent either with friendship or enmity to mankind.

3. If the injunctions of piety inculcated performance or abstinence merely according as the action specified was beneficial or injurious in the present life, religion would be precisely coincident with human laws. For these latter are destined only to ensure the same end, employing temporal instead of posthumous sanctions. Religion would command and forbid the very same action as the legislator, merely reinforcing his uncertain punishments with something more exquisite and more inevitable at the close of life. But it would give no new direction, of its own and for itself, to human conduct; it would originate no peculiar duties or crimes, but would appear

simply as an auxiliary, to second and confirm that bias which the legislator would have attempted to imprint without it.

Such would have been the case had the mandates of natural religion a tendency to produce temporal happiness. How widely different is the state of the fact! Throughout the globe, under every various system, we observe the most innocuous of human pleasures criminated and interdicted by piety; pleasures such as the worst of human legislators never forbad, and never could discover any pretence for forbidding. We observe a peculiar path of merit and demerit traced out exclusively by religion – embracing numerous actions which the law has left unnoticed, and which we may therefore infer, are not recognized as deserving either reward or punishment with reference to the present life. It is altogether impossible, therefore, that the mandates of natural religion can be directed to the promotion of temporal happiness, since they diverse so strikingly from the decrees of the legislator. Whatever other end they have in view, it cannot be the same as his.

Indeed in modern times an express discussion has arisen, whether the civil magistrate can with propriety interfere at all in matters of religion. Among the more enlightened thinkers, the doctrine of toleration, or that of leaving every man to recommend himself to God by the methods which he himself prefers, so long as he abstains from injuring others, seems to be fully recognized. Scarcely any one now is found to vindicate the exaction of a forced uniformity of worship. But the very existence of the dispute decisively implies, that religion is not naturally coincident, in her injunctions, with laws – that no pious ritual is of a character tending in itself to promote the happiness of society. The intolerant party attempted to enforce the propriety of giving to law an express extension over an apparently independent province; their opponents endeavoured to maintain this province still untouched and unregulated. If these acts could have been shown to be productive of temporal benefit or evil, this would have been the point on which the question would have been determined, as it is with regard to other cases of human conduct. No one would have contested the necessity, in the present times at least, of interdicting any acts of worship which might consist in wounding or plundering a neighbour. But the actual point in dispute was, whether out of a number of different rituals, perfectly on a level regarding temporal profit or injury, any particular one should be singly permitted and all the rest forbidden. The argument on one side was, that the Deity preferred the species of worship which they were advocating; the other side protested against this doctrine, as an unwarranted assumption of infallibility.

It is not my purpose to enter farther into this question, and I have only adduced it in order to evince, that the mandates of religion are altogether separate in their nature and application from those of law, and therefore cannot possibly be similar in the end which they are destined to ensure –

and also that this separation is virtually implied in both sides of the dispute on freedom of worship.

4. We uniformly find religious injunctions divided into two branches, the first embracing our duty to God, the second our duty to man. However beneficial may be the tendency of this latter section, it is quite impossible that the former can produce any temporal happiness. For it is, by the very definition, a rule restrictive of our conduct on those occasions when the interests of other men are not at all concerned. On these occasions the legislator would have left us unfettered, since every man naturally selects that path which is most conducive to his temporal felicity. If any other course is thrust upon him from without, it must infallibly be a sacrifice of earthly happiness.

That branch therefore, at least, of religious injunctions, which is termed *our duty to God*, must be regarded as detrimental to human felicity in this life. It is a deduction from the pleasures of the individual, without at all benefiting the species. It must be considered, so far as the present life is concerned, as a tax paid for the salutary direction which the branch termed *our duty to man* is said to imprint upon human conduct, and for the special and unequalled efficacy, with which these sanctions are alleged to operate. Supposing also the operation of this latter branch to be noxious instead of salutary, the payment of the tax will constitute so much additional evil.

CHAPTER V.

Of the Efficiency of the Inducements held out by Natural Religion. How far super-human Expectations can be regarded as likely to prove influential, where no human Inducements would be influential.

THERE is some difficulty in estimating exactly the extent of influence which the super-human inducements, held out by natural religion, actually exercise over mankind. They appear always intermixed and confounded among that crowd of motives, which in every society submitted to our experience, impel human conduct in various directions. For the solution of the present enquiry, however, it is indispensably requisite to detach from this confused assemblage the inducements of natural religion, and to measure the force of the impulse which they communicate.

There are two modes of determining this point. 1. By analysing the nature and properties of these super-human inducements, and comparing them with those human motives which commonly actuate our conduct. We shall thus discover how far those elements, which constitute and measure the force and efficiency of all human expectations, are to be found in the super-human. 2. By examining those cases where accident places them in a state of single and unassisted agency, and thus fortifying the preceding analysis with the direct certificate of experience, so far as that is attainable.

Before, however, we embark in this investigation, it will be important to examine in what degree the super-human expectations, supposing their influence purely beneficial, can be considered as indispensable instruments in the production of happiness in this life; or in other words, what is the number and importance of those cases in which human inducements would be inapplicable and inoperative, and in which posthumous expectations would effectually supply the defect.

It will be easy to see that such cases are comparatively neither numerous nor important. For wherever the legislator can distinguish what actions it is desirable either to encourage or to prevent, he can always annex to them a measure of temporal reward or punishment commensurate to the purpose. It is only necessary that he should be able to distinguish and define such actions. To affirm therefore the necessity of a recurrence to super-human agency for the repression of any definable mode of conduct, is merely to say that human laws are defective and require amendment. If this be true, let them be amended, and there will remain no ground for the complaint.

The gradations (you urge) by which guilt passes into innocence are often so nice as to be undiscoverable by the human eye, and to require the searching gaze of Omnipotence to detect their real point of separation. But if this be the case, how is it possible for the agent himself to know when he is acting well, and when he is verging towards evil? The two are undistinguishable to all men besides; why should they be otherwise to him? He knows his own intention, indeed, perfectly: it is to perform a certain action, of which no one can tell whether the tendency is beneficial or injurious. He himself cannot tell either; it is possible that he may suspect the action to be mischievous, and still intend to commit it. But he may be in error on this point, even after the most accurate consideration, and where the distinction between good and evil is so completely unassignable, the chances of error are as great as those of truth. Expectation of punishment, in case of wrong decision, could only render him more attentive in weighing the consequences, and even after this, it appears, he would be just as likely to decide wrong as right. Consequently the expectation of punishment produces no benefit whatever. Besides, if he can judge correctly, the foundations of such a judgment may be comprehended, and the offence defined, by the legislator. In all cases therefore in which guilt cannot be defined, and thence, no punishment awarded by the legislator, the apprehension of punishment from any foreign source is unproductive of any advantage.

But there are cases in which an individual may commit an act expressly forbidden by the law, relying on the impossibility or difficulty of detection. Doubtless there are such: and it is impossible to deny that on those occasions the apprehension of a posthumous verdict, from which there was no escape, *might possibly* supply an unavoidable defect in the reach of human laws. Secret crimes, however, are the only cases in which the super-human inducements can be pretended to effect an end to which human motives would be inadequate. In all other occasions, the inefficacy of human laws is merely a reproach to the legislator, who neglects to remedy a known defect. And even in the case of hidden delinquency, how frequently is the escape of the criminal owing to mistakes perfectly corrigible, such as an unskilful police, exclusion of evidence, barbarity in the punishment awarded, and other circumstances which tend to unnerve the arm of the law! Supposing these imperfections to be removed, – suppose the penal code to be comprehensive and methodical, and its execution cheap, speedy, and vigilant, it would scarcely be practicable for the criminal to escape detection, when it was known that the crime had been committed.

It is only, therefore, when a crime is known, and the criminal undiscoverable, that super-human inducements can be vindicated as indispensably necessary for the maintenance of good conduct. And as these cases must, under a well-contrived system, be uncommonly rare, the necessity and importance of such inducements must be restricted within very narrow limits.

This is a point of some consequence. For if it should appear that these posthumous expectations are on many occasions of injurious tendency, the immediate inquiry must be, what exclusive benefit this mode of operating upon human conduct presents, in preference to any other. In reply to which, we have just demonstrated, that those cases in which beneficial influence is derivable solely from this source and not from any other, are few and inconsiderable. The extent of evil in this life would therefore be trifling, were super-human inducements entirely effaced from the human bosom, and earthly institutions ameliorated according to the progress of philosophy. The pernicious tendency, which the former manifest on many occasions, will thus be compensated only by a very slender portion of essential and exclusive benefit.

These considerations also evince, that if it were practicable to supply the defect of human restrictions by recourse to a foreign world, we should be anxious to import active and faithful informers – to purchase such a revelation as would render our inferences of criminality more easy, precise, and extensive, in order that guilt might never escape our detection. We should not desire to introduce instruments for multiplying and protracting human torture. With these we are abundantly provided, if it were prudent or desirable to employ them. No earthly legislator, therefore, would attempt, if in his power, to perfect the efficacy of temporal enactments in the mode by which it is pretended that posthumous expectations accomplish this beneficial end.

CHAPTER VI.

Efficiency of super-human inducements to produce temporal Evil. Their inefficiency to produce temporal Good.

SINCE it has been shown in a former chapter that the directive rule, to which the inducements of natural religion attach themselves, will infallibly be detrimental to human happiness, it follows of course that these inducements, if they produce any effect at all, must be efficient to a mischievous purpose. I now propose to investigate the extent of influence which they exercise over mankind, as well as the manner of their operation.

All inducements are expectations either of pleasure or pain. The force with which all expectations act upon the human bosom varies according as they differ in, 1. Intensity, – 2. Duration, – 3. Certainty, – 4. Propinquity. These are the four elements of value which constitute and measure the comparative strength of all human motives.

Take for example an expected pleasure. What are the motives which govern a man in the investment of money. He prefers that mode in which the profits are largest, most certain, and quickest. Present to him a speculation of greater hazard or in which he must be kept longer out of his money; the value of such an expectation is less, and he will not embrace it unless allured by a larger profit. Deficiency in certainty and propinquity will thus be compensated by an increase of intensity and duration.

To appreciate, therefore, the sway which posthumous expectations exercise over the behaviour of mankind, we must examine to what degree they comprise these elements of value.

First, they are to the highest degree deficient in *propinquity*. Every one conceives them as extremely remote; and in the greatest number of instances, such remoteness is conformable to experience, as insurance calculations testify.

Secondly, they are also defective in *certainty*. Posthumous pleasures and pains are reserved to be awarded in the lump, after a series of years. The only possible mode of distributing them at such a period must be by reviewing the whole life of the individual – by computing his meritorious and culpable acts and striking a balance between them. It is impossible to conceive an expectation more deplorably uncertain, than that which such a scale of award must generate. In order to strip it of this character of doubt, the individual should have kept an exact journal of his debtor and creditor account with regard to post-obituary dispensations. Who ever does or ever did this? Yet if it is not done, so universal is self-deceit, that every man will unquestionably over-estimate his own extent of observance. His impression will thus be, that he has a balance in hand, and that the performance of any particular forbidden act will but slightly lessen the ample remainder which awaits him. But suppose it otherwise – let him imagine that the balance is against him. There still remains the chance of future amendment and compensation, by which it may be rendered favourable, and this prospect is incalculably more liable to exaggeration than the estimate which he forms of his past conduct.

The prodigious excess to which mankind heap up splendid purposes for the coming year, is matter of notoriety and even of ridicule. A slight accession of punishment incurred by what the individual may be about to do at the moment will be lost in the contemplation of the mass of subsequent reward. Posthumous expectations must, therefore, under every supposition, be pre-eminently defective in the element of certainty.

To make up for this want of certainty and propinquity, the pleasures and pains anticipated in a future life are (it will be urged) intense and durable to the utmost extent. Imagination, no doubt, (our sole guide under unassisted natural religion,) may magnify and protract them beyond all limit, since there is no direct testimony which can check her career. But it should be remarked that this excessive intensity and permanence can never be otherwise than purely imaginary, nor can the most appalling descriptions of fancy ever impart to them that steady and equable impressiveness which characterises a real scene subjected to the senses. As all our ideas of pleasure and pain are borrowed from experience, the most vivid anticipations we can frame cannot possibly surpass the liveliest sensation. Magnify the intensity as you will, this must be its ultimate boundary. But you never can stretch it even so high as this point: for to do this would be to exalt the conceptions of fancy to a level with real and actual experience, so that the former shall affect the mind as vividly as the latter, which is the sole characteristic of insanity, and the single warrant for depriving the unhappy madman of his liberty.

If, indeed, the expectations actually created in the mind corresponded in appalling effect to the descriptions of the fancy – and if the defects of certainty and propinquity could be so far counteracted as to leave these expectations in full possession of the mind – the result must be, absolute privation of reason, and an entire sacrifice of all sublunary enjoyment. The path of life must lie as it were on the brink of a terrific precipice, where it would be impossible to preserve a sound and distinct vision, and where the imminent and inextricable peril of our situation would altogether absorb the mind, so as to leave us no opportunity for building up any associations of comfort or delight. A man who is to have an operation performed in a short space of time, cannot dismiss it from his thoughts for an instant; how much less, if he sees, or believes that he sees, a gigantic hand, armed with instruments of exquisite torture, and menacing his defenceless frame?

Such must be the result, if these anticipations did really affect the mind in a degree proportional to their imagined intensity. They cannot be conceived as tolerably near and certain, without driving the believer mad, and without rendering it a far more desirable lot for him to have had no life at all, than the two lives taken together. Looking therefore to the happiness of the present life alone, it appears to be merely saved from complete annihilation by that diminished influence of the posthumous prospects which distance and uncertainty cannot fail to occasion. It is their inefficiency, and not their efficiency, which constitutes the safeguard of human comfort.

But what is the real value of this residuary influence? To determine this question, we must consult the analogy of human conduct and observe the effect of large expectations, when remote and uncertain, as compared with others of small amount, but close at hand and specific.

How painful are the apprehensions which the approach of death creates! To preserve the mind from being altogether overpowered by them, and to maintain a cool deportment at such an instant, is supposed to be an effort of more than human firmness. Thus terrible and overwhelming is the prospect when merely approximated to the eye. Strip it of its propinquity, and all its effects upon the mind immediately vanishes. Its real terrors, its ultimate certainty, remain unimpaired; but delay the moment, for a few years at farthest, and the whole scene is immediately dismissed from the thoughts. So confident and neglectful do we become upon the subject, that it requires more than ordinary forethought to make those provisions which a due regard to the happiness of our survivors would enjoin.

This is an illustration of peculiar value, because it is a case in which mere remoteness practically annuls the most dreadful of all expectations, without insinuating even the most transient suspicion of ultimate escape. But if distance alone will produce so striking a deduction, how much will its negative effect be heightened, when coupled with uncertainty as to the eventful fulfilment? It seems apparent that these two negative circumstances, taken together, must altogether prevent the most painful anticipations from ever affecting the mind, unless under very peculiar circumstances, which we shall presently notice.[2]

Analogy therefore seems to testify most indisputably, that sufferings so remote and so uncertain as those of a posthumous life, whatever may be

---

[2]   This important principle, that a small amount of pain, if quick and certain in its application, provides a more effectual restraint than the most painful death, when delay and the chance of complete escape is interposed – seems to be pretty generally recognized at the present day. Instruments of torture have consequently become obsolete; and most of the alterations of the legislator have been designed to cure the lame foot, and to accelerate the pace of justice. In this, indeed, his aim has been not merely to prevent in the most complete manner the commission of crime, but also to prevent it at the expense of the smallest possible aggregate of suffering. For to denounce penalties of shocking severity, but tardy and uncertain in their execution, would be to create the greatest sum of artificial pain, with the least possible preventive effect. This would be entirely at variance with the genuine spirit of legislation, whose end is the extension of human happiness by the eradication of noxious acts. This, however, cannot be the purpose of the God of natural religion; who is uniformly conceived (as I have before remarked) to delight in human misery, and who is therefore supposed, with perfect consistency, to inflict pain where the pain itself cannot produce a particle of benefit, and where the anticipation of it can have no effect whatever in repressing vicious conduct.

their fancied intensity, can scarcely affect the mind at all, in its natural state. Such anticipations can only obtain possession of it when introduced by other analogous ideas, which have previously perverted the usual current of thought, and rendered it fit for their reception. Under such circumstances, these new allies cannot fail to aggravate most powerfully that tone of sentiment to which they owe their origin. Their distance and uncertainty will be forgotten, and they will be conceived as imminent and inevitable; while the impression of their intensity will be more vehement than ever. Such will be the case in the peculiar state of mind to which we here allude; but taking mankind as they usually think and judge, it is altogether contrary to experience that posthumous expectations should ever be otherwise than nugatory.

Now, if, according to the general tenor of thought, they become thus dormant and inoperative, they cannot possibly be employed as restraints upon crime. For when crime is committed, the mind is under the sway of a present and actuating temptation. It is not only exempt from all such associations as might contribute to kindle up the thoughts of posthumous terrors; but it is under the strong grasp and impulse of a contrary passion, which fills it with ideas of a totally opposite character. So completely indeed does the temptation absorb the whole soul, that it is difficult in many cases to counteract it by the most immediate and unequivocal prospect of impending evil. But unless the punishment denounced obtrudes itself upon the delinquent with a force sufficiently pressing and inflexible to overbear the sophistry of temptation, we may be assured that he will be insensible to the threats and will commit the crime. How much more then, where the apprehended evil is so remote and uncertain, and the value of the expectation so fluctuating and occasional, as to require a peculiarly favourable tone of thought before the mind can be induced to harbour it? We are surely authorised in deeming an expectation so constituted altogether useless as a motive to resist any strong desire.

But what is that preliminary state of mind into which posthumous apprehensions find so easy an admittance? It is that in which congenial feelings have been predominant – a state of timidity and depression, when gloomy associations overspread the whole man, and cast horror and wretchedness round his future prospects. In this condition, the fountains of all painful thought are opened, and posthumous terrors present an inexhaustible fund of kindred matter. Their distance and their uncertainty are of no consequence, for the mensuration of the mental eye is at such a period confounded, and it distinguishes not the scene before it. Their indeterminate character renders them only the more appropriate, for the imagination demands but a plausible pretence and outline to conjure up the amplest detail of terrific particulars. In sickness and in nervous despondency, associations of this kind make their most disastrous inroads, and contribute most actively to plunge the mind into that state of unassuageable terror, which borders so closely on insanity, and frequently terminates in it. And in the hour of death, when these apprehensions seem on the brink of reality, they obtrude themselves in thick and appalling clouds, and aggravate that prostration both of bodily and mental faculties, which marks the close of existence.

Such is the force, and such the mode of operation, belonging to these super-human expectations, when acting singly. And it appears from hence most undeniably, that they are almost wholly inefficient on every occasion when it might have been possible for them to enlarge the sum of temporal happiness – and efficient only in cases where they swell the amount of temporal misery.

For the only benefit which they are calculated to accomplish would be the repression of crimes. To this purpose it has been shown that they are wholly inadequate; for during the influence of temptation, the only season in which a man commits crime, they find no place in the mind, and therefore can interpose no barrier. On the other hand, they act with the highest effect at a period when they cannot by possibility produce any temporal benefit – that is, at the close of life: and the extent of their influence is always in an inverse ratio to the demand for it. The greater the previous despondency, the wider the space which they occupy, and the more powerfully do they contribute to heighten those morbid associations which the overmastered reason is unable to dispel.

CHAPTER VII.
Analysis of the source from whence the real Efficiency of super-human Enjoyments is almost wholly derived.

SINCE the inducements which we have been discussing are altogether impotent as a barrier to temptation, and influential only in peculiar states of mind, how happens it (we may be asked) that their dominion in human affairs should be apparently so extensive? The cause of this seeming contrariety, which merely arises from a misconception regarding the actual motives of mankind, I shall now endeavour to unfold.

It has already been shown that the God of natural religion is uniformly conceived as delighting in the contemplation of his own superiority and in the receipt of human obedience – that is, in the debasement, the privations, and the misery of mankind. Now each man has a strong temptation to elude any payment,[3] in his own person, of these unpleasant burthens; but

---

[3]   The Reverend Mr. Colton, (in a collection of thoughts entitled 'Lacon' – Vol. 1. XXV.) says, 'Men will wrangle for religion; write for it; fight for it; die for it; *anything but – live for it.*' The same divine also asserts, in the same volume, CLXXXIX. 'Where true religion has prevented one crime, false religions have afforded a pretext for a thousand.' There cannot be a stronger acknowledgment of the enormous balance of temporal evil, which religion, considered on the whole, inflicts on mankind.

he has no temptation whatever to avert from others the necessity of paying them. On the contrary, a powerful interest inclines him to exert himself in strictly exacting from every other man the requisite quota. For the Diety, pleased with human obedience, will of course be pleased with those faithful allies who aid him in obtaining it, and will in consideration of this assistance be more indulgent towards themselves. Each man, therefore, anxious for the lighter and more profitable service, will take part with God, and will volunteer his efforts to enforce upon all other men that line of conduct most agreeable to the divine Being. This spontaneous zeal in extorting payment from his brother debtors will dispose the creditor to remit or to alleviate his own debt.

But each individual will also be perfectly conscious that these temptations are equally active in the bosoms of his neighbours. They also are upon the watch to recommend themselves to God, by avenging his insulted name, and obviating any interruptions to the leisure and satisfaction of Omnipotence. They readily bring forward their terrestrial reinforcements – abuse, hatred, and injury, against any individual who forswears his allegiance to the unseen sovereign – eulogy and veneration towards him who renders it with more than ordinary strictness. Each man is thus placed under the surveillance of the rest. A strong public antipathy is pointed against impious conduct; the decided approbation of the popular voice is secured in favour of religious acts. The praise or blame of his earthly companions will thus become the real actuating motive to religious observances on the part of each individual. By an opposite conduct it is not merely the divine denunciations that he provokes, but also the hostility of innumerable crusaders, who long to expiate their own debts by implacable warfare against the recusant.

But although thus in fact determined to a pious behaviour by the esteem and censure of his fellows, he will have the highest interest in disguising this actual motive, and in pretending to be influenced only by genuine veneration for the being whom he worships. A religious act, if performed from any other than a religious feeling, loses its character of exclusive reference to the Deity, and of course ceases to be agreeable to him. But if God is no longer satisfied with the semi-voluntary performance of the service required, neither will the neighbourhood, who take up arms in God's favour, be satisfied with it. No individual, therefore, will be able to steer clear of the public enmity, unless he not only renders these pious acts of homage, but also succeeds in convincing others that he is actuated in rendering them entirely by the fear of God. The popular sanction, therefore, not only enforces the delivery of the homage; it also compels the deliverer to carry all the marks of being influenced solely by religious inducements, and to pretend that he would act precisely in the same manner, whatever might be the sentiments of his neighbours.

The same pretence, too, will be encouraged by other considerations.

When a man is once compelled by some extraneous motive to go through the service, it will be his interest to claim all that merit in the eyes of God which a spontaneous performance of it would have insured. He will, therefore, assume all the exterior mien of a voluntary subjection to the invisible Being, and will endeavour to deceive himself into a belief that this is his genuine motive. In this self-imposition he will most commonly succeed, and his account of his own conduct, originally insincere, will in time be converted into unconscious and unintentional error.

We can now interpret this seeming contrariety between the natural impotence and the alleged apparent dominion, of religious inducements. For the real fact is, that they enlist in their service the irresistible arm of public opinion – and that too in a manner which secures to themselves all the credit of swaying mankind, while the actually determining motive is by general consent suppressed and kept out of view.

Religion is thus enabled to apply, for the encouragement and discouragement of those acts which fall within her sphere, the very same engines as morality. Moral conduct springs from the mutual wants and interests of mankind. It is each man's interest that his neighbour should be virtuous; hence each man knows that the public opinion will approve his conduct, if virtuous – reprobate it, if vicious. Religious acts, indeed, no man has any motive to approve from any benefit conferred by the actual performance of them; or, to disapprove the opposite behaviour from any injury referable to it. But every man has something to gain by being active in enforcing upon others the performance of these acts – inasmuch as this is a co-operation with the views of God, which may have the effect of partially discharging, or at least of lightening, his own obligations. The same encouragements and prohibition, therefore, which mankind apply to virtue and to vice, they will be led to annex, though from a totally opposite motive, to pious or impious behaviour.

When the public opinion has once occasioned, as it cannot fail to do, a tolerably extensive diffusion of religious practices throughout the community, the censures directed against any small remainder of nonconformists will be embittered by the concurrent action of envy. I feel myself constrained to be rigidly exact in the renewal of my pious offerings: shall my neighbour, who eludes all share in the burthen and will not deduct a moment from his favourite pursuits for similar purposes, be treated with the same courtesy and respect as myself, who expend so much self-denial in order to ensure it? Is not the labourer worthy of his hire? Being myself a scrupulous renderer of these services, it becomes my interest, even with my fellow-countrymen, to swell the merit of performing them, and the criminality of neglect, to the highest possible pitch, in order to create a proportionate distribution of their esteem. The more deeply I can impress this conviction upon mankind, the greater will be their veneration for me. All these principles conspire to sharpen my acrimony against my nonconforming neighbour, and render me doubly dissatisfied with that state of respite and impunity in which Omnipotence still permits him to live. In this condition of mind, nothing can be more gratifying than the self-assumed task of executing the divine wrath upon his predestined head.

CHAPTER VIII.
Proof of the Inefficiency of super-human Inducements, when unassisted by, or at variance with, public Opinion.

BY the preceding analysis I have attempted to show that the apparent influence of posthumous expectations is at the bottom nothing more than a disguised and peculiar agency of public opinion; and also to trace the process by which these expectations naturally and infallibly give birth to such an inflexion of the popular voice. I now propose to confirm this explanation still farther, by citing a few most convincing examples of the complete disregard with which posthumous anticipations are treated, when the voice of the public either opposes, or ceases to enforce, their influence.

For this purpose it will be absolutely necessary to allege instances from revealed religion, because it is only by means of revelation that a written, unvarying collection of precepts has become promulgated, completely independent of any variations which may take place in the national feeling. In natural religion it is impossible to discover what is the course of action enjoined, except by consulting the reigning tone of practice and sentiment; and, therefore, the two must necessarily appear harmonious and coincident, since we can only infer the former from the latter. Revelation alone communicates a known and authoritative code, with which the actual conduct of believers may be compared, and the points of conformity or separation ascertained.

1. The first practice which may be cited as manifesting the impotence of religious precepts, when opposed to public opinion, is that of duelling. Nothing can be more notoriously contrary to the divine law; which acts too on this occasion with every possible advantage, except the alliance of the popular voice. For the practice which religion here interdicts is attended with pain and hazard to the person committing it, and often with the most ruinous consequences to his surviving relatives. If ever super-human inducements could ensure obedience when opposed to the popular sanction, it would be in a case where all other motives conspire to aid them.

If posthumous enjoyments were the actual reward aimed at, and the real motive for religious conduct, this concurrence of other inducements would swell their influence and render them preponderant. But the truth is, that they are not the actual reward sought by the religionist. What he desires is, *to prove to the satisfaction of other men that they are so* – to acquire in their eyes the credit of unbounded attachment to the Deity. No man will give him credit for any such attachment, simply because he declines a duel.

He knows that the world will ascribe his refusal to cowardice – and thus the concurrence of motives abates and enfeebles, instead of confirming, the efficacy of the religious precept. He will be more ready to inflict upon himself severe bodily sufferings, in compliance with the divine code, than to follow its precepts where mankind will give him no credit for the sincerity of his obedience.

Whether, however, the justice of this solution be admitted or denied, the instance of duelling must in either case demonstrate the inefficiency of religious inducements, when opposed to public opinion.

2. *Fornication* is an act directly forbidden by the super-human code – but not forbidden by the popular voice. The latter, however, does not in this case imperatively demand the infringement of the prohibitory precept, as it did in the case of the duel; but merely leaves the divine admonition to operate unsupported. To what extent it operates thus single-handed, the state of all great cities notoriously attests.

3. *Simony*, again, is forbidden in the religious code with equal strictness, and practised with equal frequency.

4. But perhaps the case in which the impotence of posthumous apprehensions is most glaring and manifest, is that of *perjury*. The person who takes an oath solemnly calls down upon himself the largest measure of divine vengeance, if he commits a particular act. In this imprecation it is implied, that he firmly anticipates the infliction of these penalties, if he becomes guilty of this self-condemned behaviour. Yet this expectation, which he thus attests and promulgates, of posthumous inflictions, has not, when stript of the consentient impulse of public opinion, the slenderest hold upon his actions. It cannot make him forego any temptation, however small; as an appeal to unexceptionable facts will evince.

Every young man, who is entered at the University of Oxford, is obliged to take an oath, that he will observe the statutes of the University – a collection of rules for his conduct while he is a student, framed many years ago by Archbishop Laud. On this oath, after it has been once taken, not a thought is bestowed, even by the most scrupulous religionist. Its precepts are altogether unheeded and forgotten – infringed of course on every occasion when the observance of them is at all inconvenient. The conduct of all the swearers is precisely the same as it would have been had the oath never been taken. All the posthumous vengeance which they have imprecated upon themselves – all the super-human inflictions which they firmly anticipate – suffice not to produce the most trivial alteration of behaviour. Yet an adherence to some at least among the injunctions thus solemnly sealed, would entail scarcely any inconvenience at all. Slight, however, as this inconvenience is, the fear of post-obituary penalties is still slighter, and, therefore, even the easy means of averting them are altogether neglected.

The regulations prescribed by the oath, it will be said, are useless, and, therefore, there is no necessity for observing them. This may be very true, and may afford an unanswerable reason for discontinuing the form altogether: but it offers not the shadow of a plea for neglecting its dictates, when you have once gone through the ceremonial. By virtue of the oath, you have imposed upon yourself a special obligation to the performance of certain acts; you bind yourself by your apprehension of posthumous visitations in case of failure, and in order to obviate all reluctance on the part of the Almighty, you state your own fervent desire to be so treated. Whatever obligatory force was comprised in the formula, can never be impaired by your discovery that the act enjoined will produce no beneficial consequence.

The uselessness of these regulations is, indeed, the real cause why the oath to fulfil them remains universally unobserved. But why? Because the popular voice has no longer any interest in enforcing them. But the strength of the posthumous fears remains unaltered – and the result attests most strikingly *their* debility and nothingness.

As another confirmation of this doctrine, let us remark the conduct of Jurors, when they administer a law which popular opinion, as well as they themselves, condemn as sanguinary and impolitic. How undisguised is the manner in which they infringe their oaths in order to elude the necessity of passing a capital sentence! In defiance of the most irresistible testimony, they find a man guilty of stealing under the value of forty shillings, and thus consign him to the milder and more appropriate punishment. Whence comes it that the force of the oath, weighty and inflexible up to this point, suddenly dissolves into nothing and is shorn of all its credit? It is because the popular voice has ceased to uphold it. Public opinion gave, and public opinon has taken away; and all the sway, which super-human expectations possess over human behaviour, is surreptitiously procured, from their coincidence with this omnipotent sanction.

Though it is popular opinion, or the desire of temporal esteem, which forms the actuating stimulus to religious observances, yet there are unquestionably instances in which such works have been faithfully performed without any prospect of consequent credit – nay, perhaps, in spite of bitter and predominant enmity. This is perfectly conformable to the general analogy of nature. For when the associations of credit have once linked themselves with any course of behaviour, by conversation with a peculiar class, by strong personal affection, or any other cause – when the feeling of self-respect has become attached to that course – an individual will not unfrequently persevere in it, though the harvest which he reaps may not actually gratify and realize the association. What is the motive which impels the friends of mankind to exert themselves in reforming a bad government? It springs unquestionably from the desire of esteem; first the desire of obtaining it, then that of deserving it, whether it is actually attainable or not. A similar anxiety, for veneration and influence over the sentiments of others, possesses the religionist, even when he both anticipates and encounters unqualified obloquy; and the fury of proselytism, which is inseparable from his tone of feeling, attests this beyond all dispute. Even the solitary penance of the monk springs from the very same principle; for the association of credit, when once deeply implanted, will govern human conduct, though there should be no prospect of realizing the hope which originally engendered it.

In addition to this it should be remarked, that no one can question the powerful influence exercised by super-human inducements, in some peculiar cases. They sometimes produce insanity. But these are exceptions to their usual impotence, and cannot be admitted as evidence against the general conclusion which we have just established.

As it has been demonstrated that all the efficacy of posthumous inducements is in reality referable to their alliance with public opinion – we at once discover the weakness of that plea by which these inducements were asserted to affect secret crimes, uncognizable by human laws. He who entertains confident hopes of perpetrating a misdeed without detection, will of course pay no regard to the popular voice. Nor will the fear of future pains, stripped of that auxiliary which alone renders it formidable, counteract a temptation to delinquency, when we see that it cannot prevail upon an Oxford student to undergo the smallest inconvenience. That the conduct of the former is guilty and injurious – the neglect of the latter, innocent – is a distinction which does not in the least vitiate the analogy. They are both under the special and solitary restraint, whatever be its power, which super-human terrors impose. The one therefore may serve as an unexceptionable measure of the other. Nay, if anything, these fears ought to be more potent and effective in the case of the Oxford student, than in that of the secret criminal – inasmuch as the former has himself solicited and sanctioned their infliction, and has originated his own claim for their fulfilment.

But if posthumous apprehensions are inapplicable for the coercion of secret crime, it cannot be pretended that they are ever necessary – for human enactments will embrace all open and definable delinquency. To say that earthly laws do not actually perform this, is merely to affirm that governments are defective and ought to be reformed.

Recapitulation
The foregoing search into the nature and action of those posthumous expectations which unassisted natural religion furnishes, has evinced, I trust conclusively: 1. That in the absence of any authorized directive rule, the class of actions which our best founded inference would suggest as entitling the performer to post-obituary reward, is one not merely useless, but strikingly detrimental, to mankind in the present life; while the class conceived as meriting future punishment, is one always innocuous, often

beneficial, to our fellow-creatures on earth. 2. That from the character and properties of posthumous inducements, they infallibly become impotent for the purpose of resisting any temptation whatever, and efficient only in the production of needless and unprofitable misery. 3. That the influence exercised by these inducements is, in most cases, really derived from the popular sanction, which they are enabled to bias and enlist in their favour.

If these conclusions are correct, I think it cannot be denied, that the influence possessed by natural religion over human conduct is, with reference to the present life, injurious to an extent incalculably greater than it is beneficial. For if it ever does produce benefit, this must be owing to casual and peculiar associations in the minds of some few believers, who form an exception to the larger body. It is by no means my design to question the existence of some persons thus happily born or endowed. But it would be most unsafe and perilous to build our general doctrine on a few such instances of rare merit. We can only determine the general operation of these inducements, or the effect which they produce on the greatest number of minds, by analyzing their nature and properties, and by contemplating the result which these properties bring about in other known cases. This is what has been here attempted, and the inquiry has demonstrated that the agency of superhuman motives must in the larger aggregate of instances, produce effects decidedly pernicious to earthly happiness.

Having thus ascertained that the general influence of unaided natural religion is mischievous, with reference to the present life, I shall now proceed to expose the mischief more in detail, – to particularize and classify its various forms.

JEREMY BENTHAM

III

Not Paul, but Jesus (1823)

Ch. XIII
Paul's supposable *Miracles* explained

Jeremy Bentham

Note on Text III

Editorial questions similar to those which surround the publication of the *Analysis* hang over the production of *Not Paul, but Jesus* (1823). The book bore the witty if irreverent nom de plume 'Gamaliel Smith', after a New Testament teacher of Judaic law. Bentham's authorship was not long a secret. At least one critic knew that it came from the hand of 'a celebrated writer on legislation'.[1] However, according to a note by Francis Plate in his personal copy of the work 'the matter of this book was put together by me at Mr. Bentham's request in the months of August and September 1817 – during my residence with him at Ford Abbey, Devonshire'.[2] The meaning of 'put together' here is the source of whatever doubts exist about Bentham's authorship. Graham Wallas asserts that the manuscripts for *Not Paul, but Jesus* were 'rearranged, condensed and "pulled together" in making the book'.[3] It may be that Place had some hand in this, but it is difficult to substantiate what actually occurred. Unfortunately, Place's letters and diaries make no mention of the matter.[4] Entries in the diary of John Colls reveal that the manuscripts were passed to Place via Bentham's associate John Bowring in January 1821, and the *Summary View of a Work, intitled Not Paul, but Jesus*, published later that same year, announced that the work would be speedily published. Yet on 25 January 1823 Bentham was still enquiring of Place how the work was progressing.[5] Most of the manuscripts with the title 'Not Paul' were suppressed by Bentham in the hope that they would be more welcome at some future date. This material includes a 'Church History from Jesus' Ascension to Paul's Conversion';[6]

---

[1] 'Ben David' [pseudonym of the Unitarian minister John Jones], *A Reply to Two Deistical Works, entitled 'The New Trial of the Witnesses', Ec. and Gamaliel Smith's 'Not Paul, but Jesus'* (London 1824), p. 1 (later referring to Bentham by name, p. 173 note).

[2] This copy, inscribed 'From Mr. Bentham Sep. 29, 1823, FP', is in the Library at University College London.

[3] See the note attached by Wallas to Place's personal copy of *Not Paul, but Jesus* (note 2 above).

[4] As George Wallas remarked in *The Life of Francis Place 1771–1854* (1898; 4th edn., London 1951), p. 84 note, 'the whole Utilitarian circle for obvious reasons kept that side of their work rather quiet'.

[5] Bentham to Place (25 Jan. 1823), Bentham MSS, University College London, clxxiii. 92. Henceforth UCL.

[6] UCL cxxxix. 445–571, dated 1817, 1819, 1823. These dates and those in the notes below are taken from A. T. Milne, *Catalogue of the Manuscripts of Jeremy Bentham in the Library of University College* (1937; 2nd edn. London, 1962).

an unpublished appendix with the title 'Paul's Inducements';[7] material on the doctrinal differences between Paul and Jesus;[8] the intended second volume or part to *Not Paul, but Jesus*, entitled 'Sextus', which is a discussion of asceticism;[9] and, finally, the planned third part of *Not Paul, but Jesus* (a continuation of part two) with the title 'Asceticism: its repugnancy to the religion of Jesus'.[10] What remains of the material upon which the published work is based accounts for only a few of its many sections.[11] Consequently, from this evidence it is difficult to say with precision just how much of a hand Place had in the book.

In his *Autobiography* Place explicitly attributed the work to Bentham and even allowing for modesty there is no reason to doubt him.[12] As a confessed atheist Place welcomed the publication of anti-religious literature and would eagerly have assisted in any such enterprise.[13] But he was no Greek scholar (Bentham worked from a Greek Bible) and the levity with which the subject of revelation is approached is quite beyond anything Place is reputed to have been able to manage.[14] There seems little doubt that he played only a minor role, and that purely as an editor of sorts, in the publication of what the mysterious Martha Colls described in a letter to Étienne Dumont, one of Bentham's editors, as 'the comical book'.[15]

No later editions of *Not Paul, but Jesus* were published. The following extract is from the original publication of 1823, printed for John Hunt of Old Bond Street and Tavistock Street in Covent Garden, London.

---

[7]   UCL cxxxix. 332–444, dated 1816–18, 1823.
[8]   UCL clxia. 141–214, dated 1816–18.
[9]   UCL lxxiva. 35–222, dated 1814, 1816. This material harks back to some earlier fragments on 'Sexual Nonconformity' of *c.*1774 and 1785 (UCL lxxiii. 90–100 and lxxiva 1–26; lxxii. 187–205 and lxxiva. 27–34).
[10] UCL clxib. 215–523, dated 1816–18. In BL Add. Mss 29806–809, given by Bentham to Grote (see above pp. 341–43 and notes), there are sections related to the material intended for *Not Paul, but Jesus*.
[11] UCL cxxxix. 212–331, dated 1813, 1815, 1817, 1821.
[12] *The Autobiography of Francis Place (1771–1854)*, ed. Mary Thrale (Cambridge 1972), p. 8.
[13] For evidence of which see *The Autobiography of Francis Place*, pp. xxiii, 45–46, 121, 197–98 note.
[14] That Place's own writing is uniformly dull and humourless is testified on all hands (see the article on Place in the *Dictionary of National Biography*; Thrale's introduction to Place's *Autobiography*; and Wallas' *Life of Francis Place*, p. 39.
[15] Martha Colls to Dumont (29 Nov. 1823), Dumont MSS 33, iii, fol. 382, Bibliotheque Publique Universitaire, Geneva, from a transcription at the Bentham Project, UCL. The identity of Martha Colls is a mystery – it may well have been Bentham playing a practical joke on Dumont.

Not Paul, but Jesus

CHAPTER XIII.
Paul's supposable Miracles *explained.*

SECTION 1.
OBJECTIONS, APPLYING TO THEM IN THE AGGREGATE.

BUT, it may be said, Paul's alleged commission from God was certainly genuine; for it is proved by his miracles. Look at the Acts, no fewer than twelve miracles of his you will find. If then taken by themselves, for want of that accurate conception of the probative form of evidence, to which maturer ages have given birth, the account of the miracle by which his conversion was wrought fails of being completely satisfactory, – look at his miracles, the deficiency will be filled up. The man, to whom God had imparted such extraordinary powers – powers so completely matchless in these our times, – can such a man have been a liar – an impostor? a liar for the purpose of deceit – of giving support to a system of deception – and that a lucrative one? An imposition so persevering as to have been carried on, from youth to death, through, perhaps, the greatest part of his life?

The observation is plausible: – the answer will not be the less satisfactory.

The answer has two branches: one, *general,* applying to all the alleged miracles in question, taken in the lump: the other *particular,* applying to the several miracles separately considered.

Observations applying to the whole together are the following:

1. Not by Paul himself, in any one of his own Epistles, is any such general assertion made, as that he had received from God or from Jesus, – or, in a word, that he was in possession of, any such power, as the power of working miracles.

2. Nowhere in the account given of his transactions by the author of the Acts, is he in any of his speeches represented as making reference to any one act of his in the character of a miracle.

3. Nowhere in that same account, is he represented as stating himself to be in possession of any such powers.

4. Not by the author of the Acts, is he spoken of as being in possession of any such power.

5. Nowhere by the author of the Acts, is he in any general terms spoken of, as producing any effects, such as, in respect of the power necessary to

the production of them, approach to those spoken of as having been produced by Simon Magus; by that declared impostor, in whose instance, no such commission from God is represented as having been received.

6. Neither on the occasion of his conversion, nor on any other occasion, is Paul stated to have received from Jesus any such power as that of working miracles: – any such power as the real Apostles are – in Mark xvi. 15, 16, 17, 18 – stated to have received from Jesus.

Was it that, in his own conception, for gaining credence to his pretension of a commission from Jesus – from Jesus, styled by him the Lord Jesus – any need of miracles, or of a persuasion, on the part of those with whom he had to deal, of *his* having power to work miracles? By no means. Of the negative, the story told by him of the manner of his conversion is abundant proof. Of the efficient cause of this change in his mind, the account given, is plainly given in the character of the account of a miracle. But of this miracle, the proof given consists solely in his own evidence: his own statement, unsupported by that of any other person, or by reference to that of any other person: his account, of the discourse, which on the occasion of the vision, in which nothing was seen but a flood of light, he heard from the Lord Jesus: his own account, of the vision, which he says was seen by Ananias: his own account, of that other vision, which, according to Ananias, he (Paul) had had, but of which Paul himself says nothing.

In the work of his adherent and sole biographer, the author of *the Acts*, – we have five speeches, made by him, in vindication of his conduct, in the character of a preacher of the religion of Jesus; and, from his own hand, Epistles out of number: yet nowhere is any reference made, to so much as a single miracle wrought by his own hand, unless the trance which he falls into when he is alone, and the vision which he sees, when nobody else sees any thing, are to be placed to the account of miracles. Miracles? *On* him, yes; *by* him, no. True it is, that, on one occasion, he speaks in general terms of 'signs and wonders,' as having been wrought by him. But vague, in the highest degree, is the import, as well as wide the extent, of those general terms: nor is it by any means clear, that, even by himself, any such claim was meant to be brought forward, as that of having exhibited any such manifestations of supernatural power, as are commonly regarded as designated by the word *miracles*. In the multitude of the persons, whom, in places so widely distant from one another, he succeeded in numbering in the list of his followers – in the depth of the impression, supposed to have been made on the heart of this or that one of them – in all or any one of these circumstances, it was natural he should himself behold, and, whether he did or no, use his endeavours to cause others to behold, not only so many sources of wonder, but so many circumstances; all conspiring to increase the quantity of that confidence, which, with so much industry, and, as far as appears, with such brilliant success, he was labouring to plant in every breast: circumstances, serving, in the minds of his adherents in general, in the character of a sign or proof, of the legitimacy of his pretension, as above.

But, of any such supernatural power as that which is here in question, could any such loose and vague expressions be reasonably regarded as affording any sort of proof? No: – unless whatsoever, in the affairs of men, can justly be regarded as *wonderful*, ought also to be regarded as a miracle.

In one passage, and one alone, either in the Acts or in his own Epistles, is he found laying any claim, how distant and vague soever, to any such power, as having ever been exercised by him. And, in this instance, no one individual incident being in any way brought to view or referred to, what is said will be seen to amount absolutely to nothing, being nothing more than, without incurring any such interpretation as that of imposture, is at the present time continually averred by Christians of different sects.

He who makes so much of his *sufferings*, had he wrought any miracles, would he have made nothing of his *miracles*?

In the next place, although it must be admitted, that, on several occasions, by his sole biographer and professed adherent, viz. the author of the Acts, a sort of colour of the marvellous seems endeavoured to be laid on; laid on over the incident itself, and over the part, which on that occasion was taken by him; yet on no one of these occasions, unless perhaps it be the last – of which presently, – does the account, given by him of what passed, wear any such complexion as shall render it matter of necessity, either to regard it as miraculous, or to regard the biographer, as having on that occasion asserted a complete and downright untruth.

SECTION 2.
SUPPOSABLE MIRACLE I. – ELYMAS THE SORCERER BLINDED. – *Acts* xiii. 6 to 12.

1. Of these supposable miracles, the first that occurs is that which had for its subject Elymas the sorcerer.

At Paphos, in the island of Cyprus[1], Paul and his associate Barnabas are sent for, by 'the deputy of the country,' Sergius Paulus, who desires to hear the word of God. But at that same place is a certain Jew, of the name of Barjesus, alias Elymas, – a sorcerer by profession, who 'withstood them, seeking to turn away the deputy from the faith.' To this man (it is not said, either where or when) Paul is thereupon represented as making a short speech, at the end of which, after calling him a child of the devil, and so forth; he says to him, '*Thou shalt be blind, not seeing the sun for a season.*

---

[1] [*And they had also John to their minister*, xiii.5.] What *John* was this? Answer, see chap. xv. 37 to 40. This appears to have been that John, whose surname was Mark, who was the cause of the angry separation of Paul from Barnabas.

Thereupon,' (continues the story) 'immediately there fell on him a mist and a darkness; and he went about seeking some to lead him by the hand. Then the deputy,' (it concludes,) 'when he saw what was done, believed, being astonished at the doctrine of the Lord.'

Supposing this story to have had any foundation in fact, – of the appearance of blindness thus exhibited, where shall we look for the cause? In a suspension of the laws of nature, performed by the author of nature, to no other assignable end, than the conversion of this Roman governor? At no greater expense, than that of a speech from this same Paul, the conversion of a king, – King Agrippa – if the author of the Acts is to be believed, was nearly effected. 'Almost,' says Agrippa, 'thou hast persuaded me to become a Christian.' So often as God is represented, as operating in a direct – however secret and mysterious – manner, upon the heart, *i.e.* the mind, of this and that man, – while the accounts given of the suspension of the laws of nature are comparatively so few – (to speak in that sort of human language, in which alone the nature of the case admits of our speaking) if the expense of a miracle were not grudged, – might not, in the way above-mentioned, by a much less lavish use of supernatural power, the same effect have been produced? viz. by a slight influence, exercised on the heart of governor Paulus?

Whatsoever may have been the real state of the case, – thus much seems pretty clear, viz. that at this time of day, to a person whose judgement on the subject should have, for its ground, the nature of the human mind as manifested by experience, – another mode of accounting for the appearance in question will be apt to present itself as much more probable. This is – that, by an understanding between Paul and Elymas – between the ex-persecutor and the sorcerer – the sorcerer, in the view of all persons, in whose instance it was material that credence should be given to the supposed miracle, – for and during *'the season'* that was thought requisite, kept his eyes shut.

The sorcerer was a Jew: – Paul was also a Jew. Between them here was already one indissoluble bond of connexion and channel of intercourse. Elymas, by trade a sorcerer, *i.e.* an impostor – a person of the same trade with Simon Magus, by whom so conspicuous a figure is cut in the chapter of this history – was a sort of person, who, on the supposition of an adequate motive, could not naturally feel any greater repugnance, at the idea of practising imposition, at so easy a rate as that of keeping his eyes shut, than at the idea of practising it, in any of the shapes to which he had been accustomed: – shapes, requiring more dexterity, and some, by which he would be more or less exposed, to that detection, from which, in the mode here in question, it would be altogether secure.

But Paul – was he in a condition to render it worth the sorcerer's while to give this shape to his imposture? Who can say that he was not? Yes: if to a certain degree he had it in his power, either to benefit him or to make him suffer? And who can say but that these two means of operating, were one or other, or both of them, in his power? As to the sorcerer's betraying him, this is what he could not have done, without betraying himself.

True it is, that, by acting this under part, – this self-humiliating part, – so long as Paul staid, so long was the sorcerer, not the first, but only the second wonder-worker of the town. But no sooner did Paul's departure take place, than Elymas, from being the second, became again the first.

SECTION 3.
SUPPOSABLE MIRACLE II. – AT LYSTRA, CRIPPLE CURED. – *Acts* xiv. 8 to 11.

SECOND of these supposed miracles, – cure of the cripple at Lystra.

This miracle makes a bad match with the before-mentioned one.

Seeing a man at Lystra (neither man's name, nor place's, except in that general way, nor time, in any way mentioned) – seeing a man in the guise of a cripple, '*Stand upright on thy feet,*' says Paul to him with a loud voice. 'And' (continues the story) 'he leaped and walked, steadfastly beholding and perceiving that he had faith to be healed.' Chorus of the people thereupon, 'The Gods are come down to us in the likeness of men.'

To the production of an appearance of this sort, what was necessary? a real miracle? No, surely: so long as a vagrant was to be found, who, without any risk, could act a part of this sort for a few pence, in an age so fertile in imposture.

True it is, that this same man, whoever he was, is represented as being 'impotent in his feet, being a cripple from his mother's womb, who never had walked.' But these words, how much more than any other words, of the same length, in the same number, did the writing of them cost the author of this story? As to the correctness of his narratives, – of the self-contradictory accounts given by him of Paul's conversion, a sample has been already given. As to detection, supposing this circumstance false, – detection is what the account thus given of it renders impossible. For – this same cripple, what was his name? from birth to this time, where had he been living? Of this nothing is said. That, at Lystra, or any where else, the account was ever made public, is neither affirmed, nor so much as insinuated: not but that it might have been published, and, at the same time, though as to every thing but the scene that exhibited itself to outward appearance, false, – might not have found any person, at the same time able and willing to contradict the falsity, and thus naturalize the miracle.

SECTION 4.
SUPPOSABLE MIRACLE III. – DIVINERESS SILENCED. *Acts* xvi. 16–18.

WHILE Paul and his suite, – of whom, according to the author of the Acts, he himself was one, – were at Philippi, – a Roman colony, and capital of a part of Macedonia, – among their hearers, is Lydia – a purple-seller of the city of Thyatira. Being converted, she receives the whole party into her house.

From this house, in their way to prayers, – probably in a Jewish synagogue, – they are met by a certain damsel, as nameless as the lame-born cripple, who, being possessed of a spirit of divination (or of Python), brings to her masters (for masters it seems she had more than one) much gain by soothsaying. Here then is a female, who, by being possessed by or with a spirit, – a real spirit, whether devil or a spirit of any other sort, – is converted into a prophetess, and, doubtless, in the main a false prophetess.

In the present instance, however, she is a true prophetess: for, following Paul and his suite, she runs after them, saying, 'These men are the servants of the Most High God, which show unto us the way of salvation. And this did she many days.'

If, instead of a demon, it had been an angel, that took her vocal organs for the instrument of his communications, it is difficult to say, in what manner he could have deserved better at the hands of these 'servants,' real or pretended, 'of the Most High God.'

Yet, from some cause or other that does not appear, so it was it seems, – there was something about her with which Paul was not well pleased. 'Being grieved, he turns and says,' – not to the damsel herself, but to the spirit, which *possessed her*, or rather, since for the benefit of her masters, it brought her so much gain, which *she possessed*, – 'I command thee, in the name of Jesus Christ, to come out of her.'

Amongst the superstitions of that and other ages, one was – the notion of a property; possessed by such and such words – possessed, by these mere evanescent sounds – by the air of the atmosphere, when made to vibrate in a certain manner: – a property, of working effects in endless abundance and variety, and those, too, supernatural ones. In some instances, the wonders would be wrought by the words themselves; whatsoever were the mouths by which they were uttered. In other instances, they required, for the production of the effects, a person, who being possessed of a particular and appropriate power, should, for the purpose of giving exercise to such his power, give them passage through his lips. Of this latter kind was the present case. The command issued as above, 'he (for it was a he-spirit) came out of her (the damsel) the same hour.'

When the devil that Josephus saw expelled[2], came out of the man, the channel at which he made his exit, being manifest, it was accordingly specified: it was the man's *nose*. This was something to know: especially, in relation to an occurrence, the time of which was at so great a distance from our own. At the same time, however, other particulars present themselves, by which curiosity is excited, and for want of which, the information thus bestowed must be confessed to be rather imperfect. What the shape of the devil was? what the substance? whence he last came? to what place, to what occupation, after being thus dislodged, he betook himself, and so forth: not to speak of many others, which howsoever instructive and satisfactory it would have been to be acquainted with, yet now that all acquaintance with them is hopeless, it would be tedious to enumerate.

In the present instance, not only as to all these particulars, has the historian, – eye-witness as it should seem he was of every thing that passed, – left us in the dark; but, neither has he vouchsafed to afford us that single article of information, scanty as it was, for which, as above, in the case mentioned by Josephus, we are indebted to Josephus: to Josephus – that most respectable and instructive of the uninspired historians of his age.

In relation to this story, as well as to those others, the same question still presents itself: – if told of the present time, – if spoken of in some newspaper, as having happened in the present year, – exists here any person, even among the most ignorant populace, with whom it would obtain any permanent credence?

But, a reported state of things – which, if reported as having had place in the present century, would, by its disconformity to the manifest state of things, and the whole course of nature, be regarded as too absurd and flagrantly incredible to deserve to be entitled to a moment's notice, – what is there that should render it more credible, when reported as having happened in this same world of ours, at any anterior point of time?

SECTION 5.
SUPPOSABLE MIRACLE IV. – AT PHILIPPI, AN EARTHQUAKE: PAUL AND SILAS FREED FROM PRISON, A° 53.

THE passage, in which these events are related, is in Acts, chap. xvi. ver. 19 to 40 inclusive.

On this occasion three principal events are narrated; – the incarceration of Paul, an earthquake, and the liberation of Paul. Between the earthquake and the liberation of this prisoner, what was in reality the connexion? In the answer there is not much difficulty: The same as that between the earthquake and any other event that took place after it. But, by an answer

---

[2]   Supra, Ch.

thus simple, the purpose of the narrator would not have been answered: the purpose was – to induce, on the part of his readers, the belief – that it was for the purpose of bringing about the liberation of the self-constituted Apostle of Jesus, that the earth was made to shake. As to the liberation, by means altogether natural was that event produced: so he himself has the candour to inform us. Of this quasi-miracle, or of the last-mentioned one, Philippi, capital of Macedonia, was the theatre. By order of the magistrates of that town, Paul and his attendant had been beaten one evening, and thrown into prison; next morning, came to the jailor an order of these same magistrates, and in obedience to it the prisoners were discharged. That, in the minds of these magistrates, there was any connexion, between the earthquake and the treatment they had given to these adventurers, is not so much as insinuated. The purpose, which it had in view, was answered: it was the ridding the town of a pair of visitors, whose visit to it had produced disturbance to existing institutions. Acts xvi. 20–40.

Be it as it may with regard to the historiographer, – that it was an object with his hero to produce a notion of a connexion between the stripes and the imprisonment he had undergone on one hand, and the earthquake on the other, is manifest enough. The person, in whose mind the prisoner had endeavoured to produce the idea of such a connexion, was the jailor: and, for its having in this instance been successful, there seems little difficulty in giving credit to the historiographer. Every thing that appears to have been said, either of Paul or by Paul, tends to show the wonderful strength of his mind, and the facility and promptitude, with which it enabled him to gain the ascendancy over other minds. In the language of the place and time, he had bid the fortune-telling damsel *cease* her imposture, and the imposture ceased. Acts xvi. 18. Committed to prison, he formed a project for making a proselyte of the keeper: and, in this too, and in so small a compass of time as a few hours, there seems reason to believe he was successful. In his presumption, in daring to execute the sentence of the law upon so holy a person, the keeper saw the cause of the earthquake; and, whether by Paul any very strenuous endeavours were used to correct so convenient an error in geology, may be left to be imagined. Paul, when introduced into the prison, found no want of comrades: how then happened it, that it was to Paul's imprisonment that the earthquake, when it happened, was attributed, and not to any of his fellow-prisoners? Answer: It happened thus.

Of the trade, which, with such brilliant success, Paul, – with this journeyman of his, – was carrying on, a set of songs with the name of God for the burthen of them, constituted a part of the capital, and, as it should seem, not the least valuable. When midnight came, Paul – the trader in godliness – treated the company in the prison with a duet: the other prisoners, though they shared in the benefit of it, did not join in it. While this duet was performing, came on the earthquake; and Paul was not such a novice as to let pass unimproved the opportunity it put into his hand.

The historiographer, if he is to be believed, was at this time in Paul's train, as well as Silas; for so, by the word *we*, in the tenth verse of this same chapter, he, as it were, silently informs us. The beating and the imprisonment were confined to the two principals; by his comparative insignificance, as it should seem, the historiographer was saved from it. From the relation, given to him by Paul or Silas, and in particular by Paul, – must this conception, formed by the historiographer, of what passed on the occasion, have of course been derived. It was coloured of course in Paul's manner: and in his colouring, there was of course no want of the marvellous. By the earthquake, not only were 'foundations shaken' and 'doors opened,' but 'bands loosened.' The 'feet' of the two holy men had been 'made. . . . fast in the stocks,' (ver. 24): from these same stocks, the earthquake was ingenious enough to let them out, and, as far as appears, without hurt: the unholy part of the prisoners had each of them bands of some sort, by which they were confined; for (ver. 26) 'every one's bands were loosed:' in every instance if they were locked, the earthquake performed the office of a picklock. Earthquakes in these latter days, we have but too many: in breaking open doors they find no great difficulty; but they have no such nicety of touch as the earthquake, which produced to the self-constituted Apostle a family of proselytes: they are no more able to let feet out of the stocks, or hands out of hand-cuffs, than to make watches.

These elucidations being furnished, the reader is desired to turn to the text, and lay it before him: to reprint it would require more paper than he might choose to see thus employed.

As to the name of God and the name of Jesus, the two names, it should appear, were not – on the occasions in question – used at random. When the fortune-telling damsel was the subject of Paul's holy labours, she having been in some way or other already gained (ver. 17), the case was already of a sort, in which the name of Jesus Christ, the name under which the self-constituted Apostle enlisted all his followers, – might be employed with advantage. When Paul and Silas were committed to prison, no such name as that of 'Jesus Christ' would as yet have served. Of 'Jesus Christ' neither had the keeper as yet heard any thing, nor had the other prisoners. But, of God, in some shape or other, they could not but have heard, all of them: *God* accordingly was the name, by which at this time the sensibilities of the persons in question were to be worked upon. When the earth trembled, the jailor trembled likewise: he 'came trembling and fell down' (ver. 29) before Paul and Silas. And brought them out (ver. 30) and said, 'Sirs, what must I do to be saved?' Now then was the time come for the enlistment – for the enlistment in the spiritual warfare against the devil and his angels: in the as yet new name of 'the Lord Jesus Christ' were these recruits accordingly enlisted, as now, for the purpose of carnal warfare, in the name of King George. 'And they said,' (continues the narration, ver. 31) 'Believe in the Lord Jesus Christ, and thou shalt be saved, and thy house.'

SECTION 6.
SUPPOSABLE MIRACLE V. – AT CORINTH, PAUL COMFORTED BY THE LORD IN AN *UNSEEN* VISION, A° 54. – *Acts* xviii. 7–11.

A VISION, being a species of miracle, could, no more than a pantomime, have place without some expense. In the present case, as in any other, a natural question is – What was the object to be accomplished, upon which the expense – whatever it was – was bestowed? The answer is – The keeping his attendants, whoever they were, in the necessary state of obsequiousness: for no other is perceptible. To the dependants in Paul's train, it was no very uncommon sentiment to be not quite so well satisfied with the course he took, as he himself was. Corinth was at this time the theatre of his labours: of the men, whoever they were, who had staked their fortunes upon *his*, some, – the historiographer, as it should seem, of the number, – there were, whose wish it was to change the scene. In that Gentile city, – the chief ruler of the Jewish synagogue, Crispus by name – this man, besides another man, of the name of Justus, 'whose house joined hard to' that same synagogue, had become his converts: 'and many of the Corinthians hearing, believed and were baptised.' Eyes, however, there were, in which the success, whatsoever it was, was not yet enough to afford a sufficient warrant for his stay. A vision was necessary, and a vision accordingly, or at least a something which was called by that name, made its appearance. 'Thus spake the Lord,' (says the historiographer, ver. 9.) 'Thus spake the Lord to Paul in the night by a vision, Be not afraid, but speak, and hold not thy peace:—10. For I am with thee, and no man shall set on thee to hurt thee; for I have much people in this city.' Nor was the vision without its effect; for, as the next verse informs us, (ver. 11.) 'He continued *there* a year and six months, teaching the word of God among them.'

That which, on this occasion, may be believed without much difficulty is, that the word thus taught by Paul was Paul's word: and, that which may be believed with as little, by those, whoever they may be, who believe in his original conversion-vision, is – that it was God's word likewise. From Paul himself must the account of this vision have been delivered to the historiographer: for, unless at the expense of a sort of miracle, in the shape of an additional vision at least, if not in some more expensive shape, no information of any such thing could have reached him. In these latter days, no ghost is ever seen but in a *tête-à-tête*: in those days, no vision, as far as appears, was ever seen but in the same degree of privacy. A vision is the word in these pages, because such is the word in the authoritative translation made of the historiographer's. That which Paul is related to have heard, is – what we have just seen as above: but that, upon this occasion he saw any thing – that he saw so much as a flash of light, this is what we are not told: any more than by what other means he became so well assured, that the voice which he heard, supposing him to have heard a voice, was the Lord's voice. In these latter days, – inquiries, of some such sort as these, would as surely be put, by a counsel who were against the vision, – as, in the case of the Cock-lane Ghost, which gave so much exercise to the faith of the arch-lexicographer, were put by the counsel who were against the ghost; but, by a sort of general understanding, – than which nothing can be more convenient, – inquiries, such as these, – how strictly soever in season when applied to the 19th century of the vulgar ear, are altogether out of season, as often as they are applied to the commencement of it.

As to the speaking by a vision, the only intelligible way in which any such thing can really have place, is that, which under the pressure of necessity has been realized by the ingenuity of dramatists in these latter days. Such is the mode employed, when the actors, having been struck dumb by the tyranny of foolish laws, and consequently having no auditors, convey to the spectators what information seems necessary, by an appropriate assortment of gold letters on a silk ground: whether the Lord who, on this occasion, according to Paul, spoke to the eyes of Paul, came provided with any such implement, he has not informed us. Without much danger of error, we may venture to assert the negative: for, if such was the mode of converse, there was nothing but what might happen without sign or wonder: and, on this supposition, no addition was made by it, to those signs and wonders, which, as has been seen, it was his way to make reference to, in the character of evidence.

SECTION 7.
SUPPOSABLE MIRACLE VI. – AT EPHESUS, DISEASES AND DEVILS EXPELLED BY FOUL HANDKERCHIEFS. – *Acts* xix. 1–12.

AT Ephesus, Paul makes a stay of between two and three years; for 'two years' together, (Acts xix. 10.) 'disputing daily' (ver. 9.) 'in the school of one Tyrannus,' 'so that' (ver. 10.) 'all they which dwelt in Asia heard the word of the Lord Jesus, both Jews and Greeks'.

'And God' (continues the history, ver. 11.) 'wrought special miracles by the hands of Paul.'

These '*special* miracles,' what were they? Of the whole number, is there so much as a single one particularized? No; not one. *Special* as they are, the following is the account, and the only account given of them. 'So that' (continues the history) 'from his body were brought unto the sick, handkerchiefs or aprons, and the diseases departed from them, and the evil spirits went out of them.'

No circumstances whatever particularized, name of the person, name of the place, description of the time – nothing, by means of which, in case of falsity *in toto*, or incorrectness in circumstance, the mis-statement might have been exposed, – to what degree of credence, or so much as consideration with a view to credence, vague generalities such as these, can they present to much as the slightest claim? If allusions such as these are to pass proof, where is the imposture, to which proofs – proofs sufficient in number and value – can ever be wanting?

Opposed as Paul was, wherever he went, – by gainsayers or persecutors, or both – sometimes successful, sometimes altogether unsuccessful, – sometimes in a slight degree successful – in so much as any one occasion, either in this history, or in any one of his own numerous Epistles, do we find so much as a single one of these '*special miracles*,' any more than of any other miracles, brought to view by him, or so much as alluded to by him, in the character of proofs of the commission to which he pretended? Answer: No, not one.

Diseases cured, evil spirits driven out, by handkerchiefs and aprons! – by handkerchiefs and aprons brought from a man's body! Diseases cured and devils scared away by foul linen! By Jesus – by any one of his Apostles – were any such implements, any such eye-traps ever employed? No; never. As to diseases, if by such means a disease had been *propagated*, the case would have been intelligible enough. But what was wanted was a miracle: and this would have been no miracle. The price, received by the holy wearer for any of these cast-off habiliments – the price, of the precious effluvia thus conveyed – by any such little circumstance, had it been mentioned, some light might have been cast on what was done.

One thing, indeed, may be stated with some assurance: and this is – that, after a man, well or not well, had received one of these same dirty handkerchiefs, or of these same dirty aprons, no evil spirit in him was visible.

One other thing may also be stated with no less confidence: – this is that, infection out of the question, and supposing Paul free from all contagious disease, if, without handkerchief or apron, the disease would have had its exit, – by no such handkerchief or any such apron was the exit of it prevented.

Note, that all this time, according to this man (the author of the Acts), he himself was in Paul's suite. Yet, taking credit for all these miracles – taking credit thus for miracles out of number, not so much as one of them all does he take upon himself to particularize.[3].

---

[3]   Another branch of his trade, already mentioned in this same chapter, as having been carried on by him in this same place, namely, Ephesus, – and which, where circumstances

SECTION 8.
SUPPOSABLE MIRACLE VII. – AT EPILESUS, EXORCISTS SCEVAS BEDEVILED. – *Acts* xix. 13–20.

THUS it is that, as under the last head has been observed, of all these alledged successful exhibitions, not so much as a single one is particularized.

In lieu, however, of these successes of Paul's, something of a story to a certain degree particularized we have. But this is – what? a successful performance of Paul's? No: but an unsuccessful attempt of certain persons, – here termed exorcists, – who took upon themselves to act against him in the character of competitors.

Well, then: when the time came for demonstrating supernatural powers by experiment, these exorcists – these impostors, no doubt it was intended they should be deemed – made a very indifferent hand of it. Good: but the true man, Did he go beyond these same impostors? Not he, indeed: he did not so much as attempt it. But, let us hear his historiographer, who all this while was at his elbow. Acts xix. 13–20. 'Then certain of the vagabond Jews, exorcists, took upon them to call over them which had evil spirits, the name of the Lord Jesus, saying, We adjure you by Jesus, whom Paul preacheth.'

---

created a demand for the article, appears to have been more profitable than that of expelling devils or diseases, – is *that*, of which the Holy Ghost was the subject. This power of conferring – that is to say, of being thought to confer – the Holy Ghost, – such, and of such sort was the value of it, that Simon Magus, as there may be occasion to mention in another chapter, had, not less than one-and-twenty years before this, offered the Apostles money for it. (Acts viii. 18–24, A° 34.) This power, two preceding verses of the same 19th chapter, namely the 5th and 6th, represent Paul as exercising: and, whatsoever was the benefit derived, twelve is the number of the persons here spoken of as having received it.

Acts xix. 5–7. After 'they' (the above twelve (*v.* 7.) disciples, v. 9.) 'were baptized (v. 5.) in the name of the Lord Jesus;' when Paul (v. 6.) 'had laid his hands upon them, the Holy Ghost 'came on them; and they spake with tongues, and prophesied.' Here then, if, by thus laying on of hands, it is by *Paul* that any operation is performed, it is the conferring of 'the Holy Ghost.' But this power, whence had Paul received it? Not from Jesus, had the self-constituted Apostle received this gift, whatever it was, any more than he had baptism, by which ceremony, as appears from Acts viii. 16, it was regularly preceded: as in the case of the magician it actually had been. Not from Jesus: no such thing is any where so much as pretended. Not from the Apostles, or any of them; from two, for example, by commission from the rest – as in the case of Peter and John (Acts viii. 14–19.): – no such thing is any where so much as pretended. In no such persons could this – would this – their self-declared superior, have vouchsafed to acknowledge the existence, of a power in which he had no share. On this occasion, as on every other, independently of the Apostles did he act, and in spite of the Apostles.

As to the '*speaking with tongues* and *prophesying*, these are pretensions, which may be acknowledged without much difficulty. *Tongues* are the organs most men speak with. As to *prophesying*, it was an operation that might as well be performed after the fact as before the fact: witness in Luke xxii. 64, 'Prophesy, who is it that smote thee?' Read the Bible over from beginning to end, a prophet, whatever else be meant, if there be any thing else meant; you will find to have been a *politician: to prophesy* was to talk *politics*. Make a new translation, or (what would be shorter) a list of *corrigenda*, and instead of *prophet* put *politician*, – a world of labour, now employed in explanations, will be saved.

'And there were' (continues the narrative, v. 14.) 'seven sons of Sceva, a Jew, and chief of the priests, which did so.' Thus far the narrative.

The sons of the chief of the priests? Such men styled not only *exorcists* but *vagabonds?* If they are not here, in express terms, themselves styled *vagabonds*, at any rate, what is here imputed to them is the doing those same things, the doers of which have just been styled, not only *exorcists*, but at the same time *vagabonds*. But let us continue, 'And the evil spirit (v. 15.) answered and said, Jesus I know, and Paul I know, who are ye? – 16. And the man, in whom the evil spirit was, leapt on them and overcame them, and prevailed against them, so that they fled out of that house naked and wounded.' Thus far the narrative.

To whatsoever order of beings the hero of this tale may have belonged; – whatsoever may have been his proper appellative, – a man with two natures, one human, the other diabolical, – a man with a devil in him, a madman, – or a man in his sound senses counterfeiting a diabolized man or a madman, – the tale itself is surely an eminently curious one. Of these human or superhuman antagonists of his – of these pretended masters over evil spirits – the number is not less than seven: yet, in comparison of him, so feeble and helpless are they all together, that he not only masters them all seven, but gets them down, all seven together, and while they are lying on the ground in a state of disablement, pulls the clothes off their backs: but whether one after another, or all at the same time, is not mentioned. Be this as it may, hereupon comes a question or two. While he was stripping any one of them, what were the others about all that time? The beating they received, was it such as to render them senseless and motionless? No: this can scarcely have been the case; for, when the devil had done his worst, and their sufferings were at the height, out of the house did they flee, wounded as they were.

'Jesus I know, and Paul I know,' says the mysterious hero, in the fifteenth verse. Hereupon an observation or two calls for utterance. Supposing him a man, who, knowing what he was about, counterfeited the sort of being, who was half man, half devil, – one half of this speech of his, namely, *Paul I know*, may without much difficulty be believed. But, upon this supposition, forasmuch as he acted with so much effect against these rivals of Paul's, – a supposition not less natural, to say the least of it, is – that to Paul he was not unknown, any more than Paul to him: in a word, that on this occasion, between the evil spirit and the self-constituted Apostle, a sort of understanding had place. Be this as it may, how extraordinary a person must he not have been, to undertake the complete mastery of seven men at once! seven men, all of them young enough to have a father, not only living, but officiating as a priest: and at the same time, all of them old enough, if not to exercise mastery over evil spirits, at any rate to undertake it!

In Paul's suite, all this time, as far as appears, was the author of this narrative. The scene thus exhibited – was he then, or was he not, himself an eye witness of it? On a point so material and so natural, no light has he afforded us.

Another circumstance, not less curious, is – that it is immediately after the story of the unnamed multitudes, so wonderfully cured by foul clothes, – that this story of the devil-masters discomfited by a rebellious servant of theirs, makes its appearance. Turn now to the supposed true devil-master – on this score, what was it that he did? Just nothing. The devil, – and a most mischievous one he was, – *he* was doing all this mischief: – the man, who had all such devils so completely in his power, that they quit possession, and decamp at the mere sight or smell of a dirty handkerchief or apron of his; – he, though seeing all this mischief done, – done by this pre-eminently mischievous as well as powerful devil, – still suffers him to go on; – and not any the least restraint in any shape, does he impose upon him; but leaves him in complete possession of that receptacle, which, according to the narrative, he wanted neither the power nor the will to convert into an instrument of so much mischief. Was it from Paul himself, that, on this special occasion, for this special purpose, namely, the putting down these presumptuous competitors, this mysterious being received so extraordinary a gift? This is not said, but not improbably, as it should seem, this was the miracle, which it was intended by the historian should be believed.

Occasions there are – and this we are desired to believe was one of them – in which the impossibility of a thing is no bar to the knowledge of it.

'And this was known' (continues the narrative, v. 17.) 'And this was known to all the Jews and Greeks also dwelling at Ephesus: and fear fell on them all, and the name of the Lord Jesus was magnified.'

Now, supposing this thing known, the fear stated as the result of it may without difficulty be believed: – fear of being treated as those sons of the chief of the Jewish priests had been: fear of the devil, by whom those, his unequal antagonists, had been thus dealt with: fear of the more skilful devil-master, under whose eye these bunglers had been thus dealt with.

But the name here said to be *magnified* – the name of the Lord Jesus – how *that* came to be *magnified:* in this lies all the while the difficulty, and it seems no small one.

The *name*, on this occasion, and thus said to be employed, whose was it? It was, indeed, the Lord Jesus's. But was it successful? Quite the contrary. It made bad worse. In the whole of this business, what was there from which the name of Jesus could in any shape receive magnification? Yes: if after the so eminently unsuccessful use, thus made of it by those exorcists, a successful use had, on the same occasion, been made of it by Paul. But, no: no such enterprise did he venture upon. Madman, devil, counterfeit madman, counterfeit devil, – by proxy, any of these he was ready to encounter, taking for his proxy one of his foul handkerchiefs or aprons:

any of this sort of work, if his historiographer is to be believed, he was ready enough to do by proxy. But, in person? No; he knew better things.

'And many that believed' (concludes this part of the narrative, v. 18) 'came and confessed, and showed their deeds.' Yes; supposing there were any, by whom all this or any part of it was believed, – that they spoke and acted in consequence, may be believed without much difficulty: and, with this observation may the story, and the sort of elucidation endeavoured to be given of it, be left to close.

SECTION 9.
SUPPOSABLE MIRACLE VIII. – MAGICAL BOOKS BURNT BY THE OWNERS – *Acts* xix. 19, 20.

SUCH as it was, the supposable miracle last-mentioned was not without its supposed fruit: destruction of property, such as it was – destruction of property, and to an amount sufficiently wonderful for the satisfaction of any ordinary appetite for wonders. But let us see the text. It follows in the verse (19) next after that, in which mention is made, as in the last preceding section, of what was done by the 'many who believed.'

'Many of them also,' (v. 19) 'which used curious arts, brought their books together, and burned them before all men; and they counted the price of them, and found it fifty thousand pieces of silver. So mightily (v. 20.) grew the word of God, and prevailed.' And there ends the story of the books of curious arts.

As to the sum total, nothing can be more precise: as to the items, could the list of them be but produced, this would be indeed a treasure. As to the denomination *magical*, given in the title of this section to those books, styled books '*of curious arts*,' – in the text, short is the only apology that need be made for it. Of the number of those *curious arts* could not, most assuredly, have been any of the arts included at present under the name of *fine arts*; of the character of the *arts* here designated by the appellation of *curious*, a sufficient indication is afforded, by the story, by which the mention of them is, as above, immediately preceded. They were the arts, by which effects were undertaken to be produced, such as the self-consti-tuted apostle undertook to produce by so much more simple means. How vast soever were the collection, what would be the value of it, – the whole taken together, – when so much more than could be done by every thing which it professed to teach, could be done by about a score or a dozen words, on the single condition, that the lips by which they were uttered were properly commissioned lips, not to speak of the still more simple operation of the touch of a used handkerchief?

Of the state of art and science in the wake of the great temple of Diana, the representation here given is of itself no small curiosity. Books of curious arts – all of them arts of imposture – books, employed, all of them, in teaching the most secret of all secrets – books of this description, so well known to all men, as to bear a market-price! a market-price, so well known to all men, as if it were the price of bread and butcher's meat: and, in the single town of Ephesus, these books so numerous, – such the multitude or the value, – or rather the multitude as well as value, of them taken in the aggregate, that the price, that had been given for such of them as were thus given up, and which are only part, and, as it should seem by the word *many*, not the larger part, of the whole number, of those, which, at that same place, were at that same time in existence, – was, upon summing up, found actually to amount, so we are required to believe, to that vast sum.

Of the aggregate, of the prices that had been paid, we are told, for this smaller part of the aggregate number of the books, then and there existing on this single subject, – inadequate, indeed, would our conception be of it were we to regard it as not exceeding the value of the whole library collected by King George the Third, and given by his successor to the English part of his subjects. *Data*, though not for numeration, yet sufficient for conception, are by no means wanting. To consult Arbuthnot, or any successor of his, would be mere illusion: in so far as the value of money is unknown, prices in money serve but to deceive. History – and *that* the most appropriate history – has furnished us with much surer grounds. Thirty pieces of silver (Matt. xxvii. 3 to 10) was the purchase-money, of the field, called *the potters' field*, bought for a burying-ground, with the money received and returned by the traitor Judas, as the reward for his treachery. Suppose it no more than half an acre. What, in English money of the present day, would be the value of half an acre of land in or close by a closely built metropolis? A hundred pounds would, assuredly, be a very moderate allowance. Multiply the hundred pounds by fifty thousand, you have five millions; divide the five millions by thirty, you have, on the above supposition, 166,666*l.* and odd for the value of these books. Look to the English translation, look to the Greek original, the pieces of silver are the same.

SECTION 10.
SUPPOSABLE MIRACLE IX. – AT TROAS, EUTYCHUS FOUND NOT TO BE DEAD. – *Acts* xx. 7–12.

IN this story may be seen another example, of the facility with which, when men are upon the hunt for miracles, something may be made out of nothing: the most ordinary occurrence, by the addition of a loose word or two, metamorphosed into a miracle.

Paul, one evening, was treating his disciples with a sermon: he was at the same time treating them, or they him, with a supper. The architecture of the house was such, that, under favourable circumstances, a fall might be got from the top of it, or thereabouts, to the bottom, without much difficulty. If any difficulty there was, on the occasion in question it was overcome. According to circumstances, sermons produce on different minds different effects: from some, they drive sleep; in others, they produce it. On the occasion in question, the latter was the effect experienced by a certain youth. His station is represented as being an elevated one: – so elevated, that, after the fall he got from it, it may be believed without difficulty, he lay for some time motionless. Paul 'went down' to him (we are told) and embraced him. The youth received the embrace; Paul, the praise of tender-heartedness: – this is what may be asserted with a safe conscience, though it be without any special evidence. Trifling, however, is the boon he received from that congregation, in comparison of what he has been receiving from so many succeeding ones – the reputation of having made so brilliant an addition to the catalogue of his miracles. By the accident, whatever may have been the interruption, given by it to the festivity, no end was put to it. Sermon and supper ended, the rest of the congregation went their way; and with them went the youth, to whom had any thing serious happened, the historian would scarcely have left us uninformed of it.

On this occasion, between the hero and his historian, there is somewhat of a difference. The historian will have it, that when Paul reached the body he found it dead. Paul's own account of the matter is the direct contrary: so the historian himself informs us. Here then the historian and his hero are at issue. But, the historian, having the first word, makes, if we may venture to say so, a rather unfair advantage of it, and by this same first word gives a contradiction to what he makes his hero say in the next. 'He was taken up dead,' says the historian, who was or was not there: 'His life is in him,' says the preacher, who was there beyond dispute.

But let us see the text.

ACTS xx, 7–12.

7. And upon the first day of the week, when the disciples came together to break bread, Paul preached unto them, ready to depart on the morrow, and continued his speech till midnight. —8. And there were many lights in the upper chamber, where they were gathered together. —9. And there sat in a window a certain young man named Eutychus, being fallen into a deep sleep: and as Paul was long preaching, he sunk down with sleep, and fell down from the third loft, and was taken up dead. —10. And Paul went down, and fell on him, and embracing him, said, Trouble not yourselves, for his life is in him. —11. When he therefore was come up again, and had broken bread, and eaten, and talked a long while, even till break of day, so he departed. —12. And they brought the young man alive, and were not a a little comforted.

At this time of day, any such contrariety might produce some embarrassment; but, when it is considered how long ago the thing happened, no such uneasy sensation is experienced. A supposition, by which all embarrassment is excluded, is so immediately obvious, as to be scarce worth mentioning. When Paul reached the body, the soul was already in the other world; but, with the kisses goes a whisper, and the soul comes back again. Whether from indolence or from archness, there is something amusing, in the course the historian takes for enlivening his narration with these flowers: he sketches out the outline, but leaves it to our imaginations to fill it up.

SECTION 11.
SUPPOSABLE MIRACLE X. – ON SHIPBOARD, PAUL COMFORTED BY AN ANGEL.

ACTS xxvii. 20–25.

20. And when neither sun nor stars appeared for many days, and no small tempest lay on us, all hope that we should be preserved was thenceforth taken away. —21. But after long abstinence Paul stood in the midst of them, and said, Sirs, ye should have hearkened to me, and not have loosed from Crete, but have prevented this harm and damage. —22. And now I exhort you to be of good courage: for there shall be no loss of life among you, but of the ship, *there shall be loss.* — 23. For there stood by me this night an angel of that God, whose I am, and whom I serve, saying, —24. Fear not, Paul, thou must be brought before Cæsar; and lo, God hath graciously given to thee all who sail with thee. —25. Wherefore, Sirs, be of good courage; for I believe God, that it will be as it hath been told me.

THE sea being stormy, the crew are alarmed. The storm, however, is not so violent, but that Paul is able to make a speech, and they to hear it. To keep up their spirits, and, at the same time, let them see the sort of terms he is upon with the Almighty, he tells them a story about an angel. The angel had been sent to him upon a visit, and was but just gone. The business of the angel was to quiet the mind of the Apostle. The matter had been settled. The precious life was in no danger: and, not only so, but, out of compliment to him, God had been pleased to grant to him the lives of all who were happy enough to be in his company.

In the situation, in which so many lives are represented as being placed, – no very severe condemnation can easily be passed upon any little fraud, by which they might be saved. But, is it really to be believed, that this angel, whom, in a deckless vessel (for the vessels of *those* times were not like the vessels of present times) no person but Paul either saw or heard, was really sent express from the sky by God Almighty, on such an errand?

If not, then have we this additional proof, – if any additional proof can be needed, – to help to satisfy us – that, where a purpose was to be answered, falsehood, or as *he* would have called it *lying*, was not among the obstacles, by which Paul would be stopped, in his endeavours to accomplish it.

SECTION 12.
SUPPOSABLE MIRACLE XI. – AT MALTA, A REPTILE SHAKEN OFF BY PAUL WITHOUT HURT. – *Acts* xxviii. 1–6

A FIRE of sticks being kindled, a reptile, here called a viper, is represented as 'coming out of the heat,' and fastening on Paul's hand. On beholding this incident, – 'the barbarous people,' as the inhabitants are called, whose hospitality kindled the fire for the relief of the shipwrecked company, concluded that Paul was a murderer: and were, accordingly, in expectation of seeing him 'swollen, or fallen down dead suddenly.' Nothing of this sort happening, their next conclusion was, *that he was a God.* As such, did these barbarians, as did the civilized inhabitants of Lystra, sacrifice to him, or in any other way worship him? No: these conceptions of theirs reported, there the story ends.

Of this story, what is to be made? At this time of day, among Christians in general, what we should expect to find is, that it passed for a miracle. But, if by miracle is meant, not merely an accident, somewhat singular and extraordinary, – but, by a special act of Almighty power, an effect produced, by means disconformable to the uniform course of nature, – it might be too much to say, that even by the reporter himself, it is for the decided purpose of its being taken for a miracle, that it is brought to view.

If, however, the design was not here, that the incident should be taken for a miracle, – the story amounted to nothing, and was not worth the telling. But, if it *is* to be made into a miracle, where is the matter in it, out of which a miracle can be made?

The reptile – was it really a viper? Neither the barbarians of Malta, nor the reporter of this story, nor in a word, at that time of day, any other persons whatever, were either very complete or very correct, in their conception of matters belonging to the field of natural history. At present, reptiles are crawling creatures. At this time of day, when *leeches* are excepted, to fasten upon the part they have bitten is not the practice with any reptiles that we know of. If, instead of *viper*, the Greek word had been one that could have been translated *leech*, – the story would have been probable enough, but, were it only for that very reason, no miracle could have been made out of it. Shaken down into the fire, that is, into the burning fuel, – a small reptile, such as a leech, how brisk soever in the water, would be very apt to be overpowered by the heat, before it could make its escape: with a reptile of the ordinary size of a viper, this would hardly be the case.

Be this as it may, 'he felt,' – so says the story, – 'he felt no harm.' How came it that he felt no harm? Because the Almighty performed a miracle to preserve him from harm? So long as eyes are open, causes out of number – causes that have nothing wonderful in them – present themselves to view before this. 'The beast,' as it is translated, 'was not a viper:' – if really a viper, it happened, at that moment, not to be provided with a competent stock of venom: it had already expended it upon some other object: – by some accident or other, it had lost the appropriate tooth. Not to look out for others, – any mind that was not bent upon having a miracle at any price, would lay hold of some such cause as one of these, sooner than give itself any such trouble as that of torturing the incident into a miracle.

To bring under calculation the quantity of supernatural power necessary to the production of a given effect is no very easy task. At any rate, – without more or less of expense in a certain shape, nothing in that way could ever be done. In the case here in question, what could have been the object of any such expense? Was it the saving the self-constituted Apostle the pain of a bite? The expense then, would it not have been less – the operation, so to speak, more economical – had a slight turn been given to Paul's hand, or to the course of the reptile? But, in either case, neither would the name of the Lord, nor – what was rather more material – that of his Apostle, have received that glorification which was so needful to it.

Any such design, as that of giving an unequivocal manifestation of Almighty power, such as should stand the test of scrutiny, testifying the verity of Paul's commission to the end of time, – any such design could the incident have had for its final cause? A more equivocal, – a less conclusive, – proof of the manifestation of supernatural power, seems not very easy to imagine.

Here then comes once more the so often repeated conclusion: – the narrative began to be in want of a miracle, and the miracle was made.

In those days, among that people, miracles were so much in course, that without a reasonable number of them, a history would hardly have obtained credence: at any rate it would not have obtained readers, and without readers no history can ever obtain much credence.

SECTION 13.
SUPPOSABLE MIRACLE XII. – AT MALTA, DEPUTY PUBLIUS'S FATHER CURED. – *Acts* xxviii. 7–10.

'IN the same quarters' (says the story – it follows immediately upon that of the viper) 'In the same quarters were possessions of the chief man of the island, whose name was *Publius*, who received us and lodged us three days courteously. —8. And it came to pass, that the father of Publius lay sick of a fever, and of a bloody flux, to whom Paul entered in and prayed, and laid his hands on him and healed him. —9. So when this was done, others also which had diseases in the island, came and were healed. —10. Who also honoured us with many honours, and when we departed, they laded [*us*] with such things as were necessary.'

Of the fevers, which, within the compass of any given spot, and any given space of time, have place, it almost always happens, that a certain number go off of themselves. Of, perhaps, all sorts of fever, – at least of almost all sorts at present known, thus much is agreed upon by all physicians: – they have at least two regular courses, one of which terminates in death, the other or others in recovery. Supposing the person in question to have had a fever, – what is pretty clear is – that, if *of itself* it would have taken a favourable termination, there was nothing, in the forms employed by Paul, viz. utterance of prayers and imposition of hands, that could have any natural tendency to *cause* it to take an unfavourable one.

But – the course afterwards taken by the fever, was there any thing in it to distinguish it from the ordinary favourable course? If not, in that case, so far from miraculous, there is nothing that is so much as wonderful in the case.

Note here two things – the narrator one of the party; the narrative so loose and uncircumstantial. But *to see* is one thing; *to narrate*, another.

Three days, it seems, and no more, did Paul and his suite stay at the house of this Publius. Was it during that time, or not till afterwards, that Paul performed on him those ceremonies, of which healing is represented as having been the consequence? Was it within that same space of time, or not till afterwards, that the healing is supposed to have taken place? As to the English word *healing*, it cannot be accused of being indecisive. But in some languages they have words, by which a very convenient veil is thrown over the result. In the languages in question, for the endeavour to heal, whether successful or unsuccessful, the word employed is the same. The Latin affords one of these convenient words, viz. *curo*. The Greek has another, ιυσυτο, and in the Greek original of this history, this is the word employed.

In a case where a ceremony, and nothing else, is trusted to, it being supposed that the patient really has the disease, the safe and prudent course is, so to order times and seasons, that between the time of performing the ceremony, and the time at which restoration to health is expected to take place, the time shall have come for the practitioner to have shifted quarters; for, in this case, this is an interval more or less considerable, during which it being taken for granted that the desired result will take place of course, reward, in the shapes of profit and honour, will pour in upon the scientific head.

Here, as elsewhere, not only no *symptoms* are particularized, but no *place* is mentioned: no *time* is particularized, no *persons* are mentioned as *percipient witnesses:* even the individual who was the subject of the cure is not mentioned by name.

As to the givers of the supposed honours and presents – persons are indeed mentioned: – mentioned, but no otherwise than by the name of *others*. One individual alone is particularized: particularized as having received the benefit of these ceremonies. This is the father of Publius. This man, to use the phraseology of the passage, was *also healed*. But – this man, who was he? He was no less a person than the father of the chief man in the island. Well then, what are the honours, what the allotment of '*such things as were necessary?*' What were the proofs of gratitude, afforded by this man, who was so much better able to afford such presents, than any of those other persons cured? By such proofs of remuneration, some evidence – some circumstantial evidence, – supposing them exhibited at a proper time, would have been afforded, in proof of the reality of the service. But, neither by the person thus spoken of as healed, nor by his son – the chief man in the island, – is it said that any such proofs were afforded. For such a silence when the case of an individual was brought to view, coupled with the express declaration made, of gifts presented by persons unnamed, – three cases cannot but present themselves, as being any one of them more probable, than that, on this occasion, a real miracle was performed. One is – that there was no disease, perhaps no such person: another is, that though there was a disease, it went off of itself: the third is, that it never went off at all.

One thing may be asserted without much fear of contradiction: and that is, that in this country, if in terms such as these, accounts were inserted in the public prints; – accounts of diseases cured without medicine; – diseases cured, by nothing but words and gesticulations; – though the accounts given were ever so numerous, not the smallest notice would they be thought worthy of, – not the smallest attention would they receive from any one, unless it were for the joke' sake.

What is more, – numerous are the publications, in which, encompassed with circumstantiality in all manner of shapes, not only the names of the fortunate patients are mentioned, but under the signatures of those patients declarations made, assuring the public of the reality of the cure, – and yet, when at the same time, by competent persons, due inquiry has been made, it turns out after all that no such cure has been performed.

Accounts, which would not be believed were they to come out at a time of so widely diffused knowledge, are they to be believed, merely because the time they belonged to, – facts and accounts together, – was, as to all such matters, a time of universal ignorance? The less a man understands the subject, the more firmly is he to be believed, as to everything he says of it? Or is it that, between then and now, *men* and *things* have undergone a total change? and, if so, when did it take place?

SECTION 14
CONCLUSION: THE SUPPOSABLE MIRACLES CLASSED AND
SUMMED UP.

INFERENCES, – conveying more or less of instruction, – may, perhaps, be
found deducible, – at any rate our conception of the whole series taken
together, will be rendered so much the clearer, by bringing the same supposed marvels again under review, arranged in the order of time.

For this purpose, the time may be considered as divided into three
periods.

In the first are included – those, which are represented as having had
place during the time when at the outset of his missionary expedition, Paul
had Barnabas for his associate. Of these there are two, viz. 1. At Paphos,
A°. 45, Sorcerer Elymas blinded. 2. At Lystra, A°. 46, cripple cured. Of
this part of the expedition, the commencement, as in the current account,
placed in the year 45.

In the second period are included – those, which are represented as
having had place, during the time when Paul, after his separation from
Barnabas, had Silas for his associate, and the unnamed author of the Acts
for an attendant. This ends with his arrival at Jerusalem, on the occasion
of his fourth visit – the Invasion Visit.

In the current accounts, this event is placed in the year 60. Within this
period, we have the seven following supposed marvels: 1. At Philippi, A°.
53, divineress silenced. 2. At Philippi, A°. 53, earthquake: Paul and Silas
freed from prison. 3. At Corinth, A°. 54, Paul comforted by the Lord in
an unseen vision. 4. At Ephesus, A°. 56, diseases and devils expelled by
Paul's foul handkerchiefs. 5. At Ephesus, A°. 55, Exorcist Scevas bedeviled.
6. At Ephesus, A°. 56, magic books burnt by the owners. 7. At Troas, A°.
59, Eutychus found not to be dead.

In the third period are included – those which are represented as having
had place, in the interval between his forced departure from Jerusalem for
Rome, and his arrival at Rome.

In the current accounts, this event is placed in the year 62. Within
this concluding period, we have the following supposed marvels: 1. On
shipboard, A°. 62, Paul comforted by an angel. 2. At Malta, A°. 62, a
reptile shaken off by Paul without his being hurt. 3. At Malta, A°. 62,
Deputy Publius's father cured by Paul of some disorder. Year of all these
three last marvels, the same as that of Paul's arrival at Rome. Total number
of supposed marvels, twelve.

To the first of these three periods belong two supposed marvels, which,
supposing them to have any foundation in truth, present themselves as
being, in a great degree than most of the others, exposed to the suspicion
of contrivance. A moderate sum, greater or less according to the state more
or less flourishing of his practice, might suffice to engage a sorcerer, for a

few minutes or hours, to declare himself struck blind: a still more moderate sum might suffice to engage an itinerant beggar, to exhibit himself with one leg tied up, and after hearing what was proper to be heard, or seeing what was proper to be seen, to declare himself cured.

This was the period, during which Paul had Barnabas, or Barnabas Paul, for an associate. In these cases, if fraud in any shape had place, – it is not without reluctance, that any such supposition could be entertained, as that Barnabas – the generous, the conciliating, the beneficent, the persevering Barnabas – was privy to it. But, times and temptation considered, even might this supposition be assented to, on rather more substantial grounds, than that which stands in competition with it: namely, that for the production of two effects, – comparatively so inconsiderable, and not represented as having been followed by any determinate effects of greater moment, – the ordinary course of nature was, by a special interposition of Almighty power, broken through and disturbed.

Is it or is it not a matter worth remarking – that, of all these twelve supposed occurrences, such as they are, – in not more than four is the hero represented, – even by his own attendant, historian, and panegyrist, – as decidedly taking any active part in the production of the effect? These are – the blinding of the sorcerer, the cure of the cripple, the silencing of the divineress, the curing of Deputy Publius's father: the three first, at the commencement of this supposed wonder-working part of his career; the last, – with an interval of fifteen years between that and the first, – at the very close of it. In the eight intermediate instances, either the effect itself amounted to nothing, or the hero is scarcely represented as being instrumental in the production of it. These are – the being let out of prison after an earthquake had happened – being comforted, whether by God or man, in a vision or without one – having handkerchiefs, by which, when he had done with them, diseases and devils were expelled – being present when a gang of exorcists were beaten and stript by a devil, whom they had undertaken to drive out of a man – being in a place, in which some nonsensical books were burnt by their owners – being in a house, in which a youth said to be dead, was found not to be so – being comforted by an angel, who had the kindness to come on board ship uninvited – shaking off a reptile, without being hurt by it.

Whatever store may be set at this time of day upon all these marvels, less cannot easily be set upon them by any body than was by Paul himself. For proof, take the whole tenor of his own Epistles, as well as the whole tenor of his visions, as delivered by his attendant. Numberless as were the scrapes he got himself into, – numberless as were the hosts of enemies he everywhere made himself, – open as all ears were to every thing that presented itself as marvellous, – unable as men were to distinguish what could be done from what could not be done, – pressing as was at all times the need he had of evidence, that could arrest the hands of enemies, – on no occasion do we find him calling in to his aid, so much as a single one of all these supposed irrefragable evidences.

JAMES MILL

'The Church, and Its Reform' (1835)

—

James Mill (1773–1836)

Biographical Note

Mill's father, known as James Milne, was a shoemaker, and his mother, Isobel Fenton (1755–1802?), was a farmer's daughter from Kirriemuir who had worked as a domestic servant in Edinburgh. They married c. 1772 in Edinburgh and lived at Northwater Bridge, in the parish of Logie Pert, Angus, Scotland. They were probably conventional Presbyterian members of the Church of Scotland, since Bain speaks of the assistance given to Mill by the Logie Pert parish minister, Mr Peters.[1] Believing she had married beneath her, Isobel was dominating and ambitious for her first-born son, James (b. 6 April 1773). James was followed by another son, William (1775–c. 1803), and a daughter, May (1777–1837), who married her father's assistant William Greig c. 1803. After moving to England in 1802 Mill appears to have cut himself off from his family, although he helped to pay his father's debts after he fell ill and became bankrupt.

Mill was schooled at Logie Pert parish school and Montrose Academy, before attending Edinburgh University in 1790, where he was sponsored by a local landowner, Sir John Stuart (1753–1821). Mill tutored Stuart's daughter. His original plan was to become a Presbyterian minister, though his studies at Edinburgh, as suggested by books taken out from the library, were principally historical and socio-philosophical rather than theological.[2] Mill completed his arts studies in 1794 and then took a course in divinity which he completed in January 1797. The records of the Presbytery of Brechin (Mill's home presbytery) note that in October 1796 he was introduced as a future candidate to give the series of sermons and lectures required to be licensed as a preacher, known as 'trials'. On 1 February 1797 he produced for the Presbytery of Brechin the necessary certificate from the Professor of Divinity at Edinburgh that he had attended the divinity course, had passed the required exercises, and was of good moral character. In the summer and autumn of that year Mill successfully completed the 'trials', and on 4 October 1798 was examined by the Presbytery on church history, Hebrew and Greek. He was approved by the members, and subscribed to the Confession of Faith. Mill then received his licence to preach the Gospel.[3] Fenn comments, 'The university and the kirk were the

---

[1] Alexander Bain, *James Mill: A Biography* (1882; reprt. New York 1967), pp. 8–12.
[2] Bain, *James Mill*, pp. 18–19.
[3] Bain, *James Mill*, p. 22.

institutions that influenced him early in his career, and their character helped to shape his approach to the problems that concerned him.'[4]

Little is known of Mill's career between 1798 and 1802, when he moved to London. There is evidence that he acted as a preacher on becoming licensed, and is known to have officiated at Logie Pert.[5] After 1797 he may have worked as a tutor in Aberdeen to the Burnet family of Elrick.[6] In 1800–1 it seems certain he was employed as a tutor by the Marquis of Tweeddale, who had a large family of children living in East Lothian.[7] According to Ball, Mill developed 'an abiding hatred for an hereditary aristocracy' as a result of his experiences as a tutor.[8] He was defeated in his attempt to gain the patronage of the St. Andrews divinity professors, in an effort to become minister of Craig, a small parish near Montrose.[9] During the same period Mill is recorded as a member of the Select Literary Society in Edinburgh, along with James and Thomas Thomson, the anatomist John Barclay, the medical writer James Carter, and Dr James Miller, the editor of the fourth edition of the *Encyclopædia Britannica*.[10]

In 1801 Sir John Stuart was elected MP for Kincardineshire, and the following year Mill accompanied Stuart to London where he took an immediate interest in politics. He was determined to make a living by his pen but, in Ball's account, he became 'a journalistic odd-jobber and literary hack'.[11] During the next decade he turned out a huge volume of articles and reviews. Mill's doubts about religion came to the fore during this period, culminating in his complete loss of faith sometime between 1806 and 1811.[12]

In 1805 Mill married Harriet Burrow (?1783–15 June, 1854), a pretty young woman from a reasonably well off family. Within a few years the marriage became unsatisfactory, save for the production of nine children, including John Stuart Mill (b. 20 May, 1806). The younger Mill made no mention of his mother in the final draft of his *Autobiography*. In the early draft he says of his father, 'In an atmosphere of tenderness and affection he would have been tender and affectionate; but his ill-assorted marriage and his asperities of temper disabled him from making such an atmosphere.'[13] Bentham called Harriet a good creature who had 'no mind in her

4   Robert A. Fenn, *James Mill's Political Thought* (New York and London 1987), p. 2.
5   Bain, *James Mill*, p. 22.
6   Bain, *James Mill*, p. 26.
7   Bain, *James Mill*, p. 30.
8   Terence Ball (ed.), *James Mill. Political Writings* (Cambridge 1992), p. xiv.
9   Bain, *James Mill*, p. 32.
10   Bain, *James Mill*, p. 28.
11   Ball (ed.), *James Mill. Political Writings*, p. xiv.
12   Fenn, *James Mill's Political Thought*, p. 32; see above Part Two, Introduction, p. 267.
13   Jack Stillinger (ed.), *The Early Draft of John Stuart Mill's Autobiography* (Urbana, IL 1961), p. 66.

body'.[14] Mill's younger siblings were Wilhelmina Forbes (1808–61), Clara Esther (1810–86), Harriet Isabella (1812–97), James Bentham (1814–62), Jane Stuart (1816?–83), Henry (1820–40), Mary Elizabeth (1822–1913), and George Grote Mill (1825–53), several named after significant figures in Mill's life. He was generally remembered by his elder children as a stern and bad-tempered father.[15]

Mill has the reputation of being a moral puritan: 'Mill was not a worldly or self-seeking man, and his comments on society and politics often suggest the sort of puritan who disapproves of other men's pleasures from a half-conscious fear of their power over himself'.[16] Much of the moral character of his work can be traced to his Scottish Presbyterian background, which led him to question eighteenth-century scepticism, to reject established churches, to distrust art except for useful purposes, and to divide humanity into good and evil parts.[17] When he attacked the Church of England as the worst of churches in his critical attack on Robert Southey's *Book of the Church* in the *Westminster Review* (1825) and again in 'Ecclesiastical Establishments' in the same journal (1826), and later in 'The Church, and Its Reform' (1835), Mill must have remembered the profound distrust of Anglican Arminianism, ceremony and state interference which Scots Presbyterians felt. His intellectual development was also greatly influenced by his interest in church history and the Reformation as 'the great and decisive contest against priestly tyranny for liberty of thought'.[18] John Stuart Mill says that his father subscribed to the 'Manichæan theory of a Good and an Evil Principle, struggling against each other for the government of the Universe'.[19] In Stephen's account, 'His main purpose, too, was to lay down a rule of duty, almost mathematically ascertainable, and not to be disturbed by any sentimentalism, mysticism, or rhetorical foppery'.[20]

In 1808 Mill met Jeremy Bentham, and by 1810 the Mill family was living in a house provided by Bentham and spending months with him in the country during the summer. This close connection continued until Mill established a modicum of independence following the publication of *The History of British India* (1817) and the beginning of his employment at India House in 1819. Mill remained an employee of the East India Company until his death in 1836. He began as an Assistant to the Examiner of India Correspondence at India House, and in 1823 was appointed 1st Assistant Examiner. Soon after John Stuart Mill also found a place in India

---

[14]   William Thomas, *The Philosophic Radicals: Nine Studies in Theory and Practice, 1817–1841* (Oxford 1979), p. 17.
[15]   John Stuart Mill, *Autobiography*, ed. Jack Stillinger and John M. Robson, *Collected Works of John Stuart Mill* (Toronto 1981), i. 53.
[16]   Thomas, *The Philosophic Radicals*, p. 35.
[17]   Thomas, *The Philosophic Radicals*, pp. 99–101.
[18]   Mill, *Autobiography*, in *Collected Works*, i. 45.
[19]   Mill, *Autobiography*, in *Collected Works*, i. 43.
[20]   Leslie Stephen, *The English Utilitarians*, 3 vols. (London 1900), ii. 337.

House. In 1830 his father became Head Examiner, and 'acquired a very great amount of influence and authority with the Court of Directors'.[21] Mill died on 23 June 1836 'of long standing pulmonary phthisis' (probably tuberculosis) and was buried in Kensington Church.[22]

The Scottish philosophical influences shaping Mill's thought were strong. He acknowledged the influence of Dugald Stewart: 'The taste for the studies which have formed my favourite pursuits, and which will be so to the end of my life, I owe to Mr. Stewart.'[23] Mill also admired Thomas Reid, whom he followed in condemning Hume.[24] However, Fenn suggests that it was his loss of faith that led Mill to question the Reidian world view.[25] In *The History of British India* he rejected the explanation – derived from Montesquieu – of moral diversity as the consequence of culture and climate, preferring to follow John Millar in classifying nations by their level of civilization.[26] Utility was the barometer of civilization for Mill: 'Exactly in proportion as *Utility* is the object of every pursuit, may we regard a nation as civilized'.[27] He recommended Millar as essential reading to his son, John Stuart, and to the economist David Ricardo. Mill followed Adam Smith in his assessment of the East India Company's commercial monopoly.[28] The influence of Stewart and Scottish philosophy generally can also be seen in Mill's educational writing and his belief that both aristocracy and poverty were the enemies of progress.[29]

Other philosophical influences on Mill included Bacon's inductive method, which Mill applied to psychology. At first the theory of Hartley's *Observations on Man* was rejected, but by 1815 Mill considered Hartley essentially correct.[30] According to John Stuart Mill his father deemed Hartley's book 'the really master production in the philosophy of mind'.[31] Mill employed Hartley's theory in *The Analysis of the Phenomena of the Human Mind* (1828), which Fenn viewed as 'a return to the central English tradition of empirical philosophy'.[32]

The nature and degree of Bentham's influence on Mill has frequently been debated. Thomas considers that Mill, Romilly and Place were less disciples of Bentham, than men interested in his ideas but baffled by their

---

[21] Bain, *James Mill*, p. 356.
[22] Bain, *James Mill*, p. 409.
[23] Fenn, *James Mill's Political Thought*, p. 7.
[24] Fenn, *James Mill's Political Thought*, pp. 19–20.
[25] Fenn, *James Mill's Political Thought*, p. 32.
[26] See Javed Majeed, *Ungoverned Imaginings: James Mill's 'The History of British India' and Orientalism* (Oxford 1992).
[27] Quoted in Thomas, *The Philosophic Radicals*, p. 105.
[28] Thomas, *The Philosophic Radicals*, p. 114.
[29] Stefan Collini, Donald Winch, and John Burrow, *That Noble Science of Politics: A Study in Nineteenth-century Intellectual History* (Cambridge 1983), p. 123.
[30] Fenn, *James Mill's Political Thought*, pp. 25, 34.
[31] Mill, *Autobiography*, in *Collected Works*, i. 71.
[32] Fenn, *James Mill's Political Thought*, p. 41.

obscurity: 'Each of them had considerable reservations about the ultimate point of Bentham's work, and each experienced a barrier of incomprehension and distrust in their relations with him.'[33] Bain considered that while Mill followed Bentham in Law and Jurisprudence, 'he was vastly Bentham's superior in Politics strictly so called'.[34] In this area 'Mill focused his [Bentham's] activity somewhat, and gave it direction'.[35] Fenn has stated that Bentham's influence did not cause Mill to 'proceed much further than he had already gone',[36] and Ball has argued that 'Mill led Bentham to appreciate the importance of economic factors in explaining and changing social life and political institutions', and also influenced Bentham to advocate reform from a more 'democratic' than 'top down' direction.[37] More substantively, it appears Mill had a hand in Bentham's comparison between the Church of England and the Church of Scotland in *Church of Englandism and its Catechism Examined* (1818), although there is nothing quite so extreme in his own writings,[38] including the very radical 'The Church, and Its Reform'.

Certainly Mill and Bentham were fellow political radicals, though for Mill this had at its heart a belief in the progressive effects of education, derived from his reading of Locke, Hartley and Helvétius.[39] He envisaged a society dominated by an educated élite, which would provide progressive ideas in arts and science.[40] In this respect, education was the 'chief engine of progress'.[41] In spite of this belief in the intelligentsia, Macaulay attacked Mill because he disliked the intolerance of the younger utilitarians influenced by Mill: 'Philosophical pride has done for them what spiritual pride did for the Puritans in a former age; it has generated in them an aversion for the fine arts, for elegant literature, and for the sentiments of chivalry.'[42] Mill's actual utilitarian educational efforts were largely unsuccessful in the decade between 1810–20,[43] although he could take some satisfaction in the founding of the secular University College in Gower Street, London.

Mill had other important associates and connections in his later career. In 1811, probably through Bentham, he met Ricardo, to whom he was strongly attached,[44] and 'united Ricardian economics with the Benthamite

33 Thomas, *The Philosophic Radicals*, pp. 25, 26.
34 Bain, *James Mill*, p. 421.
35 Thomas, *The Philosophic Radicals*, p. 33.
36 Fenn, *James Mill's Political Thought*, p. 36.
37 Ball (ed.), *James Mill. Political Writings*, p. xv.
38 Thomas, *The Philosophic Radicals*, p. 36.
39 Thomas, *The Philosophic Radicals*, pp. 120, 121.
40 Fenn, *James Mill's Political Thought*, p. 75.
41 Ball (ed.), *James Mill. Political Writings*, p. xvii.
42 Quoted in Thomas, *The Philosophic Radicals*, p. 135. See Jack Lively and John Rees (eds), *Utilitarian Logic and Politics: James Mill's 'Essay on Government', Macaulay's Critique and the Ensuing Debate* (Oxford 1978).
43 Stephen, *The English Utilitarians*, ii. 20–22. See also W. H. Burston, *James Mill on Education* (London 1969), and *James Mill on Philosophy and Education* (London 1973).
44 Mill, *Autobiography*, in *Collected Works*, i. 31.

science of legislation.'[45] Mill was influenced by Ricardo to use political economy to help enlighten men to their own interests.[46] On the other hand, it has been said that Mill 'contributed to the formation of many of [Ricardo's] opinions'.[47] He had other friendships with reformers and radicals, including Henry Brougham, Joseph Hume (whom he met at school at Montrose), Francis Place, and Sir Samuel Romilly.

Mill's influence on the succeeding generation is also of significance. He acted as an intellectual guide to the younger utilitarians – John Stuart Mill, George Grote, and the brothers John and Charles Austin. And, in Stephen's account, 'He succeeded beyond all dispute in forcibly presenting one set of views which profoundly influenced his countrymen; and the very narrowness of his intellect enabled him to plant his blows more effectively'.[48] One modern commentator has placed Mill 'Among the most underrated and least understood of modern political thinkers'.[49]

Following the publication of the influential *The History of British India* and *Essay on Government*, Mill produced two major philosophical works: *Elements of Political Philosophy* (1821) and *The Analysis of the Phenomena of the Human Mind* (1828). Much of his best writing, however, is contained in numerous periodical essays and reviews, many of which were published anonymously.[50]

Note on the Text

'The Church, and Its Reform' (1835) was the third of Mill's critical examinations of the established Church of England. In *The Westminster Review*, No. 3 (5 Jan. 1825) he attacked Robert Southey's revisionist defence of Anglicanism in *The Book of the Church* (1824), and continued this critique in 'Ecclesiastical Establishments' in *The Westminster Review*, No. 5 (10 April, 1826). The historical approach of the first two essays is complemented by the contemporary analysis and radical prescriptions for reform contained in the third article, published in the first issue of *The London Review* in 1835. 'The Church, and Its Reform' has not appeared in any form since then, and it is this original text which follows.

[45]   Collini, Winch, and Burrow, *That Noble Science of Politics*, p. 87.
[46]   Thomas, *The Philosophic Radicals*, p. 104.
[47]   Collini, Winch, and Burrow, *That Noble Science of Politics*, p. 87.
[48]   Stephen, *The English Utilitarians*, ii. 40.
[49]   Ball (ed.), *James Mill. Political Writings*, p. xi.
[50]   See the comprehensive list in Fenn, *James Mill's Political Thought*, appendix.

The Church, and Its Reform

In the article on the State of the Nation, in the first number of this publication, it was said – 'We should now go on, and point out the reforms, which we think are needed, in the other great provinces of abuse, Law and Religion; but we have been led on so far, illustrating the spirit of reform, that we have not space for these particular subjects, and must allot to them separate articles, in the future numbers of our publication.'

This promise, in what regards the institutions appropriated to religion, we shall now endeavour to fulfil. 'Bacon says, "If St. John were to write an Epistle to the Church of England, as he did to that of Asia, it would surely contain the clause, *I have a few things against thee!*" I am not quite of his opinion. I am afraid the clause would be, *I have not a few things against thee.*' These are the words of Dr Jortin – (See his *Tracts*, vol. i. p. 350.)

'In England we certainly want a reform, both in the civil and ecclesiastical part of our constitution. Men's minds, however, I think are not yet generally prepared for admitting its necessity. A reformer of Luther's temper and talents would, in five years, persuade the people to compel the Parliament to abolish tithes, to extinguish pluralities, to enforce residence, to confine episcopacy to the overseeing of dioceses, to expunge the Athanasian Creed from our Liturgy, to free Dissenters from Test Acts, and the ministers of the establishment from subscription to human articles of faith. These and other matters, respecting the church, ought to be done,' &c.

Thus Watson, Bishop of Llandaff, delivered his sentiments, in a letter to the Duke of Grafton, in the year 1791.[1]

One of the most remarkable of the sentiments here expressed is the belief of the power, which a single advocate of reform, of the proper stamp, might exert on the public mind in England, and through the public mind on the House of Commons, and through the House of Commons on all that is faulty in our public institutions. 'A reformer of Luther's temper and talents would, in five years' (in 1791, be it observed, when the minds of men were ill-prepared) 'persuade the people to compel the Parliament,' &c. The great characteristics of Luther were courage, activity, and persever- ance; for intellectual endowments he was equalled by many of his contemporaries; and by some, Melancthon and Erasmus, for example, surpassed. We mention this, and request attention to it, as a matter of

---

[1] See Watson's Memoirs, p. 236.

encouragement to those whose minds are elevated and blessed with the love of reform. It requires, they may see, but the *will* in any individual of a class, which now is numerous, to be the author of blessings, analogous to those achieved by him who, among mortals, was the greatest benefactor of the human race.

Among the reforms which five years of proper exertion might bring about, in the ecclesiastical part of our institutions, the Bishop enumerates the abolition of tithes, the extinction of pluralities, the compulsion of residence, the confinement of episcopacy (meaning, literally, overlooking or superintending) to the appropriate function which the name denotes; besides these, erasing the Athanasian Creed from the Liturgy, abolishing the Test Acts, and subscription to Articles of Faith.

Forty-four years have passed over our heads, and, of all this, how much has been done? We have abolished the Test Acts! And yet the people are accused of being too impatient for reform; as indicating, by their impatience, a desire to destroy religion – aye, and government along with it. – And so they would be if they were only to complain of a single bad thing once in a hundred years.

The Bishop is far from intending here a systematic view of the bad things in our ecclesiastical machinery. He mentions a parcel of particulars, by way of exemplification, and ends by saying, 'these, and *other matters*,' &c. We know that he laid great stress on one thing which is here not mentioned at all; reducing the emoluments of the overpaid priests of all descriptions, and giving something more to the class whom the clergy think sufficiently paid with a beggarly pittance.

The time is come, when a service of unspeakable importance would be rendered to the community, by a full and detailed exposition of the good which *might* be done by a well-ordered and well-conducted clergy; of the want of good in any shape derivable from our present ecclesiastical corporation, while it is the perennial source of evil to an incredible amount. It is obvious, that such a work as we contemplate is not compatible with the space which could be allotted to it in this publication, or the time which could be bestowed on one of its articles. But we shall enter into some details, to give a clearer view of what we recommend to others, and earnestly desire to see accomplished.

We shall begin with some illustrations of the proposition, that the present ecclesiastical establishment in England is a perfect nullity in respect to good, but an active and powerful agent in the production of evil.

It is one of the most remarkable of all the instances which can be adduced of the power of delusion, when well supported by artifice and power – that, up to this hour, an institute, truly characterized by the terms we have just applied to it, should be still looked upon as a fabric, venerable for the benefits which it confers upon the people, at whose charge it is upheld.

It has not the look, the colour, not even one of the outward marks, of an institution intended for good.

The world, at least the Protestant world, needs no information respecting the abuses of the Romish church. That ecclesiastical establishment had been reared up into a system, most artfully contrived for rendering men the degraded instruments and tools of priests; for preventing the growth of all intellect, and all morality; for occupying the human mind with superstition; and attaching the very idea of duty to nothing but the repetition of ceremonies, for the glorification of priests.

At the time of the great revolt from the domination of the Romish priesthood, while other countries broke down and struck off, some more, some less, but all a great part of the machinery, by which the Romish church had become the curse of human nature, the English clergy embraced that machinery very nearly as it stood, have clung to it ever since with the most eager attachment, praised it to the skies, and done whatever they could in the way of persecution against all who condemned it.

Look at the facts, and see how distinctly they support this representation.

Did not our church-makers retain the same order of priests? archbishops, bishops, deans, prebendaries, rectors, vicars, curates; with the same monstrous inequality of pay?

Did they not retain the very same course of clerical service – nay, the very same book of formularies, doing little more than translate the Massbook into the English Liturgy?

Renouncing allegiance to a foreign head was the principal part of the change which took place in England, and the abolition of the religious houses, to satisfy the rapacity of the king and the nobles. But the employment and duties of the clergy remained as before, with some little alteration. The Church of England parson has less to do than the Romish priest; and being allowed to involve himself in the cares of a family, has a mind less devoted to the concerns of his place.

If the Romish establishment was not framed for the production of good, but was an exquisitely-fashioned instrument for the production of evil, is it not certain that the English establishment, which consists of the same integrant parts, must very closely resemble it in its tendencies?

Let us look at this subject a little more closely. Can any thing be a greater outrage upon the sense of propriety; a more profligate example of the contempt of public good; than to see a concatenation of priests, paid, in proportions, ranging from the height of princely revenues, down to less than the pay of a common footman; without even a pretence that the duties of the most miserably rewarded portion are less onerous or less important than those of the set who are paid with so immoral and disgraceful a prodigality?

The next thing which solicits the attention of all rational men, is the work which the English clergy are called upon to perform for this pay;

exhibiting, in their extreme, the opposite vices of extravagance, and deficiency.

We undertake to maintain the two following propositions: First, that the only services which are obligatory upon the Church of England clergy, and regularly performed, are ceremonies, from which no advantage can be derived. Secondly, that the services they might render, in raising the moral and intellectual character of the people, are not obligatory, but left wholly to their option, to do, or not to do; that they are performed always most imperfectly, and in general not at all. Let us go to the particulars.

The services obligatory on the Church of England clergymen are, the Sunday service, performing the ceremony of baptism, that of marriage, and that of the burial of the dead.

To estimate the value of them, let us see wherein they consist.

The Sunday service. That consists almost wholly in the repetition of certain formularies; read out of a book called the Book of Common Prayer. On this part of the duty (the work is actually called *duty*) of the Church of England priest, the following observations are inevitable.

1. The repetition of forms of words has a tendency to become a merely mechanical operation, in which the mind has little concern. To whatever extent the repetition of religious formularies becomes mechanical, it is converted into an unmeaning ceremony.

2. The formularies themselves are of the nature of mere ceremonies. They consist of creeds; of short sentences called collects; which are commonly words of Scripture thrown into the form of ejaculations, or petitions to God; prayers, especially the Lord's Prayer; and extracts from the Bible. It is needless to mention the Communion Service, because, excepting the purely mechanical part, handing what is to be eaten and drank, it consists of the same things.

It is necessary to bestow a short examination on each of those particulars.

Of the repetition of creeds, the best thing which can be said is, that it is purely ceremonial. If it is not ceremonial, it is far worse: it is a forced declaration of belief – in other words, an instrument for generating the worst habit which can be implanted in the human breast – the habit of saying the thing which is not – the habit of affirming as a matter of fact, that which is not a matter of fact – the habit of affirming that a man is conscious of a state of mind, when he is not conscious of it.[2] This is to

---

2   There may be chicaning on this subject; but no candid man, who really understands the human mind, will hesitate in assenting to the fact which is here affirmed, that a man is not conscious of that state of mind, called belief, with respect to every thing contained in the several creeds in the Prayer Book – perhaps in any one of them, every time he is called upon to pronounce them: above all, when he is first called upon to do so. A verbal assent is not belief. Belief implies ideas, and the perception of their being joined together according to the principles of reason. 'Strictly speaking,' says Berkeley, 'to believe that which has no meaning in it is impossible. . . . Men impose upon themselves, by imagining that they believe those propositions which they have often heard, though at bottom they have no meaning in them.' – *Principles of Human Knowledge*, § 54.

poison morality in the very fountain of life. The fine feeling of moral obligation is gone in a mind wherein the habit of insincerity is engendered: nay, more – every man who is possessed of that fatal habit possesses an instrument for the perpetration of every other crime. Mendacity is the pander to the breach of every obligation.

The collects, which are short sentences – mostly words of scripture, thrown into the form of ejaculation or petition – we may take along with the prayers; and of the whole lot together we may affirm, that if it is not ceremonial, and without meaning, it is a great deal worse.

The most important, by far, of all the religious sentiments is – the distinct, and steady, and perpetually operative conception of what is implied in the words, Almighty Being of perfect wisdom and goodness. Without this, there is no religion. Superstition there may be, in perfection. Priestism is its nature; it is a contrivance of priests, and always manufactured for their ends. When deluded people are made to think ill of the Divine Being, they are in the hands of the priests, and can be made to do whatever the cunning of the order prescribes to them.

The tendency of the Church of England prayers is to give a wrong notion of the Divine attributes; and instead of the idea of a Being of perfect wisdom and goodness, to present the idea of a being very imperfect in both. To speak of them in the most general way, we may observe, that perpetually to be asking God for things which we want, believing that this is a way to obtain them, implies the belief that God is imperfect both in wisdom and goodness. Telling God unceasingly of our wants, implies that he needs to be told them – otherwise it is an unmeaning ceremony. Asking Him continually to do things for us, implies our belief that otherwise he would not do them for us; in other words, our belief, either that God will not do what is right, if he be not begged and entreated to do so – or that, by being begged and entreated, he can be induced to do what is wrong.

In like manner, in regard to praise, which is the other element of what is called prayer: first, what use can there be in our telling the Divine Being, that he has such and such qualities; as if he was like to mistake his own qualities, by some imperfection in his knowledge, which we supply? next, what a mean and gross conception of the Divine nature is implied in supposing that, like the meanest of men, God is delighted in listening to his own praises! Surely, practices which have this tendency, if they are considered as having any meaning at all, it is much better to consider as having no meaning – that is, as being mere ceremonies.

The Divine Author of our religion every where indicates his opinion, that praying is nothing but a ceremony: he particularly marks praying, as one among the abuses of that sect among his countrymen, who carried their religious pretensions the highest, and whom he considered it his duty to reprobate as the most worthless class of men in the nation.

It is matter worthy of particular remark, that Jesus no where lays stress on prayer as a duty: he rarely speaks of it otherwise than incidentally. With that condescension to the weakness and prejudices of his countrymen, which is every where observable in his conduct, he does not reprobate a practice, to which he knew they had the attachment of an invincible habit; but by placing it among the vices of the Pharisees, he indicated with tolerable clearness what he thought of it.

It would seem, if we take his own words and example for authority, not the interested interpretation of priests – that he actually forbade the use of prayer in public worship. Let us observe how he gave warning against the abuse of this ceremony, in the sermon on the mount, and how clearly and incontrovertibly he characterized it as a ceremony, and nothing else: 'And when thou prayest, thou shalt not be as the hypocrites are: for they love to pray standing in the synagogue' (that is, in public worship) 'and in the corners of the streets, that they may be seen of men. Verily, I say unto you, they have their reward. But thou, when thou prayest, enter into thy closet; and when thou hast shut the door, pray to thy Father which is in secret, and thy Father which seeth in secret shall reward thee openly.'

Nothing can be clearer than this: all prayer is reprobated but secret prayer, and even that is not recommended. The words always are, '*when ye pray*' – that is, if ever ye do pray, do it in secret, the whole turn of the expression being permissive only, not injunctive. It is remarkable, with respect to this limitation of prayer to secret prayer only, that Jesus himself never makes a prayer on any public occasion; and as often as he is represented in the Gospels as praying, which is very rarely, he withdraws even from his disciples, and does it in absolute solitude. Jesus goes on – 'But when ye pray, use not vain repetitions, as the heathens do; for they think that they shall be heard for their much speaking. Be not ye, therefore, like unto them: for your Father knoweth what things ye have need of, before ye ask him.'

This last expression is of peculiar force and significance: Be not ye like those who think they will be heard for their much speaking; since speaking at all is of no use; 'your Father knoweth what things ye have need of, before ye ask him.' Can there be a more distinct declaration, that prayer is a ceremony only, and not very easy to be kept from being a hurtful ceremony?

Jesus subjoins to this declaration of the ceremonial nature of prayer these words – 'After this manner, therefore, pray ye;' and then comes the formulary called the Lord's Prayer, evidently intended as a pattern to prevent the excesses into which the ceremony was apt to run. And the words of the pattern itself, taken in combination with the words spoken immediately before – 'Your heavenly Father knoweth,' &c. – afford sufficient evidence, when they are minutely examined, of the character in which its Divine Author meant it should be used.

But, as it is too evident to need any illustration that the idea of the

Divine Being, as a being of perfect wisdom and goodness, so steadily and luminously fixed in the mind, as to be a principle of action, is the very essence of religion, and the sole source of all the good impressions we derive from it, it is not less evident, that every idea instilled into us, which implies imperfection in the Divine Being, is a perversion of the religious principle, and so far as it goes, converts it into a principle of evil. Because, exactly in so far as men set up for the object of their worship a being who falls short of perfect wisdom and goodness, so far they manufacture to themselves a motive for the practice of what is contrary to wisdom and goodness. Yet it is self-evident, that to offer petitions to the Divine Being, with the idea that they will have any effect – that every thing, being already ordered for the best, will not proceed in the same way exactly as if no such petition had been made, is to suppose the petitioner either wiser or better than his Maker – either knowing better what is fit to be done, or more in earnest about the doing of it.

If these observations about the ceremonial nature of prayer be admitted, there is not occasion to say much about the rest of the Sunday service. Where is the use of a priest to read a chapter of the Bible, which every head of a family does to those who live in his house? Besides, the Church of England always reads the same chapters, thereby inevitably converting the operation into a ceremony. Are these the only chapters in the Bible which deserve to be read? If not, why read them only, casting a slur upon the rest? Again, when any thing has been read sufficiently often to have fixed the purport of it indelibly in the mind, what is the use of more repetition? It is evidently ceremonial only. With regard to the Communion service, we think it is, among protestants, considered as a ceremony. Mr. Bentham has endeavoured to show that it was never intended, either by Jesus or his disciples, to be permanent, even as a ceremony, and that it is peculiarly ill-fitted for that purpose; and we have never met with any thing like an answer to his observations, which well deserve the attention of all rational and honest-minded Christians.

And now we come to the Sermon, the only part of the Sunday performance, which is not essentially ceremonial; but which may, by misperformance, become not only ceremonial, like the rest, but positively and greatly mischievous.

A celebrated wit of the last age, known by the familiar name of George Selwyn, had gone one day to church, and was asked when he returned, by some one in the family to which he was on a visit, of what sort the sermon had been? 'Oh,' said he, 'like other sermons; palavering God Almighty; and bullragging the devil.' This was said, of course, satirically; and it must be added, considering the subject, that it was said profanely. But, nevertheless, it must be confessed, that it describes with great point the character of at least one grand class of Church of England Sermons, which consist of terms of praise heaped unceasingly on the Divinity – terms of condemnation heaped as unceasingly on the Personification of Evil: as if there could be supposed to be an individual in a Christian congregation not already prepared to bestow laudatory epithets upon God, opprobrious epithets on the devil, as far as his power of language would permit him to go. As no congregation, therefore, could possibly be the better for hearing such a sermon, it is necessary to consider it as a mere ceremony.

Another grand class of Church of England sermons consists of what, to borrow (as we may here do without profaneness) the language of George Selwyn, we may call palavering the Church of England, and bullragging the Dissenters; ascribing good qualities without end to Church-of-Englandism – evil qualities, in equal proportion, to Dissenter-ism. This is not merely ceremonial, certainly; but we may safely pronounce it worse – something so bad, that hardly anything equal to it in atrocity can be conceived. It is making religion, which ought to be a principle of love among human beings, a principle of hatred; and that hatred turning upon what? The great line of distinction between moral good and evil? That by which He who is perfection is mainly distinguished from the Prince of Darkness? No, no! But upon some difference of opinion in matters of little importance, or some diversity in the use of ceremonies. Is not this to vilify, or rather to explode morality? setting above it such frivolous things, as sameness of belief in dubious matters, or sameness of performance in matters of ceremony? Is not this to renounce the good of mankind as the grand principle of action, the main point of obedience to the will of God – making the service of God a pretence for hostility to a large portion of his creatures? Is this a morality, fit to be promulgated by a man, miserably, or exorbitantly paid, in every parish in the kingdom? We restrain by punishment, and we do well, the publication of indecent books and prints, calculated to inflame the passions of the inexperienced and unwary. But these publications are innocent, compared with the sermons read to congregations, or printed for the public, to which we now allude.

The extent to which the exercise of this malignant principle is carried cannot, perhaps, be more clearly shown than by calling to mind that celebrated Charge to the clergy of London, by the then Right Reverend the Bishop of London, the present Most Reverend the Archbishop of Canterbury, to which Mr. Bentham makes such pointed allusion. 'The prostration of the understanding and the will,' there spoken of as one of the *desiderata*, one of the objects of desire, and of endeavour, to the Church of England, Mr. Bentham has commented on with his usual fulness and usual effect. And all that is necessary for us, in regard to that generous purpose, is, to refer our readers to the treat prepared for them in his comment.[3] Another expression in the said Charge – is that to which we desire to direct the reader's attention in this place. We borrow the expression from Mr.

---

[3]   Church of Englandism Examined. By Jeremy Bentham, Esq.

Bentham, other means of reference not being at hand, but with perfect confidence, knowing, as we do, what his care of accuracy in such particulars was. 'In the Charge,' says Mr. Bentham, 'we shall see Non-Church-of-Englandists marked out as "*enemies*" and men of "*guilt*." ' – Why, in the name of all that is good, should Church of England men treat as 'enemies' all men who cannot subscribe the Thirty-Nine Articles, or join in the performance of their ceremonies? Is not this to make religion the curse of human nature – the permanent fountain of discord – the extinguisher of love and of peace? Not to subscribe the Thirty-nine Articles, and not to join in certain ceremonies is 'guilt!' This is to make the Church-of-England-man the general enemy of his species. Sermons, which propagate this idea, propagate a feeling of hatred, a disposition of hostility, towards all men but those of their own particular sect. Is not this to renounce the religion of Jesus, which is a religion of peace? Is not this Antichrist? Is not this to deny the Lord that bought them? – to crucify him in the house of his friends? Assuredly sermons of this cast had better not be delivered.

Another class of sermons are the controversial: those which undertake to settle points of dogmatic divinity. We believe that all rational men are united in opinion, that such discourses, addressed to ordinary congregations, can be of no use, and have a strong tendency to be hurtful. They have a direct tendency to attach undue importance to uniformity of belief on points on which it is not necessary. They have also a direct tendency to lower men's ideas of the Divine character – representing the Almighty as favouring those who adhere to one side in the controversy, hostile to those who adhere to the other. This is to suborn belief; to create in those who yield to such teaching a habit of forcing a belief; that is, of dealing dishonestly with their own convictions. To hold out rewards for believing one way, punishment for believing another way, is to hold out inducements to resist the force of evidence, on the one side, and lend to it a weight which does not belong to it, on the other. This is a mode of attaching belief to any opinions, however unfounded; and as soon as a man is thoroughly broken in to this mental habit, not only is the power of sound judgment destroyed within him, but the moral character does not escape uninjured. The man in whose breast this habit is created, never sees anything in an opinion, but whether it is agreeable to his interest or not. Whether it is founded on evidence or not, he has been trained to neglect. Truth or falsehood in matters of opinion is no longer with him the first consideration.

This is nearly the most immoral state of mind which can have existence in a human being. No other cause of criminal actions is of equal potency with this. A man in this state of mind has an opinion ready to justify him in any profitable course of villany in which he can engage. How great a proportion of Church of England teaching, in pulpits, in schools, and in universities, has this tendency, and no other, is a subject of immense importance, and to which we must recur on future occasions. Oh, for a Pascal! Oh, for a new set of Provincial Letters!

We shall pass by the other subdivisions of sermons, and come to the moral. Though a man of the proper stamp, residing among his fellow parishioners, would have other and still more effectual means of making the impressions on their minds which lead to good conduct, we do not dispute that a discourse of the proper kind, delivered to them when assembled on the day of rest, would have happy effects. In the first place, it would establish in their minds pure ideas of the moral character of God; and would root out of them every notion which implies imperfection in the Divine Mind. This is a matter of infinite importance, though neglected, or rather trampled upon by Church of England religion; for exactly in proportion as the model which men set up for imitation is perfect or imperfect, will be the performance which takes place in consequence. It is unavailing, it is poor childishness, to call the Almighty benevolent, when you ascribe to him lines of action which are entirely the reverse. It is vain to call him wise, when you represent him as moved by considerations which have weight with only the weakest of men.

We have already seen something of the extent to which the religion of the Church of England tends to imprint the notion of imperfection, both of the moral and intellectual kind, in the character of the Deity. But there is one particular to which we have hardly as yet adverted, which deserves the deepest attention. We mean the notions propagated about punishments after death.

No wise and good man ever thinks of punishment but as an undesirable means to a desirable end; and therefore to be applied in the smallest quantity possible. To ascribe to the Divine Being the use of punishments in atrocious excess; not applying it according to the rules of the most perfect benevolence, which is its character in the hand of a virtuous man, but in the spirit of revenge, and to vindicate his dignity, is to ascribe to him, not the character of a civilized man, but of an atrocious savage. Nor is the excess of future punishments the only point of importance. The uselessness of them also deserves the utmost regard in tracing the ways in which priests, for their own ends, have perverted men's notions of the Divine character. Punishment is employed by virtuous men for the prevention of hurtful actions. But what is the use of punishment when the time of action is gone by, and when the doom of the wretched victim is fixed for ever? It is said that the apprehension of these punishments is a restraint on men during their lives. But to make this allegation is only another mode of ascribing imperfection, both intellectual and moral, to the Supreme Being.

It is a certain and undisputed principle, that proximity of punishment is necessary to its efficiency; that if a punishment is distant, and hence the conception of it faint; it loses proportionally of its force. As it is the great rule of benevolence to be sparing in the use of punishment – that is, to employ it in the smallest possible quantity which will answer the end – it is the constant aim of benevolence to make it as proximate as possible – that is, to make the smallest possible quantity suffice. What would be thought of a legislator, who should ordain, that the punishment of murder and theft should not take place till twenty years, or so, after the commission of the crime; and that, for the distance of the time, compensation should be made in the severity of the punishment? Is not this the atrocity into which those theologians sink, who tell us that the punishments of hell are intended for the prevention of evil in the present life? That this theory is not derived from the Scripture, but is the pure forgery of priests, might be inferred with certainty *à priori*, and could also be easily proved by particular evidence. But the authority of Bishop Butler will be sufficient for us on the present occasion. He has given it as his opinion, an opinion which has never been accused as unscriptural, that the change from the present to the future life will not, in all probability, be greater, than the change from the state which precedes, to that which follows the birth, that the individual will pass into the future life with all the dispositions and habits which he had acquired in his previous course, producing misery to him if they are bad, happiness if they are good; but with this advantage, that the circumstance in which he will be placed will have an irresistible tendency to correct bad habits, and encourage good ones, whence, in time, it will be brought about, that none but good habits will exist, and happiness will be universal.

Next to the propagation of correct notions regarding the character of the Supreme Being, as the perfection of wisdom and goodness, with warnings against all such notions as imply imperfection in the Divine nature, the object of discourses, calculated to be of real utility to the majority of those who compose congregations, would be, to make, and as deeply as possible, all the impressions which lead to good conduct; to give strength and constancy to the kindly and generous feelings; to stimulate the desire of doing good, by showing the value of it, and the amount of good which even a very poor man may effect, in the course of his life, if he seizes the many little occasions which he will find put in his way; to make understood and felt the value of a good name; how much of the happiness of each individual depends upon the good-will of those among whom he lives; and that the sure way of obtaining it is to show by his acts his good-will to them. Such discourses would put the people on their guard against the misleading affections; would make them understand how much is lost by giving way to them; and with what a preponderance of good, even to ourselves, they are supplanted by those which lead us to rejoice in being the instruments of happiness to others. Above all things, such discourses would make parents clearly understand, and acutely feel, the power they have over the happiness or misery of their children, during the whole course of their lives. On the mode of creating in their children the habits on which their happiness depends, such discourses would enter into the most minute detail. They would carefully warn parents against every display of feeling or passion, every thing in word, or in action, having a tendency to produce an undesirable impression on the tender mind; and would give them an habitual conviction, and, as it were, a sense, of the importance of making none but the right impressions.

It is not necessary to go farther in illustrating what sermons of the useful class would be. It is only necessary to recollect what the moral class of Church of England sermons are. Other people may have been more fortunate than we; but though we have heard a good many of that class, we never heard one which we thought good for anything. They may be characterized as a parcel of vapid commonplaces, delivered in vague and vapouring phrases, having not even a tendency to give men more precise ideas of the good they may do, or to kindle within them a more strong and steady desire of performing it. We have often asked ourselves, after hearing such a sermon, whether any human being could by possibility have received one useful impression from it; whether any one could have gone away after hearing it a better man than when he came; in the least degree more alive to the motives to good conduct, more capable of resisting the motives to bad? Never, in a single instance, do we remember having been able to make an answer in the affirmative. For a confirmation of the opinion we have thus formed of Church of England sermonizing, we appeal to the printed specimens of them, some of which are by men of considerable ability, skilful advocates of a cause, acute and eloquent controvertists, but all of them defective, or rather utterly worthless, in moral teaching.

We have now probably said enough to show how entirely of the ceremonial kind, and ceremonial with more or less of a hurtful tendency, the whole of the Sunday services obligatory on the Church of England clergyman are.

All that remains is the ceremony of baptism, the ceremony of marriage, and the ceremony of burying the dead. These services are so much regarded in the light of ceremonies, that they commonly go by that name.

The Church of England indeed pretends, that baptism washes away original sin; one of those cherished opinions by which it ascribes weakness, both intellectual and moral, to the Supreme Being. In this opinion it is reprobated by other churches, as retaining one of the errors of the Romish Church. For the rest, it cannot be pretended that it is other than ceremonial. To the infant, who knows nothing about the matter, it would be ridiculous to suppose that any good is done. And what can it be pretended is the good which it does to any other body? For a full exposure of the Church of England proceedings in respect to baptism, we refer to what is said by Mr. Bentham in his Examination of Church of England Catechism, pp. 47 to 59, where the reader will find both instruction and amusement.

About marriage it is not necessary to say much. It is in its essence a civil contract; and few rational men think that the religious ceremony is of any importance. It is very certain that nobody regards it as any security for the better performance of the duties which the contract implies.

The burial service consists in reading certain portions of Scripture and certain prayers. But to whom can this performance be considered as being of any use? Not certainly to the dead man; and certainly not to any of the living, excepting those who are present. And who are they? Hardly any body; some half-dozen of the dead man's nearest connexions being excepted. If the ceremony were believed to be of any use to those who witness the performance of it, means ought to have been employed to bring the people together for that purpose. No such means have ever been thought of. What does that declare? One of two things. Either that the Church of England clergy are utterly indifferent to the good which the witnessing of it is calculated to produce; or that they do not believe it is calculated to do any good at all.

We have thus examined in some detail the duties which are exacted of the Church of England clergy, and the only duties which they can be really considered as performing. The duties, the enforcement of which is left to conscience, to the desire of doing good, in the breast of the individual, are for the most part neglected, and never otherwise than ill-performed. We are far from denying that there are good men among the working clergy of the Church of England, notwithstanding the obstruction to goodness which their situation creates; men who reside among their parishioners, go about among them, and take pains to do them good. But these are the small number; and they never act systematically and upon a well-digested plan. They are left, unguided, to follow their own impulses; and often a great part of their well-meant endeavours is thrown away. They receive no instruction in the art of doing good. This is no part of Church of England education. Yet it is an art towards the perfection of which instruction is of first-rate importance. Few men are aware of the whole extent of their means in that respect; and still fewer judge accurately in what applications of their means they will prove the most productive. It follows, as a necessary consequence, that the amount of good which a well-intentioned man produces is often very short of what, if better directed, he would have been able to effect.

Thus employed, and thus paid, is it any wonder that the Church of England clergy should have lost their influence among a people improving, now at last improving rapidly, in knowledge and intelligence? And when a clergy have lost their influence, what is the use of them? The evidence of their total loss of influence is very striking, when it is fairly looked at and considered. The first fact is the notorious one, that one-half of the population have renounced them as utterly unfit to be their religious guides, and have chosen others of their own. This fact speaks inferences far beyond the numerical proportions. The Dissenters afford evidence of their being in earnest about their religion. The Established Church is the natural sink of all those who are indifferent about it, and belong to a church for the sake of the name, as long as there is any thing to be got by it. To this number may be added all those whose lives are too scandalous to let them be admitted into any other Christian society. Now, if we say that not more than every other man in a community is in earnest about religion, we shall not perhaps be considered as making a very unreasonable supposition. But if this be anything like an approximation to the fact, the members of the Church of England are almost wholly men who adhere to it either for the sake of the name, or for the good things which they owe to it, with a small proportion indeed of those in whose adherence to it regard for religion has any thing to do. The Church of England therefore exists in no other character than that of a state engine; a ready and ever-willing instrument in the hands of those who desire to monopolize the powers of government – that is, to hold them for the purpose of abusing them.

It is useful to mark, among the proofs that the Church of England exists for no good purpose, that those of the common people who brutalize themselves with intoxicating liquors belong almost wholly to the Church of England sect. A Dissenter is rarely a notorious drunkard, with whatever other sins he may be tainted. The coster-mongers are never Dissenters. It would be important to put means in operation to show what proportion of the people convicted of crime are Churchmen, and what Dissenters. Our conjecture would be, that nine in ten at least are of the Church of England. It would be easy to ascertain what proportion of parish paupers are Church of England men, and what Dissenters. And that, too, would be no insignificant article of evidence.

Though such, however, is the light in which the Church of England, in its present state, must appear to every intelligent and honest inquirer, we know what a clamor will be raised against us for expressing our opinion, by all those who derive their profit from what is evil in things as they are; who are therefore attached to the evil, and bitterly hostile to all who seek to expose it. With the reasonable and the sincere, we need no other protection than the evidence we adduce. With others, it may have some effect, to show them what eminent men before us have said of the clergy, and of the inevitable effect of the position in which they are placed, by a viciously constructed establishment.

Dr Middleton, one of the greatest men whom the Church of England ever produced, has spoken of one of the most deplorable of the effects of their position, their hostility to the interests of truth, in the following terms: –

'Every man's experience will furnish instances of the wretched fruits of this zeal, in the bigoted, vicious, and ignorant part, both of the clergy and the laity; who, puffed up with the pride of an imaginary orthodoxy, and detesting all free inquiry, as dangerous to their case, and sure to expose their ignorance, take pleasure in defaming and insulting men of candor, learning, and probity, who happen to be touched with any scruples, or charged with any opinions which they call heretical[4].'

One of the most respectable names to be found in the list of Church of England clergy is Jeremy Taylor. He speaks to the same effect, in the following terms: –

'Possibly men may be angry at me, and my design; for I do all them great displeasure, who think no end is then well served, when their interest is disserved[5].'
'Opinions are called heresies, upon interest, and the grounds of emoluments[6].'
'Our opinions commence and are upheld, according as our turns are served and our interests are preserved[7].'

To return again to Middleton, who saw this malignant disease of the Church of England with peculiar clearness: –

'I do not know how to account for that virulence of zeal, with which it [the Free Inquiry] is opposed by those writers, but by imputing it to their prejudices or habitual bigotry, or to some motives especially of interest; which, of course, bars all entrance to opinions, though ever so probable, if not stamped by an authority which can sweeten them with rewards[8].'

Nothing is of more importance than the repeated, and earnest, consideration of the fact, that the interest of a clergy, in the circumstances in which the Church of England clergy are placed, is in direct opposition to their duty, and makes them sworn enemies of the good of their fellow creatures. They are hired, for the purpose of propagating a certain set of opinions. They are sworn to retain them: that is, to keep their minds stationary in at least one department of thought. And it is curious to observe how far that creates a motive to exert themselves to keep the minds of other men stationary, not in that department only, but in all the departments of thought; to make the clergy the enemies of all improvement of the human mind. If one set of men stand still in this improvement, while other men

---

[4] Middleton's Works, 4to. ed., vol. ii. p. 117.
[5] Liberty of Prophesying. Epist. Ded.
[6] Ib.
[7] Ib. Introd.
[8] Preface to an intended Answer to all Objections against the Free Inquiry. Works, 4to. ed., p. 374; where there is much more to the same purpose.

go on, these men see that they will soon become objects of contempt. They are sworn to stand still; they, therefore, detest all those who go on, and exert themselves to impede their progress, and to discredit their design.

This motive has a cruel extent of operation. To be bound to stand still, in any line of mental improvement, is a state of great degradation. The progress of other men in knowledge gives them a keener sense of this degradation. The clergy therefore perceive, that, in proportion as other men grow wiser, they will sink deeper in contempt. This gives them a hatred of the pursuit of knowledge. The search of truth bodes them evil, and not good; and therefore all their art is employed to prevent it.

We think, however, that by changes – far from violent, the Church of England might be converted from an instrument of evil into an instrument of much good; and to the consideration of this part of the subject we now proceed.

We consider a local clergy, distributed everywhere among the people, as the fundamental part of an institute really intended for moulding the character of the people, and shaping their actions, according to the spirit of pure religion. The question then is, what is required towards obtaining in greatest amount the beneficial services capable of being derived from such a set of men.

The very first particular which comes to be noticed, shows in what a different spirit from that of good to the people every thing relating to the Church of England has been arranged. It is very clear, that in employing men to the best advantage in any sort of service, each individual should have enough to do, and not more than enough. This care has been wholly renounced by Church of Englandism, which exhibits the most enormous disproportions; in one place, parishes far too large for any individual to manage; in other places so small, that a man has little to do in them. A good establishment would correct this abominable instance of careless and profligate management.

Next, the men who are to direct the people in the right path, and make them walk in it as diligently as possible, should be men capable of doing their work well: that is, they should, at least, be men of good education and good character. To this end, it is absolutely necessary that they should receive sufficient pay, to be an inducement to men of that description to undertake the duties. There is evidence enough to prove that this need not be high. We do not adduce the curates; because the baneful lottery of the over-paid places in the Church draws into it too great a number of adventurers. But the medical men, of whom one is to be found in every considerable village, afford evidence to the point, and that conclusive. Besides, the situation would be one of great consideration and dignity, as soon as it came to be regarded as a source of great utility; and men with property of their own would be desirous of filling it. The situation of judges in France is strong evidence to this point. The pay is so small, that the wonder of Englishmen always is, how any body can be found to accept the situation; yet the fact is, that it is in request; and the problem is solved, by learning that men, having a moderate property of their own, covet the dignity which the office confers.

Thus far we have proceeded with no difficulty, and with very little room for doubt; but having determined the sort of men we ought to have, we come next to the question by whom, in each instance, ought they to be appointed. Three considerations obviously enter into the solution of this question – the best means of securing honesty in the selection – the best means of giving satisfaction to the parishioners, without incurring the evils of a mistaken choice – the not giving too much power to one individual. The best chance, perhaps, for having honesty and intelligence in the selection, would be to have a Minister of Public Instruction, by whom all the appointments should be made. He would act under a stronger sense of responsibility, conspicuously placed, as he would be, under the eye of the public, than any other man; and in the majority of cases, would not have any interest in acting wrong. But this would be a great amount of patronage, possibly too great to exist without danger in any single hand; and it is not easy to find an unexceptionable mode of distribution. Suppose the patronage were in each county given to the principal civil authority in the county, he would be exposed to all the local influences which are known to be so adverse to the virtuous use of patronage; and acting in a corner with very little of the salutary influence of publicity, where the choice was not made by favouritism, it would be very apt to be made in negligence.

Suppose, however, that this difficulty is got over (it would interrupt us too much at present to show that it is not insurmountable), we may assume, that where provision is made for the appointment of a fit minister in every parish, complete provision is made for the religious instruction and guidance of the people – provided we can depend upon the due discharge of the duties which those ministers are appointed to perform. It has, however, been generally believed, that the due discharge of the duties of the parochial ministers cannot be depended upon without superintendence. A question then arises, what is the best contrivance for the superintendence of a parochial clergy?

Two methods have been thought of, and are at the present hour in operation: the one is, superintendence by individual clergymen; the other is, superintendence by assemblies, in which clergy and laity are combined. One question is, which of these two methods is the best? and another question is, whether there may not be a third, which is better than either?

The two methods which are now in practice are exemplified respectively in the churches of England and Scotland. In England the scheme of superintendence by individuals has been tried, in Scotland that of superintendence by assemblies.

If we were to judge by the event, in these two instances, the question would be decided very rapidly. The Scottish system is proved by experience to have answered, and not very imperfectly, its end, while it occasions no expense whatsoever. The English system is at once disgracefully expensive, and totally inefficient to its end: it is an absolute failure, with an enormous burthen to the nation.

We hardly suppose that the proposition we have thus announced respecting those two churches will be disputed in regard to either. The general good conduct of the Scottish clergy, and the absence of flagrant abuses in that church, is matter of notoriety. The lamentable want of good conduct, though not universal, among the English clergy, and the existence of enormous abuses in their church, is matter of not less notoriety. There is no non-residence in Scotland, and no pluralities. Would such things have ever begun to exist in England, if the superintendence by bishops had been good for anything? The proportional amount of Dissenterism in Scotland is small, compared with what it is in England; and has arisen almost wholly from the people's dislike of patronage – a matter over which the clergy had no control, and of which the consequences are not to be imputed to them. There is nothing of the sort to screen the English clergy; and the enormous extent of Dissenterism in England is evidence – is *proof, invincible proof* – that the clergy have not done their duty.

It is not, however, safe to ground a general conclusion upon individual instances, unless where the reason – the *rationale* of the instances, applies to other cases. With respect to superintendence by individuals, the mode of it adopted in England is so glaringly absurd, so little reference has it to any rational purpose, that it never can have been intended to be an instrument of good – to be a means of obtaining from the local clergy the greatest amount of useful service to the people at large. The pay alone is perfect evidence to that effect. Who ever thinks of getting laborious service from a man on whom is bestowed an enormous income, which incessantly invites him to the enjoyment of voluptuous indolence, without any efficient call for exertion? Nor is this the only baneful effect of these enormous incomes: they created a line of separation between the superintending and the super-intended clergy. They constituted them two castes; and well is it known how their conduct has conformed itself to the distinction. A principle of repulsion was created between them: often enough, it is true, commuted for prostitute servility on the part of the lower caste; and thus morality, by Church of England culture, was propagated and flourished. There could rarely be any cordial communication between two classes of men placed in such relation to one another. No bishop has an intimate knowledge of the character or turn of mind of any, except an accidental individual or two, among those whom he superintends. He does not go about into the several parishes, to see and inquire how the clerical duties are performed; he knows nothing at all about the matter, unless some extraordinary instance of misconduct, which makes all the country ring, should come to his ears.

Nor could it be otherwise. Natural causes produce their natural effects. A bishop was intended to be a great lord: of course he would be governed by the impulses which govern other great lords. Not one of these impulses is to go about parishes, seeing whether clergymen have been as effectual as they might, in training the people under their tuition to bring their children up well.

The very pretext of any such duty as this is absurd, when we recollect that these reverend lords have to be absent from their business of superintendence of their clergy for one full half of their time, by attendance on their *duties* (so by an abuse of language they are called) in parliament.

As we have seen how it is with the ordinary clergy of the Church of England – that of the two classes of their duties, one the ceremonial, another the useful, it is the ceremonial only which means are used to make them perform – the useful are left to themselves to perform, or not perform, as they please; so it is exactly with the bishops. There are certain ceremonies they have to go through: these are obligatory on them. The duty of vigilantly looking after their clergy – of using means to get them to do whatever it is in their power to do, to make their people more virtuous and more happy – is left to the bishops to do, or not do, as they please; and accordingly it never is done – at least, to any purpose: by the greater part of them it is never thought of.

But it does not follow, because the plan of superintendence by individuals was so ill-constructed by the Church of England as to make it a source of evil and not of good, that therefore it is in itself, and radically, bad. We are inclined to think that it is radically good, and might be so contrived as to be superior to the Scottish method.

We do not think that an assembly is well fitted for minute inspection; and that is the only inspection which is sure of answering its end. An assembly cannot go about visiting parishes, and ascertaining on the spot where the clergyman has been to the greatest degree, where to the lowest degree, useful to his parishioners.

But if we are to employ individual inspectors (the name bishop means inspector) by what scheme is the greatest amount of good to be obtained from them?

One thing is perfectly clear: you must not over-pay them. An inspector, to be useful, must be a hard-working man: that a very rich man never is. This is an established rule, though it does not altogether exclude exceptions. They should be paid higher than the parochial clergy, because they should be men of such high character and attainments as might give weight to their decisions. Still the business of an inspecting priest is so much of the same kind, with the business of a parochial priest, that the pay of the one should be a sort of criterion by which to regulate that of the other. If the highest pay of a parish priest were, say, 500*l.* per annum, we think 1000*l.* per annum should be the highest pay of an inspector; for we allow no weight whatsoever to the pretence which is set up with characteristic impudence by the friends of public plunder, that wealth gives efficiency to superintendence. It does no such thing. A man will pull off his hat with more hurry, will bend his body lower, will speak in a softer tone, before the man of great wealth; but he will not trouble himself to do his bidding one atom the more for his riches. Is any man, so nearly deprived of intellect, as still, though grown to be a man, to need evidence on this point? Let him see how the rich are served, even in their own houses. Are they better served than those among us whose riches are less? Do we not know that the men best served in their houses are not the richest, but the most sensible men?

There is another thing to be regarded in the matter of pay, which though it appear small intrinsically, is great by its mode of operation on the human mind. It is infinitely better that the clergy should be paid in the way of salary than in the way of estate. Between the idea of salary, and the idea of service to be performed for it, the association is close and strong. Between the idea of living on the proceeds of an estate, and the idea of having nothing to do, the association is equally powerful. And so it must be. In all our experience, we regularly observe that salary and service go together. We see that commonly estate and service have no connexion. Hence it comes, that a man who lives upon an estate seems to himself to share in the common privilege of those who live upon estates; that is, to enjoy himself. No man who has studied the human mind will doubt that this is a matter of the greatest importance. If the Church of England clergy had always been paid by salary, we may be assured they would not have sunk into the state of absolute uselessness in which we now behold them.

It is unnecessary to dwell upon the scheme of paying the clergy by that particular kind of estate called tithe, because people now pretty well understand it. Of all conceivable schemes for setting the interest and the duties of the clergy in direct opposition, this is the most perfect. And it makes a fearful revelation. It proves, beyond the possibility of a doubt, that the clergy, and all those who through so long a series of ages have had in their hands the power of regulating the payment of the clergy, have been void even of the desire that the clergy should be useful. Oh, what an odious thing is the pretence of caring for religion in the mouths of such men! Contrast an establishment of men whose business it would be to go about their parishes, planting themselves in the hearts of their people, and working upon their minds to the performing of all good actions, and the acquiring of all good habits, with an establishment of men who go about their parishes, indeed, but go about raping and rending, demanding what others are unwilling to pay, carrying strife and hatred along with them, looked at by their people in the light of enemies, not of friends, the very sight of whom is odious, and in whose mouths advice to their parishioners to be mutually forbearing and helpful could only be treated with ridicule; and say if the imagination of man can present any two things of a more opposite character. Reflect also deliberately who the men are who have so long strained their lungs, and now do, proclaiming that this church is 'most excellent.' What a help-meet it must have been for misrule to earn all the protection which it has received! That on any other score it has deserved it, there is hardly impudence enough in the world now to pretend.

But if it were determined that good inspection and stimulation were more to be expected from individual superintendents, properly paid and employed, than from assemblies, another question would remain to be answered: whether these inspectors should be clergymen or laymen? There are some reasons for thinking that laymen would be the best. They would be less under the influence of that feeling which men of a class commonly contract, and which makes them willing to favour one another, to make them sympathise with their self-indulgences, and to screen their neglects. If it be surmised that such men would be less acquainted than clergymen with the supposed science of the theologians, we answer, that if it were so, and it is by no means necessary that it should be so, for that science is easily learned, it would not, upon our scheme, be a matter of much importance. For we do not mean that our parochial clergy should trouble their parishioners with dogmas. Their business will be to train them in the habits of a good life; and what is necessary to that will be judged of fully as well by a layman as by a clergyman.

We have now supposed, that a well-selected person from the class of educated men has been placed as the minister of religion in every conveniently-sized district, called a parish. This we consider as the fundamental part of a religious establishment. We have next supposed that a well-selected person from the class of men of superior acquirements and intelligence has been appointed the inspector and superintendent, of a convenient number of clergymen everywhere throughout the country. We have also spoken a little of the duties of each, but it is necessary to speak somewhat more in detail.

In the first place, it is a fundamental part of our scheme, that a clergy, paid by the state, should, in their instruction of the people, abstain entirely from the inculcation of dogmas. The reasons are conclusive. They cannot inculcate dogmas without attaching undue importance to uniformity of belief in doubtful matters; that is, classing men as good or bad on account of things which have no connexion with good conduct; that is, without derogating from morality, and lessening its influence on the minds of men.

They cannot inculcate dogmas – at least they never do – without attaching merit, and the rewards which belong to it, to belief on one side of a question; that is, without suborning belief, using means to make it exist independently of evidence; that is, to make men hold opinions without seeing that they are true – in other words, to affirm that they know to be true what they do not know to be true; that is, if we may give to the act its proper name – to lie. But a clergy, paid for teaching the people to live well, should assuredly not do what has a tendency to make them habitual liars.

To preach the importance of dogmas, is to teach men to impute imperfection to the Divine nature. It is according to the perfections of the Divine nature to approve in his rational creatures the love of truth. But the love of truth leads a man to search for evidence, and to place his belief on that side, whatsoever it be, on which the evidence appears to him to preponderate. The clergyman who tells him that God likes best belief on one side, declares to him that God does not like the honest search of truth. Oh God! with what perseverance and zeal has this representation of thy Divine nature been maintained, by men who, with the same breath, and therefore in the spirit of base adulation, were calling thee the God of truth!

Upon this ground it surely is proper to interdict the use of articles. The Articles of the Church of England are a set of propositions, the strangeness of which we shall not dilate upon. That, and the history of them, are both pretty well known. The clergy of the Church of England subscribe them as propositions which they are bound to believe. Anything more fraught with injury to the intellectual and moral parts of man's nature cannot be conceived. This is to make men enemies to truth.

We shall not repeat, what we have so immediately said, and what we are sure must make a deep impression on every untainted mind, on the atrocity of giving men inducements to make a belief, which they have not derived from evidence. The subscription of articles goes beyond this. It vouches for future belief. It is a bond, that the individual subscribing shall for ever after set his mind against the admission of evidence; that is, resist the entrance of truth; in other words, make war upon it, in the only way in which war upon truth is capable of being made.

It is a deplorable fact, – which deserves the most profound attention, though hitherto it has not received it, – that the creation of effectual motives to the hatred of truth in one department, creates effectual motives to the hatred of it generally. We have touched upon this point already. But it deserves further development; for it stands first in point of importance.

The man who is reduced to the degraded condition of resisting truth, lives under the painful assurance that he will be held to be a degraded being, by every man who sets a high value on truth, and is eager in the pursuit of it. The pursuit of truth brings thus along with it a consequence most painful to him. He therefore dislikes it. He would prevent it, if he could; and he is stimulated to do all that he can to prevent it. If the love and pursuit of truth should become general, he sees clearly that he must become an object of general contempt. What a motive is this to him to prevent its becoming general; to smother it in the very birth, if he can! – See in what perfect obedience to this impulse the Church of England has always acted! Above all, explore minutely the cruel ways in which, to this end, it has abused its power over the business of education! The whole bent of its tuition is to make its pupils acquiesce slavishly in a parcel of traditional dogmas, and instead of awakening the desire of farther progress, to frighten them at the idea of it; training them to regard it as a source of boundless evil; and all those who pursue it, as villains, aiming at the destruction of whatever is valuable among mankind.

They have thus been constituted the enemies of their species. The advance of mankind in happiness has, by a nefarious constitution of their church, been made a source of evil to them. And they have been, as it was certain they would be, its strenuous, and, to a deplorable extent, we must add, its successful opponents.

The steadiness with which the priests of this establishment have persevered in this course, is a point of great interest in their history, and should be carefully set to view. We may make it the subject of a future article. The barefacedness with which it is professed, up to the present hour, and by some of the most respectable among them, amounts to a striking phenomenon. They even reprobate Locke, the cautious, the modest, the sober-minded Locke, for that which is even *his* greatest distinction, the trusting to evidence; the seeking after truth; the desiring to know something beyond the traditional propositions of others; the taking the only course which leads to the advancement of human knowledge, the improvement of the human mind, the progress of the race in happiness and virtue. Listen to what Copleston, then Head of a House, now bishop, and peer of parliament, thought it not disgraceful to him to say a few years ago. 'His' (Locke's) 'own opinions would have been entitled to greater respect,' (observe for what) 'if he had himself treated with more respect the opinions of those who had gone before him,' (opinions, you see, are entitled to respect, not on account of the truth of them, but something else) 'and the practice of sensible men of his own time, whose judgment was worth more, in proportion as it was confirmed by experience.' – Locke misbehaved, you see, by seeking for evidence, and yielding to it when found. Had he disregarded evidence, that is truth, and taken passively the opinions given to him, he would have merited the praise of Church of England priests; by taking the course he did, no wonder he has been always unpopular among them. 'The light freedom, indeed, and the confidence with which this philosopher attacks all established notions, is one of the principal blemishes in his character.' – Is not this *instar omnium*? That is one of the principal blemishes in the character of one of the greatest philosophers who ever lived – so says Church of Englandism – which alone enabled him to do any good; namely, calling for evidence, marking where he did not find it, but only some man's *ipse ducit* instead, and then proceeding honestly in search of it himself! Good God! what sort of a place of education is it, where such a course is held up, not for imitation, but reprobation?[9]

How vividly does this call to memory the description which Pope gives of the clergy of the Church of England, as being among the most zealous of the votaries of the Goddess of Dulness, and the education they impart in their schools and colleges the most efficient of all instruments for extending her empire!

In the description given in the second book of the Dunciad of the games instituted in honour of the goddess, whereof one was swimming and plunging in Fleet Ditch, a reverend gentleman having therein distinguished himself, is thus, and his brethren along with him, held up to observation:

> 'Thence to the banks where reverend bards repose,
> They led him soft; each reverend bard arose;
> And Milbourn chief, deputed by the rest,
> Gave him the cassock, surcingle, and vest.
> "Receive," he said, "those robes which once were mine,
> Dulness is sacred in a sound divine."
>   'He ceased, and spread the robe; the crowd confess
> The reverend Flamen in his lengthen'd dress.
> Around him wide a sable army stand,
> A low-born, cell-bred, selfish, servile band,
> Prompt or to guard or stab, or saint or damn,
> Heaven's Swiss, who fight for any god or man.' – 347–358.

Such is the character of the race, drawn by the hand of our moral poet. Next we present his account of the debt of gratitude which education owes to them.

DUNCIAD, BOOK IV.

> . . . 'Since man from beast by words is known,
> Words are man's province; words we teach alone.
> When reason, doubtful, like the Samian letter,
> Points here two ways, the narrower is the better.
> Placed at the door of learning, youth to guide,
> We never suffer it to stand too wide.
> To ask, to guess, to know, as they commence;
> As fancy opens the quick springs of sense;
> We ply the memory, we load the brain,
> Bind rebel wit, and double chain on chain;
> Confine the thought, to exercise the breath,

---

[9]   See 'A Reply to the Calumnies of the Edinburgh Review against Oxford,' p. 127.

And keep them in the pale of words till death.
Whate'er the talents, or howe'er design'd,
We hang one jingling padlock on the mind.' – 149.

'Oh, cried the goddess, for some pedant reign!
Some gentle James to bless the land again!
To stick the Doctor's chair into the throne,
Give law to words, or war with words alone;
Senates and courts with Greek and Latin rule,
And turn the council to a grammar-school.
For sure, if dulness sees a grateful day,
'Tis in the shade of arbitrary sway.
O! if my sons may learn one earthly thing,
Teach but that one, sufficient for a king;
That which my priests, and mine alone, maintain,
Which, as it dies or lives, we fall or reign;
May you, my Cam and Isis, preach it long –
The right divine of kings to govern wrong!
  Prompt at the call, around the Goddess roll
Broad hats, and hoods, and caps, a sable shoal;
Thick, and more thick, the black blockade extends,
A hundred head of Aristotle's friends.
Nor wert thou, Isis, wanting to the day,
(Though Christ-Church long kept prudishly away).
Each staunch polemic, stubborn as a rock,
Each fierce logician still expelling Locke,
Came whip and spur, and dash'd through thin and thick.' – 175.

''Tis true on words is still our whole debate,
Disputes of Me or Te, or Aut or At;
To sound or sink in *Cano*, *o* or *a*,
Or give up Cicero to C or K.' – 219.

'There is the genuine head of many a house,
And much divinity without a Νοῦζ.' – 243.

'For thee we dim the eyes, and stuff the head
With all such reading as was never read;
For thee explain a thing till all men doubt it,
And work about it, goddess, and about it.' – 249.

'What though we let some better sort of fool
Thred every science, run through every school?
Never by tumbler through the hoops was shown

Such skill in passing all, and touching none.
He may, indeed (if sober all this time),
Plague with dispute, or persecute in rhyme.
We only furnish what he cannot use,
Or wed to what he must divorce, a muse.' – 255.

'With the same cement, ever sure to bind,
We bring to one dead level every mind.' – 268.

'O! would the sons of men once think their eyes
And reason given them but to study flies!
Learn but to trifle; or, who most observe,
To wonder at their Maker, not to serve.' – 453.

'First slave to words, then vassal to a name;
Then dupe to party; child and man the same:
Bounded by nature; narrow'd still by art;
A trifling mind, and a contracted heart;
Thus bred, thus taught, how many have I seen,
Smiling on all, and smiled on by a queen!' – 501.

On the above passage is the following note: 'A recapitulation of the whole course of modern education, described in this book, which confines youth to the study of words only in schools; subjects them to the authority of systems in the universities; and deludes them with the names of party distinction in the world.'

After being thus educated, they are delivered over to the magus of Dulness, Influence, 'and then admitted,' says the poet, in the Argument of the Book, 'to taste the cup of the magus, her high priest, which causes a total oblivion of all obligation, divine, civil, moral, or rational; to these, her adepts, she sends priests, attendants, and comforters, of various kinds, confers on them orders and degrees,' &c. The lines are –

'Then take them all, oh take them to thy breast!
Thy magus, Goddess! shall perform the rest.
    With that a wizard old his cup extends,
Which whoso tastes forgets his former friends,
Sire, ancestors, himself. One casts his eyes
Up to a star – and like Endymion dies:
A feather shooting from another's head
Extracts his brain, and principle is fled:
Lost is his god, his country, everything;
And nothing left but homage to a king!

> The vulgar herd turn off to herd with hogs,
> To run with horses, or to hunt with dogs.' – 515.

On the passage 'homage to a king,' is the following note: – 'So strange as this must seem to a mere English reader, the famous M. de la Bruyere declares it to be the character of every good subject in a monarchy: "Where," says he, "there is no such thing as love of our country, the interest, the glory, and service of the prince supply its place[10]" Of this duty another celebrated French author speaks, indeed, a little more disrespectfully, which, for that reason, we shall not translate, but give in his own words: "L'amour de la patrie, le grand motif des premiers heros, n'est plus regardé que comme une chimère; l'idée du service du roi, etendue jusqu'à l'oubli de tout autre principe, tient lieu de ce qu'on appelloit autrefois grandeur d'ame et fidelité[11]."

> 'But she, good goddess, sent to every child
> Firm impudence, or stupefaction mild;
> And straight succeeded, leaving shame no room,
> Cibberian forehead, or Cimmerian gloom.' – 530.

> 'Others the syren sisters warble round,
> And empty heads console with empty sound.

> 'The balm of dulness trickling in their ear.' – 541.

A note on line 567 says: 'This tribe of men, our poet hath elsewhere admirably characterized in that happy line,

> ' "A brain of feather, and a heart of lead."

For the satire takes in the whole species of those, who, with an understanding too dissipated and futile for the offices of civil life, and a heart too lumpish, narrow, and contracted for those of social, become fit for nothing, and so turn wits and critics, where sense and civility are neither required nor expected.'

There is not a finer specimen of the arts of the clergy than their newborn zeal for the religious education of the children of the poor. The religious education of the children of the poor is not among the objects of the Church of England; there is no provision for it in that establishment; it was never a practice. Though the most eminently religious of all the possible functions of a minister of religion, a clergyman of the Church of

---

[10] De la Republique, c. x.
[11] Boulainvillier's Hist. des Anc. Parl. de France.

England as little thought it belonged to him, as to make shoes for the children of his parishioners. Till the other day, there was in England no education for the children of the poor. They were absolutely uneducated, in religion, as in every thing else. During all the ages in which this state of things continued, the clergy saw no occasion for this religious education they are now so hot about. It is only when education in general, that is knowledge, begins to be, that they think education in religion is, required. Non-education in religion was not an evil, when in union with ignorance; in union with knowledge it becomes direful. – Can any body need help, in reading this passage of clergy?

So long as the people were in gross ignorance, their servility to their priests was to be depended upon. The moment light began to dawn upon them, it was, it seems, not to be expected, unless particular artifice was used. An expedient was fallen upon – that of clamouring for the union of religious education with other education.

This, in the first place, was a great impediment to education. It rendered it impossible for the children of people of different sects to be educated together. This was a capital stroke. It rendered the education of the people much more expensive, therefore much less likely to be carried into effect. It had other important consequences. It made all those benevolent individuals, whose partialities ran towards the Church, place the funds which they were disposed to contribute towards the education of the poor under the control of the Church, which was skilled in the art of giving education without instruction. From the evidence extracted by the committee of the House of Commons on Education, last year, it appears, that their endeavours in the National Schools are remarkable specimens of that art. They thus made sure of having all the children of those who nominally belong to the church in their own hands; and all the security against the desire of knowledge which education without instruction can yield.

The hollowness of the pretence is further seen in this, that all the education in religion which for ages the clergy thought necessary for the children of the poor, was only to make them able to repeat a few questions of the Catechism, before confirmation; and surely this it would not be difficult to attain, if they were educated in schools for all. What should hinder the parson of the parish (it is his business if any thing be), to assemble the children of his flock as often as needful, for the purpose of imparting to them much more religious instruction than this? That the clergy are not in earnest in their talk about the necessity of schooling in religion, is manifest from this, that they have done nothing to have it given. They have made use of the cry solely for the purpose of making schooling difficult. But where is the parson of a parish who takes the trouble to instruct the children of his parishioners in religion? Where is there one ordinance of the bishops rendering it imperative upon their clergy to fulfil the great duty of administering religious instruction to the young? The whole thing is a farce.

Having thus seen the importance of relieving the parochial ministers of religion from all concern with dogmas, we come to another question of no small importance, whether their labours of love should not also be relieved from the incumbrance of ceremonies?

The example of our Saviour shows, that in certain circumstances they cannot be dispensed with; that where the human mind is spell-bound in old habits, you cannot obtain access to it except through the medium of some of these habits.

We persuade ourselves, however, that we have attained in this country such a degree of advancement, notwithstanding the efforts of the Church of England to prevent it, that we may dispense with the performance of ceremonies on the part of those ministers of religion whom the state appoints for the pure purpose of making the people conform to the designs of a Being of perfect wisdom and goodness.

The importance would be immense of constituting a church without dogmas and ceremonies. It would be truly a Catholic church. Its ministers would be ministers of good, in the highest of all senses of the word, to men of all religious denominations. All would share in the religious services of such a church, and all would share in the blessings which would result from them. This is the true idea of a State religion; and there is no other. It ought to be stripped of all which is separating; of all that divides men from one another; and to present a point whereon, in the true spirit of reverence to the perfect being, and love to one another, they may all unite. So long as there are men who think dogmas and ceremonies a necessary part of religion, those who agree about such dogmas and ceremonies may have their separate and respective institutions of their own providing, for their inculcation and performance. But this is extraneous to the provisions which alone it is proper for the State to make, and which ought to be so contrived as to embrace, if it were possible, the whole population.

This, the scheme of which we have been endeavouring to convey the idea, we think, would effect. There is no class of Christians, who could not join in the labours of love of one who was going about continually doing good; whose more solemn addresses to his assembled parishioners would never have any other object than to assimilate them more and more in heart and mind to Him who is the author of all good, and the perfection of wisdom and benevolence. Men could not long attend a worship of this description, worship of the perfect being, by acts of goodness, without acquiring attachment to it, and learning by degrees that it is the one thing needful. All would belong to this church; and after a short time would belong to no other. Familiarized with the true worship of the Divine Being, they would throw off the pseudo worship, dogmas and ceremonies. This is the true plan for converting Dissenters. There would be no schism, if men had nothing to scind about.

If the ministers of the Established Church had nothing to do with dogmas, and nothing to do with ceremonies, how would we have them employed?

We have already expressed the general idea of their employment. It would be assiduous endeavour to make all the impressions on the minds of their parishioners which conduce to good conduct; not merely negative, in abstaining from ill; but positive, in doing all the good to one another which the means put in their power enable them to do.

It is very evident, that rules for the making of those all-important impressions cannot be given. General rules would be too vague to be of any use; and the variety of differing cases is so great, that it can only be met by the resources of zeal and discretion in the daily intercourse between the minister and the individuals of his flock. There are, however, certain things which may be assumed as tests, in each instance, of the manner in which the duties of the parochial minister are performed, and which afford a guide to the manner in which stimulants may be applied to him.

For example; we would give annual premiums to those ministers in whose parishes certain favourable results were manifested – in whose parishes there was the smallest number of crimes committed within the year – in whose parishes there was the smallest number of law-suits – in whose parishes there was the smallest number of paupers – in whose parishes there was the smallest number of uneducated children – in whose parishes the reading-rooms were best attended, and supplied with the most instructive books. We mention these as specimens. If there were any other results of the same kind, of which the evidence could be made equally certain, there would be good reason for including them in the same provision. In this manner, would pretty decisive evidence be obtained of the comparative prevalence of good conduct in the different parishes, and a motive of some importance would be applied to the obtaining of it.

We think that infinite advantage might be derived from the day of rest, if real Christian consideration, exempt from all superstitious feelings, by which the clergy have hitherto converted it to their own use, were applied to it.

We think it of great importance, that all the families of a parish should be got to assemble on the Sunday – clean, and so dressed, as to make a favourable appearance in the eyes of one another. This alone is ameliorating.

An address delivered to these assembled neighbours, by their common friend and benefactor, on their means of lessening the evils, and ensuring the happiness of one another, the motives they have to this conduct, its harmony with the laws of that benevolent Being of whom our lives are the gift, and who has made the connexion between our own happiness and the aid we afford to the happiness of others inseparable – would come powerfully in aid of all the other means employed to make salutary impressions on their minds.

When the parishioners are assembled, it is of importance to consider in what other ways the meeting can be turned to advantage.

One thing is very obvious: the opportunity would be favourable of doing something to add to their education. As often as the means were available, useful lectures on various branches of art and science might be delivered to them. Of what importance would it be to the numerous classes of workmen who make use of tools, to be made acquainted, in a general way, with the mechanical powers? What interest might be excited by chemical experiments; and what benefit derived from the knowledge of the composition and decomposition of bodies, which that science imparts. The science of botany, to all those whose employment is in the fields, and to the females whose monotonous lives are confined to their cottages, would afford a great source of interest and delight. Why should not even the wonders of the distant world – the magnitude and laws of the celestial bodies, be laid open to their minds? It will not be disputed that lectures on the art of preserving the health, pointing out the mistakes which ignorant people commit in the physical management, both of themselves and their children, and both the preventive and curative means which they might employ, would be of infinite importance to them.

It is impossible to estimate too highly the benefit which would be derived from good lectures to those parochial assemblies on the education of their children: not merely in sending them to school, and getting them taught to read and write, but in moulding their tempers; in making them gentle, moderate, forbearing, kind, and deeply impressed with the importance to themselves of habits of industry and frugality.

Not merely the mode of conducting themselves towards their children – the mode of conducting themselves towards their servants is an important topic. On the right and the wrong in this matter, in which the grossest errors are habitually committed, good teaching would be of the greatest utility. Even in the mode of training and conducting their beasts, there is great good to be done by proper instruction – in order to habituate them to the thought that gentleness is more effectual than cruelty – that when the animal disappoints our expectation, it is not by design, but by its not knowing what we desire, and that beating it for it knows not what, is no means of correction to the animal, but fuel to one of the worst of our own distempers – the disposition to inflict evil upon whatsoever or whosoever is the cause of immediate annoyance to ourselves. No man practises ferocity towards animals who would not with a little more temptation, practise it towards his fellow-men; and this is a propensity which may be effectually rooted out.

There are even branches of political science, in which it would be of importance that the people should receive instruction in their weekly assemblies. They cannot, for example, be too completely made to understand the laws which determine the rate of wages – from ignorance of which rise most of their contentions with their masters, as well as the other evils which they endure. Indeed, a knowledge of the laws of nature, by operation of which the annual produce of the labour of the community is distributed, is the best of all modes of reconciling them to that inequality of distribution which they see takes place, and which there are people ignorant or wicked enough to tell them, is all in violation of their rights, because it is by their labour that everything is produced.

We go farther: we say there is no branch of political knowledge which ought not to be carefully taught to the people in their parochial assemblies on the day of rest. If it be an established maxim of reason, that there is no security for the good use of the powers of government, but through the check imposed upon it by the representatives of the people, and no security that the representatives will duly apply that check, unless the people make them, by a right use of the power of choosing and dismissing them, it is evident how necessary a condition of good government it is that political knowledge should be diffused among the people.

And the elements of the politics are not abstruse. There is nothing in them above the comprehension of a sensible man of the most numerous class. They relate to nothing but the common-sense means for the attainment of a common-sense object – the means of compelling those in whose hands the powers of government are placed, to make the best use of them. Questions, no doubt, arise in the exercise of those powers, which are exceedingly difficult, and require the highest measure of knowledge and understanding rightly to determine them: the question of war for example. The decision whether the known calamities of war, or the evils threatened by the unchecked proceedings of another state, are, in any instance, the greatest, may require the most extensive range of knowledge, and the utmost skill and sagacity in placing the exact value on the causes of future events.

Even the elements of jurisprudence might be taught to the people with great advantage in their Sunday meetings. The art and science of protection might be opened up to them in a manner which they would find in the highest degree interesting. How usefully might they be made to perceive that to them, above all others, it is the most necessary? The rich man can always do a great deal for his own protection. The poor man – unless the means of many, combined with art, are applied to protect him – is totally deprived of it. The institution of laws and tribunals is that combination; and the essence of them it is not difficult to unfold. To protect a man in the use of what is his own – that is, a civil code must be constructed. To prevent violations of what the law has declared to be a man's own – that is, declared to be his rights – the law must determine what acts shall be considered violations of them, and what penalty shall be annexed to each:

that is, a criminal code must be made. This is all plain; and the development of it would convey, even to the common people, the most useful ideas.

The necessity of a third party, to settle disputes, and afford redress of wrongs, is a maxim of common sense, familiar to all. This is the establishment of courts of justice; and the discussion of that subject is merely the inquiry, by the instrumentality of what means can the settlement of questions of right, and the redress of wrongs, be most effectually and cheaply accomplished. Not only is there nothing abstruse in this development – it is a subject, the discussion of which, as coming home to their businesses and bosoms, is calculated to excite the most lively interest, and exceedingly to improve their minds.

So much, then, for the serious matters with which the minds of the people might be usefully engaged in their parochial meetings on the day of rest. But further than this, it is well known to those who have made the principles of human nature their study, that few things tend more effectually to make impressions on the minds of men, favourable to kindness, to generosity, to feeling joy with the joys, sorrow with the sorrows of others; from which the disposition to mutual helpfulness mainly proceeds, – than their being habituated to rejoice together – to partake of pleasures in common. Upon this principle it is that the amusements of the common people are looked upon by philosophical minds as a matter of grave importance. We think that social amusements, of which the tendency would be ameliorating with respect to the people, might be invented for the parochial meetings. They should be of a gentle character; harmonizing rather with the moderate, than the violent emotions; promoting cheerfulness, not profuse merriment. We think that sports, requiring great bodily exertion, and in which bodily strength is mainly displayed, are not well adapted to the day of rest, nor favourable to the feelings of brotherly love, to which the occupations of that day should be mainly subservient. The people of antiquity, who most encouraged sports of that description, did so with a view to war, to the evils of which they were almost incessantly exposed. We can enter but a very little way into the details of this subject. When the time shall come for thinking of it seriously, it will deserve a very careful and minute consideration.

Music and dancing, if regulated, as we think they might be, would afford an important resource. Dancing is a mimetic art, and might be so contrived as to represent all the social affections, which we most desire to implant in the breasts of the people, and to call up the trains of ideas by which they are nourished. A dance might be invented which would represent, as far as gestures and movements afford the means, the parental and filial affections; another, the fraternal affections; another, the sorrowing with those that sorrow, and rejoicing with those that rejoice. There is not any affection in itself more virtuous than that which exists between two unspotted persons of different sex, looking forward to the happiness of wedded life. But dances to represent that affection would be so apt to slide into lasciviousness, that we should be afraid to trust them. Dancing, as generally practised at present, is either a representation of profuse merriment, or of lasciviousness. In both shapes, it is altogether unfit for the moral and tranquil amusements of the day of rest. The dances which would harmonize with the tone of mind we desire to engender by everything which is done or witnessed on that day, would consist of the quiet and gentle motions, and would rather be an exhibition of grace, than of agility and strength.

The smallest tendency to exceed the bounds of decency and order in these amusements would be easily checked by a very simple expedient. The parishioners would select among themselves one of the most discreet of the elders, and one of the most discreet of the matrons, to be from time to time the master and mistress of the ceremonies, whom they would authorize to preserve regularity, and whose decisions they would firmly support.

In all ages and nations of the world, the taking of the meals together, or separately, has been considered a matter of importance. The conjunct meal has always been found a promoter of union; wherever, on the other hand, for some accursed cause, the object has been to separate men from one another, the eating and drinking together has been as carefully prevented. The institution of castes is mainly upheld by the strict separation of meals; and wherever anything partaking of the nature of the institution of castes is found to exist, as between the noble and plebeian in modern Europe, the separation in eating and drinking is more or less strictly attended to.

We are sure it would be a thing attended with the happiest effects, if the proper regulations could be enforced, that the people at their Sunday assemblings should partake of meals together, in greater or smaller parties, as convenience might direct. This would be a renewal of the social meals of the early Christians, for which the Greek language afforded an appropriate name. They were called *Agapai:* that is, friendship-meals. When the Christians of any particular place assembled to hear the instruction of an Apostle, or other teacher, it was their custom to carry with them something to eat and drink; of which they partook in common when the business of instruction was over; and thereby bound themselves to one another in stronger ties of affection.

The circumstance unfavourable to this practice in modern manners, is the prevalence of the taste for intoxicating liquors, in which there would be always some who would indulge to excess. This would produce disorder, and a spectacle far from favourable to the class of impressions which it should be the object of all the occupations of the day of rest to produce.

If there were not means by which this consequence could be prevented – and we suspect there are none but the total interdiction of intoxicating liquors – we believe it would be necessary to forego the advantages of the social meal. However, we see no reason to despair, especially under the influence of such a truly Christian pastor as we have been all along supposing, that the parishoners would come to an agreement among themselves to abstain at these meals from the use of intoxicating liquors, and not to permit any one to infringe the rule. They would have the resource of tea and coffee; and the example of the happiness of the Sunday meal would operate powerfully in weaning from the attachment to intoxicating liquors even those by whom it had been acquired.

We shall speedily hear an objector saying, 'All very fine! But how to be done? In what parish are the people to be found, who will submit to all this moral drilling?' The misfortune is, that such talk proceeds from objectors, who care not whether the work be done or not done; but they thus exempt themselves at small cost from the trouble of bearing a hand in it. However, if there were as many people in earnest about religion, as there are who pretend to be; if there were as many imbued and animated with the spirit of true religion, as there are besotted with dogmas and ceremonies, all the difficulties which present themselves would be overcome. Have not those who were interested in the work got men to submit to whatever was most repugnant to their nature and feelings? to fall in love with propositions incredible? to practise tiresome, and endless, and often painful tricks, in supposed service of the Deity, which sink the performers of them to the level of monkeys? And can we despair, if similar pains were taken, of getting them to do what, at every step, would be delightful, and from which they would derive the greatest of all conceivable pleasures, the consciousness, the heart-felt assurance, of rising higher and higher in the scale of virtue and intelligence every day! Assuredly, the best means of carrying on the moral culture of the people will not speedily present themselves to the people, if they are not aided; and if the influence of those whom they are always ready to follow is not employed to put them in the right path, and urge them forward in it to a certain extent. But for the accomplishment of all this, we should rely much on the efforts of such a class of parochial ministers as we have just been describing; who might be truly styled the servants of God, and the friends of man; who would do much, by their own influence, and much, by stimulating men of station and wealth to employ their influence in the same beneficent direction.

P. Q.

JOHN STUART MILL

'Utility of Religion' (1874)

John Stuart Mill (1806–1873)

Biographical Note

John Stuart Mill was born 20 May 1806, the son of James Mill and Harriet Burrow. Mill's early education took place under the supervision of his father and, to some degree, Jeremy Bentham. At his birth Mill's father wrote to a friend proposing an educational contest between their sons! 'I have a strong determination at present to exert myself to the utmost to see what the power of education can do.'[1] Mill began learning Greek at the age of three and Latin at seven. At the age of eleven he helped correct the proofs of his father's *The History of British India*. In 1819 he took a course in political economy, lectured by his father during their walks together.[2] Leslie Stephen remarked that Mill's education was 'One of the most singular educational experiments on record'.[3] James Mill and Bentham were consciously attempting to produce a worthy successor, tutored in utilitarian methods and theory.[4] While this education has been widely criticised, Francis Place, who was among the critics, acknowledged the younger Mill's advanced learning.[5]

Between May 1820 and July 1821 Mill was in France with Sir Samuel and Lady Bentham and their family, primarily with a view to acquiring proficiency in French. In addition, he received instruction in dancing, music, social manners, fencing, and riding. Lady Bentham wrote that they sought to give him an education 'to fit him for commerce with the world at large'.[6] At the same time Mill continued his studies, completing some nine hours of learning each day.[7] He attended lectures on chemistry, zoology and logic at the Montpellier Faculté des Sciences, received private tuition in higher mathematics and began to study botany.[8] Mill considered that the chief effect of his experience in France was 'a strong and permanent interest in Continental Liberalism, of which I ever afterwards kept myself *au courant*'.[9]

---

[1]   Jack Stillinger, 'John Mill's Education: Fact, Fiction, and Myth', in Michael Laine (ed.), *A Cultivated Mind: Essays on J. S Mill Presented to John M. Robson* (Toronto 1991), p. 23.
[2]   John Stuart Mill, *Autobiography*, ed. Jack Stillinger and John M. Robson, *Collected Works of John Stuart Mill* (Toronto 1981), i. 31.
[3]   Leslie Stephen, *The English Utilitarians*, 3 vols. (London 1950), iii. 3.
[4]   Alexander Bain, *John Stuart Mill: A Criticism with Personal Recollections* (1882; reprt. New York 1969), p. 120.
[5]   Stillinger, 'John Mill's Education: Fact, Fiction, and Myth', p. 27.
[6]   Bain, *John Stuart Mill*, p. 22.
[7]   Bain, *John Stuart Mill*, p. 23.
[8]   Mill, *Autobiography*, in *Collected Works*, i. 59, 69.
[9]   Mill, *Autobiography*, in *Collected Works*, i. 63.

Though James Mill agreed with Bentham in viewing English law as a 'chaos of barbarism',[10] between 1821 and 1823 Mill studied Roman law with John Austin. His basic utilitarian education was reinforced by his discovery that Bentham's principles were laid out clearly in Dumont's edition of the *Traité de Législation*. This was followed by a reading of Locke's *Essay concerning Human Understanding*, Helvétius' *De l'esprit*, and Hartley's *Observations on Man*.[11] Mill's botanical studies, his only recreation during this period, fostered an interest in classification, and he followed Bentham in classifying human actions according to the principle of utility.[12] In 1822 he founded the Utilitarian Society as a discussion group in emulation of the French *philosophes*, taking the society's name from Galt's *Annals of the Parish* (though Bentham had used the term as early as 1781).[13] The Society's members included William Eyton Tooke, William Ellis, George Graham, and John Arthur Roebuck. This was one of the several ways in which Mill helped to shape the thinking of the younger philosophic radicals, whose 'mode of thinking was not characterized by Benthamism in any sense which has relation to Bentham as a chief or guide, but rather by a combination of Bentham's point of view with that of the modern political economy, and with the Hartleian metaphysics.'[14]

In May 1823 Mill was appointed an Examiner of India Correspondence working under his father in the East India Company,[15] but only became a full Examiner in 1856. Nominally, he worked in his office for six hours a day, but Bain states that he actually used three of these for his own writing.[16] Mill considered this a perfect method of providing a living while allowing time for intellectual reflection and writing. Also, it afforded him an insider's view of public administration, which he found immensely beneficial in his development as a 'theoretical reformer'. The only drawbacks were being excluded from parliament and public life, and being confined to London.[17] In 1858 he refused a place on the new India Council and retired with a pension of £1500 per annum.

Mill published his first piece of journalism in the Jan–Feb. 1823 issue of the *Traveller*. The following year saw the foundation of the *Westminster Review*, the mouthpiece of philosophical radicalism, to which Mill contributed many articles. John Bowring's involvement in the Greek loans financial scandal of 1825–26 undermined the effectiveness of the *Westmin-*

---

10   Mill, *Autobiography*, in *Collected Works*, i. 67.
11   Mill, *Autobiography*, in *Collected Works*, i. 67–71.
12   Stephen, *The English Utilitarians*, iii. 13.
13   Mill, *Autobiography*, in *Collected Works*, i. 80–83, 11; Stephen, *The English Utilitarians*, iii. 16.
14   Mill, *Autobiography*, in *Collected Works*, i. 107.
15   Mill, *Autobiography*, in *Collected Works*, i. 83.
16   Bain, *John Stuart Mill*, p. 147.
17   Mill, *Autobiography*, in *Collected Works*, i. 85.

ster,[18] and this may have contributed to Mill's loss of confidence. In the same year, however, he acted as editor for Bentham's *Rationale of Judicial Evidence*, a monumental labour of five volumes. Mill maintained that this improved both his knowledge and his ability to write.[19] From 1837 to 1840 he acted as editor of the *London and Westminster Review*.

In 1826–27 Mill suffered his famous mental crisis. By his own account the crisis came when he perceived the emptiness of his dream of being a utilitarian reformer, leaving 'nothing left to live for.'[20] He found some relief in Marmontel's *Mémoires* and finally realised that 'The only chance is to treat, not happiness, but some end external to it, as the purpose of life'.[21] Hayek quotes Levi's psychoanalytic study which suggests the cause of Mill's depression was 'suppressed death wishes against his father.'[22] but concluded that it was really rooted in the effort to escape from his father's intellectual domination.[23] Mazlish tends to agree with Levi, observing that at the time of his father's death in 1836 Mill became physically ill and was unable to be present at the death-bed. Mazlish writes: 'The details are different, but the atmosphere is the same as in Marmontel's *Mémoires*. John Stuart Mill had already lived through his father's death in 1826, and he could not bear to reactivate the scene in actual fact ten years later.'[24] On the other hand, Thomas rejected any view of this episode as a total revolt against Benthamism, his education and his father.[25] Rather he believed Mill lost faith in his father's ideas of progress,[26] and began to restructure 'a deeper and more subtle version of the whole inheritance', with the same purpose, to reform the world.[27] Alexander comments that in the 1850s Mill still believed in historical progress, but along with this went 'expressions of scepticism about human nature and the moral pattern of history.'[28] During the year of crisis Mill found comfort first in music, then in poetry. He read Wordsworth, attracted by his appreciation of nature, and learned that 'there was real, permanent happiness in tranquil contemplation'.[29] He also read Byron,

---

[18] William Thomas, *The Philosophic Radicals: Nine Studies in Theory and Practice 1817–1841* (Oxford 1979), pp. 163–66.

[19] Mill, *Autobiography*, in *Collected Works*, i. 119.

[20] Mill, *Autobiography*, in *Collected Works*, i. 139.

[21] Mill, *Autobiography*, in *Collected Works*, i. 147.

[22] F. A. Hayek, *John Stuart Mill and Harriet Taylor: Their Friendship and Subsequent Marriage* (New York 1951), p. 285; A. W. Levi, 'The "Mental Crisis" of John Stuart Mill', *The Psychoanalytical Review*, 32 (1945), p. 98.

[23] Hayek, *John Stuart Mill and Harriet Taylor*, p. 31.

[24] Bruce Mazlish, *James and John Stuart Mill: Father and Son in the Nineteenth Century* (New York 1975), p. 212.

[25] Thomas, *The Philosophic Radicals*, pp. 151–55, and *Mill* (Oxford 1985), pp. 33–37.

[26] Thomas, *The Philosophic Radicals*, p. 177.

[27] Thomas, *Mill*, p. 37.

[28] Edward Alexander, 'The Principles of Permanence and Progression in the Thought of J. S. Mill', in J. M. Robson and M. Laine (eds), *James and John Stuart Mill: Papers of the Centenary Conference* (Toronto and Buffalo 1976), p. 139.

[29] Mill, *Autobiography*, in *Collected Works*, i. 153.

but 'the poet's state of mind was too like my own. . . . and I was not in a frame of mind to desire any comfort from the vehement sensual passion of his Giaours'.[30]

In the summer of 1830 Mill met Harriet Taylor, née Hardy (1807–1858), with whom he had a lengthy platonic relationship. She was the daughter of a surgeon and wife of a prosperous manufacturing chemist, John Taylor, who was eleven years her senior. Taylor was a Unitarian in religion and an active radical in politics. In 1836 he was among the founding members of the Reform Club.[31] Mill and Harriet met through the Unitarian preacher, William Johnson Fox, who edited the *Monthly Repository*, to which Harriet contributed. She thought of her relationship with Mill as 'an edifying picture for those poor wretches who cannot conceive friendship but in sex – nor believe that expediency and consideration for the feelings of others can conquer sensuality.'[32] Following the death of John Taylor in 1849, and after twenty years of platonic friendship and some degree of literary collaboration, on 21 April 1851 Mill and Harriet were married. After Bentham and his father, she was the most significant presence in his life. Bain comments that, 'He formed few close friendships, and was absorbed very early by his one great attachment.'[33] Harriet's death in Avignon, on 3 November 1858, left him in despair. Mill bought a small house and garden near the cemetery where she was buried, with the intention of spending the rest of his days there in the company of Harriet's daughter Helen Taylor, to whom he was devoted.[34]

Harriet Taylor's influence on Mill's thinking has often been debated. Mill himself gave her a large amount of credit for the development of his mature ideas, and Hayek accepts that Harriet's influence on Mill was as significant as he believed.[35] It was both an emotional and an intellectual influence, according to Thomas: 'Meeting Harriet Taylor must have made him aware that his emotions no longer needed watering with the thin nutrient of Wordsworth, and he tried to integrate his belief in poetry into a utilitarian framework.'[36] On the other hand, Robson doubted the interpretation of Harriet as a dominant influence, and downplayed her intellectual contribution: 'She was in and of his intellectual and emotional life in an unusual degree, but not in an unexampled way, and she was not, in any meaningful sense, the "joint author" of his works.'[37]

---

[30]   Mill, *Autobiography*, in *Collected Works*, i. 151.
[31]   Hayek, *John Stuart Mill and Harriet Taylor*, p. 24.
[32]   Quoted in J. M. Robson, *The Improvement of Mankind: the Social and Political Thought of John Stuart Mill* (Toronto and London 1968), p. 52.
[33]   Bain, *John Stuart Mill*, p. 150.
[34]   Hayek, *John Stuart Mill and Harriet Taylor*, p. 265.
[35]   Hayek, *John Stuart Mill and Harriet Taylor*, p. 17.
[36]   Thomas, *Mill*, pp. 39–40.
[37]   Robson, *The Improvement of Mankind*, p. 68 (see also p. 53).

Mill was raised without any religious belief,[38] though he became acutely interested in the social purpose of religion. He later commented that he found it 'profoundly immoral' to worship a being whose moral attributes we admit are unknown.[39] Britton paints a picture of a scientific agnostic who would like to believe: 'Since in every case the evidence is indecisive, we cannot go wrong in suspending judgment – although to hope is profitable.'[40]

In politics Mill was ever the radical reformer. After the perceived failure of the Great Reform Act 1832, philosophical radicalism went into decline. By 1861, however, hopes of more effective reform were renewed. In 1865 Mill was invited to stand for Westminster. He accepted but only on condition that he would not canvas and no money would be expended in the campaign. During the campaign he refused to answer questions on his religious beliefs. Once elected to parliament he became an assiduous member. He systematically voted with the radicals among the Liberals, spoke eloquently on behalf of female suffrage, and helped to pass the Reform Act 1867. In the election of 1868 for the newly reformed parliament he lost his seat and retired again to private life. He died in Avignon on 8 May, 1873.

The early influences shaping Mill's general philosophy were unsurprising, given his upbringing. Bentham, Locke, Hartley, Hume, Berkeley, Reid, Dugald Stewart and Thomas Brown are all mentioned by Mill as important reading.[41] And there was, of course, his father, Ricardo, Austin and the other young Utilitarians with whom he was in regular contact. But later on Mill sought out writers and thinkers of different views, among them the St Simonians and Auguste Comte. Mill was greatly impressed by Comte,[42] but ultimately disagreed with him over the role of the individual and about the inferiority of women.[43] Other influences came from Coleridge, John Sterling, F. D. Maurice (a critic of utilitarian ethics), and Carlyle (who frequently made fun of Benthamism). Turk sees *Three Essays on Religion* (1874) as evidence of Coleridge's influence on Mill:

> It is Coleridge's liberal interpretation of the Christian myth, and his humanist insistence on the priority of human needs as factors determining the valuation of religious ideals, that Mill's essays echo. The criteria, for both men, are human ethical ideals, not divinely imposed duties.[44]

---

[38] Mill, *Autobiography*, in *Collected Works*, i. 41; for the nature of the religious instruction Mill received see p. 45.
[39] Mill, *Autobiography*, in *Collected Works*, i. 270.
[40] Karl W. Britton, 'John Stuart Mill on Christianity', in Robson and Laine (eds), *James and John Stuart Mill*, p. 34.
[41] Mill, *Autobiography*, in *Collected Works*, i. 71.
[42] Mill, *Autobiography*, in *Collected Works*, i. 217–19.
[43] Thomas, *Mill*, p. 69.
[44] Christopher Turk, *Coleridge and Mill: A Study of Influence* (Aldershot 1988), p. 245.

De Tocqueville's *Democracy in America* left a significant impression on Mill.[45] Robson discusses this influence, noting the two men had a cordial, if distant, relationship. Mill especially approved of the scientific nature of de Tocqueville's investigations, which led him to modify his own views of democracy.[46] Stephen asserts that Mill's own approach 'was strictly scientific; it recognised the necessity of slow elaboration, but offered a sufficiently wide vista of continuous improvement to be promoted by unremitting labour.'[47]

Mill's writings helped shape the intellectual climate of his day, and works like *A System of Logic* (1843) and *The Principles of Political Economy* (1848) had a lasting influence on the following generation. *On Liberty* (1859) remains his most influential and discussed work. Cowling comments that it,

> has been one of the most influential of modern political tracts chiefly . . . because its purpose has been misunderstood. . . . [It] was not so much a plea for individual freedom, as a means of ensuring that Christianity would be superseded by that form of liberal, rationalistic utilitarianism which went by the name of the Religion of Humanity. Mill's liberalism was a dogmatic, religious one, not the soothing night-comforter for which it is sometimes mistaken.[48]

Among Mill's other major writings are *Thoughts on Parliamentary Reform* (1859), *Considerations on Representative Government* (1861), *Utilitarianism* (1863), *An Examination of Sir William Hamilton's Philosophy* (1865), *Auguste Comte and Positivism* (1865), *The Subjection of Women* (1869), and the *Autobiography* (1873).

Note on the Text

John Stuart Mill's 'Utility of Religion' is one of *Three Essays on Religion* edited by Helen Taylor and published in 1874, the year following Mill's death. A 2nd edition appeared that same year and a 3rd edition in 1885, but both are simply reprints of the 1st edition without changes. 'Nature' and 'Utility of Religion' were written in 1854 and 'Theism' sometime between 1868 and 1870. The views on religion expressed in these essays are perfectly consistent with Mill's mature thoughts on the subject expressed elsewhere, most notably in *On Liberty* (1859) and *Auguste Comte and Positivism* (1865). *Three Essays on Religion* have been reprinted many times since their original posthumous publication, most notably in *Col-*

---

[45] Mill, *Autobiography*, in *Collected Works*, i. 201.
[46] Robson, *The Improvement of Mankind*, pp. 105–14.
[47] Stephen, *The English Utilitarians*, iii. 14.
[48] Maurice Cowling, *Mill and Liberalism* (Cambridge 1963), p. xiii.

lected Works of John Stuart Mill, vol. 10, edited by J. M. Robson (Toronto 1969). The *Collected Works* edition is based on the 1874 1st edition published in London by Longmans, Green, Reader, and Dyer, and it is this edition of 'Utility of Religion' which follows.

Utility of Religion

IT has sometimes been remarked how much has been written, both by friends and enemies, concerning the truth of religion, and how little, at least in the way of discussion or controversy, concerning its usefulness. This, however, might have been expected; for the truth, in matters which so deeply affect us, is our first concernment. If religion, or any particular form of it, is true, its usefulness follows without other proof. If to know authentically in what order of things, under what government of the universe it is our destiny to live, were not useful, it is difficult to imagine what could be considered so. Whether a person is in a pleasant or in an unpleasant place, a palace or a prison, it cannot be otherwise than useful to him to know where he is. So long, therefore, as men accepted the teachings of their religion as positive facts, no more a matter of doubt than their own existence or the existence of the objects around them, to ask the use of believing it could not possibly occur to them. The utility of religion did not need to be asserted until the arguments for its truth had in a great measure ceased to convince. People must either have ceased to believe, or have ceased to rely on the belief of others, before they could take that inferior ground of defence without a consciousness of lowering what they were endeavouring to raise. An argument for the utility of religion is an appeal to unbelievers, to induce them to practise a well meant hypocrisy, or to semi-believers to make them avert their eyes from what might possibly shake their unstable belief, or finally to persons in general to abstain from expressing any doubts they may feel, since a fabric of immense importance to mankind is so insecure at its foundations, that men must hold their breath in its neighbourhood for fear of blowing it down.

In the present period of history, however, we seem to have arrived at a time when, among the arguments for and against religion, those which relate to its usefulness assume an important place. We are in an age of weak beliefs, and in which such belief as men have is much more determined by their wish to believe than by any mental appreciation of evidence. The wish to believe does not arise only from selfish but often from the most disinterested feelings; and though it cannot produce the unwavering and perfect reliance which once existed, it fences round all that remains of the impressions of early education; it often causes direct misgivings to fade away by disuse; and above all, it induces people to continue laying out their lives according to doctrines which have lost part of their hold on the mind, and to maintain towards the world the same, or a rather more demonstrative attitude of belief, than they thought it necessary to exhibit when their personal conviction was more complete.

If religious belief be indeed so necessary to mankind, as we are continually assured that it is, there is great reason to lament, that the intellectual grounds of it should require to be backed by moral bribery or subornation of the understanding. Such a state of things is most uncomfortable even for those who may, without actual insincerity, describe themselves as believers; and still worse as regards those who, having consciously ceased to find the evidences of religion convincing, are withheld from saying so lest they should aid in doing an irreparable injury to mankind. It is a most painful position to a conscientious and cultivated mind, to be drawn in contrary directions by the two noblest of all objects of pursuit, truth, and the general good. Such a conflict must inevitably produce a growing indifference to one or other of these objects, most probably to both. Many who could render giant's service both to truth and to mankind if they believed that they could serve the one without loss to the other, are either totally paralysed, or led to confine their exertions to matters of minor detail, by the apprehension that any real freedom of speculation, or any considerable strengthening or enlargement of the thinking faculties of mankind at large, might, by making them unbelievers, be the surest way to render them vicious and miserable. Many, again, having observed in others or experienced in themselves elevated feelings which they imagine incapable of emanating from any other source than religion, have an honest aversion to anything tending, as they think, to dry up the fountain of such feelings. They, therefore, either dislike and disparage all philosophy, or addict themselves with intolerant zeal to those forms of it in which intuition usurps the place of evidence, and internal feeling is made the test of objective truth. The whole of the prevalent metaphysics of the present century is one tissue of suborned evidence in favour of religion; often of Deism only, but in any case involving a misapplication of noble impulses and speculative capacities, among the most deplorable of those wretched wastes of human faculties which make us wonder that enough is left to keep mankind progressive, at however slow a pace. It is time to consider, more impartially and therefore more deliberately than is usually done, whether all this straining to prop up beliefs which require so great an expense of intellectual toil and ingenuity to keep them standing, yields any sufficient return in human well being; and whether that end would not be better served by a frank recognition that certain subjects are inaccessible to our faculties, and by the application of the same mental powers to the strengthening and enlargement of those other sources of virtue and happiness which stand in no need of the support or sanction of supernatural beliefs and inducements.

Neither, on the other hand, can the difficulties of the question be so promptly disposed of, as sceptical philosophers are sometimes inclined to believe. It is not enough to aver, in general terms, that there never can be any conflict between truth and utility; that if religion be false, nothing but good can be the consequence of rejecting it. For, though the knowledge of every positive truth is an useful acquisition, this doctrine cannot without reservation be applied to negative truth. When the only truth ascertainable is that nothing can be known, we do not, by this knowledge, gain any new fact by which to guide ourselves; we are, at best, only disabused of our trust in some former guide-mark, which, though itself fallacious, may have pointed in the same direction with the best indications we have, and if it happens to be more conspicuous and legible, may have kept us right when they might have been over-looked. It is, in short, perfectly conceivable that religion may be morally useful without being intellectually sustainable: and it would be a proof of great prejudice in any unbeliever to deny, that there have been ages, and that there are still both nations and individuals, with regard to whom this is actually the case. Whether it is the case generally, and with reference to the future, it is the object of this paper to examine. We propose to inquire whether the belief in religion, considered as a mere persuasion, apart from the question of its truth, is really indispensable to the temporal welfare of mankind; whether the usefulness of the belief is intrinsic and universal, or local, temporary, and, in some sense, accidental, and whether the benefits which it yields might not be obtained otherwise, without the very large alloy of evil, by which, even in the best form of the belief, those benefits are qualified.

With the arguments on one side of the question we all are familiar: religious writers have not neglected to celebrate to the utmost the advantages both of religion in general and of their own religious faith in particular. But those who have held the contrary opinion have generally contented themselves with insisting on the more obvious and flagrant of the positive evils which have been engendered by past and present forms of religious belief. And, in truth, mankind have been so unremittingly occupied in doing evil to one another in the name of religion, from the sacrifice of Iphigenia to the Dragonnades of Louis XIV (not to descend lower), that for any immediate purpose there was little need to seek arguments further off. These odious consequences, however, do not belong to religion in itself, but to particular forms of it, and afford no argument against the usefulness of any religions except those by which such enormities are encouraged. Moreover, the worst of these evils are already in a great measure extirpated from the more improved forms of religion; and as mankind advance in ideas and in feelings, this process of extirpation continually goes on: the immoral, or otherwise mischievous consequences which have been drawn from religion, are, one by one, abandoned, and, after having been long fought for as of its very essence, are discovered to be easily separable from it. These mischiefs, indeed, after they are past, though no longer arguments against religion, remain valid as large abatements from its beneficial influence, by showing that some of the greatest improvements ever made in the moral sentiments of mankind have taken place without it and in spite of it, and that what we are taught to regard as the chief of all improving influences, has in practice fallen so far short of such a character, that one of the hardest burdens laid upon the other good influences of human nature has been that of improving religion itself. The improvement, however, has taken place; it is still proceeding, and for the sake of fairness it should be assumed to be complete. We ought to suppose religion to have accepted the best human morality which reason and goodness can work out, from philosophical, christian, or any other elements. When it has thus freed itself from the pernicious consequences which result from its identification with any bad moral doctrine, the ground is clear for considering whether its useful properties are exclusively inherent in it, or their benefits can be obtained without it.

This essential portion of the inquiry into the temporal usefulness of religion, is the subject of the present Essay. It is a part which has been little treated of by sceptical writers. The only direct discussion of it with which I am acquainted, is in a short treatise, understood to have been partly compiled from manuscripts of Mr. Bentham,[1] and abounding in just and profound views; but which, as it appears to me, presses many parts of the argument too hard. This treatise, and the incidental remarks scattered through the writings of M. Comte, are the only sources known to me from which anything very pertinent to the subject can be made available for the sceptical side of the argument. I shall use both of them freely in the sequel of the present discourse.

The inquiry divides itself into two parts, corresponding to the double aspect of the subject; its social, and its individual aspect. What does religion do for society, and what for the individual? What amount of benefit to social interests, in the ordinary sense of the phrase, arises from religious belief? And what influence has it in improving and ennobling individual human nature?

The first question is interesting to everybody; the latter only to the best; but to them it is, if there be any difference, the more important of the two. We shall begin with the former, as being that which best admits of being easily brought to a precise issue.

To speak first, then, of religious belief as an instrument of social good. We must commence by drawing a distinction most commonly overlooked. It is usual to credit religion *as such* with the whole of the power inherent in *any* system of moral duties inculcated by education and enforced by opinion. Undoubtedly mankind would be in a deplorable state if no principles or precepts of justice, veracity, beneficence, were taught publicly or

---

[1]   'Analysis of the Influence of Natural Religion on the Temporal Happiness of Mankind.' By Philip Beauchamp.

privately, and if these virtues were not encouraged, and the opposite vices repressed, by the praise and blame, the favourable and unfavourable sentiments, of mankind. And since nearly everything of this sort which does take place, takes place in the name of religion; since almost all who are taught any morality whatever, have it taught to them *as* religion, and inculcated on them through life principally in that character; the effect which the teaching produces as teaching, it is supposed to produce as religious teaching, and religion receives the credit of all the influence in human affairs which belongs to any generally accepted system of rules for the guidance and government of human life.

Few persons have sufficiently considered how great an influence this is; what vast efficacy belongs naturally to any doctrine received with tolerable unanimity as true, and impressed on the mind from the earliest childhood as duty. A little reflection will, I think, lead us to the conclusion that it is this which is the great moral power in human affairs, and that religion only seems so powerful because this mighty power has been under its command.

Consider first, the enormous influence of authority on the human mind. I am now speaking of involuntary influence; effect on men's conviction, on their persuasion, on their involuntary sentiments. Authority is the evidence on which the mass of mankind believe everything which they are said to know, except facts of which their own senses have taken cognizance. It is the evidence on which even the wisest receive all those truths of science, or facts in history or in life, of which they have not personally examined the proofs. Over the immense majority of human beings, the general concurrence of mankind, in any matter of opinion, is all powerful. Whatever is thus certified to them, they believe with a fulness of assurance which they do not accord even to the evidence of their senses when the general opinion of mankind stands in opposition to it. When, therefore, any rule of life and duty, whether grounded or not on religion, has conspicuously received the general assent, it obtains a hold on the belief of every individual, stronger than it would have even if he had arrived at it by the inherent force of his own understanding. If Novalis could say, not without a real meaning, 'My belief has gained infinitely to me from the moment when one other human being has begun to believe the same,' how much more when it is not one other person, but all the human beings whom one knows of. Some may urge it as an objection, that no scheme of morality has this universal assent, and that none, therefore, can be indebted to this source for whatever power it possesses over the mind. So far as relates to the present age, the assertion is true, and strengthens the argument which it might at first seem to controvert; for exactly in proportion as the received systems of belief have been contested, and it has become known that they have many dissentients, their hold on the general belief has been loosened, and their practical influence on conduct has declined: and since this has happened to them notwithstanding the religious sanction which attached to them, there can be no stronger evidence that they were powerful not as religion, but as beliefs generally accepted by mankind. To find people who believe their religion as a person believes that fire will burn his hand when thrust into it, we must seek them in those Oriental countries where Europeans do not yet predominate, or in the European world when it was still universally Catholic. Men often disobeyed their religion in those times, because their human passions and appetites were too strong for it, or because the religion itself afforded means of indulgence to breaches of its obligations; but though they disobeyed, they, for the most part, did not doubt. There was in those days an absolute and unquestioning completeness of belief, never since general in Europe.

Such being the empire exercised over mankind by simple authority, the mere belief and testimony of their fellow creatures; consider next how tremendous is the power of education; how unspeakable is the effect of bringing people up from infancy in a belief, and in habits founded on it. Consider also that in all countries, and from the earliest ages down to the present, not merely those who are called, in a restricted sense of the term, the educated, but all or nearly all who have been brought up by parents, or by any one interested in them, have been taught from their earliest years some kind of religious belief, and some precepts as the commands of the heavenly powers to them and to mankind. And as it cannot be imagined that the commands of God are to young children anything more than the commands of their parents, it is reasonable to think that any system of social duty which mankind might adopt, even though divorced from religion, would have the same advantage of being inculcated from childhood, and would have it hereafter much more perfectly than any doctrine has it at present, society being far more disposed than formerly to take pains for the moral tuition of those numerous classes whose education it has hitherto left very much to chance. Now it is especially characteristic of the impressions of early education, that they possess what it is so much more difficult for later convictions to obtain – command over the feelings. We see daily how powerful a hold these first impressions retain over the feelings even of those, who have given up the opinions which they were early taught. While on the other hand, it is only persons of a much higher degree of natural sensibility and intellect combined than it is at all common to meet with, whose feelings entwine themselves with anything like the same force round opinions which they have adopted from their own investigations later in life; and even when they do, we may say with truth that it is because the strong sense of moral duty, the sincerity, courage and self-devotion which enabled them to do so, were themselves the fruits of early impressions.

The power of education is almost boundless: there is not one natural inclination which it is not strong enough to coerce, and, if needful, to destroy by disuse. In the greatest recorded victory which education has ever achieved over a whole host of natural inclinations in an entire people – the maintenance through centuries of the institutions of Lycurgus, – it was very little, if even at all, indebted to religion: for the Gods of the Spartans were the same as those of other Greek states; and though, no doubt, every state of Greece believed that its particular polity had at its first establishment, some sort of divine sanction (mostly that of the Delphian oracle), there was seldom any difficulty in obtaining the same or an equally powerful sanction for a change. It was not religion which formed the strength of the Spartan institutions: the root of the system was devotion to Sparta, to the ideal of the country or State: which transformed into ideal devotion to a greater country, the world, would be equal to that and far nobler achievements. Among the Greeks generally, social morality was extremely independent of religion. The inverse relation was rather that which existed between them; the worship of the Gods was inculcated chiefly as a social duty, in as much as if they were neglected or insulted, it was believed that their displeasure would fall not more upon the offending individual than upon the state or community which bred and tolerated him. Such moral teaching as existed in Greece had very little to do with religion. The Gods were not supposed to concern themselves much with men's conduct to one another, except when men had contrived to make the Gods themselves an interested party, by placing an assertion or an engagement under the sanction of a solemn appeal to them, by oath or vow. I grant that the sophists and philosophers, and even popular orators, did their best to press religion into the service of their special objects, and to make it be thought that the sentiments of whatever kind, which they were engaged in inculcating, were particularly acceptable to the Gods, but this never seems the primary consideration in any case save those of direct offence to the dignity of the Gods themselves. For the enforcement of human moralities secular inducements were almost exclusively relied on. The case of Greece is, I believe, the only one in which any teaching, other than religious, has had the unspeakable advantage of forming the basis of education: and though much may be said against the quality of some part of the teaching, very little can be said against its effectiveness. The most memorable example of the power of education over conduct, is afforded (as I have just remarked) by this exceptional case; constituting a strong presumption that in other cases, early religious teaching has owed its power over mankind rather to its being early than to its being religious.

We have now considered two powers, that of authority, and that of early education, which operate through men's involuntary beliefs, feelings and desires, and which religion has hitherto held as its almost exclusive appanage. Let us now consider a third power which operates directly on their actions, whether their involuntary sentiments are carried with it or not. This is the power of public opinion; of the praise and blame, the favour and disfavour, of their fellow creatures; and is a source of strength inherent in any system of moral belief which is generally adopted, whether connected with religion or not.

Men are so much accustomed to give to the motives that decide their actions, more flattering names than justly belong to them, that they are generally quite unconscious how much those parts of their conduct which they most pride themselves on (as well as some which they are ashamed of), are determined by the motive of public opinion. Of course public opinion for the most part enjoins the same things which are enjoined by the received social morality; that morality being, in truth, the summary of the conduct which each one of the multitude, whether he himself observes it with any strictness or not, desires that others should observe towards him. People are therefore easily able to flatter themselves that they are acting from the motive of conscience when they are doing in obedience to the inferior motive, things which their conscience approves. We continually see how great is the power of opinion in opposition to conscience; how men 'follow a multitude to do evil;' how often opinion induces them to do what their conscience disapproves, and still oftener prevents them from doing what it commands. But when the motive of public opinion acts in the same direction with conscience, which, since it has usually itself made the conscience in the first instance, it for the most part naturally does; it is then, of all motives which operate on the bulk of mankind, the most overpowering.

The names of all the strongest passions (except the merely animal ones) manifested by human nature, are each of them a name for some one part only of the motive derived from what I here call public opinion. The love of glory; the love of praise; the love of admiration; the love of respect and deference; even the love of sympathy, are portions of its attractive power. Vanity is a vituperative name for its attractive influence generally, when considered excessive in degree. The fear of shame, the dread of ill repute or of being disliked or hated, are the direct and simple forms of its deterring power. But the deterring force of the unfavourable sentiments of mankind does not consist solely in the painfulness of knowing oneself to be the object of those sentiments; it includes all the penalties which they can inflict: exclusion from social intercourse and from the innumerable good offices which human beings require from one another; the forfeiture of all that is called success in life; often the great diminution or total loss of means of subsistence; positive ill offices of various kinds, sufficient to render life miserable, and reaching in some states of society as far as actual persecution to death. And again the attractive, or impelling influence of public opinion, includes the whole range of what is commonly meant by ambition: for, except in times of lawless military violence, the objects of social ambition can only be attained by means of the good opinion and favourable disposition of our fellow-creatures; nor, in nine cases out of ten, would those objects be even desired, were it not for the power they confer over the sentiments of mankind. Even the pleasure of self-approbation, in the great majority, is mainly dependent on the opinion of others. Such is the involuntary influence of authority on ordinary minds, that persons must be of a better than ordinary mould to be capable of a full assurance that they are in the right, when the world, that is, when *their* world, thinks them wrong: nor is there, to most men, any proof so demonstrative of their own virtue or talent as that people in general seem to believe in it. Through all departments of human affairs, regard for the sentiments of our fellow-creatures is in one shape or other, in nearly all characters, the pervading motive. And we ought to note that this motive is naturally strongest in the most sensitive natures, which are the most promising material for the formation of great virtues. How far its power reaches is known by too familiar experience to require either proof or illustration here. When once the means of living have been obtained, the far greater part of the remaining labour and effort which takes place on the earth, has for its object to acquire the respect or the favourable regard of mankind; to be looked up to, or at all events, not to be looked down upon by them. The industrial and commercial activity which advance civilization, the frivolity, prodigality, and selfish thirst of aggrandizement which retard it, flow equally from that source. While as an instance of the power exercised by the terrors derived from public opinion, we know how many murders have been committed merely to remove a witness who knew and was likely to disclose some secret that would bring disgrace upon his murderer.

Any one who fairly and impartially considers the subject, will see reason to believe that those great effects on human conduct, which are commonly ascribed to motives derived directly from religion, have mostly for their proximate cause the influence of human opinion. Religion has been powerful not by its intrinsic force, but because it has wielded that additional and more mighty power. The effect of religion has been immense in giving a direction to public opinion: which has, in many most important respects, been wholly determined by it. But without the sanctions superadded by public opinion, its own proper sanctions have never, save in exceptional characters, or in peculiar moods of mind, exercised a very potent influence, after the times had gone by, in which divine agency was supposed habitually to employ temporal rewards and punishments. When a man firmly believed that if he violated the sacredness of a particular sanctuary he would be struck dead on the spot, or smitten suddenly with a mortal disease, he doubtless took care not to incur the penalty: but when any one had had the courage to defy the danger, and escaped with impunity, the spell was broken. If ever any people were taught that they were under a divine government, and that unfaithfulness to their religion and law would by visited from above with temporal chastisements, the Jews were so. Yet their history was a mere succession of lapses into Paganism. Their prophets and historians, who held fast to the ancient beliefs (though they gave them so liberal an interpretation as to think it a sufficient manifestation of God's displeasure towards a king if any evil happened to his great grandson), never ceased to complain that their countrymen turned a deaf ear to their vaticinations; and hence, with the faith they held in a divine government operating by temporal penalties, they could not fail to anticipate (as Mirabeau's father without such prompting, was able to do on the eve of the French Revolution) *la culbute générale*; an expectation which, luckily for the credit of their prophetic powers, was fulfilled; unlike that of the Apostle John, who in the only intelligible prophecy in the Revelations, foretold to the city of the seven hills a fate like that of Nineveh and Babylon; which prediction remains to this hour unaccomplished. Unquestionably the conviction which experience in time forced on all but the very ignorant, that divine punishments were not to be confidently expected in a temporal form, contributed much to the downfall of the old religions, and the general adoption of one which without absolutely excluding providential interferences in this life for the punishment of guilt or the reward of merit, removed the principal scene of divine retribution to a world after death. But rewards and punishments postponed to that distance of time, and never seen by the eye, are not calculated, even when infinite and eternal, to have, on ordinary minds, a very powerful effect in opposition to strong temptation. Their remoteness alone is a prodigious deduction from their efficacy, on such minds as those which most require the restraint of punishment. A still greater abatement is their uncertainty, which belongs to them from the very nature of the case: for rewards and punishments administered after death, must be awarded not definitely to particular actions, but on a general survey of the person's whole life, and he easily persuades himself that whatever may have been his peccadilloes, there will be a balance in his favour at the last. All positive religions aid this self-delusion. Bad religions teach that divine vengeance may be bought off, by offerings, or personal abasement; the better religions, not to drive sinners to despair, dwell so much on the divine mercy; that hardly any one is compelled to think himself irrevocably condemned. The sole quality in these punishments which might seem calculated to make them efficacious, their over-powering magnitude, is itself a reason why nobody (except a hypochondriac here and there) ever really believes that he is in any very serious danger of incurring them. Even the worst malefactor is hardly able to think that any crime he has had it in his power to commit, any evil he can have inflicted in this short space of existence, can have deserved torture extending through an eternity. Accordingly religious writers and preachers are never tired of complaining how little effect religious motives have on men's lives and conduct, notwithstanding the tremendous penalties denounced.

Mr. Bentham, whom I have already mentioned as one of the few authors who have written anything to the purpose on the efficacy of the religious sanction, adduces several cases to prove that religious obligation, when not enforced by public opinion, produces scarcely any effect on conduct. His first example is that of oaths. The oaths taken in courts of justice, and any others which from the manifest importance to society of their being kept, public opinion rigidly enforces, are felt as real and binding obligations. But university oaths and custom-house oaths, though in a religious point of view equally obligatory, are in practice utterly disregarded even by men in other respects honourable. The university oath to obey the statutes has been for centuries, with universal acquiescence, set at nought: and utterly false statements are (or used to be) daily and unblushingly sworn to at the Custom-house, by persons as attentive as other people to all the ordinary obligations of life. The explanation being, that veracity in these cases was not enforced by public opinion. The second case which Bentham cites is duelling; a practice now, in this country, obsolete, but in full vigour in several other christian countries; deemed and admitted to be a sin by almost all who, nevertheless, in obedience to opinion, and to escape from personal humiliation, are guilty of it. The third case is that of illicit sexual inter-course; which in both sexes, stands in the very highest rank of religious sins, yet not being severely censured by opinion in the male sex, they have in general very little scruple in committing it; while in the case of women, though the religious obligation is not stronger, yet being backed in real earnest by public opinion, it is commonly effectual.

Some objection may doubtless be taken to Bentham's instances, considered as crucial experiments on the power of the religious sanction; for (it may be said) people do not really believe that in these cases they shall be punished by God, any more than by man. And this is certainly true in the case of those university and other oaths, which are habitually taken without any intention of keeping them. The oath, in these cases, is regarded as a mere formality, destitute of any serious meaning in the sight of the Deity; and the most scrupulous person, even if he does reproach himself for having taken an oath which nobody deems fit to be kept, does not in his conscience tax himself with the guilt of perjury, but only with the profanation of a ceremony. This, therefore, is not a good example of the weakness of the religious motive when divorced from that of human opinion. The point which it illustrates is rather the tendency of the one motive to come and go with the other, so that where the penalties of public opinion cease, the religious motive ceases also. The same criticism, however, is not equally applicable to Bentham's other examples, duelling, and sexual irregularities. Those who do these acts, the first by the command of public opinion, the latter with its indulgence, really do, in most cases, believe that they are offending God. Doubtless, they do not think that they are offending him in such a degree as very seriously to endanger their salvation. Their reliance on his mercy prevails over their dread of his resentment; affording an exemplification of the remark already made, that the unavoidable uncertainty of religious penalties makes them feeble as a deterring motive. They are so, even in the case of acts which human opinion condemns: much more, with those to which it is indulgent. What mankind think venial, it is hardly ever supposed that God looks upon in a serious light: at least by those who feel in themselves any inclination to practise it.

I do not for a moment think of denying that there are states of mind in which the idea of religious punishment acts with the most overwhelming force. In hypochondriacal disease, and in those with whom, from great disappointments or other moral causes, the thoughts and imagination have assumed an habitually melancholy complexion, that topic, falling in with the pre-existing tendency of the mind, supplies images well fitted to drive the unfortunate sufferer even to madness. Often, during a temporary state of depression, these ideas take such a hold of the mind as to give a permanent turn to the character; being the most common case of what, in sectarian phraseology, is called conversion. But if the depressed state ceases after the conversion, as it commonly does, and the convert does not relapse, but perseveres in his new course of life, the principal difference between it and the old is usually found to be, that the man now guides his life by the public opinion of his religious associates, as he before guided it by that of the profane world. At all events, there is one clear proof how little the generality of mankind, either religious or worldly, really dread eternal punishments, when we see how, even at the approach of death, when the remoteness which took so much from their effect has been exchanged for the closest proximity, almost all persons who have not been guilty of some enormous crime (and many who have) are quite free from uneasiness as to their prospects in another world, and never for a moment seem to think themselves in any real danger of eternal punishment.

With regard to the cruel deaths and bodily tortures, which confessors and martyrs have so often undergone for the sake of religion, I would not depreciate them by attributing any part of this admirable courage and constancy to the influence of human opinion. Human opinion indeed has shown itself quite equal to the production of similar firmness in persons not otherwise distinguished by moral excellence; such as the North American Indian at the stake. But if it was not the thought of glory in the eyes of their fellow-religionists, which upheld these heroic sufferers in their agony, as little do I believe that it was, generally speaking, that of the pleasures of heaven or the pains of hell. Their impulse was a divine enthusiasm – a self-forgetting devotion to an idea: a state of exalted feeling, by no means peculiar to religion, but which it is the privilege of every great cause to inspire; a phenomenon belonging to the critical moments of existence, not to the ordinary play of human motives, and from which nothing can be inferred as to the efficacy of the ideas which it sprung from, whether religious or any other, in overcoming ordinary temptations, and regulating the course of daily life.

We may now have done with this branch of the subject, which is, after all, the vulgarest part of it. The value of religion as a supplement to human laws, a more cunning sort of police, an auxiliary to the thief-catcher and the hangman, is not that part of its claims which the more highminded of its votaries are fondest of insisting on: and they would probably be as ready as any one to admit, that if the nobler offices of religion in the soul could be dispensed with, a substitute might be found for so coarse and selfish a social instrument as the fear of hell. In their view of the matter, the best of mankind absolutely require religion for the perfection of their own character, even though the coercion of the worst might possibly be accomplished without its aid.

Even in the social point of view, however, under its most elevated aspect, these nobler spirits generally assert the necessity of religion, as a teacher, if not as an enforcer, of social morality. They say, that religion alone can teach us what morality is; that all the high morality ever recognized by mankind, was learnt from religion; that the greatest uninspired philosophers in their sublimest flights, stopt far short of the christian morality, and whatever inferior morality they may have attained to (by the assistance, as many think, of dim traditions derived from the Hebrew books, or from a primæval revelation) they never could induce the common mass of their fellow citizens to accept it from them. That, only when a morality is understood to come from the Gods, do men in general adopt it, rally round it, and lend their human sanctions for its enforcement. That granting the sufficiency of human motives to make the rule obeyed, were it not for the religious idea we should not have had the rule itself.

There is truth in much of this, considered as matter of history. Ancient peoples have generally, if not always, received their morals, their laws, their intellectual beliefs, and even their practical arts of life, all in short which tended either to guide or to discipline them, as revelations from the superior powers, and in any other way could not easily have been induced to accept them. This was partly the effect of their hopes and fears from those powers, which were of much greater and more universal potency in early times, when the agency of the Gods was seen in the daily events of life, experience not having yet disclosed the fixed laws according to which physical phenomena succeed one another. Independently, too, of personal hopes and fears, the involuntary deference felt by these rude minds for power superior to their own, and the tendency to suppose that beings of superhuman power must also be of superhuman knowledge and wisdom, made them disinterestedly desire to conform their conduct to the presumed preferences of these powerful beings, and to adopt no new practice without their authorization either spontaneously given, or solicited and obtained.

But because, when men were still savages, they would not have received either moral or scientific truths unless they had supposed them to be supernaturally imparted, does it follow that they would now give up moral truths any more than scientific, because they believed them to have no higher origin than wise and noble human hearts? Are not moral truths strong enough in their own evidence, at all events to retain the belief of mankind when once they have acquired it? I grant that some of the precepts of Christ as exhibited in the Gospels – rising far above the Paulism which is the foundation of ordinary Christianity – carry some kinds of moral goodness to a greater height than had ever been attained before, though much even of what is supposed to be peculiar to them is equalled in the Meditations of Marcus Antoninus, which we have no ground for believing to have been in any way indebted to Christianity. But this benefit, whatever it amounts to, has been gained. Mankind have entered into the possession of it. It has become the property of humanity, and cannot now be lost by anything short of a return to primæval barbarism. The 'new commandment to love one another;'[2] the recognition that the greatest are those who serve, not who are served by, others; the reverence for the weak and humble, which is the foundation of chivalry, they and not the strong being pointed out as having the first place in God's regard, and the first claim on their fellow men; the lesson of the parable of the Good Samaritan; that of 'he that is without sin let him throw the first stone;' the precept of doing as we would be done by; and such other noble moralities as are to be found, mixed with some poetical exaggerations, and some maxims of which it is difficult to ascertain the precise object; in the authentic sayings of Jesus of Nazareth; these are surely in sufficient harmony with the intellect and feelings of every good man or woman, to be in no danger of being let go, after having been once acknowledged as the creed of the best and foremost portion of our species. There will be, as there have been, shortcomings enough for a long time to come in acting on them; but that they should be forgotten, or cease to be operative on the human conscience, while human beings remain cultivated or civilized, may be pronounced, once for all, impossible.

On the other hand, there is a very real evil consequent on ascribing a supernatural origin to the received maxims of morality. That origin consecrates the whole of them, and protects them from being discussed or criticized. So that if among the moral doctrines received as a part of religion, there be any which are imperfect – which were either erroneous from the first, or not properly limited and guarded in the expression, or which, unexceptionable once, are no longer suited to the changes that have taken place in human relations (and it is my firm belief that in so-called christian morality, instances of all these kinds are to be found) these doctrines are considered equally binding on the conscience with the noblest, most permanent and most universal precepts of Christ. Wherever morality is

---

[2]   Not, however, a new commandment. In justice to the great Hebrew lawgiver, it should always be remembered that the precept, to love thy neighbour as thyself, already existed in the Pentateuch; and very surprising it is to find it there.

supposed to be of supernatural origin, morality is stereotyped; as law is, for the same reason, among believers in the Koran.

Belief, then, in the supernatural, great as are the services which it rendered in the early stages of human development, cannot be considered to be any longer required, either for enabling us to know what is right and wrong in social morality, or for supplying us with motives to do right and to abstain from wrong. Such belief, therefore, is not necessary for social purposes, at least in the coarse way in which these can be considered apart from the character of the individual human being. That more elevated branch of the subject now remains to be considered. If Supernatural beliefs are indeed necessary to the perfection of the individual character, they are necessary also to the highest excellence in social conduct: necessary in a far higher sense than that vulgar one, which constitutes it the great support of morality in common eyes.

Let us then consider, what it is in human nature which causes it to require a religion; what wants of the human mind religion supplies, and what qualities it developes. When we have understood this, we shall be better able to judge, how far these wants can be otherwise supplied and those qualities, or qualities equivalent to them, unfolded and brought to perfection by other means.

The old saying, *Primus in orbe Deos fecit timor,* I hold to be untrue, or to contain, at most, only a small amount of truth. Belief in Gods had, I conceive, even in the rudest minds, a more honourable origin. Its universality has been very rationally explained from the spontaneous tendency of the mind to attribute life and volition, similar to what it feels in itself, to all natural objects and phenomena which appear to be self-moving. This was a plausible fancy, and no better theory could be formed at first. It was naturally persisted in so long as the motions and operations of these objects seemed to be arbitrary, and incapable of being accounted for but by the free choice of the Power itself. At first, no doubt, the objects themselves were supposed to be alive; and this belief still subsists among African fetish-worshippers. But as it must soon have appeared absurd that things which could do so much more than man, could not or would not do what man does, as for example to speak, the transition was made to supposing that the object present to the senses was inanimate, but was the creature and instrument of an invisible being with a form and organs similar to the human.

These beings having first been believed in, fear of them necessarily followed; since they were thought able to inflict at pleasure on human beings great evils, which the sufferers neither knew how to avert nor to foresee, but were left dependent, for their chances of doing either, upon solicitations addressed to the deities themselves. It is true, therefore, that fear had much to do with religion: but belief in the Gods evidently preceded, and did not arise from, fear: though the fear, when established, was a strong support to the belief, nothing being conceived to be so great an offence to the divinities as any doubt of their existence.

It is unnecessary to prosecute further the natural history of religion, as we have not here to account for its origin in rude minds, but for its persistency in the cultivated. A sufficient explanation of this will, I conceive, be found in the small limits of man's certain knowledge, and the boundlessness of his desire to know. Human existence is girt round with mystery: the narrow region of our experience is a small island in the midst of a boundless sea, which at once awes our feelings and stimulates our imagination by its vastness and its obscurity. To add to the mystery, the domain of our earthly existence is not only an island in infinite space, but also in infinite time. The past and the future are alike shrouded from us: we neither know the origin of anything which is, nor its final destination. If we feel deeply interested in knowing that there are myriads of worlds at an immeasurable, and to our faculties inconceivable, distance from us in space; if we are eager to discover what little we can about these worlds, and when we cannot know what they are, can never satiate ourselves with speculating on what they may be; is it not a matter of far deeper interest to us to learn, or even to conjecture, from whence came this nearer world which we inhabit; what cause or agency made it what it is, and on what powers depend its future fate? Who would not desire this more ardently than any other conceivable knowledge, so long as there appeared the slightest hope of attaining it? What would not one give for any credible tidings from that mysterious region, any glimpse into it which might enable us to see the smallest light through its darkness, especially any theory of it which we could believe, and which represented it as tenanted by a benignant and not a hostile influence? But since we are able to penetrate into that region with the imagination only, assisted by specious but inconclusive analogies derived from human agency and design, imagination is free to fill up the vacancy with the imagery most congenial to itself; sublime and elevating if it be a lofty imagination, low and mean if it be a grovelling one.

Religion and poetry address themselves, at least in one of their aspects, to the same part of the human constitution: they both supply the same want, that of ideal conceptions grander and more beautiful than we see realized in the prose of human life. Religion, as distinguished from poetry, is the product of the craving to know whether these imaginative conceptions have realities answering to them in some other world than ours. The mind, in this state, eagerly catches at any rumours respecting other worlds, especially when delivered by persons whom it deems wiser than itself. To the poetry of the supernatural, comes to be thus added a positive belief and expectation, which unpoetical minds can share with the poetical. Belief in a God or Gods, and in a life after death, becomes the canvas which every mind, according to its capacity, covers with such ideal pictures as it can either invent or copy. In that other life each hopes to find the good which he has failed to find on earth, or the better which is suggested to him by the good which on earth he has partially seen and known. More especially, this belief supplies the finer minds with material for conceptions of beings more awful than they *can* have known on earth, and more excellent than they probably *have* known. So long as human life is insufficient to satisfy human aspirations, so long there will be a craving for higher things, which finds its most obvious satisfaction in religion. So long as earthly life is full of sufferings, so long there will be need of consolations, which the hope of heaven affords to the selfish, the love of God to the tender and grateful.

The value, therefore, of religion to the individual, both in the past and present, as a source of personal satisfaction and of elevated feelings, is not to be disputed. But it has still to be considered, whether in order to obtain this good, it is necessary to travel beyond the boundaries of the world which we inhabit; or whether the idealization of our earthly life, the cultivation of a high conception of what *it* may be made, is not capable of supplying a poetry, and, in the best sense of the word, a religion, equally fitted to exalt the feelings, and (with the same aid from education) still better calculated to ennoble the conduct, than any belief respecting the unseen powers.

At the bare suggestion of such a possibility, many will exclaim, that the short duration, the smallness and insignificance of life, if there is no prolongation of it beyond what we see, makes it impossible that great and elevated feelings can connect themselves with anything laid out on so small a scale: that such a conception of life can match with nothing higher than Epicurean feelings, and the Epicurean doctrine 'Let us eat and drink, for to-morrow we die.'

Unquestionably, within certain limits, the maxim of the Epicureans is sound, and applicable to much higher things than eating and drinking. To make the most of the present for all good purposes, those of enjoyment among the rest; to keep under control those mental dispositions which lead to undue sacrifice of present good for a future which may never arrive; to cultivate the habit of deriving pleasure from things within our reach, rather than from the too eager pursuit of objects at a distance; to think all time wasted which is not spent either in personal pleasure or in doing things useful to oneself or others; these are wise maxims, and the 'carpe diem' doctrine, carried thus far, is a rational and legitimate corollary from the shortness of life. But that because life is short we should care for nothing beyond it, is not a legitimate conclusion; and the supposition, that human beings in general are not capable of feeling deep and even the deepest interest in things which they will never live to see, is a view of human nature as false as it is abject. Let it be remembered that if individual life is short, the life of the human species is not short; its indefinite duration is practically equivalent to endlessness; and being combined with indefinite capability of improvement, it offers to the imagination and sympathies a

weakening of the selfish element in our nature; since they hold out to the imagination selfish good and evil of such tremendous magnitude, that it is difficult for any one who fully believes in their reality, to have feeling or interest to spare for any other distant and ideal object. It is true, many of the most unselfish of mankind have been believers in supernaturalism, because their minds have not dwelt on the threats and promises of their religion, but chiefly on the idea of a Being to whom they looked up with a confiding love, and in whose hands they willingly left all that related especially to themselves. But in its effect on common minds, what now goes by the name of religion operates mainly through the feelings of self-interest. Even the Christ of the Gospels holds out the direct promise of reward from heaven as a primary inducement to the noble and beautiful beneficence towards our fellow-creatures which he so impressively inculcates. This is a radical inferiority of the best supernatural religions, compared with the Religion of Humanity; since the greatest thing which moral influences can do for the amelioration of human nature, is to cultivate the unselfish feelings in the only mode in which any active principle in human nature can be effectually cultivated, namely by habitual exercise: but the habit of expecting to be rewarded in another life for our conduct in this, makes even virtue itself no longer an exercise of the unselfish feelings.

Secondly, it is an immense abatement from the worth of the old religions as means of elevating and improving human character, that it is nearly, if not quite impossible for them to produce their best moral effects, unless we suppose a certain torpidity, if not positive twist in the intellectual faculties. For it is impossible that any one who habitually thinks, and who is unable to blunt his inquiring intellect by sophistry, should be able without misgiving to go on ascribing absolute perfection to the author and ruler of so clumsily made and capriciously governed a creation as this planet and the life of its inhabitants. The adoration of such a being cannot be with the whole heart, unless the heart is first considerably sophisticated. The worship must either be greatly overclouded by doubt, and occasionally quite darkened by it, or the moral sentiments must sink to the low level of the ordinances of Nature: the worshipper must learn to think blind partiality, atrocious cruelty, and reckless injustice, not blemishes in an object of worship, since all these abound to excess in the commonest phenomena of Nature. It is true, the God who is worshipped is not, generally speaking, the God of Nature only, but also the God of some revelation; and the character of the revelation will greatly modify and, it may be, improve the moral influences of the religion. This is emphatically true of Christianity; since the Author of the Sermon of the Mount is assuredly a far more benignant Being than the Author of Nature. But unfortunately, the believer in the christian revelation is obliged to believe that the same being is the author of both. This, unless he resolutely averts his mind from the subject, or practises the act of quieting his conscience by sophistry, involves him in moral perplexities without end; since the ways of his Deity in Nature are on many occasions totally at variance with the precepts, as he believes, of the same Deity in the Gospel. He who comes out with least moral damage from this embarrassment, is probably the one who never attempts to reconcile the two standards with one another, but confesses to himself that the purposes of Providence are mysterious, that its ways are not our ways, that its justice and goodness are not the justice and goodness which we can conceive and which it befits us to practise. When, however, this is the feeling of the believer, the worship of the Deity ceases to be the adoration of abstract moral perfection. It becomes the bowing down to a gigantic image of something not fit for us to imitate. It is the worship of power only.

I say nothing of the moral difficulties and perversions involved in revelation itself; though even in the Christianity of the Gospels, at least in its ordinary interpretation, there are some of so flagrant a character as almost to outweigh all the beauty and benignity and moral greatness which so eminently distinguish the sayings and character of Christ. The recognition, for example, of the object of highest worship, in a being who could make a Hell; and who could create countless generations of human beings with the certain foreknowledge that he was creating them for this fate. Is there any moral enormity which might not be justified by imitation of such a Deity? And is it possible to adore such a one without a frightful distortion of the standard of right and wrong? Any other of the outrages to the most ordinary justice and humanity involved in the common christian conception of the moral character of God, sinks into insignificance beside this dreadful idealization of wickedness. Most of them too, are happily not so unequivocally deducible from the very words of Christ as to be indisputably a part of christian doctrine. It may be doubted, for instance, whether Christianity is really responsible for atonement and redemption, original sin and vicarious punishment: and the same may be said respecting the doctrine which makes belief in the divine mission of Christ a necessary condition of salvation. It is nowhere represented that Christ himself made this statement, except in the huddled-up account of the Resurrection contained in the concluding verses of St. Mark, which some critics (I believe the best), consider to be an interpolation. Again, the proposition that 'the powers that be are ordained of God' and the whole series of corollaries deduced from it in the Epistles, belong to St. Paul, and must stand or fall with Paulism, not with Christianity. But there is one moral contradiction inseparable from every form of Christianity, which no ingenuity can resolve, and no sophistry explain away. It is, that so precious a gift, bestowed on a few, should have been withheld from the many: that countless millions of human beings should have been allowed to live and die, to sin and suffer, without the one thing needful, the divine remedy for sin and suffering, which it would have cost the Divine Giver as little to have vouchsafed to all, as to have bestowed by special grace upon a favoured minority. Add to this, that the divine message, assuming it to be such, has been authenticated by credentials so insufficient, that they fail to convince a large proportion of the strongest and most cultivated minds, and the tendency to disbelieve them appears to grow with the growth of scientific knowledge and critical discrimination. He who can believe these to be the intentional shortcomings of a perfectly good Being, must impose silence on every prompting of the sense of goodness and justice as received among men.

It is, no doubt, possible (and there are many instances of it) to worship with the intensest devotion either Deity, that of Nature or of the Gospel, without any perversion of the moral sentiments: but this must be by fixing the attention exclusively on what is beautiful and beneficent in the precepts and spirit of the Gospel and in the dispensations of Nature, and putting all that is the reverse as entirely aside as if it did not exist. Accordingly, this simple and innocent faith can only, as I have said, co-exist with a torpid and inactive state of the speculative faculties. For a person of exercised intellect, there is no way of attaining anything equivalent to it, save by sophistication and perversion, either of the understanding or of the conscience. It may almost always be said both of sects and of individuals, who derive their morality from religion, that the better logicians they are, the worse moralists.

One only form of belief in the supernatural – one only theory respecting the origin and government of the universe – stands wholly clear both of intellectual contradiction and of moral obliquity. It is that which, resigning irrevocably the idea of an omnipotent creator, regards Nature and Life not as the expression throughout of the moral character and purpose of the Deity, but as the product of a struggle between contriving goodness and an intractable material, as was believed by Plato, or a Principle of Evil, as was the doctrine of the Manicheans. A creed like this, which I have known to be devoutly held by at least one cultivated and conscientious person of our own day allows it to be believed that all the mass of evil which exists was undesigned by, and exists not by the appointment of, but in spite of the Being whom we are called upon to worship. A virtuous human being assumes in this theory the exalted character of a fellow-labourer with the Highest, a fellow-combatant in the great strife; contributing his little, which by the aggregation of many like himself becomes much, towards that progressive ascendancy, and ultimately complete triumph of good over evil, which history points to, and which this doctrine teaches us to regard as planned by the Being to whom we owe all the benevolent contrivance we behold in Nature. Against the moral tendency of this creed no possible objection can lie: it can produce on whoever can succeed in believing it, no other than an ennobling effect. The evidence for it, indeed, if evidence it can be called, is too shadowy and unsubstantial, and the promises it holds out too distant and uncertain, to admit of its being a permanent substitute for the religion of humanity; but the two may be held in conjunction: and he to whom ideal good, and the progress of the world towards it, are already a religion, even though that other creed may seem to him a belief not grounded on evidence, is at liberty to indulge the pleasing and encouraging thought, that its truth is possible. Apart from all dogmatic belief, there is for those who need it, an ample domain in the region of the imagination which may be planted with possibilities, with hypotheses which cannot be known to be false; and when there is anything in the appearances of nature to favour them, as in this case there is (for whatever force we attach to the analogies of Nature with the effects of human contrivance, there is no disputing the remark of Paley, that what is good in nature exhibits those analogies much oftener than what is evil), the contemplation of these possibilities is a legitimate indulgence, capable of bearing its part, with other influences, in feeding and animating the tendency of the feelings and impulses towards good.

One advantage, such as it is, the supernatural religions must always possess over the Religion of Humanity; the prospect they hold out to the individual of a life after death. For, though the scepticism of the understanding does not necessarily exclude the Theism of the imagination and feelings, and this again, gives opportunity for a hope that the power which has done so much for us may be able and willing to do this also, such vague possibility must ever stop far short of a conviction. It remains then to estimate the value of this element – the prospect of a world to come – as a constituent of earthly happiness. I cannot but think that as the condition of mankind becomes improved, as they grow happier in their lives, and more capable of deriving happiness from unselfish sources, they will care less and less for this flattering expectation. It is not, naturally or generally, the happy who are the most anxious either for a prolongation of the present life, or for a life hereafter: it is those who never have been happy. They who have had their happiness can bear to part with existence: but it is hard to die without ever having lived. When mankind cease to need a future existence as a consolation for the sufferings of the present, it will have lost its chief value to them, for themselves. I am now speaking of the unselfish. Those who are so wrapped up in self that they are unable to identify their feelings with anything which will survive them, or to feel their life prolonged in their younger cotemporaries and in all who help to carry on the progressive movement of human affairs, require the notion of another selfish life beyond the grave, to enable them to keep up any interest in existence, since the present life, as its termination approaches, dwindles into something too insignificant to be worth caring about. But if the Religion of Humanity were as sedulously cultivated as the supernatural religions are (and there is no difficulty in conceiving that it might be much more so), all who had received the customary amount of moral cultivation would up to the hour of death live ideally in the life of those who are to follow them: and though doubtless they would often willingly survive as individuals for a much longer period than the present duration of life, it appears to me probable that after a length of time different in different persons, they would have had enough of existence, and would gladly lie down and take their eternal rest. Meanwhile and without looking so far forward, we may remark, that those who believe the immortality of the soul, generally quit life with fully as much, if not more, reluctance, as those who have no such expectation. The mere cessation of existence is no evil to any one: the idea is only formidable through the illusion of imagination which makes one conceive oneself as if one were alive and feeling oneself dead. What is odious in death is not death itself, but the act of dying, and its lugubrious accompaniments: all of which must be equally undergone by the believer in immortality. Nor can I perceive that the sceptic loses by his scepticism any real and valuable consolation except one; the hope of reunion with those dear to him who have ended their earthly life before him. That loss, indeed, is neither to be denied nor extenuated. In many cases it is beyond the reach of comparison or estimate; and will always suffice to keep alive, in the more sensitive natures, the imaginative hope of a futurity which, if there is nothing to prove, there is as little in our knowledge and experience to contradict.

History, so far as we know it, bears out the opinion, that mankind can perfectly well do without the belief in a heaven. The Greeks had anything but a tempting idea of a future state. Their Elysian fields held out very little attraction to their feelings and imagination. Achilles in the Odyssey expressed a very natural, and no doubt a very common sentiment, when he said that he would rather be on earth the serf of a needy master, than reign over the whole kingdom of the dead. And the pensive character so striking in the address of the dying emperor Hadrian to his soul, gives evidence that the popular conception had not undergone much variation during that long interval. Yet we neither find that the Greeks enjoyed life less, nor feared death more, than other people. The Buddhist religion counts probably at this day a greater number of votaries than either the Christian or the Mahomedan. The Buddhist creed recognises many modes of punishment in a future life, or rather lives, by the transmigration of the soul into new bodies of men or animals. But the blessing from Heaven which it proposes as a reward, to be earned by perseverance in the highest order of virtuous life, is annihilation; the cessation, at least, of all conscious or separate existence. It is impossible to mistake in this religion, the work of legislators and moralists endeavouring to supply supernatural motives for the conduct which they were anxious to encourage; and they could find nothing more transcendant to hold out as the capital prize to be won by the mightiest efforts of labour and self-denial, than what we are so often told is the terrible idea of annihilation. Surely this is a proof that the idea is not really or naturally terrible; that not philosophers only, but the common order of mankind, can easily reconcile themselves to it, and even consider it as a good; and that it is no unnatural part of the idea of a happy life, that life itself be laid down, after the best that it can give has been fully enjoyed through a long lapse of time; when all its pleasures, even those of benevolence, are familiar, and nothing untasted and unknown is left to stimulate curiosity and keep up the desire of prolonged existence. It seems to me not only possible but probable, that in a higher, and, above all, a happier condition of human life, not annihilation but immortality may be the burdensome idea; and that human nature, though pleased with the present, and by no means impatient to quit it, would find comfort and not sadness in the thought that it is not chained through eternity to a conscious existence which it cannot be assured that it will always wish to preserve.

INDEX